# Summary of Contents

Introduction

Chapter 1: Introducing Business Objects

Chapter 2: Application Architecture with Business Objects

Chapter 3: Business Object Analysis

Chapter 4: Designing Business Objects

Chapter 5: Implementing Business Objects using Visual Basic 6.0

Chapter 6: Implememting Business Objects Part 2-
                                        Parent and Child Objects

Chapter 7: Visual Basic Forms as a User Interface

Chapter 8: Implementing Single-Tier or Two-Tier Data Access

Chapter 9: Microsoft Office as an Interface

Chapter 10: Data-Centric Business Objects

Chapter 11: Distributing Objects using DCOM

Chapter 12: Running Server Components in MTS

Chapter 13: An Active Server Pages Interface

Chapter 14: An IIS Application Interface

Chapter 15: A DHTML Application Interface

Conclusion

Appendix A: Building Objects and Components with Visual Basic

Appendix B: Unified Modelling Language

Appendix C: Additional Code

Index

# Visual Basic 6.0 Business Objects

**Rockford Lhotka**

Wrox Press Ltd. ®

# Visual Basic 6.0
# Business Objects

Published by Wrox Press Ltd. 30 Lincoln Road, Olton, Birmingham, B27 6PA
Printed in Canada
ISBN 1-861001-4-01

# Trademark Acknowledgements

Wrox has endeavored to provide trademark information about all the companies and products mentioned in this book by the appropriate use of capitals. However, Wrox cannot guarantee the accuracy of this information.

# Credits

**Author**
Rockford Lhotka

**Development Editor**
Dominic Shakeshaft

**Editors**
Craig A. Berry
Kate Hall

**Technical Reviewers**
Richard Bonneau
Henri Cesbron
Allan Emery
Mike Erickson
Brian Francis
Richard Grimes
Christian Gross
John Harris
Mark Harrison

**Technical Reviewers**
Steve Jakab
Jesse Liberty
Boyd Nolan
Greg Peele
John Smiley
Mike Sussman
Dorai Thodla

**Design/Layout**
Frances Olesch

**Cover**
Andrew Guillaume

**Index**
Andrew Criddle
Simon Gilks

# About the Author

Rockford Lhotka has over 10 years experience in software development. He worked in Pascal, FORTRAN and Basic on VAX/VMS computers for a number of years until Windows NT and Visual Basic 1.0 first became available. Rockford has worked on many projects in various roles, including software development and design, network administration, help desk management and project management.

With the release of Visual Basic 4.0, Rockford began designing and developing n-tier client/server systems using component-based technology and has been doing so ever since. Rockford has been involved in the design and development of a number of successful, enterprise-level applications based on the techniques discussed in this book.

In addition to designing and writing software, Rockford is an avid proponent of component-oriented design using Visual Basic and COM. He regularly speaks on these topics, as well as evangelizing the concepts to friends, coworkers and clients.

Rockford currently works for BORN Information Services, an IT consulting group based out of Wayzata, Minnesota. He is a Technical Manager in the Minneapolis Microsoft Business Unit, and is responsible for managing the technical direction of the business unit.

# Dedication

To my wife, Teresa, and our sons, Timothy and Marcus.

# Acknowledgments

Writing this book has been a lot of fun, and a lot of work. Without the continued support of my family it would not have been possible, and to them I owe my greatest thanks.

Many of the ideas and concepts in this book have evolved out of discussions with a number of other people and I would like to thank them:

Thanks go to Greg Nyberg and J.C. Hamlin for the hours we spent discussing how distributed object applications are implement in Forte'. Kevin Ford has always made himself available to bounce ideas off from, and always has ideas of his own in return. Thank you to Andy Anderson for helping to solidify my arguments in favor of the n-tier architecture used in the book. Dan Boerner helped set the direction for the ASP code in the chapter with his support. Thanks also, to the BORN Information Services Visual Basic Framework Team.

My deepest thanks to the excellent team of reviewers and editors from Wrox Press. Their feedback and support have been outstanding and I appreciate them greatly!

Finally, thank YOU for purchasing this book. I sincerely hope that you find it as enjoyable and useful to read as it has been to write!

Windows programming, and more specifically Visual Basic programming has an incredibly bright future in both conventional client/server and Internet environments. I am firmly convinced that, by using object-oriented design along with COM, MTS and other Win32 services, that we'll see Visual Basic become the pre-eminent development tool for enterprise-level solutions.

Thanks, code well and have fun!

# Table of Contents

**Introduction**                                                   1
What's Covered in This Book                                        2
What You Need to Use This Book                                     3
The Source Code                                                    4
   Conventions                                      4
   Tell Us What You Think                           5

**Chapter 1: Introducing Business Objects**                       7
Overview                                                           7
What are Business Objects?                                         7
   What is an Object?                               8
   Objects and Classes                             8
      Objects Contain Data          9
      Objects Have Behaviors        10
      Objects Have Interfaces       10
         Properties   10
         Methods      11
         Events       12
      Multiple Interfaces            13
Business Objects                                                   16
Why Use Business Objects?                                          16
   Modeling Our Business                           17
   Code Reuse                                       17
   Creating Building Blocks                         18
What are Components?                                               18
   Component Interfaces                             20
   Types of Components                              21
      Standard/General Components    21
      Application-Specific Components 21
      Industry-Specific Components   22
Creating Business Components in Visual Basic                       22
   Out-of-Process Servers                           22
      The Cost of Many Processes     23
      The Cost of Cross-Process Communication   24

| | |
|---|---|
| In-Process Servers | 24 |
| ActiveX Controls | 24 |
| **Fitting Business Objects into Applications** | **25** |
| Single-Tier Applications | 25 |
| Two-Tier Client/Server | 26 |
| Three-tier Client/Server | 26 |
| Browser-based Applications | 27 |
| Traditional Browser-Based Applications | 28 |
| IIS Applications | 28 |
| DHTML Applications | 29 |
| **Object-based vs. Object-oriented Approaches** | **30** |
| Abstraction | 30 |
| Encapsulation | 31 |
| Polymorphism | 33 |
| Polymorphism through Late Binding | 33 |
| Polymorphism with Early Binding | 34 |
| Inheritance | 35 |
| Interface Inheritance | 35 |
| Containment and Delegation | 37 |
| **COM - The Plumbing Behind the Scenes** | **40** |
| **Other Industry Efforts** | **40** |
| CORBA | 40 |
| Vertical Market Groups | 41 |
| **Summary** | **41** |
| | |
| **Chapter 2: Application Architecture with Business Objects** | **43** |
| **Overview** | **43** |
| **Building Applications with Components** | **44** |
| Event-Driven Programming | 44 |
| Events and Objects | 45 |
| Code Behind Forms | 46 |
| Access to Data | 47 |
| Use of Controls | 48 |
| VBX Controls | 48 |
| ActiveX Controls | 49 |
| Use of Components | 49 |
| Reuse | 49 |
| Flexibility | 50 |
| Client/Server | 50 |
| **Introducing the Component-Based Scalable Logical Architecture (CSLA)** | **51** |
| Splitting Up a Traditional Application | 51 |
| The Application | 52 |
| The Presentation Tier | 53 |
| The Business Tier | 54 |

The Data Services Tier                                    56
The n-Tier Solution                                       56
Splitting up Business Processing                          57
Rich Interface                                            57
Batch Interface                                           58
The Best of Both Worlds                                   58
UI-Centric Business Processing                            59
Data-Centric Business Processing                          60
Tying Together the Business Logic                         61
An n-Tier Architecture                                    62
Presentation Tier                                         62
UI-Centric Business Objects                               64
Data-Centric Business Objects                             66
OLE DB Data Sources                                       66
ODBC Data Sources                                         67
Non-Relational Data Sources                               67
Minimise Licensing Costs                                  67
Data Services Tier                                        67

Summary                                                   69


**Chapter : Business Object Analysis**                    71
Overview                                                  71
Identifying and Defining Business Objects                 72
Use Case Analysis                                         73
Requirements Use Case or Scenario                         74
Use Case 1: Renting a Video                               74
Use Case 2: Problem Recording                             75
Use Case 3: Rental Analysis Reporting                     75
Identifying High-Level Requirements                       75
Identifying High-Level Objects                            76
Functional Use Case                                       76
Identifying Functionality                                 77
Identifying Business Objects                              78
Defining Object Relationships                             78
Types of Relationships                                    79
Example Relationships                                     79
Eliminating Unneeded Objects                              80
Consolidating Objects                                     81
Identifying Object Attributes (or Properties)             83
Identifying Attributes - Looking through the Use Case     83
Identifying Attributes - Looking at the Object Model Diagram  84
Identifying Object Behaviors (or Methods)                 86
Identifying Behaviors - Looking through the Use Case      86
Identifying Behaviors - Looking through the Object Model  87
Notification (or Events)                                  88
Traditional Solutions                                     88

Callbacks                                           88
   Displayer Object                                 89
   Invoice Objects                                  89
   Performing the Callback                           90
   Releasing Object References                       90
   The UI Code                                      90
Raising Events                                      91
   Invoice Objects                                  92
   The UI Code                                      92

## Other Use Case Formats                          93

## Object Relationships                             93
The Ownership Relationship - Implementing Collections   94
   The Invoice Object                               94
   The InvoiceItems Collection Object               95
   The LineItem Object                              98
   The Calling Program                              99
The User Relationship - Calling Objects             99
The Aggregate Relationship - Combining Objects      100
   Technique 1 - Simple Aggregation                 100
   Technique 2 - Combining Object Interfaces         101
   Technique 3 - Combining Data                     102
     Object Approach                           103
     Database Approach                         104
The Generalization Relationship - Containing Objects   105
   Looking for Common Ground                        106
   LineItem Class                                   107
   RentalItem Class                                 108
     Setting up the RentalItem Class           108
     Containing a LineItem Object              108
     Inheriting Behavior Using Delegation      109
     Trying It Out                             109

## Summary                                          110

## Chapter 4: Designing Business Objects            113
## Overview                                         113
## Physically Distributed Architectures             114
2-Tier Physical Architecture                        114
   Traditional 2-Tier                               114
   2-Tier with Centralized Processing               115
3-Tier Physical Architecture                        116
   Client: Presentation and UI-Centric Business Objects   116
   Application Server: Data-Centric Business Objects   117
Internet Architecture                               118
   Architecture #1                                  118
   Architecture #2                                  120

## COM/DCOM Performance                             120
Calling Single Properties                           120

| | |
|---|---|
| Passing Arguments to a Method | 121 |
| Serialization of Data | 121 |
| Directly Passing User Defined Types | 122 |
| Variant Arrays | 123 |
| Using GetRows | 124 |
| Passing User-Defined Types with LSet | 125 |
| Background | 126 |
| Visual Basic Implementation | 127 |
| Memory Alignment | 129 |
| ADO(R) Recordset with Marshaling Properties | 130 |
| Creating Recordset Objects from Data | 131 |
| Creating a Connectionless Recordset | 132 |
| Passing a Recordset by Value | 133 |
| PropertyBag Objects | 134 |
| Serializing an Object's Data | 134 |
| Deserializing an Object's Data | 135 |

## Designing Our UI-Centric Business Objects — 136

| | |
|---|---|
| The UI as a Business Object Client | 136 |
| Designing Our Objects to Support the UI | 137 |
| Business Behaviors vs. UI Behaviors | 138 |
| A Basic Object and User-Interface | 138 |
| The Person Class | 138 |
| Defining the Person Object's Interface | 139 |
| Setting up the Project | 139 |
| Coding the Person Object | 139 |
| The PersonDemo User-Interface | 141 |
| Adding the Project | 141 |
| Creating the Form | 141 |
| Referencing the PersonObjects Project | 142 |
| Adding the Code | 142 |
| Running the Program | 144 |
| Enforcing Field-Level Validation | 144 |
| Raising an Error from the Person Object | 144 |
| Trapping the Error in the UI | 145 |
| Running the Program | 145 |
| Enforcing Object-Level Validation | 146 |
| An IsValid Property | 146 |
| The BrokenRules Class | 147 |
| Creating the BrokenRules Class | 147 |
| Using the BrokenRules Object within Our Person Object | 149 |
| Handling the BrokenRule and NoBrokenRules Events | 150 |
| Implementing the IsValid Property | 151 |
| Enforcing the SSN Business Rules | 151 |
| Using the Valid Event and IsValid Property in the UI | 152 |
| Adding the EnableOK Subroutine | 152 |
| Using the IsValid Property | 152 |
| Responding to the Valid Event | 153 |
| Removing the SSN Change Event Code | 153 |
| Running the Program | 153 |

| | |
|---|---|
| Handling Canceled Edits | 153 |
| Enhancing the Person Object | 154 |
| Are We Editing the Object? | 155 |
| Saving a Snapshot of the Object's Data | 155 |
| Using the BeginEdit Method | 156 |
| Using the ApplyEdit Method | 156 |
| Using the CancelEdit Method | 157 |
| Disabling Edits when mflgEditing is False | 158 |
| Testing the Code | 158 |
| Protecting Properties and Methods | 159 |
| Read-only Properties | 159 |
| Disabling Methods | 159 |
| Write-once Properties | 160 |
| Indicating when the Object is 'New' | 160 |
| Disabling the Property | 161 |
| Testing the Code | 161 |
| Write-only Properties | 161 |

| | |
|---|---|
| **Making Objects Persistent** | **162** |
| Saving Objects within a Form or BAS Module | 163 |
| Objects that Save Themselves | 163 |
| Implementing a Load Method | 163 |
| Using the Load Method from the UI | 164 |
| Saving the Object's Data through the ApplyEdit Method | 165 |
| Objects that Save Other Objects | 167 |
| An Object Manager | 167 |
| An Object Manager as an Out-of-Process Server | 168 |
| Adding GetState and SetState Methods to Person | 168 |
| Cloning Business Objects with GetState and SetState | 170 |
| The Person Object's ApplyEdit Method | 170 |
| Creating the PersonManager Object | 170 |
| Adding a Load Method to PersonManager | 171 |
| Adding a Save Method to PersonManager | 173 |
| Adding a Delete Method to PersonManager | 175 |
| Testing the Save Method | 175 |
| Testing the Load Method | 176 |
| Data-Centric Business Objects | 177 |
| Simplifying the Code in the Form | 178 |
| Adding a Load Method to Person | 179 |
| Updating the Person Object's ApplyEdit Method | 179 |
| Adding a Delete Method to Person | 180 |
| Testing the Code | 180 |

| | |
|---|---|
| **Summary** | **181** |

| | |
|---|---|
| **Chapter 5: Implementing Business Objects Using** | |
| **Visual Basic 6.0** | **183** |
| Overview | 183 |
| Common Business Object Interface | 184 |

OK, Cancel and Apply - A Preliminary Discussion  184
Transactional Methods  184
Indicating Validity  186
Persistence: Saving/Restoring Objects  187
Load  188
ApplyEdit  188
Deleting an Object  188
IsNew  190
IsDirty  191
Creating a Class Template  193
Setting up the Class Module  193
Adding the Template Code  193
Saving the Template  195
Using the Code Template  196
The BrokenRules Class  196

Video Rental System Overview  197

Video Rental: Customer Objects  198
Customer: A Simple Object  198
Setting up the Project  198
Adding the BrokenRules Class Module  199
Adding the Customer Class Module  199
Setting up the Customer Class  199
Declarations  199
Load Method  200
BeginEdit Method  200
CancelEdit Method  201
ApplyEdit Method  201
Class_Initialize Routine  202
Customer Object Properties  202
CustomerID Property: Read-only Value  202
Name Property: Read-write Value  203
Enforcing Rules with Different Severity  204
Basic Address Properties  205
State Property: Making a Value Uppercase  206
ZipCode Property: Formatting a Value  207
Phone Property  208
Customer Object Methods  208
CreateInvoice Method: Creating Another Object  208
Testing the Customer Object  209
Customers: A Read-Only List Object  211
Read-only lists of objects  211
The CustomerDisplay Class  212
Declarations  212
Public Properties  212
Friend Properties  213
The Customers Class  214
Creating a Base Collection Object  214
Count Property  214
Supporting For...Each  214

| | |
|---|---|
| Item Method | 215 |
| Load Method | 216 |
| Using the Customers Object | 216 |

## Video Rental: Video and Tape Objects — 217

| | |
|---|---|
| TextList: a Powerful Utility Object | 217 |
| Setting up the TextList Class | 218 |
| Using an Item Value to get a Key | 219 |
| The Load Method | 220 |
| Videos: A Read-only List Object | 220 |
| Creating the Videos Object | 220 |
| Creating the VideoDisplay Object | 221 |
| Video: A Parent Object | 222 |
| Setting up the Video Class | 223 |
| Declarations | 223 |
| BeginEdit, CancelEdit and ApplyEdit Methods | 223 |
| Load Method | 224 |
| Delete Method | 225 |
| Class_Initialize Routine | 225 |
| Video Properties | 226 |
| ReleaseDate Property: Date Value | 227 |
| TextList-based Properties | 229 |
| Category Property | 230 |
| Rating Property | 231 |
| Tapes Property | 232 |

## Summary — 233

## Chapter 6: Implementing Business Objects Part 2 - Parent and Child Objects — 235

| | |
|---|---|
| Overview | 235 |
| Tape: A Child Object | 236 |
| Setting up the Tape Class | 236 |
| Updating the Template Code | 236 |
| Child Object Support | 239 |
| A Parent-Child User Interface | 240 |
| Indicating if the Tape Object is a Child | 241 |
| Enhancing BeginEdit, CancelEdit and ApplyEdit | 242 |
| BeginEdit and CancelEdit Methods | 242 |
| ApplyEdit Method | 243 |
| Delete Method | 244 |
| Load Method | 244 |
| ChildBeginEdit Method | 245 |
| ChildCancelEdit Method | 245 |
| ChildApplyEdit Method | 246 |
| ChildLoad Method | 247 |
| Tape Properties | 247 |
| Basic Properties | 247 |
| DateAcquired Property: Write Once, Read Many | 249 |
| Invoice Property: Load on Demand | 250 |

Tape Methods 251
  CheckOut Method 251
  CheckIn Method 252
Tapes: A Parent-Child Relationship Object 253
  Setting up the Tapes Class 254
  Edit Methods 255
    BeginEdit Method 255
    CancelEdit Method 256
    ApplyEdit Method 257
    Delete Method 258
  Adding Tape Objects to the Collection 259
    The Tapes Object's Add Method 260
    Modifying SetAsChild in the Tape Module 261
    Wrapping up the Add Method 261
    Modifying the Tape object's ApplyEdit Method 261
    Adding the AddTape Method to Tapes 263
  Removing Tape Objects 263
  Loading the Tape Objects 264

**Video Rental: Invoice Objects** **265**
  Late Fees: Object Interaction 265
    Adding DateDue to the Tape Object 266
    Recording the Late Fee 266
  Invoice: Another Parent Object 269
    Setting up the Invoice Object 269
      Updating the Template Code 269
      Customer Object Reference 271
    Invoice Properties 271
      Read-only Properties from Other Objects 272
      Calculated Properties 272
    Creating an Invoice Object 274
  InvoiceItem: An Interface Class 275
    Setting up the InvoiceItem Class 275
    InvoiceItem Properties and Methods 276
      Possible Set of Properties and Methods 276
      Final Set of Properties and Methods 277
      ItemType Property: Indicating the Type of Object 278
  InvoiceFee: A Read-only Child Object 278
    Setting up the InvoiceFee Class 279
      Declarations 279
      Updating the Code 280
    InvoiceFee Properties 283
    Implementing the InvoiceItem Interface 284
      Declarations 284
      Implementing the Properties and Methods 285
      Implementing the ItemType Property 286
  InvoiceTape: An Aggregate Child Object 287
    Setting up the InvoiceTape Class 287
    InvoiceTape Properties 288
    InvoiceTape Methods 289

Implementing the InvoiceItem Interface 290
InvoiceItems: A Parent-Child Collection Object 292
Setting up the InvoiceItems Class 292
BeginEdit Method 293
CancelEdit and ApplyEdit Methods 294
Delete Method 295
Load Method 296
Add Method 296
AddTape Method 298
Remove Method 298
LoadFees Method 298
SubTotal Property 299

**Summary** 300

**Chapter 7: Visual Basic Forms as a User-Interface** 303
Overview 303
VideoUI: A Visual Basic Client Project 304
Version Compatibility 304
Interface Changes 305
No Compatibility 306
Project Compatibility 306
Binary Compatibility 306
Referencing the VideoObjects Project 306
VideoMain: MDI Form 307
Edit Screens 310
Creating an Edit Form Template 310
Business Object Support 310
Declarations 311
Component Method 311
Putting the Object's Values on the Form 312
OK, Cancel and Apply Buttons 313
Data Entry Fields 314
Saving the Form Template 315
CustomerEdit: Simple Editing 316
Setting up the CustomerEdit Form 316
Customizing the Template Code 317
Adding Code Behind Controls 319
Name Text Box 319
The TextChange Routine 319
Calling the TextChange Routine 320
LostFocus Processing 321
Address, City and Phone Text Boxes 322
State and ZipCode Text Box Controls 323
Adding Code to VideoMain 324
VideoEdit: Editing a Parent Object 325
Setting up the VideoEdit Form 325
The ListView Control 327
Updating the Template Code 328

| | |
|---|---|
| Text Box Controls | 328 |
| TextBox Control with a Date Value | 329 |
| Categories and Ratings ComboBox Controls | 329 |
| Loading the ComboBox Values | 330 |
| Updating the Business Object | 331 |
| Maintaining Child Objects | 332 |
| Displaying a List of Tapes | 332 |
| Adding a Tape | 335 |
| Editing a Tape | 336 |
| Removing a Tape | 336 |
| Adding Code to VideoMain | 337 |
| TapeEdit: Editing a Child Object | 337 |
| Setting up the TapeEdit Form | 337 |
| Text Box Control | 339 |

**List Screens** — 339

| | |
|---|---|
| CustomerSearch: Criteria Entry | 339 |
| Setting up the CustomerSearch Form | 340 |
| Putting Code behind the CustomerSearch Form | 340 |
| Adding Code to VideoMain | 341 |
| CustomerList: Search Results Display | 342 |
| Setting up the CustomerList Form | 342 |
| Putting Code behind the CustomerList Form | 342 |
| Displaying the Data | 342 |
| Code behind the Controls | 344 |
| Public Property - The Selected Customer | 344 |
| Adding Code to VideoMain | 344 |
| VideoSearch: Criteria Entry | 346 |
| VideoList: Search Results Display | 347 |
| Setting up the VideoList Form | 347 |
| Main Menu Code for Video Search | 348 |

**Transaction Support** — 349

| | |
|---|---|
| InvoiceEdit | 350 |
| Setting up the InvoiceEdit Form | 350 |
| Child Object Support | 352 |
| Displaying the Child Objects | 352 |
| Adding InvoiceTape Objects | 353 |
| Editing Line Items | 355 |
| Removing Line Items | 356 |
| Setting up the Menu Option | 356 |
| Checking in a Tape | 357 |
| Running the UI | 359 |

**Summary** — 359

**Chapter 8: Implementing Single-Tier or Two-Tier Data Access** — 361

| | |
|---|---|
| Overview | 361 |
| Object State | 362 |
| An Approach to Persistence | 362 |

| | |
|---|---|
| Retrieving Data | 363 |
| Building a SQL Statement | 363 |
| Opening a Recordset | 364 |
| Copy Data Fields to the Object | 364 |
| Handling Errors | 364 |
| Adding/Updating Data | 365 |
| Adding Data | 366 |
| Updating Data | 366 |
| Copying the Field Values | 366 |
| Retrieving the New Primary Key | 366 |
| Deleting Data | 367 |
| Setting up the VideoObjects Project | 367 |
| Referencing the ADO Library | 368 |
| The Database Connection | 368 |
| Connection Variable - cnVideo | 368 |
| Opening the Database | 369 |
| Setting up the Database | 369 |
| The Customer Table | 370 |
| The LateFee Table | 370 |
| The Video Table | 371 |
| The Tape Table | 372 |
| The Categories and Ratings Tables | 373 |
| The Categories Table | 373 |
| The Ratings Table | 374 |
| The Invoice Table | 374 |
| The InvoiceTape Table | 375 |
| **Making Simple Objects Persistent** | **376** |
| The Customer Object | 376 |
| Loading the Customer Data | 377 |
| Adding/Updating the Customer Data | 378 |
| Deleting the Customer Data | 379 |
| **Making Parent and Child Objects Persistent** | **379** |
| The Video Object | 380 |
| Loading the Video Data | 381 |
| Adding, Updating and Deleting the Video Data | 381 |
| The Tapes Object | 382 |
| Loading the Tape Objects | 382 |
| The Tape Object | 384 |
| Adding the Persistence Methods to Tape | 384 |
| The Save Method | 384 |
| The DeleteObject and Fetch Methods | 385 |
| Tape as a Standalone Object | 386 |
| Tape as a Child Object | 387 |
| ChildLoad | 388 |
| ChildApplyEdit | 388 |
| Creating Late Fee Records | 389 |
| Causing a Late Fee | 389 |
| Writing the Late Fee Record | 389 |
| Calling SaveLateFee | 390 |

Persisting Polymorphic Objects                                    392
  The Invoice Object                                     392
  The Invoice Child Objects                              394
    The InvoiceItems Collection                395
      Loading the Late Fee Objects   395
      Loading the Tape Rental Objects 396
    The InvoiceFee Object                      397
      Adding the Paid Flag           397
      The Fetch Method               398
      The DeleteObject Method        399
      The Save Method                400
      Calling the Persistence Methods 400
    The InvoiceTape Object                     401
      The Save Method                401
      Checking Out a Tape            402
      DeleteObject and Fetch Methods 403
      Calling the Persistence Methods 404
Making Read-Only Objects Persistent                              405
  The Customers Object                                   405
    Loading the Customers Object's Data         405
    Updating the Customers Object's Item Method 407
  The Videos Object                                      408
    The Load Method                             408
    The Fetch Method                            408
    The Item Method                             409
  The TextList Object                                    409
    Updating the Video Object                   411
    Updating VideoEdit                          412
  Summary                                                413

**Chapter 9: Microsoft Office as an Interface**                  **415**
Overview                                                         415
Compiling the VideoObjects Project                               416
A User Form Interface                                            416
  Creating the Interface                                417
    Opening the VBA Editor                      417
    Adding a Reference to VideoObjects          418
    Adding a UserForm                           418
    Adding Our Controls                         419
    Code Behind the Form                        420
      Copying the Code from Chapter 7 420
      Adapting the Code for Excel    421
      Adding Code to a Code Module   421
  Testing the Interface                                 423
    Testing the Interface in the Editor         423
      Running the Test Routine       424
    Adding a Button to a Spreadsheet            424

| | |
|---|---|
| Adding a Button to a Worksheet | 424 |
| Setting the Button's Caption | 425 |
| Trying the Button | 426 |

| | |
|---|---|
| Using a Document to View Objects | 426 |
| Building the Report | 426 |
| Printing Column Titles | 427 |
| Clearing the Columns | 427 |
| Adding the Titles | 428 |
| Adding a Button | 428 |
| Listing the Video Titles | 429 |
| Listing the Tapes and their Status | 431 |
| The VideoList Report | 433 |
| Summary | 434 |

| | |
|---|---|
| **Chapter 10: Data-Centric Business Objects** | **437** |
| Overview | 437 |
| Splitting Out Behaviors | 438 |
| Separate UI from Persistence | 438 |
| Splitting the Object's Behavior | 439 |
| Moving the Object's State | 440 |
| Client Calling Server | 441 |
| Setting up a Server Project | 441 |
| Using ADO in VideoServer | 442 |
| Opening the Database | 442 |
| Making Simple Objects Persistent | 442 |
| Customer Object | 442 |
| Adding GetState and SetState to Customer | 443 |
| Moving the UDT | 443 |
| Adding IsNew, IsDeleted and IsDirty | 444 |
| Creating the CustomerData Type | 445 |
| The GetState Method | 445 |
| The SetState Method | 446 |
| Creating the CustomerPersist Object | 446 |
| Adding the CustomerPersist Class | 447 |
| Declaring mudtProps in CustomerPersist | 447 |
| Adding GetState to CustomerPersist | 447 |
| Adding SetState to CustomerPersist | 447 |
| Moving Save to CustomerPersist | 448 |
| Moving the DeleteObject Method | 450 |
| Moving the Fetch Method | 450 |
| Calling CustomerPersist from Customer | 451 |
| Using CreateObject | 451 |
| Calling DeleteObject from ApplyEdit | 452 |
| Calling Save from ApplyEdit | 453 |
| Calling Fetch from Load | 453 |
| Making List Objects Persistent | 454 |
| The Buffer Object | 455 |

Designing the Object                                                    455
   Focus on Performance                                   455
   String Handling in Visual Basic                        455
Creating the Buffer Class                                               456
Initializing the Buffer Object                                          456
   Declaring Variables                                    456
   The Initialize Method                                  457
Adding Elements                                                         458
   The Add Method                                         458
   Extending the Buffer                                   458
GetState and SetState Methods                                           459
   GetState Method                                        459
   SetState Method                                        459
Retrieving Elements                                                     460
   Item Property                                          460
   Informational Properties                               460
Updating Elements                                                       461
TextList Object                                                         461
Creating TextListPersist                                                462
   Adding a UDT for the TextList Data                     462
   Moving the Fetch Routine to TextListPersist            462
Updating TextList                                                       464
   Load Method in TextList                                464
   SetState Subroutine                                    465
Display Lists                                                           466
CustomersPersist Object                                                 466
   Create a UDT for each Element                          466
   The Fetch Routine                                      467
Customers Object                                                        468
   Declarations                                           468
   Load Method                                            468
   SetState Routine                                       468

**Making Child Objects Persistent**                                     **469**
Making the Video Object Persistent                                      470
Global UDTs                                                             470
   Moving the VideoProps UDT                              470
   Modifying the Property Get for ReleaseDate             471
   Adding a VideoData UDT                                 471
The VideoPersist Object                                                 471
The Video Object                                                        473
   Updating ApplyEdit in Video                           473
   Updating Load in Video                                 474
   Adding GetState to Video                               474
   Adding SetState to Video                               475
Serializing the Tape Objects                                            475
Updating the Tape Object                                                475
   Adding GetState to Tape                                475
   Adding SetState to Tape                                477
Updating the Tapes Collection Object                                    477

| | |
|---|---|
| Adding GetState to Tapes | 477 |
| Adding SetState to Tapes | 478 |
| Creating the Data-Centric Tape Objects | 479 |
| The TapesPersist Object | 479 |
| Setting up TapesPersist | 480 |
| Adding a Fetch Method to TapesPersist | 480 |
| Adding a Save Method to TapesPersist | 481 |
| The TapePersist Object | 482 |
| Setting up TapePersist | 482 |
| Adding SetState and GetState to TapePersist | 483 |
| Moving Fetch to TapePersist | 483 |
| Moving Save to TapePersist | 484 |
| Moving SaveLateFee to TapePersist | 485 |
| Moving DeleteObject to TapePersist | 486 |
| Adding SaveChild to TapePersist | 486 |
| Updating the Tapes and Tape Objects | 487 |
| The Tapes Object | 487 |
| Updating ApplyEdit in Tapes | 487 |
| Updating Load in Tapes | 487 |
| The Tape Object | 488 |
| The ChildApplyEdit method | 488 |
| The ChildLoad method | 489 |
| Making the Tape Object Make Itself Persistent | 489 |
| Make TapePersist Public | 490 |
| Updating the Scope of TapePersist | 490 |
| Updating the Scope of the TapePersist Methods | 490 |
| Updating ApplyEdit in Tape | 490 |
| Updating Load in Tape | 491 |
| Updating the Invoice Related objects | 492 |
| Removing Data Access from VideoObjects | 492 |
| **Summary** | **493** |
| | |
| **Chapter 11: Distributing Objects using DCOM** | **495** |
| **Overview** | **495** |
| Application Server Issues | 496 |
| **Building the VideoServer Project** | **497** |
| Unattended Execution | 497 |
| Multi-threading | 497 |
| Fixed Thread Pool | 498 |
| Thread per Object | 498 |
| Creating Remote Server Files | 499 |
| TLB File | 500 |
| VBR File | 500 |
| Binary Compatibility | 500 |
| Check the Database Location | 501 |
| **Installing VideoServer on the Server** | **502** |
| Installing VideoServer | 502 |

Using the Package and Deployment Wizard     503
    Remote Automation     503
    Shared Files     503
    Completing the Install     504
Manual Registration     504
    Unregister the Previous Version     504
    Copy and Register the New Version     504
DCOM Configuration     505
    Enabling DCOM     505
    Setting VideoServer Permissions     506
      Selecting the VideoServer Application     506
      Setting VideoServer Permissions     508
      Set the Identity Account     509

**Building the VideoObjects Project**     **510**
Using the TLB File from VideoServer     510
Changing the VideoObjects Server's Reference     511

**Setting up the Client**     **511**
Using the Package and Deployment Wizard     512
    Creating a Dependency File for VideoObjects     512
      Copy the VideoServer TLB File     512
      Generate Dependency File     513
      Handling dependencies for VideoServer.exe     513
      Adding the correct list of dependency files     514
      Completing the **Package and Deployment Wizard**     515
    Setup for VideoUI     515
      Listing the Included Files     515
      Setting up Remote Servers     515
      Completing the Client Install     516
Using CLIREG32     517
    Unregister VideoServer     517
    Copy VideoServer's TLB and VBR Files to \System32     517
    Register VideoServer.VBR     517

**Summary**     **519**

**Chapter 12: Running Server Components in MTS**     **521**
Overview     521
Supporting Multiple Clients     522
    Keeping Objects Alive     522
      Keeping the DLL Loaded     523
      Keeping Objects Loaded     523
      Limiting the Number of Objects     523
    Database Connections     524
Database Transactions     525
Stateless Objects     525
ActiveX DLL Servers     526
Context     526
    Transactions     526

Security 527
Object Creation and References 527
Object Lifetimes in MTS 527
Creating MTS Objects with Visual Basic 528
The New Keyword 528
The CreateObject Method 528
The CreateInstance Method 528
Error Handling 529

Getting VideoServer Ready for MTS 529
VideoServer Properties 529
Changing to an ActiveX DLL 530
Changing the Project Name 530
Unattended Execution and Threading Model 530
Compatible Server 531
Object Creation and References 532
Using CreateObject Instead of New 532
Using CreateObject 532
Calling Friend Properties and Methods 533
Using the New Keyword 533
SQL Data Sources 534
Three-tier Architecture 534
Switching from JET to SQL Server 534
Database Connections 535
Changes to VOmain 535
Updating the DeleteObject Methods 536
Updating the Fetch Methods 537
Updating the Save Methods 537

Running VideoServerMTS in MTS 538
Installing the Server in MTS 538
Copy the DLL to the Server machine 539
Using the Transaction Server Explorer 539
Adding a New Package 540
Copying the DLL into the Package 542
Creating the Client Setup 542
Making VideoObjects Use the New Server 543

MTS Transactions 545
ObjectContext Objects 545
Getting an ObjectContext Reference 545
Linking Context Objects 546
Creating Objects from the Client 546
Using CreateInstance 547
The ObjectControl interface 547
ObjectControl_CanBePooled 548
ObjectControl_Activate 548
ObjectControl_Deactivate 549
Recordset Cursor types 549
A Hierarchical View of Transactions 550
Changing the VideoPersist Save method 550

Updating the Tapes object    552
Updating the Video object    554
Indicating Transaction Status    555
Calling SetComplete and SetAbort    555
SetComplete    556
SetAbort    559
Establishing a Transaction    560
Distributed Transaction Coordinator    562
Manually Starting the DTC    562
SQL Service Manager    562
Transaction Server Explorer    563
Starting DTC as NT Boots    564
Summary    565

**Chapter 13: An Active Server Pages Interface**    **567**
Overview    567
An HTML User Interface    568
Designing for the Internet    568
Architecture of the UI    569
Active Server Pages    570
A Simple ASP Script    570
Set up the Script Directory    570
Creating a Directory for the Files    571
Microsoft Internet Service Manager    571
Create the Script    574
Simple HTML    574
Adding Code    574
Mixing Code and HTML    575
The ASP Environment    576
The Request Object    577
Request.QueryString    577
Request.Form    578
The Response Object    578
The Server Object    579
Updating our ActiveX Servers    579
ASP and Threading Models    580
Installing the VideoObjects DLL    580
Displaying Details of a Video    581
Creating the Script    581
Creating the Video Object    582
Loading the Video Object    583
Setting the Document Title    583
The Document Body    583
Displaying the Studio and Title    584
Displaying the Rating    584
Counting the Number of Tapes    585
Wrapping up the Document    585

| | |
|---|---|
| Running the Script | 586 |
| **Getting a List of Video Titles** | **586** |
| A Recursive HTML Form | 587 |
| The HTML Form | 587 |
| Handling the Recursion | 587 |
| Displaying the List of Videos | 589 |
| Creating the Videos Object | 589 |
| Loading the Object | 589 |
| Setting up the Document | 589 |
| Building the Table | 589 |
| Adding a Hyperlinked Field | 590 |
| Displaying the ReleaseDate Property | 590 |
| Wrapping up the Document | 591 |
| Running the Script | 591 |
| **Summary** | **593** |
| | |
| **Chapter 14: An IIS Application Interface** | **595** |
| **Overview** | **595** |
| **IIS Applications** | **596** |
| ASP Object Model | 596 |
| WebClass Objects | 597 |
| Hello World Example | 598 |
| WebItem Objects | 601 |
| Hello World Example | 602 |
| Tag Substitution | 604 |
| Tag Substitution Example | 605 |
| **Displaying Details of a Video** | **606** |
| Installing the VideoObjects DLL | 606 |
| Designing the Application | 607 |
| Creating our IIS Application | 607 |
| The SearchForm WebItem | 608 |
| Creating the Template | 609 |
| Updating WebClass_Start | 609 |
| Running the Application | 609 |
| The ListVideos WebItem | 610 |
| Creating the Template | 610 |
| Updating WebClass_Start | 612 |
| Loading the Videos Object | 613 |
| Building the HTML Table | 613 |
| Running the Application | 614 |
| The DisplayVideo WebItem | 615 |
| Creating the Template | 615 |
| Using the URLfor Method | 616 |
| Raising Events Using the URLfor Method | 616 |
| Adding Hyperlinks to Our Table | 617 |
| Implementing the UserEvent Procedure | 617 |

Implementing the ProcessTag Procedure 618
Running the Application 619
Summary 621

## Chapter 15: A DHTML Application Interface 623
Overview 623
DHTML Applications 624
DHTML Application Design Issues 625
Powerful Display Options 625
Built-In Objects 625
Page-Oriented Design 626
Passing Information from Page to Page 626
A Simple DHTML Application 627
Building the Page 629
Setting Document Properties 629
Adding Elements to the Page 629
Programming the Page 630
Running the Program 630
Editing the Customer Object 631
The CustSearch Page 631
Setting up the Project 632
Building the Page 632
Adding the Code 633
The CustList Page 634
Adding the Page 634
Retrieving Values from the Cookie 635
Using ActiveX Controls in a DHTML Page 635
Loading the ListView Control 636
Implementing the Cancel Button 638
Running the Program 638
Implementing the OK Button 639
The CustEdit page 639
Setting Up the Page 639
Adding Code to the Page 640
The onchange Events 640
LostFocus Functionality 643
Module-Level Variables 643
Enabling and Disabling OK and Apply 643
Loading the Customer Object 644
Coding the Buttons 645
Running the Program 646
Summary 647

## Conclusion 649

# Appendix A: Building Objects and Components with
## Visual Basic     653

## Building Objects in Visual Basic     653
Class Modules from Scratch     654
Using the Class Builder     657
## ActiveX Components     664
ActiveX EXEs     664
   Adding Our Class     664
   The Instancing Property     665
   Setting the Project Properties     666
      Project Type     666
      Project Name     666
      Unattended Execution     667
      Threading Model     667
   Compiling the Server     667
   Testing Our Server     667
ActiveX DLLs     669
   Setting up the Server     669
      The Instancing Property     669
   Project Properties     669
      Project Type     670
      Project Name     670
      Unattended Execution     670
      Threading Model     670
   Compiling the Server     670
   Testing the Server     671
      Re-referencing the Server     671
      Running the Test     671
ActiveX Controls     671
   Setting up the Server     672
      Setting up the Control     672
   Adding the CircleShape Class     672
      The Instancing Property     672
   Adding a Method to get an Object     673
   Testing the Control     673
## Summary     675

# Appendix B: Unified Modeling Language — 677

Static Class Diagram — 678
  Classes — 678
    Class Display — 678
    Property Display — 678
    Method Display — 679
  Class Relationships — 679
    General Relationship — 679
    Aggregation — 680
    Generalization (Inheritance) — 680
    Multiplicity — 680
Summary — 681

# Appendix C: Additional Code — 683

Chapter 10 — 683
  The Videos Objects — 683
  The VideosPersist Object — 684
  The Invoice Object — 685
  The InvoicePersist Object — 687
  The InvoiceItems Object — 689
  The InvoiceItemsPersist Object — 691
  The InvoiceFee Object — 693
  The InvoiceFeePersist Object — 693
  The InvoiceTape Object — 695
  The InvoiceTapePersist Object — 696
  Adding to the VideoTypes.BAS module — 697
Chapter 12 — 698
  The Invoice Object — 698
  The InvoicePersist Object — 699
  The InvoiceItems Object — 701
  The InvoiceItemsPersist Object — 702
  The InvoiceFeePersist Object — 705
  The InvoiceTapePersist Object — 707

# Index — 713

# Introduction

It seems that every time I discuss developing programs in Visual Basic using object-oriented design techniques, I'm met with skepticism or even outright disbelief. The fact is that many people have misconceptions about Visual Basic and its ability to create object-oriented applications.

However, most object-oriented design folks would agree that the language, or development tool, is secondary, and that the key to successful object-oriented design is to have the right mindset, create the design correctly, and then implement the application with the tool of your choice. Following this philosophy, it's theoretically possible to create object-oriented software using FORTRAN or COBOL. Of course, the correct choice of tool can save you many problems in the actual implementation of your design.

Fortunately, Visual Basic 6.0 provides us with almost every tool we need to implement an object-oriented design. In fact, I've developed quasi-object designs in Visual Basic 3.0, and full-blown object-oriented designs in Visual Basic 4.0. With the advent of Visual Basic 5.0, we had even more powerful object tools at our disposal, making the use of object-oriented techniques even more attractive.

This is the second edition of this book, the first was written for Visual Basic 5.0. In updating the book for Visual Basic 6.0 I have been very heartened to find that the basic concepts and architecture used in the book continue to be very appropriate with this new version of Visual Basic. This isn't terribly surprising, since the fundamental principles in the book are based more on COM than on Visual Basic itself. However, it's very reassuring to have this borne out over time, as it demonstrates that the architecture is a sound, safe approach for developing software that will continue to be valid into the future.

This book is about designing business software using Visual Basic 6.0 and following an object-oriented design philosophy. We'll be studying a number of examples to demonstrate how we can create a solid object model and implement it using Visual Basic. Along the way, we'll cover a number of specific techniques that make this whole concept work well in the Visual Basic environment. In addition, we'll demonstrate some general architectural techniques that can apply equally well to almost any tool.

First, I'll define business objects and discuss why they are so useful and important. Then we'll consider how to package these business objects into components to be reused. Once we've covered these basics, we'll look at how to build a number of user interfaces on top of the business objects, and how to provide a set of services so that the objects can be stored in a relational database.

We'll discuss different types of application design, from single-tier to multi-tier to Internet Web development. All the sample applications in this book will fit into a three-tier logical model, but the techniques can be used on one computer, on several or across the Internet.

If you're one of the skeptics I mentioned earlier, I intend to convince you that Visual Basic is entirely up to the task of creating object-oriented software, with all the benefits that entails. If, on the other hand, you're already convinced, then this book should provide you with plenty of valuable techniques and concepts about how to create distributed and object-oriented software with Visual Basic 6.0.

# What's Covered in This Book

*Visual Basic 6.0 Business Objects* will take you from a broad discussion of what business objects are, and why they're such a powerful theme in modern OO programming, through to the implementation of a full project using business objects within Visual Basic. This project will also involve some of the newest and most exciting server-side technologies, including DCOM, MTS, ASP, IIS Applications and DHTML Applications.

In Chapter 1, I present the rationale for the book, which is that object-oriented design, business objects, and Visual Basic 6 allow us to develop highly scalable and reusable code. We define what business objects are, we consider the benefits of using business objects and we begin to think about how object-oriented principles can be implemented in Visual Basic.

In Chapter 2, we review traditional Visual Basic development techniques, and see how business objects and components can improve the way we develop software. We consider various architectures that support component-based applications, and I introduce the ideas behind the component-based scalable logical architecture (CSLA) we'll be implementing. For those of you who aren't familiar with programming objects in Visual Basic, I provide an introduction in Appendix A.

In Chapter 3, we take the 'real-world' scenario of a video rental store, and analyze it in order to identify a series of representative software objects. The principles necessary to implement these objects and their interactions in Visual Basic are then introduced. Appendix B covers the details of the UML used in the design diagrams within this chapter.

In Chapter 4, we take Chapter 3's object model and apply it to possible physical architectures. We also code some examples to implement some basic business object functionality, and to highlight issues involved in coding UI and database access for these architectures.

By Chapters 5 and 6 it's time to code the video store's business objects. First we decide on some common interface elements, and then code a template class we can reuse for each business object. Chapter 5 concentrates on the simpler, standalone business objects and utility objects, while Chapter 6 implements parent-child relationships, hybrid (sometimes a child, sometimes standalone) and sibling objects.

At the end of Chapter 6, the code is functional but not very useful. It lacks both a user interface and persistence code. In Chapter 7, we code a Visual Basic client for the business objects, while in Chapter 8, we implement code to save each object's state to a local Access database.

In Chapter 9, I'll show how to implement an Excel front end to the video store project using VBA. The ease with which we accomplish this should prove just how reusable business objects can be.

In Chapter 10, I'll split off the persistence code into a separate project. This is necessary to implement a fully scalable solution, where code resides near its 'client', the database. We want to be able to put the persistence code and the database on a separate machine from the client, and ideally on separate machines themselves. The need for efficient use of the underlying transport, DCOM, drives the implementation of the communication between the business objects and their persistence counterparts. In Chapter 11, we package up the client and server code using the Package & Deployment Wizard that comes with Visual Basic.

In Chapter 12, I'll upsize the database to SQL Server, and run the persistence code within Microsoft Transaction Server. This technology simplifies issues of object management, database connection pooling and transaction management.

Finally, in Chapter 13 to 15, we implement a series of simple web interface using IIS, Active Server Pages and Dynamic HTML. This is quite easy, as we have the business objects' DLL available to the scripting code within the page.

# What You Need to Use This Book

Obviously, this book requires Visual Basic 6.0, preferably the Enterprise Edition (for the Class Wizard and the Package & Deployment Wizard).

At various times, this book requires the following Microsoft technologies:

- ❑ Visual Modeler
- ❑ Access, Excel from Office 97
- ❑ A Windows NT 4.0 Server to host DCOM Servers on a local network
- ❑ MTS 2.0
- ❑ SQL Server 6.5/7.0
- ❑ IIS 4.0 with ASP 2.0
- ❑ DHTML Applications

# The Source Code

The source code for the book is available from the Wrox web site, `http://www.wrox.com`. It focuses mainly on the `VideoStore` application discussed above.

# Conventions

We use a number of different styles of text and layout in the book to help differentiate between the various types of information. Here are examples of the styles we use along with explanations of what they mean:

Bulleted information is shown like this:

- ❑ **Important Words** are in a bold font.
- ❑ Words that appear on the screen, such as menu options, are a similar font to the one used on screen, e.g. the File menu.
- ❑ Keys that you press on the keyboard, like *Ctrl* and *Enter*, are in italics.
- ❑ All file, function names and other code snippets are in this style: `Video.mdb`.
- ❑ We've also italicized the first mention of classes like *Video*, when the discussion involves no code.

Code shown for the first time, or other relevant code, is in the following format,

```
Dim intVariable1 As Integer

intVariable1 = intVariable1 + 1
Debug.Print intVariable1
```

while less important code, or code that has been seen before, looks like this:

```
intvariable1 = intvariable1 + 1
```

Code you need to type into an Immediate window, or for a browser's URL appears like this:

```
http://www.wrox.co.uk
```

*Finally, background information will look like this,*

> **And vital, not-to-be-missed information looks like this.**

# Tell Us What You Think

We have tried to make this book accurate and enjoyable, and reading it worthwhile. But what really matters is whether or not *you* find it useful, and we would really appreciate your views and comments. You can return the the reply card in the back of the book, or contact us at:

**feedback@wrox.com**
**http://www.wrox.com**
or
**http://www.wrox.co.uk**

# Introducing Business Objects

## Overview

In the introduction, I presented the rationale for this book, which is that object-oriented design, business objects, and Visual Basic 6 allow us to develop highly scalable and reusable code. In this first chapter, we'll look at these concepts and the arguments for them in more detail. Specifically, we'll review:

- ❑ Defining objects
- ❑ Defining business objects
- ❑ Using Visual Basic 6.0 to create objects
- ❑ Re-using code with components
- ❑ Business objects in action - application types
- ❑ Object-oriented principles in Visual Basic 6.0

## What are Business Objects?

This book is about developing applications using business objects. So the first thing we need to do is define how we'll be using the term **business objects**. Since this term means different things to different people, we need to make sure that we're all talking about the same thing before proceeding any further.

Just looking at the words, you might decide that these are *objects* that reflect or represent your *business*. And you'd pretty much be right - at a high level, it really is that simple. The programs we write can be viewed as models of the real world. We create programs to simulate parts of the world around us - to record what's happening or to make predictions about what might happen.

# What is an Object?

To understand business objects, we first need to understand the concept of an **object**:

> **An object is a code-based abstraction of a real-world entity or relationship.**

In the computer, an object consists of some data (state information) and behavior (a set of routines). Our programs use an **interface** to get access to an object's data and behavior. We can represent the object as something like the following diagram:

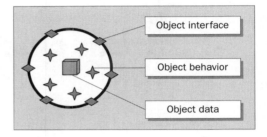

# Objects and Classes

All objects are defined by a **class**:

> **A class is essentially a template from which the object is created which means that we can create many objects based on a single class.**

Each such created object is referred to as an **instance** of the class.

The word class is pretty descriptive, since we're basically classifying our objects. For instance, if we have a couple of objects, *Squirrel* and *Rabbit*, they could be instances of a *Mammal* class.

To use a more business-like example, we may have a *Customer* class. From this class we could create instances to represent each of our customers, such as *Fred Smith* and *Mary Jones*. Each actual customer would have its own object, but all the objects would be created from the same template, the Customer class:

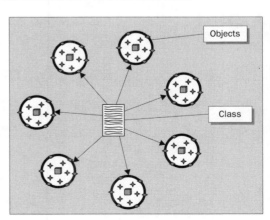

This concept is called **abstraction**, since the *Customer* is an abstract representation of both *Fred* and *Mary*. We'll discuss abstraction some more, later in this chapter.

In Visual Basic, we define classes using **class modules**. We can then create objects based on the class module, with each object being an instance of the class.

Class modules are like form or standard modules, in that they have a declaration section followed by a series of Sub, Function and Property subroutines.

> *The difference is that the variables and code in a class module can only be used by creating an instance of the class.*

Let's take a look at how Visual Basic's class modules are used to provide a template for our objects.

## Objects Contain Data

All business objects contain data about themselves. For instance, an object representing a simple cardboard box might have data about the box's height, width, and depth. The object might also know whether the box is open or closed. Furthermore, we might have many box objects, each with its own height, width and depth. Each of these objects could be an instance of a *Box* class.

Data values in objects are stored in **instance variables**. Each instance of an object has its own set of variables, separate from the variables of any other object, even those of the same class. In this way, two objects of the same class can each have their own individual data, so each of our earlier box objects can have its own height, width, and depth.

In Visual Basic, a class' instance variables are declared as module-level variables inside a class module. For example:

```
Option Explicit

Private mdblHeight As Double
Private mdblWidth As Double
Private mdblDepth As Double
Private mblnOpen As Boolean
```

As with any other module, module-level variables in a class module can be declared as either Public or Private.

Private variables are only accessible to code within the class module, and they are the preferable way to manage data within objects. For any client code to manipulate a Private variable, it must call our object's code to do the manipulation; it can't do anything directly. This gives us a lot of control, since we can implement business or validation rules against any values that the client code attempts to change.

Instance variables declared as Public are accessible to code within our object, but they are also directly accessible to any client code written to use our object. Use of Public instance variables is very bad practice. Any client code can directly manipulate a Public instance variable, without going through any of our object's code. This means our object gives up all control over the value, trusting the author of the client code not to break any rules or do anything that is invalid.

One of the primary principles of object design is **encapsulation**, a concept we'll explore throughout the rest of the book. Encapsulation means that objects should hide their internal design and data from the code that uses them.

`Private` variables help by forcing any client code to use the object's code to change our object's data. This allows us to change how the object is implemented at any time with little or no impact on other programs that use our object. `Public` variables directly break the principal of encapsulation, providing a client with direct and uncontrolled access to an object's data.

## Objects Have Behaviors

Of course, the whole idea behind having an object is so our programs can interact with it. If we're encapsulating an object's data then we need to provide the ability for the client programmer to access the information that the object holds – based on rules and conditions that we define.

The behavior of our object is defined by how we allow the client program to interact with the data – the implementation of our rules and conditions.

One way to think about our objects is to say that they provide a set of *services* that we can use. A *market fund* object, for instance, may provide services that allow us to calculate future earnings or examine what-if scenarios.

These behaviors are implemented by writing code within the class to provide the requested service. Typically our code will interact with at least some of the object's data in order to accomplish the goal.

## Objects Have Interfaces

Objects need to provide an interface to allow their client programs to gain access to these behaviors or services. Just as in the real world, where objects interact - it's our aim in programming with objects to facilitate and control their interaction - via properties, methods and events. These form the **interface** the object presents to the world.

In Visual Basic, an object's interface is composed of `Property`, `Sub` and `Function` routines, as well as any events declared using the `Event` keyword. Any of these routines declared as `Public` within the class module become part of the object's interface.

*In reality, an object can have many interfaces, allowing client code to use the object in different ways as appropriate. We'll cover this in more detail in the next section.*

### Properties

A property is an attribute that describes the object. Objects often have many properties to provide client code with access to all of their attributes.

It's important to consider that an object's properties are not the same as its data. Objects often contain data that wouldn't be considered to be an attribute of the object. For instance, a *Person* object may have an *Age* property, but the underlying data might be a birth date. The birth date itself may or may not be available as a property of the object.

Properties allow us, as the object's designer, to pick and choose which information we want to make available about our object. We can also choose which property values can be changed by our object's users. Some of that information may come directly from our object's data, while other information may come from calculated values or other sources.

So in our earlier box example we may not care to let other programs see the box's dimensions, but we may want them to be able to get at the box's volume:

```
Public Property Get Volume() As Double

   Volume = mdblHeight * mdblWidth * mdblDepth

End Property
```

Visual Basic provides us with three different types of `Property` routines. `Property Get` routines are used to retrieve a property from an object. Then there are two routines to put values into a property, depending on whether the value is a reference to an object or not. `Property Let` routines allow client code to put any value into a property other than a reference to an object, while `Property Set` routines are used only for object references.

Properties can be read-only (`Property Get`), write-only (`Property Let/Set`) or read-write (both properties). Even if we include a `Property Let` or `Property Set` routine for a property, we can include code in that routine to validate the new value or check any other business rules before allowing the client code to change the value.

## Methods

Objects, like their real-world counterparts, need to provide services (or functions) when they interact. Using their own data, or data passed as parameters to a method, they manipulate information to yield a result or to perform a service.

Methods are simply routines that we code within the class to implement the services we want to provide to the users of our object. Some methods return values or provide information back to the calling code. These are called **interrogative methods**. Others, called **imperative methods**, just perform a service and return nothing to the calling code.

In Visual Basic, methods are implemented using `Sub` (for imperative methods) or `Function` (for interrogative methods) routines within the class module that defines our object. `Sub` routines may accept parameters, but they don't return any result value when they are complete. `Function` routines can also accept parameters, and they always generate a result value that can be used by the calling code.

> *The difference between a* `Function` *routine and a* `Property Get` *routine is quite subtle. Both return a value to the calling code and, either way, our object is running a subroutine defined by our class module to return the value.*
>
> *The difference is less programmatic than it is a design choice. We could create all our objects without any* `Property` *routines at all, just using methods for all interactions with the object. However,* `Property` *routines are obviously attributes of the object, while a* `Function` *might be an attribute or a method. By carefully implementing all attributes as* `Property Get` *routines, and any interrogative methods as* `Function` *routines, we will create more readable and understandable code.*

Going back to our now familiar box example, programs may need to open or close the box - so we need to provide a way to do this:

```
Public Sub OpenBox()

   mblnOpen = True

End Sub
```

```
Public Sub CloseBox()

   mblnOpen = False

End Sub
```

With this approach, our client code might look like this:

```
Dim objBox As New Box

objBox.Open
objBox.Close
```

Where this gets more useful is when we add code to check our rules. We shouldn't be able to open an already open box, or close an already closed box. With absolutely no impact to our client code, we can add the following rules to the Box class:

```
Public Sub OpenBox()

   If mblnOpen Then Err.Raise vbObjectError, "Box already open"
   mblnOpen = True

End Sub
```

```
Public Sub CloseBox()

   If Not mblnOpen Then Err.Raise vbObjectError, "Box already closed"
   mblnOpen = False

End Sub
```

In this case, we're simply raising an error if the client code tries to call either the OpenBox method when the box is already open or the CloseBox method when it's already closed. The real key, here, is that the implementation of these methods is totally encapsulated within our class module. We were able to make these changes without having to make any changes to our client code.

### Events

In object-oriented design, the concept of an event is pervasive. In OO parlance, objects act in response to events, such as a user providing a value, or some client code calling one of our object's methods. In the Visual Basic 6.0 environment, we have access to a somewhat different type of event.

Any Visual Basic developer is used to writing code to respond to events. Controls on forms generate events continually, and we write code behind those events to take appropriate action. For instance, a CommandButton control provides a Click event, firing it every time the user clicks on the button. We then write code to respond appropriately:

```
Private Sub Command1_Click()

  MsgBox "The user clicked the button"

End Sub
```

Before Visual Basic 5.0, there was no way for a Visual Basic developer to *cause* events, only to respond to them. Now we can use the Event statement to declare an event and the RaiseEvent command to fire it off.

Going back to our Box class, let's allow the user to stretch our box by implementing a Stretch method:

```
Public Sub Stretch(Percentage As Double)

  mdblHeight = mdblHeight * Percentage
  mdblWidth = mdblWidth * Percentage
  mdblDepth = mdblDepth * Percentage

End Sub
```

As a convenience, perhaps we want to raise an event to let any client programs know that our box has a new size. Visual Basic makes this very easy. We just need to add an Event declaration in the (General) (Declarations) section of our Box class module:

```
Event Stretched()
```

Events are always Public in scope, since they're always raised back to whatever client code has a reference to our object.

With our event declared, we can now fire it off using the RaiseEvent command:

```
Public Sub Stretch(Percentage As Double)

  mdblHeight = mdblHeight * Percentage
  mdblWidth = mdblWidth * Percentage
  mdblDepth = mdblDepth * Percentage

  RaiseEvent Stretched

End Sub
```

We'll go into much more detail about events in Chapter 3.

## *Multiple Interfaces*

So far, we've looked at an object as having a single interface composed of its Public Sub, Function, and Property routines, along with any events it has declared. With Visual Basic 6.0, things are a bit more complex. Our objects can actually have many different interfaces simultaneously, although a client can only use one at a time.

If we create an object from a class we built in Visual Basic, that object will have at least the one interface we defined in our class module. In this simple case, it appears as though our program has direct access to the object, although in reality we're getting at the object through an interface defined by the class:

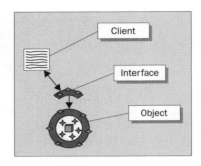

> **With Visual Basic 6.0, a client program never has direct access to an object, only to one of the object's interfaces.**

Sometimes, one interface isn't enough. Our object may represent more than one real world entity, and we need to be able to model this in Visual Basic. For instance, a *Customer* object is great, but a real customer is also a person. To model this in our application, we might need our *Customer* object to also act like a *Person* object from time to time.

To accomplish this, we can just add the *Person* interface to our object. Then a client program can use our object through the *Customer* interface with its set of properties and methods. It might also use the object through the *Person* interface, with its own separate set of properties and methods. This way, the client can use the same object in whichever way is appropriate at any given time:

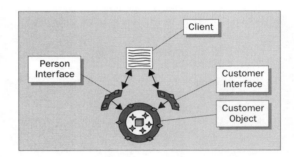

As we've seen, when we create a class in Visual Basic, its Public members comprise the interface for our object. However, we can also use the Implements statement to add another interface to our object. The Implements keyword requires that we supply a class name with which it will work.

With our Box example, for instance, we might also include an interface for a more generic Container class. To do this, we'd need to add an Implements statement in the general declarations section of our Box class module:

```
Implements Container
```

As soon as we add this line, Visual Basic will require that we add code to our class module to implement *all* the Public properties and methods from the Container class. Suppose the Container class module contains a single method, called PutIn, and a property, called IsOpen:

```
Public Sub PutIn(Item As Object)

End Sub
```

```
Public Property Get IsOpen() As Boolean

End Property
```

The property and method may or may not have code in them. Even if they have code, this code would be ignored in the classes using this implementation. We'll discuss this in more detail later when we discuss Inheritance, and we'll cover an interesting solution in the section on Containment and Delegation.

As I've shown them in this example, there's no code. It doesn't really matter to our Box class, since we need to add our own code in the Box class module regardless. For instance, the Box class' implementation of PutIn may add any new items into a Private collection variable, and IsOpen may just return our mblnOpen flag:

```
Option Explicit

Implements Container

Private colItems As New Collection
Private mdblHeight As Double
Private mdblWidth As Double
Private mdblDepth As Double
Private mblnOpen As Boolean

Public Sub OpenBox()

  If mblnOpen Then Err.Raise vbObjectError, "Box already open"
  mblnOpen = True

End Sub

Public Sub CloseBox()

  If Not mblnOpen Then Err.Raise vbObjectError, "Box already closed"
  mblnOpen = False

End Sub

Private Sub Container_PutIn(Item As Object)

  mcolItems.Add Item

End Sub

Private Property Get Container_IsOpen() As Boolean

  Container_IsOpen = mblnOpen

End Property
```

There are a couple of interesting things about these new routines that we've added. First off, they are declared as Private routines, so at first glance they don't appear to be available to any client code. This is deceptive, however, since they are available to clients through the Container interface.

If these routines were declared as `Public`, they'd be part of the `Box` interface. That's not what we are after though. Instead of declaring them as `Public`, we declare them as `Private`, and then indicate that they belong to the `Container` interface by putting `Container_` in front of the name of the routine.

We'll discuss multiple interfaces in more detail later in the book.

# Business Objects

The world around us is made up of both physical objects and abstract concepts. To effectively model or simulate the real world and human processes in our code, it would be good if our software could be made up of representations of these real-world objects. As we have seen in the previous section, object-oriented programs attempt to do just that.

Business objects are designed to represent real 'objects' and concepts in our business. Here are some examples of these real 'objects':

- ❑ An employee
- ❑ A purchased part
- ❑ A manufactured part
- ❑ A work order
- ❑ A customer

All of these are objects in the physical world, and the whole idea behind using software business objects is to create representations of these same objects inside our applications. Then our application can make these objects interact with each other just as they would in the physical world. For instance, an *employee* might create a *work order* to build a *manufactured part* from one or more *purchased parts* that are then sold to the *customer*.

Following this logic, we can create a *work order* business object that contains all the code it needs to manage itself - so we never need to replicate code to create work orders, we just use the object.

Similarly, a *customer* object contains and manages its own data. A well-designed customer object can contain all the data and routines needed to represent a customer throughout an entire business and this can be used across all the applications for that business. We may use our customer object when taking an order. We might later use it when sending out a bulk mailing and analyzing sales patterns - without effecting any of the code that uses the object to take an order. Of course, over time, the customer object may evolve: it may gain new properties or new methods to support more functionality; the point is that the previous properties and methods can and should remain the same, so that existing applications need not be changed.

# Why Use Business Objects?

Having defined the essence of a business object, let's look at the reasons we might want to use them.

# Modeling Our Business

Of course, the reason we're developing applications in the first place is to solve some problem or automate some process. Having a set of abstract objects in software that represent physical objects can simplify this whole process.

As we'll see in Chapter 3, we can identify and design our objects in such a way that they provide a model of our business domain. With our initial identification of these business objects, we can then begin to model the business process we want to automate - or the problem we need to solve.

We can draw a diagram showing how these objects relate or interact with each other in the real world. Using that diagram, we can make our software objects work with each other in the same way. Essentially, we're defining **relationships** between our various business objects, showing how each object calls methods of other objects in order to simulate the real-world process.

This is a very intuitive approach to software development, since our applications become software models of the real world.

We've already started to do this with our description of an employee creating a work order and so forth. If we break that statement down into pieces, we can see a number of similar interactions between these objects:

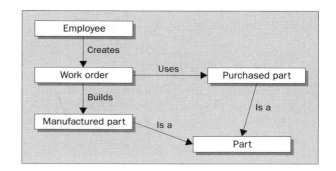

I'll demonstrate the whole process of creating and modeling objects in Chapter 3, when we get into some more specific examples.

> *It is probably worth noting that the objects we're talking about here are* business objects. *There are many other types of objects used during software development, such as database objects, utility objects and user interface objects. Where business objects represent real world concepts or entities such as customers, invoices and so forth, these other objects tend to represent* computer *concepts such as rows in a database or screen widgets.*

# Code Reuse

Most applications developed today are essentially built from scratch. Over and over, we recreate many of the same processes and procedures from earlier programs. Granted, many programmers copy code from existing programs into their new programs, and then modify the copied code to fit any new requirements. But this means that the same code is copied over and over again. If we need to change something in the original code, we'll also have to find and change that same code everywhere it's been used. Which is far from ideal.

*You've probably done this type of code reuse many times over. And you've probably spent countless hours going through dozens of programs making the same code change. Then you've spent hours debugging all the changed programs. Talk about expensive!*

In other situations, code reuse is managed through libraries of code, or maybe even precompiled routines. But even in these cases, code reuse is difficult. In one of the best environments I've ever worked, we had a large and complete library of precompiled routines. By using these routines, we were able to improve dramatically the productivity of our development team.

Still, it wasn't uncommon to run into a program that required a change to our library. Unfortunately, a change to the library required modifying and rebuilding all the applications that relied on the library. Worse yet, sometimes the new functionality required actually going back and changing all the programs that used the library to bring them up to date. This was expensive, and required us to modify what was otherwise stable program code, thereby increasing the risk of bugs.

So copying code helps, but it's far from ideal. Creating libraries of code, or pre-compiled routines, can help a lot; but both techniques still leave a lot to be desired. What we really need is a solution that allows code reuse yet retains the flexibility of selective changes based on the need of the particular application. It would be great if we could derive what we needed and modify or extend the behavior. Fortunately, objects provide just this capability.

## Creating Building Blocks

Traditional programs are centered around the processes and procedures that the program is trying to model. Object-oriented programs, on the other hand, are centered around the real-world objects that the program is trying to model. Once these objects have been identified and modeled, we can write programs that use these objects to simulate the processes and procedures in a much simpler and cleaner way than other programming approaches would accomplish.

If we base our applications on business objects then we'll create a collection of reusable building blocks that we can use time and time again in applications throughout our business. And, perhaps more importantly, we can continue to change and evolve our objects, over time, with little or no impact on the older applications that are already using those objects.

# What are Components?

If you've followed the software industry for long then you'll have realized that object-oriented technology is not exactly new any more. In fact, it's been around for many years; but only now is it really becoming a popular concept in business. Why is that?

There are probably a lot of different reasons, but there is one in particular that we need to explore. As we discussed earlier, a lot of the impetus for new development techniques is to facilitate code reuse. Unfortunately, just creating objects in code isn't enough to maximize reuse.

Until recently, if we had the code for a *Customer* object in one program, and we wanted to use that object in another application, we'd have to copy the *code* into our application. We got to reuse the code, but, if anything changed, we had to find and change each copy of the customer object in all the different applications where it could be in use.

The problem is that as soon as there are two or more different copies of the same code there's no easy way to keep them all synchronized. In many ways, we're back where we started - with simple copy-paste code reuse. At best, we've simply come up with a new way to create source code libraries:

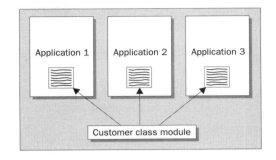

This is where **component-oriented design** comes in. Components build on object technologies to provide a better way of achieving reuse of our objects.

The term **component** is one of those overloaded words that has a different meaning to just about anyone you'd care to ask. Even within the OO community, there's a great deal of disagreement about the meaning of the term. Many people would argue that a component is nothing more than a large or complex business object.

In fact, the terms 'object' and 'component' are often used interchangeably, but there's a distinct and important difference between them:

❑    Objects are created from classes. Classes are made up of source code that defines the object's data and the routines that are needed to manipulate that data. Being made up of source code, classes are language-specific and so they can't be used by programs written in other languages.

❑    Components are precompiled *binary* code. Since components are precompiled, they are independent of the language in which they were created. Essentially a component provides a set of services that are accessed by the clients of the component through one or more interfaces. A single component may consist of a single object or can be made up of multiple objects.

Since we're using a Microsoft development tool to create software for Microsoft operating systems, we'll stick with Microsoft's definition of a component:

> **In their view, components are ActiveX servers or ActiveX controls. They are precompiled units of code that expose one or more interfaces for use by client programs:**

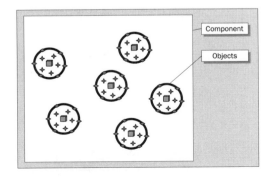

*Even within the Microsoft world you'll find some confusion. To many people, ActiveX controls and components are synonymous. In reality, however, ActiveX controls are merely one type of component, along with various other types of ActiveX servers. We'll look at all these different types of components in the next section.*

*It's even more confusing when you throw in the terms that are used in the MTS environment. Each class module is recognized as a component inside a package. In that case, your component is really what you have shown as an object and the component is the package. We'll discuss MTS and its impact in more detail in Chapter 12.*

With binary components, we can achieve a whole new level of reuse in our applications. Going back to our *Customer* object, we can put the code into our component rather than into each individual application. The applications can then use the object directly from the component:

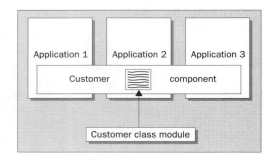

We get the same functionality as when we copied the source code into each application, but now we only need to maintain that code in a single place - the component.

# Component Interfaces

Basically, what we're saying is that a component is a pre-compiled group of objects. Some of these objects can be used by client programs, while others may be hidden from the outside world, available for use only within the component itself. In many ways, a component is like a small application, but one that makes its functionality available for use by other applications.

Earlier, we discussed object interfaces and how they are made up of the object's Public properties, methods, and events. Since a component is really a group of objects, we can then say the component's interface is made up of the public properties and methods of its public objects.

Of course, this implies that there is a way to indicate which of our objects are to be public and which are private. There's no real analog to this concept within traditional object-oriented design.

Object-oriented design typically assumes that any object can interact with any other object within our application. While there may be restrictions on which methods can be invoked on an object, the objects themselves are universally available.

Component-oriented design gives us greater control, since we can not only restrict which methods can be invoked on an object, we can also choose which of our component's objects are available for use by other applications:

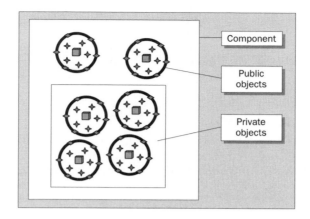

# Types of Components

Components can be designed for use in different areas within our programs. In general, there are three different types of components in an application:

- ❑ Standard/general components
- ❑ Application-specific components
- ❑ Industry-specific components

## Standard/General Components

I like to think of general components as the sort of thing you can buy out of just about any programmer's catalog. In fact, there are many components that are generally available from Windows itself or that come with Visual Basic. These are components that provide services so broadly useful that you can use them just about anywhere. Some good examples include ADO, DAO, RDO, graphing controls, grid controls and mathematical library components.

General components tend to be applicable across a great many different types of applications. For that matter, they tend to be applicable across a great many types of business or other areas where software is developed.

For the most part, we're better off purchasing general components rather than rolling our own. Most companies that sell components make their living off the sales, so the components are likely to be of pretty decent quality. Furthermore, just about any popular type of component will be developed by multiple vendors, so competition will tend to get us better quality and more features as well.

Of course, with Visual Basic 5.0 and later, we can easily create components that are quite general in nature. If we can't find a component that fits our needs then we can just create our own. Better still, if we find a component that's *close* to what we need, we can use it inside a new Visual Basic component and just build on what it provides.

## Application-Specific Components

Each application is unique, and provides some specific functionality. We can put all of those components that belong entirely to an application into the application-specific component category.

Perhaps our program needs to do some specific graphical display, or some complex calculations. These might be built as components - even though they aren't useful to any other applications.

Clearly, since we're not likely to find this type of component on the commercial market, we'll be writing our own. I'll touch on this concept here and there throughout the rest of the book, but the majority of these components will be controls to customize our interface - so they really aren't going to contain business objects.

### Industry-Specific Components

These are components that are targeted at a specific industry, or perhaps a specific area of a business. As we'll discuss later in the chapter, there are a number of efforts underway to develop vertical market components, and those efforts are almost always industry-specific.

Vertical components are less common in the commercial area. Still, if we look around we can find more and more components that fit into this area. Many standalone products are beginning to expose public object interfaces, so we can write our programs to use parts of the product as a component. Products such as accounting systems, or shop floor control systems, can be used as components if they're designed to provide a public interface.

On the other hand, we may find that there simply aren't components for our particular industry to suit our needs. In that case, we'll have to develop our own components for use in our applications.

Business objects really come into play here. By using business objects to build a model of the actual 'objects' used in our industry, we can create very powerful components. It is primarily this type of component that we'll be focusing on throughout the remainder of the book.

# Creating Business Components in Visual Basic

Hopefully, by now, you're beginning to get a solid feel for the benefits that business objects can offer. Business objects provide both code reuse and an understandable, manageable way to model our business processes in our software. With the ability to organize and group our business objects into precompiled binary components, we can fully realize the benefits of this technology.

Visual Basic allows us to create components in a variety of ways, and we can organize our business objects into these components. Using Visual Basic, we can create ActiveX servers, both in-process (DLL's) and out-of-process (EXE's). Additionally, we can create ActiveX controls (OCX's), which are another form of component. Any of these types of component can house our business objects, each type with different strengths and weaknesses.

# Out-of-Process Servers

An out-of-process server is a component that is effectively a separate program containing objects. This type of server will always run in its own process space, and will thus be largely independent from any client programs.

Out-of-process servers may be stand-alone programs that can not only be used directly by a user, but also might provide services to other programs. An excellent example of this is Microsoft Excel, which is a stand-alone application, but can also be used by other applications to provide powerful services.

We might also create out-of-process servers that can't be run directly by a user, but can only be used from other applications. This type of server is very useful if we want to package our business objects into a component, but have the objects running in a process separate from the application that is making use of them.

There are two main ways to build out-of-process servers. We can create the server so that each object runs in its own process, or we can create the server so that all the objects in the server run within a single process.

There are times when we'll want to have our objects running across a number of separate processes. This is often the case when we have a full-blown application that can also be used as a component – we probably want to isolate the objects being run in the application directly by the user from those being used by any other applications. We might also create out-of-process servers when we want to start some task and let it run in the background while the user continues to work with our application.

## *The Cost of Many Processes*

There is a cost to having our objects running across many processes. Most applications require many different business objects to be active all at the same time and, if each object runs in its own process, we'll have a lot of processes running concurrently. Having a great many processes active on a workstation can be devastating to performance.

The Windows operating system does some work every **quantum** (20 milliseconds or so) to determine which process should get to run next. Even if a process is idle, it's still in the list of processes to check, and so the operating system has to do some extra work to check our idle process. If we have a lot of processes, this can add up and become a problem:

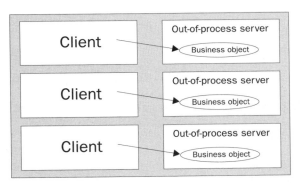

On the other hand, we can create a server where all of our objects exist inside a single process. If we put business objects inside this type of server, all of the objects can work together, sharing resources and memory. Many clients can use the objects in our server, and all the objects from all those clients can easily communicate and work with each other inside the same process:

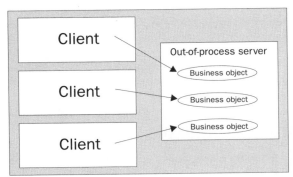

### *The Cost of Cross-Process Communication*

Either type of out-of-process server suffers from one very significant drawback: performance.

All Windows components use the Component Object Model (COM) to allow communication with objects in other processes. We'll discuss COM in more detail later in the chapter. For now, all we need to know is that COM handles all communication between objects in different processes.

Unfortunately, COM imposes a very high overhead on each call from one process to another (cross-process calls). Therefore, on each reference to a property and each call to a method, we take the hit of this overhead - and performance can suffer substantially.

There are techniques that can be used to help minimize the impact of this overhead, and I'll demonstrate those later in the book.

# In-Process Servers

An in-process server is a component where our objects run inside the *client's* process. From the client's viewpoint it has its own private copy of our component - and therefore a copy of all our objects. In reality the server's code may be shared among any number of clients running on the same machine, but each client program has its own set of data, thus giving the appearance that each client has its own copy of the server.

In-process servers avoid the overhead of running in their own process, thus conserving resources and memory for the system. Additionally, the communication between the client and our objects does not have to go from one process to another - and so we avoid almost all of the overhead imposed by COM on out-of-process server communication:

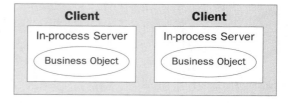

Since in-process components run inside the client's process, we use less memory and we don't create extra processes. We'll also improve performance, but we do give up some capabilities. Since each server is running in each client's process space, our business objects are effectively split up - so they can't share resources or memory with each other, but only with each client.

By judicious use of out-of-process servers combined with in-process servers, we can create applications that draw on the strengths of each. I will demonstrate this at various points throughout the book.

# ActiveX Controls

Finally, let's look at ActiveX controls. These are yet another type of component, but one that's typically used to create visual objects as part of an interface design. Some ActiveX controls are invisible; but if we get right down to it, there's very little difference between an invisible ActiveX control and a regular in-process server.

Business objects can be placed in an ActiveX control just as easily as they can be placed in an in-process server. Many developers may find it easier to work with objects packaged in this type of component, since they can literally drop the component on a form and work with it from there - just as if it were a regular control.

Also, ActiveX controls can be very powerful in a Web application. Microsoft's Internet Explorer will automatically download and install controls. This makes it easy to include a control into a Web page and then use the objects contained within the control.

One significant drawback to ActiveX controls is that they require our client programs to have at least one form that can be a container to hold the control. More than simply having to include the form in the project, we actually have to have the form loaded in memory in order to gain access to the objects inside the control. This is somewhat less efficient than getting the objects directly from an in-process server.

# Fitting Business Objects into Applications

Now that we've established what business objects are, and we've explored the different types of components that can contain them, we need to look at just where the objects fit into our typical application. We'll discuss this in much more detail in Chapter 2, but it will be useful to take a quick, high-level look at some different application models, and where business objects fit into them.

> *For the client/server experts reading this, I should point out that we're really blurring the lines between the physical and logical models in this overview. In each case, I'm really proposing a 3-tier logical model; but it is useful to see where everything falls physically regardless. In Chapter 2, we'll be more precise, as we get into more detail on the architecture we'll use throughout the book.*

## Single-Tier Applications

A single-tier application is the simplest of the models that we'll look at. This type of application is simply a program that runs on the user's machine. It might talk to a database, but that database resides on the same machine (or perhaps on a mapped network drive). The key thing, here, is that all the work takes place on the same machine: the user interface, business- and data-processing are all on the user's computer.

A diagram of this type of application would look like this:

Now let's look at where the business objects fit into the picture:

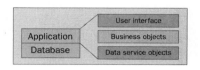

In this type of application, everything is pretty simple. Since our entire application is running on a single machine, the business objects just fit right into the application.

Don't worry about the data service objects just yet. We'll discuss what they are and what they do in Chapter 2. For now, just look at them as being the code that communicates between business objects and the database.

# Two-Tier Client/Server

The simplest type of distributed computing is two-tier client/server. In this type of application, the data processing is moved off the user's machine and on to a dedicated database server machine. The two-tier client/server is the most common type of client/server application built today. It offers significant benefits over a single-tier application, since the processing of data is centralized and becomes a shared resource between all the users:

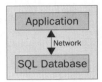

Still, with two-tier client/server, the only work that has really been moved off the user's machine is the data management - storing and retrieving data. The user-interface and any processing done by the application frequently remain pretty much where they were.

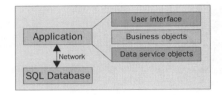

*While there are certainly applications where processing has been moved from the application to the database server, in this scenario we are relegated to using SQL to write our business code – not the most pleasant prospect when compared to more powerful languages such as Visual Basic.*

The primary difference lies in the role of the data service objects. In this model, they have to do much less work, since a lot of the data processing is moved to the database server - usually in the form of stored procedures and triggers written in SQL. Again, we'll talk in more detail about these data service objects in Chapter 2.

# Three-tier Client/Server

Over time it has become apparent that a two-tier client/server is simply not powerful enough or flexible enough to handle many larger applications. Since each client workstation maintains a dialog with the central database server, the network traffic can be quite high. Furthermore, the central database server can become a performance bottleneck - as many users try to access the same resources at the same time.

Three-tier client/server helps address these issues by putting another physical server between the users and the database. This central **application server** can more efficiently manage network traffic and the load on the database server. In many cases we also have a faster network connection between the application server and the database server, making our application even more efficient.

Better still, it's typically much easier to add more application servers than it is to add more database servers. Adding a database server would require us to split our data between the database servers, whereas adding an application server should just require some relatively minor changes to parts of our application:

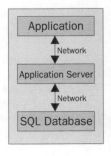

Just like two-tier client/server, the data processing is handled primarily on the database server. However, we now have an application server that can do a lot of work. This means that we can move a substantial part of our application off the user's workstation and onto the application server.

There are a number of benefits to distributed processing, including:

❑ Centralization of shared resources
❑ Rich, flexible client interfaces to the data
❑ Spreading our workload across various machines
❑ Putting processing in the most efficient location possible

How much processing is moved to the application server may vary. It depends on many factors, but mostly we need to decide how much work we want our client workstations to do. Designs range from having the client workstation do virtually nothing (a 'thin' client) to the client workstation doing almost everything (a 'fat' or 'thick' client). We'll discuss the pros and cons of each approach in Chapter 2.

As I've shown it in this diagram, much of our business logic remains on the user workstation. In Chapter 2, we'll explore why it can be very beneficial to have the business objects on the client workstation as shown here.

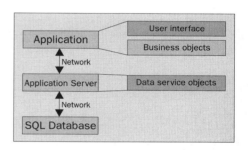

# Browser-based Applications

The models that I've presented so far leave a fair amount of the application on the client workstation. Applications designed for the World Wide Web have traditionally taken an entirely different approach. Web applications have typically put as little of the application as is physically possible on the client, and kept all the processing centralized on one or more servers:

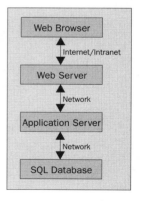

Visual Basic 6.0 provides us with powerful support for this type of application in a couple different ways. We can create components that can be used by Active Server Pages or other COM-compliant scripting tools (such as Cold Fusion). We can also create a new type of server-side application called an Internet Information Server (IIS) Application directly from within Visual Basic. IIS Applications are a very powerful approach we can use when creating server-based applications and we'll discuss them in some detail in Chapter 14.

Perhaps even more exciting, Visual Basic 6.0 allows us to create another new type of application called a DHTML Application. DHTML Applications are very similar to a traditional Visual Basic application, but instead of using Visual Basic forms as an interface, they use Internet Explorer, DHTML and the Document Object Model (DOM). This type of application allows us to leverage all the powerful capabilities of Visual Basic on the client workstation and still take advantage of the attractive capabilities we gain with a browser-based user interface. We'll discuss DHTML Applications further in Chapter 15.

## Traditional Browser-Based Applications

In a traditional browser-based application the browser has merely provided a terminal-style user-interface and so the vast bulk of our application needs to run on the server:

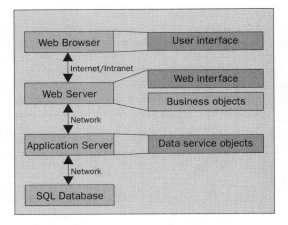

In this figure, we still have an interface, our business objects, and our services. What we've done is moved virtually everything down to the server, leaving a *very* light user interface on the user's workstation.

The big difference is that instead of a *user*-interface on top of our business objects, we now have a *web*-interface. This is a layer of code that interacts with the web server to communicate with the client. The web-interface is basically a layer of 'glue' between the business objects and the HTML that gets sent to the user's browser.

The web interface provides HTML to the browser via the web server and accepts the user's input through the browser and web-server. There are many technologies available to build this web interface - including CGI, ISAPI, Active Server Pages and others.

There are some other fairly significant issues with this type of architecture. In Chapter 13, we'll implement a browser-based user-interface using Active Server Pages as the glue between the business objects and the web server.

## IIS Applications

IIS Applications are a new way to implement browser-based applications. They provide us with the ability to create applications that run under Microsoft Internet Information Server in a manner very similar to what we may have created using Active Server Pages. With IIS Applications, however, we are creating our application entirely with Visual Basic 6.0.

In terms of our overall application architecture, IIS Applications don't appear to be much different than applications created with older technologies such as ASP. However, instead of using a mix of HTML and some scripting language to create our browser-based user interface, we can use the new capabilities provided by IIS Applications:

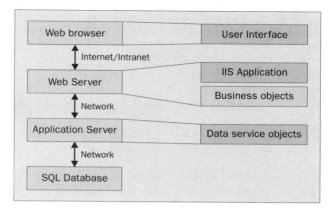

We'll cover IIS Applications in more detail in Chapter 14.

## DHTML Applications

One of the biggest limitations of browser-based applications is that the user interface has been derived almost entirely from HTML. HTML allows us to create very visually attractive interfaces, but they have the drawback of being very batch oriented. The users enter in whatever data they care to on a screen, click a button and then find out whether any of what they entered was valid. Very much like the old 3270 terminals of mainframe fame, but with more color.

Visual Basic 6.0 lets us create a new type of application to help make our browser-based user interfaces more robust: DHTML Applications. This type of application allows us to create a browser-based interface using DHTML, but with the full power and capabilities of Visual Basic running right there under the browser. This way we can take advantage of all the benefits of a DHTML interface, and all the benefits of a Visual Basic client application.

With a more advanced and capable user interface we can have access to a wide variety of architectures for our applications. One such architecture might be demonstrated by the following diagram:

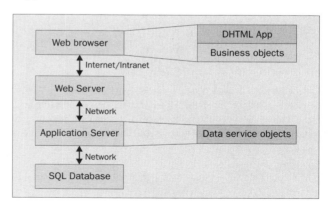

Many other possibilities exist, including the merger of DHTML Applications on the client with IIS Applications on the web server. All the possibilities are outside the scope of this book, though we will create a DHTML Application later in Chapter 15.

With all these varied architectural possibilities one thing is clear: our business logic may need to be placed on the client, an application server or even on the database server depending on our requirements. There are benefits and drawbacks to each choice we might make in this regard. In any case, to make our application perform well we'll need to make some hard design choices regarding how we implement our business objects.

# Object-based vs. Object-oriented Approaches

Visual Basic has always been object-based, meaning that we could always use objects in our programs; but the language provided no way to create objects until Visual Basic 4.0.

Perhaps it would be more accurate to say that it has always been component-based, since, until Visual Basic 4.0, we've been unable to use objects per se but rather we've used pre-built binary components.

Originally, these components came in the form of VBX's (Visual Basic Custom Controls), which really set the stage for where we are today. VBX components provided us with pre-built functionality that we could just plug into our programs and start using. They were so useful, in fact, that an entire cottage industry grew up around them - and various development tools have now been enhanced to support their use.

Unfortunately, VBX technology was pretty limiting in a number of ways. VBX controls were difficult to create, and the way they communicated with Visual Basic was strict and somewhat limited. Because of these problems, Microsoft developed a new standard for component development. These new components were called OLE Controls, and are now called ActiveX controls. Either way, they are commonly known as OCX's (OLE Custom Controls).

Visual Basic 4.0 added a number of actual object-oriented abilities to the language, by adding the *class module,* and allowing us to create objects based on our own classes. In version 5.0, we gained even more capabilities with the addition of the `Friend` and `Implements` keywords, along with the ability to raise our own events - all of which we'll discuss in detail later in the book.

We've been able to create our own components since Visual Basic 4.0. This has given us the ability to easily package our objects together into reusable binary modules, as we discussed earlier in the chapter.

Most people look at four criteria when deciding if a language is object-oriented. These criteria are **abstraction, encapsulation, inheritance** and **polymorphism**. Let's look briefly at each of these from a Visual Basic viewpoint. I don't want to get into too much detail here, since there are entire books written about this subject alone; but I do want to quickly illustrate where Visual Basic stands.

# Abstraction

Abstraction is the process by which we can think about specific properties or behaviors without thinking about a particular object that has those properties or behaviors. We know that most cars have four wheels, a steering wheel and an engine, without thinking of any particular car, or how the internals of the engine operates.

Abstraction allows us to recognize how things are similar and ignore differences - to think in general terms, and not the specifics. A TextBox control is an abstraction, because we can place it on a form, and then tailor it to our needs by setting properties. Visual Basic allows us to define abstractions using class modules.

Any language that allows a developer to create a class from which objects can be instantiated meets this criteria, and Visual Basic is no exception. We can easily create a class to represent a car, essentially providing an abstraction. We can then create instances of that class, where each object can have its own attributes such that it represents a specific automobile.

# Encapsulation

Encapsulation is the concept that an object should totally separate its interface from its implementation. Another way to put this is that an object should be a 'black box'.

This means that an object should completely contain any data it requires, and that it should also contain all the code required to manipulate that data. Programs should interact with our object through an interface, using properties and methods. Client code should never work directly with the data owned by the object.

> *In object-speak, programs interact with objects by sending messages to the object. These messages are generated by other objects, or by external sources such as the user. The way the object reacts to these messages is through methods. What Visual Basic calls properties would otherwise be called attributes.*

Visual Basic has provided full support for encapsulation through class modules since version 4.0. Using these modules, we can create classes that entirely hide their internal data and code, providing a well-established interface of properties and methods to the outside world.

For example, if we create a class module and add the following code:

```
Option Explicit

Public Property Set Form(Target As Form)

End Property

Public Property Let CurrentX(X As Single)

End Property

Public Property Let CurrentY(Y As Single)

End Property
```

Then we've created an interface for the class. From here, we could do virtually anything in terms of *implementing* the class. For instance, we could just store the values:

```
Option Explicit

Private mfrmForm As Form
Private msngX As Single
Private msngY As Single
```

```
Public Property Set Form(Target As Form)

   Set mfrmForm = Target

End Property

Public Property Let CurrentX(X As Single)

   msngX = X

End Property

Public Property Let CurrentY(Y As Single)

   msngY = Y

End Property
```

Or maybe we just want to move to the coordinates:

```
Option Explicit

Private mfrmForm As Form

Public Property Set Form(Target As Form)

   Set mfrmForm = Target

End Property

Public Property Let CurrentX(X As Single)

   mfrmForm.CurrentX = X

End Property

Public Property Let CurrentY(Y As Single)

   mfrmForm.CurrentY = Y

End Property
```

Either way, we haven't changed the *interface* of the class, and so any program working with this class would have no idea if we have switched from one implementation to the other. This is the essence of encapsulation.

> *Obviously, the user might have a problem if we made such a change to our object. If applications were developed expecting the first set of behaviors, and then we changed to the second, there could be some interesting side effects. However, the point here is that the client programs would continue to function, even if the results were quite different than when we started.*

We'll be making heavy use of encapsulation throughout this book, so you'll become very familiar with it if you haven't seen it before.

# Polymorphism

Polymorphism is often considered to be directly tied to inheritance (which we'll discuss next). In reality, however, it's independent to a large degree. Polymorphism means that we can have two classes with different implementations or code, but with the same interface. We can then write a program that operates upon that interface and doesn't care about which type of object it operates at runtime.

## Polymorphism through Late Binding

For example, if we have a class called Square and another one called Cowboy then they may both have a method called Draw. We can write a program that tells an object to draw by calling the Draw method. This program won't care if it is working with a Square or a Cowboy - even though each object must obviously implement the Draw method differently.

If the Square class contains the following code:

```
Option Explicit

Public Sub Draw(Target As Form)

  Target.Line Step(0, 0)-Step(0, 100)
  Target.Line Step(0, 0)-Step(100, 0)
  Target.Line Step(0, 0)-Step(0, -100)
  Target.Line Step(0, 0)-Step(-100, 0)

End Sub
```

And the Cowboy class contains this code:

```
Option Explicit

Public Sub Draw(Target As Form)

  Target.Print "Draw from holster"
  Target.Print "Aim"
  Target.Print "Fire"

End Sub
```

Then we can put this routine in a form:

```
Public Sub DoDraw(SomeObject As Object)

  SomeObject.Draw Me

End Sub
```

This routine doesn't care if it's passed a Square or a Cowboy, even though the two classes are implemented in an entirely different fashion. Notice that the routine accepts a parameter of type Object. By doing this, we have allowed the routine to accept literally any object we care to send it. This simple example of polymorphism works in Visual Basic 4.0 and later – including 6.0.

Visual Basic implements polymorphism in the same manner as Smalltalk, by using something called **late binding**. We've just seen an example of late binding with the Draw method of the Square and Cowboy objects.

Late binding means that the Visual Basic compiler makes no effort to determine if calls to our objects' are valid. All the checking takes place while the program is running. Each call to an object is checked as it's called, and an error is raised if the call turns out to be invalid.

## Polymorphism with Early Binding

Visual Basic not only provides this ability, but also implements a stricter form of polymorphism (similar to that found in C++) through its support of **interface inheritance** using the Implements keyword.

For example, if we create a Shape class with the following code:

```
Option Explicit

Public Sub Draw(Target As Form)

End Sub
```

Then we can use Shape as a base to create a Square class:

```
Option Explicit

Implements Shape

Public Sub Shape_Draw(Target As Form)

  Target.Line Step(0, 0)-Step(0, 100)
  Target.Line Step(0, 0)-Step(100, 0)
  Target.Line Step(0, 0)-Step(0, -100)
  Target.Line Step(0, 0)-Step(-100, 0)

End Sub
```

And we can also create a Circle class, again using the Shape class as a base class:

```
Option Explicit

Implements Shape

Public Sub Shape_Draw(Target As Form)

  Target.Circle Step(0, 0), 200

End Sub
```

With these classes defined, we can try them out. The following code accepts a parameter and then calls its Draw method:

```
Public Sub DrawShape(objSomeShape As Shape)

    objSomeShape.Draw Me

End Sub
```

Notice the difference between this example and the previous one with the `Square` and `Cowboy` classes. Instead of accepting an `Object` type as a parameter, we're now able to accept a parameter of type `Shape`. We've ensured that the only objects passed to our routine will be shapes. Since we'd probably never use the `Shape` class as a base to build a `Cowboy` class, we don't have to worry about getting a `Cowboy` when we wanted a `Square` or `Circle`.

This uses **early binding**. Early binding occurs as the program is being compiled, which means that the compiler can help us out by doing type checking and by verifying that the properties and methods we call on the object are valid.

# Inheritance

Inheritance is the concept that a new class can be based on an existing class, inheriting its interface and functionality from the original class. With inheritance, a class gains all the properties and methods that make up the interface of the base class, and it can then extend the interface by adding properties and methods of its own. The new class can also extend or change the implementation of each of the properties and methods from the original base class.

For instance, if we had a class called *Fruit* that had all the properties and methods which apply to all types of fruit, then inheritance would make it very easy to create classes for *Apple*, *Orange* and so forth. We wouldn't have to recreate all the code for an apple to be a fruit: it would get that automatically from the original *Fruit* class.

## Interface Inheritance

Visual Basic 6.0 doesn't directly support the concept of inheritance. It does provide something called **interface inheritance** using the `Implements` keyword. We've already used this keyword when we discussed polymorphism, but it can be applied here to help simulate a form of inheritance.

Interface inheritance lets us inherit the interface of one class into a new class. The downside is that all we get is the interface, not the original object's data or behavior. Worse still, we can't extend an interface created with the `Implements` keyword. One of the key benefits of inheritance is the ability to extend the base interface, so this is a substantial drawback.

If we look at a `Fruit` class, we'll find an interface that includes elements appropriate for any type of fruit. In this example, we've got a growing climate, the color for the fruit and bites:

```
Option Explicit

Public Property Get GrowingClimate() As String

End Property
```

```
Public Property Get Color() As String

End Property
```

```
Public Property Get Bites() As Integer

End Property
```

Notice that there's no code in the routines shown here. That's because all we'll be inheriting is the interface; any code in these routines wouldn't be used anyway.

Now we can create a new class, `Apple`, and inherit the interface from the `Fruit` class by using the `Implements` keyword:

```
Option Explicit

Implements Fruit

Private Property Get Fruit_GrowingClimate() As String

  Fruit_GrowingClimate = "Moderate"

End Property

Private Property Get Fruit_Color() As String

  Fruit_Color = "Red"

End Property

Private Property Get Fruit_Bites() As Integer

  Fruit_Bites = 20

End Property
```

Earlier in the chapter, we discussed multiple interfaces and how the `Implements` keyword works. Instead of declaring `GrowingClimate`, `Color` and `Bites` directly, we need to make them `Private` in scope and put `Fruit_` in front of each name so Visual Basic knows that these routines belong to the `Fruit` interface.

We might also create an `Orange` class, again based on the `Fruit` interface:

```
Option Explicit

Implements Fruit

Private Property Get Fruit_GrowingClimate() As String

  Fruit_GrowingClimate = "Warm"

End Property
```

```
Private Property Get Fruit_Color() As String

  Fruit_Color = "Orange"

End Property
```

```
Private Property Get Fruit_Bites() As Integer

  Fruit_Bites = 20

End Property
```

Now, contrary to what we'd expect, we can write code to compare apples and oranges:

```
Public Function CompareColor(AnApple As Fruit, AnOrange As Fruit)

  CompareColor = (AnApple.Color = AnOrange.Color)

End Function
```

More importantly, we've created two different classes, both having inherited the same interface from `Fruit`. This is a very powerful technique when we have otherwise dissimilar classes that have a number of the same interface elements. We can write client code to treat all the objects the same - even though they are different.

Unfortunately, this technique doesn't allow us to extend the interface, and so it's less a way to implement inheritance than it is to implement polymorphism, as in the last section. The `Orange` class can't add properties or methods to its version of the `Fruit` interface. This limits our flexibility, and really prevents us from using this to simulate full-blown inheritance.

## Containment and Delegation

Fortunately, it's possible, with a little extra work, to roll our own inheritance using Visual Basic - and thus gain many of the advantages we'd get in other languages that fully support inheritance. This is achieved by combining a concept called **containment** with another called **delegation**.

Containment is the idea that an object can have a private instance of another object inside itself. Were we to have a *Human* object, it might **contain** a *Heart* object. The *Heart* object would be private to the *Human* object, since no client code would normally interact with the *Heart*.

Delegation means that one object delegates work to another object rather than doing the work itself. If our *Human* object has a *PulseRate* property, it might ask the *Heart* object for the rate rather than figuring it out by itself. It has effectively delegated the responsibility for the *PulseRate* to the *Heart* object.

If we combine these two concepts, we can simulate inheritance. Let's look at how that can work with our fruit example.

Again, we'll create a class called `Fruit`; but this time we'll put some code in the `GrowingClimate` routine. With inheritance, we'd expect to be able to use this behavior in any new classes we create based on `Fruit`:

```
Option Explicit

Public Property Get GrowingClimate() As String

  GrowingClimate = "Moderate"

End Property
```

```
Public Property Get Color() As String

End Property
```

```
Public Property Get Bites() As Integer

End Property
```

Now we'll create an `Apple` class, but this time we won't use the `Implements` keyword. Instead, we'll manually recreate the interface from the `Fruit` class - with absolutely no changes to the declarations of either property:

```
Option Explicit

Private objFruit As New Fruit

Public Property Get GrowingClimate() As String

  GrowingClimate = objFruit.GrowingClimate

End Property
```

```
Public Property Get Color() As String

  Color = "Red"

End Property
```

```
Public Property Get Bites() As Integer

  Bites = 20

End Property
```

The first thing you might notice is that we're creating a `Private` `Fruit` object within our new class. Our new `Apple` class is using the concept of containment to have an instance of the `Fruit` class inside itself:

```
Private objFruit As New Fruit
```

In the `GrowingClimate` routine, our new `Apple` class just delegates the work down to the private `Fruit` object:

```
GrowingClimate = objFruit.GrowingClimate
```

Now let's create an `Orange` class by following the same technique:

```
Option Explicit

Private objFruit As New Fruit

Public Property Get GrowingClimate() As String

    GrowingClimate = "Warm"

End Property

Public Property Get Color() As String

    Color = "Orange"

End Property

Public Property Get Bites() As Integer

    Bites = 16

End Property

Public Property Get Slices() As Integer

    Slices = Bites / 2

End Property
```

Since the `GrowingClimate` for an `Orange` is different, it doesn't delegate that call down to the `Fruit` object. Instead, it replaces, or overrides, the functionality by implementing the routine itself.

We have also extended the interface for our `Orange` object by adding a `Slices` property. While we've simulated the inheritance of the `GrowingClimate`, `Color` and `Bites` properties, we're also able to extend the interface as needed for each specific class.

Back to our client code, which compares apples and oranges, we need to change how we accept our parameters:

```
Public Function CompareColor(AnApple As Object, AnOrange As Object)

    CompareColor = (AnApple.Color = AnOrange.Color)

End Function
```

The code within this routine is the same as we had before, but now our parameters are of type `Object` instead of type `Fruit`. Since our new classes don't use the `Implements` keyword, we can't have Visual Basic treat these objects like a `Fruit` object.

However, we do know that they have the same set of properties and methods, and so we can write our code to treat them identically. We just need to tell Visual Basic that they are generic objects rather than objects of a specific class.

# COM - The Plumbing Behind the Scenes

The Component Object Model (COM) is Microsoft's standard for object interaction.

> COM provides a standard mechanism by which objects and components can communicate, independent of the language in which the components were created.

Other major Windows technologies rely on COM to function. The two most notable of these technologies are OLE (Object Linking and Embedding) and ActiveX. These both use COM to facilitate all the interaction between objects. OLE uses COM to communicate between applications, allowing users to link or embed parts of one application's data and display into another application. ActiveX is broader, using COM to support communication between controls, in-process, and out-of-process servers.

Microsoft has designed Visual Basic to fit seamlessly into COM. Components created with Visual Basic are ActiveX components, which means that they use COM to communicate with each other and with their client programs. In many other languages, it can be very complex to create components that fit into this model, but Visual Basic takes care of all that complexity behind the scenes.

Distributed COM (DCOM) extends the communication capabilities across the network. With DCOM, any COM object can transparently communicate with COM objects on other machines over the network. This works with components created in Visual Basic as well, which means that Visual Basic developers can create objects and distribute them across the network with very little effort.

Visual Basic 6.0's object capabilities are very well matched to those of COM. COM objects typically have multiple interfaces and, as we've seen, Visual Basic objects can have multiple interfaces using the `Implements` keyword. COM, like Visual Basic, has no direct support for inheritance, but instead relies upon aggregation so we can group objects together to provide more complex functionality. Because Visual Basic 6.0's capabilities are so closely matched with COM's capabilities, it's an ideal development tool when we're working in a COM environment.

# Other Industry Efforts

DCOM isn't the only distributed object platform on the market, so we'll take a quick look at a couple of other options, mainly to try and see how important communicating components and business objects are in modern computing.

## CORBA

The Object Management Group (OMG) is a consortium of companies that have banded together to develop an object communication standard. The Common Object Request Broker Architecture (CORBA) is a standard that competes with Microsoft's Component Object Model (COM) in many ways.

The various companies involved, and the industry press, tend to dwell on the differences between the two competing standards. While it's true that there are differences, what I want to emphasize here is the similarities between these standards.

Both CORBA and COM provide standardized mechanisms for objects to communicate with each other. They specify how components and applications can be built in a distributed and organized fashion. CORBA, like DCOM, provides for communication between objects distributed across a network, providing for complex multi-tiered applications based on the standard.

Perhaps most importantly, CORBA and COM both encourage the use of business objects in their architectures. And they both advocate a separation of business rules from the presentation layer, in such a way that the main application logic is contained in an object model that's largely independent of the user-interface.

# Vertical Market Groups

Another major effort underway by various companies and organizations is the creation of business object frameworks that support specific vertical markets, such as IBM's San Francisco initiative. These are collections or groups of objects that are built to service specific business needs.

For instance, a vendor might build an object framework that encompasses the typical requirements of managing a shop floor in a factory. The vendor can then market their framework to companies who are building shop floor control software. These companies can then base their software development on the pre-existing business objects, extending or modifying them as needed to meet their specific business needs.

It remains to be seen whether this type of object framework will be viable in the marketplace. While many business processes are generally similar from company to company, it is also true that every company is unique. The level of modification required to take a framework and make it useful in a given situation could be quite large, and it could offset the benefits to be gained.

# Summary

In this chapter, we've introduced the concepts that will be covered through the remainder of the book. At this point, you should have a good understanding of what business objects are - and why they're so important to the future of software development. You should also have a general understanding of component technology and how business objects can be managed and distributed through components.

From here, we'll explore these concepts in more practical detail. We'll look at:

- ❑ The design and creation of business objects
- ❑ How these objects fit into our applications
- ❑ How business objects interact with the user-interface
- ❑ How business objects interact with the database
- ❑ How business objects can interact with each other

# Application Architecture with Business Objects

## Overview

In Chapter 1, we ran through a quick overview of what business objects are and why they're so important to software development. We also took a brief look at the concept of component-oriented design, which allows us to group business objects together into reusable binary components.

In this chapter, we'll review traditional Visual Basic development techniques, and see how business objects and components can improve the way we develop software.

Traditional Visual Basic development is very fast and very powerful, but it doesn't necessarily lend itself very well to large and complex applications. Using the capabilities of objects and components, we can more easily create and maintain very complex applications. The best part of this is that we can continue to leverage our existing Visual Basic skills, because working with business objects is really an evolutionary change rather than an entirely revolutionary approach.

The most significant change in our development, when we use objects, is that we follow a somewhat different architecture than we've used in traditional development. As we go through this chapter, we'll be looking at traditional Visual Basic architectures and the impact of business objects and binary components upon those traditional architectures.

Most large applications are implemented in a client/server environment, with the application's processing spread across a number of machines, including the user's workstation, a database server, and possibly an application server that sits in the middle. We'll look at this type of architecture, and see how we can use our business objects to take full advantage of all these machines.

# Building Applications with Components

To begin with, let's take a quick look at some of the key techniques and concepts we've used to develop applications in the past, and how these traditional techniques can be used when we're working with business objects. Most of these techniques will carry over, though sometimes there will be some subtle differences.

## Event-Driven Programming

Visual Basic programming (and Windows programming, more generally) is almost entirely geared towards event-driven programming. This means that our programs are typically composed of subroutines that are run only in response to external events - such as a mouse click. It's a rare Windows program that runs a series of procedures from top to bottom and is done.

Most mini-computer, mainframe and DOS-based applications were sequential in nature. They gathered the user's input in a specific order, processed it, and generated specific output. This was all very predictable, since the application itself was very much in control.

In an event-driven environment, such as Windows, our applications effectively give control over to the user. The user gets to choose in which order they want to enter any input, when it should be processed and often how and where the results should be displayed. Rather than being in control, our application code sits in the background waiting for the user to indicate what should be done.

For instance, let's look at how we might get input from the user. In a sequential application, we'd prompt the user for input when we needed it. In some form of DOS BASIC, that process might look like this:

```
Print "Name? ";
Input strName
Print "Age? ";
Input intAge
Call DoProcessing(strName, intAge)
```

Here, the program is in control: it asks the user for each bit of information in turn, and the user has no choice but to follow the program's flow from top to bottom.

Within Visual Basic, the approach is entirely different. We display a form to the user, allowing them to choose into which field, if any, they want to enter information:

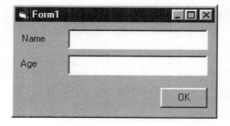

Our code, rather than being a single sequential list of commands, now becomes a series of subroutines that are only run when specific events occur. For instance, as the user enters values into each text box on the screen, we may react to the input events and store the values in variables:

```
Private Sub txtName_Change()

    strName = txtName

End Sub
```

```
Private Sub txtAge_Change()

    intAge = Val(txtAge)

End Sub
```

Then, in response to the Click event caused when the user clicks the OK button, we might perform some processing:

```
Private Sub cmdOK_Click()

    DoProcessing(strName, intAge)

End Sub
```

Either approach gets the job done, but the event-driven approach turns a lot of control back over to the user. This is, generally, a positive thing: users usually like to have a choice about how they use their applications.

## Events and Objects

Event-driven programming works well when we're dealing with objects. This is because an event is basically a type of message. When the user clicks on a button, our program gets a message saying, "*Hey, the user clicked the button*". Of course, the message comes to us in the form of an event - in this case, the Click event for our button. Still, what we basically received was a message that something happened.

When we're dealing with objects, we always interact with an object through its interface; that is, its properties and methods. When we call an object's method, we do so by *sending it a message*. This may not be very obvious, since, within our code, it looks as if we just called a method on the object. Take this line of code, for example:

```
objCustomer.CreateInvoice
```

This code *looks* like a call to the CreateInvoice subroutine within the Customer class module. However, it's important to remember, when dealing with objects, that this kind of code actually sends a CreateInvoice *message* to the objCustomer object.

Our objects react to such events in the same way that Visual Basic programs have always reacted to events: using an event-handler subroutine:

```
Public Sub CreateInvoice()

    ' create the invoice here

End Sub
```

Any time we interact with an object, we're doing so by sending it a message. From the object's perspective, a message is basically an event caused by some outside force (typically, our program's code or some other object), and so our objects are always driven by events - just like our traditional Visual Basic applications.

# Code Behind Forms

In traditional Visual Basic applications, most programs have tended to respond to the events caused by the user - through the forms and controls that we've provided on our forms. So it's been very common to find the code to handle these events directly behind the controls that raise them.

Many developers have therefore written the bulk of their code in the subroutines that run when particular events fire:

```
Private Sub cmdButton_Click()

  ' do all the work here

End Sub
```

Meanwhile, other developers have tended to call centralized subroutines in the module's General section, or subroutines that have been placed in a separate code module:

```
Private Sub cmdButton_Click()

  DoWork()

End Sub
```

```
Private Sub DoWork()

  ' do all the work here

End Sub
```

Either way, the results have been the same: Visual Basic code has been directly invoked by the events raised in the user-interface (UI).

Putting code behind events from the UI hasn't provided us with much potential for code reuse. The most that we've been able to hope for is to use code modules - so that we can call our code from multiple forms.

However, to use code in other projects, we've had to copy original code into our new projects, causing duplicate code and maintenance problems down the line. Another approach has been to include the same code module in multiple projects; but then we run the risk that modifying the code in the module will break any other programs that rely on the module. Even if we don't break the programs, they need to be recompiled and redistributed to take advantage of our changes.

By designing our applications with business objects and components, we now have the opportunity to make it significantly easier to reuse our code. Instead of trying to reuse source code, we can package that code into binary components and use those components anywhere we need them.

If we create a component that provides some key functionality - everything to do with our customers, for instance - then we can use that component in any program that needs to deal with customers. As long as we are careful not to change or remove any properties or methods from our objects, we can change or add anything we want to our customer component with little risk of breaking existing programs.

> **As long as we don't change our object's Interface, we can change its implementation all we'd like and our client programs are guaranteed to be able to continue using the object.**

# Access to Data

Most business applications deal with data. Traditional Visual Basic applications have implemented code to work directly with the database. The database could be local, or on a mapped network drive, such as a Microsoft Access database. Others would be maintained by an actual database server such as Microsoft SQL Server or Oracle.

Visual Basic hasn't always had easy access to databases. In fact, it wasn't until Visual Basic 3.0 that we had easy access to databases - through a data access model and the infamous data control. Using the JET database engine, we could finally open up databases and work with the data using native elements of the Visual Basic language. Through JET we even had access to SQL database servers through Open Database Connectivity (ODBC).

The JET engine worked well enough to create two-tier client/server applications, but it tended to be slow and inflexible. There was no easy way to tap into the power of the SQL database server from our applications. Without resorting to direct calls to the ODBC API, or using proprietary database libraries, there was no way to avoid the use of the JET engine for database access.

Visual Basic 4.0 added a couple of important capabilities: Remote Data Objects (RDO), and an enhanced data access model in the form of Data Access Objects (DAO). RDO is a thin object layer built on top of the ODBC API that provides a substantial performance boost over JET - as well as giving us more capabilities to use the power of a database server. The enhanced DAO with Visual Basic 4.0 offered powerful new capabilities for working with Access databases, but provided little help for dealing with ODBC data sources.

Visual Basic 5.0 built on the capabilities from version 4.0 with RDO 2.0 offering even more powerful and faster access to ODBC data sources. Additionally we gained ODBCDirect, which provides us with the same DAO object model we use for Access databases, but using RDO behind the scenes to provide us with significant performance benefits.

More recently developers have been increasingly faced with the need to access non-relational data as well as more traditional relational data sources. ActiveX Data Objects (ADO) is Microsoft's answer to this need. ADO is an object model that provides access to a new underlying data access technology called OLE DB. Strategically OLE DB is a replacement for ODBC, and it also provides access to non-relational data sources such as video, sound, text, etc. Likewise, ADO is a strategic replacement for DAO and RDO, since it gives us all the same capabilities plus the ability to get at any other OLE DB data source.

Visual Basic 6.0 comes with ADO 2.0, the most recent release of this new data access technology. Up to now there has been no real integration between ADO and Visual Basic. With Visual Basic 6.0 however, Microsoft has dramatically reworked Visual Basic's data access capabilities so they are fully integrated with ADO. The older capabilities to work with DAO and RDO remain, but the real power now lies in the tight integration with ADO and OLE DB.

ADO 2.0 itself provides a number of powerful new capabilities, including the ability to automatically transfer a `Recordset` object across a network, hierarchical datasets and data shaping. We can use a number of these new capabilities as we build our business objects. We'll explore some of them through the rest of the book.

Even more importantly, Visual Basic 6.0 allows us to create components. These components can be run on the user's workstation, on the database server, or on an application server sitting in the middle. Using ADO (or older technologies, such as RDO and ODBCdirect) we can create components that interact with the database. We can then use those components to develop our applications - and the application won't have to know about or deal with any database issues at all. We'll get into a lot more detail through the remainder of this chapter and at various points throughout the book.

The following table illustrates the changes in data access over time:

| Version | DAO | RDO | ODBCdirect | ADO | Component creation |
|---------|-----|-----|------------|-----|--------------------|
| 3.0 | X | | | | |
| 4.0 | X | X | | | X |
| 5.0 | X | X | X | | X |
| 6.0 | X | X | X | X | X |

# Use of Controls

As we observed in Chapter 1, controls are one of the distinguishing features of Visual Basic, and probably Visual Basic's greatest contribution to the software industry.

## VBX Controls

The first type of component available to Visual Basic programmers were VBXs, or Visual Basic Extensions. Unfortunately, VBX technology had some severe limitations. In particular, there was very little flexibility in the way that Visual Basic interacts with the controls. VBX controls had to provide a predefined list of methods, regardless of what the control actually did. Furthermore, a control developer couldn't add new methods to a control, making it very difficult to provide advanced functionality to the end developer. Instead, many controls provided an `Action` property, where the developer could set the property to a whole range of values to get different effects. This certainly didn't lead to readable code; who knows what this might do:

```
myControl.Action = 21
```

To cap it off, Microsoft chose not to support the VBX standard in the Win32 environment. This means that VBX controls are now only available to developers working in 16-bit Windows. For 32-bit development, we need to use ActiveX controls.

### *ActiveX Controls*

ActiveX controls (or OCXs) have largely removed the limitations of VBX controls by extending the VBX concept with more flexibility and more powerful capabilities. Like VBX controls, ActiveX controls typically provide a visual 'widget' for use in developing user-interfaces. However, they are also binary components; that is, they can contain multiple objects. This means that ActiveX controls can implement a complex interface, including any properties or methods that are needed to make the control useful.

Rather than implementing a generic and hard-to-read `Action` property, an ActiveX control can implement a descriptive method, for example:

```
myControl.SpinLeft
```

As the Visual Basic tool has matured, so have its capabilities with regard to controls. Today, ActiveX controls are a specialized form of component for use in building user-interfaces. As a component, ActiveX controls can contain objects, and they can make those objects available to help implement any required functionality in a program.

With Visual Basic 6.0, we have the ability to create our own ActiveX controls. We can create them as purely visual widgets for use in developing user-interfaces, or we can make them more complex by treating the control as a component and including objects.

Certainly, most controls are just visual widgets, and that is their primary function. At the same time, there are more techniques available for the distribution of controls to client workstations, or across the Internet, than there are for other ActiveX servers such as DLLs or EXEs. There are times when it's nice to be able to package objects within a control simply because that control can be automatically downloaded to a Web browser or other client where the objects are needed.

# Use of Components

Components, as I've defined them, are binary entities that contain one or more objects that can be used by applications. The components we can create with Visual Basic are always ActiveX servers: either in-process servers (DLLs) or out-of-process servers (EXEs). With the advent of Visual Basic 5.0, we were also able to create ActiveX controls, which are a more specialized form of component. Visual Basic 6.0 extends our ActiveX control creation ability, allowing us to easily create data sources, as well as both simple and complex data consumers.

Let's review the benefits of using components, which we discussed in Chapter 1.

### *Reuse*

One of the key benefits of binary components is a high level of reuse. We can use a single component in many applications, continually enhancing and improving the component without having to recompile or redistribute the client programs. For instance, we can create an application that uses version 1.0 of a component, as shown in the figure:

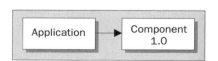

If we then find that this component would be useful in another application, with minor enhancements, we can use it as shown in the next figure:

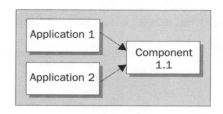

As long as we make sure the object's interface (its properties and methods) in version 1.0 of the component are not changed as we enhance it to version 1.1, our original application can continue to use the component without change. This means that we don't need to recompile or redistribute the first application - a very important consideration if our application is installed on hundreds or thousands of client workstations.

## Flexibility

The components that we create using Visual Basic are always ActiveX servers. This is important, because ActiveX servers can be used by many development languages and tools - even ones that we may not foresee, as we create our applications.

For instance, we may create an application where our business objects are in an ActiveX DLL. We could then create a user-interface for those objects using Visual Basic forms and controls, pretty much just like any other program. After we deploy our application (both the UI program and our DLL), someone else may create *their own* user interface for our DLL, perhaps using Microsoft Excel, Active Server Pages or just about any other Windows development environment.

This is a powerful advantage to us as developers. We can provide an unprecedented level of flexibility to our customers, since they can use part or all of our application as building blocks for the development of their own custom solutions. While we may provide a base application with a standard user-interface, our customers may choose to create their own user-interface - or extend our application's functionality to suit their specific needs.

## Client/Server

The ability to create components that contain one or more objects is key to the development of applications that are highly scalable. Since version 3.0, it's been practical to develop two-tier client/server applications using Visual Basic. Using components, we're now able to create more complex applications across any number of tiers.

This is true regardless of how many physical computers are involved. Even on a single machine, we can separate our application's business functionality from the user-interface through the use of components. If our business logic is contained in business objects, and those objects are in an ActiveX DLL, then we've effectively separated our objects from any user-interface that might be created to use that DLL.

Alternatively, we might put our business objects in an ActiveX EXE, or use Microsoft Transaction Server, so that they're running on another physical machine across the network. This technique allows our applications to utilize the processing power of many machines and to minimize the amount of information that's sent back and forth over the network.

In the next section, we'll look at a specific application architecture, which we'll call the **Component-based Scalable Logical Architecture** (CSLA for short), that can be used on a single workstation and yet can easily be converted to run across many machines on a network.

# Introducing the Component-Based Scalable Logical Architecture (CSLA)

To use business objects and components effectively to develop our applications, it's very helpful to start with a good **logical architecture**. This means that we want to start with a firm idea about what types of services our application will provide, and whether we want to implement them in our user-interface, in components or in a SQL database server.

In this section, we'll look in detail at the logical architecture that we'll be using throughout the remainder of the book. The CSLA is designed to work well whether it's placed entirely on a single workstation or whether it's spread across a number of machines in a network. With this type of design, we can scale an application from a single to many users with relative ease.

A logical architecture includes all the parts of an application. For instance, a typical three-tier application is composed of the following parts:

- ❑ Presentation
- ❑ Business processing
- ❑ Data processing

The following diagram shows how these parts, or tiers, work together to make up an application:

The presentation tier, or user-interface, acts as a client to our business objects. The business processing is handled by the middle tier. This tier is composed of our business objects, all working together to implement the functionality required for our application. The business objects themselves rely on the third tier to manage data processing, storing, retrieving and manipulating data within our databases.

The best way to see how an application can be divided into tiers is to look at a traditional application and break it apart - so that's what we'll do now.

## Splitting Up a Traditional Application

Let's take a simple traditional Visual Basic application, like any we may have created in Visual Basic 3.0. An application typically has at least one form for the user-interface, along with some code to do any work that needs to be done, and the application probably talks to a database to store and retrieve data.

## The Application

To keep this very simple, let's build a quick Visual Basic application that has a single form and uses a simple text file as a logical database. This example demonstrates the distinct layers of an application.

We'll just have a simple form, as shown below. The text box is called `txtName` and the command buttons are `cmdGet` and `cmdPut`:

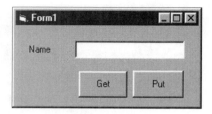

Let's suppose that we have two business rules. The first is that the name must be in uppercase, and the second is that the name is required.

To ensure that the name is uppercase, we'll add the following code:

```
Option Explicit

Private Sub txtName_LostFocus()
  txtName.Text = UCase$(txtName.Text)

End Sub
```

And to make sure we don't save a blank name, we'll add this code:

```
Private Sub cmdPut_Click()

  If Len(Trim$(txtName.Text)) = 0 Then
    MsgBox "You must enter a name", vbInformation
    Exit Sub

  End If

End Sub
```

Now let's just add some code to save the name to a file. This would normally be saving to a database, but we want to keep the program very simple to illustrate the different processes that are happening:

```
Private Sub cmdPut_Click()

  Dim lngFile As Long

  If Len(Trim$(txtName.Text)) = 0 Then
    MsgBox "You must enter a name", vbInformation
    Exit Sub

  End If

  lngFile = FreeFile
  Open "C:\TEMP.TMP" For Output As lngfile
  Print #lngFile, txtName.Text
  Close lngFile
End Sub
```

Finally, we'll add some code in behind `cmdGet` to pull the name back in from our 'database':

```
Private Sub cmdGet_Click()

   Dim lngFile As Long
   Dim strInput As String

   lngfile = FreeFile
   Open "C:\TEMP.TMP" For Input As lngFile
   Line Input #lngfile, strInput
   txtName.Text = strInput
   Close lngfile

End Sub
```

Now run the program. As you can see, we're able to store and retrieve a name. Furthermore, we won't save a blank name, and any name that we do save is stored in uppercase.

Now let's examine the program from the viewpoint of a three-tier logical model. We'll try to determine which parts of the program perform the presentation, which parts the business logic and which parts the data processing.

## The Presentation Tier

This is really the user-interface, or how the program presents information to the user and collects information from the user. In our simple example, the presentation layer certainly includes the form itself:

The presentation layer also includes some of the code that we put behind the form, but certainly not all the code is directly related to the presentation. In the following listing, the presentation code is highlighted:

```
Option Explicit

Private Sub cmdGet_Click()

   Dim lngFile As Long
   Dim strInput As String

   lngFile = FreeFile
   Open "C:\TEMP.TMP" For Input As lngFile
   Line Input #lngfile, strInput
   txtName.Text = strInput
   Close lngfile

End Sub

Private Sub cmdPut_Click()

   Dim lngFile As Long
```

```
        If Len(Trim$(txtName.Text)) = 0 Then
           MsgBox "You must enter a name", vbInformation
           Exit Sub

        End If

        lngFile = FreeFile
        Open "C:\TEMP.TMP" For Output As lngFile
        Print #lngFile, txtName.Text
        Close lngfile

     End Sub

     Private Sub txtName_LostFocus()

        txtName.Text = UCase$(txtName.Text)

     End Sub
```

Out of all that code, almost none of it is involved in actually presenting data to the user. Take a look at the lines that we've highlighted. For instance, we need to display the name after we've retrieved it from storage:

```
txtName.Text = strInput
```

Notice, however, that this line is stuck right in the middle of several other lines of code that have nothing to do with presenting the data.

Detecting that `txtName` is blank is a business rule, so that is not part of the presentation. Notifying the user that it is blank, however, is indeed part of the user interface:

```
MsgBox "You must enter a name", vbInformation
```

Again, our presentation code is in the middle of other code that is not interface-related. The upshot of this is that if we want to change the business rule, or we want to change the presentation, then we're going to be changing the same code block for either task.

That wasn't too bad, but the line in the `LostFocus` event is not so cut and dried. This line does two things: it converts the name to uppercase (a business rule), and it displays the name back into the form so that the user can see the final result (a presentation choice):

```
txtName.Text = UCase$(txtName.Text)
```

Looking at these lines of code, you can see just what a mess we've gotten ourselves into. We have no way of changing the interface without tampering with business-related code, and we can't change our business rules without affecting the interface code.

## The Business Tier

Let's now look at the parts of the program that handle the business logic or business rules. Again, it's only a part of the overall program, so we'll highlight the areas that we need to examine:

```
Option Explicit

Private Sub cmdGet_Click()

   Dim lngFile As Long
   Dim strInput As String

   lngFile = FreeFile
   Open "C:\TEMP.TMP" For Input As lngFile
   Line Input #lngFile, strInput
   txtName.Text = strInput
   Close lngfile

End Sub

Private Sub cmdPut_Click()

   Dim lngFile As Long

   If Len(Trim$(txtName.Text)) = 0 Then
      MsgBox "You must enter a name", vbInformation
      Exit Sub

   End If

   lngFile = FreeFile
   Open "C:\TEMP.TMP" For Output As lngFile
   Print #lngFile, txtName.Text
   Close lngFile

End Sub

Private Sub txtName_LostFocus()

   txtName.Text = UCase$(txtName.Text)

End Sub
```

In the `cmdPut_Click` event, we need to make sure that the name is not blank - and avoid saving the value if it is:

```
If Len(Trim$(txtName.Text)) = 0 Then
   MsgBox "You must enter a name", vbInformation
   Exit Sub

End If
```

Once again, notice how there is code managing the presentation layer right in the middle of our business processing.

The situation is worse (but now rather familiar) within the `LostFocus` event: we see the *same line* that we saw in the presentation layer, now working for our business processing to make sure that the name is in upper case:

```
txtName.Text = UCase$(txtName.Text)
```

Furthermore, suppose we need to provide access to this name for some other program, or from some other part of the same program: since the business logic is so tied into the display of this form, we'd have to duplicate the business code elsewhere.

Clearly, this is not an ideal way to organize an application.

## The Data Services Tier

In our simple example, the data service code (highlighted in the following code) is fairly straightforward:

```
Option Explicit

Private Sub cmdGet_Click()

    Dim lngFile As Long
    Dim strInput As String

    lngFile = FreeFile
    Open "C:\TEMP.TMP" For Input As lngFile
    Line Input #lngFile, strInput
    txtName.Text = strInput
    Close lngfile

End Sub

Private Sub cmdPut_Click()

    Dim lngFile As Long

    If Len(Trim$(txtName.Text)) = 0 Then
      MsgBox "You must enter a name", vbInformation
      Exit Sub

    End If

    lngFile = FreeFile
    Open "C:\TEMP.TMP" For Output As lngFile
    Print #lngFile, txtName.Text
    Close lngfile

End Sub

Private Sub txtName_LostFocus()

    txtName.Text = UCase$(txtName.Text)

End Sub
```

Still, in both the cmdGet_Click and cmdPut_Click event code, the data processing is mixed right in with the presentation and business logic, making it difficult to change the data processing without risking the other parts of the program.

## The n-Tier Solution

Certainly, there are conventional solutions to help deal with these problems - including putting code in BAS modules, or creating class modules to hold this code. Unfortunately, these solutions don't fully meet the needs of code reuse and separating (or partitioning) the various parts of the application.

The ideal solution is to pull the user-interface code into one area, the business logic into another and the data processing into a third. By breaking our application into these tiers, we can make it much easier to change any section of our program with less risk of causing bugs in the other tiers. By avoiding the case where a single routine includes code for both presentation and business logic for instance, we can change our presentation code without impacting the business code itself.

We can also facilitate code reuse. For instance, the code in the business tier may be useful to more than one form in the user-interface tier. If our business code is intermingled with the presentation code, it can be very difficult to use that business logic across various different presentations. By separating the code, we can make it very easy for our application to show the same business information through various presentations.

# Splitting up Business Processing

Developing a logical multi-tier architecture for our applications helps to partition code by separating the presentation, business and data processing. Once we've partitioned the application into manageable parts, we can build components to hold the objects at each level within the program.

Deciding exactly where to split the functionality is not easy. Even in the simple example that we just looked at, the code to convert the name to uppercase essentially belongs to both the presentation and business layers:

```
txtName.Text = UCase$(txtName.Text)
```

If we choose to put this line in the presentation tier then we're able to give the user timely feedback - indicating that the name has been converted to uppercase. But this means that we've put a business rule in the presentation tier, which is far from preferable.

We could put the code in the business tier - a good place for it, since it's a general rule that should be enforced regardless of the interface. Doing this, however, can make it much more difficult for the user-interface to provide timely feedback to the user. It's entirely possible that the business tier will be running on another machine somewhere in the network, so we could be adding a lot of network traffic if the presentation tier is asking the business layer for field-by-field information all the time.

Another possibility is to put the code in both locations. This provides timely feedback to the user, and lets the business tier centrally enforce the rule. Of course, we've duplicated the code by doing this, and so the program becomes much harder to maintain in the long run.

None of these are optimal solutions. This is one of the hardest issues we face as developers of distributed systems. It would be nice if there was a definite answer, so we could say *this is the way to do it*. Unfortunately, the choice depends on many factors, and these factors are different for each project.

So, the question remains: what are we to do about this partitioning problem? In general, there are two possible approaches: the rich (interactive) interface, and the batch interface. We'll take a look at each of these now.

## *Rich Interface*

Advocates of the rich interface look at the evolution of software from dull, non-interactive screens, to highly-interactive, graphical displays, and want to provide the latter experience for the user.

Word processing is an excellent example. Years ago, people entered their text, along with various arcane codes, into what was essentially a glorified text editor. From there, they could print their text and see what it looked like after it was formatted. User demand pressured vendors into developing what-you-see-is-what-you-get word processing, so the user eventually received a highly interactive interface with immediate feedback on appearance. Even more recently, tools such as Microsoft Word have begun to subtly provide feedback on spelling by underlining misspelled words as the user types. In short, users *like* highly interactive, well-designed interfaces.

However, there is a cost to providing this rich interface: it requires that many of the business rules be easily and quickly accessible from the presentation layer. If the rules are located on a server out on the network, then the presentation layer will have to make calls across that network - which will probably result in dismal interface performance.

The solution is to put some or all of the business rule processing on the clients, thus allowing the presentation layer to easily and quickly access those rules - which should provide a highly interactive experience for the user.

The major drawback to this solution is that it requires that we run part of our application on the client workstation. This can be a serious problem if we need to distribute the application to hundreds or thousands of client workstations. Fortunately, there are many new technologies becoming available, in the Windows environment, to automatically manage this distribution. For example, Microsoft Internet Explorer and Microsoft's Zero Administration Initiative both automate the installation of client-side components.

## Batch Interface

On-Line Transaction Processing (OLTP) developers have long subscribed to a *batch input* concept. Web browser interfaces also follow along this line, since it minimizes network traffic and leaves virtually no processing on the client.

Interfaces constructed with this technique allow the user to enter virtually anything on the screen, and perform little or no screening of input while the data is being entered. When the user accepts the screen, the business rules check all the entries and report a list of problems with the data.

The benefit to this approach is significant. All the business rules are centralized and so easily maintained. The presentation layer does virtually no work beyond that required by the controls with which the user interacts. This approach virtually eliminates the logistic problems of maintaining hundreds or thousands of clients.

The downside to batch interfaces is that the user-interface is very much non-interactive, since it gives the user no immediate feedback. In many cases, this type of interface will be unacceptable to the end users, who often want their application moved to Windows specifically to escape a batch-style interface.

## The Best of Both Worlds

The conflict between rich and batch interfaces is significant. As developers, we want to provide the user with the best, most interactive interface that we can manage. At the same time, we need to provide good performance, and design the application to be easily manageable - since it's going to be deployed to hundreds or thousands of client machines.

Visual Basic provides us with the tools to overcome these problems. To do this, we need to adopt an architecture where we split the business processing into two parts:

1.  User-Interface (UI)-centric business processing
2.  Data-centric business processing

The idea behind splitting the business processing apart is to keep processing as physically close to where it's needed as possible. This means that the processing needed by the presentation layer should be physically close, typically on the client. Processing that mostly works with data should be closer to the data source, often on a central application server.

If we look at a typical business object, we'll find that it provides some services that are only useful for developing an interface. We'll also find that it provides some services that are mostly useful for supporting data processing.

For instance, let's consider a simple *Product* object. Such an object might implement the following services:

| Service | Purpose |
|---------|---------|
| *ID* | ID value of the product |
| *Name* | Product's name |
| *Price* | Product's price |
| *QOH* | Quantity of the product on hand |
| *Receive(Quantity)* | Receive some amount of the product into the inventory |
| *Allocate(Quantity)* | Allocate some amount of the product from the inventory |
| *Load(ID)* | Load the object from the database |
| *Save()* | Save the object into the database |
| *Delete()* | Delete the object from the database |

Typically, we'd implement a *Product* object such that it implements all of these services. The problem is that we're left with a single object that needs to run on one machine - either the client or the server.

This puts us back at the rich versus batch interface crossroads. If we put the object on the client, we can provide a rich interface, but we've also put the data access methods on the client. If we put the object on the server, the client will need to go across the network to use any of the services provided by the object, so the user-interface would typically communicate with the object in a batch format; in other words, we're back to providing a batch interface for the user.

However, suppose we split our *Product* object into two separate objects: a *UI-centric Product* object, and a *data-centric Product* object. Let's consider this now.

### UI-Centric Business Processing

Our *UI-centric Product* object would provide the following services:

| Property/Method | Purpose |
|---|---|
| *ID* | ID value of the product |
| *Name* | Product's name |
| *Price* | Product's price |
| *QOH* | Quantity of the product on hand |
| *Receive(Quantity)* | Receive some amount of the product into the inventory |
| *Allocate(Quantity)* | Allocate some amount of the product from the inventory |

All these services would very likely be used only by the user-interface. By making these available in their own object, we have the option of putting that object in a component that will be installed on each client. Now the UI code will be able to interact with this object locally, without any network traffic. Any business rules that are implemented by these services will be enforced interactively. Thus we can implement a rich, highly interactive interface for the user.

There are other variations on this theme, which may be valid depending on the application's requirements. What we've discussed so far is to have these properties and methods implemented as part of the UI-centric processing. However, we may implement the QOH property and Allocation method to interact directly with the database, while the other properties and methods interact with the database in a batch mode. Or we may keep virtually no business logic in our UI-centric code, leaving all the work in the data-centric areas. Obviously the quality of our UI will degrade as we move more processing to the data-centric areas.

In general, the UI-centric business processing resides on the client machine, so it's readily accessible to the presentation layer. This is processing that does not require interaction with the database or with other centralized resources. We're including a lot of business rules and business processing in this category.

For instance, if a data field can only accept a future date, this is the place for that rule. If a series of values need to be totaled together and run through a mathematical formula, this too is where the processing belongs.

On the other hand, if a field needs to be checked against a column in a large table, or verified against some external data source (like a credit check), then this is the wrong place to do the work.

By keeping the UI-centric processing close to the client, we can build some very nice, highly interactive user-interfaces. While we can't tell the user about *every* business rule violation that they might cause, we can probably catch the majority of them and present it to the user in a timely fashion.

### Data-centric Business Processing

The *data-centric Product* object would provide the following services:

| Property/Method | Purpose |
|---|---|
| *Load(ID)* | Load the object from the database |
| *Save()* | Save the object into the database |
| *Delete()* | Delete the object from the database |

These services interact exclusively with the database to retrieve, add, update or remove our object's data. These are not the type of services that the user-interface requires on a field-by-field basis, so we won't take any serious performance hit by running them on a separate machine from the client workstation.

A lot of business rules require quick access to the data source or some other centralized resource, such as a credit checking service via TCP/IP or messaging such as a central fax service. Again, in keeping with the philosophy that processing should be performed physically close to the source, this type of business rule belongs on some central machine. Usually, this would be an application server, although that may vary. We'll discuss physical architectures more thoroughly in Chapter 4.

> It's important to understand that data-centric business processing is not the same as data services. Data services are mostly concerned with storage, retrieval and integrity of data; business processing, on the other hand, is all about enforcing business rules and performing any business logic.

A good example of a data-centric business rule is that of verifying a user's entry against a column in a very large table. It's not practical, or desirable, to download all that data to the client machine, so the rule can't be enforced there.

Such a rule might belong in the data services (implemented in SQL) if it's just a simple lookup. But suppose the business rule is more complex - such that more processing is required beyond just the lookup. This is often much easier to do in a high-level language, such as Visual Basic, than it is to do in a SQL stored procedure.

As another example, suppose we have an order entry application, and our users want automatically generated sequential order numbers that need to be displayed as soon as the order screen is presented to the user. Generating sequential order numbers is a form of business processing, but to make them sequential across all clients requires centralized processing. We *could* do this at the database level, but it would probably make more sense to handle it through our business logic. Implementing a simple business service to provide the next sequential order number is easy, and keeping it at this level can help reduce the load on the database server.

### Tying Together the Business Logic

Even though we've split the business processing into two parts, they are still integral. In fact, they *must* work together efficiently, since neither the UI-centric nor data-centric processing can, by themselves, provide all the business logic required for an application.

> What we need is for the two parts of the business processing to handle all their communications internally, so that neither the presentation layer, nor the data processing layer, is aware that the business logic has been split apart. Essentially, we want it to appear as a single layer of software.

Each UI-centric (client-side) business object must be able to efficiently communicate with any corresponding data-centric (server-side) object. The communication between these objects will typically be across a network, and so the goal is to minimize the dialog between the objects.

In Chapter 4, we'll go into the details and see how we can make this communication fast and practical.

# An n-Tier Architecture

So far, we've looked at a three-tier architecture and how we can split our business processing into two distinct parts: UI-centric and data-centric. What we've really done is move from a three-tier architecture to an **n-tier** architecture. The new architecture consists of the following four layers:

- ❏ Presentation
- ❏ UI-centric business objects
- ❏ Data-centric business objects
- ❏ Data services

If you look back at the three-tier diagram in Chapter 1 and compare it to the following figure, you'll note that all we've done is split the business tier into two parts:

This may seem like a small change, but in reality it is very significant. By splitting the UI-centric processing from the data-centric processing, we've given ourselves much more flexibility. We can now keep the UI-centric processing on the client, so we can provide a rich interface for the user. At the same time, we have the option of moving the data-centric processing away from the client to a machine with faster access to the database, so we can gain significant performance benefits.

Let's go through each part of this architecture and see how it works. We'll be using this architecture throughout the remainder of the book, so we need to make sure it's clear in our minds as we go forward.

## *Presentation Tier*

To start off, we have the most visible part of the whole application: the user-interface. Traditionally, these are the forms, menus, and controls that the user uses to interact with our program. It's quite reasonable, however, that we might need to expand this definition to fit into today's environment. The presentation layer for our application might not just be made up of Visual Basic forms anymore. Rather, it might be an HTML page, a spreadsheet, a word processor, or another entire application.

*The key thing to keep in mind about the user-interface is that it's not the application. As we'll see shortly, the business objects are the application; the user-interface is just how the user chooses to interact with our objects.*

> **The goal is to create programs that are independent of the presentation to the user. This means that our application can have many different user-interfaces implemented in different tools and technologies.**

As we discussed earlier, in a typical Visual Basic application almost all the code, and therefore almost all the processing, lives in the user-interface. Programmers put most of their code behind controls on their forms. Other programmers put the code in code modules to be called from the forms, but really the processing is still entirely centered around the interface:

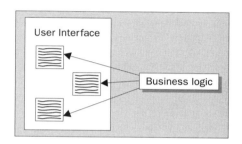

This is an ideal technique when we're writing event-driven programs, and so it has worked well for us so far. The events come from the user-interface, and so it makes perfect sense for all the code to be directly linked to that interface.

Unfortunately, this approach doesn't work nearly so well when we're trying to develop an object-oriented model for our program, since the focus of the program is on the interaction between objects rather than on an interaction with events in the interface.

Our users often want more than just a traditional user-interface; they may also want a web browser interface, for instance. A more advanced user might even want access to our application from Visual Basic for Applications (VBA), so they can work with the application from within their spreadsheet or word processor.

Also, the part of an application that typically changes the most is the user-interface. Users like to tweak their interface almost continually, and so it seems as if there is a constant stream of requests to move the controls around or replace radio buttons with a combo box and so forth. If our code is primarily placed behind the controls on forms then even an apparently simple interface change can be complex. Not only do we have to change the interface, but we probably have to rearrange the actual business logic to compensate for the changes.

This is not an easy request to fulfil if we have a substantial amount of code tied to our Visual Basic form-based interface. Even putting much of the code in **BAS** modules doesn't help, since neither Excel nor browser-based interfaces will have easy access to the code.

On the other hand, if our program is built based on components that contain business objects then we can easily write a flexible interface, or even a number of interfaces, to talk to our application:

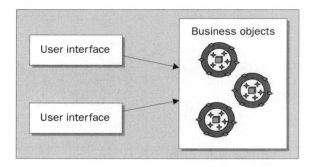

Changes to a Visual Basic form-based interface now become much simpler, and safer, since our business code is independent of the code inside the form.

Also, our application automatically supports any program that can act as a client to an ActiveX server. This includes most Windows development tools and productivity software (such as Microsoft Excel). Even the Web browser problem becomes much simpler, since we can create an IIS Application (which we'll do in Chapter 14) that manages the user interface, but has direct access to the application's business objects for business logic:

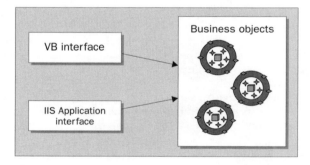

At this point, it may not be entirely clear how this architecture can be implemented with Visual Basic. As we get further into business objects, we'll delve into the details and see just how well this whole idea works out. This architecture has been used in the development of a number of large projects with great success - that's happy users, good performance and long term maintainability!

## UI-Centric Business Objects

Instead of putting the bulk of the code for our application behind Visual Basic forms, we'll move that code into business objects. By doing this, we can apply object-oriented design techniques to build an object model, and put the business rules and processing into the objects of that model.

In Chapter 1, we defined what a business object is - on a fairly high level. In summary:

> **Business objects are the core of your business solution. With Visual Basic, they are instances of class modules that are designed to represent the real-world 'objects' with which our application is dealing.**

In Chapter 3, we'll go through some techniques that we can use to identify real-world objects and translate them into software objects.

The user-interface is really a client, or user, of the business objects. While the user-interface displays and retrieves data from the user, the business objects need to provide all the business functionality and capabilities required by the user interface. At the same time, the business objects need to enforce all the business rules and relationships to meet the design requirements of our application.

> *The business objects should provide appropriate access to all the functionality of the application. The presentation tier, even including macros in other applications such as Microsoft Word, should be able to use the components containing our business objects to do their work.*

The business objects contain the business rules for the real-world entities that they represent. For instance, if a business rule says that a customer must have a last name, there should be code in the customer business object to make sure that the last name isn't blank. You might find something like the following code in the `LastName` property of a customer object:

```
Public Property Let LastName(Name As String)

   If Len(Name) = 0 Then
      Err.Raise vbObjectError + 10, "Customer class", _
         "Last name can not be blank"

   Else
      strLastName = Name

   End If

End Property
```

> *Business objects interact with each other by following the rules laid out by our object model. Business rules dictate how the objects work with, or relate to, each other.*

As an example, perhaps a customer can have many phone numbers. Translating this into business objects, our customer object will have many phone objects. There is a relationship between the customer object and each phone object, in that each phone object is owned by a customer. This relationship needs to be coded somehow into either the customer or the phone objects. For instance, the phone objects may be stored as a collection inside the customer object:

```
Option Explicit

Private mcolPhoneNumbers As Collection
```

Our UI-centric business objects should be designed to accurately reflect the real-world business entities that our application needs to model. This means that each object should represent some entity, along with any attributes, methods and business rules that affect that entity. Our overall object model should also enforce any business rules regarding how objects interact.

Any user-interface will interact exclusively with our UI-centric business objects, and so these objects must not only implement and enforce all our business rules, but they need to provide all the capabilities that the UI developer will require to create a rich, interactive interface for the user.

## Data-Centric Business Objects

By splitting the data-centric processing out of our business objects, we've provided ourselves with a great deal of flexibility in terms of how we deploy our application. We can choose to implement the data-centric business objects in a DLL, so that it runs on the client workstation, or we can put them in an EXE running on another machine on the network. We can easily compile them into a DLL and run them within Microsoft Transaction Server (as we'll see later in the book).

Our data-centric business objects typically provide certain services that are used by our UI-centric business objects. When a UI-centric business object needs some work done that it can't do by itself, it just has a data-centric object do the work.

Our UI-centric business objects should provide the UI developer with an intuitive and reliable model of the real-world objects in our business. Our data-centric objects need to provide the UI-centric objects with a robust and powerful mechanism by which data can be saved and retrieved as needed. This means that all interaction with data sources should be managed by our data-centric objects; the client-side business objects should have no idea how data is stored or retrieved.

### OLE DB Data Sources

Most applications deal with data, and quite a bit of data is stored in some type of database that we can reach using OLE DB. Because of this, most of our data-centric business objects will make heavy use of ActiveX Data Objects (ADO) to work with those OLE DB data sources.

Since our server-side business objects will handle all the database interaction, this is where we'll find all the SQL statements, recordsets, database objects and so forth. It's the job of the data-centric business objects to translate all these relational database concepts into data that is useful to our client-side business objects.

As an added bonus, our data-centric business objects can be used to shield much of our application from the differences across various SQL databases. Since all the database interaction is managed by our server-side objects, we have only one place to change code when we need to support a new database.

While it's true that we can use ADO to help minimize the differences between various databases, there is a cost. A prime example is an application that needs to run on a single workstation with an Access database *and* in a WAN environment with an Oracle database. Using ADO, we can write a single set of data-centric objects that work with both databases. Unfortunately, our code will be optimized for neither Access nor Oracle, very possibly leading to unacceptable performance.

With little or no impact to our user-interface or the UI-centric business objects, we can make our data-centric business objects smart enough to deal with both types of database. These objects can be written to detect the type of database and to run the appropriate queries and use the appropriate data access techniques for either Access or Oracle as needed.

Along the same line, if we need to migrate from one kind of database to another then we only need to change the server-side business objects, not all the business objects on the clients. Perhaps our database was a legacy system, and we used screen-scraping technology to get at the data. If we later convert to Microsoft SQL Server, we can just change the data-centric business objects to get the data from the new source - with no impact to our user-interface or the client-side business objects.

### ODBC Data Sources

Since OLE DB is relatively new on the database scene, there are quite a number of relational databases that don't yet have OLE DB providers. Fortunately almost all of these databases do have ODBC drivers that have been used to access them for a long time.

OLE DB can use ODBC to access these databases. This means that, with a small performance penalty, we can use ADO within our data-centric code to access the ODBC provider for OLE DB.

With this capability, there are very few relational databases that are not available from our programs using ADO.

### Non-Relational Data Sources

It's important to remember that data isn't always stored in a relational database. Many applications need access to specialized hardware or software. For instance, we may have objects that represent information that is stored in a proprietary laboratory information management system (LIMS) or some equivalent type of system. Perhaps our objects represent physical devices that load trucks with an appropriate mix of cement, sand and gravel to make ready-mix concrete.

As we discuss 'data-centric' business objects, we need to keep in mind that we aren't always working with relational databases, SQL, and other relatively simple data sources. Fortunately, the CSL architecture we're talking about allows us to shield our client-side business objects from all these details through the use of server-side objects. Our data-centric objects can interact with whatever data source we need to deal with, whether complex or not. At the same time, our UI-centric business objects can provide an easy, consistent interface for use by the UI developers.

### Minimise Licensing Costs

If we're implementing our architecture across multiple physical machines, we have the option of moving the data-centric objects off the client workstations and on to a central application server machine. We might do this by putting the objects in an ActiveX EXE server and using DCOM, or we might put them into an ActiveX DLL server running within Microsoft Transaction Server. We'll look at examples of each approach later in the book.

By centralizing the data-centric objects on a separate application server machine, we've also centralized all the database interaction. This means that the clients don't need to have any direct access to the database, only to the application server.

This has a couple of benefits. Logistically, we may have simplified the client desktop - since we don't need to install and maintain OLE DB providers, ADO, ODBC drivers or data connections out there. Also, suppose we have 100 client workstations: traditionally, we'd have to buy 100 client licenses for our database. By using a centralized set of data services, we can let the clients share the connections to the database, thus reducing the number of client licenses that we need to purchase. Since most database vendors charge licensing on a *per connection* basis, we can save on licensing costs.

## Data Services Tier

The final area we need to discuss is the data services tier. At a minimum, this tier is responsible for creating, updating, retrieving and deleting data from a data source. In many cases, it also includes more complex features, such as enforcement of relational integrity and other data-related rules.

In most cases, this data handling will actually take place on a database server. This allows us to put quite a bit of processing on the database server, using SQL-stored procedures and triggers. This can often provide important performance benefits, since most SQL database servers can optimize stored procedures so they run very efficiently.

It's important to note, however, that much of the work that a database server might have done in a application may actually be more appropriately placed in our data-centric business objects rather than in SQL code. SQL is notoriously difficult to work with. It doesn't compare to tools such as Visual Basic for features such as debugging and flexibility. While it's still very valid to do some SQL coding in an application, it's often much more cost effective to move the processing to a different layer of the application - where we can bring more powerful development tools to bear on the problem.

*That's not to say that stored procedures and triggers written in SQL don't have their place. There are many simple data operations that can be most efficiently performed by the SQL processing engine, since it is optimized for such work. Examples include filtering or performing minor alterations to our data as it is stored or retrieved.*

Visual Basic 6.0 provides us with some very powerful capabilities in this regard. We can now create simple OLE DB providers using Visual Basic. Such providers can be built to provide access to data sources we've been previously unable to tap, or they may be used to provide refined or more specific access to a data source we can already use. Most of these capabilities are beyond the scope of this book, but we can make thorough use of them when creating objects that need to access data.

# Summary

In this chapter, we've looked at event-driven programming, code behind forms, and other traditional design concepts. We saw how Visual Basic 6.0's object- and component-oriented features build upon older concepts to provide us with new and more powerful capabilities for software design.

We also walked through the concept of a logical three-tier application model, separating presentation, business logic and data processing. We developed a specific application model including a presentation tier, UI-centric business objects, data-centric business objects and a data services tier. We discussed how this CSL architecture can be implemented in environments ranging from a single workstation to a network where the processing is spread across multiple machines.

At this point, you should have a good understanding of how this architecture works and how business objects and binary components are used to implement it. As we progress through the remainder of the book, we'll build on these concepts and implement an application by making use of them.

From here, we'll explore these concepts in more practical detail. We'll look at:

- ❑   The design and creation of business objects
- ❑   How business objects are implemented in Visual Basic
- ❑   How business objects are used to create components
- ❑   The different types of components we can create using Visual Basic

Specifically, in the next chapter, we'll cover:

- ❑   Analysis of our business domain
- ❑   Identification of business objects
- ❑   Design of individual business objects
- ❑   How business objects interact
- ❑   Using business objects to model our business

# 3

# Business Object Analysis

## Overview

We've done some important work in the first two chapters. We've defined what we mean by business objects, we've considered the benefits of using business objects, and we've looked at some of the logical architectures that can use business objects to their best advantage. Now it's time to think about the relationship between our business objects and the real world they represent. Specifically, we're going to take a look at some of the techniques that can help us identify, in the very first instance, the actual business objects that we need to create when we're modeling business situations in the real world.

In this chapter, and through the rest of this book, we'll be creating three interrelated systems that are designed to help run a video rental store. We'll perform a detailed business object analysis of these systems within this chapter, which will provide us with a sound introduction to object analysis.

We'll be making extensive use of the **use case** technique in this chapter. This is a form of analysis that can be very useful for identifying and designing business objects. We'll also look at some of the common types of object relationships that can be found in real-world business systems, and we'll consider how we can design our business objects to support these relationships.

So here are the main business analysis themes in this chapter:

- ❑ Identifying and defining business objects
- ❑ Object attributes and behaviors
- ❑ Object relationships
- ❑ Analysis: our Video Store example project

In this chapter, we'll be focusing on the UI-centric business objects that were located within the Component-based Scalable Architecture (CSLA) that I presented in the last chapter:

The UI-centric business objects are the objects that most closely represent the real-world entities that we're trying to model with our software. As such, UI-centric objects also happen to be the heart of any application that's built upon this particular model.

> **Any presentation layer will be built directly on top of these UI-centric business objects, so a key requirement is that they provide a robust, easy-to-use model of our business processes.**

In this chapter, we'll look at real-world business entities and determine how to represent them as software objects. The technique we'll use to represent these business entities will be to model them, and the particular part of the business that we want to model will be our business **domain**. As we'll see, within this chapter, there are two major steps that we must accomplish if we are to successfully model our domain:

**1.** We need to figure out which real-world entities need to be part of our object model. From there, we can decide which attributes (properties) and behaviors (methods) these objects will need if they are to successfully represent our business entities.

**2.** We need to evaluate the relationships between our different objects. Objects can interact with or relate to each other in many different ways. We need to add properties, methods, and events to our objects so that they can work together to model our business processes.

*Another major aspect to the design comes when we decide which objects should go into different binary components, such as EXE's or DLL's. This is part of the **implementation design** of our objects, and we'll cover these issues in Chapter 4, where we discuss the creation of business object components.*

Once we've identified our business objects and their relationships, we'll have created a **logical object model**, which will help us decide how we can implement those relationships using Visual Basic.

*The relationships we'll be discussing are commonly used in object-oriented design, but exactly how we implement them in Visual Basic may vary from implementation methods commonly seen in other languages.*

# Identifying and Defining Business Objects

Here's a question that I'm often asked when I'm talking about business objects: how do you figure out what objects to create? It's a good question. Sometimes, objects are pretty obvious; a *customer* object in a sales system, for instance. Unfortunately, not all business objects are so obvious, and it can take some work to identify them.

> It's always important to do a good analysis job when we're developing any software; but it's even more critical when we're designing software using object-oriented techniques. Since one of the main aims in using objects and components is to promote reuse, it's important to identify and design our objects effectively.

There are plenty of books and articles that tell us all about rapid development and how we should quickly put together some objects and then let the object model evolve to meet future needs. This seems like an excellent idea; but unfortunately, this approach goes a long way toward defeating the reusability of the objects in the model.

> *If our evolutionary process requires that we change certain properties or methods that we've already added to an object, or that we must replace a single object with multiple objects, then we'll have to change all our client programs as well.*

While it's true that we don't have to design every detail of our objects up front, it's very important that we identify our objects carefully. It's also very important that we get to the central behaviors of each object *right from the start*. The better the job we do during the analysis and design of our objects, the less risk we run of having to make substantial and costly changes later.

There are a number of approaches we can use to analyze and identify our business objects. These techniques include:

- ❑ Decomposition of business concepts and processes
- ❑ Deriving our objects from a data model
- ❑ CRC (Class, Responsibility and Collaborator) cards
- ❑ Use cases or scenarios

In an ideal world, we'd be able to design our applications without ever having to worry about an existing data model. And if we're lucky enough to be in this situation, we can start with our business object design and then build our data model to support our objects.

Since this is rarely an ideal world, however, it's much more likely that we'll be using an existing data source with a preset structure. But even in this case, we should still start by creating a business object model - with the understanding that we may have to compromise our model later on to fit it in with the existing database.

> Using the CSLA, we can minimize the impact of the database design, since the data-centric business processing is handled separately from the objects that represent our business entities.

# Use Case Analysis

At its most basic level, a **use case** is simply a written description of a business process. We can employ this technique as a high-level analysis tool to determine overall system requirements, and to identify broad business objects that are involved in high-level processes. At the other end of the spectrum, we can get very specific in the use case description, defining detailed functionality and objects.

The process of starting with high-level use cases, and then zooming in to a number of increasingly detailed functional use cases, until we reach a set of specific objects and behaviors, is a technique known as **functional decomposition**.

This is very much a top-down approach to software analysis, and one that end users can usually relate to very well. It's easy to get a user to describe their high-level requirements, and then just continue to ask more and more questions to get a more detailed view of what they need. Usually, we can take the written use cases back to the user to make sure that what we heard and wrote down was actually what they meant.

# Requirements Use Case or Scenario

At the broadest level, we can create use cases that help to define overall system requirements. This type of use case is known as a **requirements use case**, or a **scenario**. A requirements use case can help to identify some of the more major business objects in our business domain - despite the fact that the process is actually geared more towards gathering requirements than describing any specific functionality.

Before getting into specific use cases however, it might be nice to take a quick overview of the system we'll be discussing. We'll look at a video store rental system that maintains a list of customers who shop at the store, a list of video titles and specific tapes that can be rented and handles the invoicing of the rentals. We can think of the system as having three general parts; a customer database function, an inventory function to keep track of the video tapes and an invoicing function to walk through the process of actually renting a tape to a customer and then recording when it's returned.

# Use Case 1: Renting a Video

Here's an example of a requirements use case for a common activity: renting a video. Obviously, there are a number of other high-level use cases involved in the store's overall operation, but this case covers one broad process that's central to the store's business:

### Requirements Use Case for Video Rental

The video store maintains an inventory of rentable videos for perusal by customers. A customer enters the store and browses the inventory to select any number of videos to rent.

The customer then brings the videos to the front counter where an attendant identifies the customer, makes note of each video, and calculates the total rental price. The attendant gives the customer an invoice, which lists the videos and shows the total amount due.

The customer pays for the rental and leaves with the videos. To avoid setting off the security alarm, the attendant hands the rented videos to the customer as they leave.

# Use Case 2: Problem Recording

Here's another example of some related requirements that might be implemented, in a separate system, to track problems with videos:

### Requirements Use Case for Video Problem Recording

The video store maintains an inventory of rentable videos. As the videos age they begin to have problems. By tracking the number of problems over time, the store can stop renting the videos before they get too bad.

The customer reports the problem to an attendant, either when the video is returned or sometimes over the phone. The attendant records the video's ID into the computer and indicates the nature or category of the problem, along with the date and (optionally) a text description.

# Use Case 3: Rental Analysis Reporting

Finally, here are some requirements for a system that reports an analysis of video rentals.

*Reporting requirements are often quite different from the rest of an application. Actual reporting is typically done through a reporting package that works directly against the data source. Data analysis is often best done within business objects, since there we can take full advantage of the logic we've coded into our objects.*

### Requirements Use Case for Rental Analysis

In order to decide what kinds of videos to provide for renting in the future, the store owner wants to analyze the inventory to identify which types of video make the most profit.

To do this, the computer needs to look at the number of times each video was rented and what the rental price was for each rental – essentially looking at the revenue generated by the video. This needs to be compared to the purchase cost of each video to determine whether the video recouped its cost effectively.

All this data needs to be consolidated to show the profitability of the videos - both by producing studio and by video category.

# Identifying High-Level Requirements

The requirements use case descriptions are not very specific. There are a number of areas where we've identified requirements but not specific functionality. For example, some of the requirements we can derive from the *video rental* use case could include:

❑   The store maintains an inventory
❑   The inventory must be available for browsing
❑   The store employs an attendant
❑   There is a mechanism by which the attendant can identify a specific customer
❑   The attendant can identify specific videos
❑   There is a security system triggered by videos leaving the store

# Identifying High-Level Objects

We can also pick out some potential high-level objects. This is an important step, since these objects are likely to be the ones that are shared across multiple use cases, and very likely across multiple applications within our organization.

*Basically, we just want to look through the use case and pick out all the nouns.*

Each noun has the potential to become a business object. Whether it actually ends up as a business object is something we'll determine through the rest of the process.

Here's a list of potential high-level business objects from the *video rental* use case:

| | |
|---|---|
| Store | Attendant |
| Inventory | Invoice |
| Video | Rental price |
| Customer | Payment |
| Front counter | Security alarm |

We'll use this list later on, as we go through the functional use cases and analysis. During that process, we'll identify some of the objects listed here as actual objects in our application; others, of course, won't be required. In this first phase, our objective is to identify any objects within the business domain - not just those that we'll code into our application.

# Functional Use Case

A functional use case is much more specific than the requirements use case we just saw. Most requirements use cases will actually encompass a number of more detailed functional use cases. These are used less for determining system requirements than for defining required functionality. They are also very useful for identifying business objects.

Let's use a single sentence from the *Video Rental* requirements use case, above, as an example of a functional use case:

> The customer then brings the videos to the front counter where an attendant identifies the customer, makes note of each video, and calculates the total rental price.

There are a lot of things going on here, but the description is not nearly detailed enough to fully describe the functionality. All it does describe, of course, are the requirements. So let's develop a use case that defines the functionality to support these requirements:

### Functional Use Case for Video Checkout

The customer places the videos on the counter and provides an ID card to the attendant. The attendant chooses the video rental menu option on the screen, then enters the customer's ID number by scanning the ID card with a barcode reader. This automatically retrieves the customer's name and address from the database, and displays the information on the screen. The entry point is left in position to enter the first video's ID number.

The attendant takes each video, in turn, and uses the barcode reader to enter the video's ID number by scanning the video jacket. This automatically retrieves the video's description and rental price, and displays them on the screen next to the video ID number.

As each video ID number is entered, a subtotal price is calculated and displayed at the bottom of the screen. Based on the subtotal price, the system automatically calculates and displays the tax and the end total.

Of course, this is only a small part of the whole picture. If this was more than just an example, we would continue through the requirements use case, building more functional use cases to fill in the rest of the details. But let's keep up our momentum: it's time to identify some real functionality from this use case.

# Identifying Functionality

Our functional use case for *Video Checkout*, above, is still focused on the business process; but its level of detail is sufficient for us to be able to define specific functionality - and get right to the business objects that we'll need to create. First, let's go through and list the functionality that's described:

- ❑ The customer has an ID number
- ❑ The video rental transaction is handled via a specific screen
- ❑ The customer's ID number is sufficient to retrieve the customer's information
- ❑ The customer's name and address are in the database
- ❑ Videos each have an ID number
- ❑ Once the customer data is shown, the cursor moves to the video entry field
- ❑ The video's ID number is sufficient to retrieve the video's information
- ❑ The customer and video ID numbers are scanned by a barcode reader
- ❑ The video's title and rental price are in the database
- ❑ The system must keep a running subtotal for all videos entered
- ❑ The system must calculate the tax
- ❑ The system must calculate a total rental fee

Notice that not all the functionality that's been described fits into business objects. For instance, the requirement that 'once the customer data is shown, the cursor moves to the video entry field' is not a business rule, but a presentation rule. This functionality is no less important to the end user of the system, but we do need to make sure that presentation rules are handled by the user-interface, not the business objects.

# Identifying Business Objects

Now let's find the business objects that are required to support this functionality. As before, a good technique for this process is to pick out the nouns from the use case. Of course, this could get carried to an extreme, so your judgment is required. What we need to do is to pick out possible real-world objects that might need to be modeled in the software:

| | | |
|---|---|---|
| ❑ | Customer | Video ID number |
| ❑ | Video | Barcode reader |
| ❑ | ID card | Database |
| ❑ | Attendant | Subtotal price |
| ❑ | Screen | Tax |
| ❑ | Customer ID number | Total Price |

Clearly, some of the possible objects we've listed won't end up being created as objects in the software. In fact, some will become object attributes, while others may be dropped entirely. Nevertheless, this is a good starting point. The next step is to determine how these objects relate to each other. During this process, we'll find out which of the objects are important to the software and which are not.

# Defining Object Relationships

Although it may sound old-fashioned, it can be very valuable to write the name of each object that we listed on to a small card or piece of paper, one note per object. Then we can use a white-board, or any other large surface we can draw on, and stick the objects to the surface. This lets us move the objects around as needed, and lets us draw lines between the objects to show how they're connected.

> *There are commercial case tools on the market that make this very easy to perform on a computer. Rational Rose for Visual Basic and Microsoft Visual Modeler are good examples. These programs can be very useful, as they offer the same abilities as putting cards on a white-board, but allow us to save the diagrams to disk, add comments to our objects and relationships, and sometimes even generate code based on the object design.*

Once our objects are written down and placed on a surface, we're ready to move on and figure out how they relate to each other.

> *This is fairly straightforward, since all we need to do is go back through the use case and look for verbs and other connecting phrases between the nouns.*

Again, this could get carried to an extreme, so some judgment is required!

## Types of Relationships

There are some key types of relationships that we need to find. Other relationships exist, and are important, but these are ones we need to make sure we get:

| Relationship | Description/Example |
| --- | --- |
| Ownership (owns, has) | Parent-child relationships |
| User (uses) | One object uses or employs the services of another object |
| Aggregate (contains, made of) | One object is made up of other (subordinate) objects |
| Generalization (is a) | One object is a specific type of another object |

Something else to keep in mind is that we might need to add some new objects as we go along. Picking out the nouns from the use case is great, but the use case might have *implied* some other objects that we don't have yet. For instance, we may find that we need objects to represent some of the verbs in our use cases. That's fine, just don't be surprised if it happens.

Following the same logic, there will be objects that we don't need, and we'll be getting rid of those.

## Example Relationships

So let's look through the use case and pick out some relationships:

- A customer **owns** an ID card
- An ID card **contains** a customer number
- A customer **has** an ID number
- A video **has** an ID number
- Attendant **uses** the screen
- Attendant **chooses** a menu option
- Barcode reader **scans** the ID card
- The screen **displays** (**or uses**) the customer information
- The screen **displays** (**or uses**) the video information
- The screen **displays** (**or uses**) the subtotal, tax, and total
- The subtotal price **uses** the video prices
- The tax **uses** the subtotal price
- The total is **made up of** the subtotal and tax

There are other relationships that we could identify; these are just some examples that illustrate the common relationships we'll encounter. This information is more clearly presented in diagrammatic form:

# Visual Basic 6 Business Objects

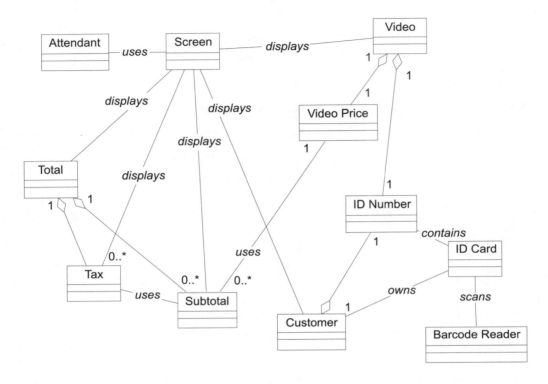

*The figure shown here was drawn using Microsoft Visual Modeler, part of the Visual Studio package. The notation used is the Unified Modeling Language (UML). Appendix B contains a brief explanation of UML as used here.*

## Eliminating Unneeded Objects

Now the challenge is to eliminate the objects that we don't need to put into our software model. There are three main things to look at:

- Objects that just aren't needed in this particular use case
- Objects that fit into other layers of the application, such as the presentation layer
- Objects which are outside the scope of the system but exist within our use case

The first thing we should do is look at those objects that don't have a lot of relationships in the diagram. Neither the *attendant* nor the *barcode reader* are well connected, so they need to be looked at carefully.

It's unlikely that we'll need to have an *attendant* object to handle the functionality in this use case, since the attendant just interacts with the screen. We won't completely write it off as an object, however, because it was also listed in the requirements use case - so it may be used to provide some other functionality. Still, we don't need it here, so we can remove it from our diagram.

The *barcode reader* is probably not required either. This is more of a common sense issue, but barcode readers usually just provide input to the software that's indistinguishable from keyboard input, so it's hard to imagine what such a business object would do for our program.

Now look at the objects that the attendant and barcode reader touched. The *screen* object is still very connected, but the *ID card* is a borderline case. Since the ID card is just a way of expressing the customer's ID number, we can probably eliminate it from the picture as well.

The next step is to look at each object and eliminate those that belong in either the presentation or data processing layers of the application. In our case, the *screen* object certainly fits the bill for belonging in the presentation layer.

> *However, it's very useful to leave something representing the presentation layer in the model, for the sake of clarity. At the same time, we don't want to mistake it to be an actual business object, so we need to keep that in mind when we look at the figure.*

After all the changes, our diagram looks like this:

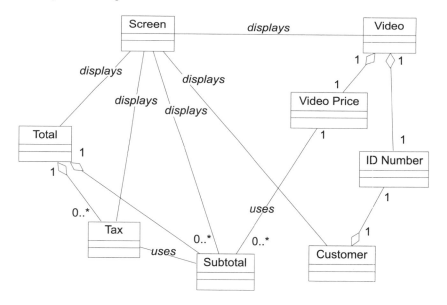

## Consolidating Objects

At this point, we've got a pretty clear picture of the objects that we need, and how they're all related to each other. Now is a good time to look at the diagram with a critical eye to determine if there are objects that can be consolidated to form a more general object.

> *There may also be objects in our diagram that are really attributes of other objects, but we won't worry about those yet. We'll discuss attributes and properties in the next section.*

Looking at the diagram, there are three objects that are all very much interrelated. The *tax* and *total* objects are both generated upon the basis on the *subtotal* object. It would make a lot of sense to add a new object to the diagram that would give us a more general view of these objects.

If we look back at our requirements use case, we'll see that there is a potential business object called an *invoice*.

> **It's important to keep looking back at the requirements use case, and to look at all the other related functional use cases, to find objects that overlap or have relationships with the objects at hand. Our functional analysis is not happening in isolation, so it's important to regularly stop and take a look at the bigger picture.**

The *invoice* object needs to display the total amount along with some other information, so it's a good candidate to use as an object to contain the *total*, *tax* and *subtotal* objects. Here's a list the relationships for our new *invoice* object:

- ❑ The invoice **has a** total
- ❑ The invoice **has a** subtotal
- ❑ The invoice **has a** tax
- ❑ The invoice **refers to** customer
- ❑ The invoice **has a** list of videos

Looking back at the previous example, we can see how complex the model is for the presentation designer. The *screen* entity is communicating with a lot of different objects in our model, so it may be very difficult for the programmer of the presentation layer to use our model effectively. In this new model, however, the UI developer only needs to worry about interacting with three objects: *invoice*, *video* and *customer*. All the other objects are available through one of these three.

If we add in the *invoice* object, we end up with the following diagram for our objects:

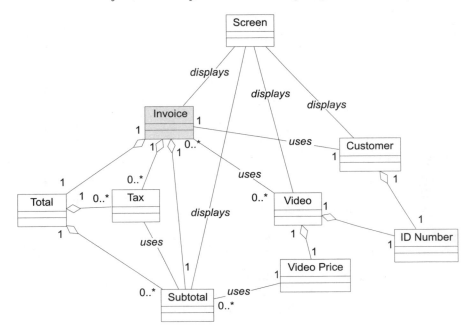

At this point, we have a pretty good understanding of the business objects that we need to handle for the functional use case. We may not be done yet, however, it's possible that we'll still need to add or remove some objects as we finish up the analysis.

Now we need to move on to figure out some specifics about the objects; in particular, we need to list the properties, methods, and events that each object needs in order to support the use case's functionality. First, let's look at the properties.

# Identifying Object Attributes (or Properties)

Our programs interact with objects using the interface (properties, methods, and events) that the object provides. Properties are the attributes, or elements, that describe an object.

> *Although the analytical processes to determine the properties and methods are similar and interrelated, it's often easier to start with the properties, keeping the behaviors in mind, and then move on to finalize the methods.*

We'll get our properties using two primary techniques:

❑ We'll go back to our functional use case to find any properties that we need to meet the requirements listed there.

❑ We'll look at the object model diagram from the previous section, since some of the objects in our model might be better expressed as attributes of other objects - something we'll cover in much more detail shortly.

Additionally, some of our objects have relationships to other objects, such as the *invoice* having a reference to a *customer* object. In this case, we'll want to add a property to the *invoice* object so that the *customer* object is accessible.

> *As well as the properties needed to fulfill the business requirements, the objects will also have properties to support the way we implement our components. We'll ignore these particular properties for now, and cover them in Chapter 5.*

## Identifying Attributes - Looking through the Use Case

So, our first technique to identify object attributes involves us going through each object in our model, and looking at the relevant use case to decide which attributes are appropriate.

A simple example is the *customer* object. Looking at the use case, we can see some fairly obvious attributes that will be required; in particular, the name and address. The customer's ID number may also be an attribute, although we've put it into our model as an object. We'll talk about the ID number shortly.

Of course, the address is likely to contain a number of attributes, such as street, city, state, and zip code.

Alternatively, we may determine that we have other addresses from other functional use cases, so perhaps the address is really a separate object. Translating from use cases into an object design is a holistic process: we need to continually look back at other use cases and related object models to see where and how they overlap. This is how code re-use is tied in to the object model we are building.

In this case, we'll just assume that a customer has a single address with a street, city, state, and zip code. Here is a list of the objects from our model, along with the properties that we're likely to derive from the use case:

| Object | Object's Attributes |
|--------|---------------------|
| Tax | Tax amount |
| Subtotal | Subtotal amount |
| Total | Total amount for invoice |
| Invoice | Since the invoice isn't actually in our use case, and we added it later, we won't get any properties from the use case |
| Customer | Name |
| | Street |
| | City |
| | State |
| | Zip |
| Video price | Rental price |
| Video | Description |
| ID number | ID Number |

### Identifying Attributes - Looking at the Object Model Diagram

Our second technique to identify object attributes involves an examination of each object in our object model to make sure that it really is an object - and not just an attribute of a related object. This distinction is somewhat subtle, and requires us to step back and look at the requirements use case and any other related functional use cases that might impact the model.

A good clue to start with is to examine the attributes we've assigned to each object at this point. Any object with just a single property is a good candidate to become a simple property of its parent object. Look at the *ID number* object. It only has a single property, so does it really warrant the status of being an object, or is it just an attribute of the *customer* and *video* objects?

This depends very much on how the *ID number* object is used in other use cases. In this particular use case, it's simply an attribute - but if it's used by other objects in other use cases we may opt to create an *ID number* object and use it across all the different objects that need it.

> *We need to keep in mind that properties are not the only thing that might define an object. As we'll discuss shortly, methods can also define an object. Before assuming that the ID number object is just an attribute, we need to ensure that it doesn't provide any behaviors that make it more appropriate to being an object.*

In going through the object model, look for objects that have a single property and those that have a parent. A parent is typically an object that *has* or *owns* or is *made up of* the object that we're looking at. Another way to look at it is that the child object *belongs to* the parent. The following objects look like good candidates to become properties of other objects:

| Object | Parent |
| --- | --- |
| Video price | belongs to the video object |
| ID number | belongs to the customer and video objects |
| Tax | belongs to the invoice object |
| Subtotal | belongs to the invoice object |
| Total | belongs to the invoice object |

At the end of this process, we have the following objects and properties:

| Object | Attributes |
| --- | --- |
| Invoice | Tax |
| | Subtotal |
| | Total |
| Customer | ID number |
| | Name |
| | Address |
| | City |
| | State |
| | Zip |
| Video | ID number |
| | Description |
| | Price |

At this point, we have properties for each of the objects individually; but, according to our diagram, the *invoice* object refers to both the *customer* and *video* objects. We need to decide how the presentation layer will get at the *customer* and *video* objects through the *invoice* object. This is a very complex issue with a lot of different solutions.

> *To give this issue the space it deserves, we'll discuss it fully in the next section of this chapter. Therefore, we'll leave the object properties as they are for now.*

Remember that everything we've done so far is tentative; we may still need some of the objects that we've eliminated if we find that they have methods in the following step. Still, it's a pretty good bet that we're close - so it is worth putting together an object model diagram that we can use to figure out the methods:

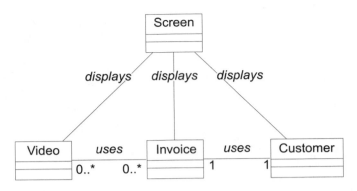

The object model has been simplified dramatically through this process. The analysis is geared toward building a simple model with just the objects that we need to represent the business process within our application. Since we chose not to remove the *screen* entity in the diagram during this process, we've also been able to simplify the model so that it will be easy to use when it's time to develop the presentation layer.

# Identifying Object Behaviors (or Methods)

Objects do not only have attributes; they also have behaviors. Our programs ask an object to act out its behaviors by using **methods**. A method is very much like a subprogram, or function, that our program can call; but whereas a subprogram is simply a routine in our program, a method is part of our object's interface and thus is available for use by our object's clients.

Objects have behaviors that help model their role in business processes. Very often, they also have behaviors, or methods, that let them interact with the other objects in the model - in ways that aren't necessarily obvious from the use cases.

> *We're going to discuss business process behaviors in this section. We'll cover object relationship behaviors in the next section.*

The technique we need to follow to determine an object's behavior is very similar to that which we've just seen for an object's properties. First, we need to go through the functional use case to find any methods that are required. Then, we need to look at our object model and add any methods that are required for objects to interact with each other.

## Identifying Behaviors - Looking through the Use Case

Let's look through each object in our object model and read through the use case to decide what behaviors or actions each object might be able to take. Many business objects primarily provide data, so don't be surprised if many of our objects don't have methods.

Looking at the *customer* object, we can see that the actual person does a lot of things, like putting the videos on the counter, and providing an ID card. However, our software doesn't need to be aware of these actions - so we don't need to provide methods for them. But our software does need to retrieve and display the customer's name and address once the ID number is entered. Now, since these are attributes of the *customer* object, it's a good bet that our *customer* object will have some behavior to load this information.

Next, let's look at the *video* object. Again, the *video* object doesn't play an active part in the use case as far as our application is concerned - other than that it needs to load the description and rental price once its ID number is entered.

Our last object is the *invoice* object. This object isn't directly in the use case at all, but it does have the subtotal, tax and total values as attributes. The use case indicates that these values are calculated, so the *invoice* object will probably need a method to support this behavior.

At this point, our objects have the following behaviors:

| Object | Behavior |
| --- | --- |
| Customer | Load customer data |
| Video | Load video data |
| Invoice | Calculate subtotal |
| | Calculate tax |
| | Calculate total |

*If we look back at the requirements use case, we can see that there are other behaviors that we are not taking into account. For instance, the invoice needs to be printed, and it's implied that the rented videos will be recorded in the inventory system. We don't need to worry about these issues at this point, since they would normally be covered by other functional use cases. This illustrates how closely all the different use cases are related to each other, and how they are all used together to come up with a comprehensive object model.*

## Identifying Behaviors - Looking through the Object Model

The *customer* and *video* objects both have behaviors that comprise loading data from a database. This type of behavior is integral in making objects persistent, as we discussed in Chapter 2. In Chapter 4, we'll get into the code for implementing this behavior. For now, however, we're just interested in defining our objects' interfaces, so we'll add a `Load` method to support this behavior, and worry about the details later.

We've listed three different calculation behaviors for the *invoice* object, all of which are closely related. This is an interesting situation that requires some thought. There are three ways to approach these behaviors:

- ❑ Implement three calculation methods
- ❑ Implement a single calculation method
- ❑ Automatically recalculate when properties are changed

When we're making decisions about our objects' interfaces, we need to keep our customer in mind. We have two main design issues: modeling the business entities, and making our objects easy to use at the presentation layer. Here, our customer is the programmer who is writing the user interface.

Implementing three different calculation methods means that the UI programmer needs to understand and call all three methods where appropriate. Since all the calculations are directly tied to each other, it would surely be much better to combine them into a single method for the programmer to call.

Better still, suppose the programmer didn't need to call *any* method to do the calculation. The calculation would only need to happen when a video was added or removed from the list of rentals. The *invoice* object owns the list of videos, so it should be able to detect when a video is added or removed - and automatically recalculate the values.

All three solutions are valid, and we could choose any of them and have a working program. We should always strive to provide the simplest object interface for the UI programmer, since it helps them to be more productive and it makes the code less prone to bugs. In this case, the upshot is that we'll opt to automatically recalculate the subtotal, tax and total, so that those values are always correct. This means we don't need any calculation methods on our *invoice* object.

Ideally, we'd be able to notify the UI when the values have been recalculated, thus making it easy for the programmer to update the display. Fortunately, Visual Basic 6.0 provides the RaiseEvent command to let us do just that.

# Notification (or Events)

There are many times when objects can perform some action in response to a property being set or a method being called. This has traditionally been difficult to implement, since an object has usually needed to notify the calling program that the action has taken place.

In the previous section, we discussed the *invoice* object and how it can detect when a video is added or removed from the list of rentals. Either of these conditions should cause the subtotal, tax and total amounts to be recalculated. The challenge is that the UI needs to be notified that these values have changed so that the display can be updated.

## Traditional Solutions

Traditionally, this would have been handled either by having the UI refresh the values when it added or removed a video, or by calling a special *Calculate* method to force the calculation.

If the UI updates the values when adding or removing a video, we've effectively coded some business logic into the UI. After all, the UI would have to know all the conditions under which the values might change, so that it could know when to refresh the display.

Using an explicit *Calculate* method is also far from ideal. If we have such a method, then we're relying on the UI code to call it, rather than recalculating our values automatically. If the UI doesn't call the method when appropriate, we could end up in a situation where the subtotal, tax, and total properties on the object would be incorrect. This solution can not only lead to bugs, but it also requires that the UI programmer must have more knowledge about how our object works than we might otherwise prefer (such as a more appropriate time to call the *Calculate* method).

## Callbacks

A more complex solution to the problem would be to have the *invoice* object call a method of another object and have that object update the UI. This solution solves most of our problems, but it's definitely harder to implement for the UI developer.

To implement this, the UI itself would have to create an object to receive the message sent by the *invoice* object. Of course, the *invoice* object would need to know about the UI's object so that it could call it; we'd therefore need to add a method to the *invoice* object so that the UI could pass a reference to its object!

Once the *invoice* object had a reference to the UI's object (let's call it *Displayer*), it could call some predefined method on the *Displayer* object whenever a message needed to be sent to the UI. This is shown in this diagram:

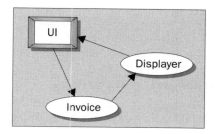

Let's look through some code that could handle this.

### Displayer Object

First off, our UI developer will need to provide an object to update the display. Create an ActiveX DLL project, create a new class module called `Displayer`, and add this sample code:

```
Option Explicit

Public Sub UpdateValues()

    ' in this routine we'd update our display
    ' with the properties from the Invoice
    ' object

End Sub
```

This example assumes that we've implemented our business objects in an ActiveX DLL, and that the UI is in a different EXE or DLL. We'll keep our `Displayer` class in a separate ActiveX DLL for now, which will allow us to create a simple UI test harness in a Standard EXE. (Alternatively, if we had created our UI in a ActiveX DLL, then the `Displayer` class could have been included within the main UI project.)

The `Displayer` class must also have its `Instancing` property set to **5 - MultiUse** so that we can make it available to the `Invoice` object.

The upshot of all this is that if we did want our `Displayer` class to be within the main UI program, then our UI project would need to be an ActiveX server - whereas it may have only needed to be a regular program prior to the introduction of the callback mechanism.

### Invoice Objects

Within the main DLL project for our business objects, the `Invoice` class also needs some special code to support the callback. It needs a method that will allow the UI to give it a reference to the `Displayer` object.

For our current example, add another ActiveX DLL project for our business objects, using the File | Add Project... menu option, then add a class module, using the Project | Add Class Module menu option, and call that class module `Invoice`. Now add the following sample code to `Invoice`:

```
Option Explicit

Private mobjCallback As Object

Public Sub SetCallback(Display As Object)

  Set mobjCallback = Display

End Sub
```

### Performing the Callback

Then, add a routine where the `Invoice` object can do its calculations. In this routine we need to call the `UpdateValues` method of the `Displayer` object so it knows that the `Invoice` object's data has been changed:

```
Public Sub Calculate()

  ' here we'd do the calculations

  mobjCallback.UpdateValues

End Sub
```

### Releasing Object References

Finally, we need to make sure that the `Invoice` object releases its reference to the `Displayer` object before the `Invoice` goes away. If we don't do this, we run the risk of having objects hanging around in memory after we've tried to close down the program:

```
Private Sub Class_Terminate()

  Set mobjCallback = Nothing

End Sub
```

### The UI Code

Now that all that has been set up, we can write some UI code that creates the `Invoice` object. Since we're going to use a Standard EXE to hold our sample UI and test our callback mechanism, add a Standard EXE project using the File | Add Project... menu option, and open the code window for `Form1`. Then enter this example code:

```
Option Explicit

Private mobjInvoice As Invoice
Private mobjDisplayer As Displayer

Private Sub Form_Load()

  Set mobjDisplayer = New Displayer
  Set mobjInvoice = New Invoice
```

```
      mobjInvoice.SetCallback mobjDisplayer
      mobjInvoice.Calculate

  End Sub
```

Notice that, as well as creating an `Invoice` object, we create a `Displayer` object, and give the `Invoice` object a reference to it.

*You'll need to make a reference to the `Invoice` object from the UI project. Select the UI project in the Project window, and use the Project | References menu option to select the project containing our `Invoice` object.*

*Since we've created a separate EXE for the UI test harness, we also need to add references to the projects containing the `Displayer` object and the `Invoice` object. Select the UI EXE project in the Project window, and use the Project | References menu option to select the appropriate references to the other projects.*

If you run the sample program as it stands, you won't see much happen: but if you step through the program execution, you'll see the callback mechanism alive and well. The UI code successfully establishes the `Displayer` callback method to itself before it calls the `Invoice` object's `Calculate` method. Within the `Calculate` method, the callback is then made to the `Displayer` class's `UpdateValues` routine.

This solves our problem, in that it allows an object to notify our program when something has happened. In our example, the `Invoice` object notifies the UI object that the `Calculate` method has been called. In some ways, this is very attractive, since the interaction between the two objects is very well defined, and the UI can give the `Invoice` object a reference to any object that implements an `UpdateValues` method. Since this technique uses regular method calls between the two objects, we can write our code to pass any parameters that our program might need.

On the other hand, this solution is somewhat complex: it forces the UI developer to add a new class to the project, or make the UI program an ActiveX server. It also tightly couples the business object to the UI implementation, since it requires that the UI provide an object with a specific method.

## Raising Events

Visual Basic 5.0 introduced the ability to raise **events** from our objects - a capability carried forward to Visual Basic 6.0. This means that we can write code in our class module that will raise an event in the calling code, just as a button control can raise a `Click` event in a form.

This is done with three related keywords within the Visual Basic language. In our class module, we need to use the `Event` and `RaiseEvent` keywords, respectively, to declare and raise events. In the calling code (Form or Class module), we need to declare the object using the new `WithEvents` keyword.

Sticking with the `Invoice` object example, we could have the `Invoice` object raise an event when the subtotal, tax and total amounts have changed. Then the UI programmer would just need to write code behind the event to update the display. This is a very nice model, since all Visual Basic programmers are familiar with writing code to respond to events - so the learning curve for the UI programmer is very small.

### Invoice Objects

Inside our `Invoice` object, we need to have a line to declare our event:

```
Option Explicit

Public Event UpdateValues()
```

Then in the routine where we calculate the amounts, we can change the code to raise the event rather than calling the method on our `Displayer` object:

```
Private Sub Calculate()
   ' here we'd do the calculations

   RaiseEvent UpdateValues

End Sub
```

All references to our `mobjCallback` object are now unnecessary, and we no longer need our `SetCallback` routine, since we've managed to create the same mechanism using events.

### The UI Code

The UI programmer just needs to make a change to the declaration of the `Invoice` object to include the `WithEvents` keyword. We'll make this change back in our Standard EXE project to the code in `Form1`:

```
Private WithEvents mobjInvoice As Invoice
```

At this point, the `mobjInvoice` object will appear in the **Object** dropdown in the upper-left of the code window, along with any other controls or objects that have events available to the module. If we choose `mobjInvoice`, then the **Procedure** dropdown in the upper right will list all the events that are declared in the `Invoice` class - just `UpdateValues` in this case. This means we can write a regular event procedure:

```
Private Sub mobjInvoice_UpdateValues()
   ' here we'd put the code to update the
   ' values on the display
End Sub
```

All references to our `mobjDisplayer` object are now unnecessary; and, since we no longer need our `Displayer` class module, the UI no longer needs to be an ActiveX server.

This solution is not very different from implementing a callback, but it does have some significant advantages. The UI programmer doesn't need to implement a special class. In fact, the UI programmer can draw on existing knowledge and techniques to write code behind the object's events - just as if they were events from a control on a form. Furthermore, the `Invoice` object author doesn't need to worry about being passed some external object, or any specifics about the calling program at all. They may appreciate that.

The bottom line is that the `RaiseEvents` command works independently of whether anyone actually receives the event that's raised. This means that we've effectively separated the UI programmer's tasks from the object developer's tasks.

# Other Use Case Formats

The concept of a use case is pretty broad. There are many different things called use cases that are written up in many different ways. That's fine - it's the concept of having a detailed description of a business process that is important.

The format that we used earlier in this chapter is a simple prose or text description of the process. A couple of other popular formats that we might encounter include: a step-by-step outline in a table format, a flowchart or a flow diagram.

Functional use cases are typically grouped together with the higher-level requirements use case from which they were derived. All of these use cases, when combined, provide a solid and traceable base of documentation for the subsequent design, development, testing and documentation of the system.

Functional use cases frequently include user-interface mock-ups or prototypes, often created in Visual Basic to look somewhat like the screen that the users will see at the end. This can be very useful, because it can help the users visualize the flow of the system as they proof our use case descriptions.

Developing prototype screens using Visual Basic can be very powerful. Not only can we create screens to assist our users in visualizing the system, but, if we're careful, we can get a significant head start on the development of the UI itself. Visual Basic is not only good for prototyping - it's also good for easily converting prototypes into full-blown applications without having to start over from scratch.

You may also notice that the object properties and methods were drawn from use cases. By covering most of the functionality with adequate number of use cases, we can get a better picture of the services required by the object.

# Object Relationships

At this point, we've gone through our use case scenarios, and we've defined all the objects that we need to model our business process. We've even gone so far as to determine how all the objects are related to each other at a high level.

Thus far, however, our objects don't have any properties or methods that actually lets them interact with each other. Essentially, we've identified relationships between objects; but we haven't added any way to implement those relationships.

Earlier in the chapter, we discussed the common types of object relationships:

| Relationship | Description/Example |
| --- | --- |
| Ownership (owns, has) | Parent-child relationships |
| User (uses) | One object uses or employs the services of another object |
| Aggregate (contains, made of) | One object is made up of other (subordinate) objects |
| Generalization (is a) | One object is a specific type of another object |

Let's go through each relationship and discuss how to implement that relationship with Visual Basic.

# The Ownership Relationship - Implementing Collections

Ownership really defines a parent-child type relationship between objects. There may be one child, or this may be a one-to-many relationship. In this section, we're going to focus on the situation where one parent has many children.

> **If there can only be one child, it's often more appropriate to view the relationship as a form of aggregation, which we'll talk about later in this chapter.**

This ownership relationship is the basis for most object hierarchies we'll find in Windows applications. It's usually viewed as a **collection** of child objects that are owned or controlled in some way by the parent. The best way to manage this type of relationship is to build a collection class to contain the child objects, and then implement a `Property Get` routine on the parent object to provide access to the collection object.

## The Invoice Object

If we consider our video store example, our `Invoice` object is likely to have a list of line items: one line item for each video that the customer rents. This is a parent-child type relationship, where it would be good to have a collection of `LineItem` objects available through the `Invoice` object.

In our `Invoice` object, we'll add a property so that the calling program can access the collection of videos. We'll call the new property `LineItems`, since it will be a list of `LineItem` objects. The code to handle this in the `Invoice` class would look something like this:

```
Option Explicit

Private WithEvents mobjLineItems As InvoiceItems

Private Sub Class_Initialize()

   Set mobjLineItems = New InvoiceItems

End Sub

Private Sub Class_Terminate()

   Set mobjLineItems = Nothing

End Sub


Public Property Get LineItems() As InvoiceItems

   Set LineItems = mobjLineItems

End Property

Private Sub mobjLineItems_AddItem(strID As String)

   CalculateAmounts

End Sub
```

```
Private Sub mobjLineItems_RemoveItem(strID As String)

  CalculateAmounts

End Sub
```

```
Private Sub CalculateAmounts()

   ' here we'd recalculate the subtotal, tax
   ' and total amounts for the invoice

End Sub
```

The LineItems property is the key, since it allows the calling program to get at the InvoiceItems collection. We've also included events so that the Invoice object will be notified when a LineItem object is added or removed from the collection. This ties in with our earlier discussion about raising events to recalculate the subtotal, tax and total amounts on the invoice.

## The InvoiceItems Collection Object

The InvoiceItems collection class is based on Visual Basic's native Collection class. Our collection uses a Visual Basic Collection object, internally, to store all the LineItem objects - but we've enhanced the Add method so that it only supports LineItem objects.

> *The normal Visual Basic* Collection *will accept just about anything to store, which doesn't bode well if we only want to allow* LineItem *objects.*

Add a new class module to the ActiveX DLL project that already contains our Invoice class. Here's what the code to support our InvoiceItems collection object might look like:

```
Option Explicit

Event AddItem(strID As String)
Event RemoveItem(strID As String)

Private mcolItems As Collection

Private Sub Class_Initialize()

  Set mcolItems = New Collection

End Sub

Private Sub Class_Terminate()

  Set mcolItems = Nothing

End Sub


Public Function Add(strID As String) As LineItem

  Dim objItem As LineItem

  Set objItem = New LineItem
```

```
    objItem.Load strID
    mcolItems.Add objItem, strID
    Set Add = objItem
    RaiseEvent AddItem(strID)

End Function
```

```
Public Sub Remove(ByVal varIndex As Variant)

  Dim strID As String

  strID = mcolItems.Item(varIndex).ID
  mcolItems.Remove varIndex
  RaiseEvent RemoveItem(strID)

End Sub
```

```
Public Function Count() As Long

  Count = mcolItems.Count

End Function
```

```
Public Function Item(ByVal varIndex As Variant) As LineItem

  Set Item = mcolItems.Item(varIndex)

End Function
```

```
Public Function NewEnum() As IUnknown

  Set NewEnum = mcolItems.[_NewEnum]

End Function
```

In this code, we've simply encapsulated a `Collection` object, `mcolItems`, by creating a `Private` variable and exposing our own `Add`, `Remove`, `Item`, and `Count` elements.

The key here is that the new `Add` method only supports `LineItem` objects, so that no unexpected object types can get into our collection. The `Add` method is also responsible for creating the `LineItem` object, and arranges to load any data based on the ID value supplied - by calling the `Load` method:

```
Set objItem = New LineItem
objItem.Load strID
```

Although we can't see it in the code, the `Item` method has been made the default by using the **Procedure Attributes** dialog for the `Item` procedure. This means that where we'd previously have written code like this:

```
Set objLineItem = objItems.Item(1)
```

We can now write the same line like this:

```
Set objLineItem = objItems(1)
```

To set a method as the default, choose the Tools | Procedure Attributes menu, and click on the Advanced button when the dialog comes up:

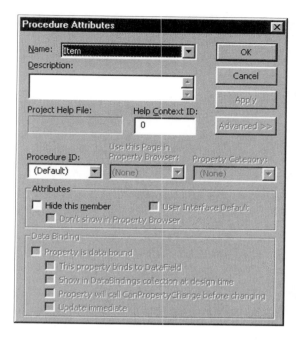

In the Name field, choose the method name to be changed. Then, in the Procedure ID field, choose the (Default) setting and click OK.

Our new class also contains a NewEnum method. This is a special method that allows the calling code to use the For Each...Next style of accessing the contents of our collection. This means that we can write client code like this:

```
For Each objLineItem In objItems
   Debug.Print objLineItem.Price
Next
```

By implementing the NewEnum method, we can make our user-defined Collection objects support the For...Each structure as well.

Our NewEnum method simply returns a hidden object within the native Visual Basic Collection class, called _NewEnum. Like the Item method, we need to use the Tools | Procedure Attributes menu option to set some special values for the NewEnum method. The following diagram shows the settings that are required:

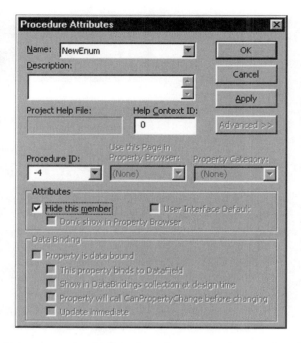

The Procedure ID field is set to −4, which is the value required to work with For...Each structures. Also, the Hide this member box is checked, to make our method hidden in the COM type library.

Notice that the InvoiceItems class declares and raises two events: AddItem and RemoveItem. These events allow the Invoice object to know when the calling program has added or removed a video from the collection, so that the invoice amounts can be recalculated.

## The LineItem Object

We'll keep the LineItem object simple. We'll just give it an ID and a Price property, along with the Load method. Add a class to our business object DLL project and name it LineItem. Here's the code:

```
Option Explicit

Private mstrID As String
Private mdblPrice As Double

Public Sub Load(ID As String)

  mstrID = ID
  ' eventually there will be code here to go
  ' load the video information from the
  ' database, but for now we'll just make up
  ' a price
  mdblPrice = 1.99

End Sub
```

```
Public Property Let ID(strValue As String)

  mstrID = strValue

End Property

Public Property Get ID() As String

  ID = mstrID

End Property

Public Property Let Price(dblValue As Double)

  mdblPrice = dblValue

End Property

Public Property Get Price() As Double

  Price = mdblPrice

End Property
```

The LineItem object has no extra code to support collections or any other relationships. The object is entirely designed around modeling the real-world video entity.

### The Calling Program

In order to bring this whole thing together, let's look at some code that will add some line items to the invoice and then interrogate the price of the first item:

```
Dim objInvoice As Invoice
Dim strPrice as String

Set objInvoice = New Invoice
objInvoice.LineItems.Add "1"
objInvoice.LineItems.Add "2"

strPrice= objInvoice.LineItems(1).Price
```

Notice how we've just used the LineItems method as though it were a collection, calling its Add method for each video.

This approach to implementing parent-child relationships is very powerful, and yet it provides a very easy interface for the end programmer who'll be using our objects to develop the application.

# The User Relationship - Calling Objects

When an object holds a reference to another object, and calls its properties or methods, we have a *uses* type relationship. Another way to look at this is as a client-server relationship between the two objects. The client calls properties or methods on the server, and gets an appropriate response.

This is the simplest of the relationships, and is one that virtually all Visual Basic programmers are familiar with - so we won't spend much time discussing it.

The user or client simply declares a variable and creates an object:

```
Dim objItem as LineItem

Set objItem = New LineItem
```

And then the user calls the object's properties or methods:

```
objItem.Load "ABC"
MsgBox objItem.Price
```

When the user is done with the object, they just release it by setting its reference to `Nothing`:

```
Set objItem = Nothing
```

Probably all of us have used objects, or at least controls, in the Visual Basic programs we've written. Having an object use another object is no more difficult than using an object from a form or code module.

# The Aggregate Relationship - Combining Objects

There are many times when an object is composed of other objects, in whole or in part. For instance, our `Invoice` object is partially composed of the `Customer` object. Without the `Customer` object, our `Invoice` doesn't have enough information to be useful. The `Customer` is subordinate to the `Invoice`, but the `Invoice` can't exist without the `Customer`.

There are two different approaches that we can use to handle this situation. The first of these is simple aggregation; the second involves combining interfaces.

Our discussion will therefore run as follows:

1. We'll look at a simple aggregation example
2. We'll alter that example to use a combined interface technique
3. We'll investigate how one object might expose another object's data as a read-only property

## Technique 1 - Simple Aggregation

The first approach we'll look at is simple aggregation. With this approach, we can simply expose the subordinate objects as properties of the top-level object. For instance, look at the following code:

```
Option Explicit

Private mobjCustomer As Customer

Private Sub Class_Initialize()

  Set mobjCustomer = New Customer

End Sub
```

```
Private Sub Class_Terminate()

   Set mobjCustomer = Nothing

End Sub
```

```
Public Function Customer() As Customer

   Set Customer = mobjCustomer

End Function
```

All we've done here, is create a private Customer object, and allowed the calling program to gain access to it through our Customer method. This is very simple to implement, and it gives the calling program full access to any of the objects we've aggregated into our top-level object.

There are, however, a couple of drawbacks to simple aggregation. The most obvious problem is that the calling program can do virtually anything to the aggregated object. In the example above, the calling program has full access to the Customer object, so it can change any properties or call any methods. In some cases, this might be fine, but we may want greater control over what the calling program can do, such as validation and error handling.

> When we're designing an object model, it's important to assume that everything will get misused or called incorrectly. Objects need to protect themselves, and if an object is composed of other objects then it needs to protect the subordinate objects as well.

## Technique 2 - Combining Object Interfaces

Now that we've seen how easy it is to implement simple aggregation, let's look at an approach that gives us more control over how the client code can use the aggregated object.

Although this doesn't follow true object-oriented design, it's often a better idea to simply merge the properties and methods of all the objects into a single object interface. With this approach, we can still have the aggregated objects instantiated inside our top-level object, but we don't make them directly available to the calling program.

Consider the following code from the Invoice class:

```
Option Explicit

Private mobjCustomer As Customer
Private mcurTax As Currency

Private Sub Class_Initialize()

   Set mobjCustomer = New Customer

End Sub
```

```
Private Sub Class_Terminate()

   Set mobjCustomer = Nothing

End Sub
```

```
Public Property Let Name(strValue As String)

   mobjCustomer.Name = strValue

End Property
```

```
Public Property Get Name() As String

   Name = mobjCustomer.Name

End Property
```

```
Public Property Get Tax() As Currency

   Tax = mcurTax

End Property
```

Note that this class is made up of both its own data and the Customer object; but rather than exposing the Customer object itself, this implementation has its own Name property that just calls the Customer object's Name property. This technique passes a lot of control to the Invoice object - at the expense of object-oriented philosophy.

Of course, this approach also has some drawbacks. If an aggregated object's interface changes, perhaps by adding a new property, then the new interface elements aren't immediately available to client programs. In that situation, we would need to add the new elements to the top-level object's interface first. With simple aggregation, on the other hand, where we would expose the aggregated object as a property, this problem would never arise.

## Technique 3 - Combining Data

As we've seen, simple aggregation and aggregation through combined interfaces are very good ways to solve the problem where one object relies on another for data or functionality. Unfortunately, neither solution is truly ideal in a client/server setting.

Let's diverge a bit from object theory, and look at a common scenario in business programming. Most of us work with data that is stored in relational tables. Even if we choose to represent that data as objects, such as Customer or Invoice, we'll often run into cases where the data needs to be consolidated (or aggregated) together across object boundaries.

With our current example, the Invoice object needs data from the Customer object to function - in our case, the Customer object's Name property. Essentially, we're trying to consolidate some of the Customer object's data into the Invoice. So far, we've done that using a couple of different techniques to implement aggregation.

Unfortunately, this can be very inefficient. In order to get the `Name` property from the `Customer` object, our `Invoice` object has to load the *entire* `Customer` object from the database. This means that we're loading two whole objects - one of them just to get a single property value. Most relational database engines can pull information together much faster than we can when we load individual objects and put them together ourselves.

Let's take an example. Here's a functional use case from the *Rental Analysis* requirements:

### Consolidated Reporting

This use case covers the specific steps used to consolidate the rental counts and prices for each video.

The system must scan all invoice detail lines for each video. Each invoice for a video will count as a single rental, and so the system must count the invoices. For this analysis, the system must also calculate an average rental price, based on each invoice for the video. Prices may change over the life of the video, and so the analysis needs to use the average price.

Once the system has calculated a video's rental count and average price, it needs to provide these numbers - along with the name of the producing studio and the video's category for analysis. The studio and category are stored with the other video information.

We'll discuss two different ways of solving this business situation. First, let's look at how we might solve it using pure aggregation of objects; then, we'll look at an alternative solution that provides much better performance.

## Object Approach

Looking at this problem with a pure object focus, we can quickly pick out the `LineItem` and `Video` objects as containing the data we need. We'll add in a `VideoData` object, which will contain the business logic to accumulate all the data together. So far, we have the objects and properties as shown in the table on the following page.

Using objects, our `VideoData` object would contain the logic to load all the `LineItem` objects for each invoice, and accumulate a rental count and average price for each `Video`. It would also aggregate the `Video` object to get the `Studio` and `Category` data.

> In Chapter 4, we'll discuss a couple of efficient techniques for loading and saving object data in a database. As good as these are, they don't compare to the performance we can get by processing a lot of data in the data tier.

| Object | Properties |
|--------|------------|
| LineItem | VideoID |
| | Price |
| Video | VideoID |
| | Studio |
| | Category |
| VideoData | VideoID |
| | RentalCount |
| | AveragePrice |
| | Studio |
| | Category |

It's relatively inefficient for the VideoData object to load all the LineItem objects from the database. The rental count and average price can be calculated with a simple SQL statement in the database itself, and this would be much faster. With an extra JOIN, the SQL statement can pull in the Studio and Category data without even having to load a separate Video object.

### Database Approach

Following a database train of thought, we would have one type of object: VideoData. This object would be loaded directly from the database using a SQL statement to pull together all the data at once, very efficiently. The following is an example SQL statement that we could use in Microsoft Access to achieve this:

```
SELECT InvoiceDetail.VideoID,
  Count(InvoiceDetail.VideoID) AS CountOfVideoID,
  Avg(InvoiceDetail.Price) AS AvgOfPrice,
  Videos.Studio, Videos.Category

FROM InvoiceDetail INNER JOIN Videos
  ON InvoiceDetail.VideoID = Videos.VideoID

GROUP BY InvoiceDetail.VideoID, Videos.Studio, Videos.Category;
```

The following figure shows this query in Access.

Of course, there are some drawbacks to building objects this way rather than through regular aggregation. Suppose the LineItem object had business logic behind the Price property. By pulling the price directly from the database, we will have bypassed that logic. This might force us to replicate the code inside the VideoData object. In that case, we'd want to think hard about which solution is the most appropriate.

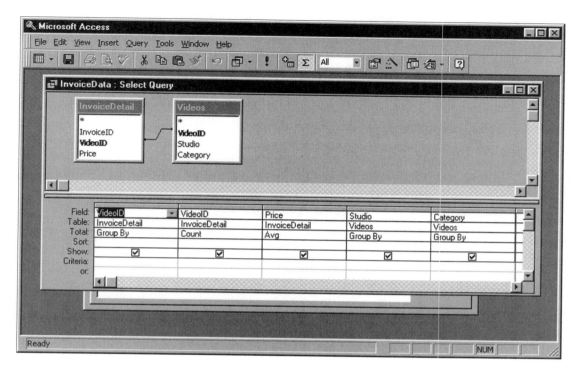

# The Generalization Relationship - Containing Objects

**Generalization** is an analysis technique used to find common ground between a number of objects. Once we've established that a group of objects have a set of common behaviors and properties, we can create a more generalized class to represent all those common elements. We can then use that generalized class as a base from which we can create all the other, more specialized, classes.

We can view this new, general class as a sort of *parent* to all the more specialized classes. The process of creating the specialized classes from the general class is called **inheritance** - something we discussed in a different context in Chapter 1. When we view our generalized class as a parent of the specialized classes, we're creating what's called a **class hierarchy**.

A class hierarchy is like a family tree for our objects. As we trace back from one object to the next, we become more and more general. Let's look at a quick example to see what this means:

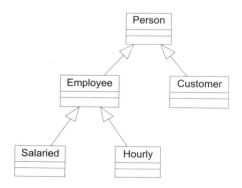

This diagram demonstrates how a class hierarchy might appear for various types of *Person*. If we look at an *Hourly* employee, we can see that they're a specialized type of *Employee*. In other words, the *Employee* class is a parent to *Hourly* and *Salaried*. We can follow the flow all the way back to the most general class, *Person*. All of these classes are derived from the *Person* class.

Generalization is a very powerful analysis technique. By identifying the commonalities between various objects, we provide ourselves with an opportunity to achieve a high level of reuse. Since we can implement all the common functionality in one class, we can then use that functionality in all the more specialized classes. The more specialized classes *inherit* the functionality from the generalized class.

Inheritance is the technique used to implement objects that are identified using the generalization technique. Visual Basic 6.0 doesn't provide a direct mechanism to support inheritance, but it's such an important concept that we need to provide it. As we discussed in Chapter 1, we can use containment and delegation together to simulate inheritance in Visual Basic.

To see how we can implement inheritance, let's use an example from our video rental store. Suppose the store decides to not only rent videos, but also to sell popcorn, candy bars and other snacks.

## Looking for Common Ground

We've already considered that our *Invoice* object has *LineItem* objects to reflect the videos that are rented. Now we're saying that we've got two different types of line item - a video rental line item and a line item for snacks the customer wants to purchase.

Let's look at the possible properties and methods for the video rental line item, which we'll call `RentalItem`:

| Properties | Methods |
|------------|-----------|
| Title | CheckOut |
| Price | MarkAsPaid |

Now let's look at the possible properties and methods we might find in the line item to purchase a snack (`PurchaseItem`):

| Properties | Methods |
|------------|-----------------|
| Price | ReduceInventory |
| TaxableFlag | MarkAsPaid |

We have a couple of indications that we may be able to come up with a more general class from these two. First off, we know they are both used in a similar way - they're both line items of an `Invoice` object. Secondly, in looking at their respective properties and methods, we can see that they share some interface elements.

Taking the common properties and methods from each, we derive the following list:

| Properties | Methods |
|:---:|:---:|
| Price | MarkAsPaid |

We can look at this as being a new, more general line item object, called LineItem. If we then use LineItem as a base from which to implement both the RentalItem and PurchaseItem objects, we'll have a class hierarchy.

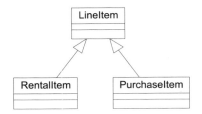

This diagram illustrates how each of our specialized line item classes, RentalItem and PurchaseItem, will inherit behaviors from the more general LineItem class.

Now let's implement this relationship using Visual Basic. To start with, we'll create our general class, LineItem. Once that's done, we'll use it as a base class to implement the RentalItem class. Once we've seen how to implement RentalItem, the implementation of the PurchaseItem class would be trivial, so we won't rehash the same material again.

## LineItem Class

Our general LineItem class will implement the properties and methods that are common to all line items. In this case, we're talking about a Price property and a MarkAsPaid method. Let's take a look at the code for the LineItem class:

```vb
Option Explicit

Private mdblPrice As Double
Private mflgPaid As Boolean

Public Property Get Price() As Double

  Price = mdblPrice

End Property

Public Property Let Price(dblValue As Double)

  mdblPrice = dblValue

End Property

Public Sub MarkAsPaid()

  mflgPaid = True

End Sub

Private Sub Class_Initialize()

  mflgPaid = False

End Sub
```

This code is very straightforward. Our `Price` property merely stores and retrieves its value from the `mdblPrice` variable, while the `MarkAsPaid` method simply sets the `mflgPaid` variable to `True`. Obviously, any real business object would be more complex, but this should be enough code to demonstrate how inheritance works.

## RentalItem Class

Now we're getting into the interesting part. Since Visual Basic doesn't directly support inheritance, we'll use a combination of containment and delegation to simulate it. We covered this briefly in Chapter 1, but we'll get a good taste for the process as we implement the `RentalItem` class.

### Setting up the RentalItem Class

Before we inherit the behaviors of the `LineItem` class, let's set up the basics of our `RentalItem` class. We don't need to worry about the `Price` property or the `MarkAsPaid` method, since we'll inherit them from the `LineItem` class. We do need to implement the `Title` property and `CheckOut` method however:

```
Option Explicit

Private mstrTitle As String
Private mflgCheckedOut As Boolean

Public Property Get Title() As String

  Title = mstrTitle

End Property

Public Property Let Title(strValue As String)

  mstrTitle = strValue

End Property

Public Sub CheckOut()

  mflgCheckedOut = True

End Sub

Private Sub Class_Initialize()

  mflgCheckedOut = False

End Sub
```

We've kept this code very simple as well. The `Title` property just stores and retrieves its value from the `mstrTitle` variable, with the `CheckOut` method setting the `mflgCheckedOut` variable to `True`.

### Containing a LineItem Object

With the basics of the class down, we can move on to inherit the `LineItem` class' functionality. The first thing we need to do is use the technique of containment to make our `RentalItem` object *contain* a `LineItem` object. This means declaring a `Private` variable to hold the reference to our `LineItem` object. Add the following line to the `RentalItem` class:

```
Option Explicit

Private strTitle As String
Private flgCheckedOut As Boolean

Private mobjLineItem As LineItem
```

We also need to create an instance of the `LineItem` class. The best place to do this is in the `Class_Initialize` routine, so the object is created right up front and is available any time we need it. Add this line to the `RentalItem` class:

```
Private Sub Class_Initialize()

   flgCheckedOut = False
   Set mobjLineItem = New LineItem

End Sub
```

## Inheriting Behavior Using Delegation

Our `RentalItem` object now has access to its own private `LineItem` object. Rather than implementing its own `Price` property, it can rely on its `LineItem` object's `Price` property to do the work. The same goes for the `MarkAsPaid` method, where the `RentalItem` object can *delegate* the work to its private `LineItem` object.

Of course, the `LineItem` object is `Private`, so any client code working with our `RentalItem` object won't be able to get at it. In order to make a `Price` property and `MarkAsPaid` method available to the client code, our `RentalItem` object will need to implement them. The implementation is simple however, since we'll just delegate the work down to our private `LineItem` object.

Add this code to the `RentalItem` class:

```
Public Property Get Price() As Double

  Price = mobjLineItem.Price

End Property

Public Property Let Price(dblValue As Double)

  mobjLineItem.Price = dblValue

End Property

Public Sub MarkAsPaid()

  mobjLineItem.MarkAsPaid

End Sub
```

When the client code calls the `MarkAsPaid` method, for instance, our `RentalItem` code merely echoes the call to the `LineItem` object's `MarkAsPaid` method, rather than trying to do any work itself.

### Trying It Out

Let's take a quick look at some client code that we might use to work with the RentalItem object at this point. Rather than creating a UI for such a simple example, let's look at how we might test this object in Visual Basic's Immediate debug window. With our two classes in place, we can enter the following into the Immediate window:

```
set x = New RentalItem
x.Price = 1.99
print x.Price
 1.99

x.MarkAsPaid
x.CheckOut

x.Title = "Video A"
print x.Title
 Video A
```

This example shows how we're able to work with the properties and methods from the RentalItem object itself, as well as those from the LineItem object. To the client code, there is no difference at all. This is exactly the behavior that we'd get using actual inheritance, were it available.

This would, of course, be a lot easier if Visual Basic directly supported inheritance; but, at the same time, this shows that we can do inheritance in Visual Basic - after a fashion. Since generalization is such an important part of object design, it's very important for us to be able to implement it in some manner.

# Summary

In this chapter, we've discussed the analysis and design process for developing a logical business object model. Our discussion included:

- ❑ Requirements use cases (or scenarios)
- ❑ Functional use cases
- ❑ How to identify objects from our use cases
- ❑ How to determine the properties, methods and events for our objects
- ❑ Object relationships and how to implement them using Visual Basic

Object-oriented analysis and design techniques provide us with very powerful and useful tools. These techniques can be useful whether we're going to implement our application using object technology or not, since they offer a general way to model our business entities and processes.

From here, we'll move on to look at implementing robust, real-world business objects and components using Visual Basic. Then, in Chapter 5, we'll start to tie everything together as we implement a full-blown example application based on the video rental store example that we studied in this chapter.

# 4

# Designing Business Objects

## Overview

In Chapter 2, we looked at the logical parts, or tiers, of a client/server application. In this chapter, we'll walk through the common *physical* architectures that we're likely to encounter as we develop our applications. We'll look at how the different logical tiers of the application fit into each physical model, and we'll discuss some different options in each case.

The physical architectures that we'll discuss include:

- ❑ 2-tier (client workstations and a database server)
- ❑ 3-tier (client workstations, application servers, and database servers)
- ❑ n-tier (traditional or browser-based client, Web server and/or application servers, and database servers)

We'll also look at some specific design concerns for our business objects. Our UI-centric business objects need to communicate with a user-interface, and there are some issues that we need to be aware of when we're designing our objects to make this work well.

We'll discuss how the Component Object Model (COM) can be used by our objects to communicate with each other. There are some serious performance concerns we need to consider as we implement our objects and their communications. Fortunately there are a number of mechanisms we can use to minimize the performance impact and we'll examine a number of them.

Additionally, our objects need to be **persistent**. This means that they must have a way to be saved and restored from a database. The CSLA (Component-based Scalable Architecture) provides for this, and in this chapter we'll get right into the details on how it's all done. As ever, what sounds easy enough in principle can be challenging in practice, so we'll take a good look at some of the techniques available in Visual Basic to make it fast and easy to persist objects.

# Physically Distributed Architectures

When we discussed the CSLA, in Chapter 2, we didn't dictate which machines were to run any particular part of our application. In this section, we're going to go through the most common physical architectures. We'll explore how we can place the logical tiers of our application on physical machines to provide a rich, interactive user-interface, good application performance, and scalability.

## 2-Tier Physical Architecture

So far, I've portrayed 2-tier applications as the 'old way' of doing things. In reality, however, this is still the most common physical client/server architecture, so it's important that we look at how we can use the CSLA within this physical 2-tier environment.

### Traditional 2-Tier

In a traditional 2-tier design, each client connects to the data server directly, and the processing is distributed between the data server and each client workstation.

Take a look at the following diagram. On the left, we can see the physical machines that are involved; on the right, we can see the logical layers - next to the machines on which they'll be running:

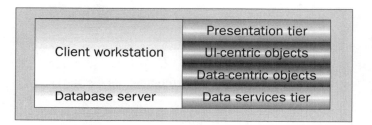

In this case, we've put virtually all the processing on the client, except for the data processing itself. This is a very typical 2-tier configuration, commonly known as an **intelligent client design,** since quite a lot of processing occurs on the client workstation.

> *Intelligent client is just another name for a* fat client, *but without the politically incorrect overtones.*

This approach makes the most use of the horsepower on the user's desktop, relying on the central database only for data services.

Just how much processing is performed on the server can have a great impact on the overall performance of the system. In many cases, the data processing can add up to a lot of work, and if the data server is being used by a great many clients then it can actually become a performance bottleneck. By moving most of the processing to the clients, we can help reduce the load on the data server.

Of course, the more processing that's moved to the client, the more data is typically brought from the server to the client to be processed. For example, suppose we want to get a list of customers in a given zip code and whose last name starts with the letter 'L'. We could have the server figure out which customers match the criteria and send over the result, or we could send over details of all the customers and have the client figure it out.

Here's the point: the more processing we move to the client, the more load we tend to put on the network. Of course, if we have *no* processing on the client, we might also have to send a lot of material over the network - since the server becomes responsible for creating each screen that's seen by the user, and those screens need to be sent across to the client.

> **Ideally, we can find a balance between the processing on the server, the processing on the client, and the load on the network, which uses each to their best advantage.**

### 2-Tier with Centralized Processing

Traditional 2-tier architectures lack one very important feature. Typically, no *business* logic runs on the server: it's all located in the clients. Certainly, there may be a fair amount of work done on the server to provide data services, but the bulk of the business processing is almost always limited to the clients.

Even in a 2-tier setting, it would be very nice if we could put some services on our database server to provide shared or centralized processing. If our data server can support the extra processing, and it's running Windows, then we can most certainly design our application to match this diagram:

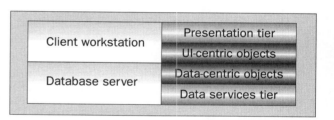

With this approach, we have objects that are running on a central server machine. This means that they can easily interact with each other, allowing us to create shared services, such as a message service, that allow a business object to send messages to other business objects on other client workstations.

This model might also reduce the network traffic. Our data-centric business objects can do a lot of preprocessing on the data from the database *before* sending it over the network - so we can reduce the load on the network.

Another benefit to this approach is that it means the database doesn't have to be a SQL database. Since the application service objects sit between the database and the actual business objects on the clients, they can allow us to use a much less sophisticated database in a very efficient manner. This could also allow us to tap into multiple data sources, and it would be entirely transparent to the code running on the client workstations.

For instance, our application may need to get at simple text files on a central server - maybe hundreds or thousands of such files. We could create an application service object that sent the data from those files to the business objects on the client workstations and updated the data when it was sent back. From the business object's viewpoint, there would be no way of knowing whether the data came from text files or from memo fields in a complex SQL database.

*Of course, this model puts a lot of extra processing on the database server. Before jumping on this as a perfect solution, we would need to evaluate whether that machine could handle both the data processing and the application service processing without becoming a bottleneck.*

## 3-Tier Physical Architecture

In a 3-tier design, the client workstations communicate with an application server, and the application server communicates with the data server that holds the database.

This is a very powerful and flexible way to set things up. If we need to add another database, we can do so without changing the clients. If we need more performance, we just add another application server - again with little or no change to the clients.

In the following diagram, the physical machines are on the left, and the various tiers of the application on the right. You can see which parts of the application would be running on the different machines:

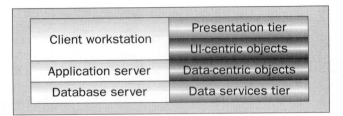

### Client: Presentation and UI-Centric Business Objects

With this approach, both the presentation layer and some objects are placed on the client workstations. This may appear a bit unusual, since it's commonly thought that the business objects go on the central application server machine.

In an ideal world, keeping all the business processing on the application server would make sense. This would put all the business rules in a central place where they would be easy to maintain. As we discussed in Chapter 2, however, this typically leads to a batch-oriented user-interface rather than the rich interface most users desire.

By moving all our processing off the client workstations, we're also failing to make good use of the powerful computers on the users' desktops. Most companies have invested immense amounts of money to provide their users with powerful desktop computers. It seems counterproductive to ignore the processing potential of these machines by moving all the applications processing to a central machine.

Another view might be that the objects should be on both the client *and* the server, moving back and forth as required. This might seem better still, since the processing could move to the machine where it was best suited at any given time. This is the basic premise of the CSLA, where we've split each business object between its UI-centric and data-centric behaviors - effectively putting half the object on the client and half on the application server.

Unfortunately, Visual Basic has no innate ability to move objects from machine to machine. From Visual Basic's perspective, once an object has been created on a machine, that's where it stays. This means we need to come up with an effective way of moving our objects back and forth between the client and the application server. We'll look at some powerful techniques for handling this later in the chapter.

Performance issues play a large role in deciding where we should place each part of our application. Let's look at our 3-tier physical model and see how the tiers of our application will most likely communicate:

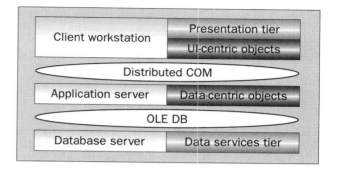

When we're using ActiveX servers like the ones we create with Visual Basic, the client workstations typically communicate with the application server through Microsoft's Distributed Component Object Model (DCOM). Our data-centric objects will most likely use OLE DB or ODBC to communicate with the database server, although this is certainly not always the case.

When we're working with DCOM, we have to consider some important performance issues. As we go through this chapter, we'll look at various design and coding techniques that we can use to achieve an excellent performance. In general, however, due to the way DCOM works, we don't want to have a lot of communication going on across the network. The problem is not that DCOM is slow, or less powerful than other network communication alternatives, such as Distributed Computing Environment (DCE) or Common Object Request Broker Architecture (CORBA). The bottom line is that this problem happens to be common to all of these related technologies.

> **It is always important to minimize network traffic and calls to objects or procedures on other machines.**

Regardless of performance arguments, we should always keep our objects phyically close to whatever it is that the objects interact with the most. The user-interface should be close to the user, and the data processing should be close to the data. This means that the user-interface should be on the client, and the data services should be on the data server. By keeping the objects in the right place we can avoid network communication and gain a lot of performance.

Our UI-centric business objects primarily interact with the user-interface, so they belong as close to that interface as possible. After all, the user-interface is constantly communicating with the business objects to set and retrieve properties and to call methods. Every now and then, a business object talks to its data-centric counterpart, but the vast bulk of the interaction is with the user-interface.

### Application Server: Data-Centric Business Objects

As we discussed in the last section, the data-centric business objects run on the application server. Typically, these objects will communicate with the database server using OLE DB or possibly ODBC:

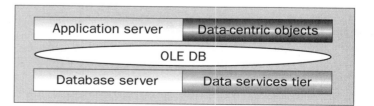

We'll probably use ActiveXData Objects (ADO) to interact with OLE DB. If we are using a common relational database such as SQL Server or Oracle we may use any one of the database technologies available within Visual Basic 6.0. The most common technologies include:

- ActiveX Data Objects (ADO)
- Remote Data Objects (RDO)
- ODBCDirect

In general, ADO is the preferred data access technologies. All of the other data technologies (RDO, ODBC or ODBCDirect) continue to be supported, but Microsoft is putting their development efforts entirely toward improving and enhancing ADO (and OLE DB, its underlying technology). The version of ADO (2.0) included with Visual Basic 6.0 provides relatively comparable or even better performance when compared to technologies such as RDO.

If we choose not to use ADO and we're working with a typical database server, such as Oracle or SQL Server, then RDO is probably the next choice. It provides very good performance, and allows us to tap into many of the features of the database server very easily. RDO is just a thin object layer on top of the ODBC API, so there's very little overhead to degrade performance.

ODBCDirect should be avoided if at all possible, since it is a technology that Microsoft recommends against using. As part of the push toward ADO and OLE DB, ODBCDirect is already considered obsolete.

Something to keep in mind is that the application server can talk to the data server in whatever way really works best. For instance, our application server may use TCP/IP sockets, some form of proprietary DLL, or screen-scraping technology, to interact with the data source:

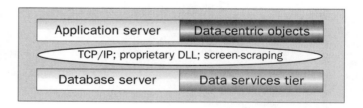

This illustrates a major benefit to this whole design, and one that a lot of companies can use. If our data is sitting on some computer that's hard to reach, or expensive in terms of licensing or networking, then we can effectively hide the data source behind the application server and still let our UI-centric business objects work with the data, regardless of how we accessed it.

## Internet Architecture

Now that we've looked at a fairly traditional 3-tier physical architecture, let's examine a couple of different architectures for Internet/Intranet development. These architectures are not the typical Web browser-based designs that most people are familiar with. Instead, we're going to blur the browser approach together with the CSLA to demonstrate a multi-tier architecture with a browser interface.

### Architecture #1

The first architecture we'll look at is the closest to today's typical Web development. On the left is the physical layout, which is very typical of a Web environment. On the right, though, we're using our now familiar CSLA, with one exception:

| Web browser | Presentation tier |
|---|---|
| Web server | IIS Application |
| | UI-centric objects |
| | Data-centric objects |
| Database server | Data services tier |

One of the primary goals for Internet development is to keep the client as thin as possible to provide compatibility across all the different Web browsers out there. This means that we should avoid putting any processing on the client if at all possible.

Ideally, all we'd ever send to a client would be pure HTML, since that would let any browser act as a client to our program. Of course, HTML provides no ability to do any processing of program logic on the client side, and so this provides the ultimate in thin clients.

Since the Web browser client provides no real processing capabilities, we need a layer of code to run within Microsoft Internet Information Server (IIS) to act as a surrogate or proxy user-interface for the business objects.

> *Similar capabilities are available for other web servers, but we'll stick with IIS in this book because it is the easiest to work with from Visual Basic.*

We could actually implement this layer using a variety of technologies, but we've shown it here using a new type of project in Visual Basic 6.0: an IIS Application. IIS Applications provide us with very powerful capabilities when it comes to building applications on the web server. They are a successor to Active Server Pages (ASP) based applications, providing similar capabilities, but within the context of a full-blown Visual Basic application.

Our newly added IIS Application interface layer accepts input from the browser and uses it to act like a traditional business object client. What this really means is that the Visual Basic code in this layer takes the place of the Visual Basic forms that we'd normally be using as an interface to the business objects.

Our IIS Application can access COM objects as easily as any other Visual Basic application. However, IIS Applications have special capabilities that make it very easy for us to send HTML out to the user's browser. Thus, IIS Applications make an excellent surrogate for a forms-based user interface since we can tap into the power of our UI-centric business objects and use that information to generate the appropriate interface for the user.

With this technology, and a good set of components containing business objects, we can build an application based on business objects and then use IIS Applications to create the user-interface. We'll cover this in more detail in Chapter 14, where we'll build an IIS Application interface. This interface will use the same underlying business objects as the Visual Basic form-based interface that we'll create in Chapter 7 and the Microsoft Excel interface that we'll create in Chapter 9.

### Architecture #2

The second design that we'll look at here is very similar to the first, but it's more scalable. In this design, we retain the application server from the 3-tier model that we discussed earlier to offload some of the processing from the web server:

| Web browser | Presentation tier |
|---|---|
| Web server | IIS Application |
|  | UI-centric objects |
| Application server | Data-centric objects |
| Database server | Data services tier |

In this diagram, we've moved the data-centric business objects off the Web server and back on to the application server. This can be particularly useful if we have a mixed environment where we're providing a browser interface for some users and a Visual Basic forms interface to others.

The code running in the IIS Application takes the place of the Visual Basic forms in a more traditional user-interface. This means that any code that would have been behind our Visual Basic forms, to format data for display, or to modify any user input, will be coded within the IIS Application – generating HTML to be sent to the user's browser. Either way, this code should be pretty minimal, since any actual business logic should always be placed in the business objects or application services.

> *If we want to get real fancy, we can use the new DataFormat object capability of Visual Basic 6.0 to create an ActiveX DLL that contains objects that know how to format our data for display. These objects could then be used when we're developing our forms based interface as well as our IIS Application interface.*

The IIS Application also needs to generate the HTML responses for the user, essentially creating a dynamic display of our data. Since IIS Applications are written in Visual Basic there's a very small learning curve to move from traditional Visual Basic development to developing Web pages using IIS Applications.

# COM/DCOM Performance

Most of the physical architectures that we've been looking at use DCOM (Distributed Component Object Model) for communication between machines on the network. But even with the speed improvements over Remote Automation, DCOM can still be pretty slow. In particular, there is substantial overhead on a *per call basis*.

Each time our program calls an object's property, or method, there's a speed hit. We get pretty much the same speed regardless of whether our call sends a single byte to the object or a thousand bytes. Sure, it takes a little longer to send a thousand bytes than a single byte, but the COM *overhead* is the same either way - and that overhead is far from trivial.

## Calling Single Properties

From a high-level view, each time we access a property or call a method, COM needs to find the object that we want to talk to; and then it needs to find the property or method. Once it's done all that work, it moves any parameter data over to the other process, and calls the property or method. Once the call is done, it has to move the results back over to our process and return the values.

Take the following code, for example:

```
Set objObject = CreateObject("MyServer.MyClass")

With objObject
  .Name = "Mary"
  .Hair = "Brown"
  .Salary = 31000
End With
```

This code has four cross-process or cross-network calls (depending on whether `MyServer` is on the same machine or across the network). The `CreateObject` call is remote and has overhead. Each of the three property calls is also remote, and each has similar overhead. For three properties, this might not be too bad; but suppose our object had 50 properties, or suppose that our program was calling these properties over and over in a loop. We'd soon find this performance totally unacceptable.

# Passing Arguments to a Method

Passing multiple arguments to a method, rather than setting individual properties, is significantly faster. For example:

```
Set objObject = CreateObject("MyServer.MyClass")

objObject.SetProps "Mary", "Brown", 31000
```

But too much overhead still remains, because of the way COM and DCOM process the arguments on this type of call. Furthermore, this technique doesn't allow us to design our business objects in the way we discussed in Chapter 3. With this technique, we'd end up designing our object interfaces around technical limitations.

# Serialization of Data

Many programmers have tried the techniques we've just seen, and they've eventually given up, saying that COM is too slow to be useful. This is entirely untrue. Like any other object communication technology, COM provides perfectly acceptable performance, just as long as we design our applications using an architecture designed to work with it.

Due to COM's overhead, when we're designing applications that communicate across processes or across the network we need to make every effort to minimize the number of calls between objects. Preferably, we'll bring the number of calls down to one or two, with very few parameters on each call.

> **Instead of setting a series of parameters, or making a method call with a list of parameters, we should try to design our communication to call a method with a single parameter that contains all the data we need to send.**

There are five main approaches we can take to move large amounts of data in a single method call:

- ❑ Directly passing user defined types
- ❑ `Variant` arrays

- ❑ User defined types with the `LSet` command
- ❑ ADO(R) `Recordset` with marshalling properties
- ❑ PropertyBag objects

In any case, what we're doing is **serializing** the data in our objects. This means that we're collecting the data into a single unit that can be efficiently passed to another object and then pulled out for use by that object.

## Directly Passing User Defined Types

Visual Basic 6.0 provides us with a new capability, that of passing user defined types (UDTs) as parameters – even between different COM servers. This means we can easily pass structured data from one object to another object, even if the objects are in different Visual Basic projects, running in different processes or even running on different computers.

For instance, suppose we create a class named `SourceClass` in an ActiveX server (DLL or EXE):

```
Option Explicit

Public Type SourceProps
  Name As String
  BirthDate As Date
End Type
```

```
Private mudtProps As SourceProps
```

```
Public Property Let Name(ByVal Value As String)

  mudtProps.Name = Value

End Property
```

```
Public Property Get Name() As String

  Name = mudtProps.Name

End Property
```

```
Public Property Let BirthDate(ByVal Value As Date)

  mudtProps.BirthDate = Value

End Property
```

```
Public Property Get BirthDate() As Date

  BirthDate = mudtProps.BirthDate

End Property
```

```
Public Function GetData() As SourceProps

  GetData = mudtProps

End Function
```

This class is fairly straightforward, simply allowing a client to set or retrieve a couple of property values. Note how the UDT, `SourceProps`, is declared as `Public`. This is important, as declaring it as `Public` makes the UDT available for use in declaring variables outside the object. The other interesting bit of code is the `GetData` function:

```
Public Function GetData() As SourceProps

   GetData = mudtProps

End Function
```

Since the object's property data is stored in a variable based on a UDT, we can provide the entire group of property values to another object by allowing it to retrieve the UDT variable. The `GetData` function simply returns the entire UDT variable as a result, providing that functionality.

Now we can create another class named `ClientClass`:

```
Option Explicit

Private mudtProps As SourceProps

Public Sub PrintData(ByVal Source As SourceClass)

   mudtProps = Source.GetData
   Debug.Print mudtProps.Name
   Debug.Print mudtProps.BirthDate

End Sub
```

This class simply declares a variable based on the same UDT from our `SourceClass`. Then we can retrieve the data in the `SourceClass` object by using its `GetData` function. Once we've retrieved the data and stored it in a variable within our new class we can use it as we desire. In this case we've simply printed the values to the Immediate window, but we could do whatever is appropriate for our application.

This mechanism allows us to pass an object's data to any other code as a single entity. By serializing our object's data this way, we can efficiently pass the data between processes or even across the network.

## Variant Arrays

The `Variant` data-type is the ultimate in flexibility. A `Variant` variable can contain virtually any value of any data-type - including numeric, string, or even an object reference. As you can imagine, an *array* of `Variants` extends that flexibility so that a single array can contain a collection of values, each of a different data-type.

For instance, consider this code:

```
Dim vntArray(3) As Variant

vntArray(0) = 22
vntArray(1) = "Fred Jones"
vntArray(2) = 563.22
vntArray(3) = "10/5/98"
```

Inside the single array variable `vntArray` we've stored four different values, each of a different type. We can then pass this entire array as a parameter to a procedure:

```
PrintValues vntArray
```

In a single call, we've passed the entire set of disparate values to a procedure. Since methods of objects are simply procedures, we could also pass the array to a method:

```
objMyObject.PrintValues vntArray
```

The `PrintValues` procedure or method might look something like this:

```
Public Sub PrintValues(Values() As Variant)

  Dim intIndex As Integer

  For intIndex = LBound(Values) To UBound(Values)
    Debug.Print Values(intIndex)
  Next intIndex

End Sub
```

This simple code just prints the values from the array to the immediate window in the Visual Basic development environment. It does, however, illustrate how easy it is to get at the array data within an object's method.

Of course, the `Variant` data-type is highly inefficient compared to the basic data-types, such as `String` or `Long`. Using a `Variant` variable can be many times slower than a comparable variable with a basic type. For this reason, we need to be careful about how and when we use `Variant` arrays to pass data.

The `Variant` data-type is generic, meaning that a `Variant` variable can hold virtually any piece of data we provide. The downside to this is that, each time we go to use the variable, Visual Basic needs to check and find out what kind of data it contains. If it isn't the right type of data then Visual Basic will try to convert it to a type we can use. All this adds up to a lot of overhead, and thus our performance can suffer.

If our object's data is stored in a `Variant` array, we'll incur this overhead every time we use any of our object's data from that array. The code in most objects work with data quite a lot, so we really do run the risk of creating objects with poor performance if we use `Variant` arrays.

## Using GetRows

Many of our objects will need data from a database. If we're going to use a `Variant` array to send this data across the network, we'll need some way to get the data from the database into the array. Usually, we'll get the data from the database in the form of an ADO `Recordset`.

`Recordset` objects provide us with an easy way to copy the database data into a `Variant` array. This is done using the `GetRows` method that's provided by the object. The `GetRows` method simply copies the data from the object into a two-dimensional `Variant` array.

The following code, for instance, copies the entire result of a query into a `Variant` array named `vntArray`:

```
Dim vntArray As Variant

rsRecordset.MoveFirst
vntArray = rsRecordset.GetRows(rsRecordset.RecordCount)
```

`vntArray` now contains the contents of the recordset as a two-dimensional array. The first dimension indicates the column or field from the recordset; the second dimension indicates the row or record:

```
vntMyValue = vntArray(intColumn, intRecord)
```

Of course, the subscripts for the column are numeric, so they aren't as descriptive as the field name would be if we had access to the actual recordset. Instead of the following:

```
vntValue = rsRecordset("MyValue")
```

We're reduced to using something like this:

```
vntValue = vntArray(2)
```

The order of columns is entirely dependent upon the field order returned in the recordset. This means that if we add a field to our SQL `SELECT` statement, in the middle of other fields that we're retrieving, then we'll have to change all of our programs that rely on `Variant` arrays to pass data.

## Passing User-Defined Types with LSet

Many people store their object's data in a variable based on a UDT, because it's a very concise and convenient way to handle the values. While Visual Basic allows us to pass UDT variables as parameters, there are some serious drawbacks to this approach.

In particular, we need to make the UDT `Public` in order to pass it as a parameter. This feature can't be used if our objects are not part of an ActiveX server – for instance from a **Standard EXE** project. Additionally, this approach makes it very easy for someone to write a client program that retrieves our object's data, manipulates it without our business logic and places it back in the object. Finally, VB passes UDT variables in a way not supported by other tools or languages. Using this technique prevents us from passing the data to routines written in other languages or through other tools such as Microsoft Message Queue.

The ideal would be if we could use a UDT to store our object's data, but also be able to retrieve that data as a single stream of data – say in a `String` variable.

Luckily, there is a very nice solution that enables us to efficiently convert a UDT variable to a `String` variable so we can pass its data to another ActiveX component. We'll take a good look at this solution, but first let's put it in perspective.

### Background

Many languages have some equivalent to Visual Basic's UDT. For instance, C has the `struct`, and both FORTRAN and Pascal have similar constructs. Some languages natively support multiply-defined structures, where the programmer can define two different variable definitions for the same chunk of memory. FORTRAN implements `COMMON` memory blocks, while C uses a `union` keyword within a `struct`:

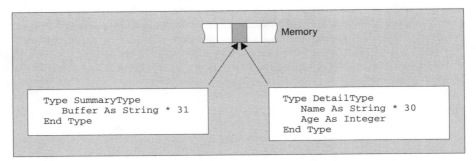

Multiply-defined structures are very powerful. They allow us to set up a user-defined type like this:

```
Private Type DetailType
  Name As String * 30
  Age As Integer
End Type
```

Then we can set up another user-defined type that is exactly as long as `DetailType`:

```
Private Type SummaryType
  Buffer As String * 31
End Type
```

> Remember that in Win32 environments such as Windows 98 and Windows NT, strings are all Unicode; therefore, each character in a string will actually consume 2 bytes of memory. This is so Windows can support more complex character sets, such as those required by Arabic or languages in the Far East.
>
> So `DetailType` is a total of 62 bytes in length: 60 for the `Name` field and 2 for the `Age` field. This means that `SummaryType` also needs to be 62 bytes in length. With Unicode, a 62 byte `String` is actually half that many characters. Therefore, dividing 62 by 2, we find that `SummaryType` needs to be 31 characters long.
>
> It's worth noting that if `DetailType` were 61 bytes in length (say `Age` was a `Byte`) then `SummaryType` would still need to be 31 characters long, since we must round up. If we didn't round up, then `SummaryType` would be just 30 characters long and could only hold 60 of the 61 characters: we'd lose one byte at the end.

FORTAN, C, and some other languages would allow a single variable to be referenced as `DetailType` or `SummaryType`. In other words, they would let us get at the same set of bytes in memory in more than one way. This means that we could set the `Name` and `Age` values with `DetailType`, and also treat the memory as a simple String without having to copy any values in memory.

Since Visual Basic doesn't allow us to pass a UDT variable as a parameter to an object, we need some way to convert our UDT variables to a data-type that can be passed. The ideal situation would be one in which we could simply define the same chunk of memory as both a UDT and a simple String variable, as shown above.

Although Visual Basic doesn't allow us to do this, it does provide us with a very efficient technique that we can use to provide an excellent workaround.

### Visual Basic Implementation

Visual Basic's approach does require a memory copy, but it's performed with the `LSet` command, which is very fast and efficient. Let's take a look at how `LSet` works.

Open a Standard EXE project and type in the `DetailType` and `SummaryType` UDT's that we just looked at. They need to be entered in the **General Declarations** section of our form. Then add the following code to the `Form_Click` event:

```
Private Sub Form_Click()

  Dim udtDetail As DetailType
  Dim udtSummary As SummaryType

  With udtDetail
    .Name = "Fred Jones"
    .Age = 23
  End With

End Sub
```

This code simply defines a variable, using each UDT, and then loads some data into the `udtDetail` variable, which is based on the `DetailType` type. So far, this is pretty simple - so here comes the trick. We'll add a line using the `LSet` command:

```
Private Sub Form_Click()

  Dim udtDetail As DetailType
  Dim udtSummary As SummaryType

  With udtDetail
    .Name = "Fred Jones"
    .Age = 23
  End With

  LSet udtSummary = udtDetail

End Sub
```

This new line uses the LSet command to do a direct memory copy of the contents of udtDetail into udtSummary. Visual Basic doesn't perform any type checking here; in fact, it doesn't even look at the content of the variables; it just performs a memory copy. This is very fast and very efficient: substantially faster than trying to copy individual elements of data, for instance.

The result of this code is that the Name and Age values are stored in the udtSummary variable, and can be accessed as a string using udtSummary.Buffer. Of course, the values stored aren't all printable text, so if we try to print this value we'll get garbage. That's OK though: the objective was to get the data into a single variable. Now we can pass that string to another procedure using the following code:

```
Private Sub Form_Click()

  Dim udtDetail As DetailType
  Dim udtSummary As SummaryType

  With udtDetail
    .Name = "Fred Jones"
    .Age = 23
  End With

  LSet udtSummary = udtDetail
  PrintValues udtSummary.Buffer

End Sub
```

The PrintValues subroutine just accepts a simple String as a parameter. Of course, we're really passing a more complex set of data, but it's packaged into a simple String at this point so it's easy to deal with. Let's look at the PrintValues routine:

```
Private Sub PrintValues(Buffer As String)

  Dim udtDetail As DetailType
  Dim udtSummary As SummaryType

  udtSummary.Buffer = Buffer
  LSet udtDetail = udtSummary

  With udtDetail
    Debug.Print .Name
    Debug.Print .Age
  End With

End Sub
```

Again, we declare variables using DetailType and SummaryType for use within the routine, and we copy the parameter value into udtSummary.Buffer. Both values are simple Strings, so this isn't a problem. We do need to get at the details of Name and Age, though, so we use the LSet command to perform a memory copy and get the data into the udtDetail variable:

```
  LSet udtDetail = udtSummary
```

Once that's done, we can simply use udtDetail as normal: in this case, for just printing the values to the Immediate window in the Visual Basic IDE.

**128**

If you run this program, and click on the form, the appropriate output will appear in the Immediate window accordingly.

### Memory Alignment

In most languages, including Visual Basic, the compiler will align certain user-defined data-types in memory so that they fall on longword boundaries. This means that the compiler inserts filler space if an element won't start on an even 4-byte boundary.

This slightly complicates how we determine the length of our string buffer UDT. While this memory alignment problem adds some complexity to our use of LSet to copy a UDT, it's not hard to overcome. Let's look at the details of the problem, and then we'll see how easy it is to solve.

Consider the following user-defined type:

```
Private Type TestType
  B1 As Byte
  L1 As Long
End Type
```

If we assume that the compiler starts the type on a memory boundary, then B1 will be at the start of a 4-byte boundary. But B1 is only a single byte long, and it's required that L1 start on a longword boundary; so that leaves 3 bytes of space, between B1 and L1, which need to be taken up. This is where the compiler inserts the filler space.

One way to quickly check the actual length (in bytes) of a UDT is to declare a variable based on the UDT in question and use the LenB function. This function will return the length, in bytes, of any variable - including one based on a UDT. For instance, we could write the following code:

```
Private Sub TypeLength()

  Dim udtTest As TestType

  MsgBox LenB(udtTest)

End Sub
```

If we run this subroutine, we get a message box showing the total number of bytes in the TestType UDT, which in this case is 8.

Not all data-types are longword-aligned. Some are word-aligned, meaning that they'll fall on 2-byte boundaries. To accurately determine where the compiler will be adding filler space, we need to know which data-types will be word-aligned and which will be longword-aligned. The following data-types are always aligned to a word (2 byte) boundary:

```
Byte
Integer
Boolean
String
```

The following data-types are longword aligned by the compiler:

```
Long            Single
Double          Date
Currency        Decimal
Object          Variant
```

The compiler will add space as needed in front of any of these data-types, so they always start on a longword boundary.

When the compiler adds these filler spaces, it makes our UDT that much longer. Of course, we're creating another UDT to copy our data into, so we need to know exactly how long to make that UDT so that it can fit all the data. Here's our problem: the length of the string needs to be inflated to include the filler spaces - otherwise it will be too short, and the last few bytes of data will be lost during the copy.

The following UDT will hold 6 bytes of data:

```
Private Type StringType
   Buffer As String * 3
End Type
```

At first glance, we might expect `StringType` to be able to contain the `TestType` elements shown above, since a `Byte` and `Long` combined are only 5 bytes in length. But because L1 (the Long) needs to be longword-aligned, the compiler inserts 3 filler bytes before L1; therefore, the total length of `TestType` is actually 8 bytes. This means that we need the following UDT to hold all the data from `TestType`:

```
Private Type StringType
   Buffer As String * 4
End Type
```

While the issue of longword alignment makes it more complicated to determine the length of the buffer UDT, it is a predictable behavior, and it isn't really very hard to ensure we get the length correct.

## ADO(R) Recordset with Marshaling Properties

ADO 2.0 provides us with some powerful new capabilities that we can use to help us serialize an object's data and transfer it from one process to another or across the network from one computer to another. The core of this capability lies with ADO's support for batch mode updating of a `Recordset` object. With this capability, ADO is able to not only provide a reference to a `Recordset` object, but it can actually copy the object's data from one process to another or from one machine to another – essentially allowing us to pass ADO `Recordset` objects by value rather than by reference.

Couple the ability to move `Recordset` objects across the network with ADO 2.0's support for `Recordset` objects that are disconnected from any database connection. This means we can create a `Recordset` object out of thin air – no database required. We can define the columns of data we want to provide, then add or manipulate rows of data at will.

Between these two capabilities, we can use ADO 2.0 to create an arbitrary Recordset object to store any data we'd like and then pass that Recordset from process to process or machine to machine as we choose. ADO takes care of all the details of serializing the Recordset itself, allowing us to simply interact with a Recordset object to view, update or add our data.

Before we can pass a Recordset around our network we need to create it. There are two ways to create a Recordset object for serializing our object's data – creating the Recordset from a database, or creating a connectionless Recordset through code.

## Creating Recordset Objects from Data

The most common way to create a Recordset object is to select some data from a database to be loaded into the object. However, if we're going to pass that Recordset around the network we do need to take some extra steps as we open it.

In particular, we need to set the CursorLocation property of our Connection or Recordset object must be set to adUseClient. This causes ADO to use a cursor engine located on the client machine rather than one within the database server itself. Since the cursor engine is local to the client, we can send the Recordset's data to any machine where ADO or ADOR (the light-weight client version of ADO) is installed.

We also need to specify the LockType property of our Recordset as adLockBatchOptimistic. This causes ADO to build our Recordset object in a batch update mode, allowing us to manipulate the Recordset and its data even if it is not currently connected to the data source.

By setting these two properties as we initialize our Recordset object we will cause ADO to automatically support batch processing of our data, and to automatically pass the Recordset object's *data* to any process that interacts with the object.

There is one caveat to this approach. Our CursorType property can only be one of adOpenKeyset or adOpenStatic when we are using a batch mode Recordset. If we are passing the Recordset to a machine that only has ADOR installed (such as a thin client workstation), then we can only use the adOpenStatic setting for the CursorType property.

Let's take a look at some code that opens a Recordset and returns the object upon request:

```
Public Function GetData() As Recordset

  Dim rs As Recordset
  Dim strConnect As String

  Set rs = New Recordset

  strConnect = "Provider=Microsoft.Jet.OLEDB.3.51;" & _
     "Persist Security Info=False;Data Source=c:\Wrox\VB6 Pro Objects\Video.mdb"

  With rs
    .CursorLocation = adUseClientBatch
    .Open "SELECT * from customer", strConnect, adOpenStatic, _
          adLockBatchOptimistic
  End With

  Set GetData = rs
  Set rs = Nothing

End Function
```

This code doesn't look much different than what we'd expect to see any time we open a Recordset based on some data in a database. However, there are a couple interesting things to note. First off, before calling the Open method we set the CursorLocation property of the object:

```
.CursorLocation = adUseClientBatch
```

Then, in the call to the Open method we set the LockType to adLockBatchOptimistic. We also set the CursorType to adOpenStatic. We could have set it to adOpenKeyset if we'd chosen, but by choosing adOpenStatic we know we can pass the Recordset to a client that might only have ADOR installed without having ADO convert our cursor type during that process

### Creating a Connectionless Recordset

While we can create Recordset objects from a database, that often won't work well for serializing data from our objects. It is not at all unusual for an object's state to include information that isn't necessarily stored in a database. For instance, we may wish to pass a flag indicating whether our object is new or other types of information between our client workstation and the application server. If our Recordset object is generated directly from a database query we are restricted to only passing information that comes from that database.

Fortunately ADO 2.0 provides a very elegant solution to this problem by allowing us to create a Recordset object that is totally unrelated to any data source. The steps involved in this process are quite straightforward:

- ❑ Create the Recordset object
- ❑ Add columns to the Recordset using the Fields object's Append method
- ❑ Open the Recordset
- ❑ Add or manipulate data in the Recordset

As an example, the following code creates a connectionless Recordset with two columns of data: Name and BirthDate. We then add a couple rows of information to the Recordset object and return it as a result of the method:

```
Public Function MakeData() As Recordset

  Dim rs As Recordset

  Set rs = New Recordset

  With rs
    .Fields.Append "Name", adBSTR
    .Fields.Append "BirthDate", adDate

    .Open

    .AddNew
    .Fields("Name") = "Fred"
    .Fields("BirthDate") = "1/1/88"
    .Update

    .AddNew
    .Fields("Name") = "Mary"
    .Fields("BirthDate") = "3/10/68"
    .Update
  End With
```

```
    Set MakeData = rs

    Set rs = Nothing

  End Function
```

The first couple lines simply declare and create an instance of a `Recordset` object. Once that's done we can move on to adding columns to the empty `Recordset` by calling the `Append` method of the `Fields` object:

```
.Fields.Append "Name", adBSTR
.Fields.Append "BirthDate", adDate
```

After we have columns defined, all that remains is to load our object with some data. This is as simple as calling the `AddNew` method, loading some data and calling `Update` to store the data into the `Recordset`. Of course the data isn't stored into any database, since this `Recordset` exists only in our computer's memory.

### Passing a Recordset by Value

We've now looked at two different ways to create a `Recordset` object that we can pass to another process or across the network. Both of the routines shown above are written as `Function` methods, returning the `Recordset` object as a result.

ADO itself handles all the details of moving the `Recordset` object's data to the client process or computer, so we really don't need to do any extra work at all beyond setting the properties as we did to create the `Recordset`. Our client code can be quite simple as shown by the following fragment:

```
Dim objServer As Object
Dim rs As Recordset

Set objServer = CreateObject("MyDataServer.DataMaker")

Set rs = objServer.GetData

Set objServer = Nothing
```

Once this code fragment is complete, we have a `Recordset` object to work with. This code assumes that the code to create the `Recordset` is in an ActiveX server named `MyDataServer` and in a class named `DataMaker`. This ActiveX server could be running in another process, or on another machine on the network.

Regardless, once we've got the `Recordset` through this code, the `MyDataServer` ActiveX server can be totally shut down – the machine it is running on could even be shut off – and our code can still continue to work with the `Recordset` and its data.

The program running this code fragment does require a reference to either the ADO or ADOR library in order to function. In many cases the lighter-weight ADOR library is sufficient, as it provides basic support for interacting with `Recordset` object's that are created and updated by another process or machine.

## *PropertyBag Objects*

A property bag is an object that supports the concept of a key-value pair. The idea is that the property bag can store a value associated with a key, or name, for that value. For instance, we might store the value 5 along with the key Height. At any point we can also retrieve the Height value from the property bag.

Visual Basic 5.0 introduced the concept of a PropertyBag object as part of the ability to create ActiveX controls. While the concept was useful when storing properties of our control that the developer set at design time, we couldn't take advantage of the PropertyBag object outside of control creation.

Visual Basic 6.0 extends the PropertyBag object such that we can use it anywhere we choose within our applications. Basically, anywhere that we need to manage key-value pairs, we can make use of the PropertyBag object provided by Microsoft.

Better still, the PropertyBag object implements a Contents property that allows us to access the entire contents of the object as a single Byte array – essentially it provides built-in support for streaming its own data. We can retrieve the data, send the Byte array as a parameter to another process or across the network, and then place it into a PropertyBag object, giving us an exact duplicate of the object we started with.

Of course Byte arrays aren't nearly as easy to manipulate or work with as a String variable would be. Fortunately this isn't a serious problem either, as Visual Basic makes it very easy for us to convert a Byte array to a String and then back to a Byte array.

### *Serializing an Object's Data*

Let's take a look at some simple code that illustrates how we can use a PropertyBag to serialize the data in an object.

Suppose we've got an object with two pieces of data: Name and BirthDate. We can store this data in a PropertyBag object with code similar to this:

```
Public Function GetObjectData() As String

  Dim pbData As PropertyBag

  Set pbData = New PropertyBag

  With pbData
    .WriteProperty "Name", mstrName
    .WriteProperty "BirthDate", mdtmBirthDate
  End With

End Function
```

Once we've created the PropertyBag object, we can simply use its WriteProperty method to store the values from our object into the property bag. In this case, we're assuming that the name and birth date data are stored in the variables mstrName and mdtmBirthDate.

After our property bag has our object's data, we can retrieve all the data in a single Byte array using the PropertyBag object's Contents property.

```
Public Function GetObjectData() As String
  Dim pbData As PropertyBag

  Set pbData = New PropertyBag

  With pbData
    .WriteProperty "Name", "Fred"
    .WriteProperty "BirthDate", "5/14/77"
  End With

  GetObjectData = pbData.Contents
End Function
```

With this simple code we've converted our object's data into a single `String` variable that we can easily pass as a parameter to another object, even across the network.

### Deserializing an Object's Data

Now that we've seen how we can take data from an object and use a `PropertyBag` to serialize that data into a simple `String` variable, let's take a look at how we can use that `String` variable to load another object with the data.

Since we know we'll be receiving a `String` value, the first step is to convert that `String` into a `Byte` array so we can place it into the `PropertyBag` object's `Contents` property. While we're doing this, we'll also need to create a `PropertyBag` object to work with:

```
Public Sub LoadObject(StringBuffer As String)
  Dim arData() As Byte
  Dim pbData As PropertyBag

  Set pbData = New PropertyBag

  arData = StringBuffer

  pbData.Contents = arData

End Sub
```

Once we've converted the `String` to a `Byte` array, we simply set the `Contents` property of our `PropertyBag` using that value. This causes the `PropertyBag` object to contain the exact data that was contained in the other `PropertyBag` object that we used to create the `String` variable.

Now that the `PropertyBag` object has been populated we can use the `ReadProperty` method to retrieve the individual data values for use by our object:

```
Public Sub LoadObject(StringBuffer As String)
  Dim arData() As Byte
  Dim pbData As PropertyBag

  Set pbData = New PropertyBag

  arData = StringBuffer

  pbData.Contents = arData
```

```
    With pbData
      mstrName = .ReadProperty("Name")
      mdtName = .ReadProperty("BirthDate")
    End With

  End Sub
```

In many ways the use of a `PropertyBag` object for serializing our object's data is comparable to how we used the `LSet` command to convert a UDT to a `String`. Either approach results in our object's data being converted into a single `String` value that we can pass as a parameter, store in a database or send as the body of an email or Microsoft Message Queue (MSMQ) message. Once the data reaches the other end of its journey we can easily reconstitute our object by converting the `String` value back into its original form.

# Designing Our UI-Centric Business Objects

So far, we've looked at how the logical tiers of our application can be deployed across various physical machines. We've also looked at the performance ramifications of using COM and Distributed COM to communicate between our objects.

In this section, we'll go through a number of key concepts that are critical to our business objects and the creation of Visual Basic user-interfaces to our objects. Here are the major themes we'll be considering:

- ❑ The UI as a business object client
- ❑ Field-level validation
- ❑ Object-level validation
- ❑ Canceled edits
- ❑ Protecting properties and methods

In the sections that follow, we'll be developing a small project to help us discuss these main themes. And in Chapters 5 through 7, where we'll expand upon this discussion, we'll implement a full set of major business objects and a corresponding user-interface that will become the core of our video rental store project.

## The UI as a Business Object Client

One of the primary tenants of the CSLA is that the user-interface will rely on our business objects to provide all the business rules and business processing. This implies that there will be a fair amount of communication between our UI-centric business objects and the user-interface itself:

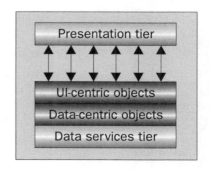

In the CSLA, the UI-centric business objects typically reside on the same machine as the user-interface. In the first section of this chapter, we looked at 2-tier, 3-tier, and Internet physical architectures - so we've seen where the Presentation tier and UI-centric objects may reside.

In a conventional client/server setting (2-tier or 3-tier), we can put these Presentation tier objects and UI-centric objects directly on the client workstations. If we were developing a browser-based user-interface, we'd put these objects on a Web server using an IIS Application.

The following figure shows how all the logical tiers of our application can be deployed across the physical machines in both a 3-tier and Internet scenario:

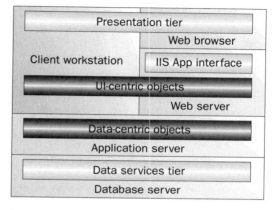

By keeping the UI-centric business objects as close to the user-interface as possible, we can make the development process as easy as possible for the UI developer. If the UI-centric objects are right there on the client machine then they're easy and safe to work with. This means quick development and a higher quality application.

Most larger projects will be developed in a team setting. Typically, the team will be divided into developers who manage the data, developers who construct the business objects, and developers who develop the user interface (UI) by using the business objects. The people in each of these groups need different skills and a different focus.

The UI developers are those who use the business objects. Ideally, they don't need to understand OO analysis or design; nor do they need to have full knowledge of the complexities of DCOM, network traffic, or implementing inheritance with Visual Basic. Instead, these people should have skills geared toward creating an intuitive user-interface. Their focus is on providing the user with the best possible experience when using the application.

## Designing Our Objects to Support the UI

It's our job, as business object designers and builders, to make the UI developer's job as easy as possible. We need to design our business objects so that they are powerful and provide all the features and functionality that the UI developer will need. At the same time, our objects have to be robust and self-protecting.

> If an object can be misused, it will be misused. If an object can be created outside of its proper place in an object hierarchy, it will be. In short, if our business objects don't protect themselves then the resulting application will be buggy.

> *What this really boils down to is that the UI is just a client of the business objects. The business objects are the core of the application, and the UI is secondary. This makes it very easy to change the UI without risking the business logic stored in the business objects.*

It also means that we can change our business logic in one place and, by simply upgrading the ActiveX components that contain our business objects, we can change the application's behavior. Often this can be done with little or no impact on the user-interface itself.

We need to make sure that our objects provide sufficient functionality so that we don't limit the capabilities of the UI. At the same time, we need to make sure that our functionality is not tied to any single UI or interface concept. If we compromise our objects for a specific UI then we set a precedence that might mean we'll change our objects any time the UI is changed - and that is exactly what we want to avoid.

Ideally, we should design our UI-centric business objects so they provide a robust and consistent set of services for use by the user-interface. It isn't enough that the objects simply represent real-world entities; they also need to make it easy for the UI developer to create rich and interactive user-interfaces.

## Business Behaviors vs. UI Behaviors

The business-related behaviors of each object will vary - depending on the real-world entity that each object represents. At the same time, we should be able to provide a consistent set of behaviors, across all our business objects, to support the user-interface. We don't want the UI developer to have to learn a whole new set of rules to work with each and every business object. Instead, we want all our business objects to basically behave in the same manner.

As we've already seen, our objects provide an interface that is composed of properties, methods, and events that represent real-world objects. This is sufficient to create a simple UI that just lets the user enter information in the hope that it's correct. However, there are a couple other types of interaction that a UI will need if we want to provide more feedback to the user. These include raising errors and having some way to indicate when an object is in a valid state.

We also need to take steps to ensure that the UI developer can't easily break our objects by calling inappropriate methods or setting inappropriate properties. And we need to prevent the UI from creating or accessing objects that need to be protected.

# A Basic Object and User-Interface

We've just covered a number of concepts that are very important if we're going to provide a consistent set of behaviors to the users of our objects. To illustrate these concepts, we'll use a simple example. This will let us try out each concept in turn.

## The Person Class

For our example, let's create a single class that represents a person. It's going to be easy to work with this class, because we can all understand the properties and behaviors that might make up a *Person* object. This class also makes a good example for us because there isn't very much difference between a person, a customer, and an employee - and the latter two are both typical business objects that we might need to create.

### Defining the Person Object's Interface

We won't get too carried away with the attributes of a person. Certainly we could list hundreds, if not thousands, of attributes, but we'll limit the list to four:

- ❑ SSN (social security number)
- ❑ Name
- ❑ Birthdate
- ❑ Age

In Chapters 1 and 3, we discussed events and how they could be used to allow our objects to indicate when certain things happened. In our Person object, we'll implement an event to indicate when the person's age has been changed:

- ❑ NewAge

As we'll see, this event will need to be fired any time the BirthDate property is set, since that is when the person will get a new Age property value.

### Setting up the Project

If we're going to do some coding, we'll need to set up a project in Visual Basic where we can work. Following the CSLA, we'll actually want to create two different projects: one for our business object (Person), and one for the user-interface.

Putting the UI in a separate project from the business object will help enforce the separation between the presentation and business tiers. The UI itself will be in a program that the user can run, just like any other program we'd normally create. For our business objects, we'll use an ActiveX DLL, since we don't want the overhead of running a whole other EXE for our Person object.

Right now, we're going to concentrate on the Person object. We'll create a project for the UI once we're done with the Person object. So create a new ActiveX DLL project, and change the name of the project to PersonObjects using its **Properties** window.

### Coding the Person Object

Once we've opened our new PersonObjects project, we should see the code window for Class1. Use the **Properties** window for the class to change the name of the class to Person.

Here is the code for the Person class:

```
Option Explicit

Event NewAge()

Private Type PersonProps
    SSN As String * 11
    Name As String * 50
    Birthdate As Date
End Type

Private mintAge As Integer
Private mudtPerson As PersonProps
```

```vb
Public Property Let SSN(Value As String)

  mudtPerson.SSN = Value

End Property

Public Property Get SSN() As String

  SSN = Trim$(mudtPerson.SSN)

End Property

Public Property Let Name(Value As String)

  mudtPerson.Name = Value

End Property

Public Property Get Name() As String

  Name = Trim$(mudtPerson.Name)

End Property

Public Property Let Birthdate(Value As Date)

  Static intOldAge As Integer

  mudtPerson.Birthdate = Value

  CalculateAge

  If mintAge <> intOldAge Then
    intOldAge = mintAge
    RaiseEvent NewAge

  End If

End Property

Public Property Get Birthdate() As Date

  Birthdate = mudtPerson.Birthdate

End Property

Public Property Get Age() As Integer

  Age = mintAge

End Property

Private Sub CalculateAge()

  If DatePart("y", mudtPerson.Birthdate) > DatePart("y", Now) Then
    mintAge = DateDiff("yyyy", mudtPerson.Birthdate, Now) - 1

  Else
```

```
        mintAge = DateDiff("yyyy", mudtPerson.Birthdate, Now)

    End If

End Sub
```

This class contains a very straightforward set of code. We just accept the values for properties and return them when requested. The exception being that we call the `CalculateAge` method to recalculate the `mintAge` value each time the `Birthdate` property is set, so that it can be returned in the read-only `Age` property.

Also notice that we have code to raise the `NewAge` event in the `Property Let` routine for the `BirthDate` property. When we get a new birth date for the person, we always need to check to see if we've changed the person's age. If we have changed their age, we can raise this event to indicate to our client program that the age is now different.

That's all there is to this class, for the moment. We'll expand on its functionality shortly, but right now we need make sure that we can create a user-interface to work with this simple version.

## The PersonDemo User-Interface

### Adding the Project

Let's put together a very simple form to act as an interface for a `Person` object. We'll build this in a new **Standard EXE** project called `PersonDemo`. We can add this project to the same Visual Basic session that we used to build the `PersonObjects` project: simply choose the <u>F</u>ile|<u>A</u>dd Project... option, rather than <u>F</u>ile|<u>N</u>ew Project, and choose **Standard EXE**. Don't forget to change the name of this second project to `PersonDemo` using its **Properties** window.

> *When we run our project with other projects loaded inside the IDE, Visual Basic will break us into the debugger in any of the projects that are loaded, making this a very attractive feature for debugging. It hasn't always been this easy - in Visual Basic 4.0, we would have had to run a copy of Visual Basic for each project we wanted to debug interactively.*

### Creating the Form

Select `Form1` and change its name to `EditPerson`. Here's what we'll want this form to look like:

141

The form has three text boxes so that the user can supply values for the social security number (txtSSN), name (txtName), and birth date (txtBirthDate). It also has a label set up to display the person's age (lblAge), as well as standard **OK**, **Cancel** and **Apply** buttons (cmdOK, cmdCancel and cmdApply). Set the **Enabled** properties of cmdOK and cmdApply to False, and set the **BorderStyle** property of lblAge to 1 - Fixed Single.

## Referencing the PersonObjects Project

Before we start putting code behind the form, we need to make sure our new project has access to our Person class. Even though both projects are running within the same Visual Basic window, we still need to add a reference from our UI project back to the ActiveX DLL we created.

To do this, we need to choose the **Project|References** menu option to bring up the **References** dialog window. Then find the entry for **PersonObjects** and check the box to the left:

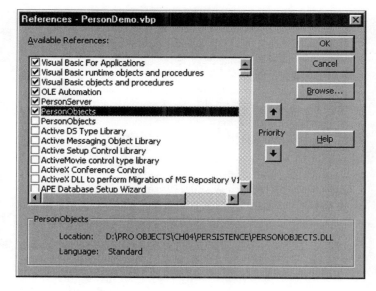

When we click OK, we'll establish a reference from our UI project back to our in-process server, PersonObjects. This will give our program access to all the public classes in that project. In this case, we'll get access to the Person class.

## Adding the Code

Now let's put some code behind the **Edit Person** form:

```
Option Explicit

Private WithEvents mobjPerson As Person

Private Sub cmdApply_Click()

    ' save the object

End Sub

Private Sub cmdCancel_Click()

    ' do not save the object
    Unload Me
```

```
    End Sub

    Private Sub cmdOK_Click()

        ' save the object
        Unload Me

    End Sub

    Private Sub Form_Load()

        Set mobjPerson = New Person

    End Sub

    Private Sub mobjPerson_NewAge()

        lblAge = mobjPerson.Age

    End Sub

    Private Sub txtBirthdate_Change()

        If IsDate(txtBirthdate) Then mobjPerson.Birthdate = txtBirthdate

    End Sub

    Private Sub txtName_Change()

        mobjPerson.Name = txtName

    End Sub

    Private Sub txtSSN_Change()

        mobjPerson.SSN = txtSSN

    End Sub
```

There's nothing terribly complex going on here.

At the top, we declare a variable to hold our Person object and then, in the Form_Load event, we create a Person object and store a reference to it in the mobjPerson variable. The only point worth making, here, is that we're using the WithEvents keyword as we declare the mobjPerson variable. This is what allows our program to receive the NewAge event that the Person object might raise. We don't have to use the WithEvents keyword, but without it we won't be able to receive the event.

If we do receive a NewAge event, it will be handled in the mobjPerson_NewAge routine. In this case, we want to update the age value that's displayed in lblAge with the mobjPerson.Age property.

Each text box has a Change event subroutine that simply takes the value from the control and puts it into the corresponding property of our Person object. We are trusting the business object, Person, to handle any validation or business rules, so there's no reason to worry about that here in the UI.

*While we could use the new* Validate *event that was introduced in Visual Basic 6.0, the* Change *event allows us to apply our business logic as the user enters each keystroke, providing the richest possible feedback to the user. Additionally, the* Validate *event suffers from the same limitation as the* LostFocus *event, in that it won't be fired if the user presses* Enter *to take the default button action or* Escape *to take the cancel button action. The* Change *event is the only way to ensure beyond all doubt that our business logic is applied to each field as the data is entered by the user.*

The OK, Cancel and Apply button code is intentionally vague. How we support these buttons from within our business object is tricky. The solution we're going to see is both elegant and powerful, but we'll need to beef up our Person object a bit before we're ready to cover it.

### Running the Program

Since it is from the PersonDemo project that our UI calls the business objects, we need to make sure that it's from the PersonDemo project that the program starts to run. To set this up, select the PersonDemo project in the **Project Group** window, right-click the mouse to get the context menu, and select **Set as Start Up**. Now, when we run the program, Visual Basic will begin execution within the PersonDemo project.

At this point, we should be able to choose the Run|Start menu option or press *F5* to run the program and interact with our Person object.

This seems like a pretty nice, straightforward solution. However, we'll soon find that we have a couple problems with our implementation, so let's take a look at them.

# Enforcing Field-Level Validation

Looking at the Person class, we see that it should only store 11 characters for the SSN and 50 characters for the Name - at least according to our user-defined type, PersonProps:

```
Private Type PersonProps
    SSN As String * 11
    Name As String * 50
    Birthdate As Date
    Age As Integer
End Type
```

Here's the situation: if we run the program and enter text into the SSN or Name fields on the form, we'll find that we can enter as many characters as we like. This is obviously a problem.

While we could simply set the MaxLength property on the form's fields, we haven't solved the underlying problem. After all, suppose the next interface is an Excel spreadsheet, where we don't have a MaxLength property. This is a clear case where the object needs to protect itself.

### Raising an Error from the Person Object

The easiest way for the object to indicate that it has a problem with a value is just to raise an error. So let's alter the SSN Property Let in our Person class as follows:

```
Public Property Let SSN(Value As String)

    If Len(Value) > 11 Then _
      Err.Raise vbObjectError + 1001, "Person", "SSN too long"
    mudtPerson.SSN = Value

End Property
```

Now the form will be notified if the user's entry is invalid. We might still want to set the MaxLength property on the form's field but, if we don't, then at least there will be some indication that there was a problem - and the object will have protected itself.

## Trapping the Error in the UI

Of course, the form will need some extra code to handle the error that's raised. How that error is handled is up to the individual UI designer. It could be handled as simply as sounding a beep and resetting the displayed value. Add this code to the txtSSN_Change routine in the EditPerson form:

```
Private Sub txtSSN_Change()

    On Error GoTo HandleError
    mobjPerson.SSN = txtSSN
    Exit Sub

HandleError:
    Beep
    txtSSN = mobjPerson.SSN
    txtSSN.SelStart = Len(txtSSN)

End Sub
```

*Since we're handling our own error situation here, it's necessary to set the Visual Basic environment to break only on those errors that we aren't handling ourselves. To set this up, we need to make sure that the Visual Basic environment will only* Break on Unhandled Errors. *In Visual Basic, choose the* Tools|Options *dialog, select the* General *tab, and make sure that* Break on Unhandled Errors *is selected.*

*Also note that we didn't use* On Error Resume Next, *but instead used a labeled error handler. With Visual Basic 5.0 and later, this is an important performance consideration, since the native code compiler adds a lot of extra code to support* On Error Resume Next, *so a labeled error handler is much more efficient.*

### Running the Program

At this point, we should be able to run our program and see how this works. Go to the SSN field and try to enter a value longer than 11 characters. The code we just added should prevent us from entering any value longer than 11 characters.

The beauty of this solution is that the code in the form only deals with the presentation; it doesn't enforce any business rules. We could add extra checks in the Person class to prevent entry of alpha characters in the field, or change the maximum length, and there would be no impact on the code in the form.

# Enforcing Object-Level Validation

By raising errors when a field is given an invalid value, we've provided **field-level validation** through our business object. It's also important to provide **object-level validation** to the largest degree possible.

Object-level validation checks the entire object - all the properties and internal variables - to make sure that everything is acceptable and all business rules have been met. This is important to the UI developer, since they may want to disable the OK and Apply buttons when the object is not valid and cannot be saved.

Object-level validation is more difficult to implement than field-level validation, since it depends upon more factors. An object might be valid only when all fields have values filled in; or perhaps a field is required only when another field contains a specific value. Virtually anything is possible, since the rules are dictated by the business requirements for the object.

Worse still, some object-level validation may not be possible in the business object on the client. Some business rules might really be relational rules in the database, so it's possible that we won't know they aren't being met until we try to save the object's data.

Granted, we can't guarantee that an object is valid according to rules enforced by the application services; but that shouldn't stop us from indicating whether the object meets all the conditions that *can* be checked right there on the client workstation. If we do that, then at least the UI can disable the OK and Apply buttons most of the time it's actually appropriate to do so, and we'll be moving towards a better interface.

## *An IsValid Property*

To provide this functionality for the UI, let's just add a single `Boolean` property to the `Person` object, called `IsValid`. This property will return a `True` value if all the business rules are met (or at least, as far as our object can tell that they've all been met).

If our object has an `IsValid` property, then the form can check to see if the object is valid at any point. If the `IsValid` property returns `False` then the form knows that the object has at least one broken business rule, and the OK and Apply buttons can be disabled.

This implies that the `IsValid` property's value is based on *all* the business rules in the object. That can make things pretty complex, since an object might have a lot of business rules to check. For instance, we may have rules specifying which properties are required. We may also have rules that specify that a field must be blank if another has a value - or just about anything else we can think up.

There are a number of ways to implement an `IsValid` property. For instance, we could code all the business rules into the `IsValid` routine itself. Then, every time the property was checked, we'd just run through a series of checks to make sure all the conditions were met. This approach can be a serious performance problem, however, if we have a lot of rules - or if some of our rules are complex and hard to check.

Another possibility is to keep a `Private` variable to keep track of the number of rules that are broken at any given time. As property values change, we can check all the appropriate rules and change this counter as needed. This solution can provide better performance, but can be very difficult to implement.

In particular, when we check a rule we have no way of knowing if it was already broken or if it's newly broken due to some new data. If it was already broken then we don't want to increment our rule-broken count; but if it's a newly broken rule, then the rule-broken count needs to be upped by one.

One very good way to implement the IsValid property is to keep a collection of the rules that are broken within the object. If there are no broken rules in our collection, then we know the object is valid. As we check each rule, we can also use the collection to track whether the rule was already broken, is broken now, or is unbroken. This is a very useful concept, and one that we'll use in Chapter 5 - where we implement quite a number of business objects.

To make all this easier, let's create a BrokenRules class to help manage this collection for us. We'll then be able to use this class whenever we need to implement an object-level IsValid property in our business objects. We'll certainly be seeing it in action when we implement the objects for our video rental store application, in Chapter 5.

## The BrokenRules Class

The BrokenRules class has one purpose, and that is to make it easy for our business objects to keep track of their business rules and how many are broken at any given time. If there are no broken business rules then our business object can return a True value from its IsValid property.

### Creating the BrokenRules Class

Since this class will be used exclusively by our business objects as they keep track of their broken business rules, we'll need to add the BrokenRules class module to any business object projects we may be developing.

For instance, in the Person project that we've been developing in this chapter, we will need to add the BrokenRules class to our PersonObjects project - since that's where our business object resides in this example.

So add a new class module to the PersonObjects project, using the Project|Add Class Module menu option, and change the name of the new class module to BrokenRules using its **Properties** window.

Go ahead and enter the following code for the BrokenRules class, and then we'll walk through how it works.

```
Option Explicit

Event BrokenRule()
Event NoBrokenRules()

Private mcolBroken As Collection

Private Sub Class_Initialize()

  Set mcolBroken = New Collection

End Sub

Public Sub RuleBroken(Rule As String, IsBroken As Boolean)
```

```
      On Error GoTo HandleError

    If IsBroken Then
      mcolBroken.Add True, Rule
      RaiseEvent BrokenRule

    Else
      mcolBroken.Remove Rule
      If mcolBroken.Count = 0 Then RaiseEvent NoBrokenRules

    End If

HandleError:

End Sub
```

```
Public Property Get Count() As Integer

    Count = mcolBroken.Count

End Property
```

*Once you've entered this code, make sure you save it, because we'll be using it throughout the development of our video rental project.*

Our BrokenRules class first declares a collection variable and two events:

```
Event BrokenRule()
Event NoBrokenRules()

Private mcolBroken As Collection
```

The mcolBroken collection will be used to store exactly which rules have been broken; meanwhile, the events that we've declared will be raised when a rule is broken or when the broken-rule count goes to zero.

The real work in the class is done in the RuleBroken routine:

```
Public Sub RuleBroken(Rule As String, IsBroken As Boolean)

    On Error GoTo HandleError

    If IsBroken Then
      mcolBroken.Add True, Rule
      RaiseEvent BrokenRule

    Else
      mcolBroken.Remove Rule
      If mcolBroken.Count = 0 Then RaiseEvent NoBrokenRules

    End If

HandleError:

End Sub
```

The calling code, in our `Person` object, just passes this routine a label for the rule and a `Boolean` flag to indicate whether the rule was broken or not. Then, we just check that `Boolean` flag: if it's `True` then the rule was broken, so we make sure it's in the collection:

```
If IsBroken Then
    mcolBroken.Add True, Rule
    RaiseEvent BrokenRule
```

If it is already in the collection, we'll get an error and exit the routine via the `HandleError` label; but if it isn't already there, then we'll not only add it to the collection but also raise the `BrokenRule` event so the calling program knows that at least one rule has been broken.

Likewise, if `IsBroken` is `False` then we'll remove the entry from the collection:

```
Else
    mcolBroken.Remove Rule
    If mcolBroken.Count = 0 Then RaiseEvent NoBrokenRules
```

If the entry is not in the collection, an error will occur and we'll exit the routine via the `HandleError` label. If the entry was in the collection, then we'll see if the overall count of broken rules is down to zero. When the count reaches zero, the `NoBrokenRules` event will be fired so the calling code can tell that everything is valid.

> *Of course, events aren't universally supported: we can't get them just anywhere within Visual Basic itself, and we can't necessarily use them in all other environments. Other environments can still use this class, but if they don't support events then they'll need to check the* `Count` *property for these event conditions: when* `Count` *is zero, there are no broken rules and everything should be valid.*

## Using the BrokenRules Object within Our Person Object

Now let's see how we can use this `BrokenRules` class in our `Person` object. To keep this fairly simple, let's just enforce a rule that states that the `SSN` field is required and must be exactly 11 characters in length. We've already implemented code to prevent the user from entering more than 11 characters in this field; but now we're making the rules even more restrictive.

In order to use the `BrokenRules` object within our `Person` object, we need to declare and create a `Private` variable to hold the new object. Add the following line of code to the **General Declarations** section of our `Person` class module:

```
Private WithEvents mobjValid As BrokenRules
```

We also need to add code in the `Person` object's `Class_Initialize` routine to create an object for this variable:

```
Private Sub Class_Initialize()

  Set mobjValid = New BrokenRules
  mobjValid.RuleBroken "SSN", True

End Sub
```

Notice, here, that we're forcing the `"SSN"` rule to be considered broken straight away. This is important, because, as the programmer, we know that the value is blank to begin with, so we need to make sure the business rule is enforced right from the start by indicating that it's broken.

> **An important note about events. An object can't raise events until it has been fully instantiated, and an object isn't instantiated until *after* the** `Class_Initialize` **routine is complete. This means that any** `RaiseEvent` **statements called during the** `Class_Initialize` **routine won't actually raise any events – which is what we'd really like to have happen.**
>
> **In this example, we're indicating that a rule is broken, so the** `BrokenRule` **event should fire; but it won't, because we're still in the** `Class_Initialize` **routine.**

### Handling the BrokenRule and NoBrokenRules Events

Our `Person` object needs to handle the events that will be created by the `BrokenRules` object we just created. To make it easier for the UI developer, we'll also have our `Person` object raise an event to let the UI know when the `Person` object becomes valid or invalid.

This first line that we'll add to handle these events goes in the General Declarations section of the `Person` class module, and it declares the `Valid` event. We'll use this event to indicate when our `Person` object switches between being valid and invalid:

```
Event Valid(IsValid As Boolean)
```

As we've seen, our `BrokenRules` object raises two events of its own: `BrokenRule` and `NoBrokenRules`. The `BrokenRule` event will be fired whenever a new rule is broken, while the `NoBrokenRules` will be fired any time the number of broken rules reaches zero.

By adding the following code to our `Person` object, we'll be able to react to these events by raising our own `Valid` event to tell the UI whether the `Person` object is currently valid:

```
Private Sub mobjValid_BrokenRule()

  RaiseEvent Valid(False)

End Sub
```

```
Private Sub mobjValid_NoBrokenRules()

  RaiseEvent Valid(True)

End Sub
```

If the `BrokenRule` event is fired then we know that at least one of our `Person` object's rules is broken. We can then raise our `Valid` event with a `False` parameter to indicate to the UI that the `Person` object is currently invalid. Likewise, when we receive a `NoBrokenRules` event, we can raise our `Valid` event with a `True` parameter to indicate to the UI that there are no broken rules and that our `Person` object is currently valid.

## Implementing the IsValid Property

When we started this discussion, it was with the intent of creating an `IsValid` property on our `Person` object so that the UI could check to see if the object was valid at any given point. By implementing the `Valid` event in the previous section, we've actually provided a better solution; but we can't assume that the UI can actually receive events, since not all development tools provide support for them. The `IsValid` property therefore remains very important.

Fortunately, our `BrokenRules` object makes implementation of the `IsValid` property very trivial. The `BrokenRules` object provides us with a count of the number of broken rules, and if that count is zero then we know that there are no rules broken. No broken business rules translates very nicely into a valid `Person` object.

To implement our `IsValid` property, let's enter the following code into the `Person` class module:

```
Public Property Get IsValid() As Boolean

  IsValid = (mobjValid.Count = 0)

End Property
```

This property simply returns a `Boolean` value that's based on whether the broken rule count equals zero or not.

## Enforcing the SSN Business Rules

In our `Person` object's `Class_Initialize` routine, we added a line to indicate that our `SSN` field was invalid. Since we're making it a required field, and all fields in a brand new object are blank, we know that the rule is broken during the initialization of the class.

We can therefore finish the job by adding some code to check our business rules within the `Person` object's `Property Let` routine for our `SSN` property:

```
Public Property Let SSN(Value As String)

  If Len(Value) > 11 Then _
    Err.Raise vbObjectError + 1001, "Person", "SSN too long"

  mudtPerson.SSN = Value
  mobjValid.RuleBroken "SSN", (Len(Trim$(mudtPerson.SSN)) <> 11)

End Property
```

What we've done, here, is simply call the `RuleBroken` method of our `BrokenRules` object, passing it the name of our rule "SSN" and a `Boolean` to indicate whether the rule is currently broken. In this case, the rule just checks to make sure the value is exactly 11 characters long.

Anywhere that we need to enforce a rule in our object, we just need to add a single line of code with the rule's name and a `Boolean` to indicate if it's broken or unbroken. All the other details are handled through the `BrokenRules` object and the events that it fires.

## Using the Valid Event and IsValid Property in the UI

At this point, we've implemented the `BrokenRules` object to keep track of how many business rules are broken within a business object. We've also enhanced our business object, `Person`, to take advantage of the new `BrokenRules` object. All that remains is to enhance our user interface to take advantage of the `Valid` event and `IsValid` property that we just added to our `Person` object.

A rich user-interface should be able to enable or disable the OK and Apply buttons as appropriate, so that they're only available to the user if the object is actually valid at the time. Most users dislike clicking on a button only to be told that the requested operation can't be performed. Ideally, when an operation can't be performed, the associated buttons should be disabled.

In our case, the OK and Apply buttons are only valid if the business object itself is valid. If the business object isn't valid then we can't save it, so both the OK and the Apply button should be disabled.

### Adding the EnableOK Subroutine

The easiest way to manage the enabling and disabling of these buttons is to put the code in a central routine in the form. In our case, we'll need to add the following routine to our `EditPerson` form in the `PersonDemo` project:

```
Private Sub EnableOK(IsOK As Boolean)

  cmdOK.Enabled = IsOK
  cmdApply.Enabled = IsOK

End Sub
```

### Using the IsValid Property

When the Edit Person form loads, the first thing it needs to do is make sure that the buttons are enabled properly. We need to check the `Person` object's `IsValid` property in our `Form_Load` routine to find out if the business object is valid at this point. Add this line of code to the `EditPerson` form's `Form_Load` routine:

```
Private Sub Form_Load()

  Set mobjPerson = New Person
  EnableOK mobjPerson.IsValid

End Sub
```

All we need to do is call our `EnableOK` subroutine, passing the `Person` object's `IsValid` property value as a parameter. If the object is valid, we'll be passing a `True` value, which will indicate that the OK and Apply buttons are to be enabled.

> *It might look as if we could rely on the* `Person` *object's* `Valid` *event to fire as the object was created. We could then act on that event to enable or disable the two buttons on our form. Unfortunately, objects can't raise events as they are being created, so there is no way for our* `Person` *object to raise its* `Valid` *event while it's starting up. This means we can't rely on the* `Valid` *event to tell us whether the object is valid as our form is first loading.*

### Responding to the Valid Event

Once the EditPerson form is loaded and the user is interacting with it, we can rely on the Person object to raise its Valid event to tell the form whether it is currently valid. In our EditPerson form, we can add code to respond to this event, enabling and disabling the **OK** and **Apply** buttons as appropriate:

```
Private Sub mobjPerson_Valid(IsValid As Boolean)

   EnableOK IsValid

End Sub
```

Since the object will raise this event any time it changes from valid to invalid or back, the UI developer can rely on this event to enable or disable the buttons for the life of the form. All we need to do is call our EnableOK subroutine, passing the IsValid parameter value to EnableOK to indicate whether to enable or disable the two buttons.

### Removing the SSN Change Event Code

As our form currently stands, we have code in the Change event of the txtSSN control to trap any error raised by our business object. Now that we've enhanced the business object to utilize the BrokenRules object, we don't need this code in the form. Change the Change event code as shown:

```
Private Sub txtSSN_Change()

   mobjPerson.SSN = txtSSN

End Sub
```

With this change we're allowing the user to enter any value into the TextBox control and thus into our object. We're relying in the business logic in the object to raise the Valid event to inform the UI when the user has entered valid data.

### Running the Program

We can now run our program and see how well this works. When the EditPerson form first appears, the **OK** and **Apply** buttons are disabled. As a result of the code we've just entered, these buttons will only be enabled when there are exactly 11 characters in the SSN field.

# Handling Canceled Edits

Most forms have **OK** and **Cancel** buttons, and many have an **Apply** button as well. We've included these on our sample form to illustrate how to support them within the object, since there have been some extra steps involved.

So far, we've left the code in the buttons' Click events somewhat vague. Now let's think through the behaviors we require of the business object to support **OK**, **Cancel** and **Apply**.

We've implemented our form so that our Person object's properties are being set every time a field changes on the form. This is important, because it means that any business rules are validated as the user presses each key. A further ramification is that the business object's internal variables are always changing as the user changes values on the screen.

If the OK button is clicked, we just need to save the Person object's variables - and the form goes away. We'll cover different ways of saving the object later in the chapter, but the point here is that the OK button is pretty easy. After all, the object already has its internal variables set and ready to be saved. Since the form goes away when OK is clicked, we don't have to worry about any subsequent editing of the data.

The Cancel button is a different story. When the user clicks this button, the form goes away, but the Person object might have different data stored in its variables, since the user may well have been typing into some fields before they clicked the Cancel button.

On the surface, this might not seem like a problem: the form holds a reference to the Person object and, when it releases that reference, the object, along with its changed data, will just go away – or will it? Unfortunately, the object won't go away if some other form or object also holds a reference to it. Perhaps we have a Family object that holds references to a number of Person objects. If we were editing one of those Person objects and we clicked Cancel, we'd expect the Person object itself to stick around as part of the Family object; but we'd also expect any changes to its data to be reset to the original values.

The Apply button ties in here as well. When the user clicks Apply, the Person object's variables will be saved (as we'll see later). However, the user can keep editing the object - because the form doesn't get unloaded by the Apply button.

To make matters just a bit more complicated, there are also combinations: the user might do some editing, then Apply the edits, do some more work, and then click Cancel. Given that sequence of events, we'd need to keep all the changes up to when the Apply was clicked.

## Enhancing the Person Object

Let's look at how we can make it easy for a UI developer to support these three buttons. What we're talking about, here, is the ability to start editing the object, and then either **commit** (Apply) or **roll back** (Cancel) the edits that were made.

Let's add three methods to our Person object: BeginEdit, ApplyEdit and CancelEdit:

```
Public Sub BeginEdit()

  LSet mudtSaved = mudtPerson
  mflgEditing = True

End Sub
```

```
Public Sub ApplyEdit()

' data would be saved here
  mflgEditing = False

End Sub
```

```
Public Sub CancelEdit()

  LSet mudtPerson = mudtSaved
  mflgEditing = False

End Sub
```

We'll walk through the details of these routines over the next few pages.

> *The* `ApplyEdit` *routine contains a comment to indicate where we need to add some code to save the object to a database. In the section on* Making Objects Persistent, *later in this chapter, we'll discuss saving objects to a database and we'll get into more details about this process.*

Right now, let's see how these three new routines provide support for the OK, Cancel and Apply buttons. The code in these routines makes use of two new module-level variables that we need to add to the General Declarations section of the `Person` class module:

```
Private mudtSaved As PersonProps
Private mflgEditing As Boolean
```

### Are We Editing the Object?

The `mflgEditing` variable is easy to follow: we just set it to `True` when we start editing the object and `False` when we're done.

We do need to initialize this variable up front, however; so add the following line to the `Class_Initialize` method of the `Person` class module:

```
Private Sub Class_Initialize()

    mflgEditing = False


    Set mobjValid = New BrokenRules
    mobjValid.RuleBroken "SSN", True

End Sub
```

By keeping track of whether our object is currently being edited or not, we can make sure that our object's data is only changed when appropriate. We can use this flag to disable all the `Property Let` routines in our object, so the only time a value can be changed is when the object is in **edit mode**. By edit mode, I mean when the `mflgEditing` flag is set to `True` by the `BeginEdit` method.

> *Essentially, we are making the object somewhat self-aware. The object will* know *whether it should allow any client code to change its data. The technique of viewing an object as a self-aware entity is called anthropomorphization. The term is derived from anthropus for human, and morph for change; we are changing our view of the object from a chunk of code to an intelligent entity. This is one of the core tenants of object-oriented design.*

### Saving a Snapshot of the Object's Data

The `mudtSaved` variable deserves a bit of explanation. Here's how we declare it:

```
Private mudtSaved As PersonProps
```

Within our `BeginEdit` routine, above, the `Person` object's data is stored in this `mudtSaved` variable, which is based on the user-defined type `PersonProps`:

```
LSet mudtSaved = mudtPerson
```

There are a couple of important reasons for doing this, one of which is to make it easy to handle canceled edits, since we've stored a version of the Person's object data prior to the edit. The other reason is to make it easy to save the object to a database - but again, we'll discuss this later on in the "Making Objects Persistent" section of this chapter.

The `Person` object uses the `mudtPerson` variable to store all its data values. The `mudtSaved` variable is a snapshot of the object's state at the time the `BeginEdit` method was called. The copy is very fast and simple, since we use the `LSet` command to copy one user-defined variable directly into another very efficiently. Visual Basic does virtually no extra work during this call: it is, essentially, a memory copy function, and so it's incredibly fast.

> *It is certainly possible to store an object's data in `Private` variables, then declare a second set of the variables, and copy them all one by one to create a snapshot. But the technique we're using with the `LSet` command is far faster, and it's easier to code.*

### Using the BeginEdit Method

The `BeginEdit` method starts the editing process for the object:

```
Public Sub BeginEdit()

  LSet mudtSaved = mudtPerson
  mflgEditing = True

End Sub
```

The routine simply copies the object's current data into the `mudtSaved` variable, in case we need to get back to where we started. It also sets the `mflgEditing` variable to `True`, to establish that the object is being edited.

This method needs to be called by the UI before any editing takes place, so we'll now add a line to call it from the `EditPerson` form's `Load` routine:

```
Private Sub Form_Load()

  Set mobjPerson = New Person
  EnableOK mobjPerson.IsValid
  mobjPerson.BeginEdit

End Sub
```

### Using the ApplyEdit Method

Once the `EditPerson` form has called the `BeginEdit` method on the `Person` object, the object knows that it's being edited. The user can change data on the form to their heart's content, but they'll eventually have to either save any changes or try to cancel them.

If the user clicks either **OK** or **Apply**, we need to save the changes in the object. Therefore, we'll also add these lines to the **Edit Person** form:

```
Private Sub cmdApply_Click()

  ' save the object
```

```
    mobjPerson.ApplyEdit
    mobjPerson.BeginEdit

End Sub

Private Sub cmdOK_Click()

    ' save the object
    mobjPerson.ApplyEdit
    Unload Me

End Sub
```

Both routines call the `ApplyEdit` method, and the **Apply** button's code also calls the `BeginEdit` method to resume the editing process for the object. We need to do this because the **Apply** button doesn't make the form unload, so the user must be able to continue editing the data at this point.

As you can see from the code above, the `ApplyEdit` routine sets the `mflgEditing` variable to `False`, indicating to the `Person` object that editing is complete. The `ApplyEdit` method is also responsible for saving the object's data to the database: once again, a topic we'll cover in more detail in the section on "Making Objects Persistent".

### Using the CancelEdit Method

The user might also click the **Cancel** button, so we'll add the following line to the `EditPerson` form:

```
Private Sub cmdCancel_Click()

    ' do not save the object
    mobjPerson.CancelEdit
    Unload Me

End Sub
```

All this line does is call the `CancelEdit` method within our `Person` business object. Here's that `CancelEdit` method again:

```
Public Sub CancelEdit()

    LSet mudtPerson = mudtSaved
    mflgEditing = False

End Sub
```

This routine does a couple things, including setting the `mflgEditing` variable to `False`, because the editing process is over, and restoring the `Person` object's data to the values stored in `mudtSaved`:

```
    LSet mudtPerson = mudtSaved
```

Again, this is essentially a memory copy of the data that was saved in the `BeginEdit` routine back into the object's central repository of data, `mudtPerson`.

> It's important to remember that for this to work, all the object's data must be in the user-defined type. If data values were kept in module-level variables, we'd need some extra code to save and restore those values.

### Disabling Edits when mflgEditing is False

The final set of changes we need to make to the `Person` object are to make sure that the object doesn't allow itself to be edited until the `BeginEdit` method has been called. We just need to add a line to each `Property Let` and `Property Set` to raise an error unless we're in the middle of editing. We may also choose to disable certain methods; in particular, those methods that impact our object's internal variables.

For example, we'd add this line to the `Property Let Name` routine:

```
Public Property Let Name(Value As String)

    If Not mflgEditing Then Err.Raise 383
    mudtPerson.Name = Value

End Property
```

Error 383 is an error that indicates a property is read-only, so if we don't want our property to be editable we can just raise that error. Of course, we only need to raise it if `mflgEditing` is `False`, so once the `BeginEdit` method has been called the error won't be raised.

This line just needs to be added to the top of each `Property Let` in the `Person` class module. And we'll do essentially the same thing with the `ApplyEdit` and `CancelEdit` methods in the `Person` class module, but we'll use error 445 for these instead. This error is 'Object doesn't support this action' and it's more appropriate for disabling methods:

```
Public Sub CancelEdit()

    If Not mflgEditing Then Err.Raise 445
    LSet mudtPerson = mudtSaved
    mflgEditing = False

End Sub
```

### Testing the Code

These changes are easy enough to test by slightly breaking the code in our `EditPerson` form. Just comment out the call to `BeginEdit` that we put in the `Form_Load` routine and then run the program.

Now, any attempt to change values in the form's fields will result in error 383 being raised. Clicking the Cancel button should result in error 445.

*When you've finished this test, don't forget to uncomment the call to BeginEdit!*

While a well-behaved form will never actually encounter these errors, they are vitally important during development of the UI. Again, our objects must be written with the assumption that the UI developer is not going to write the perfect set of code on the first pass, so what we're doing here is helping the UI developer do their job while protecting our objects from errant code.

# Protecting Properties and Methods

In the previous section, we effectively switched some properties from read-write to read-only, based on whether the object is flagged as editable. We also disabled some methods using a similar technique.

In this section, we'll quickly run through the reasons why we might want to disable properties or methods. We'll also consider exactly how to implement this disabling.

## Read-only Properties

There are various reasons why we might need a read-only property. The most common is where we have a property that's calculated from other data within the object. A good example of this is the `Age` property in our `Person` object, which is read-only and is based on the `Birthdate`.

Other properties might switch between read-write and read-only, depending upon business rules or other criteria. We saw an example of this behavior in the previous section, where we made properties read-only when the object was not in an editable state.

There are two techniques available to us for creating read-only properties. The simplest technique is to provide no `Property Let` or `Property Set` routines for the property. Of course, this technique allows no flexibility, in that we can't then make the property read-write at runtime. The second technique available to us is to still create the `Property Let` or `Property Set` routines, but to raise error 383 'Set not supported (read-only property)' at the top of the routine when we want to make the property read-only:

```
Public Property Let X(Value As Integer)

    If condition_met Then Err.Raise 383

    Regular code goes here

End Property
```

## Disabling Methods

As we've seen, there are situations where we need to temporarily disable methods, `Sub`, or `Function` code within our object. Depending on the state of the object, or various business rules, we may need to effectively turn off a method.

Disabling a method is as simple as generating error 445 'Object doesn't support this action' at the top of a method's code when we want that method disabled:

```
Public Sub X()

    If condition_met Then Err.Raise 445

    Regular code goes here

End Sub
```

We did this earlier, in the `ApplyEdit` and `CancelEdit` methods of our `Person` class. They weren't appropriate unless the object was currently being edited and the `mflgEditing` flag was set to `True`.

## *Write-once Properties*

There are also cases where we may wish to create a property that is only written once. This is an excellent technique to use for unique key values that identify an object, and for those situations where business rules dictate that data can not be changed once entered. Real-world examples of this would include an electronic signature or an identity stamp where an object is stamped with a security code that must not be changed.

Write-once properties are implemented using the same error raising technique as a read-only property, but with a bit more logic to support the concept. As an example, let's enhance our `Person` object's `SSN` property to be write-once. After all, once a person gets assigned a social security number, they've got it for life.

### *Indicating when the Object is 'New'*

We can't consider the SSN to be entered until the object is first saved by the user when they click the OK or Apply buttons. At that point, we need to lock down the `Property Let SSN` and any other write-once properties.

To lock down the value, we'll add a module-level variable to our `Person` class module to indicate whether the `Person` object is 'new'. This same variable will come in useful, later, when we talk about saving and restoring objects from a database, since a restored object also needs its write-once properties locked out. Add this variable declaration to the General Declarations section of our `Person` class module:

```
Private mflgNew As Boolean
```

Since the UI might also care to know if an object is new or not (so it can alter its appearance appropriately), we'll also create a read-only property for this purpose by adding the following code to the `Person` object:

```
Public Property Get IsNew() As Boolean

  IsNew = mflgNew

End Property
```

Now let's implement the `mflgNew` variable's operation. We need to start out assuming the object is indeed new:

```
Private Sub Class_Initialize()

  mflgEditing = False
  mflgNew = True
  Set mobjValid = New BrokenRules
  mobjValid.RuleBroken "SSN", True

End Sub
```

Then we just need to flip the switch, when the `Person` object is saved, via the `ApplyEdit` method:

```
Public Sub ApplyEdit()

    If Not mflgEditing Then Err.Raise 445
    mflgEditing = False
    mflgNew = False
    ' data would be saved here

End Sub
```

### Disabling the Property

All that remains is to change the `Property Let SSN` routine to become disabled when the object is no longer considered new:

```
Public Property Let SSN(Value As String)

    If Not mflgEditing Then Err.Raise 383
    If Not mflgNew Then Err.Raise 383

    If Len(Value) > 11 Then _
        Err.Raise vbObjectError + 1001, "Person", "SSN too long"

    mudtPerson.SSN = Value
    mobjValid.RuleBroken "SSN", (Len(Trim$(mudtPerson.SSN)) <> 11)

End Property
```

With these changes, the SSN can be entered and changed by the user up to the point where they click OK or Apply. At that point, the `Person` object will be saved to the database, the `mflgNew` flag would be set to `False`, and the user will no longer be able to edit the SSN field.

### Testing the Code

We can test this in our program, even though the data isn't actually saved to the database, since the `ApplyEdit` method still sets the `mflgNew` flag to `False` when the Apply button is clicked.

Run the program, enter 11 characters into the SSN field, and click the Apply button. Now try to change the SSN field again. As a result of the code we've just entered, you'll find that the SSN is fixed. Once the data is saved to the database our object won't allow it to be edited.

*Of course the use of write-once properties isn't without risk. After all, this technique means that the user can't change the SSN value after it's been saved to the database – even if it is incorrect.*

## Write-only Properties

Write-only properties are less common than read-only properties, but they do have their uses. A good example of a write-only property is a password property on a security object. There's no reason to read the password back, but we would, sometimes, want to set it.

As with read-only properties, there are two ways to create write-only properties. If we don't need to dynamically change the status at run-time, we can implement a write-only property by simply not writing a `Property Get` routine for the property.

However, if we do need to dynamically change a property from read-write to write-only for some reason, we just need to raise error 394 'Get not supported (write-only property)' at the top of the Property Get when the property needs to be write-only:

```
Public Property Get X() As Long

    If condition_met Then Err.Raise 394

    Regular code goes here

End Property
```

# Making Objects Persistent

Throughout our discussion, so far, we've danced around the idea of making an object persistent. Objects are great, but if we can't save an object into a database and then retrieve it later, they're somewhat limited in their use.

As we've seen, business objects are intended to represent real-world entities. An entity in the real world, such as a customer, has no concept of saving, adding, updating, or deleting itself - those things just don't make sense. However, when we create an object in software to model a customer or product, we need to compromise the model slightly in order to handle these activities.

> **A primary goal in making business objects persistent is to minimize the impact to the logical business model. We want a customer object to be a model of a customer, not a model of a database record.**

In this section, we'll discuss a couple of techniques that we can use to efficiently save business objects to a database without compromising the integrity of the CSLA. Then, we'll talk about what part of our program should actually do the work of saving and retrieving the data. Finally, we'll look at the details of the persistence service that we'll be using through the rest of the book.

The first thing we need to look at is exactly how are we're going to save an object to the database. Virtually all the databases used today are relational databases, although there are exceptions - such as hierarchical databases and object databases. Because of the prevalence of relational databases, however, we're going to focus on saving and restoring objects from that type of database, leaving the others to be covered elsewhere.

It's important to decide where to locate the code that takes care of saving or updating an object in the database. The specifics of how to save an object's data will depend upon where we put this code. There are three basic approaches:

- ❑   Saving/restoring is handled by user-interface code
- ❑   Business objects save/restore themselves
- ❑   A specialized object manages the saving/restoring of business objects

The first solution may be valid in certain cases, but we won't cover it in any detail, because it's directly opposed to an object-oriented solution. The second solution is very valid, but not terribly scalable. In the end, we'll settle on the last solution: it works well with our object-oriented design, and yet provides good scalability for our applications.

But let's take a good look at each of these options, and consider their pros and cons in more detail.

# Saving Objects within a Form or BAS Module

In keeping with a more traditional Visual Basic development approach, it's possible to put the persistence code in the form itself, or in a **BAS** module called by the form. Of course, this means putting quite a bit of logic into the user-interface - something that I don't recommended, since it makes our code much less general.

With this approach, every form that wants to use a given object will need the code to save and restore that object from the database. This almost guarantees duplication of code, and largely defeats the goals that we're trying to achieve by using object-oriented design in our applications.

We're not going to go into the details of any code to support this solution, since it's so directly in conflict with the principles we're trying to follow in this book.

# Objects that Save Themselves

I've made it very clear, so far, that the business objects are the application, and the user-interface is pretty expendable. Thus it seems quite logical to assume that each object should know how to save itself to the database. By just adding some form of Load and Save methods to each object, it would appear that we've pretty much solved all our persistence issues. Let's consider this approach.

## Implementing a Load Method

We'll consider, as an example, the Person object that we developed in the previous section.

> *Don't actually make any of these changes to the PersonObjects project, however, because this is not yet the optimal solution to our problem. I'll clearly signal when we have found the best solution.*

Were we to implement a solution where objects saved themselves, we could add a Load method like this (assuming we have a JET database with a Person table for our data):

```
Public Sub Load(SSN As String)

  Dim rsPerson As Recordset
  Dim strConnect As String
  Dim strSQL As String

  strConnect = "Provider=Microsoft.Jet.OLEDB.3.51;" & _
    "Persist Security Info=False;" & _
    "Data Source=C:\Wrox\VB6 Pro Objects\Person.mdb"
  strSQL = "SELECT * FROM Person WHERE SSN='" & SSN & "'"
  Set rsPerson = New RecordSet
  rsPerson.Open strSQL, strConnect
```

```
With rsPerson
  If Not .EOF And Not .BOF Then
    mudtPerson.SSN = .Fields("SSN")
    mudtPerson.Name = .Fields("Name")
    mudtPerson.Birthdate = .Fields("Birthdate")

  Else
    rsPerson.Close
    Err.Raise vbObjectError + 1002, "Person", "SSN not on file"

  End If

End With

rsPerson.Close
Set rsPerson = Nothing

End Sub
```

This code would simply open the database, perform a lookup of the person (based on the supplied social security number), and put the data from the recordset into the object's variables. Also, note that the path we've used when opening our database is an absolute one; you'll need to change it to point to your own database.

> *Since this code makes reference to a* `Recordset` *object, you would need to add a reference in your project to ADO. Using the* Project|References *menu option you would select the most up-to-date ADO reference, such as* Microsoft ActiveX Data Objects 2.0 Library.

## Using the Load Method from the UI

From the UI developer's perspective, this would be pretty nice, since all they'd need to do would be to get the user to enter the social security number. Let's assume the UI programmer stored this SSN number in a variable called `strSSN`. Some simple code to achieve this (which ignores any input validation concerns right now), which could be placed in a button event or the `Form_Load` routine, might run as follows:

```
Dim strSSN As String

strSSN = InputBox$("Enter the SSN")
```

> *Remember that we're not actually making these changes to our Person project and PersonDemo UI, because this is not the optimal solution to our problem.*

The working UI code would then follow:

```
With mobjPerson
  .Load strSSN
  txtSSN = .SSN
  txtName = .Name
  txtBirthdate = .Birthdate
  lblAge = .Age
End With
```

Of course, this code would not only put the values from the object into each field on the form, but it would also trigger each field's `Change` event. These events are set up to put the values right back into the object, which is a rather poor solution. We could, perhaps, overcome this with a typical UI trick: a module-level flag to indicate that we were loading the data:

```
Private mflgLoading As Boolean
```

Then, at the top of each `Change` event, we'd just add the following line of code:

```
If mflgLoading Then Exit Sub
```

And finally, we'd slightly alter the code that copied the values to the form's fields:

```
mflgLoading = True
With mobjPerson
  .Load strSSN
  txtSSN = .SSN
  txtName = .Name
  txtBirthdate = .Birthdate
  lblAge = .Age
End With
mflgLoading = False
```

## Saving the Object's Data through the ApplyEdit Method

Back in the `Person` object, we already have a method, `ApplyEdit`, to handle updating the object; so we would just add some code to that routine:

```
Public Sub ApplyEdit()

  Dim rsPerson As Recordset
  Dim strConnect As String
  Dim strSQL As String

  If Not mflgEditing Then Err.Raise 445
  mflgEditing = False
  mflgNew = False

  strConnect = "Provider=Microsoft.Jet.OLEDB.3.51;" & _
    "Persist Security Info=False;" & _
    "Data Source=C:\Wrox\VB6 Pro Objects\Person.mdb"
  strSQL = "SELECT * FROM Person WHERE SSN='" & SSN & "'"
  Set rsPerson = New Recordset
  rsPerson.Open strSQL, strConnect

  With rsPerson
    If Not .EOF And Not .BOF Then
      .Edit

    Else
      .AddNew

    End If

    .Fields("SSN") = mudtPerson.SSN
```

```
        .Fields("Name") = mudtPerson.Name
        .Fields("Birthdate") = mudtPerson.Birthdate
        .Update

    End With

    rsPerson.Close

End Sub
```

Since this would just update an already existing routine, we wouldn't need to make any changes to our form's code to support the new functionality.

This solution is pretty nice. Probably the biggest benefit of objects that save themselves is that they are very easy for the UI developer to understand. They simply need to have some code to support the `Load` method, and they're all set.

> *It's worth noting that the way we would have coded the `Load` and `ApplyEdit` methods essentially employed **optimistic locking**. This means that no lock is held on the data in the database, so many users may bring up the same row of data at the same time.*
>
> *Since no database connection was maintained once the data was loaded or saved, there was no lock on the data in the database while the object was in memory.*
>
> *We could very easily modify the code to maintain an open recordset as long as the object existed, thus converting this to use **pessimistic locking**. This means that a lock would be held on any data that is brought into our objects, preventing more than one user from ever attempting to view or alter the same set of data.*
>
> *This could become very resource intensive if there were a lot of objects, however, since each object would have to maintain its own reference to a recordset.*

There are a couple of drawbacks to this approach of objects saving themselves. One of our primary goals in creating objects is to make them accurate models of the business entities they represent. By putting all the data-handling code into the objects themselves, we've effectively diluted the business logic with the mechanics of data access. While we can't make our objects pure models of the business entities, it's important to keep as close to that ideal as possible.

Another drawback is that we've tied the data handling and the business handling together in a single object. If our intent is to distribute processing following the CSLA then this approach doesn't help us meet that goal. What we really want is to separate the data access code from the code that supports the business rules - so they can be distributed across multiple machines if need be.

On the upside, this technique of objects saving themselves is very good for applications where we know that the solution doesn't need to scale beyond a physical 2-tier setting. If the application will always be communicating with an ISAM database, such as Microsoft Access, or directly with a SQL database, such as Oracle, then this may be an attractive approach. Be warned, however: applications rarely stay as small as they were originally designed, and it may be wise to consider a more scalable solution.

# Objects that Save Other Objects

Now that we've discussed how the UI could directly save an object, and how an object might directly save itself, we'll look at how we can design our business objects to rely on another object to manage their data access. This approach has a couple of very important benefits and is the one we'll use to write our video rental store application through the book.

An important benefit of having an object save itself, as in the previous section, is that the UI developer has a very simple and clear interface for loading and saving an object. At the same time, we really don't want the data access code to be located in the object itself, since that doesn't provide a very scalable solution.

One way to design an application's persistence is to create an object that the UI can call when it needs to save a business object to the database. This new object is designed to manage the persistence of the business object, and so it's called an **object manager**. The object manager contains all the code to retrieve, store, and delete a business object from the database on behalf of the UI.

Another alternative utilizes **data-centric business objects**. This is basically the concept that we can take objects as we saw in the previous section, "Objects that Save Themselves", and pull only the data-centric processing out into a new object. Then the UI-centric business object can make use of the data-centric business object as needed to retrieve, store, and delete its data from the database.

The object manager solution is a valid approach to designing an application with distributed objects, and so we'll walk through how it could be implemented. Once we've coded this solution, we'll see how easy it is to move from an object manager solution to one using data-centric business objects.

## An Object Manager

One approach to persisting business objects is to create an object manager object for use by the UI developer. The UI code would simply ask the object manager to load and save objects on its behalf, typically passing the business objects themselves as parameters to the Load and Save methods of the object manager.

This design is illustrated in the following figure:

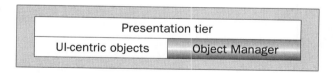

As shown, the presentation tier, or UI, will interact with both our UI-centric business objects, such as our Person object, and the object manager that knows how to retrieve, save, and delete our business objects.

Sticking with the Person object we've used so far, let's take a look at a PersonManager class. The PersonManager will handle all the details of retrieving, saving, and deleting Person objects from the database. The UI code will ask the PersonManager to retrieve a Person object when it wants one loaded from the database. The UI will also use it to save a Person object back to the database or to delete a Person object.

### An Object Manager as an Out-of-Process Server

One of our goals is to be able to put the PersonManager object on a separate machine from the client workstation. This will allow us more flexibility in how we deploy our application, as we can put this object manager on an application server machine and increase the scalability of our application:

| Client workstation | Presentation tier |
|---|---|
| | UI-centric objects |
| Application server | Object Manager |
| Database server | Data services tier |

This figure shows where an object manager, such as PersonManager, would fit into the CSLA. It also shows how the PersonManager can be run on an application server machine separate from the client workstation.

> *We don't have a 'data-centric' object in this case, as the Object Manager fills that role under this scenario. In many ways the Object Manager is analogous to a data-centric business object, but we use the Object Manager in a different manner than we would a data-centric business object.*

For us to be able to run the PersonManager object on a separate machine, we'll need to implement this class in a separate Visual Basic project from the Person class.

As we discussed earlier in this chapter, there are serious performance concerns when communicating between processes or across a network. Since we're designing the PersonManager to be at least out-of-process, and very likely on another machine across the network, we need to take steps to make sure that our communication is very efficient.

### Adding GetState and SetState Methods to Person

To this end, we'll use the user-defined type and LSet technique discussed earlier in this chapter. In order to implement this in the Person object itself, we need to add a couple of new methods: GetState and SetState.

To use the LSet technique, we need to make sure our object's data is stored using a user-defined type. Then we need to create a second user-defined type of the same length to act as a buffer for all the detailed **state data** from our object.

> We'll use the word *state* to describe the core data that makes up an object. An object can be viewed as an interface, an implementation of that interface (code), and state (data). An object could have a lot more data than is really required to define its state. The state data includes only that which must be saved and restored to return an object to its original state.

Our Person object already stores its state data in a user-defined type, PersonProps. However, this type will be needed by both the Person object and the PersonManager object, so we'll want to make it available to both. The easiest way to do this is to add a new code module to the PersonObjects project and move the PersonProps type from the Person class module into this code module. We'll call this new code module PersonUDTs:

```
Public Type PersonProps
    SSN As String * 11
    Name As String * 50
    Birthdate As Date
    Age As Integer
End Type
```

Notice that we've also changed the scope of the user-defined type from `Private` to `Public` so that it will be available outside this code module.

Now we can add the following user-defined type to the `PersonUDTs` code module:

```
Public Type PersonData

    Buffer As String * 68

End Type
```

This type will act as a buffer for the `PersonProps` data, allowing us to use the `LSet` command to easily copy the detailed information from `PersonProps` into the simple string buffer declared here.

With the user-defined types set up, we're all ready to add the `GetState` and `SetState` methods to our `Person` class module:

```
Public Function GetState() As String

    Dim udtBuffer As PersonData

    LSet udtBuffer = mudtPerson
    GetState = udtBuffer.Buffer

End Function
```

To get the object's state, we just copy the detailed `mudtPerson` variable into `udtBuffer`. The `udtBuffer` variable is just a `String`, so we can return it as the result of the function:

```
Public Sub SetState(ByVal Buffer As String)

    Dim udtBuffer As PersonData

    udtBuffer.Buffer = Buffer
    LSet mudtPerson = udtBuffer
    CalculateAge

End Sub
```

To set the object's state, we simply reverse the process: accepting a string buffer and copying it into `udtBuffer`. Then we just `LSet udtBuffer`'s data into `mudtPerson`, and the object is restored.

We also make a call to the `CalculateAge` method to ensure that the read-only `Age` property will return the correct value. Since the data that is passed into our object via the `SetState` method bypasses all our `Property Let` routines we need to make sure that any required processing (such as calculating the age) are performed as part of the `SetState` method.

Given these methods, our `PersonManager` object needs to make only one call to retrieve all of the data from our object, and make only one other call to send all the object's data back. As we discussed earlier, this is very fast and efficient, even over a network connection.

### Cloning Business Objects with GetState and SetState

Since `GetState` and `SetState` simply copy and restore the object's state data, we can use them for other purposes than persistence. They make a built-in cloning capability for each object, since we can write code like this:

```
Dim objPerson1 As Person
Dim objPerson2 As Person

Set objPerson1 = New Person
Set objPerson2 = New Person
objPerson1.SetState objPerson2.GetState
```

The `GetState` method of `mobjPerson2` simply converts that object's data into a string buffer. That buffer is then passed to the `SetState` method of `mobjPerson1`, which converts it back into detailed state data. We've moved all the detailed state data from `mobjPerson2` to `mobjPerson1` in one line of code.

### The Person Object's ApplyEdit Method

In our original `Person` object's `ApplyEdit` method, we inserted a comment to indicate that this routine would be responsible for saving the object's data:

```
Public Sub ApplyEdit()

  If Not mflgEditing Then Err.Raise 445
  mflgEditing = False
  mflgNew = False
  ' data would be saved here

End Sub
```

This isn't actually true if we intend to use an object manager like `PersonManager`. Instead, the `PersonManager` object itself will be responsible for saving the `Person` object's data. We don't need to make any changes to the `ApplyEdit` method, but it's important to recognize that the work involved in saving the `Person` object won't be done here and that it will be handled by the `PersonManager`.

It could be argued that it's possible to merge the code from `ApplyEdit` into the `GetState` method, since the `GetState` method will be called by `PersonManager` when it's saving the object - so the edit process must be complete. Unfortunately, this would introduce a side-effect into the `GetState` method that isn't intuitive. From the outside, just looking at the name `GetState`, you'd never guess that it also ends the editing process. To avoid confusion, methods should always be as descriptive as possible without unexpected side-effects, and merging these two routines could easily cause such confusion.

### Creating the PersonManager Object

Now that we've got the `Person` object ready to go, let's build the `PersonManager` object. To start off, make sure you've saved the `PersonObjects` project and, with the **File|New** Project menu option, start a new **ActiveX EXE** project. Set the project's **Project Name** to `PersonServer` under the Project|Properties menu option.

Change the name of `Class1` to `PersonManager` and make sure its Instancing property is set to 5-Multiuse.

Since we'll be sending data back and forth between our `Person` object and the `PersonManager` object through the use of the `LSet` technique, it's important that both objects have access to the `PersonProps` and `PersonData` user-defined types. Fortunately, we've put those types into the code module named `PersonUDTs`, so we can choose Project|Add File and add that code module to our new `PersonServer` project. Now both the `PersonObjects` and `PersonServer` projects have access to the exact same code module containing our user-defined types.

Now we're ready to add some code to the `PersonManager` class.

### Adding a Load Method to PersonManager

The UI code will use the `PersonManager` object to load object data from the database into a new `Person` object. To do this, we'll implement a `Load` method on the `PersonManager` object for use by the UI developer. This is where things get interesting.

At the very least, we need to pass the `Load` method an identifier so that it can retrieve the right person. In this example, we'll pass the social security number, with the assumption that it provides a unique identifier for an individual.

Now we need to figure out how to get the data back to the client and into an object. Ideally, we'd like to make the `Load` method a function that returns a fully loaded `Person` object. This would mean our UI client code could look something like this:

```
Dim objPersonManager As PersonManager
Dim objPerson As Person

Set objPersonManager = New PersonManager
Set objPerson = objPersonManager.Load(strSSN)
```

Unfortunately, this is difficult at best. In order to return an object reference, the `Load` method needs to create an object. When an object is created, using either `New` or `CreateObject`, it's instantiated in the same process, and on the same machine, as the code that creates it. This means that a `Person` object created by the `PersonManager`'s `Load` method would be created, in the `PersonManager` object, on whatever machine that code is running.

We need the `Person` object to be created on the client machine, inside our client process. This means that the code to instantiate the object needs to be in that process as well. As a compromise, let's make our client code look something like this:

```
Dim objPersonManager As PersonManager
Dim objPerson As Person

Set objPersonManager = New PersonManager
Set objPerson = New Person
objPersonManager.Load strSSN, objPerson
```

This way, the object is created in the client, but we'll pass it as a reference to the `PersonManager` object to be loaded with data.

Given this approach, let's enter the following code, for the Load method itself, into the PersonManager class module:

```
Public Sub Load(ByVal SSN As String, Person As Object)

   Dim rsPerson As Recordset
   Dim strConnect As String
   Dim strSQL As String
   Dim udtPerson As PersonProps
   Dim udtBuffer As PersonData

   strConnect = "Provider=Microsoft.Jet.OLEDB.3.51;" & _
     "Persist Security Info=False;" & _
     "Data Source=C:\Wrox\VB6 Pro Objects\Person.mdb"
   strSQL = "SELECT * FROM Person WHERE SSN='" & SSN & "'"
   Set rsPerson = New Recordset
   rsPerson.Open strSQL, strConnect

   With rsPerson
     If Not .EOF And Not .BOF Then
       udtPerson.SSN = .Fields("SSN")
       udtPerson.Name = .Fields("Name")
       udtPerson.Birthdate = .Fields("Birthdate")

       LSet udtBuffer = udtPerson
       Person.SetState udtBuffer.Buffer

     Else
       rsPerson.Close
       Err.Raise vbObjectError + 1002, "Person", "SSN not on file"

     End If

   End With

   rsPerson.Close

End Sub
```

*Once again, this code makes reference to a* Recordset *object, so you may need to add a reference in your project to the ADO. Use the* Project/References *menu option and select the most up-to-date ADO reference, such as* **Microsoft ActiveX Data Objects 2.0 Library.**

For the most part, this is pretty straightforward database programming, but let's walk through the routine to make sure everything is clear.

The code opens the database and builds a recordset based on a SQL statement using the social security number:

```
   strConnect = "Provider=Microsoft.Jet.OLEDB.3.51;" & _
     "Persist Security Info=False;" & _
     "Data Source=C:\Wrox\VB6 Pro Objects\Person.mdb"
   strSQL = "SELECT * FROM Person WHERE SSN='" & SSN & "'"
   Set rsPerson = New Recordset
   rsPerson.Open strSQL, strConnect
```

If we successfully retrieve the data, we just load that data into our user-defined type and use `LSet` to copy the detailed data into a user-defined type that represents a single string buffer:

```
udtPerson.SSN = .Fields("SSN")
udtPerson.Name = .Fields("Name")
udtPerson.Birthdate = .Fields("Birthdate")

LSet udtBuffer = udtPerson
```

Now that we've got all the data in a single string, we can just make a single call to the `Person` object's `SetState` method, as discussed above:

```
Person.SetState udtBuffer.Buffer
```

*This technique does require that both the detail and buffer user-defined types be available to both the business object project and the `PersonManager` object. The best way to handle this is to put the UDT definitions in a BAS module and include that module in both projects. Better yet, if you're using source code control such as Visual SourceSafe then you can link the file across both projects and allow the source control software to keep them in sync.*

Once we've called the `Person` object's `SetState` method to pass it the data from the database, the UI will have a reference to a fully loaded `Person` object. Then the UI code can use that `Person` object through its properties and methods.

## Adding a Save Method to PersonManager

At some point, the UI will need to save a `Person` object's data to the database. To do this, it will use the `PersonManager`, so we'll add a `Save` method to the `PersonManager` object to handle the add and update functions.

The `Save` method can have a fairly simple interface, since all we really need to do is send down a reference to the object itself. The code can then directly call the `GetState` method of the `Person` object to retrieve its data. Here is the code:

```
Public Sub Save(Person As Object)

  Dim rsPerson As Recordset
  Dim strConnect As String
  Dim strSQL As String
  Dim udtPerson As PersonProps
  Dim udtBuffer As PersonData

  udtBuffer.Buffer = Person.GetState
  LSet udtPerson = udtBuffer

  strConnect = "Provider=Microsoft.Jet.OLEDB.3.51;" & _
    "Persist Security Info=False;" & _
    "Data Source=C:\Wrox\VB6 Pro Objects\Person.mdb"
  strSQL = "SELECT * FROM Person WHERE SSN='" & udtPerson.SSN & "'"
  Set rsPerson = New Recordset
  rsPerson.Open strSQL, strConnect, adLockOptimistic

  With rsPerson
    If Person.IsNew Then .AddNew
```

```
        .Fields("SSN") = udtPerson.SSN
        .Fields("Name") = udtPerson.Name
        .Fields("Birthdate") = udtPerson.Birthdate
        .Update

    End With

    rsPerson.Close

End Sub
```

*A good question, at this point, might be: why pass the object reference when we could just pass the state string returned by* GetState*? In this case, it would accomplish the same thing, but with one less out-of-process or network call.*

*Suppose, however, that the* Person *object also included a comment field, a dynamic string in the object, and a memo or long text field in the database. Since this variable would be dynamic in length, we couldn't put it into a user-defined type, and so we couldn't easily pass it within our state string.*

*In a case like this, the* Save *method may not only need to use the* GetState *method, but it may also have to use a* GetComment *method - which we'd implement in the* Person *object to return the comment string.*

*Basically, by passing the object reference, rather than just the state string, we've provided ourselves with virtually unlimited flexibility in terms of communication between the* PersonManager *and* Person *objects.*

To save a Person object, the code in our form's cmdOK_Click and cmdApply_Click event routines will need to be updated. Open our PersonDemo project and bring up the form's code window. Change these two routines as shown:

```
Private Sub cmdApply_Click()

    Dim objPersonManager As PersonManager

    ' save the object
    Set objPersonManager = New PersonManager
    objPersonManager.Save mobjPerson
    mobjPerson.ApplyEdit
    mobjPerson.BeginEdit

End Sub

Private Sub cmdOK_Click()
    Dim objPersonManager As PersonManager
    ' save the object
    Set objPersonManager = New PersonManager
    objPersonManager.Save mobjPerson
    mobjPerson.ApplyEdit
    Unload Me

End Sub
```

Since we're passing the Save method a reference to the mobjPerson object, it can retrieve the data from the Person object and write the data out to the database.

### Adding a Delete Method to PersonManager

At this point, our UI code can use the PersonManager object's Load method to retrieve a Person object and the Save method to add or update a Person object into the database. The only remaining operation we need to support is removal of a Person object from the database.

To provide this support, we'll add a Delete method to the PersonManager object. We can use the same identity value for the Delete that we used for the Load; in this case, the social security number. And since we don't need the object's data, we don't need to worry about passing the object reference at all:

```
Public Sub Delete(SSN As String)

  Dim cnPerson As Connection
  Dim strConnect As String
  Dim strSQL As String

  strConnect = "Provider=Microsoft.Jet.OLEDB.3.51;" & _
    "Persist Security Info=False;" & _
    "Data Source=C:\Wrox\VB6 Pro Objects\Person.mdb"
  strSQL = "DELETE * FROM Person WHERE SSN='" & SSN & "'"
  Set cnPerson = New Connection
  cnPerson.Open strConnect
  cnPerson.Execute strSQL
  cnPerson.Close
  Set cnPerson = Nothing

End Sub
```

To delete a Person object, the UI code would look like this:

```
Dim objPersonManager As PersonManager

Set objPersonManager = New PersonManager
objPersonManager.Delete mobjPerson.SSN
```

This might be implemented behind a **Delete** button or a menu option - whatever is appropriate for the specific user-interface.

### Testing the Save Method

We should be able to immediately try out the PersonManager object's Save method. To do this, we'll need to compile our PersonServer project into an EXE. This is done using the File|Make PersonServer.exe menu option from within Visual Basic.

Once the PersonServer project has been compiled, we're almost ready to run our PersonDemo program. Load up the PersonDemo project again, and just add a reference to the PersonServer using the Project|References menu option.

Now run the PersonDemo program. The form will come up as always, allowing us to enter information into our Person object. However, with the changes we just made to the code behind the **OK** and **Apply** buttons, clicking either one should cause our Person object's data to be saved to the database by our PersonManager object.

## *Testing the Load Method*

The `Load` method is a bit trickier, since we need to come up with some way to get the SSN value from the user before we can call the method. The UI code we looked at for calling the `Load` method assumed we already had the SSN value.

Enter the following lines into our `EditPerson` form's `Form_Load` routine; this way, we can load a `Person` object as the form loads:

```vb
Private Sub Form_Load()

    Dim objPersonManager As PersonManager

    Set mobjPerson = New Person
    Set objPersonManager = New PersonManager

    objPersonManager.Load strSSN, mobjPerson

    EnableOK mobjPerson.IsValid
    mobjPerson.BeginEdit

End Sub
```

We can easily enhance this by using the `InputBox$` function to ask the user for the SSN. In the `PersonDemo` project, add the following to the `Form_Load` method:

```vb
Private Sub Form_Load()

    Dim strSSN As String
    Dim objPersonManager As PersonManager

    Set mobjPerson = New Person
    Set objPersonManager = New PersonManager
    strSSN = InputBox$("Enter the SSN")
    objPersonManager.Load strSSN, mobjPerson

    EnableOK mobjPerson.IsValid
    mobjPerson.BeginEdit

End Sub
```

This gets us almost there. If the user supplies a valid SSN value then our `Person` object will be loaded with the data from the database. All that remains is to update the display on the form, so let's add these lines to the `Form_Load` routine:

```vb
Private Sub Form_Load()

    Dim strSSN As String
    Dim objPersonManager As PersonManager

    Set mobjPerson = New Person
    Set objPersonManager = New PersonManager
    strSSN = InputBox$("Enter the SSN")
    objPersonManager.Load strSSN, mobjPerson

    mflgLoading = True
```

```
    With mobjPerson
      txtSSN = .SSN
      txtName = .Name
      txtBirthDate = .BirthDate
      lblAge = .Age
    End With
    mflgLoading = False

    EnableOK mobjPerson.IsValid
    mobjPerson.BeginEdit

End Sub
```

Notice, here, that we're using the module-level variable trick we saw in an earlier discussion where we looked at objects that save themselves: we set `mflgLoading` to `True` while we're loading information into our form, so that we can switch off the form's `Change` events of the text fields.

Therefore, we also need to declare this module-level variable in the General Declarations area of our `EditPerson` form:

```
    Private mflgLoading As Boolean
```

and we need to add this line to all the `Change` events in the `EditPerson` form:

```
    Private Sub txtName_Change()

      If mflgLoading Then Exit Sub
      mobjPerson.Name = txtName

    End Sub
```

If we run our `PersonDemo` program now, we'll be prompted for an SSN value. Entering a valid SSN should cause that `Person` object to be displayed. Of course, we don't have any error trapping for invalid SSN entries, but this demonstrates the basic concepts of saving and restoring an object from the database. We'll build a more robust application based on these general techniques starting in Chapter 5.

## Data-Centric Business Objects

The use of an object manager makes the process of retrieving, saving, and deleting an object pretty straightforward. However, compared to having an object save itself, this is a bit more complex from the UI developer's viewpoint. The UI developer not only needs to understand how to create and use the business objects themselves, but they need to understand how to create and use the objects that manage the persistence. This seems like extra work for little gain.

On the other hand, it's a small step from having the UI developer call the persistence manager object, as we've just seen, to having the business object itself call the persistence manager object:

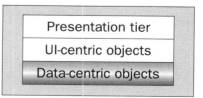

This figure indicates that the presentation tier, or UI, only needs to interact with our UI-centric business objects. The UI developer just uses simple `Load` and `ApplyEdit` methods on the UI-centric business object, and lets the UI-centric business object take care of asking the data-centric object to actually retrieve, save, or delete the data. The UI developer doesn't have to worry about any of the code to persist the object. At the same time, we get the benefit of having the persistence code in a separate object that can be distributed across the network.

Let's look at how we can modify the previous example to use this new and improved technique. Fortunately, the changes aren't too difficult, so this will go quickly.

### Simplifying the Code in the Form

First, let's look at the UI code. The whole idea is to simplify it, and we can easily do that. In fact, we can return it to the form it was in earlier in the chapter, before we implemented the `PersonManager`. The `Apply` and `OK` button code needs to be changed to appear as follows:

```
Private Sub cmdApply_Click()

  mobjPerson.ApplyEdit
  mobjPerson.BeginEdit

End Sub
```

```
Private Sub cmdOK_Click()

  mobjPerson.ApplyEdit
  Unload Me

End Sub
```

We also have code in the `Form_Load` routine to get an SSN value from the user and to load our `Person` object using the `PersonManager` object. We'll need to simplify that code as well:

```
Private Sub Form_Load()

  Dim strSSN As String

  Set mobjPerson = New Person
  strSSN = InputBox$("Enter the SSN")

  mobjPerson.Load(strSSN)

  mflgLoading = True
```

In all three routines, the big difference is that our form's code doesn't need to create or deal with a `PersonManager` object. All the UI developer needs to be concerned with are the basic methods provided by the UI-centric business object, which is our `Person` object.

Since we no longer need to use the `PersonServer` project from the `PersonDemo` UI project, we need to use the <u>P</u>roject|Refere<u>n</u>ces menu option and remove the reference to the `PersonServer` project.

### Adding a Load Method to Person

The changes to the Person object itself are a bit more extensive. Earlier in the chapter, we discussed having business objects save themselves to the database. To do this, we created a Load method for the object and enhanced the ApplyEdit method. Basically, we want to do the same thing here, except that the actual database code will be in a separate object, PersonManager.

First, let's add a Load method to the Person object. Enter the following code into the Person class module in the PersonObjects project:

```
Public Sub Load(SSN As String)

    Dim objManager As PersonManager

    Set objManager = New PersonManager
    objManager.Load SSN, Me
    Set objManager = Nothing

End Sub
```

This should look familiar, as it's pretty much the same code we just dealt with when having the client talk to the PersonManager. The code simply creates a PersonManager object, and then asks it to retrieve the object's data by passing the social security number and Me, a reference to the current object.

> You'll now need to add a reference to the PersonServer project from within your PersonObjects project. Use the **Project|References** menu option, and select PersonServer.
>
> It's worth noting, at this point, that the PersonManager object itself is entirely unchanged from our previous example. By simply adding a few extra lines of code into our business objects, we've dramatically simplified the UI developer's job, and we don't even have to change the objects that contain the data access code.

### Updating the Person Object's ApplyEdit Method

Back to the Person object, we also need to change the ApplyEdit method to talk to the PersonManager:

```
Public Sub ApplyEdit()

    Dim objManager As PersonManager

    If Not mflgEditing Then Err.Raise 445

    Set objManager = New PersonManager
    objManager.Save Me
    Set objManager = Nothing

    mflgEditing = False
    mflgNew = False

End Sub
```

Again, all we've done is created a `PersonManager` object, just like we did in the UI of the previous example. Then we just call its `Save` method passing `Me`, a reference to the current object, as a parameter. Of course, the UI developer simply calls `ApplyEdit` to save the object to the database; they don't need to worry about any of these details.

## Adding a Delete Method to Person

Finally, let's add a `Delete` method to the `Person` business object. After all, we've already got that capability built into `PersonManager`; we just need to make it available to the UI developer via the business object:

```
Public Sub Delete()

  Dim objManager As PersonManager

  Set objManager = New PersonManager
  objManager.Delete mudtPerson.SSN
  Set objManager = Nothing

End Sub
```

*The only real drawback to this implementation of a* `Delete` *method is that the UI code may cheat and continue to retain a reference to the* `Person` *object after the* `Delete` *method has been called. This can make it much harder to debug the UI, since the developer may not immediately spot the fact that they are still using an object that has theoretically been deleted. One solution to this problem is to maintain a* `Boolean` *variable inside the object to indicate that the object has been deleted. Using this variable, we can add a line at the top of every property and method to raise the appropriate error to disable them, as discussed earlier in the chapter.*

This final approach to object persistence is a combination of the other techniques. It takes the best from each and puts them together to create an object to manage our data access that is transparent to the UI developer, easy to use for the business object developer, and that can be distributed to a central application server machine.

## Testing the Code

The project should now run just as it did when we ran it under the full auspices of the `PersonManager` - we're able to perform deletions and apply edits as normal.

This is as far as we shall pursue our `PersonDemo` project. It's still in a pretty rough form, and there are lots of things we could do to improve it, of course; but the main functionality is in place, and it's served our purposes as we've explored a number of key concepts in this chapter. We're now ready to move on to bigger and better things - such as our video rental store project, where we'll develop the techniques we've learnt with our `PersonDemo` project to produce a sophisticated set of business objects and UI.

# Summary

In this chapter, we returned to the CSLA. We looked at how that logical architecture can be implemented on a single machine and across multiple machines. As the number of physical tiers is increased, we can gain better distribution of the processing - increasing our flexibility and scalability with each layer. Of course, each extra layer of hardware can add communications overhead to our application.

We explored some of the business object design issues that impact user-interface developers. One of the primary goals of a business object developer is to make it easy for UI developers to work with the objects. At the same time, the business objects must protect themselves. Essentially, the business object developer must assume that the user-interface code will do something to break the objects - and the developer must take steps to prevent that from happening.

We wrapped up the chapter by looking at different techniques that we can use to save and restore object data in a database, or make objects persistent. Making objects persistent is the key to creating client/server applications using business objects. Most of an application's performance issues surround the techniques used to persist objects in a database, so it's important to choose the appropriate technique for each application.

We'll continue to explore the concepts from this chapter throughout the remainder of the book. Using the video store example from Chapter 3, we'll walk through the development of a series of applications by applying the CSLA to each typical physical model. Here's what we'll be looking at through the next few chapters:

Chapter 5     Build the simpler objects for a Video store
Chapter 6     Build more complex parent-child objects for a Video store
Chapter 7     Create a UI using Visual Basic forms
Chapter 8     Add code to our objects to save themselves to the database
Chapter 9     Create a UI using Microsoft Excel
Chapter 10    Using data-centric business objects over Distributed COM
Chapter 11    Distributing objects over DCOM
Chapter 12    Using data-centric business objects with Microsoft Transaction Server
Chapter 13    Active Server Pages and HTML as a front end
Chapter 14    Using an IIS Application as a front end
Chapter 15    Create a UI using a DHTML Application

# 5

# Implementing Business Objects Using Visual Basic 6.0

## Overview

So far, we've looked at business objects, distributed computing and various physical and logical architectures. We've also taken a fairly in-depth look at some techniques for identifying and designing business objects. At the end of Chapter 4, we also examined a number of approaches to making objects persistent by saving and restoring their core data, or state, within a relational database.

In Chapters 5 through to 13, we're going to build and modify an application to operate a fictitious video rental store. Of course, the whole idea behind using business objects is to conserve code by encapsulating our core business processes within the business objects themselves. This should make it easy to create subsequent applications with minimal changes to the business object code.

It therefore makes sense to implement our business objects first - and then add the user-interface and object persistence based on the physical requirements of the application. When we talk about physical requirements we're referring to whether the application will be running on a single workstation or in either a two- or n-tier client/server setting.

In this chapter, we'll go through the process of implementing all the business objects that will be required to develop the applications in the remaining chapters.

Along the way we'll also look at some ways to increase our productivity. We'll use Visual Basic's capability to create template modules to create some reusable code. We'll also create a `TextList` object to help us manage data used to populate `ComboBox` or `ListBox` controls.

# Common Business Object Interface

In Chapter 4, we talked about common interface elements that objects should provide the UI developer. Let's quickly refresh that now, because all the business objects that we're about to implement need to provide those interface elements. Along the same lines, all our business objects need to implement certain behaviors so that they're consistent and easy to understand and use from the UI developer's viewpoint.

We won't go into this in great detail, as we covered all of this in Chapter 4. On the other hand, we were talking theory, earlier, and here we're getting down to brass tacks - so we need to be clear on what needs to be done.

## OK, Cancel and Apply - A Preliminary Discussion

To support a robust user-interface, including OK, Cancel and Apply buttons, we need to provide support for beginning edits, canceling edits and applying edits. We also need to indicate if the object can be saved or not at any given point in time, so the OK and Apply buttons can be enabled and disabled as needed.

> **Don't worry about typing this code in yet. After we review the concepts, we'll enter this code into a code template. Code templates make it easy to create new code modules that start out with a lot of basic code already entered into the module.**

### Transactional Methods

All our public objects need to support methods to be called from the OK, Cancel and Apply buttons:

- ❑ BeginEdit
- ❑ CancelEdit
- ❑ ApplyEdit

Part of the implementation of these methods requires that the object keep track, internally, of whether it can be edited at any given point. This can be handled through a private mflgEditing variable.

The basic code to support these methods is pretty simple. Of course, each object will have its own private variables to store its state data, but the following code contains the essence of what each object must do:

```
Option Explicit

Private mflgEditing As Boolean

Public Sub BeginEdit()

  If mflgEditing Then Err.Raise 445
' save object state
  mflgEditing = True

End Sub
```

*Remember, don't worry about entering this code yet. Later in the chapter, we'll enter this code into a code template, which will make it easier for us to create new code modules to add to our video rental store project. For now, we're just looking at the ideas behind the code being presented.*

`BeginEdit` is only valid if the object is not already being edited, so it raises an error if it's called while editing is taking place.

If the object is not already being edited, we need to save the object's core data - whatever that may be. This is indicated by the comment in this code, since the specific code will be different for each object. Finally, we just need to set the `mflgEditing` variable to `True`, since everything is now set for editing the object's data.

Here is the code for `CancelEdit`:

```
Public Sub CancelEdit()

  If Not mflgEditing Then Err.Raise 445

  mflgEditing = False
' restore object state

End Sub
```

The `CancelEdit` method is not valid unless `mflgEditing` is true, since we can't cancel an edit if the object is not being edited. If this rule is broken, the method just raises an error to the calling code.

If the object was being edited, we just need to set the `mflgEditing` flag to `False` to indicate that the editing is done. Then we must restore the object's state to the copy we made in the `BeginEdit` method. Again, the code for this will be different for each object, depending upon the nature of the data involved; so we've just put a comment here to show where that code would be located.

Here's the code for `ApplyEdit`:

```
Public Sub ApplyEdit()

  If Not mflgEditing Then Err.Raise 445

' save object state
  mflgEditing = False

End Sub
```

As with `CancelEdit`, this method is not valid unless the object is being edited, and, rather like applying a database transaction, applying the edits to an object ends the editing session by setting `mflgEditing` to a value of `False`.

Virtually all the code in this method will be customized for each object. To apply the edits we need to save the object's current data just as we did in the `BeginEdit` method. A good approach is to create a common private subroutine to hold this code, and then just call that routine from both `BeginEdit` and `ApplyEdit`.

As we'll discuss shortly, `ApplyEdit` is also responsible for saving the object's data to the database. As we saw in Chapter 4, the database code might be right here, or this routine might call a method on an object on another machine to talk to the database instead.

## Indicating Validity

Our business objects also need to provide mechanisms for the user-interface to know when the object is valid. That is, the UI needs to know when to enable and disable the OK and Apply buttons on the screen. This can be done through:

- ❑ A `Valid` event
- ❑ An `IsValid` property

As we saw in Chapter 4, a very good way to implement the `Valid` event and `IsValid` property is to use a `BrokenRules` object. Using the `BrokenRules` object, we'll have code in all our business objects to manage those rules.

First, we need to declare a variable for the `BrokenRules` object:

```
Private WithEvents mobjValid As BrokenRules
```

Then we need to add code to the `Class_Initialize` event to create the object. We also need to initialize the list of broken rules with any rules that we know are broken when an object is blank. Examples of this might include a required field that starts out blank, and thus breaks the rule immediately upon creating the object.

Here's the `Class_Initialize` code:

```
Private Sub Class_Initialize()

  Set mobjValid = New BrokenRules
  ' if we know any rules are broken on startup
  ' then add code here to initialize the list
  ' of broken rules

  ' mobjValid.RuleBroken "RuleName", True

End Sub
```

Of course, we want to expose a property to allow the UI to find out if the object can be saved, or is valid. We'll call that property `IsValid`:

```
Public Property Get IsValid() As Boolean

  IsValid = (mobjValid.Count = 0)

End Property
```

Along the same lines, the `BrokenRules` object raises a couple of events indicating when a rule is broken and when there are no broken rules. We thus also declare our own `Valid` event which can be raised when we need to indicate a change in the state of the object's validity:

```
Event Valid(IsValid As Boolean)
```

When the `BrokenRules` object raises events we need to intercept them and raise our `Valid` event up to the UI - so that the UI developer can easily enable or disable the OK and Apply buttons if desired. Here's the code to raise those two events:

```
Private Sub mobjValid_BrokenRule()

   RaiseEvent Valid(False)

End Sub

Private Sub mobjValid_NoBrokenRules()

   RaiseEvent Valid(True)

End Sub
```

We can also use the object's `IsValid` property, within the object itself, to disable any properties or methods that shouldn't be called when the object is not in a savable state. One obvious example of this is the `ApplyEdit` method. If the object shouldn't be saved, we want to make sure the `ApplyEdit` method returns an error when called:

```
Public Sub ApplyEdit()

   If Not mflgEditing Then Err.Raise 445
   If Not IsValid Then Err.Raise 445

' save object state
   mflgEditing = False

End Sub
```

Any other properties or methods that we need to disable can be handled by adding the same line of code at the top of those routines.

# Persistence: Saving/Restoring Objects

Most of our business objects will have data that's stored and retrieved from a database. While the actual implementation of this persistence can vary, as we saw in Chapter 4, the business objects can provide a consistent interface to the UI developer regardless of the underlying code.

We need to provide support for retrieving, saving and deleting an object's data. It's also very useful for the UI developer to know whether the object can be considered new and whether it's been changed since it was loaded.

> **Don't worry about typing this code in anywhere. After we review the concepts we'll enter this code into a code template. Code templates make it easy to create new code modules that start out with a lot of basic code already entered into the module.**

## Load

In order to get data from the database into our object, we'll implement a Load method in all our objects. As we discussed in Chapter 4, there are a number of different ways to implement such a method, so the code here will be fairly light. We'll expand on this code in Chapter 8, then again in Chapters 10 and 12.

```
Public Sub Load(KeyValue As Variant)

  If mflgEditing Then Err.Raise 445

' code to load the object goes here

End Sub
```

Typically, the Load method will accept one or more parameters. After all, we need to provide enough information to uniquely identify the object's data within the database.

Also, this method needs to be disabled if the object is already being edited. We don't want a developer to accidentally reload an object after the user has already started entering values into it. To prevent this, the routine just checks mflgEditing and raises an error if the value is True.

## ApplyEdit

We've already discussed the ApplyEdit method in the context of supporting the OK, Cancel and Apply buttons. This method is also the key to saving our object's data. When we apply the edits, we not only want to update the object's internal state, but we also want to update its data in the database:

```
Public Sub ApplyEdit()

  If Not mflgEditing Then Err.Raise 445
  If Not IsValid Then Err.Raise 445

' save object to database if appropriate
' save object state
  mflgEditing = False

End Sub
```

As with the Load method, the specific implementation of saving the data to the database can vary greatly. More important is that we know that the ApplyEdit method is a consistent place to locate whatever implementation we choose.

## Deleting an Object

To facilitate deletion of an object's data from the database, we'll add a Delete method to all the persistent objects. Ideally, our CancelEdit and ApplyEdit methods will also cover deleting an object - so that the UI developer can have maximum control over the behavior.

It isn't difficult to work the Delete method into the existing methods. First, we need to add a module-level variable to indicate whether the object has been deleted:

```
Private mflgDeleted As Boolean
```

The `Delete` method itself should only be called after a call to `BeginEdit`, but beyond that it will just set `mflgDeleted` to a value of `True`:

```
Public Sub Delete()

  If Not mflgEditing Then Err.Raise 445

  mflgDeleted = True

End Sub
```

Finally, we need to change `CancelEdit` and `ApplyEdit`. `CancelEdit` merely needs to restore `mflgDeleted` to a `False` value. This effectively cancels the delete operation, since the flag is reset and the data hasn't been removed from the database.

```
Public Sub CancelEdit()

  If Not mflgEditing Then Err.Raise 445
  If Not IsValid Then Err.Raise 445

  mflgEditing = False
  mflgDeleted = False
' restore object state

End Sub
```

The changes to `ApplyEdit` are a bit more extensive, since this method needs to actually commit any data changes. In this case, it needs to commit the delete operation:

```
Public Sub ApplyEdit()

  If Not mflgEditing Then Err.Raise 445

  If mflgDeleted Then
    ' code to delete the object's data goes here
    mflgDeleted = False

  Else
    If Not IsValid Then Err.Raise 445
    ' save object to database if appropriate
    ' save object state

  End If

  mflgEditing = False

End Sub
```

If `mflgDeleted` is `True` then the code to delete the object's data will be run. At the risk of being repetitive, the implementation of this code can vary depending on the persistence strategy we choose. The routine also resets the `mflgDeleted` flag back to `False`, since the delete is now complete and the object is almost like a new object that has yet to be saved to the database.

If `mflgDeleted` was `False`, on the other hand, we just need to add or update the object's data as we were doing before these changes were made. The trick is that we move the line that checks `IsValid` into this area along with the code that saves the object's state data. Neither of these activities is appropriate when deleting an object - only when we are updating the data in the database.

As a last step, we'll add an `IsDeleted` property to each object. This is mostly a convenience to developers using our objects, as they may have a need to determine if the object will be deleted if they call `ApplyEdit`. This way, the UI code doesn't need to track whether the `Delete` method has been called; we do it instead:

```
Public Property Get IsDeleted() As Boolean

    IsDeleted = mflgDeleted

End Property
```

## IsNew

It can be very useful to the UI developer to know when an object is new. Frequently, the programmer will choose to adapt the interface to indicate that an object is new. For instance, it may be possible to enter some data fields only on a new object.

To implement this property, we'll simply keep a `Boolean` flag within the object:

```
Private mflgNew As Boolean
```

Then, in the `Class_Initialize` method, we'll set this flag to `True`, indicating that the object has not been loaded with any data from the database:

```
Private Sub Class_Initialize()

    mflgNew = True
    Set mobjValid = New BrokenRules
    ' if we know any rules are broken on startup
    ' then add code here to initialize the list
    ' of broken rules

    ' mobjValid.RuleBroken "RuleName", True

End Sub
```

Of course, as soon as we load data into the object from the database, we know that the object is no longer new. Handling this is as simple as adding a line to our `Load` method:

```
Public Sub Load()

    If mflgEditing Then Err.Raise 445
    If Not mflgNew Then Err.Raise 445

    ' code to load the object goes here
    mflgNew = False

End Sub
```

We've also added a line to prevent the Load method from being run unless the object is new. This is just a bit of protection for developers using our objects. After an object has been loaded with data, we don't want them accidentally reloading the object with other data from the database.

Even if our object starts out new, as soon as we save it to the database with the ApplyEdit method, the object is really no more new than if we'd loaded it from the database with the Load method.

Of course, ApplyEdit might also delete the object if the mflgDeleted flag is True. In this case, the object basically becomes new once again. The definition of a new object is one where the object's data doesn't exist in the database, and by removing the object's data from the database we sure meet that condition.

All we need to do is add a couple lines to the ApplyEdit method:

```
Public Sub ApplyEdit()

  If Not mflgEditing Then Err.Raise 445

  If mflgDeleted And Not mflgNew Then
    ' code to delete the object's data goes here
    mflgNew = True
    mflgDeleted = False

  Else
    If Not IsValid Then Err.Raise 445
    ' save object to database if appropriate
    ' save object state
    mflgNew = False

  End If

  mflgEditing = False

End Sub
```

With these changes, we now have a mflgNew variable that always indicates whether our object is new or whether it came from data that is stored in the database or that was entered by the user and saved to the database. All that remains is to implement a simple IsNew property so that the UI developer has access to this information as well:

```
Public Property Get IsNew() As Boolean

  IsNew = mflgNew

End Property
```

## IsDirty

Along the same lines as knowing when an object is new, it can be very useful to know when the object's data has been changed. This, too, can be implemented by simply adding a Boolean variable to the object and setting it to true any time the object's data is changed:

```
Private mflgDirty As Boolean
```

By default, the variable will start out with the value of `False`, which is just fine, since a new, empty object is obviously not dirty. To indicate that an object has been changed, we need to add the code inside any `Property Let` routines to set `mflgDirty` to `True`:

```
mflgDirty = True
```

If we subsequently save the data out to the database then we have synchronized the object with the database, and so we can consider the object to no longer be dirty. This is another line in the `ApplyEdit` method, where we save the object's data. Better still, we only need to save the object's data to the database if `mflgDirty` is `True`, so we'll add a check for that as well:

```
Public Sub ApplyEdit()

  If Not mflgEditing Then Err.Raise 445

  If mflgDeleted And Not mflgNew Then
    ' code to delete the object's data goes here
    mflgNew = True
    mflgDeleted = False

  ElseIf mflgDirty Or mflgNew Then
    If Not IsValid Then Err.Raise 445
    ' save object to database if appropriate
    ' save object state
    mflgNew = False

  End If

  mflgDirty = False
  mflgEditing = False

End Sub
```

In the `Delete` method of each object, the `mflgDirty` flag should be set to `True`. We'll need to do this so that when we try to delete an object that is a child of another, the child object will show up as dirty - otherwise the child object isn't necessarily sent to the server to be deleted.

```
Public Sub Delete()

  If Not mflgEditing Then Err.Raise 445

  mflgDeleted = True
  mflgDirty = True


End Sub
```

The final modification we need to make to our existing code involves the `CancelEdit` method. If the user has canceled the editing process we revert our object's state to the stored values. We also need to reset the `mflgDirty` flag to `False`, since we're now back at the state we were to start with.

```
Public Sub CancelEdit()

  If Not mflgEditing Then Err.Raise 445
  If Not IsValid Then Err.Raise 445
```

```
    mflgEditing = False
    mflgDeleted = False
    mflgDirty = False
' restore object state

End Sub
```

At this point, we have a `mflgDirty` variable that continually indicates whether our object's data has been changed since it was last loaded from or saved to the database. By adding an `IsDirty` property, we can give the UI developer access to this information as well:

```
Public Property Get IsDirty() As Boolean

    IsDirty = mflgDirty or mflgNew

End Property
```

It is important to note that we are also returning a True value if the `mflgNew` variable is True. It only stands to reason that any brand new object is 'dirty' – especially if we define dirty as being different from the last time it was loaded from the database. Since a new object has never been loaded from a database it must be different.

# Creating a Class Template

As you can see, just creating a simple business object can involve quite a lot of code. No one likes typing the same stuff over and over again. Fortunately, Visual Basic provides a way to get a jump-start on coding by letting us add our own templates to the development environment.

In this section we'll create a code template for our UI-centric business objects based on the concepts we just reviewed. We'll use this template through the remainder of this chapter, as we build the business objects for our video store application.

## Setting up the Class Module

First, open a new ActiveX DLL project in Visual Basic. This should put us right into a new class module named `Class1`. In the properties window we need to set the Name and Instancing properties of `Class1`. Set the Name to `Business` and the Instancing to 5-Multiuse.

## Adding the Template Code

Now we need to add the template code. The code we need is all the code we just discussed for OK, Cancel and Apply along with the object persistence and all the related properties. Enter this code into the module:

```
Option Explicit

Event Valid(IsValid As Boolean)

Private mflgNew As Boolean
Private mflgDeleted As Boolean
Private mflgDirty As Boolean
Private mflgEditing As Boolean
Private WithEvents mobjValid As BrokenRules
```

```vb
Public Sub BeginEdit()

  If mflgEditing Then Err.Raise 445

  ' save object state
  mflgEditing = True

End Sub
```

```vb
Public Sub CancelEdit()

  If Not mflgEditing Then Err.Raise 445

  mflgEditing = False
  mflgDeleted = False
  mflgDirty = False
  ' restore object state

End Sub
```

```vb
Public Sub ApplyEdit()

  If Not mflgEditing Then Err.Raise 445

  If mflgDeleted And Not mflgNew Then
    ' code to delete the object's data goes here
    mflgNew = True
    mflgDeleted = False

  ElseIf mflgDirty Or mflgNew Then
    If Not IsValid Then Err.Raise 445
    ' save object to database if appropriate
    ' save object state
    mflgNew = False

  End If

  mflgDirty = False
  mflgEditing = False

End Sub
```

```vb
Private Sub Class_Initialize()

  mflgNew = True
  Set mobjValid = New BrokenRules
  ' if we know any rules are broken on startup
  ' then add code here to initialize the list
  ' of broken rules
  '
  ' mobjValid.RuleBroken "RuleName", True

End Sub
```

```vb
Public Property Get IsValid() As Boolean

  IsValid = (mobjValid.Count = 0)

End Property
```

```
Private Sub mobjValid_BrokenRule()

  RaiseEvent Valid(False)

End Sub

Private Sub mobjValid_NoBrokenRules()

  RaiseEvent Valid(True)

End Sub

Public Sub Load()

  If mflgEditing Then Err.Raise 445
  If Not mflgNew Then Err.Raise 445

  ' code to load the object goes here

  mflgNew = False

End Sub

Public Sub Delete()

  If Not mflgEditing Then Err.Raise 445

  mflgDeleted = True
  mflgDirty = True

End Sub

Public Property Get IsDeleted() As Boolean

  IsDeleted = mflgDeleted

End Property

Public Property Get IsNew() As Boolean

  IsNew = mflgNew

End Property

Public Property Get IsDirty() As Boolean

  IsDirty = mflgDirty or mflgNew

End Property
```

## Saving the Template

Now we need to save the class module into the `Template\Classes` directory under the directory where Visual Basic itself is installed. Typically this will be something like:

```
C:\Program Files\Microsoft Visual Studio\Vb98
```

Right-click on the Business class in the Project window and choose the Save Business As... option from the menu; then use the Save File As dialog to save the class module into the Template\Classes directory.

That's it, we now have a template ready to use. We'll want to close the current project (or remove the Business template class module) before trying to use the template to avoid accidentally saving over the file we just created. We don't need to save the project itself, it's only the template module that we're concerned with at this point.

## Using the Code Template

To see how it works, create an new ActiveX DLL project if you closed down the previous project, just choose the Project | Add Class Module menu option. The Add Class Module dialog will appear, with our new Business template listed as an option:

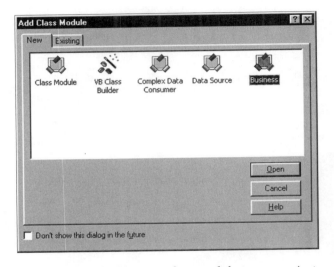

Choose the Business option and click Open. Visual Basic will add a new class module to our project, called Business, that contains all the code we entered earlier. From now on, any time we need to add a new business object class to our projects we can just use this template.

# The BrokenRules Class

The template we just created relies on the BrokenRules class being available to the project. We created the BrokenRules class in Chapter 4 to simplify the process of tracking which business rules are broken at any given point in time.

We can either add the BrokenRules class to every project, or we can compile it into a DLL and just reference it in each project that needs it. The optimum solution is to put it into a Utility.dll or Common.dll along with any other classes our developers create that are useful to many different applications.

However, in our video store application, our business objects will all be in one Visual Basic project, so we'll just include the BrokenRules.cls file into that project.

# Video Rental System Overview

If we were developing an application for real, either for our employer, a client or for retail sale, we'd want to do a full analysis of the business requirements and functional requirements. We looked at some techniques for doing this back in Chapter 3.

Of course, these documents tend to be very long and very dry. While they are invaluable in developing an application, they'd make pretty boring material for a technical book. Because of this, we're just going to run through a very quick overview of the application's requirements - so we can see how the various objects fit into the picture - and leave it at that.

As this is a video rental store application, we'll obviously have customers coming in to rent the videos. And we'll have videos for them to rent, probably with a number of tapes for each video title - especially the popular ones. The rental itself is a transaction, and so we'll express it as an invoice, with line items for each tape that gets rented.

In general, then, we have the following objects:

- ❑ Customer
- ❑ Video
- ❑ Tape
- ❑ Invoice
- ❑ InvoiceItem

When we go through each of these business functions, there will be a number of supporting objects that need to be created. Mostly, these will be collection objects, or objects that represent a series of related business objects. For instance, we will have a *Tapes* object that represents all the *Tape* objects for a specific video title.

The following diagram provides an overview of the main objects we'll be implementing for this system. The arrows indicate an ownership or parent-child type relationship between the objects.

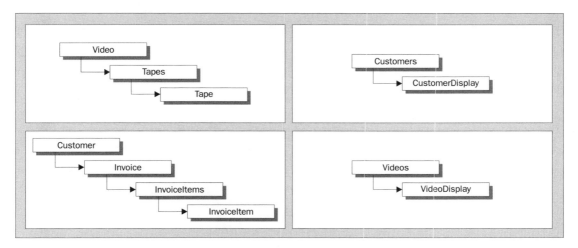

We'll be implementing a few other objects along the way, but this should provide a good picture of all the major objects that are needed to support a video rental store.

# Video Rental: Customer Objects

In any retail system, there's always a customer of some sort. Our video store is no exception; someone needs to pay the bills after all. Our customer object needs to contain some pretty basic information about a person - including their name, address and phone number.

We also need to provide a way to find a customer. A typical application would provide some search facility so that the user can enter criteria and get back a list of customers to choose from. The easiest way to support this concept, with objects, is to provide a collection object to contain the list of customers. For this purpose, we'll create a `Customers` object.

In the implementation we'll do here, there is no real relationship between a `Customer` object and a `Customers` object. The `Customer` object will represent a real-world customer. Our `Customers` object will represent a customer list, such as a paper ledger listing some or all of our customer's names.

# Customer: A Simple Object

Since this is the first real business object we're creating, we'll go through the process in detail. After this object, we'll gloss over the more repetitive steps so we can focus in on the differences between the objects.

## Setting up the Project

To start with, open up a new ActiveX DLL project in Visual Basic. Change the project name to `VideoObjects` by choosing Project | ProjectX Properties... and changing the Project Name field on the Project Properties dialog:

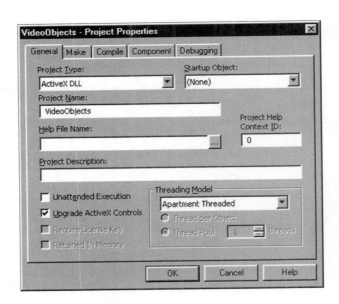

Now right-click on the `Class1` item in the Project window and choose the Remove Class1 option. Answer No when prompted to save any changes.

We'll be adding our classes using the Business class template we created earlier in this chapter.

## Adding the BrokenRules Class Module

We'll also need the BrokenRules class from earlier in the book. Choose the Project | Add File... menu option and just include the class module directly into this project.

## Adding the Customer Class Module

Now we're ready to add our Customer class module. Choose the Project | Add Class Module menu option. From the dialog, choose the Business class template that we created earlier and click Open:

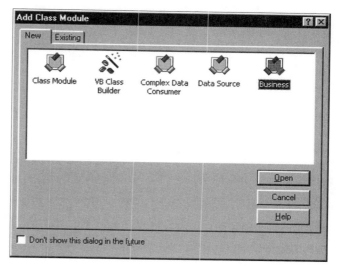

We should be looking at a ready-to-go class module with all the template code we built earlier in the chapter. Change the Name property of the class to Customer in the Properties window, and make sure that the Instancing property is 5-Multiuse.

> *It's important to restrict the creation of objects, when appropriate, by setting the Instancing property to 1-Private or 2-PublicNotCreatable. In the case of the* Customer *object, however, we want the UI developer to be able to create new* Customer *objects as needed. Later in the chapter, we'll see some objects that can't be directly created from the UI.*

## Setting up the Customer Class

Now it's down to adding the code for the class. The first thing we need to do is set up variables to store the object's data. As we discussed earlier in the book, it's a good idea to use user-defined types (UDTs) to store the data, because it makes it easier to save and restore the object's core data - as well as to implement distributed database load and save operations.

### Declarations

In the (Declarations) section of the code module, let's add a UDT, CustomerProps, to store the object's data. We'll also add declarations for a couple of variables based on this type. The first, mudtProps, will store the object's properties. The other, mudtSave, will be the copy we'll use when we need to save or restore the object's data within the BeginEdit, CancelEdit and ApplyEdit methods:

```
Option Explicit

Event Valid(IsValid As Boolean)

Private Type CustomerProps
  CustomerID As Long
  Name As String * 50
  Phone As String * 25
  Address1 As String * 30
  Address2 As String * 30
  City As String * 20
  State As String * 2
  ZipCode As String * 10
End Type

Private mudtProps As CustomerProps
Private mudtSave As CustomerProps

Private mflgNew As Boolean
Private mflgDeleted As Boolean
Private mflgDirty As Boolean
Private mflgEditing As Boolean
Private WithEvents mobjValid As BrokenRules
```

Now we need to go through the template code and update it in a few places. In particular, we need to add code to save and restore the object's data as needed.

### Load Method

Our template supplied a basic `Load` method, but we need to customize it to suit our needs. In particular, it needs to accept a parameter to uniquely identify the customer data to be loaded. The `CustomerID` field is the unique identifier for our customer objects, so that's the parameter we'll need to accept:

```
Public Sub Load(CustomerID as Long)

    If mflgEditing Then Err.Raise 445
    If Not mflgNew Then Err.Raise 445

    ' code to load the object goes here

    mflgNew = False

End Sub
```

There's not much else we can customize in the `Load` method at this point, since the actual data loading code will depend on the data access implementation we choose. Through the remaining chapters of this book, we'll be implementing this method in a couple of different ways.

### BeginEdit Method

In the `BeginEdit` method, we need to add a line to save the data in `mudtProps` to the `mudtSave` variable:

```
Public Sub BeginEdit()

  If mflgEditing Then Err.Raise 445

  ' save object state
  LSet mudtSave = mudtProps
  mflgEditing = True

End Sub
```

### CancelEdit Method

In the `CancelEdit` method, we need to do the reverse, copying the data in `mudtSave` back into `mudtProps` to restore the object to the last data that was saved:

```
Public Sub CancelEdit()

  If Not mflgEditing Then Err.Raise 445

  mflgEditing = False
  mflgDeleted = False
  ' restore object state
  LSet mudtProps = mudtSave

End Sub
```

### ApplyEdit Method

Similar to the `BeginEdit` method, the `ApplyEdit` method also copies the `mudtProps` data into the `mudtSave` variable using the `LSet` command:

```
Public Sub ApplyEdit()

  If Not mflgEditing Then Err.Raise 445

  If mflgDeleted And Not mflgNew Then
    ' code to delete the object's data goes here
    mflgNew = True
    mflgDeleted = False

  ElseIf mflgDirty Or mflgNew Then
    If Not IsValid Then Err.Raise 445
    ' save object to database if appropriate
    ' save object state
    LSet mudtSave = mudtProps
    mflgNew = False

  End If

  mflgDirty = False
  mflgEditing = False

End Sub
```

Note that we're not touching the parts of the code that will eventually save and restore the data from the database. For now, we're just leaving the comments there to remind us that we need to add that code later.

### Class_Initialize Routine

Let's say that, at the very least, any customer needs to have a name and a phone number. With a new object, we know that these fields will be blank, and so we need to initialize the BrokenRules object to know that these rules are broken. We'll do this by adding a couple of lines to the Class_Initialize routine:

```
Private Sub Class_Initialize()

    mflgNew = True
    Set mobjValid = New BrokenRules
    ' if we know any rules are broken on startup
    ' then add code here to initialize the list
    ' of broken rules
    '
    ' mobjValid.RuleBroken "RuleName", True
    mobjValid.RuleBroken "Name", True
    mobjValid.RuleBroken "Phone", True

End Sub
```

That's it for the basics. Virtually every business object we create will need the same changes we just made - tailored for that object's specific properties, of course.

Now we can move on to implement any specific properties and methods that the Customer object will need. These properties and methods are fairly obvious, since they correspond to the data elements in the UDT that we declared.

## Customer Object Properties

Let's go through each property in turn. Most of them will be very similar, but we do have some required fields and one read-only property.

### CustomerID Property: Read-only Value

The CustomerID property is primarily a key value for the database. Customer numbers are often displayed on forms, or shown on reports, however; so we need to make this available to the UI developer - at least on a read-only basis.

Implementing key values like the CustomerID can be a tricky business. We need to decide if the user can enter the initial value, and whether we want to let them change it after it has been entered. The easiest solution, of course, is for the key value to be generated automatically by the computer.

Even if the computer automatically generates the key value, we still need to decide if it should be generated right away when the object is created, or perhaps if it should be generated when the object is first saved to the database. Most databases provide some facility to generate sequential numbers for key values, such as the AutoNumber type in Microsoft Access. If we need to provide a key value before saving the object to the database, things get more complex - as we need to generate the number on our own.

For our Customer object, we'll assign the key value when the object is saved to the database the first time. If the object is new, we'll just return an ID value of zero. Since we'll be generating the value in code, there is no reason for the UI to ever set the value in our object, and so we'll make it a read-only property - by just implementing a Property Get without any Property Let procedure:

```
Public Property Get CustomerID() As Long

   CustomerID = mudtProps.CustomerID

End Property
```

## Name Property: Read-write Value

The `Name` property is read-write, since the user will need to enter a name for the customer, and the UI developer will need to read the `Name` property, later, to display it on any forms.

So here's the `Property Let` procedure for the `Name` property. It accepts a parameter that will contain the name - as entered by the user:

```
Public Property Let Name(Value As String)

  If Not mflgEditing Then Err.Raise 383

  If Len(Value) > Len(mudtProps.Name) Then _
    Err.Raise vbObjectError + 1001, "String value too long"
  mobjValid.RuleBroken "Name", (Len(Trim$(Value)) = 0)

  mudtProps.Name = Value
  mflgDirty = True

End Property
```

The first thing we do in this procedure is check the `mflgEditing` flag:

```
  If Not mflgEditing Then Err.Raise 383
```

If we aren't editing the object, because the UI developer hasn't yet called the `BeginEdit` method, then we need to raise an error. This is less for the end user's benefit than to help the UI developer during the debugging process.

If it's OK to edit the object's data, we need to check any business rules for this field:

```
  If Len(Value) > Len(mudtProps.Name) Then _
    Err.Raise vbObjectError + 1001, "String value too long"
  mobjValid.RuleBroken "Name", (Len(Trim$(Value)) = 0)
```

*We'll use the `BrokenRules` object that we set up earlier to record and track the rules that are broken. The `RuleBroken` method of the `BrokenRules` object accepts the rule name as the first parameter and a `Boolean` for the second. If we pass it a `True` value, it records the rule as being broken, while a `False` value indicates that the object's data is valid for this rule.*

One rule that we obviously have is that the field length can't exceed the length of our fixed length `Name` field in the user-defined type. The other rule we have for this field is that it is a required field, so the length can't be zero.

## Enforcing Rules with Different Severity

Here's where we can get into a bit of discussion about business rules and their interaction with the UI code. Looking at the code, we can see that we raise an error if the data length is too long, but not when the length is zero. In a sense, we can look at these rules as having two levels of severity. To decide whether to raise an error when a business rule is broken, we need to look at two criteria:

❑ First, we need to see if it is possible for our code to even handle the value that we were passed. If the parameter we are passed is too long then we can't even store it, since the UDT's Name field can't hold more than fifty characters - and so we have little choice but to raise an error. On the other hand, if the value we are passed is a zero-length string, we can store it without a problem - so we aren't forced to raise an error; instead, we can use the BrokenRules object to record the broken business rule.

❑ The other criterion we need to consider is what works best for the UI developer. We need to put ourselves in the UI developer's shoes and think about what makes their life easier. If a field is required, the UI needs to disable the OK and Apply buttons, but probably doesn't need to do anything else especially. If the data in the field is too long, however, the UI probably needs to beep or take some other action to let the user know they have typed too much.

If we get past the business rule checks without raising an error, we need to assign the parameter value to the Name field of the mudtProps variable:

```
mudtProps.Name = Value
```

This updates the 'live' copy of our data. We also set mflgDirty to True in this routine to ensure that our object is aware that at least one data field has been changed.

```
mflgDirty = True
```

Since we've required that BeginEdit be called before we can edit this field, we know that the original value is stored in the mudtSave variable - and we can get back to it if the CancelEdit method is called later.

We also need to provide a Property Get routine for the Name property:

```
Public Property Get Name() As String

  Name = Trim$(mudtProps.Name)

End Property
```

The routine returns a string value. In this code we're using the Trim$() command to trim off any spaces from the mudtProps.Name value. This is important, as mudtProps.Name is a fixed length string and would normally return a value out to its full length, padding the end with spaces. This is typically not the expected behavior for a string property on an object; normally, we'd expect to just get the data without trailing spaces. Adding in the Trim$() call removes those spaces and gives us the desired result.

## Basic Address Properties

The `Address1` property contains the first address line for the customer. It, too, is a read-write property, since the user needs to enter the address and the UI will need to display it. This one is somewhat simpler, since it has no associated business rules beyond simply enforcing the maximum field length. It is about as basic as we're likely to get:

```
Public Property Let Address1(Value As String)

  If Not mflgEditing Then Err.Raise 383

  If Len(Value) > Len(mudtProps.Address1) Then _
    Err.Raise vbObjectError + 1001, "String value too long"

  mudtProps.Address1 = Value
  mflgDirty = True

End Property
```

Again, we make sure that it's OK to edit the object's data before doing any real work. If editing is allowed, we check the length of the value to make sure it isn't too long - and raise an error if there is a problem. Finally, we store the parameter value into the UDT variable and we're on our way.

The `Property Get` is also as simple as we'll get. It just returns the value from the UDT, after calling the `Trim$()` command to remove those pesky spaces from the fixed length string:

```
Public Property Get Address1() As String

  Address1 = Trim$(mudtProps.Address1)

End Property
```

The `Address2` and `City` properties work the same way:

```
Public Property Let Address2(Value As String)

  If Not mflgEditing Then Err.Raise 383

  If Len(Value) > Len(mudtProps.Address2) Then _
    Err.Raise vbObjectError + 1001, "String value too long"

  mudtProps.Address2 = Value
  mflgDirty = True

End Property

Public Property Get Address2() As String

  Address2 = Trim$(mudtProps.Address2)

End Property

Public Property Let City(Value As String)

  If Not mflgEditing Then Err.Raise 383
```

```
   If Len(Value) > Len(mudtProps.City) Then _
     Err.Raise vbObjectError + 1001, "String value too long"

   mudtProps.City = Value
   mflgDirty = True

End Property
```

```
Public Property Get City() As String

   City = Trim$(mudtProps.City)

End Property
```

### State Property: Making a Value Uppercase

With the `State` property, we have an extra bit of work. The codes for states are always shown in upper case, so we essentially have a business rule that says that this field is always uppercase. It would be an easy thing to have the UI just make them uppercase for us, but it's very important for business objects to protect themselves, and assume that the UI won't necessarily take care of such details:

```
Public Property Let State(Value As String)

   If Not mflgEditing Then Err.Raise 383

   If Len(Value) > Len(mudtProps.State) Then _
     Err.Raise vbObjectError + 1001, "String value too long"

   mudtProps.State = UCase$(Value)
   mflgDirty = True

End Property
```

The difference between this and the previous `Property Let` routines is subtle but nevertheless important. We use the `UCase$()` command to make the value uppercase before storing it in the UDT variable:

```
mudtProps.State = UCase$(Value)
```

*Our other options are to raise an error if the value isn't already uppercase, or to use the `BrokenRules` object to record this as a broken rule. Raising an error seems like a severe response to the user simply missing the Shift key. Even recording it as a broken rule makes the UI developer do more work that might be needed.*

*Instead, by simply ensuring the object has the correct value at any time we've protected our data. We also enable the UI to simply use the `LostFocus` event on the field to refresh the display with whatever is stored in the business object. This means that the user can enter whatever they like, and the display will be updated with the uppercase version as they leave the field.*

This is a pretty nice compromise for this type of business rule, since it doesn't force the UI developer to do any extra work or worry about errors, but the business rule is still enforced and the display does get updated for the user.

The State property also has a Property Get, which is no more complex than any of the others:

```
Public Property Get State() As String

   State = Trim$(mudtProps.State)

End Property
```

### ZipCode Property: Formatting a Value

Like the State property, the ZipCode property has some extra processing to ensure that it appears correctly:

```
Public Property Let ZipCode(Value As String)

   Dim intDash As Integer

   If Not mflgEditing Then Err.Raise 383

   If Len(Value) > Len(mudtProps.ZipCode) Then _
     Err.Raise vbObjectError + 1001, "String value too long"

   intDash = InStr(1, Value, "-")

   If intDash > 0 Then
     mudtProps.ZipCode = _
       Format$(Val(Mid$(Value, 1, intDash - 1)), "00000") & _
       "-" & Format$(Val(Mid$(Value, intDash + 1)), "0000")
   Else
     mudtProps.ZipCode = _
       Format$(Val(Mid$(Value, 1, 5)), "00000") & _
       "-" & Format$(Val(Mid$(Value, 6)), "0000")
   End If

   If Right$(mudtProps.ZipCode, 5) = "-0000" Then _
     mudtProps.ZipCode = Left$(mudtProps.ZipCode, 5)

   mflgDirty = True

End Property

Public Property Get ZipCode() As String

   ZipCode = Trim$(mudtProps.ZipCode)

End Property
```

Zip codes are 5 digits, a dash and then 4 digits. If the last 4 digits are all zeros then the dash and zeros are suppressed.

*This routine is built with US zip codes in mind. We'd need to implement a different set of business logic to handle zip codes from other countries, but the concept of reformatting the user's input remains valid regardless.*

While the display format data is often controlled within the UI code, it's the business object's job to make sure that the data inside each object is consistent and useful. If we choose to enforce the official zip code format in the UI and the database, then the business object must consider that to be a business rule.

With a method like this, where there is a bit of code to handle the proper formatting of the zip code, it's advantageous to put the logic into the business object. If this field were displayed in a variety of locations in the UI, we would have to duplicate the code in this method in all those places. This way, the code is centralized and easily maintained.

### Phone Property

The final property is the Phone property. Like the Name property, this is a required field, and so we check the length of the parameter value and use the BrokenRules object to track whether the field has data:

```
Public Property Let Phone(Value As String)

  If Not mflgEditing Then Err.Raise 383

  If Len(Value) > Len(mudtProps.Phone) Then _
    Err.Raise vbObjectError + 1001, "String value too long"

  mobjValid.RuleBroken "Phone", (Len(Trim$(Value)) = 0)

  mudtProps.Phone = Value
  mflgDirty = True

End Property
```

```
Public Property Get Phone() As String

  Phone = Trim$(mudtProps.Phone)

End Property
```

## Customer Object Methods

In the real world, just about everything centers around a customer. Customers rent the videos in the store, return the videos when they are done and pay for any fees that are incurred. Our object's methods need to mimic these activities.

### CreateInvoice Method: Creating Another Object

The first method we'll add is CreateInvoice. This method will enable the business process where a customer wants to rent one or more videos, since that process is primarily handled through an Invoice. We'll create the Invoice object later in the chapter, but that doesn't mean we can't add some code to the Customer object now:

```
'Public Function CreateInvoice() As Invoice
'
'   Dim objInvoice As Invoice
'
'   Set objInvoice = New Invoice
'   objInvoice.Initialize Me
```

```
'   Set CreateInvoice = objInvoice
'   Set objInvoice = Nothing
'
'End Function
```

*Since we haven't added the* `Invoice` *class module to our project yet, we'll comment out the routine for now. Once we've added the* `Invoice` *class to the project we can come back and uncomment those lines.*

This routine is a function that returns the `Invoice` object as a result. This means that the calling code will use something like this to create an invoice:

```
Set objInvoice = objCustomer.CreateInvoice
```

We've put in some extra code beyond simply creating the object. At the very least, we can assume that the new `Invoice` object will need to know information about the customer that created it, so we're also assuming that the `Invoice` object will have an `Initialize` method that accepts a `Customer` object as a parameter:

```
objInvoice.Initialize Me
```

We'll need to remember to add this method when we build the `Invoice` object later.

*This* `Initialize` *method is very different from the* `Class_Initialize` *routine available to all class modules. Visual Basic doesn't provide us with any mechanism by which we can pass parameters to an object as it is being created. However, with our* `Invoice` *object we need to pass it a reference to the* `Customer` *object, so we'll use our own* `Initialize` *method to do this.*

Beyond this code, all the routine does is create a new, blank `Invoice` object, and assign the function's result to be that object:

```
Set CreateInvoice = objInvoice
```

Then we set our local reference to the new object equal to `Nothing`. This leaves it up to the calling code to maintain a reference to the new object or it will simply disappear.

## Testing the Customer Object

At this point, the customer object should be done and ready to use. Basic testing of business objects can be done very simply using Visual Basic's interactive debugging capabilities. We can just run an ActiveX DLL project in the IDE and use the Immediate window to test the object's methods and properties.

Press *F5* to run the project. We'll be presented with a dialog with various options for running our DLL:

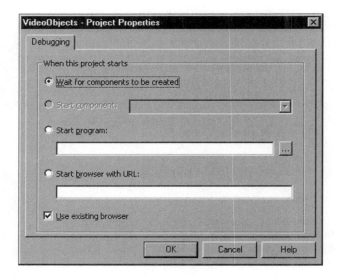

In this case we'll just accept the default. The other options provide for more complex debugging capabilities that we won't be using just at the moment.

Now press *Ctrl-Break* to stop the program. If the Immediate window is not visible, use the View | Immediate Window menu option to display it.

We can now create an instance of the Customer class with the following line:

Set x = New Customer

x is now a late-bound variable pointing to our new Customer object. We can use it to call the object's methods and set and retrieve its properties. For instance, to start an edit of the object type:

x.BeginEdit

Then we can set and check a property value:

x.ZipCode = "123456789"
? x.ZipCode
12345-6789

If we now cancel the edit process, we should be able to prove that the ZipCode property gets reset to a blank:

x.CancelEdit
? x.ZipCode
                    <blank space>

It's very easy to work with our objects within the Immediate window for simple debugging. Better still, this ease of use carries up to the UI developer, since they just need to use similar code within the interface to accomplish the same work.

**210**

# Customers: A Read-Only List Object

The `Customer` object was a good example of a very simple business object that represents a single real-world entity. Many business processes, and thus many applications, also need to deal with lists of things - such as a list of customers. Typically, these lists are generated based on some criteria, either because all the items are directly related to each other (such as all the invoices for a customer) or because they share some common data field (such as a zip code).

With a video store application, the user will need a way to search the database for the right customer. They probably won't want to page through individual customers hoping to find the right one; instead, they'll expect to see some sort of search window displaying a list of customers that match a set of search criteria they've supplied.

## *Read-only lists of objects*

There are three ways to approach a list object like this. This object can be a collection of `Customer` objects, or it can just be a list of the information that needs to be displayed in the search results window. Each has its benefits and drawbacks:

❑ We may choose to simply return a `Recordset` object back to the UI and allow the UI developer to display it as they choose. This is often the best performing solution, and may be appropriate where performance is the primary concern. However, this approach really defeats the purpose of using objects to abstract our data from our business logic. We're returning to the mode where the UI is developed to interact directly with data rather than with an object-oriented abstraction of the data.

❑ If we choose to make our list object a collection of `Customer` objects, we have a very elegant and simple solution. All the data for each customer will be available for our use, including all the business rules and everything that comes with the `Customer` class. The drawback is a serious one, however: performance. Instead of just retrieving the minimum data required to be displayed, and storing it in an efficient format, we need to retrieve all the data about each customer and create an object for each one. This can turn out to be pretty slow if we are dealing with many customers.

❑ We could choose our list object to contain simpler data. In this case it would be a list of only the information that needs to be displayed for the search results. This would, typically, be much faster, since we wouldn't need to retrieve as much data, and we wouldn't need to store it in full-blown `Customer` objects. On the other hand, we'd lose a lot of flexibility, since we'd be tailoring our list object for this one search window. If the UI designer later decides to have a different customer list display, we could end up either extending this object or creating a different customer list object.

This is one of those cases where there is no right answer for all situations. Typically, the third option will be best, since better performance is almost always very important for an application.

> **Objects representing lists of other objects or data can be the biggest performance problems in any client/server application. It's very important to weigh performance concerns heavily when deciding how to design your list objects.**

For this example, then, we'll use the third option, just in case our video application ends up having a large number of customers. This option will give us the better performance, though it will require a bit more work to implement. We'll name our new list object `Customers` (note the plural), since it will contain a list of information about multiple customers.

We need to identify the criteria that the user will be supplying to our new list object. Our object will expose properties to the UI developer so they can supply the criteria we'll use when searching for matching Customer objects. Since we're going with the option of providing only the required result data (rather than the entire customer object), we also need to identify which fields will be available to the UI developer for display.

For this example, the search criteria will include the customer's name and phone number - our two required fields from the Customer class.

Since the Customers class represents a list of customer data, it's very much like a Collection object. However, unlike a standard Visual Basic Collection object, it's a read-only list. Our object won't allow the UI developer to add or remove customers, instead it will just retrieve a list of customers that meet the supplied criteria.

For each item in our read-only collection, we'll be making a number of data elements available: CustomerID, Name and Phone. The easiest way to do this is to add a worker class containing read-only properties for those elements. We'll call this class CustomerDisplay.

## The CustomerDisplay Class

Using the current project, choose Project | Add Class Module to add a class.

As a simple read-only list of properties, the CustomerDisplay class is a far cry from a persistent business class. So, from the Add Class Module dialog, choose the Class Module option and click Open.

Change the Name property for the class to CustomerDisplay. Change the Instancing property to 2-PublicNotCreatable. We want this class to be visible and useful to the UI developer, but we don't want the UI to be able to create instances of this object. Instead, we'll rely on the Customers object to actually create any of these objects that we need and supply those instances to the UI developer upon request.

### Declarations

Like most objects, CustomerDisplay will need a place to store its data. Let's set up a user-defined type to hold the three data elements we'll be using. We'll also declare a variable of this new type, mudtProps, for use throughout the class module:

```
Option Explicit

Private Type DisplayProps
   CustomerID As Long
   Name As String * 50
   Phone As String * 25
End Type

Private mudtProps As DisplayProps
```

### Public Properties

Similar to the Customer object itself, we need to provide Public properties so that the calling code can retrieve the values from our object. These properties just return the values from the UDT variable upon request:

```
Public Property Get CustomerID() As Long

    CustomerID = mudtProps.CustomerID

End Property

Public Property Get Name() As String

    Name = Trim$(mudtProps.Name)

End Property

Public Property Get Phone() As String

    Phone = Trim$(mudtProps.Phone)

End Property
```

## Friend Properties

At this point, we've defined the object's data storage and public interface. We still need to provide some way to get the data into the object without exposing any new properties or methods to the client code. Fortunately, Visual Basic provides the `Friend` keyword, allowing us to create `Property Let` routines that are visible only to other code inside our Visual Basic project:

```
Friend Property Let CustomerID(Value As Long)

    mudtProps.CustomerID = Value

End Property

Friend Property Let Name(Value As String)

    mudtProps.Name = Value

End Property

Friend Property Let Phone(Value As String)

    mudtProps.Phone = Value

End Property
```

These property routines look and work just like a regular property routine, except that their scope is limited to the current Visual Basic project. The UI developer will never know that these properties even exist.

Since these properties will only ever be called from the `Customers` class, we don't need to put in any code to catch data errors or broken business rules. The data that will be placed in these properties will come right from the database, through another business object, into the `CustomerDisplay` object. Any data in the database should have gotten there through the `Customer` object, where any business rules would have been enforced before the data could be saved.

## The Customers Class

To add the Customers class to our project, choose Project | Add Class Module from the menu. Since the Customers class won't be a typical persistent business object, but will instead be a form of collection object, choose the Class Module option from the dialog and click Open.

Change the Name property of the class to Customers and make sure the Instancing property is set to 5-Multiuse. The UI developer should be able to create a Customers object whenever they want to get a list of customers from the database.

Earlier in the book, we went through the steps to create a full-blown collection class. The Customers class will be similar, but it will be read-only, and will have data loaded from the database.

### Creating a Base Collection Object

Let's now go through the code that is basic to virtually any collection class. The heart of any collection class is a local variable that contains the actual underlying Collection object. We'll start by entering the following:

```
Option Explicit

Private mcolDisplay As Collection
```

It's important to remember that we must create an instance of the collection in the Class_Initialize routine so we have it ready for use throughout the rest of the module:

```
Private Sub Class_Initialize()

  Set mcolDisplay = New Collection

End Sub
```

### Count Property

Collections also provide a Count method which we can provide by simply echoing the Count value of the underlying Collection object:

```
Public Function Count() As Long

  Count = mcolDisplay.Count

End Function
```

### Supporting For...Each

We also want to enable the use of the For...Each statement against our collection object. We can do this by implementing a NewEnum method on our object:

```
Public Function NewEnum() As IUnknown

  Set NewEnum = mcolDisplay.[_NewEnum]

End Function
```

*Our* NewEnum *method returns a reference to an* IUnknown *type object. More accurately, it returns a reference to the* IUnknown *interface of an object. In this case we're returning the interface to whatever is behind the* NewEnum *method of a Visual Basic* Collection *object. We don't need to worry about the composition of this return value, it comes from a Visual Basic object and will be used by Visual Basic to support our* For...Each *functionality – we're just acting as a go-between.*

Choose the Tools | Procedure Attributes... menu option. Under the Advanced button, tick the Hide this member option and set the Procedure ID to −4. If we forget this step, the NewEnum method will be visible to client programs and won't be recognized for use with the For...Each statement by Visual Basic.

## Item Method

In a regular collection class, we'd implement Add and Remove methods. Since the Customers object is read-only, we won't be allowing the client code to add or remove items from our list - and so we don't want to implement those methods. However, we do need to provide the Item method - to allow the client code to retrieve the data from our collection.

This is where things get more interesting. The implementation of the Item method can vary quite a lot, depending on how the data was retrieved from the database and loaded into the Customers object. It's this process of loading data into the object and making it available, via the Item method, that dictates the performance of this type of object. We'll look at a couple of different implementations later: one for use with a local database in Chapter 8, and one for use in a multi-tiered application design in Chapter 10.

Since the implementation can vary so greatly, we'll just put comments in the routine for now. Regardless of the implementation, however, the method's name, parameter and return value will remain constant:

```
Public Function Item(ByVal Index As Variant) As CustomerDisplay

  ' find or build a CustomerDisplay object
  ' then return it as a result

End Function
```

The Item method, in a normal collection, is the default method. We'll want to emulate that behavior to keep our object as close as possible to a regular collection. To make this property the default, choose the Tools | Procedure Attributes... menu option and click the Advanced button.

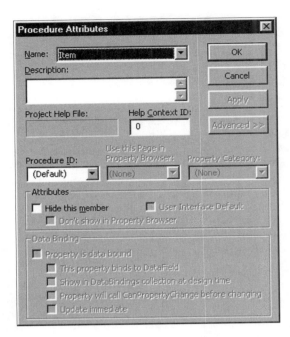

Make sure the Item method is selected in the **Name** option at the top of the dialog. Then just set the **Procedure ID** field to **(Default)** as shown in the screenshot and click **OK**.

> *The* Index *parameter is passed to the* Item *method using the* ByVal *keyword. This is done because the* Index *parameter on a regular Visual Basic* Collection *object is declared using the* ByVal *keyword and we need to make sure to fully emulate the interface provided by the regular* Collection *object.*

## Load Method

One big similarity that the Customers object does have with other business objects is that it needs to provide some way to load the data from the database. To be consistent with other business objects, we'll do this through the use of a Load method that accepts the criteria as parameters:

```
Public Sub Load(Optional Name As String, Optional Phone As String)

  ' load data from database

End Sub
```

Like the Item method, the Load method's implementation will vary greatly depending on the data access technique we choose. A lot of performance can be gained or lost depending on this implementation, so it's important to make the appropriate choice. In Chapters 8 and 10, we'll implement this method in a couple of different ways - so we can see how they differ.

## Using the Customers Object

Finally, let's consider how the UI developer will use the object. Of course, we can't actually get anything from the object yet, since we don't have any data access code to get data from the database. However, the UI code might look like this:

```
Dim objCustomers As Customers
Dim objDisplay As CustomerDisplay

Set objCustomers = New Customers
objCustomers.Load Phone:="555-1234"

For Each objDisplay In objCustomers

   With objDisplay
     Debug.Print .CustomerID
     Debug.Print .Name
     Debug.Print .Phone
   End With

Next

Set objCustomers = Nothing
```

With similar code, the UI developer could load a list control, such as a `ListView`, to display this information.

# Video Rental: Video and Tape Objects

Now that we've got objects to represent our customers, we can move on to the videos that they'll be renting. Video stores typically have a number of tapes for each video title that they rent out. The video itself has a title, rating, production studio and other relevant information. Each individual tape has little more than a unique barcode number, but since it's the tapes that we actually rent out, it's important to keep track of each one individually.

Since we've already gone through the creation of basic business objects with the `Customer` and `Customers` objects, we'll try not to be too repetitive regarding the basic creation process. Instead, we'll focus on those elements and concepts that are new. In particular, the relationship between the object representing a video title and the objects representing the individual tapes.

We'll also introduce a generic class to retrieve lists of text - for use both in validating user input and populating controls like the `ComboBox`. We'll use this class to build the video object.

## TextList: a Powerful Utility Object

We'll get to the actual video title object shortly, but first let's go through the more generic class that can be used to represent a list of text items. One of the most common types of entry field is one where the user selects an option from a list. In the case of our video object, we'll have a list of movie ratings and a list of video categories.

Strictly speaking, a list of text fields is probably not analogous to any real-world business entity. At the same time, it's one of the most common concepts that we, as programmers, have to deal with - both from a UI and an object perspective. Most forms have `ComboBox` controls for users to select values, and any underlying business object needs to provide the content for those controls and also screen the supplied values to make sure they're valid. After all, we can't assume that the client code in the UI is going to send us a valid option, since that would break our tenet that the code calling our object will eventually do something that will cause problems in our object.

Like the Customers object, the TextList object will be read-only. Any calling code will just get the object loaded from the database and then use the object's properties to get at the data. As a collection-style object, our TextList will have both text data and a key value for each entry in the list.

## Setting up the TextList Class

In our VideoObject project, choose the Project | Add Class Module option. As this isn't our basic business object, we'll just use the Class Module option and click Open.

Set the Name property to TextList and the Instancing to 2-PublicNotCreatable. Objects of this class will be created within the context of actual business objects, and so we won't allow the UI developer to create them directly.

Again, our collection object will be based on a normal Visual Basic Collection object:

```
Option Explicit

Private mcolList As Collection
```

In a normal collection, we can do a look-up based on the key value to quickly retrieve an item's value. That is all very useful, but this class will also be used to translate item values back to the original key. The reason for this is because relational databases typically store key values rather than any item's text value. Since the user will be choosing a text value on the screen, at some point we'll need to translate that back to a key value.

To make this easy, we're going to include a second Collection object in the class to store the key and item values in reverse - making it possible to use the item's value to quickly do a look-up and retrieve the key value.

```
Option Explicit

Private mcolList As Collection
Private mcolKeys As Collection
```

In the Class_Initialize we need to create instances of these collections:

```
Private Sub Class_Initialize()

  Set mcolList = New Collection
  Set mcolKeys = New Collection

End Sub
```

As with any read-only collection object, we won't have Add or Remove methods, but we will provide an Item method to retrieve the item values based on the keys. In this case, all we need to do is echo the value out of the mcolList collection upon request. The return type is String since this object is set up to manage lists of text data:

```
Public Function Item(ByVal Index As Variant) As String

   Item = mcolList.Item(Index)

End Function
```

Use the Tools | Procedure Attributes... menu option to make the Item method the default for this object.

To support the For...Each concept, we also need to provide the NewEnum method with its Procedure ID set to −4 and the Hide this member option checked:

```
Public Function NewEnum() As IUnknown

   Set NewEnum = mcolList.[_NewEnum]

End Function
```

## Using an Item Value to get a Key

Note that both the Item and NewEnum methods are based on the mcolList collection. This works great when we use the TextList object as a regular collection, but it doesn't give us the ability to do the reverse; that is to easily use a text value to find a key.

So, in addition to the Item method, we'll add a corresponding Key method. This method works the same as Item, but uses the mcolKeys collection instead of mcolList. All we need to do is make sure to load mcolKeys with the item and key values reversed. We'll cover this in more detail shortly:

```
Public Function Key(ByVal Text As String) As String

   Key = mcolKeys.Item(Text)

End Function
```

Now the user can not only get at an item with this code:

```
strItem = objTextList.Item(strKey)
```

but they can also get at a key value with this code:

```
strKey = objTextList.Key(strItem)
```

The ability to retrieve a key value when provided with a text value is a nice feature. There are many cases where a UI developer has to implement extra code to track not only the items they've listed in a ListBox or ComboBox, but also the key values corresponding to those items. If we can easily provide support to translate a text value back to its key value, then the UI developer may not have to take these extra steps.

## The Load Method

All that remains is to provide a way to get the data from the database into the object. Like our other objects, we'll add a `Load` method to take care of these details. To keep it simple, this `Load` method will just accept a `String` parameter. We can use this parameter to indicate which data should be loaded from the database:

```
Friend Sub Load(ListName As String)

  ' load data from database
  '
  'mcolList.Add strItem, strKey
  'mcolKeys.Add strKey, strItem

End Sub
```

Like the other `Load` methods we've looked at, we've commented out the code because it's very much dependent on the persistence model we choose. At the same time, there are a few things that we can take note of here.

First off, this method is declared as `Friend` rather than `Public`. Since we set the Instancing property to PublicNotCreatable, the UI code can't create a `TextList` object directly. By the time they get one of these objects, it should already be populated with data. Our business objects will create `TextList` objects and call their `Load` methods all within the same DLL - so `Friend` is the way to go.

We've also put in comments showing how the two collections will be loaded with data:

```
'mcolList.Add strItem, strKey
'mcolKeys.Add strKey, strItem
```

Remember, here, that `mcolList` is loaded with the item and key values in the proper order, while `mcolKeys` is loaded with the values in reverse order. This code enables our `Key` method to function properly. Although this technique consumes more memory than a normal collection, because it's storing everything twice, we do get the benefit of being able to quickly retrieve a key value when supplied with an item, as well as just being able to retrieve an item when supplied with a key.

# Videos: A Read-only List Object

We need to take one more quick detour before getting into the meat of the `Video` and `Tape` objects. As with customers, the system will need to provide a lookup function for video tapes. To take care of this, we'll implement a `Videos` object along the same lines as the `Customers` object we put together earlier.

## Creating the Videos Object

We won't spend much time discussing this object, since it's virtually identical to the `Customers` object. The bulk of the code for objects of this type comes when we implement the database access - so we'll look more closely at it in subsequent chapters.

Add a class module to the `VideoObjects` project, call it `Videos`, and make sure its Instancing property is set to 5-Multiuse so the UI code can create and use the object. Then enter the following code:

```
Option Explicit

Private mcolDisplay As Collection

Private Sub Class_Initialize()

    Set mcolDisplay = New Collection

End Sub

Public Sub Load(Optional Title As String, Optional Studio As String)

    ' load data from database

End Sub

Public Function Item(ByVal Index As Variant) As VideoDisplay

    ' find or build a VideoDisplay object
    ' then return it as a result

End Function

Public Function Count() As Long

    Count = mcolDisplay.Count

End Function

' NewEnum must return the IUnknown interface of a
' collection's enumerator.
Public Function NewEnum() As IUnknown

    Set NewEnum = mcolDisplay.[_NewEnum]

End Function
```

As with the Customers object, our new Videos object is based on a Visual Basic Collection object. However, since it's a read-only list we haven't included Add or Remove methods in our object. The client code can use the Item method to retrieve individual elements from our list. In this case, each element will be a new type of object named VideoDisplay.

> *Don't forget to choose the Tools | Procedure Attributes... menu option to make the* Item *method the default; also, for the* NewEnum *method, change the Hide this member option and set the Procedure ID to -4.*

## Creating the VideoDisplay Object

In the same way the Customers object used a CustomerDisplay object to return individual items, the Videos object will use a VideoDisplay object. As with CustomerDisplay, this object is a simple read-only object that contains only the fields we'll be retrieving for the UI to display. Add another Class Module, set its Instancing property to 2-PublicNotCreatable, and enter this code for the VideoDisplay object:

```
Option Explicit

Private Type DisplayProps
  VideoID As Long
  Title As String * 30
  ReleaseDate As Variant
End Type

Private mudtProps As DisplayProps

Public Property Get VideoID() As Long

  VideoID = mudtProps.VideoID

End Property

Public Property Get Title() As String

  Title = Trim$(mudtProps.Title)

End Property

Public Property Get ReleaseDate() As Variant

  ReleaseDate = Trim$(mudtProps.ReleaseDate)

End Property

Friend Property Let VideoID(Value As Long)

  mudtProps.VideoID = Value

End Property

Friend Property Let Title(Value As String)

  mudtProps.Title = Value

End Property

Friend Property Let ReleaseDate(Value As Variant)

  mudtProps.ReleaseDate = Value

End Property
```

# Video: A Parent Object

We need to have an object to represent each video title. This object will be a bit different from those we've looked at so far. This is the parent object to one or more objects representing the actual tapes of that title. It will also contain a couple of the TextList objects that we just defined.

Of course, it will also have regular properties for things like the title of the video and the studio where it was produced.

## Setting up the Video Class

In the `VideoObjects` project, add a new class module using the `Business` template we built earlier in this chapter. Change the **Name** property to `Video` and make sure the **Instancing** is set to 5-Multiuse.

### Declarations

As usual, we'll set up a UDT to store the object's data, and we'll declare `mudtProps` and `mudtSave` as variables of that type. In this case, we'll also declare `mobjCategories` and `mobjRatings` as type `TextList` to store the lists of valid category and rating codes.

Each `Video` object will also need to have a list of the physical tapes for the title, so we'll declare a variable of type `Tapes` as well. We'll cover the `Tapes` object a bit later, but it's basically a collection object containing all the related `Tape` objects.

Here's what the code for our `Video` object now looks like (remember there's already a lot of code from our `Business` object template):

```
Option Explicit

Event Valid(IsValid As Boolean)

Private Type VideoProps
    VideoID As Long
    Title As String * 30
    ReleaseDate As Variant
    Studio As String * 30
    Category As String * 20
    Rating As String * 5
End Type

Private mudtProps As VideoProps
Private mudtSave As VideoProps

Private mobjCategories As TextList
Private mobjRatings As TextList
Private mobjTapes As Tapes

Private mflgNew As Boolean
Private mflgDeleted As Boolean
Private mflgDirty As Boolean
Private mflgEditing As Boolean
Private WithEvents mobjValid As BrokenRules
```

### BeginEdit, CancelEdit and ApplyEdit Methods

As usual, we need to update the `BeginEdit`, `CancelEdit` and `ApplyEdit` methods to manage the object's state:

```
Public Sub BeginEdit()

    If mflgEditing Then Err.Raise 445

    ' save object state
    LSet mudtSave = mudtProps
```

```
      mobjTapes.BeginEdit
      mflgEditing = True

End Sub

Public Sub CancelEdit()

  If Not mflgEditing Then Err.Raise 445

  mflgEditing = False
  mflgDeleted = False
  mflgDirty = False
  ' restore object state
  LSet mudtProps = mudtSave
  mobjTapes.CancelEdit

End Sub

Public Sub ApplyEdit()

  If Not mflgEditing Then Err.Raise 445

  If mflgDeleted And Not mflgNew Then
    ' code to delete the object's data goes here
    mflgNew = True
    mflgDeleted = False

  ElseIf mflgDirty Or mflgNew Then
    If Not IsValid Then Err.Raise 445
    ' save object to database if appropriate
    ' save object state
    LSet mudtSave = mudtProps
    mflgNew = False

  End If

  mobjTapes.ApplyEdit mudtProps.VideoID
  mflgDirty = False
  mflgEditing = False

End Sub
```

We don't need to worry about keeping copies of the mobjCategories or mobjRatings objects, as they are essentially static lists of text representing the valid options for those fields.

> *The list of tapes contained in a* Tapes *collection object could be a concern. If we have added a tape to that collection, and then we cancel editing on the parent object,* Video, *we need to remove that new tape from the list. Rather than trying to track all that detail here in the* Video *class, we'll let the* Tapes *class manage it. All we need to do in the* Video *code is call the* Tapes *object's* BeginEdit, CancelEdit *and* ApplyEdit *methods. Later in the chapter, we'll need to make sure that we implement those methods properly in the* Tapes *class.*

### Load Method

Our Load method will be implemented based on whatever persistence approach we choose later. However, we do need to add a bit of code now to support the loading of the Tapes object:

```
Public Sub Load(VideoID As Long)

    If mflgEditing Then Err.Raise 445
    If Not mflgNew Then Err.Raise 445

    ' code to load the object goes here
    mobjTapes.Load mudtProps.VideoID

    mflgNew = False

End Sub
```

At some point, the list of tapes for this video needs to be loaded from the database. We can let the Tapes object's Load method do the actual work of loading the data, but that method needs to be called somewhere.

We have two basic options for loading the list of tapes. Firstly, we can load them when the Video object itself is loaded, as shown here. This slows down the overall data load process, but gets all the data loaded for use right up front. If we know that the client code is likely to use the collection, it probably makes sense to load it right up front.

Alternatively, we can wait until the first time the UI code tries to access the list of tapes and load the list at that point. This speeds up the loading of the Video object itself, but incurs a delay the first time the client code tries to get at a Tape object. If the collection data may or may not be used by the client code then we may want to wait to load it. That way, the data won't ever get loaded if the client code doesn't use it - and so we'll get an overall performance gain.

### Delete Method

Continuing through the template code, the next method to look at is the Delete method. Like the Load method, we need to make sure all the related Tape objects get deleted if the Video object is deleted:

```
Public Sub Delete()

    If Not mflgEditing Then Err.Raise 445

    mflgDeleted = True
    mflgDirty = True
    mobjTapes.Delete

End Sub
```

Like the previous methods we've looked at, the Delete method just calls the Delete method on the Tapes collection object, and we'll implement it in the Tapes class to manage deleting all the associated Tape objects.

### Class_Initialize Routine

We also need to modify our Class_Initialize routine:

```
Private Sub Class_Initialize()

    mflgNew = True
    Set mobjValid = New BrokenRules
```

```
    Set mobjCategories = New TextList
    mobjCategories.Load "Categories"

    Set mobjRatings = New TextList
    mobjRatings.Load "Ratings"

    Set mobjTapes = New Tapes

    ' if we know any rules are broken on startup
    ' then add code here to initialize the list
    ' of broken rules
    '
    mobjValid.RuleBroken "Title", True

End Sub
```

The first change in this routine is to create `TextList` objects for the `mobjCategories` and `mobjRatings` variables. Once each of these are created, we call the `TextList` object's `Load` method to load the category and rating lists respectively.

We'll also put some commented lines into this code, which will remind us, when we write our persistence code, to add code to put the first items from the database tables into our respective `mudtProps` variables, as default values:

```
    Set mobjCategories = New TextList
    mobjCategories.Load "Categories"
  ' code to assign mudtProps.Category with database information

    Set mobjRatings = New TextList
    mobjRatings.Load "Ratings"
  ' code to assign mudtProps.Rating with database information
```

Now we need to create an instance of the `Tapes` object for the `mobjTapes` variable. We don't need to load this object right now, as we'll load it in the `Video` object's `Load` method, as we've already seen:

```
    Set mobjTapes = New Tapes
```

The last change is one we've seen before. In the `Video` object, the `Title` property is a required field - and so we assume that we start out with a broken rule for the `Title` since we know that the field is blank in a new object like this:

```
    mobjValid.RuleBroken "Title", True
```

## Video Properties

Most of the properties implemented in the `Video` object use the concepts we looked at with the `Customer` object. The `VideoID` will be a read-only field with a system-generated value, just like `CustomerID`. The `Title` and `Studio` properties are basic text properties, with the `Title` being a required field:

```
Public Property Get VideoID() As Long

   VideoID = mudtProps.VideoID

End Property


Public Property Let Title(Value As String)

   If Not mflgEditing Then Err.Raise 383

   If Len(Value) > Len(mudtProps.Title) Then _
      Err.Raise vbObjectError + 1001, "String value too long"
   mobjValid.RuleBroken "Title", (Len(Trim$(Value)) = 0)

   mudtProps.Title = Value
   mflgDirty = True

End Property


Public Property Get Title() As String

   Title = Trim$(mudtProps.Title)

End Property


Public Property Let Studio(Value As String)

   If Not mflgEditing Then Err.Raise 383

   If Len(Value) > Len(mudtProps.Studio) Then _
      Err.Raise vbObjectError + 1001, "String value too long"

   mudtProps.Studio = Value
   mflgDirty = True

End Property


Public Property Get Studio() As String

   Studio = Trim$(mudtProps.Studio)

End Property
```

### ReleaseDate Property: Date Value

The ReleaseDate field bears some examination, since it's the first date field we've encountered so far in this chapter. Since Visual Basic provides a Date data type, it would seem that implementing a date property would be trivial. After all, if the Property Let just accepts a Date parameter and the Get returns a Date data type, we don't even have to screen the values - since Visual Basic does it for us (*Please don't enter this code*):

```
Public Property Let ReleaseDate(Value As Date)

   If Not mflgEditing Then Err.Raise 383

   mudtProps.ReleaseDate = Value
   mflgDirty = True

End Property
```

```
Public Property Get ReleaseDate() As Date

  ReleaseDate = mudtProps.ReleaseDate

End Property
```

If there were any business rules, such as requiring the date to be in the past or future, then we'd need to add an extra line or two of code, but, otherwise, one might be tempted to say that there's nothing to it.

Unfortunately, this implementation won't always work. The problem is that Date type variables *always* contain some value. As soon as a Date variable is created it contains 12/30/1899 12:00:00 AM.

In many cases, it's important to know whether the date property is blank or whether the user has given it a value. The Date datatype doesn't provide us with any way to detect this, and so we need an alternative solution.

Instead of using the Date data type, we'll use a Variant. Then we'll have to add extra code to the Property Let to ensure that we really did get passed a valid date. The ReleaseDate routine we'll use looks like this:

```
Public Property Let ReleaseDate(Value As Variant)

  If Not mflgEditing Then Err.Raise 383

  If Len(Trim(Value)) = 0 Then
    mudtProps.ReleaseDate = ""
    mobjValid.RuleBroken "ReleaseDate", False

  ElseIf IsDate(Value) Then
    mudtProps.ReleaseDate = CVDate(Value)
    mobjValid.RuleBroken "ReleaseDate", False

  Else
    mobjValid.RuleBroken "ReleaseDate", True

  End If

  mflgDirty = True

End Property
```

In this version of the routine, we accept a Variant parameter instead of a Date data type. This means the calling code can send us virtually any value - so we need to take some extra steps.

Let's look at this code. Since we want to allow entry of a blank, or empty string value, we check for that. We use the Trim() command to remove any leading or trailing spaces, and then we check the resulting length. If the length turns up zero then we can just assign an empty string to the ReleaseDate variable, and we're all done. We also make sure that the BrokenRule object knows that we have a valid value:

```
If Len(Trim(Value)) = 0 Then
  mudtProps.ReleaseDate = ""
  mobjValid.RuleBroken "ReleaseDate", False
```

On the other hand, if the parameter value has a length of greater than zero then we need to find out if it can be translated to a date value. This is easily accomplished by using the `IsDate()` function. `IsDate()` has the benefit of recognizing any date format that Visual Basic can possibly understand, so it provides a great amount of flexibility - with virtually no code:

```
ElseIf IsDate(Value) Then
  mudtProps.ReleaseDate = CVDate(Value)
  mobjValid.RuleBroken "ReleaseDate", False
```

If the parameter value is a valid date then we just need to assign the value to the `ReleaseDate` variable. To make sure that it's stored as a date, we run it through the `CVDate()` function to translate the parameter value to a valid date. `CVDate` returns an error if it can't do the translation, but we don't need to worry about that since we've already used `IsDate()` to make sure it is valid. Once again, we also need to make sure that the `BrokenRule` object knows that we have a valid value.

If both of the previous checks fail then the parameter is neither an empty string nor a valid date. In this case, we'll use the `BrokenRule` object to indicate that a business rule is broken. The business rule that applies here is that we need a valid date and we don't have one:

```
mobjValid.RuleBroken "ReleaseDate", True
```

Moving on, the `Property Get` for `ReleaseDate` changes very little from our first attempt (which used the `Date` type, as above). We just need to return a `Variant` instead of a `Date` type value, but beyond that there is no change.

Since the `mudtProps.ReleaseDate` variable will always contain either an empty string or a valid date value, we can just return whatever it contains without having to perform any conversions to the value:

```
Public Property Get ReleaseDate() As Variant

  ReleaseDate = mudtProps.ReleaseDate

End Property
```

## TextList-based Properties

Now let's look at some more interesting code. We've already built a general utility class named `TextList` and, within our `Video` object, we have two variables, `mobjCategories` and `mobjRatings`, based on that class. We now need to implement some properties to make these variables useful.

There are two main reasons for implementing text list properties with `TextList` objects contained inside a business object:

❑   The business object needs to validate any data supplied through a `Property Let`. To validate data against a list of values, the business object needs to have the list available.

❑ The UI will probably want to display the list to the user in a ListBox or ComboBox control. Since the business object already needs to load the list for validation purposes, we don't want to take the performance hit of having the UI load it a second time.

Another possibility is to load the list in the UI and have the UI supply the data to the business object for validation. This keeps performance acceptable, since we don't need to load the list twice; and it does make the list available to the object. This is not a good solution for a couple reasons:

❑ The business object becomes dependent on the UI developer. If the UI developer introduces a bug such that the list doesn't load properly, it may be the business object that appears to have a bug rather than the UI.

❑ The UI developer is forced to do some extra work and for no benefit. Every part of the UI that uses our business object would need to load the text list data, so there'd be a lot of redundant code and effort.

## Category Property

So let's look at the `Category` property and see how this works. We've already loaded the `mobjCategories` TextList object, back in the `Class_Initialize` routine, so we're all ready to go at this point:

```
Public Property Let Category(Value As String)

  If Not mflgEditing Then Err.Raise 383

  mudtProps.Category = mobjCategories.Key(Value)
  mflgDirty = True

End Property
```

When the user chooses an option from the ComboBox control we'll get the text chosen by the user passed as a parameter to our `Property Let` routine. What we need to store in our UDT variable, `mudtProps.Category`, is the key value, not the text value.

To convert from a text value back to a key value we can use the `TextList` object's `Key` method. We implemented this method specifically to accept a text value and to return the corresponding key. If the supplied value isn't found, it will result in an error in the `TextList` object - and we'll just let that error raise right up to the calling code.

*The reason we want to store the key value in our internal variable is because that's typically the value we'd find in a database. Most tables containing a list of text values also contain an associated list of key values to be used as foreign keys in other tables.*

*This design makes it easy to change the text values in the table without worrying about losing connections with data in other tables. By structuring our business objects to store these same key values in our object, we make it very easy to load and save the objects from a database. The value we are storing in our object's internal variable is the same as that stored in the database table.*

*In some more complex scenarios, it's even possible that the content of the list could be different depending on the object's current state. For instance, consider a list of possible surnames on a* Person *object. If the* Person *object's* Gender *property is* Male *then the list might contain* Mr, Dr, Sir *and so forth; meanwhile, a* Female Gender *property might reconfigure the list to contain* Mrs, Ms, Dr *and so on. In this case, the content of the list is dictated by business rules - and that code needs to reside inside the business object.*

The `Property Get` method employs a similar technique:

```
Public Property Get Category() As String

  Category = Trim$(mobjCategories.Item(Trim$(mudtProps.Category)))

End Property
```

Since we stored the key value in our internal variable, we just need to call the `TextList` object's `Item` method to translate the key back into a text value to return to the UI.

Note that we need to use `Trim$()` to remove the trailing spaces from the key value before sending it to the `Item` method. Since the value was stored in a fixed length string, it has trailing spaces - and those would prevent it from matching the key values in the collection.

*Interestingly enough, the UI developer in a traditional application would need to know all about the relationship between key values and item values, since they'd be directly reading the tables. The business objects hide the key values entirely, making the UI developer's job much easier - since they just need to load their list control with item values and return the item value chosen by the user, without worrying about translating it to a key value.*

The `Property Let` and `Property Get` routines allow the UI developer to give us a value and retrieve the current value. We still need to provide some way for the UI developer to get at the list of valid options. After all, a typical UI will provide the user with this list to make it easy to choose an option that won't generate an error. To do this, we'll implement a `Categories` property that exposes the `mobjCategories` variable:

```
Public Property Get Categories() As TextList

  Set Categories = mobjCategories

End Property
```

As we discussed during the implementation of the `TextList` class, the object that the UI developer will get is totally read-only. The UI developer won't even have access to the object's `Load` method, since it's declared as a `Friend` method and is only available within the same Visual Basic project.

The UI developer will be able to retrieve the object's item values, however, by using the property just like a regular Visual Basic `Collection` object. The code might look something like this:

```
For Each vntItem in objVideo.Categories
   cboComboBox.AddItem vntItem
Next
```

### Rating Property

Moving on, we can see that the `Rating Property Let` and `Property Get` are virtually identical to the `Category` property routines:

```
Public Property Let Rating(Value As String)

  If Not mflgEditing Then Err.Raise 383
```

```
    mudtProps.Rating = mobjRatings.Key(Value)
    mflgDirty = True

End Property

Public Property Get Rating() As String

    Rating = Trim$(mobjRatings.Item(Trim$(mudtProps.Rating)))

End Property
```

Likewise, the `Ratings` property is a near carbon copy of the `Categories` routine:

```
Public Property Get Ratings() As TextList

    Set Ratings = mobjRatings

End Property
```

## Tapes Property

The final property that we need to worry about is the `Tapes` property. This one is separated from the others not because it's complex, but because it's very different in concept. This property implements a Parent-Child relationship, making the `Video` object a parent to any number of `Tape` objects:

```
Public Property Get Tapes() As Tapes

    Set Tapes = mobjTapes

End Property
```

This is a very simple bit of code for such a complex concept. The complexity will come in the `Tapes` object itself, which we'll look at shortly. It's important that this is simple, to help keep the focus of the `Video` object on representing a video. If we'd included a lot of extra code to manage `Tape` objects - adding and removing them from a collection - we would have introduced a lot of code that really had nothing to do with modeling a video - but had everything to do with modeling the relationship.

By pulling the complexity of adding and removing objects from a list out of `Video` and putting it into a specialized `Tapes` object, we have abstracted the relationship management into its own little container.

Don't forget to save the project at this point.

# Summary

In this chapter we've started to code our video rental store example, putting some of the concepts and ideas we've discussed in previous chapters into action. Specifically we've created:

- ❑  A common interface for our code
- ❑  A Business template class
- ❑  The start of the video rental system

The VideoStore example now has the following defined classes:

- ❑  Customer
- ❑  Customers
- ❑  CustomerDisplay
- ❑  TextList
- ❑  Videos
- ❑  VideoDisplay
- ❑  Video
- ❑  BrokenRules

This is a good place to take a break. In the next chapter, we'll continue our development of the VideoStore set of business objects, but there we need to consider how to handle child objects properly.

# Implementing Business Objects Part 2 - Parent and Child Objects

## Overview

In Chapter 5, we started to build up the business objects we needed for our `VideoStore` example. We're about halfway through the initial implementation now - there will be persistence code to add in Chapters 8 and 10. This chapter will be concerned mainly with the more complicated object relationships:

- ❑ Parent-child
- ❑ Hybrid - both child and standalone
- ❑ Polymorphism

We'll implement the following classes:

- ❑ `Tape`
- ❑ `Tapes`
- ❑ `Invoice`
- ❑ `InvoiceItem`
- ❑ `InvoiceFee`
- ❑ `InvoiceTape`
- ❑ `InvoiceItems`

As we build these classes we'll explore some important concepts, including implementation of multiple interfaces using the `Implements` keyword. We'll also explore some basic issues surrounding transaction processing in our object model and how to manage object state with cascading parent-child relationships.

# Tape: A Child Object

Before we get into the `Tapes` object, we should really put together the `Tape` object. After all, it's a lot easier to build a collection object when we have something to put into it!

The `Tape` object has some extra complexity when compared to the `Video` or `Customer` objects. Neither `Video` nor `Customer` are child objects, but `Tape` is a child object of `Video`, and so we need to do a fair amount of extra work for `Tape` to work smoothly. We'll get into the details after we get the basic object laid out.

The `Tape` object doesn't have a lot of properties: just a `TapeID`; a flag indicating if it's currently rented out; and the date the tape was acquired. When we rent out a tape to a customer we do it through an invoice. To make it easy to find the invoice on which a tape is rented, we'll also throw in a property to return a reference to the `Invoice` object.

> *Something to keep in mind is that the* `Tape` *object could also be a parent of other objects. For instance, in Chapter 3 we discussed objects to record problems with tapes. All the* `Problem` *objects for a tape would be child objects of that particular* `Tape` *object. To support this, we'd have a* `Problems` *property and a private* `Problems` *object to manage the list of child objects.*

The `Tape` object will also have a couple of methods, `CheckOut` and `CheckIn`, to facilitate the rental process. When a tape gets added to an invoice, we'll use the `CheckOut` method to mark it as rented; and then the `CheckIn` method will be used when the tape is returned - so we know it's available for renting again.

## Setting up the Tape Class

In the `VideoObjects` project, choose the <u>P</u>roject | Add <u>C</u>lass Module menu option and use the `Business` class template to add a new class. Change its **Name** property to `Tape`.

We'll be instantiating `Tape` objects from the `Tapes` collection and from the `Invoice` object. Additionally, we'll allow the UI to instantiate a `Tape` object directly - to facilitate the process of returning the tape after it has been rented.

> *When the customer returns the tape, the user simply enters the* `TapeID` *(typically via a barcode reader) and the tape is recorded as being checked back in.*

To support this, make sure the **Instancing** property is set to **5-Multiuse**.

### Updating the Template Code

We'll go through the usual steps of altering the template code to customize it for this object. Rather than walking through the code in detail, I'll just list it here with the alterations highlighted. Then we'll go through the changes we need to make to support the parent-child relationship with the `Video` object.

```vb
Option Explicit

Event Valid(IsValid As Boolean)

Private Type TapeProps
  TapeID As Long
  VideoID As Long
  Title As String * 30
  CheckedOut As Boolean
  DateAcquired As Variant
  InvoiceID As Long
End Type

Private mudtProps As TapeProps
Private mudtSave As TapeProps

Private mflgDirty As Boolean
Private mflgNew As Boolean
Private mflgDeleted As Boolean
Private mflgEditing As Boolean
Private WithEvents mobjValid As BrokenRules

Public Sub BeginEdit()

  If mflgEditing Then Err.Raise 445

  ' save object state
  LSet mudtSave = mudtProps
  mflgEditing = True

End Sub

Public Sub CancelEdit()

  If Not mflgEditing Then Err.Raise 445

  mflgEditing = False
  mflgDelected = False
  mflgDirty = False
  ' restore object state
  LSet mudtProps = mudtSave

End Sub

Public Sub ApplyEdit()

  If Not mflgEditing Then Err.Raise 445

  If mflgDeleted And Not mflgNew Then
    ' code to delete the object's data goes here
    mflgNew = True
    mflgDeleted = False

  ElseIf mflgDirty Or mflgNew Then
    If Not IsValid Then Err.Raise 445
    ' save object to database if appropriate
    ' save object state
    LSet mudtSave = mudtProps
    mflgNew = False
```

```vb
      End If

      mflgDirty = False
      mflgEditing = False

  End Sub

  Private Sub Class_Initialize()

      mflgNew = True
      Set mobjValid = New BrokenRules

      ' if we know any rules are broken on startup
      ' then add code here to initialize the list
      ' of broken rules
      '
      ' mobjValid.RuleBroken "RuleName", True
      mobjValid.RuleBroken "DateAcquired", True

  End Sub

  Public Property Get IsValid() As Boolean

      IsValid = (mobjValid.Count = 0)

  End Property

  Private Sub mobjValid_BrokenRule()

      RaiseEvent Valid(False)

  End Sub

  Private Sub mobjValid_NoBrokenRules()

      RaiseEvent Valid(True)

  End Sub

  Public Sub Load(TapeID As Long)

      If mflgEditing Then Err.Raise 445
      If Not mflgNew Then Err.Raise 445

  ' code to load the object goes here

      mflgNew = False

  End Sub

  Public Sub Delete()

      If Not mflgEditing Then Err.Raise 445

      mflgDeleted = True
      mflgDirty = True

  End Sub

  Public Property Get IsDeleted() As Boolean
```

```
        IsDeleted = mflgDeleted

    End Property

    Public Property Get IsNew() As Boolean

        IsNew = mflgNew

    End Property

    Public Property Get IsDirty() As Boolean

        IsDirty = mflgDirty Or mflgNew

    End Property
```

We just set up our UDT and the normal `mudtProps` and `mudtSave` variables. We'll make the `DateAcquired` property a required field - and so the `Class_Initialize` has code to record the field as being invalid using the `BrokenRules` object.

Two of the data elements in the UDT are of particular note. The `VideoID` value is our object's link to its parent. Since `Tape` objects are children of `Video` objects, each child needs to have some mechanism to refer back to its parent.

Even more interesting is the `Title` field. The `Video` object represents a specific video title, with all the related `Tape` objects obviously having the same title as the parent `Video` object. There's a good reason why we've added a `Title` field to our UDT: performance.

There are many cases where an object will need to provide fields that are normally part of another object; in this case, we'll be wanting to display a `Tape` object, including the tape's title. One way to approach this is to instantiate the `Video` object and get the `Title` from that object; and it's a very elegant object-oriented solution. Unfortunately, it also means that to get one simple bit of information we would have to instantiate an entire object, thus incurring the related database and network traffic.

Instead, it's often easier to include data like this as read-only properties of several objects. This way, the data can be loaded and sent over the network all at once, along with the other data belonging to the object. It's much more efficient to do a table join and retrieve the video's title along with the `Tape` object's data than it would be to get the `Tape` object and then turn around and get the entire `Video` object in a separate step.

Since the UI will only deal with our business objects in either case, we can change the underlying implementation regarding how the data is collected at any time. This illustrates the power and flexibility available through the CSLA approach.

## Child Object Support

The `Tape` object is a bit different from `Video` or `Customer`, since it's a child of the `Video` object. This makes things more complex, since there are some extra behaviors we need to support. Let's look at where this complexity comes from.

### A Parent-Child User Interface

Imagine a screen that displays a `Video` object's properties in the top half of the form, and which has a list of the associated `Tape` objects at the bottom. This screen would have OK, Apply and Cancel buttons as we'd expect:

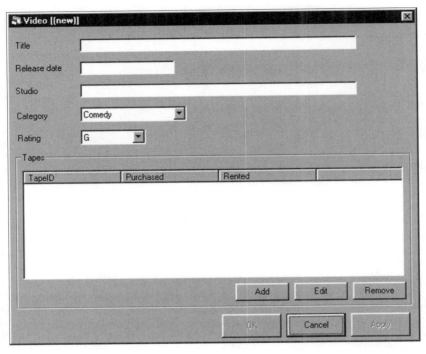

These buttons call the `CancelEdit` and `ApplyEdit` methods of the `Video` object, since that's the object this screen is editing. Calling `ApplyEdit` should cause the `Video` object's data to be saved to the database like normal.

The screen would also have Add, Edit and Remove buttons for the `Tape` objects in the list. If the user clicks Add or Edit then a second screen pops up showing the `Tape` object's data:

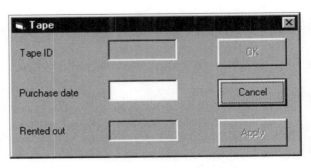

This screen would also have OK, Apply and Cancel buttons, each of which would call `CancelEdit` and `ApplyEdit` as we've done so far. But this is where the difference comes in, because the `ApplyEdit` call on the `Tape` object should *not* save the data to the database.

When the user clicks OK or Apply on the tape-editing screen, we still don't know that the user won't click Cancel on the Video screen and cancel the entire set of changes. This means that the Tape object's ApplyEdit method can't work like a normal ApplyEdit. Instead, we need to figure out some way for the Video object to tell all its children to save their data to the database when its own ApplyEdit is called.

The same principal applies to the CancelEdit method. When the user clicks Cancel on the Video screen, all the child Tape objects need to reset their internal state to the values they held back when the Video object's BeginEdit was called - even if the user brought up a Tape screen, edited a Tape object and clicked the OK button on that screen.

To make things even more complex, the Tape object can be brought up directly by the user - since its Instancing is 5-Multiuse. So if the user directly creates the object, it's not part of a Tapes collection - and thus is not a child object. We need to implement the Tape object such that it knows whether or not it is a child object - so that it can behave properly in either setting.

## Indicating if the Tape Object is a Child

Let's update the code for our Tape object accordingly. The first thing we'll do is add a module-level variable to indicate whether the object is a child. We can use this flag throughout the class to change the behavior of the methods, depending on the mode of the object:

```
Private mflgEditing As Boolean
Private mflgChild As Boolean
Private WithEvents mobjValid As BrokenRules
```

By default, this flag will have the value of False, which works well since we don't want the UI developer to have to worry about calling extra properties or methods when using a Tape object. Instead, we'll have the parent object call an extra method on the Tape object to set the flag's value to True. This SetAsChild method has a Friend scope, so it isn't visible to the UI developer and thus won't be called by accident:

```
Friend Sub SetAsChild()

    mflgChild = True

End Sub
```

This will require that we add an extra line of code inside our Tapes collection object's Add method when it creates a new Tape object. We'll actually code this in the next section when we create the Tapes object. The code might look something like this:

```
Set objTape = New Tape
objTape.SetAsChild
objTape.Load lngTapeID
```

So, now we have a way for the object to know whether it's actually a child at any time. We're now ready to go through the code and make it act properly - depending on the value of mflgChild. This is where things get really interesting!

### Enhancing BeginEdit, CancelEdit and ApplyEdit

It's important to preserve the same public interface as a normal business object - so that the UI developer doesn't have to worry about an object being a child or not. It shouldn't matter to them what is going on behind the scenes in our object. This means that we need to keep the `BeginEdit`, `CancelEdit` and `ApplyEdit` methods, and make them work basically the same way from the UI developer's viewpoint.

At the same time, we need to build a way for the parent object to tell the child when to save its state (`BeginEdit`), restore its state (`CancelEdit`), or keep any updates (`ApplyEdit`). Basically, we're looking at creating a new set of transaction methods that are only for use by the parent object. This is on top of altering the original three methods so they work properly with the new methods.

> *This stuff can really twist a person's brain. Especially when you consider that we could have* `Problem` *objects as children of a* `Tape` *object. When the user clicks* Cancel *on the* Video *screen, not only do all the* `Tape` *objects need to be reset, but all their respective* `Problem` *objects would need to be reset as well. We'd have to provide for cascading transactional support throughout all the children. Fortunately, the solution I'm presenting here will cover that, hopefully while keeping everyone's sanity.*

Our `Tape` object already has a great deal of code for managing whether it's valid, dirty, new and so forth. Rather than reinventing all of this, we want to tap into it and, with slight alterations, make it work in this new setting. The only new thing we need to keep track of is whether the parent has told us we are editing:

```
Private mflgChild As Boolean
Private mflgChildEditing As Boolean
Private WithEvents mobjValid As BrokenRules
```

Along these same lines, we'll be creating a second set of transaction methods to save and restore our object's core data. In the `Tape` object, this means a new variable based on the `TapeProps` UDT:

```
Private mudtProps As TapeProps
Private mudtSave As TapeProps
Private mudtChild As TapeProps
```

### BeginEdit and CancelEdit Methods

Before we get into the new methods, let's look at the changes to the existing ones. `BeginEdit` and `CancelEdit` are virtually unchanged from our earlier code; there are just a couple of exceptions:

```
Public Sub BeginEdit()

    If mflgChild Then If Not mflgChildEditing Then Err.Raise 445
    If mflgEditing Then Err.Raise 445

    ' save object state
    LSet mudtSave = mudtProps
    mflgEditing = True

End Sub

Public Sub CancelEdit()
```

```
      If mflgChild Then If Not mflgChildEditing Then Err.Raise 445
      If Not mflgEditing Then Err.Raise 445

      mflgEditing = False
      mflgDeleted = False
      mflgDirty = False
      ' restore object state
      LSet mudtProps = mudtSave

    End Sub
```

Both routines have a new line at the top that disables them if the object is a child, and the new
`ChildBeginEdit` hasn't been called. What we're doing here is preventing the object from being
edited - unless the parent has initiated an editing session as well. We don't want children being edited
without the parent's knowledge, since it's the parent that calls the routines to save the data to the
database. If the parent is unaware of edits then the save methods won't get called and the data won't
be saved.

The nice thing about this approach is that no one can call `BeginEdit` unless the parent has given
permission. Since almost everything else in the object's code requires `BeginEdit` to be called, so
`mflgEditing` is `True`, we essentially make the object read-only until the `ChildBeginEdit`
method gets called.

The second change we're going to make will only apply if this object had child objects of its own. As
we discussed earlier, we'd need to echo all the `BeginEdit`, `CancelEdit` and `ApplyEdit` calls
down to our child collection object. If the `Tape` object itself is a child then those calls should only get
echoed when the parent object calls them, not when a screen calls them.

> *This is the part that enables cascading transaction support throughout all our children. Suppose
> we did implement child `Problem` objects with a `Problems` collection to hold them. Then the
> collection objects, `Tapes` and `Problems`, would both call the `ChildBeginEdit`,
> `ChildCancelEdit` and `ChildApplyEdit` methods on all their child objects. These
> methods should only be called by a parent object - never in response to some UI code behind a
> button.*

> *Right now we're implementing the changes so the `Video` object can tell the `Tapes` object to echo
> the calls to all its child objects. We also need to make sure that each child `Tape` object would
> also echo the call down to any of its child objects.*

### ApplyEdit Method

The `ApplyEdit` method's changes are very similar in concept:

```
    Public Sub ApplyEdit()

      If mflgChild Then If Not mflgChildEditing Then Err.Raise 445
      If Not mflgChild And mflgNew Then Err.Raise 445
      If Not mflgEditing Then Err.Raise 445

      If Not mflgChild Then
        If mflgDeleted And Not mflgNew Then
          ' code to delete the object's data goes here
          mflgNew = True
          mflgDeleted = False
```

```
      ElseIf mflgDirty Or mflgNew Then
        If Not IsValid Then Err.Raise 445
        ' save object to database if appropriate
        ' save object state
        LSet mudtSave = mudtProps
        mflgNew = False

      End If

      mflgDirty = False

    End If

    mflgEditing = False

  End Sub
```

Again, we have the line at the top of the routine to prevent it from being called unless the ChildBeginEdit method has been called and set the mflgChildEditing flag to True.

The second new line addresses a more complex concern. We don't want to let the UI code add Tape objects without going through a Video object. Without going through the Video object, the UI could add Tape objects with no valid parent, thus creating orphan objects. This means that we need to add a check to disable the routine in the case where the UI has created a new Tape object that isn't a child - and then tries to save that object.

Almost all the code in a normal ApplyEdit method is geared around deleting an object from the database, or updating the object's data in the database. Since we want all of this activity to happen in the ChildApplyEdit method, we need to prevent it from happening here. Basically, this means we've put an If...Then check around everything except the code to reset the mflgEditing flag.

### Delete Method

Along with the other transactional methods, the Delete method needs some slight alteration:

```
  Public Sub Delete()

    If mflgChild Then If Not mflgChildEditing Then Err.Raise 445
    If Not mflgEditing Then Err.Raise 445

    mflgDeleted = True
    mflgDirty = True

  End Sub
```

Since the Delete method just sets its flags and lets ApplyEdit, or in this case ChildApplyEdit, actually do the delete operation, we don't need to change much. Like the other methods, we need to make sure that the method can't be called until ChildBeginEdit has 'unlocked' the object.

### Load Method

Before moving on to the new methods, we'll visit the Load method for a moment. If an object is a child of another object, we can't let the UI code load just anything into that child object. In fact, the data loaded into the child object should be under the control of the parent object. What we really want, is to disable the Load method if the object is a child. We'll go through a new ChildLoad method for use by the parent in a bit. Right now, let's disable the Load method:

```
Public Sub Load(TapeID As Long)

    If mflgChild Then Err.Raise 445
    If mflgEditing Then Err.Raise 445
    If Not mflgNew Then Err.Raise 445

' code to load the object goes here

    mflgNew = False

End Sub
```

Now let's look at the new methods. All of these methods will have `Friend` scope, so they won't be available to any client code; but they will be usable by the object's parent.

### ChildBeginEdit Method

The first is `ChildBeginEdit`, which is called by the parent when an editing session is started:

```
Friend Sub ChildBeginEdit()

    If mflgChildEditing Then Err.Raise 445

    ' save object state
    LSet mudtChild = mudtProps
    mflgChildEditing = True

End Sub
```

> *What will really happen is that the* `Video` *object's* `BeginEdit` *will call* `BeginEdit` *on the* `Tapes` *object that we'll implement shortly. The* `Tapes` *object's* `BeginEdit` *will then go through all the* `Tape` *objects in its collection and call* `ChildBeginEdit`.

Notice how similar this new method is to the original `BeginEdit`. The only differences are that it uses the new `mflgChildEditing` variable instead of `mflgEditing` to avoid confusion with the original `BeginEdit` method, and it stores the object's data in `mudtChild` instead of `mudtSave`.

### ChildCancelEdit Method

Likewise, `ChildCancelEdit` is very similar to the original `CancelEdit` method:

```
Friend Sub ChildCancelEdit()

    If Not mflgChildEditing Then Err.Raise 445

    mflgChildEditing = False
    mflgDeleted = False
    ' restore object state
    LSet mudtProps = mudtChild

End Sub
```

Again, the only significant differences are that the `mflgChildEditing` variable is used instead of `mflgEditing`, and the object's data is restored from `mudtChild` instead of `mudtSave`.

Our object's `BeginEdit`, `ApplyEdit` and `CancelEdit` store a copy of the object's data in `mudtSave` as they've always done. By storing a copy of the object's data in `mudtChild`, in addition to `mudtSave`, we have allowed the user to bring up the `Tape` object and edit it multiple times, getting the normal Cancel and Apply effects they'd expect through the `mudtSave` copy.

If the user clicks Cancel on the `Video` object's screen, we're able to ignore all the intervening edits and get back to the `mudtChild` copy we made in `ChildBeginEdit`.

> Basically, we've implemented `mudtChild` for the express purpose of being able to roll back our child object's state to what it was when the user started editing the *parent* object. This way the user can cancel the edits on the parent object and we can make sure all the edits on any child objects are rolled back as well.

### ChildApplyEdit Method

The `ChildApplyEdit` method is also closely based on the original `ApplyEdit` method, so it should look pretty familiar:

```
Friend Sub ChildApplyEdit(VideoID As Long)

  If Not mflgChildEditing Then Err.Raise 445

  If mflgDeleted And Not mflgNew Then
    ' code to delete the object's data goes here
    mflgNew = True
    mflgDeleted = False

  ElseIf mflgDirty Or mflgNew Then
    If Not IsValid Then Err.Raise 445
    mudtProps.VideoID = VideoID
    ' save object to database if appropriate
    ' save object state
    LSet mudtChild = mudtProps
    mflgNew = False

  End If

  mflgDirty = False
  mflgChildEditing = False

End Sub
```

Like the other new methods, this method uses `mflgChildEditing` instead of `mflgEditing` and stores the object's state data in `mudtChild` instead of `mudtSave`.

One significant difference is the `VideoID` parameter that this routine expects. Since each `Tape` object is a child of a `Video` object, the `Tape` object needs to have some mechanism to know the identity of the parent `Video` object.

The `Video` object's ID number will be assigned as the object is being saved to the database, so the ID number won't be available until after the object has been saved. At this point the `Video` object itself has its ID number, but we still need to provide it to the child `Tape` objects.

The easiest solution is to have the Video object pass the ID number as a parameter to the ApplyEdit method of the Tapes object. That method can then pass the ID number as a parameter to the ChildApplyEdit methods of each child Tape object.

The rest of the code is identical to a normal ApplyEdit method, in that the value of the mflgDeleted flag is queried and, if it's True, the data is deleted. Otherwise, the mflgDirty flag is queried and, if it turns out to be True, then the data is saved in the database.

### ChildLoad Method

When the Tape object is a child rather than a standalone object, the only place that any data is loaded from or saved to the database is in the ChildLoad and ChildApplyEdit methods. The Load is entirely disabled, and the ApplyEdit method is relegated to setting some flags and storing an intermediate state value.

Let's take a look at the ChildLoad method:

```
Friend Sub ChildLoad(TapeID As Long)

    If mflgChildEditing Then Err.Raise 445
    If Not mflgNew Then Err.Raise 445

' code to load the object goes here

    mflgNew = False

End Sub
```

As with the other child methods, this one relies on mflgChildEditing as a master flag to indicate whether it is a valid method. Beyond that, this routine is identical to a regular Load method, which is important, since the Load method itself will be disabled if this Tape object is a child of a Video object (and yet the code to load data from the database is identical either way).

In the final analysis, by adding a couple of Boolean variables, slightly modifying some existing routines, and adding four new methods, we've altered the Tape object so that it can behave as a standalone object or a child object equally well.

*If our application were to have several child objects, it would be wise to create a BusinessChild class template, along the lines of the Business class template we created earlier in this chapter, to save all the typing involved in doing these changes.*

## Tape Properties

Now that the basic operation of the object has been coded, we can move on to the object's properties.

### Basic Properties

Like the other ID properties so far, the TapeID value will be generated by the database, so it's a simple read-only property in our object:

```
Public Property Get TapeID() As Long

    TapeID = mudtProps.TapeID

End Property
```

In our UDT, we have a slot for the title of the tape. As we've discussed, this field is actually part of the `Video` object, but it's more efficient to have a read-only copy here. This way, the UI can display the tape's title without having to go to the expense of instantiating an entire `Video` object.

Now let's look at our `Title` code:

```
Public Property Get Title() As String

  If mflgNew Then Err.Raise 445

  Title = Trim$(mudtProps.Title)

End Property
```

It's important to note that we load the `Title` data into our object when the object's data is retrieved from the database. Because of this, the `Tape` object's `Title` field needs to be disabled while the object is new.

*Alternatively, we could have implemented code to update all the* `Tape` *objects whenever the* `Video` *object's* `Title` *field changed; but this could have serious performance ramifications of its own - as you can probably imagine!*

We'll also implement a `Boolean` property called `CheckedOut` to indicate if the tape is currently checked out on an invoice:

```
Public Property Get CheckedOut() As Boolean

  CheckedOut = mudtProps.CheckedOut

End Property
```

Later on, we'll go through a couple of methods that maintain the `mudtProps.CheckedOut` variable's value. Since this value will be controlled through these methods, we don't want the calling code to be able to directly alter it - and so this needs to be a read-only property.

*Object purists may argue that* all *properties should be read-only and that only methods should alter property values. While there is something to be said for this approach, from a strict OO viewpoint, it doesn't fit with the historical philosophy of Visual Basic. Visual Basic programmers are used to being able to set properties on forms, controls and other built-in Visual Basic objects. One of our goals with business objects is to make it easy for a Visual Basic UI developer to get up to speed using our objects. So it makes a lot of sense for Visual Basic business objects to follow in Visual Basic's footsteps and provide read-write properties when appropriate.*

*Additionally, Visual Basic* Property *routines are really just methods. This is often confusing to OO developers coming from other languages, as they use the words attribute and property interchangeably. Within Visual Basic however, an attribute is a module-level variable in a class, while a property is a specific type of method that we may use to provide access to attributes or other data.*

### DateAcquired Property: Write Once, Read Many

The `DateAcquired` property is a bit more interesting. Since it's a date property, it will have extra code along the lines of the `ReleaseDate` property in the `Video` object. Also, as we've seen, this will be a required field in the object - so there'll be code to support that as well.

To add another twist to this property, we're going to make it a **WORM** (write once, read many) property. This means that the property can only be set when the object is new, and it becomes a read-only property once the object is saved to the database. While this can be a fairly restrictive business rule, it's nevertheless quite common. In this case, we're assuming that the tape's acquired date will be set when the tape's purchase is recorded into the system - and it shouldn't be changed after that point. Another example of a WORM property might be a digital signature, or personal ID code that's set on an object when it is created. Here's our code for `DateAcquired`:

```
Public Property Let DateAcquired(Value As Variant)

  If Not mflgEditing Then Err.Raise 383
  If Not mflgNew Then Err.Raise 383

  If Len(Trim(Value)) = 0 Then
    mudtProps.DateAcquired = ""
    mobjValid.RuleBroken "DateAcquired", True

  ElseIf IsDate(Value) Then
    mudtProps.DateAcquired = CVDate(Value)
    mobjValid.RuleBroken "DateAcquired", False

  Else
    mobjValid.RuleBroken "DateAcquired", True

  End If

  mflgDirty = True

End Property
```

In order to implement the WORM concept, we must only allow the `Property Let` code to run if the object is new. Fortunately, our template code already maintains the `mflgNew` variable, which indicates whether the object is new or not. All we need to do is add a line at the top of the routine to disable it if `mflgNew` is `False`:

```
If Not mflgNew Then Err.Raise 383
```

Like the `ReleaseDate` property in the `Video` class, this routine accepts a `Variant` parameter, and checks to make sure that it's either an empty string or a valid date. In this case, however, an empty string breaks the business rule that this field is required, so we need to record that:

```
mobjValid.RuleBroken "DateAcquired", True
```

Likewise, if the parameter is a valid date then we'll record that the requirement was met, so the object's `IsValid` property returns `True`:

```
mobjValid.RuleBroken "DateAcquired", False
```

The `Property Get` is quite simple, just like the routine from `ReleaseDate` in the `Video` class:

```
Public Property Get DateAcquired() As Variant

  DateAcquired = mudtProps.DateAcquired

End Property
```

### Invoice Property: Load on Demand

We'll also implement a read-only `Invoice` property to return a reference to the `Invoice` object - in case this `Tape` object is marked as `CheckedOut`. In the `TapeProps` UDT, at the top of the class, we included an `InvoiceID` variable to store the ID number of the `Invoice` object that represents the transaction that rented out this tape.

This property is a good place to apply a new concept called **load on demand**. Loading an entire object, such as an `Invoice` object, can be very expensive in terms of performance. It would be a shame to take all the time to load the `Invoice` object - unless the calling code actually used the `Invoice` property. Instead, we'll only create an instance of the object when the client code calls the `Property Get Invoice` routine:

```
Public Property Get Invoice() As Invoice

  Dim objInvoice As Invoice

  If Not mudtProps.CheckedOut Then Err.Raise 445

  Set objInvoice = New Invoice
  objInvoice.Load mudtProps.InvoiceID
  Set Invoice = objInvoice
  Set Invoice = Nothing

End Property
```

The first thing that this routine does is declare a placeholder variable for the `Invoice` object we'll be creating:

```
Dim objInvoice As Invoice
```

Then we need to check to see if the current tape is actually rented out. If the `CheckedOut` value is `False` then the tape isn't rented out and so it can't be associated with an invoice. Conversely, if `CheckedOut` is `True` then there must be an invoice associated with the tape, since it can only be checked out through an invoice. We'll implement the `Invoice` object later in the chapter.

```
If Not mudtProps.CheckedOut Then Err.Raise 445
```

If the tape is not checked out then we just disable the property by raising an error to the calling code.

All that remains is to create an instance of the `Invoice` class and call its `Load` method with our `InvoiceID` value. As we'll see later, with the implementation of the `Invoice` class, its `Load` method will accept an ID value as a parameter.

```
Set objInvoice = New Invoice
objInvoice.Load mudtProps.InvoiceID
```

The final line of the routine assigns the newly loaded `Invoice` object to be the return value of the property:

```
Set Invoice = objInvoice
```

An alternative approach to this routine would be to make `objInvoice` a module-level variable and change the routine to load the object once - and then retain a reference to it from that point forward (*don't enter this code*):

```
Public Property Get Invoice() As Invoice

  Static mflgLoaded As Boolean

  If Not mudtProps.CheckedOut Then Err.Raise 383

  If Not mflgLoaded Then
    Set mobjInvoice = New Invoice
    mobjInvoice.Load mudtProps.InvoiceID
    mflgLoaded = True
  End If

  Set Invoice = mobjInvoice

End Property
```

This has the advantage of loading the `Invoice` object less often if it's heavily used by the client code. The drawback to it is that the `Invoice` object will remain in memory until the `Tape` object is terminated; if the `Invoice` object is only used a couple times by the calling code, this could be a waste of memory. Either approach works fine - just choose the one that fits the way the property will be used by the client code.

## Tape Methods

The `Tape` object will need a couple of methods to interact with the `Invoice` object. As a tape is added to an `Invoice`, the `CheckOut` method will be called to mark the `Tape` object as being checked out. Likewise, when the tape is returned, the `CheckIn` method needs to be called to record that the tape has been checked back in.

### CheckOut Method

The only way to check out a tape is to add it to an invoice. Because of this, the UI developer shouldn't be able to call the `CheckOut` method directly, but should instead have to go through the `Invoice` object. This means the routine will be declared with the `Friend` keyword - so that only our other business objects can call it.

The routine will accept the ID value of the invoice to which it's being added as a parameter. We'll store this value in our `mudtProps` for use in implementing the `Property Get Invoice` we looked at earlier:

```
Friend Sub CheckOut(InvoiceID As Long)

  If Not mflgEditing Then Err.Raise 445

  With mudtProps
    .CheckedOut = True
    .InvoiceID = InvoiceID
  End With

  mflgDirty = True

End Sub
```

The first thing that this routine does is to make sure that the object is being edited. Basically, this means that the method can't be called unless the `BeginEdit` method has been called first. The `CancelEdit` and `ApplyEdit` methods will roll back or commit this method's activities - just as they would with a change to a property value.

> *This is not necessarily a requirement for all methods, but this method will be changing property values in our object, so the ability to support canceling or applying the method is useful to have. Consider the case where the user adds a list of tapes to an invoice, resulting in each tape's* `CheckOut` *method being called as it's added. Then suppose the user clicks the* Cancel *button on the screen, canceling the invoice. All of the* Tape *objects need to reset their values now too, since they are no longer on an invoice. If this can be done by simply calling* `CancelEdit` *on each* Tape *object the process becomes very easy to implement.*

The rest of the code is not complex. Since we're checking out this tape, we'll just set the `mudtProps.CheckedOut` variable to `True`:

```
.CheckedOut = True
```

The parameter to this routine was the `InvoiceID` of the invoice to which the tape is being added. We'll record this value in the UDT as well, so we can use it in the `Invoice` property routine we looked at earlier:

```
.InvoiceID = InvoiceID
```

### CheckIn Method

The `CheckIn` method is the reverse of `CheckOut`. When a tape is returned to the store, the system shouldn't require the user to bring up the invoice in order to check in the tape. That would be awkward, so the system needs to allow the UI to directly call the `CheckIn` method on a tape. The UI code would then look something like this:

```
' get the TapeID from a barcode reader
Set objTape = New Tape

With objTape
  .Load lngTapeID
  .BeginEdit
```

```
    .CheckIn
    .ApplyEdit
End with

Set objTape = Nothing
```

For this to work, the CheckIn method needs to be Public in scope rather than the Friend scope of CheckOut. Beyond that, it just needs to reset the CheckedOut and Invoice properties to indicate that the tape is checked in:

```
Public Sub CheckIn()

  If Not mflgEditing Then Err.Raise 445

  With mudtProps
    .CheckedOut = False
  End With

  mflgDirty = True

End Sub
```

To be consistent with the behavior of CheckOut, this method does require that BeginEdit be called first. For all we know, the UI developer might want to build an entire list of tapes to check in, calling the CheckIn method on each one. If the UI includes a Cancel button, it might be important to be able to use CancelEdit to safely undo all those calls to CheckIn.

# Tapes: A Parent-Child Relationship Object

In the Video object, we implemented a Tapes property to contain all the specific Tape objects that are children of a specific Video object. The Tapes property simply exposed a Tapes object to the calling code. Now we need to implement the Tapes class to support the requirements of the Video object's property.

The Tapes object is highlighted in the following diagram:

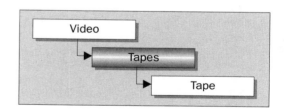

In many cases, collection objects don't represent any real-world entity as much as they represent a real-world relationship between entities. For instance, it's difficult to envision a real-world entity for a Tapes object to model. The Tapes object will model the parent-child relationship between a video title and all the physical tapes of that title in the store.

When we implemented the Tape object itself, we added a bit of extra code so it can act as a standalone object as well as a child object. When we're using Tape objects within this new Tapes collection object, they'll be child objects - so we'll need to make use of the SetAsChild, ChildLoad, ChildBeginEdit, ChildCancelEdit and ChildApplyEdit methods.

he Tapes object when we implemented the Video object earlier. The
d methods need to make it appear as a collection of Tape objects, but we
ethods that will be implemented with Friend scope for use by the

## Setting up the Tapes Class

Add a standard class module to the VideoObjects project. Set its **Name** property to Tapes and its **Instancing** property to 2-PublicNotCreatable. This object will only be created as a part of the Video object, so it shouldn't be creatable by outside code; however, it will be exposed via the Video object's Tapes property, so it needs to be publicly available.

As with any other collection object, we'll need an actual Collection object to build our code around:

```
Option Explicit

Private mcolTapes As Collection
```

And, of course, the Class_Initialize needs to create an instance of a Collection object for this variable:

```
Private Sub Class_Initialize()

  Set mcolTapes = New Collection

End Sub
```

Since this is a collection type object, we'll have the standard Item, Count and NewEnum methods. Don't forget to use **Tools | Procedure Attributes...** to make the Item method the default and the NewEnum method have a **Procedure ID** of −4 and **Hide this member** attribute.

```
Public Function Item(ByVal Index As Variant) As Tape

  Set Item = mcolTapes(Index)

End Function
```

```
Public Function Count() As Long

  Count = mcolTapes.Count

End Function
```

```
Public Function NewEnum() As IUnknown

  Set NewEnum = mcolTapes.[_NewEnum]

End Function
```

As a collection of Tape objects, it's no surprise that the Item method returns a Tape object when called:

```
Public Function Item(ByVal Index As Variant) As Tape
```

The rest of the code in this object will be a bit different from what we've seen in past collection objects, such as `Customers`. As the owner of a group of child `Tape` objects, the `Tapes` object needs to contain code to manage starting, canceling and applying edits, as well as adding and deleting `Tape` objects.

## Edit Methods

When we implemented the `Video` object, we added code in its `BeginEdit`, `CancelEdit` and `ApplyEdit` to call routines of the same names in the `Tapes` object. Now we need to implement those methods so they act as expected.

Since our object will have its own set of these methods, we'll need a module-level variable to make them interact properly, just like all the other objects with these methods:

```
Option Explicit

Private mcolTapes As Collection
Private mflgEditing As Boolean
```

### BeginEdit Method

When the `Video` object calls the `BeginEdit` method on the `Tapes` object, it isn't merely indicating that the collection should become editable; but it's also indicating that all the child `Tape` objects should become editable. When we implemented the `Tape` class, we added a `ChildBeginEdit` method for this very purpose. So here's the `BeginEdit` routine for our `Tapes` object:

```
Public Sub BeginEdit()

  Dim objTape As Tape

  If mflgEditing Then Err.Raise 445

  For Each objTape In mcolTapes
    objTape.ChildBeginEdit
  Next

  mflgEditing = True

End Sub
```

This routine is a bit different from any other `BeginEdit` methods we've seen so far. The first couple of lines are pretty simple, just declaring a local variable of type `Tape` and disabling the routine if the editing flag is already set to `True`:

```
Dim objTape As Tape

If mflgEditing Then Err.Raise 445
```

The next thing we do is use a `For...Each` to loop through all the items in the `mcolTapes` collection:

```
For Each objTape In mcolTapes
  objTape.ChildBeginEdit
Next
```

For each of the `Tape` objects in the collection, we just call `ChildBeginEdit`. This means that when the `Tapes` object's `BeginEdit` method is called by the parent `Video` object, this routine just turns around and calls `ChildBeginEdit` for every child `Tape` object in the collection. Essentially, we've just echoed the `Video` object's `BeginEdit` call down to every child `Tapes` object.

The final line just sets the `mflgEditing` flag to `True` so that the `Tapes` object knows it is being edited:

```
mflgEditing = True
```

### CancelEdit Method

The `CancelEdit` method is quite similar in concept, but it does have an extra twist:

```
Public Sub CancelEdit()

  Dim objTape As Tape
  Dim lngIndex As Long

  If Not mflgEditing Then Err.Raise 445

  mflgEditing = False
  For lngIndex = mcolTapes.Count To 1 Step -1
    Set objTape = mcolTapes.Item(lngIndex)
    With objTape
      If .IsNew Then _
        mcolTapes.Remove lngIndex
      .ChildCancelEdit
    End With

  Next lngIndex
End Sub
```

Here, again, we just declare a couple of local variables and disable the routine unless the `BeginEdit` method has been called and set `mflgEditing` to `True`. Of course, we then set `mflgEditing` to `False`, since we're canceling the edit process:

```
Dim objTape As Tape
Dim lngIndex As Long

If Not mflgEditing Then Err.Raise 445

mflgEditing = False
```

Then the real fun begins. Like the `BeginEdit` method, this routine loops through all the items in the `mcolTapes` collection, calling each object's `ChildCancelEdit` method. However, this loop looks quite a bit different:

```
For lngIndex = mcolTapes.Count To 1 Step -1
  Set objTape = mcolTapes.Item(lngIndex)
  With objTape
    If .IsNew Then _
      mcolTapes.Remove lngIndex
    .ChildCancelEdit
  End With
Next lngIndex
```

If the user has added any new `Tape` objects to the collection during this editing session, we need to make sure that they're removed if the edit is canceled. After all, canceling the edit should effectively reset all the child `Tape` objects, and the collection itself, back to where they were when the `BeginEdit` method was called. If new `Tape` objects have been added since the call to `BeginEdit`, they need to be removed to get us back to where we were.

This removal is not complex, since each `Tape` object knows if it's new or not, and we can find out by using the object's `IsNew` property. If a `Tape` object is new, we can simply remove it from the collection:

```
If .IsNew Then _
    mcolTapes.Remove lngIndex
```

Unfortunately, the `Remove` method on a collection requires the index value of the item to be removed. Using `For...Each` to go through a collection, there is no way to find out the index for the current item, and so we'd have no way to call `Remove`. Instead, we have to loop through the collection using a numeric index variable, `lngIndex`.

It's also important to note that all the index values of items in a collection move up by one when an item is removed with the `Remove` method. If we start at index 1 and end up removing it, all the subsequent item index values will be off by one, and we'll have a bug. Instead, we need to start with the bottom item and move back to the top:

```
For lngIndex = mcolTapes.Count To 1 Step -1
```

The other bit of complexity is that all objects in a collection are effectively late-bound. To get the performance and debugging benefits of early-binding, we need to `Set` each item into our `objTape` variable so that we can use it as an early-bound `Tape` object:

```
Set objTape = mcolTapes.Item(lngIndex)
```

In the end, our `CancelEdit` routine loops through all the child `Tape` objects and calls `ChildCancelEdit` on each one - so they each reset to the values they held when the `ChildBeginEdit` methods were called. It also removes any new `Tape` objects from the collection, thereby returning the collection itself back to the state it was in when the `BeginEdit` method was called.

### ApplyEdit Method

`ApplyEdit` works the same as `CancelEdit`, though instead of removing new `Tape` objects from the collection, it removes any `Tape` objects that are marked as deleted:

```
Public Sub ApplyEdit(VideoID As Long)

    Dim objTape As Tape
    Dim lngIndex As Long

    If Not mflgEditing Then Err.Raise 445
```

```
      For lngIndex = mcolTapes.Count To 1 Step -1
        Set objTape = mcolTapes.Item(lngIndex)
        With objTape
          If .IsDeleted Then _
              mcolTapes.Remove lngIndex
          .ChildApplyEdit VideoID
        End With

      Next lngIndex

      mflgEditing = False

    End Sub
```

The routine loops through the items in the collection from bottom to top:

```
    For lngIndex = mcolTapes.Count To 1 Step -1
      Set objTape = mcolTapes.Item(lngIndex)
```

Since we're committing to the changes at this point, we no longer need any deleted objects. In fact, we want to remove them from our collection since, at the end of `ApplyEdit`, our collection should reflect the contents of the database, and any deleted objects have been removed from the database by the `ChildApplyEdit` code:

```
    If .IsDeleted Then _
        mcolTapes.Remove lngIndex
```

For each child object we also call the `ChildApplyEdit` method. This will cause each `Tape` object to delete or save itself in the database, as appropriate.

```
      .ChildApplyEdit VideoID
```

When we implemented the `Tape` object's `ChildApplyEdit` method earlier, we built it to expect the `VideoID` value to be passed. This `ApplyEdit` method accepts that value from the `Video` object and relays it to each `ChildApplyEdit` call.

The end result of the `ApplyEdit` method is that all the child `Tape` object's `ChildApplyEdit` methods have been called, so each one of them has been updated in the database as appropriate. Additionally, any `Tape` objects that were deleted from the database have also been removed from our `Tapes` collection.

### Delete Method

The `Video` object's `Delete` method calls a `Delete` method on the `Tapes` object. Of course, the `Video` object's `Delete` method marks the `Video` object itself for deletion, and so we'd expect that all the parent object's children would also get marked for deletion. If the parent is deleted and the children are not, we'd have orphan child objects - and that could be a big problem.

```
    Public Sub Delete()

      Dim objTape As Tape
```

```
    If Not mflgEditing Then Err.Raise 445
    ' code to delete the object's data goes here

    For Each objTape In mcolTapes
      With objTape
        .BeginEdit
        .Delete
        .ApplyEdit
      End With

    Next

  End Sub
```

Like the `BeginEdit` method, our `Delete` method uses a `For...Each` to loop through all the child `Tape` objects and call each of their individual `Delete` methods. Of course, the `Delete` method can't be called without calling `BeginEdit` first, and the deletion won't stick unless the `ApplyEdit` method is called as well.

As with the `Tape` object, the `Delete` method just sets `mflgDeleted` to `True`, so the `Tapes` object isn't really deleted at this point, just flagged for deletion. Nothing, including the `Video` object itself, is actually deleted until the `Video` object's `ApplyEdit` method is called. Then, the `Tape` object's `ChildApplyEdit` method will be called and the `Tape` actually deleted.

## Adding Tape Objects to the Collection

We need to provide a mechanism for the UI code to add new, blank `Tape` objects to our collection. This capability will be required when the video store purchases a new tape for a video title and needs to add it to the list of tapes to be rented.

Before we launch into the code however, we need to think a bit about how this process will work. At first glance it seems that adding a `Tape` object should be pretty straightforward, perhaps by using a routine similar to the following (*do not enter this code*):

```
Public Function Add() As Tape

  Dim objTape As Tape

  Set objTape = New Tape
  mcolTapes.Add objTape
  Set Add = objTape

End Function
```

While the general concept is valid: creating a new `Tape` object and adding it to our internal collection, there is a problem here that may not be immediately obvious. In particular, since the `Tape` object we're dealing with is brand new and blank, it's probably not a valid object until the user has had a chance to add some data to it. Our user interface will probably support the adding of this data – but suppose the user clicks the Cancel button and *doesn't* add any valid data? If the user, for whatever reason, doesn't add valid data to our new `Tape` object we'll find that our internal collection contains a bad object.

What we need to do is figure out a way to create a new Tape object when the Add method of our Tapes object is called, but only add that new Tape object to our internal collection if the user provides valid data for the object. This will require a couple small changes to our existing Tape object, as well as a little more complexity within our Tapes object's Add method.

The solution we'll implement will create a Tape object when the Tapes object's Add method is called, but it won't add it to the collection at that time. Instead, we'll enhance the Tape object so it can tell the Tapes object to add it to the collection after the user accepts the Tape object. To do this, we'll implement a new method on the Tapes object, AddTape. In order to call this method, the Tape object will need to have a reference back to the Tapes object.

We'll write our code to support the following flow of events:

Create a new Tape object
Give the Tape object a reference to the Tapes object
Allow the user to manipulate the Tape object
If the user accepts the Tape object, the Tape object calls the AddTape method
If the user cancels the Tape object we can simply forget about it

### The Tapes Object's Add Method

Typical collection objects have an Add method, and our Tapes object will be no exception. The Add method is the accepted interface for adding new elements to a collection, and so we'll implement an Add method to create a new Tape object. Once we have a new Tape object we'll also make sure it has a reference to the Tapes object so it can call the AddTape method (which we'll implement shortly). Open the code window for the Tapes object and add the following code:

```
Public Function Add() As Tape

  Dim objTape As Tape

  If Not mflgEditing Then Err.Raise 445

  Set objTape = New Tape
  objTape.SetAsChild Me
  objTape.ChildBeginEdit
  Set Add = objTape
  Set objTape = Nothing

End Function
```

This code creates a new Tape object:

```
Dim objTape As Tape

If Not mflgEditing Then Err.Raise 445

Set objTape = New Tape
```

There's also the check in here to make sure we don't allow the addition of a Tape object unless we're editing the Tapes object. This makes sense – since the Tapes object is really made up of the individual Tape objects, so we shouldn't allow the edit unless we are in the process of editing the Tapes object itself.

Next we need to tell this new `Tape` object that it is currently a child object rather than a standalone object. We've already created a `SetAsChild` method in our `Tape` object to support this capability. However, we also need to provide the `Tape` object with a reference to the `Tapes` object and the `SetAsChild` method seems like an appropriate method for this purpose as well. Since this is the case, we'll pass a reference to the `Tapes` object as part of the method call:

```
objTape.SetAsChild Me
```

## Modifying SetAsChild in the Tape Module

We do need to modify the `SetAsChild` method to accept this parameter. Bring up the `Tape` object's code window and navigate to the `SetAsChild` routine. This method is called not only when we are creating a new `Tape` object like now, but also whenever we are loading existing objects from the database. The only time that we need to worry about having a reference to the `Tapes` object is when the `Tape` object is new, so we'll check the `mflgNew` flag before storing the value:

```
Friend Sub SetAsChild(objTapes As Tapes)

  If mflgNew Then Set mobjParent = objTapes
  mflgChild = True

End Sub
```

We'll also need to declare the `mobjParent` variable in the declarations section of the `Tape` code module:

```
Private mobjParent As Tapes
```

## Wrapping up the Add Method

OK, so with that set up we can return to the `Tapes` object and our `Add` method. Having created a new `Tape` object and both made sure it acts as a child object and has a reference to our `Tapes` object, we are ready to move on and finish the `Add` routine.

Since we know the `Tapes` object's `BeginEdit` has been called and all the existing `Tape` objects have therefore had their `ChildBeginEdit` methods invoked, we need to make sure to do the same thing with our new `Tape` object:

```
objTape.ChildBeginEdit
```

Finally, we need to set the `Add` method's return value to the new object, so that the calling code can get a direct reference, if so desired. We'll then release our local reference to the `Tape` object, making it the responsibility of the calling code to retain a reference to the new object:

```
Set Add = objTape
Set objTape = Nothing
```

## Modifying the Tape object's ApplyEdit Method

Now we've got everything set up so the `Tapes` object will create the `Tape` object such that the `Tape` object has a reference back to its parent. We now need to alter the `Tape` object so it makes sure it gets added to the collection if the user enters valid data and then accepts the object. To do this, bring up the `Tape` object's code module and move to the `ApplyEdit` method.

The user interface that requested the Tape object in the first place will need to allow the user to enter data to populate the object. Once that's complete, either the CancelEdit or ApplyEdit method will be called.

If CancelEdit is called then we don't need to do anything to add the Tape object to its parent Tapes object's collection of children – after all, the user is effectively discarding the Tape object itself.

However, if the ApplyEdit method is called we know that the user has provided valid data and wants to save the new Tape object. This means we need to make sure it gets added to the Tapes object's collection of child objects.

The ApplyEdit method is almost entirely wrapped in an If..Then block so very little is done if the object is a child. However, we'll only want to add the Tape object to its parent's collection if it is a child. This means we'll place our new code in an Else block. Make the following changes:

```
Public Sub ApplyEdit()

    If mflgChild Then If Not mflgChildEditing Then Err.Raise 445
    If Not mflgChild And mflgNew Then Err.Raise 445
    If Not mflgEditing Then Err.Raise 445

    If Not mflgChild Then
       If mflgDeleted And Not mflgNew Then
          ' code to delete the object's data goes here
          mflgNew = True
          mflgDeleted = False

       ElseIf mflgDirty Or mflgNew Then
          If Not IsValid Then Err.Raise 445
       ' save object to database if appropriate
       ' save object state
          LSet mudtSave = mudtProps
          mflgNew = False
       End If

       mflgDirty = False

    Else
       If Not mobjParent Is Nothing Then
         mobjParent.AddTape Me
         Set mobjParent = Nothing
       End If

    End If

    mflgEditing = False

End Sub
```

Not only will this code only be run if the Tape object is a child, but it also will only be run if the mobjParent variable contains a reference to the Tapes object. If the mobjParent variable has the value Nothing then we won't attempt to use it to call a method.

This works pretty well, since the only time we are putting a value into `mobjParent` is when we've created a new `Tape` object and called the `SetAsChild` method. If our `Tape` object isn't new then the `mobjParent` variable will not have been set and so this new code won't be run.

The new code itself calls an `AddTape` method from the `Tapes` object, passing the `Tape` object itself as a parameter:

```
mobjParent.AddTape Me
```

We'll create this new `AddTape` method shortly. For now it's enough to know that the method will add the `Tape` object to the `Tapes` object's internal collection of child objects.

Once we've added the `Tape` object to its parent via the `AddTape` method, we need to set the `mobjParent` variable to `Nothing`.

```
Set mobjParent = Nothing
```

This is important, as it's possible for the client code to call `ApplyEdit`, then `BeginEdit` and call `ApplyEdit` a second time. However, we want to only add the `Tape` object to its parent one time. If we set `mobjParent` to `Nothing` on the first time `ApplyEdit` is called, then this code won't be run on subsequent calls to `ApplyEdit`.

### Adding the AddTape Method to Tapes

Since we've just added code to the `Tape` object's `ApplyEdit` method to call an `AddTape` method from the `Tapes` object, we'd better return to the `Tapes` object's code and create that method. Open the code window for the `Tapes` object and add the following code:

```
Friend Sub AddTape(Child As Tape)

   mcolTapes.Add Item:=Child

End Sub
```

This is pretty simple code. All we need to do at this point is add the `Tape` object to the internal collection within the `Tapes` object. Once this is done our 'new' `Tape` object will be treated just like any other child `Tape` object – including being saved to the database, removed from the collection via the `Remove` method or any other valid operation.

## Removing Tape Objects

The `Remove` method on our `Tapes` object is fairly straightforward. Our `Tape` objects themselves already have the functionality required to delete themselves, so we just need to call the appropriate `Tape` object's `Delete` method:

```
Public Sub Remove(ByVal Index As Variant)

   If Not mflgEditing Then Err.Raise 445

   With mcolTapes(Index)
     .BeginEdit
```

```
        .Delete
        .ApplyEdit
    End With

End Sub
```

Of course we can't just call `Delete`. First we need to call `BeginEdit` to tell the `Tape` object that we're going to alter it, then we need to call `ApplyEdit` once the delete is done to commit the change. Remember that the `Tape` object isn't really deleted at this point, simply marked for deletion.

## Loading the Tape Objects

The only remaining issue is how to get all of the child `Tape` objects loaded with data and put into our collection. The `Video` object's `Load` method calls the `Tapes` object's `Load` method, passing it the `VideoID` of the parent object.

Using that ID value, we should be able to write database code to retrieve data for all the `Tape` objects that belong to that `VideoID`. Then, all that remains is to loop through all the retrieved database records, creating a `Tape` object for each one that we can add to our collection.

Like all the other data-related code in this chapter, the actual implementation will vary greatly depending on the physical architecture we choose. We'll go through various approaches to loading this data in chapters 8 and 10. For now, we'll just add some comments to remind us how to loop through the data:

```
Friend Sub Load(VideoID As Long)

    If mflgEditing Then Err.Raise 445

    ' here we'll put looping code to load
    ' each of the Tape objects for the VideoID

    ' For Each TapeID
    '     Set objTape = New Tape

    '     With objTape
    '         .ChildLoad TapeID
    '         .SetAsChild Me
    '     End With

    '     mcolTapes.Add Item:=objTape

    ' Loop

End Sub
```

Notice that all we need to retrieve from the database up front is a list of `TapeID` values that correspond to the tapes we need. Then we just loop through the list, creating a new `Tape` object and calling its `ChildLoad` method with each `TapeID` value. Of course, we also call each object's `SetAsChild` method to make sure it knows it's a child object, as we discussed when we implemented the `Tape` class.

*It's important to note that this approach will work quite well in a single-tier and many two-tier physical architectures, but it will have dismal performance in some two-tier and all three-tier implementations. When we get to a three-tier implementation, we'll see how we can rewrite this* Load *method so that it's very efficient in that setting.*

# Video Rental: Invoice Objects

Now we've established our building blocks. We have objects to represent the store's customers, and we have objects to represent the tapes that the store rents out.

So far, our objects have been largely independent of each other. The only relationship that we've looked at in any depth has been the parent-child relationship between the Video and Tape objects. But the objects that support invoicing will tie the customer objects together with the video tape objects, and so we'll get an opportunity to explore some more complex relationships.

By thinking about how an invoice is put together, a couple of objects readily come to mind. Of course, there's an object representing the invoice itself, but an invoice is really composed of a series of line items - in this case, one for each tape being rented. To represent these line items, we'll have an InvoiceItem object that is a child of the Invoice object itself: Since there may be more than one InvoiceItem object for an Invoice, we'll also implement an InvoiceItems object to manage these child objects as shown in the following diagram:

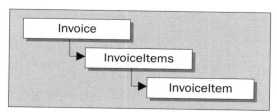

This is a good opportunity to explore **polymorphic** objects and the use of **multiple interfaces** with the Implements keyword. To this end, we'll have two types of invoice line items: one for rental of a tape, and one for late fees. Both will be InvoiceItem objects, so they'll implement that interface, but they are each unique and different objects - and so we'll create a separate class for each one.

# Late Fees: Object Interaction

Before we get too far into the invoicing itself, we should take a short detour to discuss some issues regarding interaction between objects. Late fees provide a good forum for this discussion, since they are the result of some objects interacting with each other.

When someone rents a video tape, there's a specific date by which they need to return the tape, otherwise they're charged a late fee. Typically, rental stores put this late fee on an invoice the next time the customer goes in to rent a tape.

This scenario suggests that each customer has an associated list of late fees that may be outstanding. These fees are added to the list during the process of checking in a tape that is overdue. We have a CheckIn method on our Tape object, so this seems to be a natural place to add the code to record the late fee.

## Adding DateDue to the Tape Object

First, we need to add a `DateDue` property to our `Tape` object. Since it will be automatically calculated, it needs to be a read-only property. We'll add the value to our UDT:

```
Private Type TapeProps
  TapeID As Long
  VideoID As Long
  Title As String * 30
  CheckedOut As Boolean
  DateAcquired As Variant
  DateDue As Variant
  InvoiceID As Long
End Type
```

And we'll add a read-only property in case anyone is interested in using the date to display somewhere:

```
Public Property Get DateDue() As Variant

  If Not mudtProps.CheckedOut Then Err.Raise 438

  DateDue = mudtProps.DateDue

End Property
```

The first line of code just makes sure that the property is disabled unless the tape is checked out. After all, if the tape isn't checked out it sure doesn't make sense to see when it's due back in. Otherwise, this routine simply returns the date stored in our object.

OK, now for the more interesting part. When the tape is checked out, we need to make sure to calculate the due date. Most video stores let the customer keep some videos longer than others, but we don't want this to get too confusing. We'll make all the videos in this store two-day rentals.

We already have a `CheckOut` routine, so all we need to do is add a bit of code to calculate the due date and store it:

```
Friend Sub CheckOut(InvoiceID As Long)

  If Not mflgEditing Then Err.Raise 445

  With mudtProps
    .CheckedOut = True
    .DateDue = DateAdd("d", 2, Now)
    .InvoiceID = InvoiceID
  End With

  mflgDirty = True

End Sub
```

## Recording the Late Fee

With this code, we've got everything set up to maintain the due date in each `Tape` object. All that remains is to add any late fees to the customer's list of fees.

The first instinct, at this point, is to create a `LateFee` object as a child of the `Customer` object. This makes a lot of sense, and fits very well into the whole object design concept. The trick is to not only look at this from the object perspective, but also to analyze this from a client/server perspective. This means we need to make sure that the UI processing is in the UI and the data processing is close to the database.

What really happens when we add a late fee during the check in process? It actually boils down to adding a record in a table somewhere to record that fee. To do this with objects, we'd probably have the following steps:

- Instantiate the `Invoice` object to find the customer ID
- Instantiate the `Customer` object
- Add a `LateFee` object to the `LateFees` collection
- Call `ApplyEdit` on the `Customer` object to save it and its children

When we consider that a fair amount of network traffic occurs to load the invoice, the customer, and then all the old late fee objects, it sure seems like a lot of work just to add one record to a table. And it is. If there's no compelling reason to create these objects, we can come up with a much more efficient solution.

The closer to the database that we can get the process of adding a record to a table, the faster things will run. Following this train of thought, it would be best if the code that stores the `Tape` object into the database could also just add this late fee record into the appropriate table. This code is already interacting with the database, and so it can directly access data from the invoice and customer - without the overhead of instantiating entire objects.

This means that we'll just add a flag to our UDT so we know enough to apply the late fee when needed.

```
Private Type TapeProps
    TapeID As Long
    VideoID As Long
    Title As String * 30
    CheckedOut As Boolean
    DateAcquired As Variant
    DateDue As Variant
    LateFee As Boolean
    InvoiceID As Long
End Type
```

This flag will start out `False` in any new object, so all we need to do is set it to `True` when appropriate:

```
Public Sub CheckIn()

    If Not mflgEditing Then Err.Raise 445

    With mudtProps
        .CheckedOut = False
        If DateDiff("d", .DateDue, Now) > 0 Then _
            .LateFee = True
```

```
    End With

      mflgDirty = True

  End Sub
```

The final change we'll make is in the `ApplyEdit` and `ChildApplyEdit` methods. Here are the `ApplyEdit` changes:

```
Public Sub ApplyEdit()

    If mflgChild Then If Not mflgChildEditing Then Err.Raise 445
    If Not mflgChild And mflgNew Then Err.Raise 445
    If Not mflgEditing Then Err.Raise 445

    If Not mflgChild Then
      If mflgDeleted And Not mflgNew Then
        ' code to delete the object's data goes here
        mflgNew = True
        mflgDeleted = False

      ElseIf mflgDirty Or mflgNew Then
        If Not IsValid Then Err.Raise 445
        ' save object to database if appropriate
        If mudtProps.LateFee Then
          ' add the late fee to the customer
        End If
        ' save object state
        LSet mudtSave = mudtProps
        mflgNew = False

      End If

      mflgDirty = False

    Else
      If Not mobjParent Is Nothing Then
        mobjParent.AddTape Me
        Set mobjParent = Nothing
      End If   End If

    mflgEditing = False

  End Sub
```

As usual, we just have a comment anywhere there might be database code. The actual code to add the late fee record will vary depending on the physical architecture of the application, so we'll look at some specific examples in chapters 8 and 10.

The `ChildApplyEdit` changes are just as exciting:

```
Friend Sub ChildApplyEdit(VideoID As Long)

    If Not mflgChildEditing Then Err.Raise 445
    If Not IsValid Then Err.Raise 445
```

```
If mflgDeleted And Not mflgNew Then
  ' code to delete the object's data goes here
  mflgNew = True
  mflgDeleted = False

ElseIf mflgDirty Or mflgNew Then
  mudtProps.VideoID = VideoID
  ' save object to database if appropriate
  If mudtProps.LateFee Then
    ' add the late fee to the customer
  End If
  ' save object state
  LSet mudtChild = mudtProps
  mflgNew = False

End If

mflgDirty = False
mflgChildEditing = False

End Sub
```

Once we've added the database handling code in these two methods, we have everything all set to handle the recording of late fees for a customer. That's only half the battle, though, since we still need to implement a special line item on our invoices to charge the customer for the late fee on their next videotape rental.

# Invoice: Another Parent Object

Let's now implement the `Invoice` object itself. Like the `Video` object, this is a parent object, and so we have to add a little code to manage our child objects. Still, we went over all the concepts involved when we implemented the `Video` object, so we can fly through the code here.

## Setting up the Invoice Object

As usual, add a `Business` class module to the `VideoObjects` project. Set its **Name** property to `Invoice` and its **Instancing** property to **5-Multiuse**.

The UI will be creating `Invoice` objects using the `Customer` object's `CreateInvoice` method, but the user may still choose to pull up an invoice after it has been added to the system, so **Multiuse** is appropriate.

### Updating the Template Code

Now run through the template code, and make the following changes. By now, these should be old hat - with one exception! (I haven't listed the areas of code that don't need changing.)

```
Option Explicit

Event Valid(IsValid As Boolean)

Private Type InvoiceProps
  InvoiceID As Long
  CustomerID As Long
```

```vb
   CustomerName As String * 50
   CustomerPhone As String * 25
End Type

Private mudtProps As InvoiceProps
Private mudtSave As InvoiceProps

Private mobjItems As InvoiceItems

Private mmflgNew As Boolean
Private mflgDeleted As Boolean
Private mflgDirty As Boolean
Private mflgEditing As Boolean
Private WithEvents mobjValid As BrokenRules

Public Sub BeginEdit()

  If mflgEditing Then Err.Raise 445

  ' save object state
  LSet mudtSave = mudtProps
  mflgEditing = True
  mobjItems.BeginEdit

End Sub

Public Sub CancelEdit()

  If Not mflgEditing Then Err.Raise 445

  mflgEditing = False
  mflgDeleted = False
  ' restore object state
  LSet mudtProps = mudtSave
  mobjItems.CancelEdit

End Sub

Public Sub ApplyEdit()

  If Not mflgEditing Then Err.Raise 445

  If mflgDeleted And Not mflgNew Then
    ' code to delete the object's data goes here
    mflgNew = True
    mflgDeleted = False

  ElseIf mflgDirty Or mflgNew Then
    If Not IsValid Then Err.Raise 445
    ' save object to database if appropriate
    ' save object state
    LSet mudtSave = mudtProps
    mflgNew = False

  End If

  mflgDirty = False
  mflgEditing = False
```

```
      mobjItems.ApplyEdit mudtProps.InvoiceID

End Sub

Private Sub Class_Initialize()

  mflgNew = True
  Set mobjValid = New BrokenRules

  Set mobjItems = New InvoiceItems

  ' if we know any rules are broken on startup
  ' then add code here to initialize the list
  ' of broken rules
  '
  ' mobjValid.RuleBroken "RuleName", True
  mobjValid.RuleBroken "Customer", True

End Sub

Public Sub Load(InvoiceID As Long)

  If mflgEditing Then Err.Raise 445
  If Not mflgNew Then Err.Raise 445

' code to load the object goes here

  mflgNew = False

  mobjValid.RuleBroken "Customer", False
  mobjItems.Load mudtProps.InvoiceID

End Sub
```

### Customer Object Reference

The only new concept here is the use of `mobjValid`, the `BrokenRules` object, to track whether the `Invoice` has a valid `Customer` object associated with it. In the `Class_Initialize` routine, we assume that we don't have a valid `Customer` object, since when we first create an `Invoice` object it won't have any `Customer` object associated with it.

In the `Load` method, however, we have some code that assumes we *do* have a valid `Customer`. After all, if the `Invoice` object was saved, it must have had a valid `Customer` object - and so when we're restoring it from the database it should still be valid.

## Invoice Properties

Our invoice object has a number of properties. The `InvoiceID` property is the same as all the other ID properties we've implemented so far: it relies on the ID value being set when the object is first saved to the database:

```
Public Property Get InvoiceID() As Long

  InvoiceID = mudtProps.InvoiceID

End Property
```

We discussed, earlier, how the `Invoice` is a parent object having line items as child objects. In order for the UI to add line items to the invoice, we need to expose the `InvoiceItems` collection for its use:

```
Public Property Get InvoiceItems() As InvoiceItems

  Set InvoiceItems = mobjItems

End Property
```

As with the `Video` and `Tapes` objects, the `Invoice` object will rely heavily on the `InvoiceItems` object to manage the child objects.

### Read-only Properties from Other Objects

The next few properties are more interesting. A couple of times, earlier in the chapter, we discussed how valuable it can be to include read-only properties on an object that provides data belonging to another object. These properties are actually part of the `Customer` object, but they're virtually always used on any invoice display - so we'll make them read-only properties for ease of use and performance reasons. Add these properties to the `Invoice` class:

```
Public Property Get CustomerID() As Long

  CustomerID = mudtProps.CustomerID

End Property

Public Property Get CustomerName() As String

  CustomerName = Trim$(mudtProps.CustomerName)

End Property

Public Property Get CustomerPhone() As String

  CustomerPhone = Trim$(mudtProps.CustomerPhone)

End Property
```

We'll go into how these fields are initially loaded in a short while. In Chapters 8 and 10, we'll see how these fields are actually brought in from the database.

### Calculated Properties

Any invoice involves the collection of money. In our case, the invoice needs to have a total amount for all the line items, plus any applicable sales tax amount, and then a final total to charge the customer. All three values hinge, almost entirely, on getting a total amount for all the line items: a value we'll refer to as a **subtotal** for the invoice.

This is one of those cases where the `Invoice` object will let the `InvoiceItems` collection object do quite a lot of the work. We'll discuss this collection object in a bit, and we'll take a closer look at the implementation of its `SubTotal` method. Suffice it to say that it calculates the total amount due for all the line items, and returns it for our use here:

```
Public Property Get SubTotal() As Double

   SubTotal = mobjItems.SubTotal

End Property
```

Once we have a subtotal for the invoice, the rest is easy. Sales tax is simply a percentage calculation based on the subtotal and rounded to the nearest penny:

```
Public Property Get Tax() As Double

   Tax = Val(Format$(mobjItems.SubTotal * 0.065 + 0.0005, "0.00"))

End Property
```

> *The rounding technique we're using here is quite common in dealing with financial values, although it looks a bit odd at first glance. In particular, you may be wondering why we're adding .0005 to the value before rounding it with* Format$(). *To see why it's important, try running the following line of code in the Immediate window:*
>
> ```
> ? Format$(.0045,"0.00")
> ```
>
> *We'd expect to get a result of 0.01, since the 5 should round up the 4 to a 5 and that should, in turn, round up the right-most 0 to a 1. This doesn't happen; instead, the result is 0.00.*
>
> *Now try this line:*
>
> ```
> ? Format$(.0045+.0005,"0.00")
> ```
>
> *Now we get the desired result of 0.01. Just one of those little tricks that comes in useful from time to time.*
>
> *Visual Basic 6.0 provides a new* Round *method. Unfortunately, this method doesn't provide appropriate rounding functionality for financial amounts either, so we've opted against its use in this case.*

With both a subtotal and a tax amount, calculating the total due in an invoice is as simple as adding the two together:

```
Public Property Get Total() As Double

   Total = SubTotal + Tax

End Property
```

Notice how we use the SubTotal and Tax properties themselves within this property. This is intentional: we want to ensure that any business rules or processing that happens in those properties is also applied to the calculation of the total. So in this case, we're getting the same rounding effect on the tax amount as when the UI code retrieved it via the Tax property, without duplicating the code to do the rounding.

## Creating an Invoice Object

Our `Invoice` object so far has only one method outside the ones from the business object template code and that's the `Initialize` method. This method is called in the `Customer` object's `CreateInvoice` routine that we created in Chapter 5, though we left it commented out at that time. Since we'll be building the code to create the Invoice now, let's open the `Customer` class module and uncomment that method:

```
Public Function CreateInvoice() As Invoice

  Dim objInvoice As Invoice

  Set objInvoice = New Invoice
  objInvoice.Initialize Me
  Set CreateInvoice = objInvoice
  Set objInvoice = Nothing

End Function
```

The only way to add a new invoice to the system is through this method on the `Customer` object. This is important, since any invoice must have a customer, and this mechanism determines that we have one to work with when we're setting up the `Invoice` object.

The `Customer` object calls our `Invoice` object's `Initialize` method, passing itself as a parameter. This means that our method can pull any information it needs right off the `Customer` object - very slick. Add this code to the `Invoice` code module:

```
Friend Sub Initialize(Renter As Customer)

  With Renter
    mudtProps.CustomerID = .CustomerID
    mobjValid.RuleBroken "Customer", .IsNew
    mudtProps.CustomerName = .Name
    mudtProps.CustomerPhone = .Phone
    mobjItems.LoadFees .CustomerID
  End With

End Sub
```

Of course, the routine is set up as `Friend`, since it will only be called from the `Customer` object. After all, we don't want to let the UI developer call this routine directly, we want to make sure they've identified a valid customer first.

The routine is not complex: it simply copies the `CustomerID`, `Name` and `Phone` properties from the `Customer` object into the `Invoice` object itself.

There is also a check that the `Customer` object really is valid:

```
  mobjValid.RuleBroken "Customer", .IsNew
```

Obviously, we have a `Customer` object; but to be truly valid it can't be a new customer. We need to make sure the customer data is in the database. Fortunately, that's easily determined by checking the `IsNew` property of the object, since `IsNew` will always return `False` if it's been saved to the database.

Also notice the call to `mobjItems.LoadFees`:

```
mobjItems.LoadFees .CustomerID
```

We'll look more closely at this method when we implement the `InvoiceItems` collection object. Its purpose is to ensure that we add line items to the invoice for all outstanding late fee records associated with the customer. This routine accepts the `CustomerID` field as a parameter so that it can find those records and create line item objects for them.

Once the `Initialize` method has been called, the `Invoice` object is all set. Of course, the user will undoubtedly add some line items for the tapes that are being rented, but that's handled through the `InvoiceItems` collection object.

# InvoiceItem: An Interface Class

Before we get into the collection object itself, let's take a look at the child objects that it will contain. These are a bit more complex than the simple `Tape` object that we implemented earlier in the chapter, since we now have two different things we need to represent.

Our line items will be either a tape that's being rented (`InvoiceTape`) or a late fee (`InvoiceFee`) that needs to be paid. This is shown in the following figure:

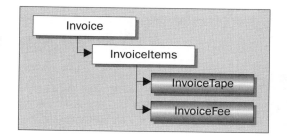

Each object is different, but they do have substantial similarities.

In Chapter 1, we discussed how objects can have multiple interfaces. All objects have their default interface, composed of the `Public` properties and methods we implement. Objects can also have other interfaces, created through the use of the `Implements` keyword. This technique is called **interface inheritance**.

Now we're going to use some of that background to add a common interface, `InvoiceItem`, to both of our new invoice line item objects. The `InvoiceItem` interface will have all the properties and methods that are common to both types of line item, while each line item object's default interface will have properties and methods specific to that type of item.

We'll also discuss some limitations that Visual Basic has imposed on the `Implements` keyword. While it's very powerful, there are some things it doesn't handle as well as we might hope.

## *Setting up the InvoiceItem Class*

Add a generic class module to the `VideoObjects` project. Change its **Name** property to `InvoiceItem` and set its **Instancing** property to 2-PublicNotCreatable.

Interface objects typically need to have their **Instancing** property set to something other than **Private**. If we attempt to set the property to 1-Private then we can't use the `InvoiceItem` class name in any **Public** property or method on any other object. If we do so, we'll get a compile error:

'User-defined types and fixed-length strings not allowed as the type of public member of an object module; private object modules not allowed as the type of a public member of a public object module'

## InvoiceItem Properties and Methods

The idea behind an interface class like `InvoiceItem` is to build an interface so that many of the operations we'll need to perform on the child objects are included. For instance, we know that we'll need to run through all the child objects adding up the total amount due for each one, indicating a `Total` property. Without a common interface containing this property, we'd have to use late-binding to run through all the child objects.

In such a case, our client code could look something like this:

```
Dim objItem As Object

For Each objItem In mcolItems
   dblTotal = dblTotal + objItem.Total
Next
```

While this code looks simple enough, it has declared `objItem` as type `Object` - and so it's using late-binding. Not only do we get a serious performance hit, but we've lost the ability to have Visual Basic perform compile-time checking on our call to the `Total` method.

If all the child objects implement the `InvoiceItem` interface, we can use early-binding to accomplish the same thing much faster - and with full compile-time checking by Visual Basic:

```
Dim objItem As InvoiceItem

For Each objItem In mcolItems
   dblTotal = dblTotal + objItem.Total
Next
```

### Possible Set of Properties and Methods

Since `InvoiceItem` is just an interface class, there won't be any code included. The only thing that's important in an object of this type is the declaration of all the properties and methods. As we discussed in Chapter 1, the purpose of an interface class is merely to define the properties and methods that make up the interface - each object implementing that interface needs to supply the code behind each property and method.

We know that `InvoiceFee` and `InvoiceTape` will be child business objects, so we know they'll both have the set of child methods and properties that entail:

```
BeginEdit        CancelEdit
ApplyEdit        Delete
IsValid          IsNew
IsDirty          IsDeleted
ChildBeginEdit   ChildCancelEdit
ChildApplyEdit   ChildLoad
```

Here's where one of the major limitations of Implements comes into play. When an object Implements the interface of another object, only the Public properties and methods come across. Anything declared as Friend or Private won't show up. At the same time, we have good reasons for declaring a number of these elements using Friend; in particular, we don't want them available to any client code!

### Final Set of Properties and Methods

This leaves us with a smaller set of interface elements that we can include in our InvoiceItem interface object:

```
Option Explicit

Public Sub BeginEdit()

End Sub

Public Sub CancelEdit()

End Sub

Public Sub ApplyEdit()
End Sub

Public Sub Delete()
End Sub

Public Property Get IsValid() As Boolean

End Property

Public Property Get IsNew() As Boolean

End Property

Public Property Get IsDirty() As Boolean

End Property

Public Property Get IsDeleted() As Boolean

End Property
```

Of course, we know that we'll have a couple of less generic properties in these objects as well. We'll now add the Total property to this object; we've already discussed this property and its role, and all we need to include here is its declaration:

```
Public Property Get Total() As Double

End Property
```

To make it easy to display the list of line items, we should also include some form of description for each item:

```
Public Property Get ItemDescription() As String

End Property
```

### ItemType Property: Indicating the Type of Object

When we're dealing with a common interface and multiple objects that use that interface, it's often very useful to be able to find out just what type of object we're talking to. Once we know what type of object is actually behind the common interface, we can then write code that talks to that object's native interface - in case we need to do anything that isn't supported by the more generic common interface we're implementing here.

For instance, we may want to treat an `InvoiceTape` object differently than an `InvoiceFee` object at times. If we're using the `InvoiceItem` interface to walk through all the line items on an `Invoice`, we'll need some way to find out which type of object we're really working with at any given time.

To support multiple object types, we'll add a property to return the value:

```
Public Property Get ItemType() As ItemTypes

End Property
```

Notice that this property returns a value of type `ItemTypes`. A good way of implementing this as an Enum, or as a set of enumerated values. We can simply add the declaration of the list at the top of the `InvoiceItem` class module:

```
Option Explicit

Public Enum ItemTypes
   ITEM_TAPE = 0
   ITEM_FEE = 1
End Enum
```

Since this Enum is `Public`, it will be available for our use throughout our project, so we can use it to determine the type of each object without resorting to cryptic numeric values like 0 and 1. We could write code such as this:

```
If objItem.ItemType = ITEM_FEE Then

   Set objFee = objItem
   ' now we can use the native interface of objFee
End If
```

Now that we have a common interface to implement within each actual child object, it's time to move on. We'll have two child classes, `InvoiceFee` and `InvoiceTape`. Each will have its own native interface, and each will use `Implements` to include the `InvoiceItem` interface as well.

# InvoiceFee: A Read-only Child Object

As a child object, `InvoiceFee` will be very similar to the `Tape` object that we implemented earlier:

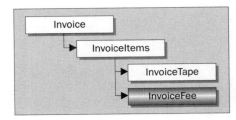

Fortunately, though, the `InvoiceFee` object will never be used as a standalone object like `Tape`. The UI code will never be able to directly create an `InvoiceFee` object; instead, it will need to get at the objects through the `Invoice` object.

This simplifies things, since we need a little less code to keep track of whether or not the object is a child at any given point. At the same time, however, we do still need to provide support for the parent-child relationship - just as we did with the `Tape` object - and so the code will be very similar overall.

## Setting up the InvoiceFee Class

Add a new class to the `VideoObjects` project. It's easiest to make it a generic class module to start off. Then just copy the template routines plus the module-level declarations from the `Tape` class into this class, since the differences between these two classes will be fairly minor. These routines are:

| | | |
|---|---|---|
| `BeginEdit` | `CancelEdit` | `ApplyEdit` |
| `Delete` | `IsValid` | `IsDirty` |
| `IsNew` | `IsDeleted` | `ChildBeginEdit` |
| `ChildCancelEdit` | `ChildApplyEdit` | `ChildLoad` |
| `Class_Initialize` | `mobjValid_BrokenRule` | `mobjValid_NoBrokenRules` |

Set the **Name** property to `InvoiceFee`, and make the **Instancing** property 2-PublicNotCreatable.

Rather than going back through all the parent-child relationship code that we covered with the `Tape` object, I'll just highlight the differences in this code as compared to the `Tape` class. Then we'll go through the properties that are specific to this object, and, finally, we'll implement the `InvoiceItem` interface.

### Declarations

We'll need to replace the UDT from the `Tape` class with one appropriate for our new object. All the variable declarations for that UDT will need to be updated as well.

```
Option Explicit

Event Valid(IsValid As Boolean)

Private Type FeeProps
  InvoiceID As Long
  FeeID As Long
  VideoTitle As String * 30
  EnteredDate As Date
  DaysOver As Integer
End Type

Private mudtProps As FeeProps
Private mudtSave As FeeProps
Private mudtChild As FeeProps

'Private mobjParent As Tape

Private mflgNew As Boolean
Private mflgDeleted As Boolean
Private mflgDirty As Boolean
Private mflgEditing As Boolean
Private mflgChildEditing As Boolean
Private WithEvents mobjValid As BrokenRules
```

Like any other business object, we've added in a UDT, and the variables based on that type. We'll use these throughout the rest of the code, and we'll review the elements of the UDT as we use each one.

It's also worth noting that the `mflgChild` variable is not declared here. Since this object is always a child object, we don't need that variable to keep track of whether or not we are a child.

Additionally, this object will never be created directly by the user, only via the process of checking in a tape after its due date. This means we won't need the `mobjParent` variable and so we can remove its declaration. I've commented it out in the code above.

### Updating the Code

These routines ought to be very familiar by now. They are almost the same as the `Tape` object's implementation. The highlighted lines all have a common theme, in that with the `Tape` object they had an extra check to determine if the object was a child or not. In this case, we can assume that we're always a child - so those checks have been removed:

```
Public Sub BeginEdit()

    If Not mflgChildEditing Then Err.Raise 445
    If mflgEditing Then Err.Raise 445

    ' save object state
    LSet mudtSave = mudtProps
    mflgEditing = True

End Sub

Public Sub CancelEdit()

    If Not mflgChildEditing Then Err.Raise 445
    If Not mflgEditing Then Err.Raise 445

    mflgEditing = False
    mflgDeleted = False
    ' restore object state
    LSet mudtProps = mudtSave

End Sub

Public Sub Delete()

    If Not mflgChildEditing Then Err.Raise 445
    If Not mflgEditing Then Err.Raise 445

    mflgDeleted = True
    mflgDirty = True

End Sub
```

The `ApplyEdit` method is simplified even more:

```
Public Sub ApplyEdit()

    If Not mflgChildEditing Then Err.Raise 445
    If Not mflgEditing Then Err.Raise 445
```

```
    mflgEditing = False

End Sub
```

In the `Tape` object, this routine had a fair amount of code, but it was all there for when `mflgChild` was set to `False`. In this case, `InvoiceFee` is always a child, and so we can remove that entire code block.

There's been no `Load` method so far either. The `Load` method exists in the other objects - so that the client code can create the object and then call `Load` to have the object loaded from the database. This entire sequence of events is invalid if the object is only a child, and so we don't need a `Load` method. We'll still have a `ChildLoad` method, though, which we'll look at in this next bit of code:

```
Friend Sub ChildLoad(FeeID As Long)

    If mflgChildEditing Then Err.Raise 445
    If Not mflgNew Then Err.Raise 445

' code to load the object goes here

    mflgNew = False

End Sub
```

The modifications to this code are pretty simple, just making the code readable by changing the parameter name. The `ChildBeginEdit` and `ChildCancelEdit` routines are unchanged from the code we've copied:

```
Friend Sub ChildBeginEdit()

    If mflgChildEditing Then Err.Raise 445

    ' save object state
    LSet mudtChild = mudtProps
    mflgChildEditing = True

End Sub

Friend Sub ChildCancelEdit()

    If Not mflgChildEditing Then Err.Raise 445

    mflgChildEditing = False
    mflgDeleted = False
    ' restore object state
    LSet mudtProps = mudtChild

End Sub
```

Again, these routines ought to be very familiar, as they are directly out of the `Tape` object. The `ChildApplyEdit` routine needs a bit of alteration to fit into our new object. We need to change the parameter that the routine expects from `VideoID` to `InvoiceID` and make sure that a value is placed into the UDT variable. Also we need to comment out or remove the code that deals with the late fee, as it only applies to the `Tape` object. Otherwise, the code remains the same:

```
   Friend Sub ChildApplyEdit(InvoiceID As Long)

     If Not mflgChildEditing Then Err.Raise 445

     If mflgDeleted And Not mflgNew Then
       ' code to delete the object's data goes here
       mflgNew = True
       mflgDeleted = False

     ElseIf mflgDirty Or mflgNew Then
       If Not IsValid Then Err.Raise 445
       mudtProps.InvoiceID = InvoiceID
       ' save object to database if appropriate
'        If mudtProps.LateFee Then
'          ' add the late fee to the customer
'        End If
       ' save object state
       LSet mudtChild = mudtProps  .
       mflgNew = False

     End If

     mflgDirty = False
     mflgChildEditing = False

   End Sub
```

The `Tape` object implemented a `SetAsChild` method so that we could tell it to become a child by setting `mflgChild` to `True`. `InvoiceFee` is always a child, so we need neither the `mflgChild` variable nor the `SetAsChild` method.

The `Class_Initialize` routine needs a minor change. In the `Tape` object, we had some code to indicate that the `DateAcquired` field was invalid. This line of code needs to be removed from the `InvoiceFee` object's code, since it doesn't even have a `DateAcquired` field. I've shown the offending line, here, commented out:

```
Private Sub Class_Initialize()

  mflgNew = True
  Set mobjValid = New BrokenRules
  ' if we know any rules are broken on startup
  ' then add code here to initialize the list
  ' of broken rules
  '
  ' mobjValid.RuleBroken "RuleName", True
  ' mobjValid.RuleBroken "DateAcquired", True

End Sub
```

The remaining business object routines from the business object template are totally unchanged - so I won't repeat their code here.

## *InvoiceFee Properties*

The InvoiceFee object is a read-only representation of a late fee. A customer gets a late fee when they return a tape after its due date. We implemented this in the Tape object by adding code to the CheckIn method that checks the due date. Then, in the code to save the Tape object to the database, we noted that we would need some code to add a record in a late fee table associated with the customer.

Since that is the only way a late fee can be added to our system, there will be no mechanism for the UI code to add an InvoiceFee object directly. Therefore, each InvoiceFee object will be loaded from the database to represent one of those late fee records. Essentially, we're creating objects so that they can be viewed or displayed, but not created or edited.

This property, roughly corresponds to the Property Get TapeID that we implemented in the Tape class:

```
Public Property Get FeeID() As Long

  FeeID = mudtProps.FeeID

End Property
```

Like all the other objects, these will have had an ID value assigned when the record was added to the database. Now we add a VideoTitle property that is synonymous with the Title property in the Tape class:

```
Public Property Get VideoTitle() As String

  VideoTitle = Trim$(mudtProps.VideoTitle)

End Property
```

In our UDT, we included a field for the video's title. This is primarily because the system will need to put something on the invoice so that the customer knows what the late fee is for. When we added the late fee record, we knew how many days late the tape was being returned. This property just returns the number of days that were recorded at that time:

```
Public Property Get DaysOver() As Integer

  DaysOver = mudtProps.DaysOver

End Property
```

The InvoiceFee object represents a fee for some tape that was returned late. In this case, we've put in code to charge $1.50 for each day the tape was late. A full-blown video rental system might have some more complex calculation here, but we'll keep things as simple as possible.

```
Public Property Get Fee() As Double

  Fee = DaysOver * 1.5

End Property
```

Our Fee routine calls the DaysOver property to get the number of days the tape was overdue. While we could get the same value from mudtProps.DaysOver, it's always wise to use the object's properties, since we might add some business rules into the property, and then we'd want to make sure that those properties were used in calculating the fee, without duplicating the code.

*At the same time, keep in mind that performance can be much better when accessing a simple variable rather than calling a property routine. While calling a property routine ensures that our business logic is enforced, it is faster to work directly with the variables. If, for your application, performance is more critical than easily maintained code you may need to think carefully about how to implement this type of code.*

The first question that a lot of customers will ask is when the late fee occurred. To answer that question, we'll add an EnteredDate property:

```
Public Property Get EnteredDate() As Date

  EnteredDate = mudtProps.EnteredDate

End Property
```

The date returned, here, is the date that the late fee was recorded in the database. We'll get into the actual database design in Chapter 8, but trust me, this field will be in there.

## Implementing the InvoiceItem Interface

Now that we've got the InvoiceFee object implemented, we can add in the code that we need to support the InvoiceItem interface. Because we've already implemented the entire object, adding this interface will be quite simple.

### Declarations

First, add the Implements InvoiceItem line to the top of the InvoiceFee class module:

```
Option Explicit

Implements InvoiceItem

Event Valid(IsValid As Boolean)
```

Looking at the Object list in the upper-left of the code window, we find that InvoiceItem is one of the options. Choose it as an option, and then look at the Procedure list in the upper-right of the code window. This list now shows all the properties and methods that we added to the InvoiceItem class earlier.

The trick in implementing an interface like this is that Visual Basic *requires* that all the properties and methods of that interface are coded within your module. This can be limiting if we don't actually *want* all of them in our new object. Fortunately, we've planned ahead and only included the interface elements that are common to both our child objects in our InvoiceItem class.

## Implementing the Properties and Methods

Now let's look at the implementation of those interface elements. Many of these properties and methods are duplicated in the object's native interface. What we've done here is to implement the native interface so all those properties and methods contain the code. With those routines already coded, we can just have each routine in the `InvoiceItem` interface call the corresponding routine that we've already written.

For instance, let's look at `InvoiceItem_BeginEdit`:

```
Private Sub InvoiceItem_BeginEdit()

   BeginEdit

End Sub
```

The fact that this routine is declared as `Private` and that the routine name includes `InvoiceItem_` before the normal name is quite usual and normal itself. We discussed how this works in Chapter 1, and it may be worth referring back to that if this seems confusing.

The most interesting aspect of this routine is that it has virtually no code. Instead, we're just deferring the call to the `BeginEdit` method that we've already implemented. There is no sense in duplicating code here to do the same thing, so this makes good sense.

An alternative would be to add a third routine to contain the implementation and have both `BeginEdit` and `InvoiceItem_BeginEdit` call that routine. This is perfectly valid, but adds a lot of extra procedures to the module to accomplish the same goal.

Most of the remaining interface elements are implemented the same way:

```
Private Sub InvoiceItem_ApplyEdit()

   ApplyEdit

End Sub

Private Sub InvoiceItem_CancelEdit()

   CancelEdit

End Sub

Private Sub InvoiceItem_Delete()

   Delete

End Sub

Private Property Get InvoiceItem_IsDeleted() As Boolean

   InvoiceItem_IsDeleted = IsDeleted

End Property
```

```
Private Property Get InvoiceItem_IsDirty() As Boolean

  InvoiceItem_IsDirty = IsDirty

End Property
```

```
Private Property Get InvoiceItem_IsNew() As Boolean

  InvoiceItem_IsNew = IsNew

End Property
```

```
Private Property Get InvoiceItem_IsValid() As Boolean

  InvoiceItem_IsValid = IsValid

End Property
```

We haven't implemented an `ItemDescription` or a `Total` property in our `InvoiceFee` object so far. Instead, we've implemented `Title` and `Fee` properties that do essentially the same function but have more descriptive names. This is still no problem: we'll just call the appropriate property from within the `ItemDescription` and `Total` properties:

```
Private Property Get InvoiceItem_ItemDescription() As String

  InvoiceItem_ItemDescription = VideoTitle

End Property
```

```
Private Property Get InvoiceItem_Total() As Double

  InvoiceItem_Total = Fee

End Property
```

### Implementing the ItemType Property

The only remaining property to be implemented is `ItemType`. This property is a bit different, since it has no analogous property within `InvoiceFee` so far. It doesn't make sense for the `InvoiceFee` interface to include an `ItemType` property, however, since if we have a reference to an `InvoiceFee` object using its native interface then we know what kind of object we have.

`ItemType` is only useful within the `InvoiceItem` interface, because otherwise we have no way of knowing what kind of object is actually behind the interface. Thus the implementation of this property within the `InvoiceFee` object is simple: it just needs to return `ITEM_FEE` to indicate that it is an `InvoiceFee` object:

```
Private Property Get InvoiceItem_ItemType() As ItemTypes

  InvoiceItem_ItemType = ITEM_FEE

End Property
```

With this simple code, we've added an entire second interface to our `InvoiceFee` object. Any code using our object can now get at it through either the native `InvoiceFee` interface or through the `InvoiceItem` interface, whichever is more appropriate.

# InvoiceTape: An Aggregate Child Object

The `InvoiceTape` object is very similar to `InvoiceFee` in most respects. Sure, it has some different properties in its native interface but it, too, will implement the `InvoiceItem` interface - and so client code can use it in exactly the same way as it would use `InvoiceFee`.

## Setting up the InvoiceTape Class

We can take advantage of the similarity between the `InvoiceFee` object and what we need for the `InvoiceTape` object. Using the `VideoObjects` project, add a generic class module and copy the business object template routines plus the declarations from `InvoiceFee` into this new module. We won't be changing those very much, so that makes a good start.

This is the list of routines that should be copied:

| | | |
|---|---|---|
| BeginEdit | CancelEdit | ApplyEdit |
| Delete | IsValid | IsDirty |
| IsNew | IsDeleted | ChildBeginEdit |
| ChildCancelEdit | ChildApplyEdit | ChildLoad |
| Class_Initialize | mobjValid_BrokenRule | mobjValid_NoBrokenRules |

Set the **Name** property to `InvoiceTape` and the **Instancing** property to **2-PublicNotCreatable**. The UI code will need access to the object, but only through the `Invoice` object, so we don't want to make the routine publicly creatable:

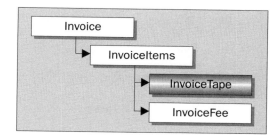

Of course, this object will have its own UDT, but beyond that the general declarations section of the module will be the same as `InvoiceFee`. Here's the UDT for `InvoiceTape`:

```
Private Type InvoiceTapeProps
   InvoiceID As Long
   ItemID As Long
   TapeID As Long
   Title As String * 30
   Price As Double
End Type

Private mudtProps As InvoiceTapeProps
Private mudtSave As InvoiceTapeProps
Private mudtChild As InvoiceTapeProps
```

In our `Tape` object we added code so a new `Tape` object would add itself to the `Tapes` collection in the `ApplyEdit` method. We need to do the same thing here in the `InvoiceTape` object. When a new `InvoiceTape` object is created by the `InvoiceItems` object it isn't automatically added to the collection. Instead, we need to make sure it gets added to the collection when the `InvoiceTape` object is accepted by the user.

To do this we'll change the `ApplyEdit` method as shown:

```
Public Sub ApplyEdit()

  If Not mflgChildEditing Then Err.Raise 445
  If Not mflgEditing Then Err.Raise 445

  If Not mobjParent Is Nothing Then
    mobjParent.AddTape Me
    Set mobjParent = Nothing
  End If

  mflgEditing = False

End Sub
```

This is the same code we added to the Tape object's `ApplyEdit` method, so it should be pretty familiar. We also need to declare the `mobjParent` variable in the declarations section of the `InvoiceTape` object's code module:

```
  Private mobjParent As InvoiceItems
```

We'll implement the remainder of the code relating to the `mobjParent` variable as we go through the rest of this code module.

The only change to the remainder of the template code is that we need to modify the `ChildLoad` method. This is the same as the `ChildLoad` method from the `Tape` object, except we need to pass an appropriate parameter to identify the specific invoice line item:

```
  Friend Sub ChildLoad(ItemID As Long)

    If mflgChildEditing Then Err.Raise 445
    If Not mflgNew Then Err.Raise 445

  ' code to load the object goes here

    mflgNew = False

  End Sub
```

## InvoiceTape Properties

The `InvoiceTape` object's properties are different from `InvoiceFee`, although there are similarities. Still, the fact that they are different highlights the reason it made sense to implement a common interface using `InvoiceItem`.

As usual, this object will have an ID value that's assigned when it is first saved to the database:

```
  Public Property Get ItemID() As Long

    ItemID = mudtProps.ItemID

  End Property
```

To make it easy to display the line item on a screen, we need to make sure that the video tape's title is available. Even though this field originated on the `Video` object, we'll duplicate it here to prevent us from having to instantiate an entire `Video` object just to get it. This is our new version:

```
Public Property Get Title() As String

  Title = Trim$(mudtProps.Title)

End Property
```

When a tape is rented, we need to establish a price. In the `Initialize` method, we'll take the simple approach of making the default price be $1.99 for all tapes. Still, there are cases where a price needs to be overridden - and so we'll make the `Price` property read-write by implementing a `Property Let`:

```
Public Property Let Price(Value As Double)

  mudtProps.Price = Value
  mobjValid.RuleBroken "Price", (Value < 0 Or Value > 4)
  mflgDirty = True

End Property
```

A fair amount of the template code that we included in both `InvoiceFee` and `InvoiceTape` is unused in this program. As we discussed earlier, when we were working with the `InvoiceTape` object, there are certain advantages to leaving this unused code within our objects, such as the facility to enhance our objects at a later date.

It would be quite possible to go through and remove a lot of the code in these objects, since they are very simple.

> *Applications tend to evolve over time. An object that starts out very simple may become more and more complex, to support new application functionality. Were we to strip each object down to its barest code, eliminating all support for concepts like business rules, editing, and so forth, we'd end up with objects that were difficult to enhance later. While there is some cost associated in having this extra code in each object, it's usually well worth it later when the object needs to be enhanced.*

The `Property Get Price` routine just returns the value stored in `mudtProps`, whether that be the $1.99 from the `Initialize` method, or a value entered by the user through the `Property Let` we just implemented:

```
Public Property Get Price() As Double

  Price = mudtProps.Price

End Property
```

## InvoiceTape Methods

The `InvoiceTape` object represents a tape that is being rented via this invoice. One line item will be added to the invoice for each tape that the customer is renting, so we need to make sure we provide a mechanism for the UI code to easily add new line items.

The `InvoiceItems` collection object will provide an `Add` method, so the UI code can add a line item. The only line items that can be added are those to rent a tape; all the late fee items come from previous tape returns, as we discussed earlier.

Since the line items we'll be adding revolve around a specific tape that's being rented, it makes sense to use a `Tape` object to get any information we'll need for our new line item. To this end, we'll add an `Initialize` method that accepts a `Tape` object as a parameter. The `Tape` object itself will be created in the `InvoiceItems` object's `Add` method, based on the `TapeID` of the tape chosen by the user.

```
Friend Sub Initialize(RentalTape As Tape, Parent As InvoiceItems)

  If mflgNew Then Set mobjParent = Parent

  With RentalTape
    mudtProps.TapeID = .TapeID
    mudtProps.Title= .Title
    mudtProps.Price = 1.99
  End With

End Sub
```

The `Initialize` method itself just copies the properties of interest from the `RentalTape` object into the `mudtProps` variable within `InvoiceTape`.

In this case, we've just fixed the price at $1.99 to rent a tape for simplicity. A more comprehensive application might store the price on the `Tape` object, or perhaps base the price on some other more complex criteria.

This method also accepts a `Parent` parameter which we'll store if the `InvoiceTape` object is new. This fills the same role as the `SetAsChild` method in our `Tape` object, where we need to have a reference back to the parent object. In this case we need a reference back to the `InvoiceItems` object that created the `InvoiceTape` object so we can call the `AddTape` method of that object if the user accepts the `InvoiceTape` object.

## Implementing the InvoiceItem Interface

As with the `InvoiceFee` object, the code to implement the `InvoiceItem` interface is very straightforward. All the routines, except `ItemType`, just call the appropriate property or method from the `InvoiceTape` object's native interface.

Most of this code is identical to the `InvoiceItem` interface we created for the `InvoiceFee` object:

```
Private Sub InvoiceItem_ApplyEdit()

  ApplyEdit

End Sub

Private Sub InvoiceItem_BeginEdit()

  BeginEdit

End Sub
```

```
Private Sub InvoiceItem_CancelEdit()

  CancelEdit

End Sub

Private Sub InvoiceItem_Delete()

  Delete

End Sub

Private Property Get InvoiceItem_IsDeleted() As Boolean

  InvoiceItem_IsDeleted = IsDeleted

End Property

Private Property Get InvoiceItem_IsDirty() As Boolean

  InvoiceItem_IsDirty = IsDirty

End Property

Private Property Get InvoiceItem_IsNew() As Boolean

  InvoiceItem_IsNew = IsNew

End Property

Private Property Get InvoiceItem_IsValid() As Boolean

  InvoiceItem_IsValid = IsValid

End Property

Private Property Get InvoiceItem_ItemDescription() As String

  InvoiceItem_ItemDescription = Title

End Property

Private Property Get InvoiceItem_Total() As Double

  InvoiceItem_Total = Price

End Property
```

The `InvoiceFee` object's `ItemType` property returned `ITEM_FEE`, and the `InvoiceTape` object will have the same code, just returning `ITEM_TAPE` instead:

```
Private Property Get InvoiceItem_ItemType() As ItemTypes

  InvoiceItem_ItemType = ITEM_TAPE

End Property
```

# InvoiceItems: A Parent-Child Collection Object

Now that we have the child objects ready to go, all that remains is to put together the collection object to manage them. This object is just like the `Tapes` object we implemented earlier, but with one twist: this collection will contain two types of child objects.

There are a number of routines in a parent-child collection object like this that loop through all the child objects. Where possible, we'll use the `InvoiceItem` interface to the child objects for this. Unfortunately, it is a rare case that we can do this, since a lot of the methods we need to call are implemented as `Friend` - so they aren't available to the UI developer; but this also prevented us from making them part of the `InvoiceItem` interface.

## Setting up the InvoiceItems Class

Add a new class module to the `VideoObjects` project. Make it a generic class module, then copy all the code from the `Tapes` class into this one. We'll use that code as a base, since it gets us most of the way there.

Set the **Name** property to **InvoiceItems** and the **Instancing** property to **2-PublicNotCreatable**. The only time this object should be created is within an `Invoice` object, although it will be used by the UI code through the `Invoice` object's `InvoiceItems` property.

The (General) (Declarations) section should be fine; just change `mcolTapes` to `mcolItems` for clarity:

```
Option Explicit

Private mcolItems As Collection
Private mflgEditing As Boolean
```

As usual, we'll have a `Class_Initialize` to create the `Collection` object itself:

```
Private Sub Class_Initialize()

    Set mcolItems = New Collection

End Sub
```

Since this is a collection, we've got the standard `Item`, `Count` and `NewEnum` methods. These are essentially unchanged but for the name of the collection variable:

```
Public Function Item(ByVal Index As Variant) As InvoiceItem

    Set Item = mcolItems(Index)

End Function

Public Function Count() As Long

    Count = mcolItems.Count

End Function
```

```
Public Function NewEnum() As IUnknown

    Set NewEnum = mcolItems.[_NewEnum]

End Function
```

*Again, remember to use the Tools | Property Attributes menu option to set* Item *to be the default method and* NewEnum *with a Procedure ID of –4 and to be hidden.*

## BeginEdit Method

The BeginEdit method needs some work. This is the first case where we loop through all the child objects, so it would be nice to use the InvoiceItem interface. Unfortunately, the method we need to call is ChildBeginEdit, and it is declared as a Friend within each child class. Still, we'll use the InvoiceItem interface to get at the ItemType property, so it's not a total loss:

```
Public Sub BeginEdit()

    Dim objInvoiceItem As InvoiceItem
    Dim objTape As InvoiceTape
    Dim objFee As InvoiceFee

    If mflgEditing Then Err.Raise 445

    For Each objInvoiceItem In mcolItems
       If objInvoiceItem.ItemType = ITEM_FEE Then
          Set objFee = objInvoiceItem
          objFee.ChildBeginEdit

       Else
          Set objTape = objInvoiceItem
          objTape.ChildBeginEdit

       End If

    Next

    mflgEditing = True

End Sub
```

We put each item from the collection into a variable, called objInvoiceItem, which is declared as type InvoiceItem. This variable uses the InvoiceItem interface to whatever child object we're looking at, regardless of whether it is an InvoiceFee or InvoiceTape. This means that we can use the ItemType property to find out with which type of object we are dealing:

```
If objInvoiceItem.ItemType = ITEM_FEE Then
```

From there, we are able to use either objFee or objTape to get at the native interface of the object. For instance, if we have an InvoiceFee object, we just set the objFee variable to point to the current item:

```
Set objFee = objInvoiceItem
```

Since `objFee` is declared as type `InvoiceFee`, that's the interface it will use to get at the object. This means that we can now call the native properties and methods from the `InvoiceFee` interface, including those declared as `Friend`:

```
objFee.ChildBeginEdit
```

> The only way to call a property or method declared as `Friend` is to use the default interface. Interface elements declared as `Friend` are not available through other interfaces; nor can they be used through any late-bound variable.
>
> Thus, we can't just declare `objInvoiceItem` as type `Object` and call these methods. If we're going to use the power of the `Friend` keyword then we're going to have to do this extra work.

## CancelEdit and ApplyEdit Methods

`CancelEdit` and `ApplyEdit` run along the same principle, using the `InvoiceItem` interface to find out what type of object we have, and then using a variable of that type to get at the native interface for the object:

```vb
Public Sub CancelEdit()

    Dim objInvoiceItem As InvoiceItem
    Dim objTape As InvoiceTape
    Dim objFee As InvoiceFee
    Dim lngIndex As Long

    If Not mflgEditing Then Err.Raise 445

    mflgEditing = False

    For lngIndex = mcolItems.Count To 1 Step -1
      Set objInvoiceItem = mcolItems.Item(lngIndex)
      If objInvoiceItem.ItemType = ITEM_FEE Then
        Set objFee = objInvoiceItem

        With objFee
          If .IsNew Then _
            mcolItems.Remove lngIndex
          .ChildCancelEdit
        End With

      Else
        Set objTape = objInvoiceItem

        With objTape
          .ChildCancelEdit
          If .IsNew Then _
            mcolItems.Remove lngIndex
        End With

      End If

    Next lngIndex

End Sub
```

```
Public Sub ApplyEdit(InvoiceID As Long)

  Dim objInvoiceItem As InvoiceItem
  Dim objTape As InvoiceTape
  Dim objFee As InvoiceFee
  Dim lngIndex As Long

  If Not mflgEditing Then Err.Raise 445

  For lngIndex = mcolItems.Count To 1 Step -1
    Set objInvoiceItem = mcolItems.Item(lngIndex)
    If objInvoiceItem.ItemType = ITEM_FEE Then
      Set objFee = objInvoiceItem

      With objFee
        If .IsDeleted Then _
          mcolItems.Remove lngIndex
        .ChildApplyEdit InvoiceID
      End With

    Else
      Set objTape = objInvoiceItem

      With objTape
        If .IsDeleted Then _
          mcolItems.Remove lngIndex
        .ChildApplyEdit InvoiceID
      End With

    End If

  Next lngIndex

  mflgEditing = False

End Sub
```

### Delete Method

The Delete method is a bit easier. The InvoiceItem interface has a Delete method and so we don't need to do all that work to find out what type of object we're dealing with. Instead, we'll just declare a variable of type InvoiceItem, and use it within the routine.

```
Public Sub Delete()

  Dim objInvoiceItem As InvoiceItem

  If Not mflgEditing Then Err.Raise 445

  ' code to delete the object's data goes here
  For Each objInvoiceItem In mcolItems
    With objInvoiceItem
      .BeginEdit
      .Delete
      .ApplyEdit
    End With

  Next

End Sub
```

### Load Method

Our `Load` method is as generic as ever. As with the other objects, the code for this method will be fleshed out in chapters 8 and 10. The only real difference here is that the `InvoiceID` is passed as a parameter, so we can easily find the appropriate records to load into our child objects:

```
Friend Sub Load(InvoiceID As Long)

  If mflgEditing Then Err.Raise 445

  ' here we'll put looping code to load
  ' each of the InvoiceItem objects for the InvoiceID

  ' For Each InvoiceItemID
  '   Set objInvoiceItem = New InvoiceItem
  '   objInvoiceItem.ChildLoad InvoiceItemID
  '   mcolItems.Add Item:=objInvoiceItem

  ' Loop

End Sub
```

Even though the pseudo-code is commented out, it's a good idea to update the comments to reflect the new variable names as shown here. This makes it easier to implement the code when we do add in database access.

## Add Method

Remembering back to earlier discussions about adding child objects to the invoice, we decided that it wasn't possible for the UI to add `InvoiceFee` objects. Only `InvoiceTape` objects can be added, one for each tape that the customer is going to rent.

Most video stores have barcode scanners to scan in the video tape's ID number right off the tape case. Following this line of thought, it seems reasonable to expect the UI developer to get this ID value and pass it to our `Add` method when a new line item is to be added to the invoice. So we'll change our `Add` method now:

```
Public Function Add(TapeID As Long) As InvoiceItem

  Dim objInvoiceTape As InvoiceTape
  Dim objTape As Tape

  If Not mflgEditing Then Err.Raise 445

  Set objTape = New Tape
  objTape.Load TapeID

  If objTape.CheckedOut Then
    Set objTape = Nothing
    Err.Raise vbObjectError + 1100, _
      "InvoiceItems", "Tape already checked out"
    Exit Function
  End If

  Set objInvoiceTape = New InvoiceTape
  objInvoiceTape.Initialize objTape, Me
  If mflgEditing Then objInvoiceTape.ChildBeginEdit
```

```
      Set Add = objInvoiceTape
      Set objInvoiceTape = Nothing
```

```
  End Function
```

To start with we need to make a couple of simple changes to the method declaration and variable declarations:

```
  Public Function Add(TapeID As Long) As InvoiceItem

    Dim objInvoiceTape As InvoiceTape
```

As we've already implemented the `InvoiceTape` object, we know it has an `Initialize` method that expects a `Tape` object as a parameter. Now that we've got the `TapeID` value, it should be easy enough to instantiate the appropriate object:

```
    Dim objTape As Tape

    If Not mflgEditing Then Err.Raise 445

    Set objTape = New Tape
    objTape.Load TapeID
```

We then perform a check to see if the tape has already been checked out. If it is, then we raise the error we were expecting from the code in Chapter 7 and exit the function:

```
  If objTape.CheckedOut Then
     Set objTape = Nothing
     Err.Raise vbObjectError + 1100, _
       "InvoiceItems", "Tape already checked out"
     Exit Function
  End If
```

Of course, we need to create an `InvoiceTape` child object as well:

```
    Set objInvoiceTape = New InvoiceTape
```

Since we already have a `Tape` object, we can just call our new object's `Initialize` event and use `objTape` as a parameter:

```
    objInvoiceTape.Initialize objTape
```

The remainder of the routine simply returns the value to the calling code, and cleans up. Pretty much the same as the `Tapes` object from before:

```
    If mflgEditing Then objInvoiceTape.ChildBeginEdit

    Set Add = objInvoiceTape
    Set objInvoiceTape = Nothing

  End Function
```

## AddTape Method

In the Tapes object we implemented a Friend method that is called from a new Tape object when that object needs to be added to the parent collection. We'll need to modify this method for our InvoiceItems object:

```
Friend Sub AddTape(Child As InvoiceTape)

    mcolItems.Add Item:=Child

End Sub
```

As in the Tapes object, this method simply accepts the child object as a parameter and adds it to the internal collection object. Once that's done the new child object will be treated just like any other child object that is part of the collection.

## Remove Method

As with all collection-oriented objects, we should provide the ability to remove an item from our list. Our Remove method in this case will be virtually identical to the one we implemented for the Tapes collection object:

```
Public Sub Remove(ByVal Index As Variant)

    If Not mflgEditing Then Err.Raise 445

    With mcolItems(Index)
        .BeginEdit
        .Delete
        .ApplyEdit
    End With

End Sub
```

To mark the item as deleted we simply call BeginEdit, then delete the item and call ApplyEdit to commit the change. The item isn't really deleted until the parent object, Invoice, is committed of course.

## LoadFees Method

We do have a variation on the Load method that we need to add to this object. In the Invoice object, we have an Initialize method that is called by the Customer object's CreateInvoice routine. This method's purpose is to load the customer's data into a newly created Invoice object.

All the late fees for a customer are essentially customer data, and so it's important that, when the customer's data is loaded into the Invoice object, the late fees get loaded too. We realized this earlier, and made the Invoice object's Initialize method call a LoadFees method to get those late fee records into the collection:

```
Friend Sub LoadFees(CustomerID As Long)

    If mflgEditing Then Err.Raise 445
```

```
    ' here we'll put looping code to create
    ' each of the InvoiceFee objects for the CustomerID

    ' For Each InvoiceFeeID
    '   Set objInvoiceFee = New InvoiceFee
    '   objInvoiceFee.ChildLoad InvoiceFeeID
    '   mcolItems.Add Item:=objInvoiceFee
    ' Loop

End Sub
```

As with the other data access routines in this chapter, it's just a few comments. The implementation will vary, and we'll take a look at it later in the book. We do get the `CustomerID` as a parameter, and that should be sufficient to find all unpaid late fees for that customer - so we can load them into `InvoiceFee` objects and add them to the collection.

## SubTotal Property

The last thing we need to do with this object is add a `SubTotal` property. The `Invoice` object also has a `SubTotal` property, but it relies on this property to do all the work of adding up the amount due from each line item.

Fortunately, we included a `Total` property on the `InvoiceItem` interface, and so this routine needs merely to loop through all the child objects using the `InvoiceItem` interface to get at that `Total` property.

By adding together all the `Total` properties, we'll arrive at a total due for all the line items on the entire invoice:

```
Friend Property Get SubTotal() As Double

  Dim objItem As InvoiceItem
  Dim dblAmount As Double

  For Each objItem In mcolItems
    If Not objItem.IsDeleted Then _
      dblAmount = dblAmount + objItem.Total
  Next

  SubTotal = dblAmount

End Property
```

# Summary

In this chapter we've looked at how business objects sharing a parent-child relationship can be implemented to give transactional support to the UI, so that no child's state is committed until the parent's state is saved. We've also looked at hybrid child and standalone objects, and at using shared code interfaces to take advantage of the early-binding.

These have been two long chapters, covering many issues specific to the implementation of business objects. Some key types of objects that we have created include:

- Simple business objects
- Objects returning search results for display
- Objects representing a list of text and key values
- Parent business objects
- Child business objects
- Hybrid child and standalone business objects
- Parent-child relationship objects

A lot of the routines in these objects were left with comments to indicate where database access code needs to be added. In the remaining chapters, we will use these objects to illustrate various techniques for database access using the different physical architectures covered in Chapter 4.

Here are the remaining chapters what we'll cover within them:

Chapter 7     Create a UI using Visual Basic forms
Chapter 8     Add code to our objects to save themselves to the database
Chapter 9     Create a UI using Microsoft Excel
Chapter 10    Using data-centric business objects over Distributed COM
Chapter 11    Distributing objects over DCOM
Chapter 12    Using data-centric business objects with Microsoft Transaction Server
Chapter 13    Active Server Pages and HTML as a front end
Chapter 14    Using an IIS Application as a front end
Chapter 15    Create a UI using a DHTML Application

# 7

# Visual Basic Forms as a User-Interface

## Overview

In Chapters 5 and 6, we built a fairly simple application to operate a video rental store. Of course, the application was entirely composed of business objects, with no user-interface or data access of any sort. Those were left out intentionally - to illustrate how easy and important it is to design an application's objects first, and deal with the other aspects later.

Throughout the remaining chapters, we'll be looking at how to build a variety of user-interfaces, and how to implement various different data access techniques. Probably the most common style of user-interface will be one built using Visual Basic and regular everyday Visual Basic forms. That's what we're going to cover in this chapter.

While it's certainly possible to create very rich and complex user-interfaces using Visual Basic's forms and an application designed with business objects, we're going to keep the interface in this chapter fairly simple. The logic here is quite straightforward: the most important thing, at this stage, is for us to take a clear look at the basic techniques available when we're designing a UI on top of our business objects. Once we've got the concepts down, we'll be in a position to build new and exciting interfaces for our programs.

> As we build the code in this chapter, you'll notice that we're dealing specifically with the details of this, our main example UI, and how our video objects interact with this UI. At the end of this chapter, we'll be able to compile both the business objects and an empty interface shell. In the next chapter, we'll go ahead and implement the object persistence routines that will allow our objects to interact with a database.

# VideoUI: A Visual Basic Client Project

The first thing we need to do is put together a Visual Basic project for our forms. All our business objects are contained in the `VideoObjects` project.

As we created it in Chapters 5 and 6, `VideoObjects` is an ActiveX DLL project. While we can add forms to this type of project, the user can't directly run it. We need an **EXE** project of some sort for the user to run.

It's also important to implement the UI outside of the business object DLL, to help maintain the separation of the user-interface from the application itself.

> We need to keep in mind that the business objects are the application; there may be a number of different user-interfaces that use those objects.

Our new project has no reason to be an ActiveX server of any sort. All it will contain are code modules that are to be used locally within the UI. That's not to say that it might not contain class modules: it's just that those classes would be for the use of the UI itself, not other applications.

This all boils down to our project being a Standard EXE project. So let's set one up and keep moving.

Open up Visual Basic, choose **Standard EXE** from the **New Project** dialog. Then open up the **Project Properties** window by choosing the **P**roject | Prop**e**rties menu option to change the **Project Name** field to `VideoUI`.

The easiest way to implement our user-interface program is to actually add the `VideoObjects` project right into the development environment using a project group. To do this, choose the **F**ile | A**d**d Project menu option. Use the **Add Project** dialog window to select the `VideoObjects` project, and click **OK**. This will add the `VideoObjects` project to the project window, along with our `VideoUI` project.

The `VideoUI` project should be shown in bold, with the `VideoObjects` shown in a regular font. The bold indicates which project will be run when we press the *F5* key or choose the **R**un | **S**tart menu option.

## Version Compatibility

We're going to add a reference from our `VideoUI` project to the `VideoObjects` project, but before we do this, it's very important that the **Version Compatibility** setting in the **Component** tab of the `VideoObjects` **Project Properties** dialog be set to either **Project Compatibility** or **Binary Compatibility**. In this section, we're going to take a good look at why we need to do this:

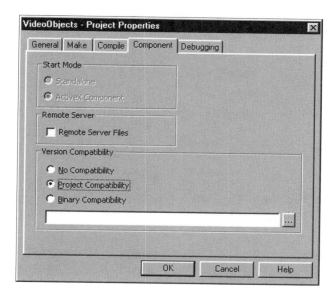

When we add a reference to an ActiveX Server, Visual Basic records the **global unique ID** (GUID) of the server, and uses it for future references. This GUID value may change each time we recompile the ActiveX server project, causing any client programs to lose their reference to the server.

> *A GUID is a 128-bit structure generated by the Win32 API. The value is created by combining the current date and time with either the ID number from the computer's ethernet card or a randomly-generated value. Microsoft has developed the GUID to provide identification values that are unique in time and space.*

A complex set of rules control how and when the GUID changes, and the Version Compatibility setting is at the heart of these rules. Let's consider this a bit further now.

### Interface Changes

We'll talk about the various Version Compatibility settings in a moment, but first let's look at the conditions under which the GUID will change. We can consider an ActiveX server's interface as being composed of all the public interface elements of all the public classes in the server. The interface is basically a contract with all our server's clients. If any part of that interface changes, then the contract could be broken - in which case there is the possibility of a GUID change on the server itself:

| Activity | Effect on server GUID |
|---|---|
| Adding a public class | Depends on Version Compatibility |
| Adding a public property/method to a public class | Depends on Version Compatibility |
| Changing a public property/method on a public class | New GUID |
| Removing a public class | New GUID |
| Removing a public property/method from a public class | New GUID |

### No Compatibility

When the Version Compatibility setting is No Compatibility, Visual Basic will generate a new GUID value for the ActiveX server each time the project is recompiled. This setting is very difficult to work with when we're testing our server, since each time we recompile the server (ActiveX EXE or DLL) any client projects will lose their reference to the server.

### Project Compatibility

With Project Compatibility selected, Visual Basic will generate a GUID the first time the project is compiled, and will attempt to use that same GUID for subsequent compiles, based on the conditions in the table above.

To throw in an extra twist, each public class in the project has a **class ID** (CLSID). A CLSID is a GUID value that represents a class rather than the entire ActiveX server. When we're using the Project Compatibility setting in Visual Basic 6.0, the CLSIDs for the project's classes are generated the first time the project is compiled and Visual Basic will attempt to use that same GUID for subsequent compiles.

Project Compatibility is a very good setting to use during the debugging process. Since the server's GUID and the CLSIDs remain largely constant, the client programs won't lose their reference to the server.

This setting is inappropriate once we've released our ActiveX server to users, or we've moved beyond initial debugging and testing. Project Compatibility doesn't provide enough overall stability for the GUIDs in our project to ensure that clients will continue to work as we change the ActiveX server. This can prove to be a serious logistic problem.

### Binary Compatibility

Of the three settings, Binary Compatibility is the strictest. With this setting, Visual Basic will make every effort to retain both the server's GUID and all the CLSIDs on each compile. However, changing existing interface elements or removing a class, property, or method, will still result in a new GUID, even with Binary Compatibility selected.

Binary Compatibility is the most appropriate setting for servers that have moved beyond initial debugging and are in production. As long as we don't alter the interface to existing properties and methods, or remove any classes, the server's GUID and CLSIDs will remain constant - so any client programs we've distributed will continue to work with the server as it is updated. We can change all the code we want *inside* our properties and methods, we just can't change the declarations, or interface, to them.

## Referencing the VideoObjects Project

Now that we've got a handle on GUIDs, CLSIDs, and the various project compatibility settings, we're ready to move on and add a reference from our `VideoUI` project to the `VideoObjects` server.

For a client program to use business objects from an ActiveX server using early-binding, we need to add a reference to the server within the client project. By adding this reference, we're telling the client project to load the server's public interface information from the server's type library.

A type library is a file that contains the definitions for all the public classes (and their public properties and methods) in an ActiveX server. ActiveX EXE and DLL files created by Visual Basic contain this information right inside the EXE or DLL file, but it's still fully accessible to programs that want to communicate with it via COM.

To add a reference to the
VideoObjects project, select the
VideoUI project in the Project
window and choose the Project |
References... menu option:

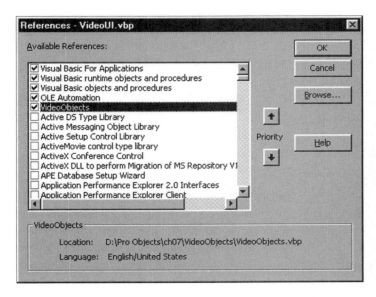

Find the VideoObjects item in the list and check the box to add a reference to it within the project.

Once we've compiled the VideoObjects DLL, there will be two VideoObjects entries in the list.
Make sure the Location shown near the bottom of the window is the .VBP file rather than the .DLL
file.

> *If we select the .dll file, Visual Basic won't use the project contained in the Visual Basic
> environment - and so we won't be unable to step through the code when we're debugging.*

# VideoMain: MDI Form

Most users are very familiar with MDI (multiple document interface) style applications due to the
popularity of office suites - almost all of which employ this design. We'll build this interface using an
MDI design as well, since it works well to illustrate a number of important concepts about an
application built with business objects.

The program will have a main form, VideoMain, which is the MDI parent. All the other forms in the
application will be either child windows within this form or modal dialog windows to solicit user
input. We'll use menus from this main window to give the user access to all the functionality that we'll
implement.

To get started, let's add the main form to the project. Choose Project | Add MDI Form. The Add MDI
Form dialog should appear. Just click Open to add a regular MDI form to the project:

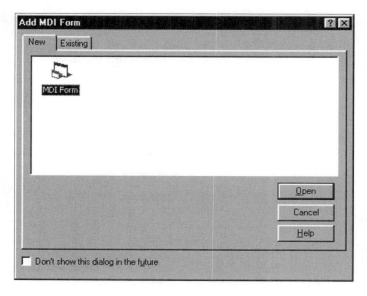

In the form's Properties window, set the Name property to VideoMain.

Now let's add the menus for the user. We'll put code behind all the menu options through the rest of the chapter, but it's nice to get them set up now so we don't have to worry about it as we go.

Choose the Tools | Menu Editor menu option to bring up the Menu Editor dialog. We won't walk through the details of adding each menu option. As far as the top-level menus go, just set up File (mnuFile) and Window (mnuWindow). Make the Window menu option a WindowList by checking the option in the dialog.

Under the File menu, set up the following options:

| Menu | Sub-menu | Name |
|------|----------|------|
| Customers | | mnuFileCust |
| | Search | mnuFileCustSearch |
| | - | mnuFileCustLine1 |
| | New customer | mnuFileCustNew |
| Videos | | mnuFileVideo |
| | Search | mnuFileVideoSearch |
| | - | mnuFileVideoLine1 |
| | New video | mnuFileVideoNew |
| - | | mnuFileLine1 |

| Menu | Sub-menu | Name |
|------|----------|------|
| New invoice | | mnuFileInvoiceNew |
| Check in tape | | mnuFileCheckIn |
| - | | mnuFileLine2 |
| Exit | | mnuFileExit |

Click OK to save the menus.

*It would be good to save the project at this point as well. To keep things straight, always save each Visual Basic project in its own directory. This avoids confusion as to which files belong to which projects. When dealing with business object-based applications, it's even more important to keep client applications, such as VideoUI, separate from the project containing the business objects - since various other client applications may exist beyond the Visual Basic forms application.*

The only menu item that we can really implement at this point is the code for File | Exit. The rest of the options will require us to design some forms and tap into the business objects. The code behind File | Exit is very simple:

```
Private Sub mnuFileExit_Click()

   Unload Me

End Sub
```

Since `VideoMain` is the parent form, and therefore the first form that we want to get running, we'll set it to be the Startup Object for our UI project. Select the Project | Properties menu option for the UI project, and set the Startup Object to `VideoMain`.

# Edit Screens

Our application will need to provide screens so that the user can add and edit the main objects we developed in Chapters 5 and 6. The objects that our users will need to edit are:

- ❑ `Customer`
- ❑ `Video`
- ❑ `Tape`

All of these edit screens will be very similar. However, each one illustrates some differences. `Customer` is a simple business object, while `Video` is a parent of the `Tape` objects. As a result, there are subtle differences involved in developing a form for each type of object.

# Creating an Edit Form Template

Just like the business objects themselves, there's a set of code that is essentially common to all the forms that work with our business objects. Rather than starting from scratch with each form we need to create, let's put together that common code - just as we did with the common business object code at the beginning of Chapter 5.

### Business Object Support

Compared to the amount of code in the business object, a Visual Basic form will be pretty simple. In fact, that's the whole idea: since the program code itself should be mostly contained within the business objects, the forms should be pretty lightweight.

As a simple template, our form will be pretty bare. We'll build our template using the `Form1` that should already be part of our `VideoUI` project. All it really needs to have are the three buttons, OK, Cancel and Apply. Any data entry and display fields will need to be added based on the properties of each specific business object:

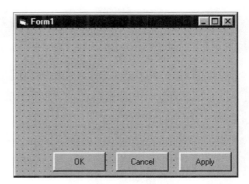

We do need to set some properties to make everything work the way we'd like. Set the Form's Name property to `BusForm` to indicate it is for use with a business object.

Name the three buttons `cmdOK`, `cmdCancel`, and `cmdApply`, respectively. Of course, we'll also want to set their captions as shown in the figure. We can leave all their other properties alone: we'll control anything we need to through code.

*If you have other application requirements for your forms, you may want to add them to your template as well. For instance, if all your forms have a similar color scheme or graphic image, you can set those properties at this point.*

### Declarations

Now let's get down to the form's code. We need to declare a business object variable to use within the form. Throughout this code, we'll be using the `Business` class that we'd get by adding a class based on the `Business` template we created in the last chapter.

```
Option Explicit

Private mflgLoading As Boolean

Private WithEvents mobjBusiness As Business
```

The `Business` variable is declared using the `WithEvents` keyword, because we know that our business object will raise at least the `Valid` event that we created. We'll get to the code for that event shortly.

We also declare a `Boolean` variable, `mflgLoading`. We'll use this to suppress any activities that we don't want to happen while the object's values are loaded into the form's controls. By setting `mflgLoading` to `True` as the form is being loaded, we can code a check in each routine to avoid any processing that isn't appropriate during the load process. This technique will become very familiar as we go through the template.

### Component Method

The form needs a business object to work with. There are two approaches that we can take to this:

1.  The form can create the object itself

2.  The form can get the object passed to it from some other code

Which approach should we choose?

Having each form create its business object directly seems like a very elegant solution. It means that the code to display the form doesn't need to worry about the object: it can just load and display the form. The problem with this approach is that we have no direct way for our form to edit an existing object that was created from some other source.

Following the second approach, we could write code outside the form to create both the business object and the form. Then we could have that code provide the form with a reference to the business object. Since our form is getting the object passed to it from outside code, it doesn't care if the object is brand new or if it already existed. This provides us with much more flexibility and control.

In this chapter, we'll take this second approach by implementing code behind the MDI form's menu items to create the appropriate business object, load the form, and connect the two together. Our individual forms won't have any code to create objects; instead, they'll rely on our MDI form's code to pass a reference to the object.

This implies that we need to provide a way for the code in the MDI form to pass an object reference to each of our forms. To facilitate this, we'll add a `Component` method to each form:

```
Option Explicit

Private mflgLoading As Boolean

Private WithEvents mobjBusiness As Business

Public Sub Component(BusinessObject As Business)

  Set mobjBusiness = BusinessObject

End Sub
```

The method is quite simple: all we want to do is receive and store a reference to the business object. Once we've got that reference in mobjBusiness, we'll be able to use the object throughout the rest of the form's code.

### Putting the Object's Values on the Form

The first thing we'll probably do with any business object is display the object's property values in controls that are on the form. The best place to do this is in the Form_Load routine, since this event fires when the form is loaded but *before* it's actually visible to the user. This means that the values will be in the controls by the time the user sees the form, so there won't be any flickering in the display as the values are copied.

The code we're adding will copy values from the object into the form, and each control's Change event will fire as we load it with a value. As we'll see shortly, the Change event is the perfect place to put code to copy the control's value into the business object.

The problem, here, is that we're pulling the values directly from the object and into each control. It makes no sense for the control's Change event to turn around and copy each value back into the business object. This can become a performance problem. Rather than simply displaying the values in the form, we're also copying the value back into the object - invoking any business rules or other business processing contained within the object.

When we set up the declarations section of our form, we declared a variable named mflgLoading. If we have our Form_Load set mflgLoading to True, then we can add a line at the top of each Change routine to exit that routine before the value is copied back into the business object. This way, we won't waste the effort of copying the value out of the business object just to copy it back in:

```
Private Sub Form_Load()

  mflgLoading = True

  With mobjBusiness
    ' load object values into form controls
    ' txtText = .Property
    .BeginEdit
  End With

  mflgLoading = False

End Sub
```

Notice we make a call to the object's `BeginEdit` method. Since the purpose of this form is to allow the user to edit the object's data, we might as well start off assuming that we'll be doing some edits by calling this method right away.

### OK, Cancel and Apply Buttons

We need to add code behind the OK, Cancel and Apply buttons to call the appropriate methods on the business object. The OK button needs to apply any changes and then get rid of the form:

```
Private Sub cmdOK_Click()

    mobjBusiness.ApplyEdit
    Unload Me

End Sub
```

The Cancel button also gets rid of the form, but first it needs to tell the business object to cancel any edits that have been done - by calling the `CancelEdit` method:

```
Private Sub cmdCancel_Click()

    mobjBusiness.CancelEdit
    Unload Me

End Sub
```

Finally, the Apply button just needs to tell the business object to apply any changes to date. This is as simple as calling the `ApplyEdit` method on the business object. Of course, the `ApplyEdit` method also ends the editing session, and a typical Apply button leaves the user ready to continue editing - so we need to also call the `BeginEdit` method to resume the editing session again:

```
Private Sub cmdApply_Click()

    mobjBusiness.ApplyEdit
    mobjBusiness.BeginEdit

End Sub
```

Ideally, the OK and Apply buttons would only be enabled if the object could be saved. We've already implemented an `IsValid` property and a `Valid` event on our business objects, so all we actually need to do is tap into them from our form.

Since there are a couple of places in the form where we'll need to enable or disable these buttons, the easiest thing to do is create a local subprocedure to contain this code. Let's call it `EnableOK`:

```
Private Sub EnableOK(flgValid As Boolean)

    cmdOK.Enabled = flgValid
    cmdApply.Enabled = flgValid

End Sub
```

Now all we need to do is call this routine and send it either a `True` or a `False` to indicate whether the OK and Apply buttons should be enabled or disabled.

We're expecting that our business object has been passed to our form via the `Component` method before the form is loaded. By the time the `Form_Load` event is run we already have a reference to a business object so we can add code to find out if that business object is valid. Many objects have required fields that will start out at zero length, so they aren't initially valid. The only way to know for sure is to check the object's `IsValid` property:

```
Private Sub Form_Load()

  mflgLoading = True

  With mobjBusiness
    EnableOK .IsValid
      ' load object values into form controls
      ' txtText = .Property
    .BeginEdit
  End With

  mflgLoading = False

End Sub
```

From this point forward, the business object will raise the `Valid` event any time the object switches from being valid to invalid or vice versa. We therefore need to add some code behind this event to call `EnableOK`. This code is quite simple, since the `Valid` event supplies us with a `Boolean` parameter that indicates whether the object is valid or not - and we just need to pass that along to our local routine:

```
Private Sub mobjBusiness_Valid(IsValid As Boolean)

  EnableOK IsValid

End Sub
```

### Data Entry Fields

Since this is a generic template form, we don't have any data entry fields. Still, it can't hurt to throw in a quick comment to remind ourselves what the code would look like to handle these fields.

While we don't really have any such control on our form, let's add commented code to react to the `Change` event of a fictitious `TextBox` control, `Text1`. This will act as a prototype for any code we add when we're creating a real form based on this template.

At the very least, we want to use the `Change` event of our control to update the business object with the current data in the entry field. This allows the business object to continually be aware of whether that particular property contains a valid entry - so that the `Valid` event can be raised as needed:

```
'Private Sub Text1_Change()
'
'   If mflgLoading Then Exit Sub
'
'   mobjBusiness.Text1 = Text1.Text
'
'End Sub
```

We already largely defined the Tapes object when we implemented the Video object earlier. The object's public properties and methods need to make it appear as a collection of Tape objects, but we also know there are some methods that will be implemented with Friend scope for use by the Video object itself.

## Setting up the Tapes Class

Add a standard class module to the VideoObjects project. Set its **Name** property to Tapes and its **Instancing** property to 2-PublicNotCreatable. This object will only be created as a part of the Video object, so it shouldn't be creatable by outside code; however, it will be exposed via the Video object's Tapes property, so it needs to be publicly available.

As with any other collection object, we'll need an actual Collection object to build our code around:

```
Option Explicit

Private mcolTapes As Collection
```

And, of course, the Class_Initialize needs to create an instance of a Collection object for this variable:

```
Private Sub Class_Initialize()

   Set mcolTapes = New Collection

End Sub
```

Since this is a collection type object, we'll have the standard Item, Count and NewEnum methods. Don't forget to use Tools | Procedure Attributes... to make the Item method the default and the NewEnum method have a **Procedure ID** of −4 and **Hide this member** attribute.

```
Public Function Item(ByVal Index As Variant) As Tape

   Set Item = mcolTapes(Index)

End Function
```

```
Public Function Count() As Long

   Count = mcolTapes.Count

End Function
```

```
Public Function NewEnum() As IUnknown

   Set NewEnum = mcolTapes.[_NewEnum]

End Function
```

As a collection of Tape objects, it's no surprise that the Item method returns a Tape object when called:

```
Public Function Item(ByVal Index As Variant) As Tape
```

```
    .CheckIn
    .ApplyEdit
End with

Set objTape = Nothing
```

For this to work, the `CheckIn` method needs to be `Public` in scope rather than the `Friend` scope of `CheckOut`. Beyond that, it just needs to reset the `CheckedOut` and `Invoice` properties to indicate that the tape is checked in:

```
Public Sub CheckIn()

  If Not mflgEditing Then Err.Raise 445

  With mudtProps
    .CheckedOut = False
  End With

  mflgDirty = True

End Sub
```

To be consistent with the behavior of `CheckOut`, this method does require that `BeginEdit` be called first. For all we know, the UI developer might want to build an entire list of tapes to check in, calling the `CheckIn` method on each one. If the UI includes a Cancel button, it might be important to be able to use `CancelEdit` to safely undo all those calls to `CheckIn`.

# Tapes: A Parent-Child Relationship Object

In the `Video` object, we implemented a `Tapes` property to contain all the specific `Tape` objects that are children of a specific `Video` object. The `Tapes` property simply exposed a `Tapes` object to the calling code. Now we need to implement the `Tapes` class to support the requirements of the `Video` object's property.

The `Tapes` object is highlighted in the following diagram:

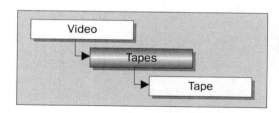

In many cases, collection objects don't represent any real-world entity as much as they represent a real-world relationship between entities. For instance, it's difficult to envision a real-world entity for a `Tapes` object to model. The `Tapes` object will model the parent-child relationship between a video title and all the physical tapes of that title in the store.

When we implemented the `Tape` object itself, we added a bit of extra code so it can act as a standalone object as well as a child object. When we're using `Tape` objects within this new `Tapes` collection object, they'll be child objects - so we'll need to make use of the `SetAsChild`, `ChildLoad`, `ChildBeginEdit`, `ChildCancelEdit` and `ChildApplyEdit` methods.

Here, again, is the `mflgLoading` variable. Notice how we check the value at the top of the routine, and just exit immediately if it's `True`. This way, the `Form_Load` routine can copy the object's values into the form's controls without invoking the code that copies the form's values back into the business object.

It's also not a bad idea to refresh the form's display, based on the business object's data, in each control's `LostFocus` event. Refreshing the display in the `Change` event is not very practical, since it can wreak havoc with the user's cursor position; but we may still want to keep the display in sync with the object:

```
'Private Sub Text1_LostFocus()
'
'   Text1.Text = mobjBusiness.Text1
'
'End Sub
```

A good example of where this is useful is some field where a business rule dictates that the characters should all be uppercase. The business object would contain code to uppercase the data as it was supplied. Unless the form refreshes the display using the business object's copy of the data, the user may be unaware that their entry was uppercased.

### Saving the Form Template

At this point, our form is all set and ready to go. To make it into a template, we need to save the form into the `Template\Forms` directory, under the directory where Visual Basic is installed.

Right-click on `BusForm` in the **Project** window, and choose the **Save BusForm As...** menu option. Use the **Save File As** dialog to save the form into the `Template\Forms` directory wherever Visual Basic itself was installed on the system.

Once our new template form has been saved, make sure to remove it from the current project by right-clicking on `BusForm` in the Project window and choosing **Remove BusForm.frm**.

We can test the template by choosing the **Project | Add Form** menu option. The `BusForm` template should be an option in the **Add Form** dialog that appears:

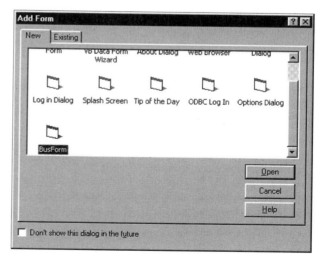

Choose **BusForm** and click **Open** to add a new form to our `VideoUI` project - with the buttons and all the code we just added.

# CustomerEdit: Simple Editing

Creating the screen to edit the Customer object is a good place to begin, since the Customer object is pretty basic - being neither a parent nor a child object.

Since this is the first form we've looked at which will communicate with a business object, we'll study it in some detail. For the rest of the forms in the chapter, however, we'll skip over this detail and focus only on the differences.

Since our BusForm form template contains the basic code to deal with business objects, we'll use it now to simplify the process of building our CustomerEdit form.

## Setting up the CustomerEdit Form

In the VideoUI project in Visual Basic, use the BusForm form that we just created from the template.

Set this new form's **Name** property to CustomerEdit and the **MDIChild** property to True.

Now add the following controls, as shown in the diagram:

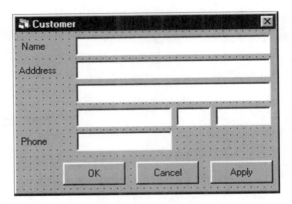

| Control | Caption | Name |
|---------|---------|------|
| Label | Name | |
| TextBox | | txtName |
| Label | Address | |
| TextBox | | txtAddr1 |
| TextBox | | txtAddr2 |
| TextBox | | txtCity |
| TextBox | | txtState |
| TextBox | | txtZipCode |
| Label | Phone | |
| TextBox | | txtPhone |

## Customizing the Template Code

The template code handles most of the basic operations we'll need to perform on an object, such as loading its data, and the OK, Cancel, and Apply buttons. All we really need to do is change the generic `mobjBusiness` reference to something more meaningful - such as `mobjCustomer`, and change the `Business` reference to `Customer`. The easiest way to do this is to use a couple of quick global replace operations using the Edit | Replace menu option.

The following code indicates the lines that are changed by two such global replacements:

```
Option Explicit

Private mflgLoading As Boolean

Private WithEvents mobjCustomer As Customer

Public Sub Component(CustomerObject As Customer)

  Set mobjCustomer = CustomerObject

End Sub

Private Sub Form_Load()

  mflgLoading = True

  With mobjCustomer
     EnableOK .IsValid
     ' load object values into form controls
     ' txtText = .Property
     .BeginEdit
  End With

  mflgLoading = False

End Sub

Private Sub cmdOK_Click()

  mobjCustomer.ApplyEdit
  Unload Me

End Sub

Private Sub cmdCancel_Click()

  mobjCustomer.CancelEdit
  Unload Me

End Sub

Private Sub cmdApply_Click()

  mobjCustomer.ApplyEdit
  mobjCustomer.BeginEdit

End Sub
```

```
Private Sub EnableOK(flgValid As Boolean)

  cmdOK.Enabled = flgValid
  cmdApply.Enabled = flgValid

End Sub

Private Sub mobjCustomer_Valid(IsValid As Boolean)

  EnableOK IsValid

End Sub

'Private Sub Text1_Change()
'
'  If mflgLoading Then Exit Sub
'
'  mobjCustomer.Text1 = Text1.Text
'
'End Sub

'Private Sub Text1_LostFocus()
'
'  Text1.Text = mobjCustomer.Text1
'
'End Sub
```

The only other thing we need to do is extend the `Form_Load` routine that came with the template. It would be nice if we could set the form's caption based on the business object. If the object is new, then the caption is set to a generic value; otherwise, the customer's name is placed in the caption. We also need some extra code added to copy the object's properties to the appropriate fields on the form:

```
Private Sub Form_Load()

  mflgLoading = True

  With mobjCustomer
    EnableOK .IsValid

    If .IsNew Then
      Caption = "Customer [(new)]"

    Else
      Caption = "Customer [" & .Name & "]"

    End If

    txtName = .Name
    txtAddr1 = .Address1
    txtAddr2 = .Address2
    txtCity = .City
    txtState = .State
    txtZipCode = .ZipCode
    txtPhone = .Phone

    .BeginEdit
  End With
  mflgLoading = False

End Sub
```

## Adding Code Behind Controls

With the basics of our form all set, we can move on and put code behind each of our controls.

### Name Text Box

We're going to put a fair amount of code behind the `Text Box` controls to illustrate how we can create a responsive interface. You'll then be free to choose to implement a simpler or a more complex interface, simply by eliminating code or extending some of these concepts.

In order to provide the user with instant feedback as they press each key, we could put some code behind the `txtName_Change` event (*don't enter this code*):

```
Private Sub txtName_Change()

    Dim intPos As Integer

    If mflgLoading Then Exit Sub

    On Error GoTo INPUTERR
    mobjCustomer.Name = txtName
    Exit Sub

INPUTERR:
    Beep
    intPos = txtName.SelStart
    txtName = mobjCustomer.Name
    txtName.SelStart = intPos - 1

End Sub
```

In general, this routine copies the value of the control into the business object, allowing the business object to validate the entry with each change. In Chapter 5, we made our business objects either raise an error or raise the `Valid` event when an invalid entry is made. For instance, if the field has a length limit, and the new value exceeds that limit, then our business object raises an error back to the form.

### The TextChange Routine

However, virtually every text box we'll ever use will have this same code. It makes a lot more sense to put this code into a central routine that we can call – making our program much more maintainable and saving us from writing a lot of code.

Add a BAS module to our `VideoUI` project. We'll put this new routine in a BAS module so it can be used from any of the forms we'll be adding to our project – after all, a lot of them will contain text boxes.

The routine we'll add will basically contain the same code we just looked at for the `txtName` control, except that it will be generalized to work with any text box. Prior to Visual Basic 6.0 creating such a routine was a virtual impossibility, since there was no way to pass a reference to a specific property on an object. Visual Basic 6.0 introduces a new language keyword, `CallByName`, which allows us to call any method or property on an object by using a string representation of that method or property.

Add the following code to the new BAS module:

```
Public Sub TextChange(Ctl As TextBox, Obj As Object, Prop As String)

    Dim lngPos As Long

    On Error GoTo INPUTERR
    CallByName Obj, Prop, VbLet, Ctl.Text
    Exit Sub

INPUTERR:
    Beep
    lngPos = Ctl.SelStart
    Ctl = CallByName(Obj, Prop, VbGet)
    Ctl.SelStart = lngPos - 1

End Sub
```

The new TextChange routine accepts three parameters. The first is the TextBox control who's Change event just fired. The second is a reference to the business object the control needs to interact with and the third is the name of the property on our business object.

The first couple of lines enable error trapping in the routine, and copy the control's current value into the business object. However, instead of directly setting the property value on the object, we are using the new CallByName method to call the Property Let routine for the property name that was passed as a parameter:

```
On Error GoTo INPUTERR
CallByName Obj, Prop, VbLet, Ctl.Text
Exit Sub
```

By using the On Error GoTo statement we ensure that any error will cause our error handler, below the INPUTERR label, to be run:

```
INPUTERR:
    Beep
    lngPos = Ctl.SelStart
    Ctl = CallByName(Obj, Prop, VbGet)
    Ctl.SelStart = lngPos - 1
```

If an error occurs, such as the field length being too long or some other immediate error raised by the business object, we just beep the workstation's speaker and restore the control's value to the value contained in the object. Again we're using the CallByName method to call the appropriate property on our business object rather than calling the property directly. This way our routine is entirely dynamic and can work with any business object and any property.

We use the lngPos variable to keep the cursor's position within the text in the same location that it was before the user pressed the last key.

### Calling the TextChange Routine

Now that we've got a centralized routine to handle the functionality we want for a text box, we simply need to call it from our control's Change event. Return to the txtName_Change routine and enter the following code:

```
Private Sub txtName_Change()

  If Not mflgLoading Then _
     TextChange txtName, mobjCustomer, "Name"

End Sub
```

When the form is loading, and all the object's values are being copied into each control for display, we don't want to be copying the value right back into the object. As we discussed earlier, our solution is to set a flag, `mflgLoading`, to be `True` at the start of our `Form_Load`, and then `False` at the end. This way, we can check `mflgLoading` to find out if we're currently loading values in during the `Form_Load` - or if we've actually gone past that point. If `mflgLoading` is `True` then we know that values are still being loaded into the form.

This code simply calls our new routine, passing a reference to the `txtName` control, a reference to the business object and the name of the property we want to set.

### LostFocus Processing

Although it isn't required in the `txtName` control, it's always wise to use the `LostFocus` event to copy the business object's value into the control. As with the `Change` event processing, we'll create a centralized routine to handle this work so we can make our code more maintainable.

The reason for this will become more apparent with some of the other controls we'll look at in this section. It's a good idea to always include this code in the `LostFocus` event to be consistent across all controls. If, at a later stage, some processing is added to the `Name` property of the `Customer` object, the form will already have the code in this event to properly present the user with the results of the processing. For example, perhaps we later decide to add code to capitalize the first letter of each word. This code would copy the changed value from the business object to the form as the user leaves the field.

Open the code window for the BAS module that contains the `TextChange` routine and enter the following code:

```
Public Function TextLostFocus(Ctl As TextBox, Obj As Object, Prop As String)

  TextLostFocus = CallByName(Obj, Prop, VbGet)

End Function
```

As with the `TextChange` routine, this one accepts three parameters. We need a reference to the control we're dealing with so we can retrieve its value, then we need a reference to the business object and the name of the property to pull back. Using that information we simply call the `CallByName` method to get the value from the business object's property and place it into the `TextBox` control.

We can now use this routine from each text box control's `LostFocus` event. Return to the `txtName` control's code and add a `txtName_LostFocus` routine as shown:

```
Private Sub txtName_LostFocus()

  txtName = TextLostFocus(txtName, mobjCustomer, "Name")

End Sub
```

We'll add similar code to all the LostFocus events for our TextBox controls as we build the rest of the UI.

### Address, City and Phone Text Boxes

The two Address text box controls, the City text box control, and the Phone text box control, all work exactly like the Name text box we just looked at. I'll include the code here, but we won't go through it in detail as it is just calling the TextChange and TextLostFocus routines we just wrote:

```
Private Sub txtAddr1_Change()

  If Not mflgLoading Then _
    TextChange txtAddr1, mobjCustomer, "Address1"

End Sub
```

```
Private Sub txtAddr1_LostFocus()

  txtAddr1 = TextLostFocus(txtAddr1, mobjCustomer, "Address1")

End Sub
```

```
Private Sub txtAddr2_Change()

  If Not mflgLoading Then _
    TextChange txtAddr2, mobjCustomer, "Address2"

End Sub
```

```
Private Sub txtAddr2_LostFocus()

  txtAddr1 = TextLostFocus(txtAddr2, mobjCustomer, "Address2")

End Sub
```

```
Private Sub txtCity_Change()

  If Not mflgLoading Then _
    TextChange txtCity, mobjCustomer, "City"

End Sub
```

```
Private Sub txtCity_LostFocus()

  txtCity = TextLostFocus(txtCity, mobjCustomer, "City")

End Sub
```

```
Private Sub txtPhone_Change()

  If Not mflgLoading Then _
    TextChange txtPhone, mobjCustomer, "Phone"
```

```
End Sub

Private Sub txtPhone_LostFocus()

  txtPhone = TextLostFocus(txtPhone, mobjCustomer, "Phone")

End Sub
```

### State and ZipCode Text Box Controls

Not surprisingly, the code for the State and ZipCode text box controls is no different from what we've seen so far:

```
Private Sub txtState_Change()

  If Not mflgLoading Then _
    TextChange txtState, mobjCustomer, "State"

End Sub

Private Sub txtState_LostFocus()

  txtState = TextLostFocus(txtState, mobjCustomer, "State")

End Sub

Private Sub txtZipCode_Change()

  If Not mflgLoading Then _
    TextChange txtZipCode, mobjCustomer, "ZipCode"

End Sub

Private Sub txtZipCode_LostFocus()

  txtZipCode = TextLostFocus(txtZipCode, mobjCustomer, "ZipCode")

End Sub
```

You may remember that, in Chapter 5, we added code in the Customer business object to make sure that the State value was uppercased. This is a good illustration of why we have the code in the LostFocus event. Suppose we enter a value into the form as shown in this screenshot:

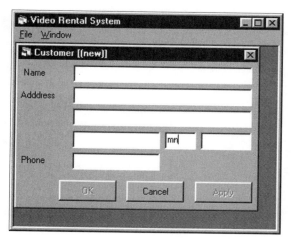

Notice that the value entered by the user is in lowercase. Now, when the user moves to another field, the `LostFocus` event will fire, copying the object's data back into the form's text box:

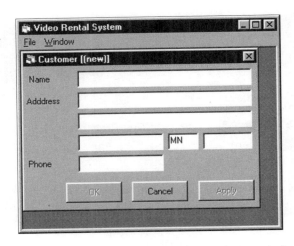

Similarly, the `ZipCode` field is reformatted by the `Customer` object's code, and the result is copied into the control within the `LostFocus` event.

## Adding Code to VideoMain

For now, we'll just look at the code for the File | Customers | New Customer menu option.

> *The Search menu option will invoke a different form, which will use our* `Customers` *collection object. We'll deal with that later.*

Here's the code for the File | Customers | New Customer menu option:

```
Private Sub mnuFileCustNew_Click()

  Dim objCustomer As Customer
  Dim frmCustomer As CustomerEdit

  Set objCustomer = New Customer
  Set frmCustomer = New CustomerEdit

  frmCustomer.Component objCustomer
  frmCustomer.Show

End Sub
```

This code is wonderfully simple. We just declare two variables: one for the form, and the other for the `Customer` object. Then we simply create instances of the form and object, using the `New` keyword:

```
Set objCustomer = New Customer
Set frmCustomer = New CustomerEdit
```

We're creating an *instance* of the form here, not directly showing the form itself. This is important since we're building an MDI application. Were we to show the form itself we'd only be able to allow the user to work with a single customer at a time. By creating a new instance of the form each time we're allowing the user to work with many customers in different windows. Essentially what we're doing is treating the form module just like a class module and creating different instances of the form just like we create instances of a class.

All that remains is for us to use the form's `Component` method to provide the form with a reference to the new object, and then to show the form to the user:

```
frmCustomer.Component objCustomer
frmCustomer.Show
```

If we look back at the `Component` method in the form, it just stores the object reference in a form-level variable for later use. The `Show` method causes the `Form_Load` event routine to be run, and the code we put in that `Form_Load` routine copies the object's data into the form's controls before the user gets to see the form itself.

# VideoEdit: Editing a Parent Object

The `Video` object is more complex than the `Customer` object in a couple different ways. First, it's a parent object, having `Tape` objects as children. Second, it contains two `TextList` objects that are available through the `Categories` and `Ratings` properties.

Accordingly, the `VideoEdit` form will also need to be a bit more complex. It will need to provide an interface to list, add, edit and remove the `Tape` objects. Additionally, it will have a couple of ComboBox controls so that the user can choose a category and a rating from the list of valid options provided by the `Video` object.

## Setting up the VideoEdit Form

The process of adding any edit form is virtually identical to what we've seen for the `Customer` form. We won't go through an explanation of the code in detail, since it's now well within our grasp to set up the basic form and functionality.

Add a form to the `VideoUI` project using the **BusForm** template. Set the **Name** property to `VideoEdit` and the **MDIChild** property to **True**. Use **Edit | Replace** to replace `mobjBusiness` with `mobjVideo` and to replace `Business` with `Video`.

Now add controls as shown in the following figure:

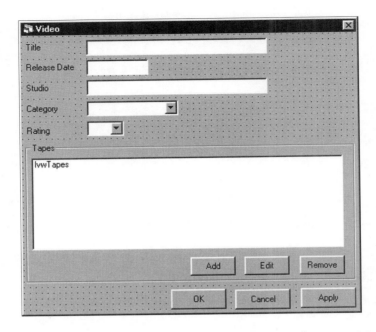

*This form uses the* `ListView` *control, which is not available on the ToolBox by default. To add it to your toolbox, right-click on the ToolBox and choose the* Components *option. Then find and include the* Microsoft Windows Common Controls 6.0 *option from the list.*

| Control | Caption | Name |
|---|---|---|
| Label | Title | |
| Text Box | | `txtTitle` |
| Label | Release date | |
| Text Box | | `txtRelease` |
| Label | Studio | |
| Text Box | | `txtStudio` |
| Label | Category | |
| ComboBox | | `cboCategory` |
| Label | Rating | |
| ComboBox | | `cboRating` |
| Frame | Tapes | |

| Control | Caption | Name |
|---|---|---|
| ListView | | `lvwTapes` |
| Command Button | Add | `cmdAdd` |
| Command Button | Edit | `cmdEdit` |
| Command Button | Remove | `cmdRemove` |

### The ListView Control

We need to set up the `ListView` control's properties.

*If there is one control that causes Visual Basic to crash frequently, it's the `ListView` control. It's a good idea to always save immediately before and after doing anything with this control, to prevent a lot of frustration over lost work.*

*Another possibility would be to build a user interface based on a grid control instead of a `ListView` and editing forms. This would allow in-place editing by the user within the grid, but is typically a much more complex type of interface to implement than the one we're building here.*

Open up the `VideoEdit` form. Right-click on the `lvwTapes` control, and choose the Properties menu option. On the General tab, we need to change the View property to 3-lvwReport:

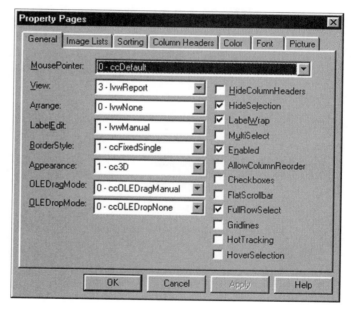

While we're on this tab, also change the LabelEdit property to 1-lvwManual. This will prevent the user from changing the TapeID column on the screen. Also check the FullRowSelect option from the list at the right. This is a new feature in Visual Basic 6.0 that will make the entire row show as selected when the user clicks on it.

Then use the Column Headers tab to add the column titles TapeID, Purchased, and Rented.

## *Updating the Template Code*

The only routine that needs to be changed from the template code, at this point, is the `Form_Load` routine. We'll add some code to display the title of the video in the form's caption, and we'll load the video object's properties to the appropriate fields on the form:

```
Private Sub Form_Load()

  mflgLoading = True

  With mobjVideo
    EnableOK .IsValid

    If .IsNew Then
      Caption = "Video [(new)]"

    Else
      Caption = "Video [" & .Title & "]"

    End If

    txtTitle = .Title
    txtRelease = .ReleaseDate
    txtStudio = .Studio

    .BeginEdit
  End With

  mflgLoading = False

End Sub
```

## *Text Box Controls*

The `Title` and `Studio` fields will have code that's very similar to the code for the text box controls in the `CustomerEdit` form. The logic of this code should therefore be familiar:

```
Private Sub txtTitle_Change()

  If Not mflgLoading Then _
    TextChange txtTitle, mobjVideo, "Title"

End Sub
```

```
Private Sub txtTitle_LostFocus()

  txtTitle = TextLostFocus(txtTitle, mobjVideo, "Title")

End Sub
```

```
Private Sub txtStudio_Change()

  If Not mflgLoading Then _
    TextChange txtStudio, mobjVideo, "Studio"

End Sub
```

```
Private Sub txtStudio_LostFocus()

  txtStudio = TextLostFocus(txtStudio, mobjVideo, "Studio")

End Sub
```

## TextBox Control with a Date Value

At first glance, the `txtRelease` control would appear to be just another text box. It is, however, quite different: the underlying property in the `Video` object is a date, and our date properties behave a bit differently than simple text fields.

In particular, the user can enter virtually anything into the field and the business object won't raise an error. Instead, the business object validates the entry each time to see if it is a valid date. As we coded it in Chapter 5, we used the `IsDate()` method to determine if the value could be converted to a date or not.

The business object raises the `Valid` event to tell the form whether all the values in the object are okay. The template code for this form handles the `Valid` event by enabling or disabling the OK and Apply buttons, so the user can't try to accept the form if the `Video` object isn't valid.

Basically however, we need to do the same thing here as with any other text box, so we'll call the `TextChange` routine to handle everything:

```
Private Sub txtRelease_Change()

  If Not mflgLoading Then _
    TextChange txtRelease, mobjVideo, "ReleaseDate"

End Sub
```

Of course, the `Video` object converts the value into a `Variant` with a `Date` data type, so in our `LostFocus` event we need to copy that value out of the object and into the control by using the `TextLostFocus` routine:

```
Private Sub txtRelease_LostFocus()

  txtRelease = TextLostFocus(txtRelease, mobjVideo, "ReleaseDate")

End Sub
```

*By default, Visual Basic displays values of type* `Date` *using the system's predefined 'Short Date' setting. Typically, this is good, because it provides a localized display for the date, based on the user's preferences.*

*If our application has different needs for date displays then this would be an appropriate place to use the* `Format$()` *method to convert the date into the format we require.*

## Categories and Ratings ComboBox Controls

As we've discussed, the `Video` business object implements a couple of list-based properties: `Categories` and `Ratings`. These properties both require that the UI provide a valid entry; that is, one contained within the `Categories` or `Ratings` lists respectively.

To make it easy for the UI developer to implement a robust interface, we implemented the Categories and Ratings properties so that the UI can get access to these lists of valid options. These lists are stored in objects of type TextList, which provides a read-only list of the values, and their keys, for use by the UI developer.

### Loading the ComboBox Values

The first thing we need to do is load the two ComboBox controls with the values from the TextList objects. Once this is done, things get easy, because the user can only select options from the list - so we don't have to worry about them choosing a value that the business object will reject.

> **This does mean that the two ComboBox controls must have their Style property set to 2-Dropdown List.**

To minimize the amount of code in the form, it's a good idea to implement a LoadCombo method with the code we need to copy the contents of a TextList object into a ComboBox control:

```
Private Sub LoadCombo(Combo As ComboBox, List As TextList)

  Dim vntItem As Variant

  With Combo
    .Clear
    For Each vntItem In List
      .AddItem vntItem
    Next
    If .ListCount > 0 Then .ListIndex = 0
  End With

End Sub
```

This routine clears the control's contents, then uses a For Each to loop through all the items in the TextList object, adding each one to the control with the AddItem method. Once the control is loaded, and if it contains any elements, we set the ListIndex to 0 so that the user sees the first element in the list right away.

> *This routine is generally useful in many applications. It may be a good idea to put it into a code module so you can easily reuse it. Better still, you could include it as a method of a custom ComboBox control. For more information about creating such controls, see the Wrox Press book* Instant Visual Basic 5 ActiveX Control Creation *(ISBN 1-861000-23-5).*

Now we just need to add some code in the Form_Load routine to load the two controls (I'll explain why they're commented out straight after the code):

```
Private Sub Form_Load()

  mflgLoading = True

  With mobjVideo
    EnableOK .IsValid

    If .IsNew Then
      Caption = "Video [(new)]"
```

```
      Else
        Caption = "Video [" & .Title & "]"

      End If

      txtTitle = .Title
      txtRelease = .ReleaseDate
      txtStudio = .Studio

  '   LoadCombo cboCategory, .Categories
  '   LoadCombo cboRating, .Ratings

      .BeginEdit
    End With

    mflgLoading = False

  End Sub
```

These lines just use the `LoadCombo` routine to copy the values from the `Video` object into the form's controls.

> *We'll comment these lines out, for now, because we haven't implemented the persistence code which we'll do in Chapter 8. Only when the persistence code is in place will* `mobjVideo.Categories` *and* `mobjVideo.Ratings` *have been initialized from the database.*

If this is an existing object, the `Category` and `Rating` properties will have specific values. Our `LoadCombo` routine defaults the values to the first item in each list, but that won't be valid if the business object already has a value. As with the other controls on the form, we need to add code to set the ComboBox controls to the current value from the business object. Add these lines to the `Form_Load` event:

```
  '   LoadCombo cboCategory, .Categories
  '   cboCategory.Text = .Category
  '   LoadCombo cboRating, .Ratings
  '   cboRating.Text = .Rating
```

### Updating the Business Object

Since the list that the user can choose from comes directly from the business object, we don't need to worry about screening the values or having the `Video` object reject the value due to a business rule. This makes the code behind the controls very simple.

With the ComboBox `Style` property set to **2-Dropdown List**, the `Change` event never fires. Instead, the `Click` event fires any time the value in the control is changed; so we'll just put the code behind the `Click` event instead:

```
Private Sub cboCategory_Click()

  If mflgLoading Then Exit Sub
  mobjVideo.Category = cboCategory.Text

End Sub
```

```
Private Sub cboRating_Click()

  If mflgLoading Then Exit Sub
  mobjVideo.Rating = cboRating.Text

End Sub
```

When we authored the Video business object, we wrote it to accept the text value from the list rather than the key value. This was intentional, so that the UI developer doesn't have to worry about maintaining both a list of text values and corresponding keys. This way, the UI code can just put the text values into the list and return those values to the business object - very simple.

We also don't need to worry about the LostFocus event, since the values are predetermined by the TextList object, so the Video object won't have altered the values in any way that would need to be refreshed on the screen.

## Maintaining Child Objects

Perhaps the most interesting thing about the Video object is that it's the parent of zero or more Tape objects. We implemented this by adding a Tapes object, which is a customized collection object that manages the parent-child relationship between Video and Tape.

The Video object provides a property, Tapes, that can be used by the UI developer to gain access to the child objects. Through the Tapes property, the Video object provides a reference to the Tapes object containing its children.

Using the Tapes object, the UI code can display, add, or remove Tape objects. All of these activities are controlled by the Tapes object, so it shouldn't be possible for the UI code to create invalid child objects.

### Displaying a List of Tapes

Earlier, we configured a ListView control named lvwTapes. Now we'll use this control to display the list of Tape objects owned by the Video object.

Let's create a routine to display the Tape objects' values in the ListView. There will be a number of places within the program where we'll want to refresh the list of items in the view, so it makes a lot of sense to put this code in a central routine within the form:

```
Private Sub LoadTapes()

  Dim objTape As Tape
  Dim itmList As ListItem
  Dim lngIndex As Long

  lvwTapes.ListItems.Clear
  For lngIndex = 1 To mobjVideo.Tapes.Count
    Set itmList = lvwTapes.ListItems.Add _
      (Key:=Format$(lngIndex) & "K")
    Set objTape = mobjVideo.Tapes(lngIndex)

    With itmList
      If objTape.IsNew Then
        .Text = "(new)"
```

```
        Else
          .Text = objTape.TapeID

        End If

        If objTape.IsDeleted Then .Text = .Text & " (d)"
        .SubItems(1) = objTape.DateAcquired
        .SubItems(2) = IIf(objTape.CheckedOut, "Yes", "No")
      End With

    Next

  End Sub
```

The first thing we do here is clear the contents of the ListView:

```
lvwTapes.ListItems.Clear
```

Since we'll be calling this routine repeatedly within the form's code, we need to make sure that we're starting with a blank slate each time.

Then we loop through each item in the `Tapes` collection using a `For Next` loop:

```
For lngIndex = 1 To mobjVideo.Tapes.Count
```

We want to store the index value for each `Tape` object in the ListView control's `Key` value so that we can use it later to easily get at the specific element in the list. If we used a `For Each`, then there would be no way to access each element's index value, so we're reduced to using this slower approach.

In order to display each line in a ListView control, we need to create `ListItem` objects for each line. This is done through the `Add` method of the `ListItems` object owned by the `ListView` control:

```
Set itmList = lvwTapes.ListItems.Add _
  (Key:=Format$(lngIndex) & "K")
```

The `Add` method returns a reference to the new `ListItem` object. It also accepts various parameters; in our case, we're setting the object's `Key` value. The key value we're providing is the index of the item from the `Tapes` collection, in a string format, with the letter 'K' appended to the end.

> *Even if we convert a numeric value to a string when setting a* `ListItem` *object's* `Key` *value, it will convert it back to a number, making it difficult to deal with later. To prevent this conversion, we can stick a letter on the end of the numeric value so that the overall value appears to be alphanumeric. Later on, we'll use the* `Val()` *command to easily pull the numeric value back out of the key when needed, since* `Val()` *converts all numbers until it hits the first non-numeric character.*

Now that we have a `ListItem` object ready to be loaded with values for display, we need to get the `Tape` object so that we have the actual values. The easiest way to do this is to use a local variable to store the reference to the `Tape` object:

```
Set objTape = mobjVideo.Tapes(lngIndex)
```

Now we're ready to load the values for display:

```
With itmList
  If objTape.IsNew Then
  .Text = "(new)"

  Else
    .Text = objTape.TapeID

  End If

    If objTape.IsDeleted Then .Text = .Text & " (d)"
    .SubItems(1) = objTape.DateAcquired
    .SubItems(2) = IIf(objTape.CheckedOut, "Yes", "No")
End With
```

If the `Tape` object is new, we put (new) in the **Tape ID** column; otherwise, we use the object's ID value. In either case, if the `Tape` object's `IsDeleted` property is set to `True` we know that the object has been marked for deletion. In this case we'll simply mark this fact with a '(d)' after the ID value.

Finally we load the `DateAcquired` value into the display, and put either **Yes** or **No** in the **Rented** column, based on the `Tape` object's `CheckedOut` property.

That pretty much wraps up the routine. Let's go through the rest of the code and insert the calls to load the display where needed. The most obvious place is in the `Form_Load`, since that's where we copy all the other values from the `Video` object on to the form:

```
Private Sub Form_Load()

  mflgLoading = True

  With mobjVideo
    EnableOK .IsValid

    If .IsNew Then
      Caption = "Video [(new)]"

    Else
      Caption = "Video [" & .Title & "]"

    End If

    txtTitle = .Title
    txtRelease = .ReleaseDate
    txtStudio = .Studio

    ' LoadCombo cboCategory, .Categories
    ' cboCategory.Text = .Category
    ' LoadCombo cboRating, .Ratings
    ' cboRating.Text = .Rating
    .BeginEdit
  End With
  LoadTapes
```

```
      mflgLoading = False

  End Sub
```

As the user adds new Tape objects, they'll be displayed in the list with a **Tape ID** value of (new). When the user clicks the **Apply** button, these objects will be saved to the database, and they'll be assigned actual ID values. We need to refresh the display once this is complete, so the user can see the new ID values displayed - rather than (new):

```
  Private Sub cmdApply_Click()

     mobjVideo.ApplyEdit
     mobjVideo.BeginEdit
     LoadTapes

  End Sub
```

We'll also need to call LoadTapes when we add, edit, or remove a tape from the list. Let's go through and look at the code to handle these functions.

### Adding a Tape

The user indicates that they want to add a new tape by clicking on the **Add** button:

```
  Private Sub cmdAdd_Click()

    Dim frmTape As TapeEdit

    Set frmTape = New TapeEdit
    frmTape.Component mobjVideo.Tapes.Add
    frmTape.Show vbModal
    LoadTapes

  End Sub
```

The code behind this button creates a TapeEdit form (which we'll look at next) for the user to work with. It then creates a new Tape object and provides a reference to the new object for the TapeEdit form, using the form's Component method:

```
  frmTape.Component mobjVideo.Tapes.Add
```

To create a new Tape object, we need to use the Tapes object's Add method. This function creates and initializes a new Tape object and returns a reference to that object for our use.

In Chapter 6, we implemented this process in such a way that the object wasn't actually added to the Tapes collection until the new Tape object's ApplyEdit method was called. This way, if the user clicks the **Cancel** button on the TapeEdit form, the blank Tape object won't be added to the Tapes collection accidentally.

The routine then shows the TapeEdit form:

```
  frmTape.Show vbModal
```

**335**

When the user is done, having clicked either the OK or Cancel button, the LoadTapes routine is called to refresh the list and display the newly added Tape object.

### Editing a Tape

Editing a Tape object is just as easy:

```
Private Sub cmdEdit_Click()

  Dim frmTape As TapeEdit

  Set frmTape = New TapeEdit
  frmTape.Component _
    mobjVideo.Tapes(Val(lvwTapes.SelectedItem.Key))
  frmTape.Show vbModal
  LoadTapes

End Sub
```

In this case, we don't need to create a new Tape object; instead, we use the Key value we stored in the ListView control to quickly retrieve the appropriate object from the Tapes collection:

```
frmTape.Component _
  mobjVideo.Tapes(Val(lvwTapes.SelectedItem.Key))
```

When we loaded the key value into the ListItem object, we concatenated the numeric ID value with the letter 'K' to force it to be an alphanumeric value. Fortunately, the Val() function returns the numeric value of all the characters in a string until it finds a non-numeric character. This makes it easy to retrieve the numeric index value of the item the user selected - so we can use it to pull out a reference to the underlying Tape object within the collection.

### Removing a Tape

Removing a tape from the list is even easier:

```
Private Sub cmdRemove_Click()

  mobjVideo.Tapes.Remove Val(lvwTapes.SelectedItem.Key)
  LoadTapes

End Sub
```

Again, we use the Val() function to retrieve the index value of the item the user selected. Using this index value, we just need to call the Remove method on the Tapes collection object, and it will remove the Tape object from the list. We then call LoadTapes so that our list is updated on the form.

The removal of an item from the list will be undone if the user then clicks the Cancel button on the VideoEdit screen. This is because, in Chapter 6, we built the Tapes object so that it didn't actually remove any objects until the ApplyEdit method was called. So now, when the user clicks Cancel, we'll cause the CancelEdit method to be called, which will restore any deleted Tape objects to the collection.

### Adding Code to VideoMain

Back in the `VideoMain` form, the <u>F</u>ile | <u>V</u>ideos | <u>N</u>ew Video menu option needs to contain the following code:

```
Private Sub mnuFileVideoNew_Click()

  Dim objVideo As Video
  Dim frmVideo As VideoEdit

  Set objVideo = New Video
  Set frmVideo = New VideoEdit

  frmVideo.Component objVideo
  frmVideo.Show

End Sub
```

Like the <u>N</u>ew Customer menu option, this code creates an instance of the `VideoEdit` form and a new instance of a `Video` object. It then uses the `VideoEdit` form's `Component` property to provide the form with a reference to the new object, and shows that form to the user.

## TapeEdit: Editing a Child Object

In the `VideoEdit` form's code, we provided support for adding and editing `Tape` objects. This was done with a `TapeEdit` form, so we'd best build that form at this point.

The `TapeEdit` form will be child's play compared to the others we've looked at. Excuse the pun, but this works out well since it's designed to edit a child object.

### Setting up the TapeEdit Form

As with the other forms, add a new form to the `VideoUI` project using the `BusForm` template. Set its **Name** property to `TapeEdit`. Since we'll be displaying this form in a modal fashion, set its **BorderStyle** to 3-Fixed Dialog. Add controls to make the form appear as shown here:

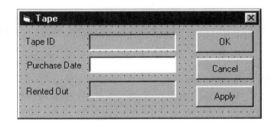

| Control | Caption | Name |
|---|---|---|
| Label | Tape ID | |
| Label | | lblTapeID |
| Label | Purchase date | |
| TextBox | | txtAcquired |
| Label | Rented out | |
| Label | | lblRented |

Make sure to set the `BorderStyle` property to **1-Fixed single** on the `lblTapeID` and `lblRented` controls to get the proper appearance.

As with the other forms, change the template code to work with the relevant business object; in this case, globally change `mobjBusiness` to `mobjTape`, and change every instance of the `Business` data type to `Tape`. Then change the `Form_Load` method as follows:

```
Private Sub Form_Load()

  mflgLoading = True

  With mobjTape
    EnableOK .IsValid

    If .IsNew Then
      Caption = "Tape [(new)]"

    Else
      Caption = "Tape [" & .Title & "]"
      txtAcquired.Locked = True
      txtAcquired.BackColor = lblTapeID.BackColor

    End If

    lblTapeID = .TapeID
    txtAcquired = .DateAcquired
    lblRented = IIf(.CheckedOut, "Yes", "No")
    .BeginEdit
  End With

  mflgLoading = False
End Sub
```

For the most part, this should look very familiar at this point - with one exception. In Chapter 6, we implemented the `Tape` object's `DateAcquired` property to be editable only when the object is new. This means that when an existing `Tape` object is brought up to be edited, this field can't be altered.

To make this visually apparent to the user, we've added some code to change the behavior of the `txtAcquired` control when the `Tape` object is not new:

```
txtAcquired.Locked = True
txtAcquired.BackColor = lblTapeID.BackColor
```

This code sets the control's `Locked` property to `True`, preventing the user from editing the field in any way. We also set the `BackColor` property to the background color of one of the label controls (typically gray), making it very apparent to the user that the field can't be edited.

This code may appear to replicate some business logic in the form. Why did we go through the work of making the property only editable when the object is new only to turn around and put similar code into the form?

We've considered this question once or twice already in earlier chapters. Ultimately, the answer is that we want to make the UI very friendly. We could just allow the business object to enforce the rule, but that would leave the user with no visual way to know that the field wasn't editable. They wouldn't know there was a problem until they tried to edit the field and got an error message.

Another alternative would be to *only* enforce the business rule in the UI, leaving the business object out of the picture. The problem with this approach is that our Visual Basic UI may not be our only user-interface using the business object. Some other UI developer might not be as thorough in implementing this rule - meaning that we could easily end up with the value being changed when it shouldn't be.

By keeping the business rule in our object, we can prevent the user from editing this field when it is inappropriate, regardless of the particular UI being used. At the same time, it makes a lot of sense for our UI to provide the user with a visual indication that the field isn't editable, thus providing a more friendly and pleasant user experience.

> **Just because a business rule is implemented in the object, that doesn't mean we shouldn't take steps to make the user's interface as rich and friendly as possible.**

### Text Box Control

The `txtAcquired` control represents a date property, just like the `txtRelease` control did on the `VideoEdit` form. The code is virtually identical; only the object and control names have changed:

```
Private Sub txtAcquired_Change()

  If Not mflgLoading Then _
    TextChange txtAcquired, mobjTape, "DateAcquired"

End Sub
```

```
Private Sub txtAcquired_LostFocus()

  txtAcquired = TextLostFocus(txtAcquired, mobjTape, "DateAcquired")

End Sub
```

# List Screens

Now that we've implemented all the functionality to add customers, videos, and tapes, we need to let the user bring up existing data to be viewed or edited. In Chapter 5, we built a couple of list objects to make this as easy as possible: `Customers` and `Videos`.

The objects' `Load` methods accept search criteria as parameters. They then act as collection objects, returning `CustomerDisplay` or `VideoDisplay` objects as elements of the collection as appropriate.

# CustomerSearch: Criteria Entry

Before we can display the content of the `Customers` object, we need to load it with values from the database. This is done using the object's `Load` method, which accepts search criteria as parameters: either `Name` or `Phone` or both.

## Setting up the CustomerSearch Form

Add a new form to the VideoUI project. Don't use the business form template in this case, as the form we're building now will be much simpler than that template would create. Set the Name property to CustomerSearch and the BorderStyle to 3-Fixed Dialog.

Add controls to make the form appear as shown:

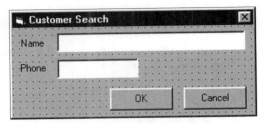

| Control | Caption | Name |
|---------|---------|------|
| Label | Name | |
| Text Box | | txtName |
| Label | Phone | |
| Text Box | | txtPhone |
| Command Button | OK | cmdOK |
| Command Button | Cancel | cmdCancel |

## Putting Code behind the CustomerSearch Form

We want to make forms that just retrieve criteria from the user to work as much like an object as possible. This will allow us to just show the form to the user, let them enter their input, and click either OK or Cancel. Either way, the form won't unload; rather, it will just hide itself and expose some Public properties so that the client code can find out what the user did on the form:

```
Option Explicit

Private mflgOK As Boolean

Private Sub cmdCancel_Click()

  mflgOK = False
  Hide

End Sub

Private Sub cmdOK_Click()

  mflgOK = True
  Hide

End Sub
```

In this case, we expose an OK property so that the client code can find out if the user clicked OK or Cancel:

```
Public Property Get OK() As Boolean

  OK = mflgOK

End Property
```

We'll also expose `Name` and `Phone` properties to return the values that the user entered into the form's controls:

```
Public Property Get ResultName() As String

  ResultName = txtName

End Property
```

```
Public Property Get ResultPhone() As String

  ResultPhone = txtPhone

End Property
```

## Adding Code to VideoMain

To see how this form is used, let's look at some of the code behind the <u>F</u>ile | <u>C</u>ustomers | <u>S</u>earch menu option within the `VideoMain` form:

```
Private Sub mnuFileCustSearch_Click()

  Dim frmSearch As CustomerSearch
  Dim objCustomers As Customers

  Set frmSearch = New CustomerSearch
  With frmSearch
    .Show vbModal

    If .OK Then
      Set objCustomers = New Customers
      objCustomers.Load .ResultName, .ResultPhone
      ' display the Customers object in a display form
      Set objCustomers = Nothing
    End If

  End With

  Unload frmSearch
  Set frmSearch = Nothing

End Sub
```

This code creates an instance of our criteria form, `CustomerSearch`, and shows it to the user. Using the values entered by the user, we create a `Customers` object and pass those values to its `Load` method. At this point, our `Customers` object should contain a list of all the customers who match the criteria supplied by the user.

# CustomerList: Search Results Display

Now that we have the user's search criteria, and we've used the Customers object's Load method to retrieve the list of matching data, we can display the information. We'll keep this as simple as possible. In some applications, we may need to build a more sophisticated form, but this will illustrate the basic principals that will be used.

## Setting up the CustomerList Form

Add a new form to the VideoUI project. Again, don't use the business form template, as this form will be quite simple. Name the form CustomerList and set its BorderStyle to 3-Fixed Dialog.

Add controls to make the form appear as follows:

| Control | Caption | Name |
|---|---|---|
| ListView | | lvwItems |
| CommandButton | OK | cmdOK |
| CommandButton | Cancel | cmdCancel |

Use the ListView control's properties window to change the View to 3-lvwReport, LabelEdit to 1-lvwManual and check FullRowSelect. Use the Column Headers tab to set up two columns: Name and Phone.

## Putting Code behind the CustomerList Form

In a very real sense, a form that displays a list of values so that the user can select one is basically just another way of gathering criteria - or user input. Whichever customer the user selects, in this window, that information will just be used as input to the Load method of a Customer object so that it can be edited.

Based on this view of the form, we'll treat it just like we did the CustomerSearch form in terms of implementation. When the user clicks OK or Cancel, the form won't Unload, but instead Hide itself - and the calling code can find out what the user chose by using Public properties on the form.

### Displaying the Data

Add the following code to the CustomerList form:

```
Option Explicit

Private mobjCustomers As Customers
Private mlngID As Long

Public Sub Component(objComponent As Customers)

  Dim objItem As CustomerDisplay
  Dim itmList As ListItem
  Dim lngIndex As Long

  Set mobjCustomers = objComponent
  For lngIndex = 1 To mobjCustomers.Count
    With objItem
      Set objItem = mobjCustomers.Item(lngIndex)
      Set itmList = _
        lvwItems.ListItems.Add(Key:= _
        Format$(objItem.CustomerID) & " K")

      With itmList
        .Text = objItem.Name
        .SubItems(1) = objItem.Phone
      End With

    End With

  Next

End Sub
```

This code implements a `Component` method to allow the client code to provide a reference to a `Customers` object. Within this method, we've put the code to copy the items from the `Customers` collection into the ListView control for display to the user.

Each item returned from the `Customers` object is a `CustomerDisplay` object, which provides `Name` and `Phone` properties.

The code to load the `ListView` control is virtually identical to the code we used to load the `Tape` objects into the `VideoEdit` form. However, with the `Tape` objects we simply used the index value of each object from the collection as the `Key` value in our `ListView` control. Here, we're going to store the `CustomerID` value as the `Key` value instead. This way, when the user selects an item from our list, we can easily retrieve the `CustomerID` value from the control and use it to load the appropriate `Customer` object.

The item's `Name` and `Phone` properties are placed in the `ListItem` object to be displayed:

```
Set itmList = _
  lvwItems.ListItems.Add(Key:= _
  Format$(objItem.CustomerID) & " K")

With itmList
  .Text = objItem.Name
  .SubItems(1) = objItem.Phone
End With
```

### Code behind the Controls

The OK and Cancel buttons hide the form rather than unloading it. They also set a module-level variable, mlngID, to hold the ID value of the object chosen by the user. The Cancel button stores a 0 to indicate no selection, while the OK button stores the index value of the item from the Customers collection object - by retrieving the value from the key value of the ListView control:

```
Private Sub cmdCancel_Click()

  mlngID = 0
  Hide

End Sub
```

```
Private Sub cmdOK_Click()

  On Error Resume Next
  mlngID = Val(lvwItems.SelectedItem.Key)
  Hide

End Sub
```

### Public Property - The Selected Customer

This form only needs to provide the ID value for the Customer object that the user has selected:

```
Public Property Get CustomerID() As Long

  CustomerID = mlngID

End Property
```

Since we stored the CustomerID property value as the key for each item in the ListView control, we were easily able to retrieve that value when the user clicked the OK button. That code stored the value in the module-level variable mlngID, so all we need to do within this property is provide that value to the client code.

## Adding Code to VideoMain

Now we can look at the entire code behind the File | Customers | Search menu option, back in our VideoMain form. We've already looked at the code to bring up the criteria form, so we can move on to add the code to bring up the CustomerList form:

```
Private Sub mnuFileCustSearch_Click()

  Dim frmSearch As CustomerSearch
  Dim frmList As CustomerList
  Dim objCustomers As Customers
  Dim objCustomer As Customer

  Set frmSearch = New CustomerSearch
  With frmSearch
    .Show vbModal
    If .OK Then
      Set frmList = New CustomerList
      Set objCustomers = New Customers
      objCustomers.Load .ResultName, .ResultPhone
```

```
        With frmList
          .Component objCustomers
          .Show vbModal

          If .CustomerID > 0 Then
            Set objCustomer = New Customer
            objCustomer.Load .CustomerID
            ' create and set up a CustomerEdit form
            Set objCustomer = Nothing
          End If

        End With

        Unload frmList
        Set frmList = Nothing
        Set objCustomers = Nothing

      End If

    End With

    Unload frmSearch
    Set frmSearch = Nothing

  End Sub
```

This new code creates an instance of the `CustomerList` form and uses its `Component` property to provide it with a reference to the `Customers` object we'd already loaded. The code then checks the resulting `CustomerID` property on the form to see if the user selected a valid customer to be edited.

If the user selected a customer from the list, then the `CustomerID` value will be greater than zero. In this case, we create a new `Customer` object and pass its `Load` method the ID value from the `CustomerList` form:

```
Set objCustomer = New Customer
objCustomer.Load .CustomerID
```

All that remains now is to add some extra code to bring up the `CustomerEdit` form and give it a reference to the `Customer` object we just loaded:

```
Private Sub mnuFileCustSearch_Click()

  Dim frmSearch As CustomerSearch
  Dim frmList As CustomerList
  Dim frmCustomer As CustomerEdit
  Dim objCustomers As Customers
  Dim objCustomer As Customer

  Set frmSearch = New CustomerSearch
  With frmSearch
    .Show vbModal
    If .OK Then
      Set frmList = New CustomerList
      Set objCustomers = New Customers
      objCustomers.Load .ResultName, .ResultPhone
```

```
    With frmList
      .Component objCustomers
      .Show vbModal

      If .CustomerID > 0 Then
        Set frmCustomer = New CustomerEdit
        Set objCustomer = New Customer
        objCustomer.Load .CustomerID
        frmCustomer.Component objCustomer
        frmCustomer.Show
        Set objCustomer = Nothing
      End If

    End With

    Unload frmList
    Set frmList = Nothing
    Set objCustomers = Nothing

  End If

End With

Unload frmSearch
Set frmSearch = Nothing

End Sub
```

With the completion of this code, the user can now add and edit customers at will.

*We could easily base a Delete menu option on the code for the search menu option. Instead of bringing up the* `CustomerEdit` *form, we'd just call the* `Customer` *object's* `Delete` *method, and away it would go.*

# VideoSearch: Criteria Entry

The `VideoSearch` form should work just like the `CustomerSearch` form. We won't go through this form in any detail, as it's very straightforward.

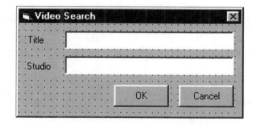

The two text boxes are called `txtTitle` and `txtStudio`, respectively. Here's the code to support this form:

```
Option Explicit

Private mflgOK As Boolean

Public Property Get OK() As Boolean

  OK = mflgOK
```

```
End Property

Public Property Get ResultTitle() As String

  ResultTitle = txtTitle

End Property

Public Property Get ResultStudio() As String

  ResultStudio = txtStudio

End Property

Private Sub cmdCancel_Click()

  mflgOK = False
  Hide

End Sub

Private Sub cmdOK_Click()

  mflgOK = True
  Hide

End Sub
```

# VideoList: Search Results Display

Again, the `VideoList` form is virtually identical to the `CustomerList` form. The primary difference is that the `Videos` object returns `VideoDisplay` objects for each item in the list whereas the `Customers` object returned `CustomerDisplay` objects. Beyond that, the form's code performs the same function, displaying the list to the user and providing a Public property so that the client code can retrieve the user's selection.

## Setting up the VideoList Form

Create the form to appear as
shown here:

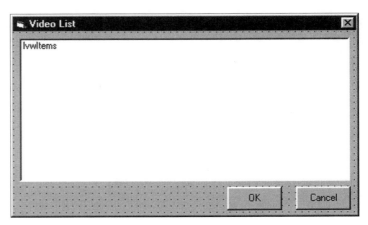

The column headers for the `ListView` control should be set to Title and Release date, with the View, LabelEdit and FullRowSelect properties set the same as with the `CustomerList` form. The code behind this form is shown here:

```
Option Explicit

Private mobjVideos As Videos
Private mlngID As Long

Public Sub Component(objComponent As Videos)

  Dim objItem As VideoDisplay
  Dim itmList As ListItem
  Dim lngIndex As Long

  Set mobjVideos = objComponent
  For lngIndex = 1 To mobjVideos.Count
    With objItem
      Set objItem = mobjVideos.Item(lngIndex)
      Set itmList = _
        lvwItems.ListItems.Add(Key:= _
        Format$(objItem.VideoID) & " K")

      With itmList
        .Text = objItem.Title
        .SubItems(1) = objItem.ReleaseDate
      End With

    End With

  Next

End Sub

Public Property Get VideoID() As Long

  VideoID = mlngID

End Property

Private Sub cmdCancel_Click()

  mlngID = 0
  Hide

End Sub

Private Sub cmdOK_Click()

  On Error Resume Next
  mlngID = Val(lvwItems.SelectedItem.Key)
  Hide

End Sub
```

## Main Menu Code for Video Search

We also need to add some code to the `VideoMain` form behind the File | Video | Search menu option. This code will make use of both the `VideoSearch` and `VideoList` forms, as well as the `Videos` object:

```
Private Sub mnuFileVideoSearch_Click()

  Dim frmSearch As VideoSearch
  Dim frmList As VideoList
  Dim frmVideo As VideoEdit
  Dim objVideos As Videos
  Dim objVideo As Video

  Set frmSearch = New VideoSearch
  With frmSearch
    .Show vbModal

    If .OK Then
      Set frmList = New VideoList
      Set objVideos = New Videos
      objVideos.Load .ResultTitle, .ResultStudio

      With frmList
        .Component objVideos
        .Show vbModal

        If .VideoID > 0 Then
          Set frmVideo = New VideoEdit
          Set objVideo = New Video
          objVideo.Load .VideoID
          frmVideo.Component objVideo
          frmVideo.Show
          Set objVideo = Nothing
        End If

      End With

      Unload frmList
      Set frmList = Nothing
      Set objVideos = Nothing

    End If

  End With

  Unload frmSearch
  Set frmSearch = Nothing

End Sub
```

This code is very similar to that used for the File | Customers | Search menu option. We use the
VideoSearch form to get the search criteria from the user, and we then provide the criteria to the
Videos object's Load method. Once the Videos object has retrieved the data from the database, we
create an instance of the VideoList form and use its Component method to give it a reference to
the Videos object.

# Transaction Support

So far, we've seen how to create forms that work with our business objects to add new objects, edit
existing objects, and display lists of data. All the objects we've worked with so far represent simple
business entities: a customer, a video title, a tape.

In addition to our simple business entities, we have a set of objects that support the concept of an invoice. Adding an invoice is typically considered a transaction, so the Invoice object represents a transaction rather than a simple business entity. We also need to support the concept of checking in a tape when the customer returns it - which also qualifies as a form of transaction.

Let's look at how we can create a UI to support these two transactions.

# InvoiceEdit

While adding an Invoice object is considered to be a transaction, there is no difference in code from the UI developer's viewpoint. We can treat this like any other form that edits a business object. This means that the InvoiceEdit screen will work just like the CustomerEdit and VideoEdit forms that we implemented earlier in the chapter.

## Setting up the InvoiceEdit Form

Since this form will primarily be editing a business object, use the business object form template to add a form to the VideoUI project. Set the Name property to InvoiceEdit and the MDIChild property to True.

Now add controls to the form as shown here:

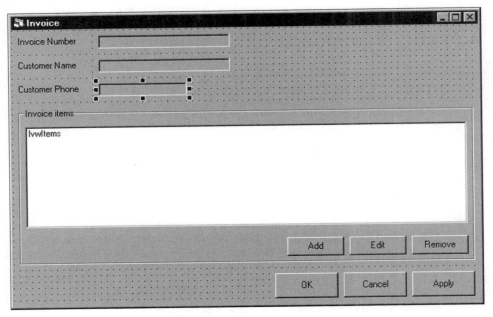

| Control | Caption | Name |
|---------|---------|------|
| Label | Invoice Number | |
| Label | | lblInvoiceID |
| Label | Customer Name | |

| Control | Caption | Name |
|---|---|---|
| Label | | lblName |
| Label | Customer Phone | |
| Label | | lblPhone |
| Frame | Invoice Items | |
| ListView | | lvwItems |
| Command Button | Add | cmdAdd |
| Command Button | Edit | cmdEdit |
| Command Button | Remove | cmdRemove |
| Command Button | OK | cmdOK |
| Command Button | Cancel | cmdCancel |
| Command Button | Apply | cmdApply |

Set the **BorderStyle** property of the `lblInvoiceID`, `lblName` and `lblPhone` controls to 1-Fixed Single.

We also need to set some of the properties of the ListView control in this form. Right-click on the control and choose **P**roperties from the context menu. Now set the **V**iew property to 3-lvwReport , the Label**E**dit property to 1-lvwManual, check the **FullRowSelect** option and, under the **Column Headers** tab, add the column titles **Type, Description** and **Amount**.

As with the edit screens we built earlier, we need to change all instances of `mobjBusiness` to refer to the relevant business object. In this case, globally change `mobjBusiness` to `mobjInvoice` and change all the instances of `Business` to `Invoice` in the template code. The `Form_Load` method will also need to be modified to copy the `Invoice` object's property values into the form's controls:

```
Private Sub Form_Load()

  mflgLoading = True

  With mobjInvoice
    EnableOK .IsValid

    If .IsNew Then
      lblInvoiceID = "(new)"

    Else
      lblInvoiceID = .InvoiceID

    End If

    lblName = .CustomerName
    lblPhone = .CustomerPhone
```

```
      .BeginEdit
    End With

    mflgLoading = False

  End Sub
```

Other than the line items on the invoice, there aren't any fields for the user to edit. The `Customer` object's `CreateInvoice` method not only creates the `Invoice` object, but it also provides it with the basic information that's displayed on the screen. The rest of the information is based on the `InvoiceItem` child objects that the user adds later.

## Child Object Support

Like the `Video` object, the `Invoice` object is a parent to other objects. The `Invoice` object is a bit more complex, however, since the child objects might be both `InvoiceFee` and `InvoiceTape` objects. Using traditional programming techniques, we'd probably need extra code to deal with this case. Since we're using object-oriented techniques, however, we can avoid any extra work.

When we implemented these objects, we created them both to provide an `InvoiceItem` interface. This means that each of these objects has two interfaces. The `InvoiceFee` object has an `InvoiceFee` interface *and* an `InvoiceItem` interface. Likewise, the `InvoiceTape` object has both an `InvoiceTape` interface and an `InvoiceItem` interface. Since both objects have an `InvoiceItem` interface, we can create code to work with just that interface - and we won't care what particular type of object it really is. This is an application of both multiple interfaces and polymorphism, all in one shot.

### Displaying the Child Objects

As with the `VideoEdit` form, we'll add a `LoadItems` routine to copy the child object's properties into the `ListView` control for display:

```
  Private Sub LoadItems()

    Dim objItem As InvoiceItem
    Dim itmList As ListItem
    Dim lngIndex As Long

    lvwItems.ListItems.Clear

    For lngIndex = 1 To mobjInvoice.InvoiceItems.Count
      Set itmList = lvwItems.ListItems.Add _
        (Key:=Format$(lngIndex) & "K")
      Set objItem = mobjInvoice.InvoiceItems(lngIndex)

      With itmList
        .Text = IIf(objItem.ItemType = ITEM_FEE, _
          "Late fee", "Rental")
        If objItem.IsDeleted Then .Text = "(deleted)"
        .SubItems(1) = objItem.ItemDescription
        .SubItems(2) = Format$(objItem.Total, "0.00")
      End With

    Next

  End Sub
```

Notice that the `objItem` variable is declared as type `InvoiceItem`. Even though the child objects will be of either the `InvoiceFee` or `InvoiceTape` types, we can treat them all as `InvoiceItem` objects because they implemented that interface. The beauty of this is that we could add more types of child business objects and we wouldn't have to change this display routine at all – beyond perhaps adding some new description text.

We'll need to call the `LoadItems` routine from a number of places within the form, starting with the `Form_Load` routine:

```
Private Sub Form_Load()

  mflgLoading = True

  With mobjInvoice
    EnableOK .IsValid

    If .IsNew Then
      lblInvoiceID = "(new)"

    Else
      lblInvoiceID = .InvoiceID

    End If

    lblName = .CustomerName
    lblPhone = .CustomerPhone
    .BeginEdit
  End With

  LoadItems
  mflgLoading = False

End Sub
```

We'll add the call to `LoadItems` elsewhere as we get to each routine.

### Adding InvoiceTape Objects

Unlike the display routine, we do need to have different support for each type of child object that we need to add to the `Invoice` object. This is because we'll need to provide an interface for the user to add the information that's customized to the child business object.

We'll keep the code behind the `Add` button as simple as possible. The only type of line item the user can add to the invoice is a tape rental. To add this line item, the only piece of information that is absolutely required is the tape's ID value. This would probably be scanned off the tape with a barcode reader, so we'll just prompt the user for this value using the `InputBox$()` command:

```
Private Sub cmdAdd_Click()

  Dim frmItem As InvoiceTapeEdit
  Dim strID As String

  strID = InputBox$("Scan the tape ID", "Tape ID")
  If Val(strID) = 0 Then Exit Sub
```

If no number is supplied, we'll just exit the subroutine. The typical reason this value would be 0 is if the user clicked the Cancel button in the input box.

Now that we've got a tape's ID value, we can create an instance of a form to edit the line item:

```
Set frmItem = New InvoiceTapeEdit
```

This form's name is `InvoiceTapeEdit`. It's another basic business object edit form, so use the `BusForm` template and add the controls as shown here:

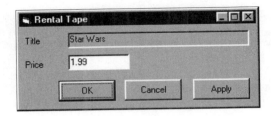

| Control | Caption | Name |
|---------|---------|------|
| Label | Title | |
| Label | | lblTitle |
| Label | Price | |
| TextBox | | txtPrice |

Set the BorderStyle property of the `lblTitle` control to 1-Fixed Single and that of the form itself to 3 - Fixed Dialog.

As with the edit screens we built earlier, we need to change the code behind it so that all instances of `objBusiness` refer to the relevant business object.

In this case, globally change `mobjBusiness` to `mobjInvoiceTape`, and change all the instances of `Business` to `InvoiceTape` in the template code. The `Form_Load` method will also need to be modified to copy the `Invoice` object's property values into the form's controls:

```
Private Sub Form_Load()

  mflgLoading = True

  With mobjInvoiceTape
    EnableOK .IsValid
    lblTitle = .Title
    txtPrice = .Price
    .BeginEdit
  End With

  mflgLoading = False

End Sub
```

Back in the `cmdAdd_Click` event of `InvoiceEdit` we can use our new form's `Component` method and provide it with a reference to a new `InvoiceTape` line item:

```
    On Error GoTo ADDERR
    frmItem.Component mobjInvoice.InvoiceItems.Add(Val(strID))
    frmItem.Show vbModal
    LoadItems
    Exit Sub
```

The new object is created using the Add method of the InvoiceItems object from the InvoiceEdit form's Invoice object. We implemented this Add method in Chapter 6 so that it accepts a Tape ID value as a parameter and builds the line item based on that ID.

If we didn't get an error when calling the Add method, we show the form to the user so they can edit the line item as needed. In this case, all they can change is the price. As with the other child objects we've worked with, if they click the Cancel button then the object won't be added to the InvoiceItems collection. Once the user has completed their editing of the object we'll call the LoadItems routine to refresh the display of child information on the form.

The On Error GoTo ADDERR is important, since the Add method we've called might raise an error. In particular, if the ID value entered by the user is invalid, we'll get an error; equally, if the tape has already been rented out on another invoice, we'll get another error. The following code checks to see if there was an error, and responds appropriately for each error:

```
  ADDERR:
    If Err = vbObjectError + 1100 Then
      MsgBox "Tape is already checked out", vbExclamation

    Else
      MsgBox "Invalid tape id", vbExclamation

    End If

    Set frmItem = Nothing

  End Sub
```

### Editing Line Items

As with adding items, we need to check the line item's type when editing. The only type of line item the user can edit are the InvoiceTape items. With the ListView control the user might select an InvoiceFee line item to edit, so we need to check for this and handle it appropriately.

The first thing we need to do is get a reference to the object corresponding to the item the user selected on the screen. We'll put the reference to the object in objItem, which is of type InvoiceItem:

```
  Private Sub cmdEdit_Click()

    Dim frmItem As InvoiceTapeEdit
    Dim objItem As InvoiceItem

    Set objItem = _
      mobjInvoice.InvoiceItems(Val(lvwItems.SelectedItem.Key))
```

The `InvoiceItem` interface provides an `ItemType` property that we can use to determine the type of the object the user selected. If it's of type `ITEM_TAPE`, we can use the `InvoiceTapeEdit` form to allow the user to edit the object; otherwise, we'll just display a message so the user knows they can't edit late fee line items:

```
    If objItem.ItemType = ITEM_TAPE Then
      Set frmItem = New InvoiceTapeEdit
      frmItem.Component _
        mobjInvoice.InvoiceItems(Val(lvwItems.SelectedItem.Key))
      frmItem.Show vbModal
      LoadItems

    Else
      MsgBox "Only tape rental items can be edited", _
        vbInformation

    End If

  End Sub
```

### Removing Line Items

Both the `InvoiceTape` and `InvoiceFee` objects provide support for being deleted, so the code behind the **Remove** button won't have to care which type of line item the user selected. This means the code is pretty much identical to the code we used on the `VideoEdit` form:

```
  Private Sub cmdRemove_Click()

    mobjInvoice.InvoiceItems.Remove Val(lvwItems.SelectedItem.Key)
    LoadItems

  End Sub
```

## Setting up the Menu Option

As with the forms we've put together earlier in the chapter, the `InvoiceEdit` form expects to be provided with an `Invoice` object through its `Component` method. In Chapter 6, we implemented the `Invoice` object as **PublicNotCreatable**, with the intent that the UI code would be using the `CreateInvoice` method of the `Customer` object to add any `Invoice` objects.

This makes sense, since the typical video rental transaction starts by identifying the customer and then adding the invoice. Our application should follow this model to make it as easy as possible for the user. When the user chooses the File | New invoice menu option, they should be prompted to choose a customer; then the `InvoiceEdit` form should come up.

This whole process is very similar to what happens with the File | Customers | Search menu option. We need to present the criteria screen and then the CustomerList screen. Where we displayed the `CustomerEdit` before, we'll change the code to create a new `Invoice` object and bring up the `InvoiceEdit` screen.

All of the following code is new to our `VideoMain` form, so it all needs to be entered. However, I've only highlighted those lines that are different from the code for our File | Customers | Search menu option; this way, you can see the similarity between them more easily:

```
Private Sub mnuFileInvoiceNew_Click()

    Dim frmSearch As CustomerSearch
    Dim frmList As CustomerList
    Dim objCustomers As Customers
    Dim objCustomer As Customer
    Dim objInvoice As Invoice
    Dim frmInvoice As InvoiceEdit

    Set frmSearch = New CustomerSearch

    With frmSearch
      .Show vbModal

      If .OK Then
        Set frmList = New CustomerList
        Set objCustomers = New Customers
        objCustomers.Load .ResultName, .ResultPhone

        With frmList
          .Component objCustomers
          .Show vbModal
          If .CustomerID > 0 Then
            Set frmInvoice = New InvoiceEdit

            Set objCustomer = New Customer
            objCustomer.Load .CustomerID
            Set objInvoice = objCustomer.CreateInvoice

            frmInvoice.Component objInvoice
            frmInvoice.Show
          End If

        End With

        Unload frmList
        Set frmList = Nothing
        Set objCustomers = Nothing

      End If

    End With

    Unload frmSearch
    Set frmSearch = Nothing

End Sub
```

# Checking in a Tape

Our menu also provides a File | Check in tape menu option to allow the user to check in a tape that has been rented. When the customer returns a tape, the user should just have to enter the tape's ID value into the system to have it recorded as returned.

To keep this as simple as possible, we'll just use the InputBox$() command to prompt the user for the tape's ID value. If the user clicks the Cancel button, we'll get a value of 0; and if we do get a 0 result, we'll just exit the subroutine:

```
Private Sub mnuFileCheckIn_Click()

   Dim strID As String
   Dim objTape As Tape

   strID = InputBox$("Scan tape ID", "Check in tape")
   If Val(strID) = 0 Then Exit Sub
```

Once we have an ID value, we can create a `Tape` object and use its `Load` method to retrieve the object's data from the database:

```
   Set objTape = New Tape
   On Error Resume Next
   objTape.Load Val(strID)
```

The `Load` method could return an error if the user has provided an ID value that is invalid. By using `On Error Resume Next` before calling the `Load` method, we can then check the `Err` value to see if an error occurred. If we do get an error, we can react by informing the user that the supplied ID value isn't valid:

```
   If Err Then
      MsgBox "Invalid tape ID", vbExclamation
      Exit Sub

   End If

   On Error GoTo 0
```

If we don't get an error then we know we have a `Tape` object that's loaded with information from the database. At this point, we can use the `CheckIn` method to indicate that the tape is no longer rented out to a customer.

We'll also include some code to make sure the tape is in fact checked out by using the `CheckedOut` property. While this is a business rule that is enforced within the business object, we'll add code in the form as well - just to make sure the user has a more pleasant experience with our application. The `Tape` object will raise an error if we call the `CheckIn` method on an object that isn't checked out; but, rather than trapping that error, we'll head it off by using the `CheckedOut` property:

```
   With objTape
      If .CheckedOut Then
         .BeginEdit
         .CheckIn
         .ApplyEdit

      Else
         MsgBox "Tape is not checked out", vbExclamation

      End If

   End With

   Set objTape = Nothing

End Sub
```

The calls to BeginEdit and ApplyEdit are necessary because we built the CheckIn method, in Chapter 6, to provide some support for being rolled back by the CancelEdit method.

## Running the UI

We've finished developing our UI for the moment, and we should be able to compile both the business objects and the empty interface shell that we've developed in this chapter.

If you run the VideoUI project, you'll see the VideoMain MDI form load, and various menu options are available from the program's menu bar.

Of course, these menu items won't be very active, at the moment, because we haven't implemented any persistence code behind them. Nevertheless, we've really achieved something in this chapter: we now have a full UI, our business objects are interacting with that UI, and we're ready to bring our Video Rental system to life in the next chapter.

## Summary

In this chapter, we've covered some basic concepts behind building a user-interface to work with our business objects. This interface was constructed with Visual Basic forms. We looked at a number of different types of interface:

- ❑   Editing simple business objects
- ❑   Editing parent objects
- ❑   Editing child objects
- ❑   Transaction objects

We also saw how we can easily add form templates to our Visual Basic environment. We used one such template to build a number of the forms that edit business objects.

We can use this interface as we go through the remaining chapters and implement data access code for our objects. Once we've finished the next chapter, we'll have a fully working single-tier application. In addition, we'll be able to use the code we've developed here to create another interfaces using Microsoft Excel.

# Implementing Single-Tier or Two-Tier Data Access

## Overview

So far, in our journey through business objects for Visual Basic, we've built an application from business objects and we've created a user-interface to work with those objects. Of course, the application isn't very useful yet, since none of the business objects have any code to retrieve or save their state in a database.

In Chapter 4, we discussed a number of different physical architectures. The simplest architecture we've identified is a single-tier where the client directly accesses the files that contain the database. Using Visual Basic, this type of access is typically done using ADO (ActiveX Data Objects). Fortunately for us, as Visual Basic programmers, ADO is also a practical technology we can use when we're developing two-tier applications, where the client communicates directly with a data server such as Microsoft SQL Server.

Also, in Chapter 4, we looked at the various techniques we can use to implement object persistence, including:

- ❑ Putting the data access code in each object
- ❑ Using an object manager to provide data access
- ❑ Putting the data access in a data-centric business object

Of these techniques, the first is the simplest: to include the data access code within each business object. This technique is only useful in single-tier or two-tier physical architectures, but it does have the advantage of being the easiest to implement and understand.

As a great introduction to implementing object persistence, in this chapter we'll keep the data access code inside the business objects themselves and use ADO to work with the database. We'll use a Microsoft Access database, so that anyone with Visual Basic can implement this code.

The techniques and principals that we'll use here are easily adaptable to a two-tier setting. The ADO code will need virtually no change as we move to a 2 or even an n-tier solution.

# Object State

One of the key concepts in making an object persistent is the concept of *state*. We discussed this earlier in the book, but a quick refresher is probably in order, since this concept is so important.

Objects are composed of three basic concepts:

- ❑ **Interface** - The interface is composed of the object's public properties and methods.
- ❑ **Implementation** - The implementation is basically the code that makes the interface work. This is the code behind each property or method that implements the desired behaviors.
- ❑ **State** - The object's state is the core set of data values that make up the object. These are the values that must be saved to and restored from a database, such that the object can be destroyed and recreated based on those values. Note that the object may well have other data values and properties that are derived from these core data values.

Each individual object is unique and has an underlying set of data that makes it so. Often an object can be represented by a single row of data within a table, although there are exceptions. An object's state must always contain a unique identifier that can be used as a primary key value when retrieving the object's data from the database. This unique identifier may not always be made available to client programs through the object's interface, although we did make it available in all the business objects we built in Chapter 5.

# An Approach to Persistence

In this chapter, all the objects will contain the code they need to retrieve, add, update, and delete themselves from within the database. We've already implemented Load, Delete and ApplyEdit methods in our objects, with the intent of making it easy to add this database code.

All the data access code will be hidden from the UI code. The business objects will manage all database activity behind the scenes. In our video rental store example, the VideoUI interface project won't even have a reference to the ADO library: it will let the VideoObjects DLL handle all the details of data access.

In Chapter 10, we'll see how the database code can be moved out of the UI-centric business objects and into data-centric objects. This will allow us to make the data access code run on an application server rather than directly on the client workstation. As we discussed in Chapter 4, this is a much more scalable solution than including the code directly in the objects, since it puts the data access code much closer to the data source.

Keeping scalability in mind, it's a good idea to put all the data access code in private routines within each object rather than directly in the Load, Delete and ApplyEdit methods. This not only makes the code clearer overall, but will make it easier to take the data access code out of the business objects and move them to an application server later.

## Retrieving Data

All of our objects need to be able to load their state from the database. We'll create a private `Fetch` routine in each object to contain the code to retrieve the data.

Earlier, we defined an object's state as being its core data. We also noted that each object's state includes a unique identifier that can be used as the primary key when retrieving the object's data from the database. Our `Fetch` routine will accept this key value as a parameter, making it very easy to go to the database and find the correct data to bring back.

The following is an example of a very basic `Fetch` method for an object with an `ID` and a `Name` field. All the `Fetch` methods that we'll implement in our objects will follow this basic pattern.

Don't worry about entering this code, we'll get around to that when we make our video rental store objects persistent later in the chapter.

```
Private Sub Fetch(ObjectID As Long)

  Dim rsObject As Recordset
  Dim strSQL As String

  strSQL = "SELECT NAME FROM TABLE WHERE OBJECTID=" & ObjectID
  Set rsObject = New Recordset
  rsObject.Open strSQL, cnVideo

  With rsObject
    mudtProps.ObjectID = ObjectID
    mudtProps.Name = .Fields("Name")

    mobjValid.RuleBroken "Name", False

    .Close
  End With

  rsObject.Close
  Set rsObject = Nothing

End Sub
```

The subroutine accepts an `ObjectID` value as a parameter. In this example, the value is of type `Long`, but it could be of any data type able to represent the primary key that we'll use to find the data in the database.

### Building a SQL Statement

The next thing we need to do is use this `ID` value to build a SQL statement so we can retrieve the appropriate data from the database.

```
strSQL = "SELECT NAME FROM TABLE WHERE OBJECTID=" & ObjectID
```

This example SQL statement is not complex; it just retrieves the data from the table using a simple `WHERE` clause. If our object's data is scattered across multiple tables, we might have to join the tables together to get at all the fields.

## Opening a Recordset

Now that we have a SQL statement, we can use it to create a recordset using the object's `Open` method and using a pre-existing `Connection` object. We'll discuss how to open the connection itself in our `VideoObjects` project later in the chapter, but for now we'll just use a `Connection` variable named `cnVideo`:

```
Set rsObject = New Recordset
rsObject.Open strSQL, cnVideo
```

> *It's best to put the SQL statement into a string variable and then use it to create a recordset. This makes debugging easier, since we can set a breakpoint on this line and very easily use the Immediate window to look at the full SQL statement. It's certainly possible to build the SQL statement right in the Open statement, but then it would be very difficult to use the Immediate window to see the SQL statement.*
>
> *From a performance perspective it's also typically best to use a parameterized query or stored procedure rather than passing a straight SQL query. Most database engines compile and/or optimize parameterized queries and stored procedures, allowing them to run faster within the database.*

Since the only thing we're going to do with the data in this recordset is to store it in the object's local variables, we don't need read-write access to the data. Fortunately, the OLE DB provider for Jet databases defaults to creating read-only `Recordset` objects.

## Copy Data Fields to the Object

Using the recordset we just created, we can easily write code to copy the data from the recordset into the object's local variables. All our objects store their state in a variable named `mudtProps`, which is based on a user-defined type (UDT); so we've followed that implementation here:

```
With rsObject
  mudtProps.ObjectID = .Fields("ObjectID")
  mudtProps.Name = .Fields("Name")
```

If we assume that the data loaded from the database is valid then we can also run through any rules that we marked as broken in the object's `Initialize` subroutine and mark them as unbroken. This is pretty typical, since usually the only way the data gets into the database is through our objects; so when the data is read back in, it's fair to assume that it's still as valid as when it was written out:

```
mobjValid.RuleBroken "Name", False

.Close
```

## Handling Errors

We have no error-trapping code in this routine. Believe it or not, this is intentional, since if an error is encountered while loading the object's data, we'll want to raise the error up to the UI code. That way, an appropriate message can be displayed to the user. Visual Basic's default behavior for unhandled errors in an object is to raise it up to the calling code, so the easiest thing we can do is just take the default.

The most likely error we'll get in this code is if the `ObjectID` value doesn't return a record in the database. As soon as we try to use the recordset we'll get an error, and that error will be automatically raised by Visual Basic right back up to the code in the UI. This makes it very easy for the UI developer to trap that error and let the user know what happened in whatever way is appropriate for the interface.

## Adding/Updating Data

Not every object needs to be able to save itself to the database. Some objects are read-only and typically come from data entered through other objects or from other applications. On the other hand, many objects do need to be able to save themselves in the database. To support this operation we'll add a `Private Save` subroutine to those objects.

We're combining the add and update operations together because the code required for them is so similar. When using the data object models such as ADO or RDO, the difference between adding a record or updating a record is just a couple lines. The vast bulk of the code is identical either way, since both operations need to copy the object's values into the record and call an update method on the data object.

The basic structure of the `Save` routine is pretty straightforward. The following example is based on the same simple object we looked at with the `Fetch` subroutine, where the object's data is composed of an `ID` value and a `Name` field:

```
Private Sub Save()

  Dim rsObject As Recordset
  Dim strSQL As String

  Set rsObject = New Recordset
  rsObject.LockType = adLockPessimistic
  strSQL = "SELECT * FROM TABLE WHERE OBJECTID=" & ObjectID
  rsObject.Open strSQL, cnVideo
  If mflgNew Then rsObject.AddNew

  With rsObject
    .Fields("Name") = mudtProps.Name
    .Update
    If mflgNew Then mudtProps.ObjectID = .Fields("ObjectID")
    .Close
  End With

  Set rsObject = Nothing

End Sub
```

The first thing we need to do is create a `Recordset` object with read-write access to our database. To do this we'll create a new `Recordset` object and use its `Open` method. First though, we make sure to set the object's `LockType` to something other than the default read-only setting. In this example we've set it to `adLockPessimistic`, for pessimistic locking.

In traditional applications setting the `LockType` to `adLockPessimistic` would imply that our program will maintain a lock on the record we've accessed – allowing us to edit that data without fear of some other user gaining access and editing it at the same time.

With the way we're building our application, the business object will retrieve the data and immediately release any reference to the database. This means that we are always employing optimistic locking, regardless of the setting for this recordset. Thus any lock we might have had is destroyed immediately, so actual pessimistic locking only exists during the time it takes to copy the data from the recordset into our internal variables.

### Adding Data

The next thing we need to do is determine whether we're adding or updating the object to the database. Fortunately, our object maintains the `mflgNew` variable to indicate whether it represents data in the database or whether it contains data that's not in the database yet. If `mflgNew` is `True`, we can call the `AddNew` method to add a new record to the table:

```
If mflgNew Then rsObject.AddNew
```

### Updating Data

If `mflgNew` turns out to be `False`, we are updating existing data in the database. Since we've already opened our recordset to be read-write and to select the correct row of data with the `WHERE` clause we don't need to do any more work. We can simply proceed to change the data in the recordset and then call the `Update` method when we're done.

### Copying the Field Values

Using the recordset we just opened, we can simply copy the object's internal data values into the recordset:

```
With rsObject
  .Fields("Name") = mudtProps.Name
  .Update
```

We don't want to copy the `ObjectID` value, of course, since it's the primary key and thus can't be changed. We do, however, need to copy all the other data elements that comprise the object's state.

After the data values are copied into the recordset, we can call the recordset's `Update` method to actually put the data into the database. If we're updating the database then we're pretty much all done; but if we're adding data, there's a bit more work to do.

### Retrieving the New Primary Key

All of the objects we created in Chapter 5 were designed with a numeric ID value. In all these objects, the assumption we made was that the ID value would be assigned by the database when the object was first saved out. This is easily accomplished with most databases, since they almost all provide a mechanism to automatically generate a sequentially ascending number. In Microsoft Access, this type of field is called an Autonumber.

> *In case your database does not support this Autonumber capability, you can easily simulate it. How this is done can vary by database type. For instance, in Oracle you would use a trigger and leverage the Sequence object inherent in that database. If your database has no native support for generating unique values you can simulate an Autonumber by creating a table with two columns – table name and sequence number field. Every time you need a sequence number, access the specific table entry, retrieve the current sequence number, increment the value and update the record. You may want to abstract this behavior by a function if you want portability across different types of databases.*

By making each object's ID field an **Autonumber** within the database, we ensure that the database will provide a unique numeric ID value when a new record is added to the table. The trick is that this ID value is *in the database*, not in our object. Once the object has been saved to the database, it's no longer a 'new' object, so all our code assumes that the object knows its ID value.

Using ADO with the Jet provider, this is easy to accomplish. Once we've called the `Update` method on our `Recordset` object, ADO leaves us on the current record with any changed values updated into the object. Thus, we can simply retrieve the `ObjectID` field's value back from our `Recordset` object and we're on our way:

```
If mflgNew Then mudtProps.ObjectID = .Fields("ObjectID")
```

This way the object's internal state should completely match the data stored in the database, right down to the newly created primary key value.

### Deleting Data

Many of our objects will also need to be removed from the database through their `Delete` methods. This means we need to provide a routine along the lines of `Fetch` and `Save` to manage the removal of an object's data from the database. Of course, `Delete` is a reserved word, so we need to choose a different name. Instead, we'll use the name `DeleteObject` within these objects.

Of the operations we've looked at so far, the delete operation is typically the simplest:

```
Private Sub DeleteObject(ObjectID As Long)

  cnVideo.Execute "DELETE FROM TABLE WHERE OBJECTID=" & ObjectID

End Sub
```

Like the `Fetch` subroutine, this one requires that the object's ID value be passed as a parameter. From there it's easy, since all we need to do is use the `Connection` object's `Execute` method to run a SQL `DELETE` statement.

# Setting up the VideoObjects Project

Now that we've looked at the basic approach and concepts that we'll use to save each object to the database, let's move on to apply them to our sample application.

One of the biggest benefits in using component-oriented design is that we can isolate many application changes to a specific component, leaving the others unchanged and perhaps even unaware that anything has been changed. While this isn't always possible, we can certainly minimize the impact of changes and even eliminate them in some cases.

To illustrate how this is possible, in this chapter we'll add the code to make our objects persistent by altering just the `VideoObjects` component, leaving the `VideoUI` interface project entirely alone and unaware of the changes.

Therefore, all the changes we'll be making to the code through the rest of this chapter will be within the `VideoObjects` project. The `VideoUI` project that we created in Chapter 7 will continue to work without change - but we'll see our UI becoming more effective as we implement the code that will allow our business objects to begin saving and retrieving data.

## Referencing the ADO Library

ADO may be fairly new to many Visual Basic developers, as Visual Basic 6.0 is the first time ADO and OLE DB have been included directly with the product. Some Visual Basic developers may have started using ADO when developing Active Server Pages or even from within Visual Basic 5.0 if they installed the ADO libraries themselves. In any case, using ADO is really no more difficult than using DAO – a technology with which virtually all Visual Basic developers are very familiar.

Both ADO itself and full support for Access databases via OLE DB are provided with Visual Basic 6.0 right out of the box. This should make it fairly easy for us to implement everything in this chapter.

To use ADO within a Visual Basic project, we need to add a reference to the ADO object library. Open up the `VideoObjects` project and make sure the Microsoft ActiveX Data Objects 2.0 Library is selected within the Project | References menu option.

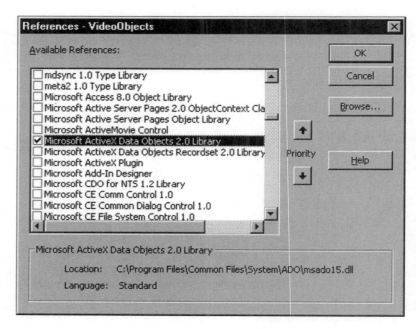

Now we'll be able to use all the objects and constant values from the ADO library within the `VideoObjects` project.

## The Database Connection

In the `Fetch`, `Save` and `DeleteObject` routines that we examined earlier in this chapter, the code assumed that there was a pre-existing database connection. In our example code, this was a variable named `cnVideo`. We'll want to provide the same persistent data connection within our `VideoObjects` project. Opening a database through ADO can be an expensive operation in terms of performance. Ideally we'd open a connection to the database when the program starts up and leave it open until the program is closed.

### Connection Variable - cnVideo

For a variable to be available across all modules within a Visual Basic project, it must be declared as a `Public` variable in a `BAS` module. Normally it's best to avoid such global variables, but there are a few cases where they are required- and this is one of those cases.

Open the `VideoObjects` project, add a standard code module and name it `VOmain`. Then add a declaration for a `cnVideo` variable as type `Connection`:

```
Option Explicit

Public cnVideo As Connection
```

### Opening the Database

Now that we have a database variable, all that remains is to open the database when the program starts up. More accurately, we need to open the database before any objects inside our `VideoObjects` ActiveX DLL are created. After all, if the client program never uses any of our objects we don't need to worry about opening the database.

Fortunately for us, Visual Basic makes this very easy to implement. An ActiveX DLL can have a `Main` subroutine in a code module, and that subroutine can be set as the project's startup routine. Then, when the client program attempts to create the first object from the DLL, Visual Basic will run the `Main` subroutine before the object is created. If we open the database at that time, we can keep it open until the last object from the DLL is terminated.

Within the `VOMain` code module we just created, add a `Public Sub Main` subroutine and have it open a connection to the database:

```
Public Sub Main()

   Set cnVideo = New Connection
   cnVideo.Provider = "Microsoft.Jet.OLEDB.3.51"
   cnVideo.Mode = adModeReadWrite
   cnVideo.Open "C:\Wrox\VB6 Pro Objects\Video.mdb"

End Sub
```

In this case we're using the OLE DB Jet provider and setting the connection to be read-write rather than read-only. The `Open` method accepts the filename as a parameter. This may require changing depending on where the file actually resides.

Make sure to choose the Project | VideoObjects Properties... menu option and change the Startup Object to Sub Main, otherwise this routine won't ever be run.

# Setting up the Database

Data access code is pretty useless without a database to work with. We won't go into detail on how to create a Microsoft Access database, although I will lay out the table definitions clearly.

The best approach is to create the database using Microsoft Access itself. This is by far the easiest tool to use when creating Access databases. Alternatively, Visual Basic comes with VisData, the Visual Data Manager. To use this tool, choose the Add-Ins | Visual Data Manager... menu option within Visual Basic.

It's worth noting that we have the luxury of creating the database based on the objects we designed in Chapter 5. This is an ideal situation, since our objects are dictating the design of the database.

In many cases, we'll find that we need to work with a database that already exists. When this happens, we'll need to make the Fetch, Save and DeleteObject methods more complex so they can retrieve and update each object's data in the appropriate fields in the appropriate tables in the database. The reason this might be more complex is that an object's data might be scattered across multiple tables in an existing database, or even across multiple data sources such as Microsoft SQL Server for some data and DB2 on a mainframe for some other data – all for the same object.

## The Customer Table

The Customer table will be used to store our Customer objects' data. The fields in the table will reflect the elements of the CustomerProps UDT we implemented in the Customer object:

```
Private Type CustomerProps
   CustomerID As Long
   Name As String * 50
   Phone As String * 25
   Address1 As String * 30
   Address2 As String * 30
   City As String * 20
   State As String * 10
   ZipCode As String * 10
End Type
```

Here are the fields for the Customer table:

| Field Name | Data Type | Field Size |
|---|---|---|
| CustomerID | AutoNumber | Long Integer |
| Name | Text | 50 |
| Phone | Text | 25 |
| Address1 | Text | 30 |
| Address2 | Text | 30 |
| City | Text | 20 |
| State | Text | 10 |
| ZipCode | Text | 10 |

The CustomerID field should be set up as the primary key for the table. Optionally, we might also choose to add indexes for the Name and Phone numbers, since we know they'll be used as search criteria by the Customers object.

## The LateFee Table

The only data elements directly subordinate to the Customer table are the late fees. While we didn't create a LateFee object per se, we did set up the Tape object to add records to a list of late fees for the customer and we designed the invoice objects to work with these late fees as well.

| Field Name | Data Type | Field Size |
|---|---|---|
| FeeID | AutoNumber | Long Integer |
| CustomerID | Number | Long Integer |
| TapeID | Number | Long Integer |
| FeeDate | Date/Time | |
| PaidDate | Date/Time | |
| DaysOver | Number | Integer |
| Paid | Yes/No | |
| Deleted | Yes/No | |

This table's primary key is the FeeID field. There should also be an index for the CustomerID field since we know this will be the field used by the invoice process to retrieve records. The Paid field will also be used, since we'll only be pulling non-paid records into the invoice.

The CustomerID field is important, as it's the link between this table and the parent Customer table. Had we created a LateFee object, it would have been a child of the Customer object, and the tables in the database reflect this relationship as well.

The TapeID field is important since we'll need to provide the tape's title as a property on the InvoiceFee object. The DaysOver field is also used by the InvoiceFee object so it can calculate the total amount due the customer because of the late fee.

The two date fields, FeeDate and PaidDate, have been added to illustrate that the database may contain information that is not directly used by an object's logic. The FeeDate field will correspond to the EnteredDate property of the InvoiceFee object, but other than filling in the date, our object has no use for the PaidDate field.

Even if the store decides not to charge a customer for a late fee, they probably want to know how many times a customer returned tapes late. Because of this, we've added a Deleted flag to the table. This way we'll never actually delete a late fee record, but instead we'll mark it as deleted. Then the customer won't have to pay the fee, but the record remains in the table for later reporting.

## The Video Table

Like the Customer table, this table will hold objects. In this case, it will hold the Video object, whose state is contained in a type named VideoProps:

```
Private Type VideoProps
   VideoID As Long
   Title As String * 30
   ReleaseDate As Variant
   Studio As String * 30
   Category As Long
   Rating As Long
End Type
```

The table layout corresponds to the UDT:

| Field Name | Data Type | Field Size |
|---|---|---|
| VideoID | AutoNumber | Long Integer |
| Title | Text | 30 |
| ReleaseDate | Date/Time | |
| Studio | Text | 30 |
| Category | Number | Long Integer |
| Rating | Number | Long Integer |

As usual, the VideoID field is the primary key. Our Videos object uses the Title and Studio fields as criteria so we'll want to create indexes for them.

## The Tape Table

Like the LateFee table, the Tape table is a child of another table. In this case, it's a child of the Video table, so it will contain a VideoID field to link the two together. The table's fields are based on the Tape object's state:

```
Private Type TapeProps
    TapeID As Long
    VideoID As Long
    Title As String * 30
    CheckedOut As Boolean
    DateAcquired As Variant
    DateDue As Variant
    LateFee As Boolean
    InvoiceID As Long
End Type
```

This table has a couple of changes to what we've seen so far. The Title field in the UDT will actually come from the Video table, as the Tape table doesn't contain a Title field. As we implemented it in Chapter 5, the Title property on the Tape object is read-only, specifically because it's a value that really comes from another object's table.

The LateFee variable is also a change. While we have included it in the object's state, it won't actually be saved to, or restored, from the database. While this might not make a lot of sense now, it will when we move the persistence code to an application server in Chapter 9.

The rest of the fields map directly to the table:

| Field Name | Data Type | Field Size |
|---|---|---|
| TapeID | AutoNumber | Long Integer |
| VideoID | Number | Long Integer |

| Field Name | Data Type | Field Size |
|---|---|---|
| CheckedOut | Yes/No | |
| DateAcquired | Date/Time | |
| DateDue | Date/Time | |
| InvoiceID | Number | Long Integer |

The `TapeID` is the primary key for each record.

Our `Tape` objects always have a `Video` object as their parent. Our database needs to reflect this relationship as well. To support this we include the `VideoID` value in this table as well. It's a foreign key to the `Video` table, allowing us to easily determine which `Tape` objects belong to a given `Video` object.

The `InvoiceID` field doesn't need an index, since it shouldn't be used as a lookup into this table; rather, our code will use this value to find the corresponding invoice record.

## The Categories and Ratings Tables

The `Categories` and `Ratings` tables are used to load the two `TextList` objects within the `Video` object. As such, they are simple tables with just an ID value and a field for the text label.

The `TextList` object is read-only, so these tables will need to be edited through some other mechanism. For instance, we might choose to create business objects to represent a `Category` and a `Rating` and use those objects to support editing of the tables. Alternatively, we can just use Microsoft Access to directly edit the tables, since they are so simple and change so rarely.

It doesn't matter much whether we create a primary key or any indexes for these tables, since we'll always be pulling in their entire contents to populate the `TextList` object.

### The Categories Table

| Field Name | Data Type | Field Size |
|---|---|---|
| CategoryID | Number | Long Integer |
| Category | Text | 20 |

Using Microsoft Access or any other data tool of your choice, add some data to this table. This would be pretty static data in a regular application, so we won't worry about building an editor. In a real-world application you might need to build such an editor, but here we'll simply add some data similar to the following:

| CategoryID | Category |
|---|---|
| 1 | Comedy |
| 2 | Drama |

*Table Continued on Following Page*

| CategoryID | Category |
|------------|----------|
| 3 | Horror |
| 4 | SF |
| 5 | Action |
| 6 | Children |

### The Ratings Table

| Field Name | Data Type | Field Size |
|------------|-----------|------------|
| RatingID | Number | Long Integer |
| Rating | Text | 5 |

As with the Categories table, we'll take this opportunity to use Microsoft Access or any other tool you prefer to add some data to this table. Add data similar to the following:

| RatingID | Rating |
|----------|--------|
| 1 | G |
| 2 | PG |
| 3 | PG-13 |
| 4 | R |
| 5 | NC-17 |
| 6 | NR |

## The Invoice Table

Our Invoice object will need a table to store its state. Like most of our other objects, the Invoice object stores its state in a UDT variable:

```
Private Type InvoiceProps
   InvoiceID As Long
   CustomerID As Long
   CustomerName As String * 50
   CustomerPhone As String * 25
End Type
```

Like the LateFee table, this table will contain some fields that aren't included directly in the object's UDT. Our Invoice object has properties for Subtotal, Tax and Total to indicate the monetary amounts due on the invoice. While we don't need to store these values in the table for the Invoice object's use, they are very valuable in case the user wants to create reports directly from the database. This is not uncommon, and so many objects will save out information that will never be read back into the object just to make it easier for reporting or other applications:

| Field Name | Data Type | Field Size |
|---|---|---|
| InvoiceID | AutoNumber | Long Integer |
| CustomerID | Number | Long Integer |
| Subtotal | Number | Double |
| Tax | Number | Double |
| Total | Number | Double |

The InvoiceID field should be set as the primary key. Our objects don't provide any mechanism to look up all invoices for a customer, so we may not need to create an index for the CustomerID field. On the other hand, such an index would probably be used by any reporting that the user might want and so, in that light, it may be valuable. So we'll make CustomerID an index.

Our object's Save subroutine will store the appropriate values in the Subtotal, Tax and Total fields. The Fetch subroutine won't need to load them back in, however, since we implemented the Invoice object to recalculate those values each time the properties are accessed.

## The InvoiceTape Table

Our final table is a child table of the Invoice table. Our Invoice object actually supports two types of child objects, InvoiceFee and InvoiceTape. The InvoiceFee objects are based on the LateFee table we already created, so all that remains is to provide a table to store the InvoiceTape objects:

```
Private Type InvoiceTapeProps
   ItemID As Long
   TapeID As Long
   Title As String * 30
   Price As Double
End Type
```

Like the Tape object, this object's UDT contains a Title field that won't actually be stored in the table. The Title property on the object is read-only as the value comes from the Video table, even though it is part of this object's state:

| Field Name | Data Type | Field Size |
|---|---|---|
| ItemID | AutoNumber | Long Integer |
| InvoiceID | Number | Long Integer |
| TapeID | Number | Long Integer |
| Price | Number | Double |

The primary key for this table is the ItemID field. There should be an index for the InvoiceID field since that is the field that we'll use to retrieve the records for a specific invoice.

The `TapeID` field will be used to find the appropriate record in the `Tape` table, so it won't be used as criteria when retrieving records from this table. Thus no index should be required on that field.

# Making Simple Objects Persistent

Now that we've established the basic concepts and the database design is out of the way, we should be ready to move on to modifying our objects from Chapter 5 and 6. To start with, we'll go through the simplest object, `Customer`. Then we'll move on to look at some of the more complex objects, such as the `Tape` and `InvoiceTape` child objects.

## The Customer Object

The simplest business object we created in Chapter 5 was the `Customer` object. This object is neither a parent nor a child: it's a standalone object that needs to be added, updated, and removed from the database as appropriate.

We've already looked at the basic `Fetch`, `Save` and `DeleteObject` methods, so we won't rehash the details of how they work. Here's the code for these routines in the `Customer` business object:

```vb
Private Sub Save()

  Dim rsCustomer As Recordset
  Dim strSQL As String

  Set rsCustomer = New Recordset
  strSQL = "SELECT * FROM CUSTOMER WHERE CUSTOMERID=" & _
    CustomerID
  rsCustomer.Open strSQL, cnVideo, , adLockOptimistic
  If mflgNew Then rsCustomer.AddNew

  With rsCustomer
    .Fields("Name") = mudtProps.Name
    .Fields("Address1") = mudtProps.Address1
    .Fields("Address2") = mudtProps.Address2
    .Fields("City") = mudtProps.City
    .Fields("State") = mudtProps.State
    .Fields("ZipCode") = mudtProps.ZipCode
    .Fields("Phone") = mudtProps.Phone
    .Update

    If mflgNew Then mudtProps.CustomerID = .Fields("CustomerID")

    .Close
  End With

  Set rsCustomer = Nothing

End Sub

Private Sub DeleteObject(CustomerID As Long)

  cnVideo.Execute "DELETE FROM CUSTOMER WHERE CUSTOMERID=" & _
    CustomerID

End Sub
```

```
Private Sub Fetch(CustomerID As Long)

  Dim rsCustomer As Recordset
  Dim strSQL As String

  strSQL = "SELECT * FROM CUSTOMER WHERE CUSTOMERID=" & _
    CustomerID
  Set rsCustomer = New Recordset
  rsCustomer.Open strSQL, cnVideo

  With rsCustomer
    mudtProps.CustomerID = .Fields("CustomerID")
    mudtProps.Name = .Fields("Name")
    mudtProps.Address1 = .Fields("Address1")
    mudtProps.Address2 = .Fields("Address2")
    mudtProps.City = .Fields("City")
    mudtProps.State = .Fields("State")
    mudtProps.ZipCode = .Fields("ZipCode")
    mudtProps.Phone = .Fields("Phone")

    mobjValid.RuleBroken "Name", False
    mobjValid.RuleBroken "Phone", False

    .Close
  End With

  Set rsCustomer = Nothing

End Sub
```

The more interesting parts of this are the changes we need to make to the code we put together in Chapter 5 - so that these three new subroutines get called at the appropriate times.

## Loading the Customer Data

The Fetch subroutine retrieves the object's data from the database and copies it into the object's local variables. This routine requires a parameter be passed; in particular, it requires the CustomerID value, so that it can be used to create a SQL SELECT statement to find the record in the Customer table.

From the UI developer's viewpoint, the Customer object gets its data when the object's Load method is called. Not coincidentally, the Load method also requires that the CustomerID value be passed as a parameter.

We'll add a call to the Fetch subroutine within the Customer object's Load method. We need to relay the CustomerID parameter supplied by the UI code down into the Fetch routine:

```
Public Sub Load(CustomerID As Long)

  If mflgEditing Then Err.Raise 445
  If Not mflgNew Then Err.Raise 445

  Fetch CustomerID

  mflgNew = False
End Sub
```

It is important that `mflgNew` be set to `False` *after* the `Fetch` subroutine is complete. This is because the `Fetch` routine could raise an error in the case that the supplied ID value doesn't correspond to a customer record. If this happens, we don't want to erroneously mark the object as having been loaded by setting the `mflgNew` variable to `False`.

Again note that we don't have any error handling of our own in this routine. If an error occurs during the call to the `Fetch` routine, Visual Basic will raise it back to our `Load` routine. Since our `Load` routine has no error trapping code, Visual Basic will then raise the error back to the code that called the `Load` routine. This should be the UI code, where the UI developer should be trapping the error.

By trapping the error in the UI, we can most easily handle it in whatever way is appropriate for the particular UI. For instance, we may want to show the error in a message box, or write it to a log file or entirely ignore it - all of which is up to the specific UI.

## Adding/Updating the Customer Data

Just as the UI developer expects that the object's data will be loaded by the `Load` method, they also expect that the object's data will be stored when the `ApplyEdit` method is called. This will get more complicated with child objects, but with a simple object such as `Customer`, we'll want to call the `Save` routine within the `ApplyEdit` method's code:

```
Public Sub ApplyEdit()

If Not mflgEditing Then Err.Raise 445

   If mflgDeleted And Not mflgNew Then
      ' code to delete the object's data goes here
      mflgNew = True
      mflgDeleted = False

   ElseIf mflgDirty Or mflgNew Then
      If Not IsValid Then Err.Raise 445
      ' save object to database if appropriate
      Save
      ' save object state
      LSet mudtSave = mudtProps
      mflgNew = False

   End If

   mflgDirty = False
   mflgEditing = False

End Sub
```

Notice that the `Save` method is called before we save the object state by copying `mudtProps` into `mudtSave`. There is a good reason for this.

Look back at the `Save` routine we just implemented. Near the bottom of the routine, we have code to copy the `CustomerID` back into the object from the database when the object is new:

```
If mflgNew Then mudtProps.CustomerID = .Fields("CustomerID")
```

Since this actually made a change to the object's state, we'll want to make sure it gets saved into the `mudtSave` variable along with all the other data in `mudtProps`.

If we don't do this, and the UI code calls the `CancelEdit` method, we'd lose the `CustomerID` value when `mudtSave` was copied back into `mudtProps`. This would lead to a bug, since the UI code could then call `ApplyEdit` and our object would not know its own ID value- so it would try to update the wrong customer record in the database.

### *Deleting the Customer Data*

The question of where to call the `DeleteObject` routine is a bit trickier. Our object has a `Delete` method, and it might seem appropriate to just delete the object using that method. We discussed this a little in Chapter 5, however, where we wanted to make sure that the `CancelEdit` method would undo the `Delete` operation.

In order to support the ability to cancel the `Delete` method, we chose to set a flag, `mflgDeleted`, within the `Delete` method, and hold off actually deleting any data until the `ApplyEdit` method was called. That way, the `CancelEdit` method can just reset `mflgDeleted` back to `False` and it will be as though the `Delete` method were never called:

```
Public Sub ApplyEdit()

  If Not mflgEditing Then Err.Raise 445

  If mflgDeleted And Not mflgNew Then
    ' code to delete the object's data goes here
    DeleteObject mudtProps.CustomerID
    mflgNew = True
    mflgDeleted = False

  ElseIf mflgDirty Or mflgNew Then
    If Not IsValid Then Err.Raise 445
    ' save object to database if appropriate
    Save
    ' save object state
    LSet mudtSave = mudtProps
    mflgNew = False

  End If

  mflgDirty = False
  mflgEditing = False

End Sub
```

As the `DeleteObject` method may result in an error for some reason, it's important not to reset the `mflgNew` and `mflgDeleted` variables until after the call to `DeleteObject`. By resetting `mflgNew` to `True`, we're indicating that the object doesn't correspond to any data in the database. Therefore, we've effectively got a brand new object, though one loaded with some pre-existing data. Since the object is basically new, we'll also want to reset the `mflgDeleted` variable to `False` to make it practical to continue using the object.

# Making Parent and Child Objects Persistent

Now that we've seen how to make a simple business object persistent, let's move on to something more complex. The `Video` object is a parent to `Tape` objects. This parent-child relationship is managed by the `Tapes` object, as we discussed in Chapter 5.

The `Video` and `Tape` objects are both persistent business objects, while the `Tapes` object is merely a collection of individual `Tape` objects. This means that both the `Video` and `Tape` objects will contain `Fetch`, `Save` and `DeleteObject` routines. The `Tapes` object doesn't have a corresponding table, so it doesn't need these routines. Instead, it needs to make sure to call the appropriate methods on the child `Tape` objects so they each get saved out to the `Tape` table.

# The Video Object

The `Video` object is a parent to `Tape` objects. We implemented this relationship by having the `Video` object own a `Tapes` object and having that `Tapes` object manage all the child `Tape` objects.

Since we moved most of the complexity of dealing with the child objects off to the `Tapes` object, the `Video` object doesn't have to worry about these details. We've already altered the `Video` object's `BeginEdit`, `CancelEdit`, `ApplyEdit`, `Delete` and `Load` methods so they make appropriate calls to the same routines within the `Tapes` object. The `Tapes` object then worries about getting the appropriate action taken care of in all the child objects.

Therefore, the `Video` object's `Fetch`, `Save`, and `DeleteObject` routines only need to deal with the `Video` object itself, so they are virtually no different from the basic routines we looked at earlier in the chapter:

```
Private Sub Save()

  Dim rsVideo As Recordset
  Dim strSQL As String

  Set rsVideo = New Recordset
  strSQL = "SELECT * FROM Video WHERE VideoID=" & VideoID
  rsVideo.Open strSQL, cnVideo, , adLockOptimistic
  If mflgNew Then rsVideo.AddNew

  With rsVideo
    .Fields("Title") = mudtProps.Title
    .Fields("ReleaseDate") = mudtProps.ReleaseDate
    .Fields("Studio") = mudtProps.Studio
    '.Fields("Rating") = mudtProps.Rating
    '.Fields("Category") = mudtProps.Category
    .Update
    If mflgNew Then mudtProps.VideoID = .Fields("VideoID")
    .Close
  End With

  Set rsVideo = Nothing

End Sub
```

```
Private Sub DeleteObject(VideoID As Long)

  cnVideo.Execute "DELETE FROM Video WHERE VideoID=" & VideoID

End Sub
```

```
Private Sub Fetch(VideoID As Long)

  Dim rsVideo As Recordset
  Dim strSQL As String
```

```
    strSQL = "SELECT * FROM Video WHERE VideoID=" & VideoID
    Set rsVideo = New Recordset
    rsVideo.Open strSQL, cnVideo

    With rsVideo
      mudtProps.VideoID = .Fields("VideoID")
      mudtProps.Title = .Fields("Title")
      mudtProps.ReleaseDate = .Fields("ReleaseDate")
      mudtProps.Studio = .Fields("Studio")
      mudtProps.Rating = .Fields("Rating")
      mudtProps.Category = .Fields("Category")

      mobjValid.RuleBroken "Title", False

      rsVideo.Close
    End With

    Set rsVideo = Nothing

  End Sub
```

Notice that the code to save the `Rating` and `Category` fields is commented out. This is because we haven't implemented the `Ratings` or `Categories` object's persistence yet. We'll uncomment these lines once that functionality is in place.

## Loading the Video Data

As with the `Customer` object, we'll call the `Fetch` routine from within the `Load` method.

```
    Public Sub Load(VideoID As Long)

      If mflgEditing Then Err.Raise 445
      If Not mflgNew Then Err.Raise 445

      Fetch VideoID
      mobjTapes.Load mudtProps.VideoID

      mflgNew = False

    End Sub
```

Notice how we load the `Video` object's data, then the `Tapes` object is told to load all the child objects, and finally we set `mflgNew` to `False`. This way, if the `Video` object fails to load, we won't waste effort in trying to load all the child objects; and if any of the load process fails, we won't indicate that the object represents data from the database by changing the value of `mflgNew`.

## Adding, Updating and Deleting the Video Data

Likewise, the `Save` and `DeleteObject` methods will be called from within the `ApplyEdit` method, as they were within the `Customer` object.

```
    Public Sub ApplyEdit()

      If Not mflgEditing Then Err.Raise 445
```

```
        If mflgDeleted And Not mflgNew Then
            ' code to delete the object's data goes here
            DeleteObject mudtProps.VideoID
            mflgNew = True
            mflgDeleted = False

        ElseIf mflgDirty Or mflgNew Then
            If Not IsValid Then Err.Raise 445
            ' save object to database if appropriate
            Save
            ' save object state
            LSet mudtSave = mudtProps
            mflgNew = False

        End If

        mobjTapes.ApplyEdit mudtProps.VideoID
        mflgDirty = False
        mflgEditing = False

    End Sub
```

The call to `ApplyEdit` is echoed to the `Tapes` object so it can make sure the appropriate method is called on all the child objects as well.

# The Tapes Object

The `Tapes` object is not a persistent business object. That is, the `Tapes` object doesn't save itself to any table in the database. Instead, its job is to manage all the child `Tape` objects, making sure they are loaded, saved and deleted as appropriate.

We just saw how the `Video` object echoes the calls to the `Load`, `ApplyEdit` and `Delete` methods down to the `Tapes` object. The `Tapes` object just turns around and calls the appropriate methods on each child object in the collection.

We covered this process in great detail in Chapter 5, so we won't revisit it here. The key thing to keep in mind is which methods get called on the `Tape` objects when each method is called on the `Tapes` collection object.

When the `Load` method is called on the `Tapes` object, it calls the `ChildLoad` method for each child object. The `ApplyEdit` method calls `ChildApplyEdit` on each child, and the `Delete` method calls the `Delete` method on each child.

## Loading the Tape Objects

The `Tapes` object's `Load` method bears some further examination. In Chapter 5, we just put comments into this routine, since its actual implementation was dependent on having a database. Now we'll replace those comments with some code.

The `ChildLoad` method of the `Tape` object requires that the `TapeID` value be passed as a parameter. This implies that the `Tapes` object's `Load` method must have a list of `TapeID` values to use when calling each of the child object's `ChildLoad` methods. Add the following code to the `Load` method of the `Tapes` object:

```
Friend Sub Load(VideoID As Long)

    Dim rsTape As Recordset
    Dim strSQL As String
    Dim objTape As Tape
    If mflgEditing Then Err.Raise 445

    strSQL = "SELECT TapeID FROM Tape WHERE VideoID=" & VideoID
    Set rsTape = New Recordset
    rsTape.Open strSQL, cnVideo

    Do While Not rsTape.EOF
      Set objTape = New Tape

      With objTape
        .ChildLoad rsTape("TapeID")
        .SetAsChild Me
      End With

      mcolTapes.Add Item:=objTape
      rsTape.MoveNext

    Loop

    rsTape.Close
    Set rsTape = Nothing

End Sub
```

Getting these values isn't difficult. We can simply create a recordset that contains the `TapeID` values for all the tape records that have the right `VideoID`:

```
strSQL = "SELECT TapeID FROM Tape WHERE VideoID=" & VideoID
Set rsTape = New Recordset
rsTape.Open strSQL, cnVideo
```

Then we can loop through this recordset, creating a new `Tape` object for each record:

```
Do While Not rsTape.EOF
  Set objTape = New Tape
```

We can then tell each `Tape` object that it's a child using the `SetAsChild` method, as we discussed in Chapter 5. Once we've made it a child object, we can call its `ChildLoad` method with the `TapeID` value to load that object with the right data from the `Tape` table:

```
With objTape
  .SetAsChild Me
  .ChildLoad rsTape("TapeID")
End With
```

All that remains is to add the fully loaded child object to the `Tapes` object's internal collection and move on to the next record:

```
    mcolTapes.Add Item:=objTape
    rsTape.MoveNext
Loop
```

# The Tape Object

The Tape object is probably our most complex object. It's a child object, each one being owned by a Video object. But to make things even more difficult, the Tape object can be used as a standalone object like the Customer object, so it not only has code to support being a child, but also code to support being a standalone entity.

## Adding the Persistence Methods to Tape

Either way, the Fetch, Save and DeleteObject routines are required. The process of loading and saving data to the database isn't affected by how the object is being used. In either case, the object's state is being written out to the database or read back in. At the same time, the Tape object has some special requirements in these routines.

### The Save Method

Add the following code to the Tape object:

```
Private Sub Save()

    Dim rsTape As Recordset
    Dim rsVideo As Recordset
    Dim strSQL As String

    strSQL = "SELECT * FROM Tape WHERE TapeID=" & TapeID
    Set rsTape = New Recordset
    rsTape.Open strSQL, cnVideo, , adLockOptimistic
    If mflgNew Then rsTape.AddNew

    With rsTape
        .Fields("VideoID") = mudtProps.VideoID
        .Fields("CheckedOut") = mudtProps.CheckedOut
        .Fields("DateAcquired") = mudtProps.DateAcquired
        .Fields("DateDue") = mudtProps.DateDue
        .Fields("InvoiceID") = mudtProps.InvoiceID
        .Update
        If mflgNew Then mudtProps.TapeID = .Fields("TapeID")
        .Close
    End With

    Set rsTape = Nothing
    If mflgNew Then
        strSQL = "SELECT TITLE FROM Video WHERE VideoID=" & _
            mudtProps.VideoID
        Set rsVideo = New Recordset
        rsVideo.Open strSQL, cnVideo
        mudtProps.Title = rsVideo("Title")
        rsVideo.Close
        Set rsVideo = Nothing
    End If

End Sub
```

When we designed the Tape table, we intentionally didn't provide fields in the table to store the Title or LateFee elements from the TapeProps UDT. The LateFee variable is a flag to indicate whether to create a late fee record, something we'll talk about shortly.

The `Title` value actually comes from the `Video` table. It's a read-only property of the `Tape` object, so it can't be changed through the `Tape` object. Therefore, we have no reason to write out the `Title` value from the object to the database.

If our object is new then we do need to read the `Title` value in from the database to get it into our object. For an existing object we've already loaded that value in the `Load` method, but for a new object we need to retrieve it as we save the data to the database:

```
strSQL = "SELECT TITLE FROM Video WHERE VideoID=" & _
    mudtProps.VideoID
  Set rsVideo = New Recordset
  rsVideo.Open strSQL, cnVideo
  mudtProps.Title = rsVideo("Title")
  rsVideo.Close
```

This process is not unlike reading in the primary key value generated by the database after we've added a new record, but in this case we're doing the lookup against a different table. The end result is that we retrieve the video's title and put it into the `Tape` object's state, `mudtProps`.

### The DeleteObject and Fetch Methods

Now add the following code to our `Tape` object:

```
Private Sub DeleteObject(TapeID As Long)

  cnVideo.Execute "DELETE FROM Tape WHERE TapeID=" & TapeID

End Sub
```

```
Private Sub Fetch(TapeID As Long)

  Dim rsTape As Recordset
  Dim strSQL As String

  strSQL = "SELECT Tape.*,Video.Title " & _
    "FROM Tape INNER JOIN Video ON " & _
    "Tape.VideoID = Video.VideoID " & _
    "WHERE TapeID=" & TapeID
  Set rsTape = New Recordset
  rsTape.Open strSQL, cnVideo

  With rsTape
    mudtProps.TapeID = .Fields("TapeID")
    mudtProps.VideoID = .Fields("VideoID")
    mudtProps.Title = .Fields("Title")
    mudtProps.CheckedOut = .Fields("CheckedOut")
    mudtProps.DateAcquired = .Fields("DateAcquired")
    mudtProps.DateDue = .Fields("DateDue")
    mudtProps.InvoiceID = .Fields("InvoiceID")

    mobjValid.RuleBroken "DateAcquired", False

    rsTape.Close
  End With

  Set rsTape = Nothing

End Sub
```

The `Fetch` routine is a bit different to anything we've seen so far. Again we come back to the read-only `Title` property on the `Tape` object. There is no field on the `Tape` table for `Title`, because this value actually comes from the `Video` table. To load this value into the `Tape` object's state, we need to get it from that table; in this case, we add a `JOIN` to the SQL statement we're using to retrieve the object's data:

```
strSQL = "SELECT Tape.*,Video.Title " & _
   "FROM Tape INNER JOIN Video ON " & _
   Tape.VideoID = Video.VideoID " & _
   "WHERE TapeID=" & TapeID
```

If we were trying to stick with a pure object-oriented design, this would be a problem. From an object-oriented viewpoint, it's far better to create an instance of a `Video` object and get the `Title` value from that object rather than directly reading it from the database. By getting the value from a `Video` object, we'll automatically get the benefit of any business logic that the `Video` object might contain for dealing with the `Title` field.

Unfortunately, there can be a very serious performance hit for loading up an entire object just to get at one field, especially when we compare it to the quick performance of adding a simple `JOIN` to our SQL statement to get the same result. The easiest way to create these SQL statements is to use the query designer in Microsoft Access; otherwise, they'll need to be written by hand.

> **The trick is to remember that we're creating a client/server application using objects. If we put object-oriented design ahead of the client/server constraints we'll create an elegant but exceedingly slow application.**

## Tape as a Standalone Object

When the `Tape` object is being used as a standalone object, the `mflgChild` variable is set to `False`. In this case, the object will be used by the UI code just like any other standard business object, and the calls to `Fetch`, `Save` and `DeleteObject` will be made in the `Load` and `ApplyEdit` methods as normal. Of course, they can only be called if `mflgChild` is `False`:

```
Public Sub Load(TapeID As Long)

   If mflgChild Then Err.Raise 445
   If mflgEditing Then Err.Raise 445
   If Not mflgNew Then Err.Raise 445

' code to load the object goes here
   Fetch TapeID
   mflgNew = False

End Sub


Public Sub ApplyEdit()

   If mflgChild Then If Not mflgChildEditing Then Err.Raise 445
   If Not mflgChild And mflgNew Then Err.Raise 445
   If Not mflgEditing Then Err.Raise 445
```

```
      If Not mflgChild Then
        If mflgDeleted And Not mflgNew Then
          ' code to delete the object's data goes here
          DeleteObject mudtProps.TapeID
          mflgNew = True
          mflgDeleted = False

        ElseIf mflgDirty Or mflgNew Then
          If Not IsValid Then Err.Raise 445
          ' save object to database if appropriate
          Save
          If mudtProps.LateFee Then
            ' add the late fee to the customer
          End If
          ' save object state
          LSet mudtSave = mudtProps
          mflgNew = False

        End If

        mflgDirty = False

      Else
        If Not mobjParent Is Nothing Then
          mobjParent.AddChild Me
          Set mobjParent = Nothing
        End If

      End If

      mflgEditing = False

    End Sub
```

## Tape as a Child Object

If `mflgChild` is `True` then the `Tape` object is acting as a child to a `Video` object. In this case the behavior of the object changes. In particular, the `Load` method disables itself entirely by raising an error:

```
    If mflgChild Then Err.Raise 445
```

The `ApplyEdit` method isn't disabled, but the majority of its code is contained within an `If...Then` statement that checks `mflgChild`:

```
    If Not mflgChild Then
```

These behavioral changes prevent the UI code from directly causing the `Tape` object to interact with the database when it's acting as a child of a `Video` object.

> **The underlying principle is that child objects should only interact with the database when their parent object tells them to do so.**

As we've just seen, the `Tapes` object calls the `ChildLoad` and `ChildApplyEdit` methods to make each child `Tape` object interact with the database. The code in each of these routines is very similar to the `Load` and `ApplyEdit` methods in a normal object, but they are only called by the parent collection object.

### ChildLoad

The `ChildLoad` method calls the `Fetch` routine to load the object's data:

```
Friend Sub ChildLoad(TapeID As Long)

   If mflgChildEditing Then Err.Raise 445
   If Not mflgNew Then Err.Raise 445

   ' code to load the object goes here
   Fetch TapeID

   mflgNew = False

End Sub
```

This is no different than when `Fetch` is called from the `Load` method; however, this call is invoked by the `Tapes` object rather than the UI code.

### ChildApplyEdit

The `ChildApplyEdit` method makes appropriate calls to `DeleteObject` or `Save`:

```
Friend Sub ChildApplyEdit(VideoID As Long)

   If Not mflgChildEditing Then Err.Raise 445
   If Not IsValid Then Err.Raise 445

   If mflgDeleted And Not mflgNew Then
      ' code to delete the object's data goes here
      DeleteObject mudtProps.TapeID
      mflgNew = True
      mflgDeleted = False

   ElseIf mflgDirty Or mflgNew Then
      ' save object to database if appropriate
      mudtProps.VideoID = VideoID
      Save
      If mudtProps.LateFee Then
         ' add the late fee to the customer
      End If
      ' save object state
      LSet mudtChild = mudtProps
      mflgNew = False

   End If

   mflgDirty = False
   mflgChildEditing = False

End Sub
```

Before we call the `Save` routine, the `VideoID` that was passed as a parameter is copied into `mudtProps` so it's part of the object's state. This is important, since this value is the primary key of the parent object and thus is a key part of our object's identity. With this value set, we're able to call the `Save` routine knowing that our object contains all the information needed to save the data into the database.

## Creating Late Fee Records

The `Tape` object has another unique feature. When a `Tape` object's `CheckIn` method is called, it indicates that the tape has been returned by the customer and is being checked back in, to be available for rental.

### Causing a Late Fee

This routine checks the current date against the date the tape was due back from the customer, and, if the tape is overdue, it sets a flag to indicate that a late fee record needs to be created. The code that we entered to handle this in Chapter 5 is highlighted here:

```
Public Sub CheckIn()

  If Not mflgEditing Then Err.Raise 445

  With mudtProps
    If Not .CheckedOut Then _
      Err.Raise vbObjectError + 1101, "Tape", _
      "Tape is not checked out"
    .CheckedOut = False
    If DateDiff("d", .DateDue, Now) > 0 Then _
      .LateFee = True
  End With

  mflgDirty = True

End Sub
```

The code only sets a flag, it doesn't create the late fee record on the spot. This is because the user might click Cancel when the late fee shouldn't be saved. Instead, it sets a flag so we can create the late fee record when the `ApplyEdit` method is called.

### Writing the Late Fee Record

Before we get into those details, we should look at the code that actually creates the late fee record. We need to put all this code into the `Tape` class module in a routine called `SaveLateFee`:

```
Private Sub SaveLateFee()

  Dim rsLateFee As Recordset
  Dim rsInvoice As Recordset
  Dim strSQL As String

  strSQL = "SELECT CUSTOMERID FROM INVOICE WHERE INVOICEID=" & _
    mudtProps.InvoiceID
  Set rsInvoice = New Recordset
  rsInvoice.Open strSQL, cnVideo
  strSQL = "LateFee"
  Set rsLateFee = New Recordset
```

```
    rsLateFee.Open strSQL, cnVideo, , adLockOptimistic
    rsLateFee.AddNew

    With rsLateFee
      .Fields("CustomerID") = rsInvoice("CustomerID")
      .Fields("TapeID") = mudtProps.TapeID
      .Fields("FeeDate") = Now
      .Fields("DaysOver") = DateDiff("d", mudtProps.DateDue, Now)
      .Fields("Paid") = False
      .Update
      .Close
    End With

    rsInvoice.Close
    Set rsInvoice = Nothing
    Set rsLateFee = Nothing

  End Sub
```

This routine is just regular ADO code. Since the late fee is for a customer, the `LateFee` table has a `CustomerID` field that we need to fill in. Our `Tape` object has no `CustomerID` field, but it does have an `InvoiceID` and we can find out which customer is recorded on that invoice. To do this, we simply retrieve the `CustomerID` field from the `Invoice` table:

```
strSQL = "SELECT CUSTOMERID FROM INVOICE WHERE INVOICEID=" & _
   mudtProps.InvoiceID
Set rsInvoice = New Recordset
rsInvoice.Open strSQL, cnVideo
```

Then we can move on to create a new record in the `LateFee` table:

```
strSQL = "LateFee"
Set rsLateFee = New Recordset
rsLateFee.Open strSQL, cnVideo, , adLockOptimistic
rsLateFee.AddNew
```

Given the new record, all that remains is to set the appropriate values into the recordset's fields and call the `Update` method to write them to the database:

```
With rsLateFee
  .Fields("CustomerID") = rsInvoice("CustomerID")
  .Fields("TapeID") = mudtProps.TapeID
  .Fields("FeeDate") = Now
  .Fields("DaysOver") = DateDiff("d", mudtProps.DateDue, Now)
  .Fields("Paid") = False
  .Update
```

### Calling SaveLateFee

The `SaveLateFee` routine we just created will create the late fee record with all the right data. Of course, we need to make sure to call the `SaveLateFee` routine at the appropriate points in the `ApplyEdit` and `ChildApplyEdit` methods.

The only time we need to worry about late fees is when the customer has returned a video tape and it is being checked in. We implemented a `CheckIn` method in the `Tape` object in Chapter 5.

The `Tape` object's `CheckIn` method is available when the `Tape` object is not a child. In fact, this is the intended purpose behind allowing the object to be used in a standalone fashion. We want to make it easy for the user to supply the tape's ID value, load the tape from the database and check it in.

The `Tape` object's `CheckIn` method determines whether a late fee needs to be applied. If it does, the `mudtProps.LateFee` variable is set to `True`.

In the `Tape` object's `ApplyEdit` method we can see if the tape has been checked in by using the `mudtProps.LateFee` variable. In this case, we know that we need to call the `SaveLateFee` method to create the late fee record:

```
Public Sub ApplyEdit()

    If mflgChild Then If Not mflgChildEditing Then Err.Raise 445
    If Not mflgChild And mflgNew Then Err.Raise 445
    If Not mflgEditing Then Err.Raise 445

    If Not mflgChild Then
      If mflgDeleted And Not mflgNew Then
        ' code to delete the object's data goes here
        DeleteObject mudtProps.TapeID
        mflgNew = True
        mflgDeleted = False

      ElseIf mflgDirty Or mflgNew Then
        If Not IsValid Then Err.Raise 445
        ' save object to database if appropriate
        Save
        If mudtProps.LateFee Then
          ' add the late fee to the customer
          SaveLateFee
        End If
        ' save object state
        LSet mudtSave = mudtProps
        mflgNew = False

      End If

      mflgDirty = False

    Else
      If Not mobjParent Is Nothing Then
        mobjParent.AddChild Me
        Set mobjParent = Nothing
      End If

    End If

    mflgEditing = False

End Sub
```

Although we don't envision the user checking in a tape by bringing it up as a child object, it doesn't hurt to add the code to support such an action. Where it is easy to provide flexibility to the UI developer it's usually a good idea to do so. It's hard to envision how our objects will be used somewhere down the line, so the more flexible they are, the easier it will be to get them to meet future requirements.

To this end, we'll also add the call to `SaveLateFee` in the `ChildApplyEdit` method:

```
Friend Sub ChildApplyEdit(VideoID As Long)

   If Not mflgChildEditing Then Err.Raise 445
   If Not IsValid Then Err.Raise 445

   If mflgDeleted And Not mflgNew Then
      ' code to delete the object's data goes here
      DeleteObject mudtProps.TapeID
      mflgNew = True
      mflgDeleted = False

   ElseIf mflgDirty Or mflgNew Then
      ' save object to database if appropriate
      mudtProps.VideoID = VideoID
      Save
      If mudtProps.LateFee Then
         ' add the late fee to the customer
         SaveLateFee
      End If
      ' save object state
      LSet mudtChild = mudtProps
      mflgNew = False

   End If

   mflgDirty = False
   mflgChildEditing = False

End Sub
```

Now when the `Tape` object is saved, either through `ApplyEdit` or `ChildApplyEdit`, a late fee record will be created if necessary.

# Persisting Polymorphic Objects

The `Invoice` object and its child objects, `InvoiceTape` and `InvoiceFee`, are similar to the `Video` and `Tape` objects, but with a twist. Where the `Video` object has only one type of child object, the `Invoice` object has two.

The `Invoice` object's children are managed by the `InvoiceItems` collection object. As with the `Video` object, this means that pretty much all the complexity of handling the child objects has been moved out of the `Invoice` object. The `Invoice` object just calls methods on the `InvoiceItems` object, as appropriate, to get all the child objects loaded, deleted or saved.

## The Invoice Object

As with our other objects, the `Invoice` object implements the `Fetch`, `Save` and `DeleteObject` subroutines. Since each child object will handle its own data access, the `Invoice` object's subroutines only need to deal with the `Invoice` object itself:

```
Private Sub Save()

  Dim rsInvoice As Recordset
  Dim strSQL As String

  strSQL = "SELECT * FROM Invoice WHERE InvoiceID=" & InvoiceID
  Set rsInvoice = New Recordset
  rsInvoice.Open strSQL, cnVideo, , adLockOptimistic
  If mflgNew Then rsInvoice.AddNew

  With rsInvoice
    .Fields("CustomerID") = mudtProps.CustomerID
    .Fields("Subtotal") = Me.SubTotal
    .Fields("Tax") = Me.Tax
    .Fields("Total") = Me.Total
    .Update
    If IsNew Then mudtProps.InvoiceID = .Fields("InvoiceID")
    .Close
  End With

  strSQL = "SELECT NAME,PHONE FROM Customer " & _
    "WHERE CustomerID=" & mudtProps.CustomerID
  rsInvoice.Open strSQL, cnVideo
  mudtProps.CustomerName = rsInvoice("Name")
  mudtProps.CustomerPhone = rsInvoice("Phone")
  rsInvoice.Close
  Set rsInvoice = Nothing

End Sub


Private Sub DeleteObject(InvoiceID As Long)

  cnVideo.Execute "DELETE FROM Invoice WHERE InvoiceID=" & _
    InvoiceID

End Sub


Private Sub Fetch(InvoiceID As Long)

  Dim rsInvoice As Recordset
  Dim strSQL As String

  strSQL = "SELECT Invoice.*,Customer.Name,Customer.Phone " & _
    "FROM Invoice INNER JOIN Customer ON " & _
    "Invoice.CustomerID = Customer.CustomerID " & _
    "WHERE InvoiceID=" & CStr(InvoiceID)
  Set rsInvoice = New Recordset
  rsInvoice.Open strSQL, cnVideo

  With rsInvoice
    mudtProps.InvoiceID = .Fields("InvoiceID")
    mudtProps.CustomerID = .Fields("CustomerID")
    mudtProps.CustomerName = .Fields("Name")
    mudtProps.CustomerPhone = .Fields("Phone")
    .Close
  End With

  Set rsInvoice = Nothing
  mobjValid.RuleBroken "Customer", False
End Sub
```

As with the `Video` object, the `Invoice` object will call the `Fetch` routine in its `Load` method. It calls the `Save` and `DeleteObject` routines from within the `ApplyEdit` method:

```
Public Sub Load(InvoiceID As Long)

   If mflgEditing Then Err.Raise 445
   If Not mflgNew Then Err.Raise 445

   Fetch InvoiceID
   mflgNew = False

   mobjValid.RuleBroken "Customer", False
   mobjItems.Load mudtProps.InvoiceID

End Sub


Public Sub ApplyEdit()

   If Not mflgEditing Then Err.Raise 445

   If mflgDeleted And Not mflgNew Then
      ' code to delete the object's data goes here
      DeleteObject mudtProps.InvoiceID
      mflgNew = True
      mflgDeleted = False

   ElseIf mflgDirty Or mflgNew Then
      If Not IsValid Then Err.Raise 445
      ' save object to database if appropriate
      Save
      ' save object state
      LSet mudtSave = mudtProps
      mflgNew = False

   End If

   mflgDirty = False
   mflgEditing = False
   mobjItems.ApplyEdit mudtProps.InvoiceID

End Sub
```

Each routine also echoes the method call down to the `InvoiceItems` collection object, just as we did with the `Video` object.

# The Invoice Child Objects

The `InvoiceItems` collection can contain two different types of object, `InvoiceTape` and `InvoiceFee`. However, both of these objects implement the `InvoiceItem` interface, so we're able to use them as though they were the same class when we can use them as `InvoiceItem` objects - which is where polymorphism comes into play.

Unfortunately, a shared interface such as `InvoiceItem` can't contain anything other than `Public` properties and methods. This is because the `Implements` keyword only brings the `Public` properties and methods from the base class into the class implementing the interface.

In the child objects, the `ChildLoad`, `Delete` and `ChildApplyEdit` methods aren't `Public`, since we don't want the UI code to have access to them. Therefore, we were unable to include them in the `InvoiceItem` interface.

## The InvoiceItems Collection

What this boils down to is that, in Chapter 5, we did some extra work in the `InvoiceItems` collection object to handle each type of child object differently.

We covered this in great detail in Chapter 5, so we won't go over it again here. In the end, the `InvoiceItems` object directly calls each child object's `ChildLoad`, `Delete` and `ChildApplyEdit` method when its `Load`, `LoadFees` and `ApplyEdit` methods are called by the `Invoice` object.

As with the `Tapes` object, the `InvoiceItems` object doesn't implement the `Fetch`, `Save` or `DeleteObject` routines. It doesn't have any data of its own that needs to be saved to the database; instead, it just needs to make sure all the child objects interact with the database as appropriate.

The `Tapes` object's `Load` method contained code to get the ID values for each child and then to create each child object using those ID values. We need to do the same thing with the `InvoiceItems` object, but with a bit more complexity since we have two types of child objects.

### Loading the Late Fee Objects

Within the `InvoiceItems` object, we have a `LoadFees` method to load all the late fee objects. In Chapter 6, we simply put comments in this routine, as it can't be implemented without access to a database. We'll replace those comments here with the following code:

```
Friend Sub LoadFees(CustomerID As Long)

    Dim rsItems As Recordset
    Dim objInvoiceFee As InvoiceFee
    Dim strSQL As String

    If mflgEditing Then Err.Raise 445

    strSQL = "SELECT FEEID FROM LATEFEE " & _
        "WHERE DELETED=FALSE AND PAID=FALSE AND " & _
        "CUSTOMERID=" & CustomerID
    Set rsItems = New Recordset
    rsItems.Open strSQL, cnVideo

    Do While Not rsItems.EOF
        Set objInvoiceFee = New InvoiceFee
        objInvoiceFee.ChildLoad rsItems("FeeID")
        mcolItems.Add Item:=objInvoiceFee
        rsItems.MoveNext
    Loop

    rsItems.Close
    Set rsItems = Nothing

End Sub
```

This routine gets the `CustomerID` value as a parameter. The `Invoice` object provides this `CustomerID` when it calls the `LoadFees` method, since it knows which customer owns the invoice. The late fee records are all owned by a customer, so this field is used in the `WHERE` clause of the SQL statement to retrieve the correct records:

```
strSQL = "SELECT FEEID FROM LATEFEE " & _
    "WHERE DELETED=FALSE AND PAID=FALSE AND " & _
    "CUSTOMERID=" & CustomerID
```

The `WHERE` clause also contains checks to make sure we don't retrieve records for late fees that have already been paid, or for those that have been deleted. On an invoice we only want to include late fees that need to be paid by the customer.

Using the resulting list of `FeeID` values, we can loop through the recordset, creating and loading an `InvoiceFee` object for each record:

```
Do While Not rsItems.EOF
   Set objInvoiceFee = New InvoiceFee
   objInvoiceFee.ChildLoad rsItems("FeeID")
   mcolItems.Add Item:=objInvoiceFee
   rsItems.MoveNext
Loop
```

Unlike the `Tape` object, the `InvoiceFee` object has no `SetAsChild` method, since the `InvoiceFee` objects are always child objects.

### Loading the Tape Rental Objects

Similarly, we need the `Load` method to load the `InvoiceTape` objects. Again, in Chapter 5 we commented the pseudo-code for this routine; now we'll replace that with actual code.

This method would only be used to bring up an old `Invoice` object, perhaps for display or reporting reasons:

```
Friend Sub Load(InvoiceID As Long)

   Dim rsItems As Recordset
   Dim objInvoiceTape As InvoiceTape
   Dim strSQL As String

   If mflgEditing Then Err.Raise 445

   strSQL = "SELECT ITEMID FROM INVOICETAPE " & _
       "WHERE INVOICEID=" & InvoiceID
   Set rsItems = New Recordset
   rsItems.Open strSQL, cnVideo

   Do While Not rsItems.EOF
      Set objInvoiceTape = New InvoiceTape
      objInvoiceTape.ChildLoad rsItems("ItemID")
      mcolItems.Add Item:=objInvoiceTape
      rsItems.MoveNext
   Loop
```

```
      rsItems.Close
      Set rsItems = Nothing

   End Sub
```

Like the other `Load` methods we've looked at, this one creates a recordset containing all the primary key values for the child objects; in this case, `InvoiceTape` objects. Then each child object's `ChildLoad` method is called, and the loaded object is added to the `InvoiceItems` object's collection.

## The InvoiceFee Object

The `InvoiceFee` object is rather interesting. This object represents data in a table that is not so much related to an invoice as it is related to a customer. `InvoiceFee` illustrates how powerful this whole object-oriented approach can be, since we are able to create an object model that makes a set of data, a customer's unpaid late fees, appear to be part of an invoice.

To pull this off, we need to take extra care to build the `Fetch`, `Save` and `DeleteObject` so they work with the data correctly. First though, we need to update the object's `FeeProps` UDT.

### Adding the Paid Flag

When we created our table earlier in the chapter, we added a field to indicate if the late fee had been paid. While this field is not part of the object's interface, it's part of the implementation. The `InvoiceFee` object needs to update this field as it is saved, to indicate that the late fee has been paid via an `Invoice` object.

The `FeeProps` UDT needs to have a `Paid` variable added to track the current value of the field. We'll also add a `PaidDate` field to match the one we added to the table earlier. Again, this field will be updated as the `InvoiceFee` object is saved to indicate when the late fee was paid:

```
   Private Type FeeProps
      InvoiceID As Long
      FeeID As Long
      VideoTitle As String * 30
      EnteredDate As Date
      DaysOver As Integer
      Paid As Boolean
      PaidDate As Date
   End Type
```

We'll use these fields in the `Fetch` and `Save` methods we're about to implement. We'll also create a new method in our object, `Pay`, which will allow us to indicate that the late fee has been paid. Add the following code:

```
   Private Sub Pay()

   With mudtProps
      .Paid = True
      .PaidDate = Now
   End With

   mflgDirty = True
   End Sub
```

This routine is `Private`, since it will only be called from within the object itself. In reality, our `InvoiceFee` object will only be loaded as part of an `Invoice` object – basically meaning that the customer is at the counter ready to rent a tape and/or pay for a late fee. Because of this we can automatically assume that when an `InvoiceFee` object is instantiated and then saved that we are paying a late fee.

We'll call this new `Pay` method from the `ChildApplyEdit` routine. When the user clicks OK on the screen to tell the `Invoice` object to save itself, the `Invoice` object will in turn tell the `InvoiceItems` collection to save itself. `InvoiceItems` will then call each child object, including `InvoiceFee` object, to tell it to save. This is done by calling the `ChildApplyEdit` method. Add the following code to that method:

```
Friend Sub ChildApplyEdit(InvoiceID As Long)

  If Not mflgChildEditing Then Err.Raise 445

  If Not mflgDeleted And Not mflgNew Then _
    Pay
  If mflgDeleted And Not mflgNew Then
    ' code to delete the object's data goes here
    mflgNew = True
    mflgDeleted = False

  ElseIf mflgDirty Or mflgNew Then
    If Not IsValid Then Err.Raise 445
    mudtProps.InvoiceID = InvoiceID
    ' save object to database if appropriate
    ' save object state
    LSet mudtChild = mudtProps
    mflgNew = False

  End If

  mflgDirty = False
  mflgChildEditing = False

End Sub
```

All we need to do is make sure the object isn't being deleted and that the object isn't new. This means that we're dealing with an existing object that needs to be saved – thus we can make sure it's paid by calling the `Pay` method.

This provides a good illustration of how our objects sometimes perform entirely data-centric activities. Setting the `Paid` and `PaidDate` fields is a consequence of adding the `InvoiceFee` object to an `Invoice` object, but the process is not something the UI is directly involved with. Instead, it's entirely handled by our object behind the scenes.

### The Fetch Method

Let's look at the `Fetch` routine first:

```
Private Sub Fetch(FeeID As Long)

  Dim rsLateFee As Recordset
  Dim strSQL As String
```

```
    strSQL = "SELECT LateFee.*, Video.Title " & _
      "FROM (LateFee INNER JOIN Tape ON " & _
      "LateFee.TapeID = Tape.TapeID) " & _
      "INNER JOIN Video ON Tape.VideoID = Video.VideoID " & _
      "WHERE LateFee.FeeID=" & Format$(FeeID)
    Set rsLateFee = New Recordset
    rsLateFee.Open strSQL, cnVideo

    With rsLateFee
      mudtProps.FeeID = .Fields("FeeID")
      mudtProps.VideoTitle = .Fields("Title")
      mudtProps.EnteredDate = .Fields("FeeDate")
      mudtProps.DaysOver = .Fields("DaysOver")
      mudtProps.Paid = .Fields("Paid")
      If Not IsNull(.Fields("PaidDate")) Then _
        mudtProps.PaidDate = .Fields("PaidDate")
      .Close
    End With

    Set rsLateFee = Nothing

  End Sub
```

Overall, this routine is not much different from what we've seen in the other objects. The big difference is in the SQL statement, since this object has a `Title` property that needs to come from the `Video` table:

```
    strSQL = "SELECT LateFee.*, Video.Title " & _
      "FROM (LateFee INNER JOIN Tape ON " & _ .
      "LateFee.TapeID = Tape.TapeID) " & _
      "INNER JOIN Video ON Tape.VideoID = Video.VideoID " & _
      "WHERE LateFee.FeeID=" & Format$(FeeID)
```

The only field we have to work with is the `TapeID` field, but that only gets us to the `Tape` table. From there, we need to use the `VideoID` field on the tape record to do a `JOIN` on the `Video` table so we can get the `Title` value.

### The DeleteObject Method

The `DeleteObject` routine is even more different than the others we've seen. Instead of removing a record from the table, this routine just changes the `Deleted` field on the record to `True` so the late fee is marked as being deleted but still exists in the table for later reporting:

```
    Private Sub DeleteObject(FeeID As Long)

      Dim rsLateFee As Recordset
      Dim strSQL As String

      strSQL = "SELECT DELETED FROM LateFee WHERE FeeID=" & FeeID
      Set rsLateFee = New Recordset
      rsLateFee.Open strSQL, cnVideo

      With rsLateFee
        .Fields("Deleted") = True
```

```
      .Update
      .Close
   End With

End Sub
```

### The Save Method

The `Save` routine for this object doesn't actually save the object's state as much as it sets a couple fields on the related `LateFee` record. The overall structure of the routine is the same as we've seen before:

```
Private Sub Save()

  Dim rsLateFee As Recordset
  Dim strSQL As String

  strSQL = "SELECT * FROM LateFee WHERE FeeID=" & _
     mudtProps.FeeID
  Set rsLateFee = New Recordset
  rsLateFee.Open strSQL, cnVideo, , adLockOptimistic
  If mflgNew Then rsLateFee.AddNew

  With rsLateFee
     .Fields("Paid") = mudtProps.Paid
     .Fields("PaidDate") = mudtProps.PaidDate
     .Update
     If mflgNew Then mudtProps.FeeID = .Fields("FeeID")
     .Close
  End With

  Set rsLateFee = Nothing

End Sub
```

The difference is more a philosophical one than a physical one. The `InvoiceFee` object doesn't directly represent the `LateFee` table's data; it's more a user of the record. So the `Save` method is less saving the object's state to a table than it is updating the table to reflect the results of a transaction where the late fee was paid by the customer.

### Calling the Persistence Methods

The `InvoiceFee` object's `Fetch` routine will be called by a `ChildLoad` method. We've already added code in the `InvoiceItems` object's `LoadFees` method to call the `ChildLoad` method as it creates each `InvoiceFee` object. Now we need to update our code to call the `Fetch` routine:

```
Friend Sub ChildLoad(FeeID As Long)

   If mflgChildEditing Then Err.Raise 445
   If Not mflgNew Then Err.Raise 445

   Fetch FeeID
   mflgNew = False

End Sub
```

The `DeleteObject` and `Save` routines will be called, as usual, from within the `ChildApplyEdit` method:

```
Friend Sub ChildApplyEdit(InvoiceID As Long)

  If Not mflgChildEditing Then Err.Raise 445
  If Not IsValid Then Err.Raise 445

  If mflgDeleted And Not mflgNew Then
    ' code to delete the object's data goes here
    DeleteObject mudtProps.FeeID
    mflgNew = True
    mflgDeleted = False

  ElseIf mflgDirty Or mflgNew Then
    mudtProps.InvoiceID = InvoiceID
    ' save object to database if appropriate
    Save
    'If mudtProps.LateFee Then
    '   ' add the late fee to the customer
    'End If
    ' save object state
    LSet mudtChild = mudtProps
    mflgNew = False

  End If

  mflgDirty = False
  mflgChildEditing = False

End Sub
```

The `ChildApplyEdit` method is called for each child object by the `InvoiceItems` collection object.

## The InvoiceTape Object

The `InvoiceTape` object is very much a typical child object. It has an `InvoiceTape` table to hold each object's state data, and its `Fetch`, `Save` and `DeleteObject` routines work primarily with that table. Since this object is always a child object, there is no `SetAsChild` method as with the `Tape` object, so things are somewhat simpler.

The `Fetch`, `Save` and `DeleteObject` routines work primarily with the `InvoiceTape` table, although the `Title` field is brought in from the `Video` table as it was in the `InvoiceFee` object.

### The Save Method

Let's start with the `Save` method:

```
Private Sub Save(InvoiceID As Long)

  Dim rsInvoiceTape As Recordset
  Dim strSQL As String

  strSQL = "SELECT * FROM InvoiceTape WHERE ItemID=" & _
    Format$(ItemID)
  Set rsInvoiceTape = New Recordset
```

```
    rsInvoiceTape.Open strSQL, cnVideo, , adLockOptimistic
    If mflgNew Then rsInvoiceTape.AddNew

    With rsInvoiceTape
        .Fields("InvoiceID") = InvoiceID
        .Fields("TapeID") = mudtProps.TapeID
        .Fields("Price") = mudtProps.Price
        .Update
        If IsNew Then mudtProps.ItemID = .Fields("ItemID")
        .Close
    End With

    strSQL = "SELECT Video.Title " & _
        "FROM Tape INNER JOIN Video ON " & _
        "Tape.VideoID = Video.VideoID " & _
        "WHERE Tape.TapeID=" & mudtProps.TapeID
    rsInvoiceTape.Open strSQL, cnVideo
    mudtProps.Title = rsInvoiceTape("Title")
    rsInvoiceTape.Close
    Set rsInvoiceTape = Nothing

End Sub
```

This `Save` routine is a bit different from others we've seen, in that it accepts a parameter. This is typical of `Save` routines for child objects, since they need to receive the primary key value of their parent object. In this case, the parent object is the `Invoice` and so the `InvoiceID` is the parameter.

The `InvoiceID` is then stored in the table so we can use it later to retrieve the child record within the `Fetch` routine:

```
.Fields("InvoiceID") = InvoiceID
```

This code takes care of saving each line item into the `InvoiceTape` table. Of course, each invoice line item refers to a specific tape that's being rented. We also need to make sure and update that tape's data.

### Checking Out a Tape

In Chapter 6, we implemented a `CheckOut` method on our `Tape` object. This method takes care of indicating that the `Tape` object is currently checked out to a `Customer`. With the `Save` method we just implemented, our `InvoiceTape` object takes care of creating an invoice line item, but it should also make sure to call the `Tape` object's `CheckOut` method so the `Tape` object knows it has been rented.

Since this process involves a bit of code, we'll create a small subroutine in the `InvoiceTape` object to take care of checking out the tape:

```
Private Sub CheckOut(InvoiceID As Long)

    Dim objTape As Tape

    Set objTape = New Tape
    objTape.Load mudtProps.TapeID
```

```
    With objTape
        .BeginEdit
        .CheckOut InvoiceID
        .ApplyEdit
    End With

    Set objTape = Nothing

End Sub
```

This routine creates an instance of the appropriate `Tape` object by using the `TapeID` field from the line item. It then puts the `Tape` object in edit mode with `BeginEdit`, calls the `CheckOut` method, and applies the change with the `ApplyEdit` method.

We just need to call this routine from the `InvoiceTape` object's `Save` method. We'll add this call near the bottom of the `Save` method we just implemented in the `InvoiceTape` object:

```
    rsInvoiceTape.Close
    Set rsInvoiceTape = Nothing
    CheckOut InvoiceID

End Sub
```

With this code, our `InvoiceTape` objects now not only create an invoice line item, but they also make sure the `Tape` object is checked out. This is a good example of object interaction, in that we are able to take advantage of the `CheckOut` behavior of the `Tape` object from within the `InvoiceTape` object.

### DeleteObject and Fetch Methods

The `DeleteObject` code for our object is quite straightforward, and so is the `Fetch` routine:

```
Private Sub DeleteObject(ItemID As Long)

  cnVideo.Execute "DELETE FROM InvoiceTape WHERE ItemID=" & _
    CStr(ItemID)

End Sub
```

```
Private Sub Fetch(ItemID As Long)

  Dim rsInvoiceTape As Recordset
  Dim strSQL As String

  strSQL = "SELECT InvoiceTape.*, Video.Title " & _
    "FROM (InvoiceTape INNER JOIN Tape ON " & _
    "InvoiceTape.TapeID = Tape.TapeID) " & _
    "INNER JOIN Video ON Tape.VideoID = Video.VideoID " & _
    "WHERE InvoiceTape.ItemID=" & ItemID
  Set rsInvoiceTape = New Recordset
  rsInvoiceTape.Open strSQL, cnVideo
```

```
    With rsInvoiceTape
      mudtProps.ItemID = .Fields("ItemID")
      mudtProps.TapeID = .Fields("TapeID")
      mudtProps.Title = .Fields("Title")
      mudtProps.Price = .Fields("Price")
      .Close
    End With

    Set rsInvoiceTape = Nothing

  End Sub
```

These routines are called from within the `InvoiceTape` object's `ChildLoad` and
`ChildApplyEdit` methods.

### Calling the Persistence Methods

We don't have to worry about the `Load` or `ApplyEdit` methods at all with this object, since these
are always child objects, and those two methods will never cause the objects to interact with the
database:

```
  Friend Sub ChildApplyEdit(InvoiceID As Long)

    If Not mflgChildEditing Then Err.Raise 445
    If Not IsValid Then Err.Raise 445

    If mflgDeleted And Not mflgNew Then
      ' code to delete the object's data goes here
      DeleteObject mudtProps.ItemID
      mflgNew = True
      mflgDeleted = False

    ElseIf mflgDirty Or mflgNew Then
      ' save object to database if appropriate
      Save InvoiceID
      'If mudtProps.LateFee Then
      '  ' add the late fee to the customer
      'End If
      ' save object state
      LSet mudtChild = mudtProps
      mflgNew = False

    End If

    mflgDirty = False
    mflgChildEditing = False

  End Sub
```

The `Fetch` routine will be called from a `ChildLoad` method. We've already added code in the
`Load` method of the `InvoiceItems` object to call this method, but we still need to add some code to
this method in the `InvoiceTape` class:

```
  Friend Sub ChildLoad(ItemID As Long)

    If mflgChildEditing Then Err.Raise 445
```

```
        If Not mflgNew Then Err.Raise 445

        Fetch ItemID
        mflgNew = False

    End Sub
```

This method is essentially the same as any of the other `Load` or `ChildLoad` methods we've implemented so far in this chapter.

# Making Read-Only Objects Persistent

The final set of objects we need to cover are the read-only objects that we built in Chapter 5. The `Customers` and `Videos` objects are designed to return lists of information to the UI so the UI developer can create a screen displaying a list of the items.

This list might be used either for simple display or as selection criteria to load a `Customer` or `Video` object. The UI we designed in Chapter 6 uses these objects to provide a list of items for the user to choose from for editing.

The `TextList` object is more generic, providing a list of text values for use in populating `ComboBox` or `ListBox` controls. The list of values is also used to validate data entry into certain properties on an object. For instance, our `Video` object provides `Categories` and `Ratings` properties for the UI to populate `ComboBox` controls, and also uses the `TextList` objects to make sure the `Category` and `Rating` values entered by the user are valid.

In all of these cases, the data in the objects is provided in a read-only fashion. The UI code can't change or update any of the data. This means that we won't need to provide `Save` or `DeleteObject` routines within these objects. All we'll be doing is loading information into the object from the database, so the only routine that we need to worry about is the `Fetch` routine.

## The Customers Object

In Chapter 5, we implemented what was essentially a skeleton of the `Customers` object. Much of this object relies on the data access code to actually operate, so we'll really flesh it out in this section.

### Loading the Customers Object's Data

The `Customers` object provides a `Load` method with two optional parameters, `Name` and `Phone`. The UI developer can call this method to cause the object to load itself with data matching those parameters, with the expectation that they'll be used as matching criteria to return a list of customer information. This is where we'll call our `Fetch` routine, relaying the two parameters along as well. Add this line to the `Customers` object:

```
    Public Sub Load(Optional Name As String, Optional Phone As String)

        ' load data from database
        Fetch Name, Phone

    End Sub
```

*We're not using the* IsMissing() *function to check to see if both* Name *and* Phone *were supplied. This is because both parameters are typed as* String, *and* IsMissing() *is only valid for optional parameters of type* Variant. *With optional parameters of other data types the function will always return* False, *even if the client code didn't actually supply a value. Just one of those idiosyncrasies of Visual Basic...*

The Customers object's Fetch routine takes the parameters and uses them to build a SQL SELECT statement to find any matching customer data in the Customer table:

```
Private Sub Fetch(Name As String, Phone As String)

  Dim rsCustomer As Recordset
  Dim strSQL As String
  Dim strWHERE As String
  Dim objDisplay As CustomerDisplay

  strSQL = "SELECT CUSTOMERID, NAME, PHONE FROM CUSTOMER"
  If Len(Name) > 0 Then _
    strWHERE = "NAME LIKE '" & Name & "%' "

  If Len(Phone) > 0 Then

    If Len(strWHERE) > 0 Then
      strWHERE = strWHERE & " AND PHONE LIKE '" & Phone & "%'"

    Else
      strWHERE = "PHONE LIKE '" & Phone & "%'"

    End If

  End If

  If Len(strWHERE) > 0 Then _
    strSQL = strSQL & " WHERE " & strWHERE
  Set rsCustomer = New Recordset
  rsCustomer.Open strSQL, cnVideo

  Do While Not rsCustomer.EOF
    Set objDisplay = New CustomerDisplay

    With objDisplay
      .CustomerID = rsCustomer("CustomerID")
      .Name = rsCustomer("Name")
      .Phone = rsCustomer("Phone")
      mcolDisplay.Add objDisplay
      Set objDisplay = Nothing
      rsCustomer.MoveNext
    End With

  Loop

  rsCustomer.Close
  Set rsCustomer = Nothing

End Sub
```

We're not doing anything particularly fancy here. If the user supplied a Name value, we add it to the WHERE clause along with a wildcard character. The same goes for the Phone value: if the user supplied a value, we stick a wildcard on the end and add it to the clause. In both cases, we use the LIKE keyword to cause the JET engine to do a wildcard match against the field values in the table.

> *For those new to ADO, it may seem odd to be using the '% ' character as a wildcard match.*
> *However, this is the typical wildcard character for ANSI SQL and so that's why ADO makes use*
> *of it.*

The SELECT statement only returns the three values that we'll be providing through the CustomerDisplay object's properties, CustomerID, Name and Phone. While restricting the number of fields returned in a SELECT statement doesn't impact performance much when dealing with an Access database, it's critical in a two-tier setting using an ODBC data source.

Once we've got a SQL statement to work with, we open a recordset; in this case, a Snapshot to retrieve the data:

```
Set rsCustomer = New Recordset
rsCustomer.Open strSQL, cnVideo
```

At this point, the Fetch routine looks a lot like the others we've built in this chapter. The code loops through the recordset, creating a CustomerDisplay object for each record in the list:

```
Do While Not rsCustomer.EOF
   Set objDisplay = New CustomerDisplay
```

The CustomerDisplay object has no Load method and, in fact, we've already retrieved all the data we need to populate the CustomerDisplay objects. In Chapter 5, we implemented Property Let routines for each Property Get, but we made them all with Friend scope. That way, they can be given values by the Customers object, but the values can't be changed by the UI code, since Friend properties aren't available outside the ActiveX server itself:

```
With objDisplay
  .CustomerID = rsCustomer("CustomerID")
  .Name = rsCustomer("Name")
  .Phone = rsCustomer("Phone")
  mcolDisplay.Add objDisplay
  Set objDisplay = Nothing
  rsCustomer.MoveNext
End With
```

This code sets the CustomerDisplay object's properties from the recordset, adds the object to the Customers object's collection, and moves on to the next record.

## Updating the Customers Object's Item Method

The Customers object, as we implemented it in Chapter 5, has only comments in its Item method. This is because we didn't know, at the time, how the CustomerDisplay objects would be loaded, since the implementation can vary depending on how we handle persistence.

Now that we've implemented the `Customers` object's `Fetch` routine, we know how it works. Our new `Fetch` routine loads the data from the database and creates a `CustomerDisplay` object for each record from the database. In the end, the `mcolDisplay` collection contains a list of `CustomerDisplay` objects, all ready for use.

With this implementation, our `Customers` object's `Item` method is very simple, since all it needs to do is return the appropriate item from `mcolDisplay`:

```
Public Function Item(ByVal Index As Variant) As CustomerDisplay

    Set Item = mcolDisplay(Index)

End Function
```

# The Videos Object

The `Videos` object has a `Load` method and a `Fetch` routine just like the `Customers` object. We'll include the code here, but we won't go through it in detail since the process is identical to what we just implemented with the `Customers` object.

## The Load Method

Again, the `Load` method accepts parameters to be used as criteria to find any matching records. These parameters are relayed to the `Fetch` subroutine for its use.

```
Public Sub Load(Optional Title As String, Optional Studio As String)

    ' load data from database
    Fetch Title, Studio

End Sub
```

## The Fetch Method

The `Fetch` routine takes the parameters and builds a SQL `SELECT` statement that is used to open a recordset with all the matching records. A `VideoDisplay` object is created for each row in the recordset, its properties are loaded from the recordset's data, and the object is added to the collection:

```
Private Sub Fetch(Title As String, Studio As String)

    Dim rsVideo As Recordset
    Dim strSQL As String
    Dim strWHERE As String
    Dim objDisplay As VideoDisplay

    strSQL = "SELECT VideoID, TITLE,RELEASEDATE FROM Video"
    If Len(Title) > 0 Then _
        strWHERE = "TITLE LIKE '" & Title & "%' "

    If Len(Studio) > 0 Then

        If Len(strWHERE) > 0 Then
            strWHERE = strWHERE & " AND STUDIO LIKE '" & Studio & "%'"
```

```
        Else
          strWHERE = "STUDIO LIKE '" & Studio & "%'"

        End If

      End If

      If Len(strWHERE) > 0 Then _
        strSQL = strSQL & " WHERE " & strWHERE
      Set rsVideo = New Recordset
      rsVideo.Open strSQL, cnVideo

      Do While Not rsVideo.EOF
        Set objDisplay = New VideoDisplay

        With objDisplay
          .VideoID = rsVideo("VideoID")
          .Title = rsVideo("Title")
          .ReleaseDate = rsVideo("ReleaseDate")
          mcolDisplay.Add objDisplay
          Set objDisplay = Nothing
          rsVideo.MoveNext
        End With

      Loop

      rsVideo.Close
      Set rsVideo = Nothing

    End Sub
```

## The Item Method

As with the `Customers` object, we need to update the `Item` method of our `Videos` object. In Chapter 5, we just put comments in this routine, but here we'll put in some code:

```
Public Function Item(ByVal Index As Variant) As VideoDisplay

    Set Item = mcolDisplay(Index)

End Function
```

Our `Fetch` routine creates a `VideoDisplay` object for each record retrieved from the database. It then loads each `VideoDisplay` object into the `mcolDisplay` collection, so our `Item` method merely needs to return the appropriate `VideoDisplay` object from the collection on request.

# The TextList Object

The `TextList` object is a bit different, though still quite similar to what we've seen. Like all the other objects, it has a `Load` method that calls the `Fetch` routine:

```
Friend Sub Load(ListName As String)

    Fetch ListName

End Sub
```

It may seem odd that we bother to have a separate `Fetch` routine if the `Load` method is only a single line of code to call that routine. Why not include the code from the `Fetch` routine right into the `Load` method? If we had no intention of moving the data access code to an application server later, it might make sense to put the code into the `Load` method. However, we'll be moving this code to another object in Chapter 10, so we're doing this to make it easier later.

In writing this routine, we've made some specific assumptions that are very important. We're assuming that the `ListName` parameter will be the same as the name of the table containing the data. We're also assuming that the table's layout has a first column with a unique ID value and a second column where the text value is displayed.

Since we designed both the `Categories` and `Ratings` tables this way, we can make these assumptions. If we have a more complex data design we may have to make this routine more complicated to compensate.

Like most of our other `Fetch` subroutines, this one opens a recordset to retrieve a list of values from the table. In this case, we're opening the whole table as a Snapshot by using the `ListName` parameter in the `Open` statement:

```
Private Sub Fetch(ListName As String)

   Dim strSQL As String
   Dim rsList As Recordset

   Set rsList = New Recordset
   rsList.Open ListName, cnVideo

   Do While Not rsList.EOF
      mcolList.Add Format$(rsList(1)), Format$(rsList(0))
      mcolKeys.Add Format$(rsList(0)), Format$(rsList(1))
      rsList.MoveNext
   Loop

   rsList.Close
   Set rsList = Nothing

End Sub
```

Then we loop through all the elements in the recordset, loading both the `mcolList` and `mcolKeys` collections. The `mcolList` collection is loaded with the text values being the Item and the ID value from the table being the collection's Key:

```
Do While Not rsList.EOF
   mcolList.Add Format$(rsList(1)), Format$(rsList(0))
```

The `mcolKeys` collection is loaded with the ID value from the table as the collection's Item and the text value from the table as the Key. This is exactly the reverse of the `mcolList` collection:

```
   mcolKeys.Add Format$(rsList(0)), Format$(rsList(1))
   rsList.MoveNext
Loop
```

```
        rsList.Close
        Set rsList = Nothing

    End Sub
```

After all the values have been loaded into both collections, we close the recordset and the object is ready for use.

## Updating the Video Object

Now that we've implemented the persistence code for our `TextList` object, we can update some code that we began to develop in Chapter 5 that was dependent upon this persistence. In the `Video` object's `Class_Initialize` method, we noted that we needed to set our `mudtProps.Category` and `mudtProps.Rating` variables with data from the database. We've had to wait until now to update this code, because we read the data from the `TextList` objects within the `VideoEdit` form. So add the following lines to the `Class_Initialize` method of the `Video` object:

```
        Set mobjCategories = New TextList
        mobjCategories.Load "Categories"
        mudtProps.Category = mobjCategories.Key(mobjCategories(1))

        Set mobjRatings = New TextList
        mobjRatings.Load "Ratings"
        mudtProps.Rating = mobjRatings.Key(mobjRatings(1))
```

These lines store the first item from the `Category` and `Rating` tables within our `mudtProps.Category` and `mudtProps.Rating` variables by reading the data we've just read in from the `Load` method of our `TextList` variables.

Earlier in the chapter we left a couple lines from the `Video` object's `Save` method commented out because the `Ratings` and `Categories` objects weren't being populated. Now that we've got that covered, we can uncomment these lines of code:

```
    Private Sub Save()

        Dim rsVideo As Recordset
        Dim strSQL As String

        Set rsVideo = New Recordset
        strSQL = "SELECT * FROM Video WHERE VideoID=" & VideoID
        rsVideo.Open strSQL, cnVideo, , adLockOptimistic
        If mflgNew Then rsVideo.AddNew

        With rsVideo
          .Fields("Title") = mudtProps.Title
          .Fields("ReleaseDate") = mudtProps.ReleaseDate
          .Fields("Studio") = mudtProps.Studio
          .Fields("Rating") = mudtProps.Rating
          .Fields("Category") = mudtProps.Category
          .Update
          If mflgNew Then mudtProps.VideoID = .Fields("VideoID")
          .Close
        End With

        Set rsVideo = Nothing

    End Sub
```

## *Updating VideoEdit*

Now that we have our `Video` and `TextList` persistence code in place, we can implement some code that we put on hold from within our UI. You may recall, from Chapter 7, how we commented out some lines from the `VideoEdit` form that accessed information that would only become available once object persistence was implemented. The code we can enable is within the `Form_Load` method of the `VideoEdit` form. Change the following lines:

```
Private Sub Form_Load()

  mflgLoading = True

  With mobjVideo
    EnableOK .IsValid
    If .IsNew Then
      Caption = "Video [(new)]"

    Else
      Caption = "Video [" & .Title & "]"

    End If

    txtTitle = .Title
    txtRelease = .ReleaseDate
    txtStudio = .Studio
    LoadCombo cboCategory, .Categories
    cboCategory.Text = .Category
    LoadCombo cboRating, .Ratings
    cboRating.Text = .Rating
    .BeginEdit
  End With

  LoadTapes
  mflgLoading = False

End Sub
```

# Summary

Given the material we've covered in this chapter (as well as Chapters 5 and 6), we now have a fully functional application - which is no small achievement. The business objects provide the application's logic, and we have a user-interface developed with Visual Basic forms.

In this chapter, we added the final piece of the puzzle, giving the objects the ability to save and restore themselves from the database.

We looked at techniques to persist a number of different types of object:

- ❏ Simple objects
- ❏ Parent objects
- ❏ Child objects
- ❏ Parent-child relationship objects
- ❏ Read-only objects

The techniques that we've used in this chapter are fairly limiting in terms of scalability, since the data access code is right inside each object and thus would be running on each client workstation. On the other hand, the approach is very simple to implement, so it can be a good solution for a single-tier or 2-tier setting.

There are some flaws in this approach when it comes to database transactions. It is technically possible to save a `Video` record, then have one of the `Tape` objects saves fail, leaving us with questionable data in the tables. This can be overcome by adding *BeginTrans* and *CommitTrans* statements in strategic locations within our objects. We didn't address this issue within the chapter, so we could keep the focus on the process of saving and restoring the objects' data.

In Chapter 10, we'll revisit object persistence, moving the `Fetch`, `Save` and `DeleteObject` routines for each object off to an application server. We will further address performance, scalability, and transactional support in that chapter.

# 9

# Microsoft Office as an Interface

## Overview

One of the major benefits of designing our application as a component that contains business objects is that we can easily change the user-interface. We can even go so far as to have multiple user-interfaces to the same application code.

In Chapters 5 and 6, we built an application using business objects, and in Chapter 8 we added code so that those objects can save and restore themselves from a database. In Chapter 7, we implemented a user-interface to the application using Visual Basic forms and controls.

To illustrate just how powerful component-oriented application design can be, in this chapter we'll build a user-interface to some of our objects from within Microsoft Office 97. We'll be using Microsoft Excel as our environment, but most of the concepts we'll cover in this chapter can be easily translated to Microsoft Word, PowerPoint and Project. This provides very powerful capabilities, since we can create various types of user interface that leverage the unique capabilities of each part of Microsoft Office. By using Excel, for instance, we may allow the user to leverage the analytical capabilities of Excel against the data from our objects in ways unforeseen when the application is originally developed.

We won't be replacing the entire user-interface that we built in Chapter 7; instead, we'll focus on some of the specific approaches that we can take when we're using Excel as an interface to our application's business object components.

# Compiling the VideoObjects Project

In Chapter 7, we used Visual Basic 6.0's ability to load multiple projects into a single environment using a project group. If we want to develop user-interfaces using tools other than Visual Basic 6.0, however, we'll need to compile our project into an actual binary component so that the other tool can access it. With the VideoObjects project, we compile it into an ActiveX DLL.

To compile the project, open up Visual Basic and load the VideoObjects project into the environment. Then choose the File | Make VideoObjects.dll... menu option:

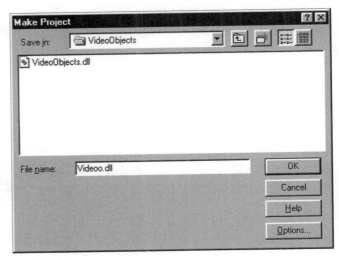

In this example, we'll name the DLL VideoObjects.dll.

Once you've compiled the DLL, make sure to save the VideoObjects project. It will have recorded the location of the file we just created and will use that file to maintain project compatibility - as we discussed in Chapter 7.

# A User Form Interface

Microsoft Office 97 comes with VBA (Visual Basic for Applications) built right into all its applications.

> **Creating an interface using VBA is very similar to creating an interface with Visual Basic itself.**

This shouldn't be surprising, since VBA is a subset of Visual Basic. The underlying language used by all VB programmers is the language supported by VBA.

In this section, we'll see how to create an interface to our business objects using Excel. The other applications in the Microsoft Office suite have the ability to create the same interface just as easily, so we could easily apply the same concepts to Word or PowerPoint and develop a similar interface, if that was required.

# Creating the Interface

We'll walk through the process of adding a form within Excel, so we can add a customer using our `Customer` business object. As we'll see, the process is remarkably similar to adding such a form to our `VideoUI` project from Chapter 7.

Once we've built the form, we'll see how we can make that form available to the user from within Excel. There are many ways to do this but, to keep things fairly simple, we'll just add a button to a spreadsheet that brings up the form - so the user can add a customer to the database.

## Opening the VBA Editor

To use VBA within Excel, we need to open up the Visual Basic Editor. First things first, though; you'll need to open up Excel before we can go any further.

Within Excel, choose the <u>T</u>ools | <u>M</u>acro | <u>V</u>isual Basic Editor menu option or press *Alt-F11*. Either way, after a short pause you should see the editor appear on your screen:

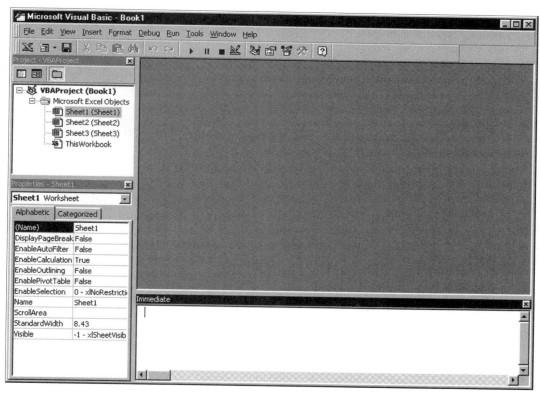

Not surprisingly, it looks very similar to the familiar Visual Basic 6.0 interface that we work in all the time. It has a Project window, a Properties window, and even an Immediate window for use with debugging.

We'll use this environment to develop an interface to our `Customer` business object.

## Adding a Reference to VideoObjects

As with the `VideoUI` project we developed in Chapter 7, we'll need to add a reference to the `VideoObjects` server. Earlier in this chapter, we compiled the `VideoObjects` project into a DLL - so we should be all ready to add a reference to our `VideoObjects` from within this new environment.

> *If you are developing this user interface on a machine other than the one where you developed the VideoObjects DLL itself you may need to copy the DLL and register it on the new workstation. This process is covered in detail in Chapter 11, when we explore how to deploy applications and application components on different machines.*

Choose the Tools | References... menu option to bring up the References dialog:

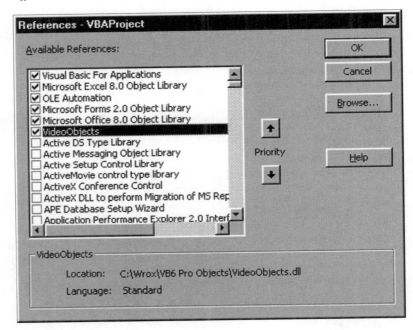

Find the VideoObjects entry in the list and check the box to its left. Then click OK to add a reference to the server.

## Adding a UserForm

Now that we have a reference to our server, we can move on to building the interface itself. The VBA Editor environment is not as advanced or friendly as the Visual Basic 6.0 IDE, but it does provide the basic functionality that we'll need to build the interface.

Choose the Insert | UserForm menu option to add a form to the project:

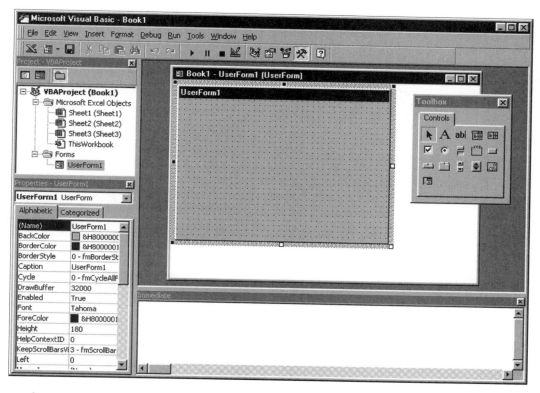

A new form, UserForm1, is added to the Project window and is displayed in the edit area. A Toolbox, similar to the Visual Basic Toolbox, will appear - so we have a palette from which we can add controls to the form.

Using the Properties window, change the Name of the form to CustomerEdit and the Caption property to Add a customer.

## Adding Our Controls

Within the new form, we need to add controls so that the user can enter the customer information. To continue my emphasis on the similarity between forms within Office and forms within Visual Basic itself, let's make this form look as close as possible to the CustomerEdit form we created in Chapter 7:

Add the controls as shown, using the following naming scheme.

| Control | Caption | Name |
|---------|---------|------|
| Label | Name | |
| Text Box | | txtName |
| Label | Address | |
| Text Box | | txtAddr1 |
| Text Box | | txtAddr2 |
| Text Box | | txtCity |
| Text Box | | txtState |
| Text Box | | txtZipCode |
| Label | Phone | |
| Text Box | | txtPhone |
| Command Button | OK | cmdOK |
| Command Button | Cancel | cmdCancel |
| Command Button | Apply | cmdApply |

Click on the OK button and change its Default property to True. Then click on the Cancel button and change its Cancel property to True. This will make the buttons respond appropriately to the *Enter* and *Escape* keys if they are pressed by the user.

## Code Behind the Form

If you glance back at the CustomerEdit form in Chapter 7, you will notice that this form looks virtually identical. Even more importantly, all the controls are laid out the same and have the same names. This is far from coincidental, and we'll make use of these similarities right now.

### Copying the Code from Chapter 7

Bring up Visual Basic itself and open up the VideoUI project. In the Project window, click on the CustomerEdit form and open up its code window.

Select all the text behind the CustomerEdit form and choose Edit | Copy. To quickly select all the text, you can use the Edit | Select All menu option. Note that you'll need Full Module View on to see all the code in the class at once.

Now switch back to the Visual Basic Editor and double-click on the CustomerEdit form there to bring up its code editing window. Highlight all the code and select Edit-Copy to put the code into the clipboard. Paste the contents of the clipboard, the code from Chapter 7, into this new form's code window.

I won't repeat the code here; you can look back to Chapter 7 to see what it looks like, how it works, and why we did things the way we did.

## Adapting the Code for Excel

The events behind the UserForm are not identical to those behind a regular Form. This is also true of the controls. These controls are different from their Visual Basic counterparts; there are also some different events, some with different names.

The biggest difference that affects us is that there is no Load event for the form. Without this event, there's no easy way to know when to load the object's property values into the form's controls. The best compromise, in this case, is to load the controls when the form's Component property is set:

```
Public Sub Component(CustomerObject As Customer)

    Set mobjCustomer = CustomerObject
    mflgLoading = True

    With mobjCustomer
       EnableOK .IsValid
       If .IsNew Then
          Caption = "Customer [(new)]"

       Else
          Caption = "Customer [" & .Name & "]"

       End If

       txtName = .Name
       txtAddr1 = .Address1
       txtAddr2 = .Address2
       txtCity = .City
       txtState = .State
       txtZipCode = .ZipCode
       txtPhone = .Phone
       .BeginEdit
    End With

    mflgLoading = False

End Sub
```

This is the code that was in the Form_Load routine. Of course, that routine is no longer needed - since there's no Load event to fire it.

All the events used by our controls still exist, except for LostFocus on the TextBox controls. This event does still exist; but in VBA it's called AfterUpdate instead. If we perform an Edit | Replace and change all the occurrences of _LostFocus to _AfterUpdate this problem will be fixed as well. For instance, the txtName_LostFocus routine should become:

```
Private Sub txtName_AfterUpdate()
```

## Adding Code to a Code Module

We need to open a code window in which to enter the TextChange and TextLostFocus methods from the code module in our VideoUI project. This is easy: choosing the Insert | Module menu option. The result should be an empty code window named Book1.xls – Module1 (code). Rename the module VUIMain. Copy and paste all the code from the module in the VideoUI project into VUIMain.

VBA does not recognize the `TextBox` object, so we have to use the general `Object` instead.

```
Public Sub TextChange(Ctl As Object, Obj As Object, Prop As String)

   Dim lngPos As Long

   On Error GoTo INPUTERR
   CallByName Obj, Prop, "VbLet", Ctl.Text
   Exit Sub

INPUTERR:
   Beep
   lngPos = Ctl.SelStart
   Ctl = CallByName(Obj, Prop, "VbGet")
   Ctl.SelStart = lngPos - 1
End Sub

Public Function TextLostFocus(Ctl As Object, Obj As Object, Prop As String)
   TextLostFocus = CallByName(Obj, Prop, "VbGet")

   End Function
```

In addition, we can not use the `CallByName` function with VBA. To replicate `CallByName`, add a reference to the project for the **TypeLib Information Library:**

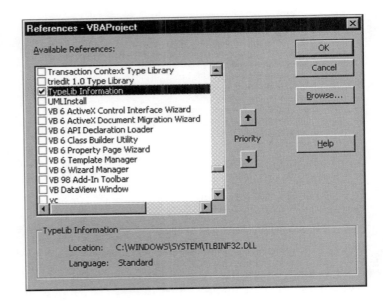

Then put the following into the `VUIMain` module:

```
Public Function CallByName(Object As Object, ProcName As String, _
   CallType As String, Optional Args As Variant) As Variant
   Dim tliApp As TLIApplication

   Set tliApp = New TLIApplication

   Select Case CallType
      Case "VbGet"
         CallByName = tliApp.InvokeHook(Object, ProcName, INVOKE_PROPERTYGET)
      Case "VbLet"
```

```
        tliApp.InvokeHook Object, ProcName, INVOKE_PROPERTYPUT, Args
    End Select

    Set tliApp = Nothing

End Function
```

With those small changes, we have brought an entire form's worth of code from Visual Basic 6.0 into a Form in Microsoft Office. Pretty incredible.

# Testing the Interface

At this point, we've got a form in Excel that lets us add and edit `Customer` objects. Now we need to test it, and also come up with a way for users to bring up the form.

## Testing the Interface in the Editor

It's quite easy to test a form from within the VBA Editor, although it may not be very obvious where to start, since our form requires that the `Component` property be set to a new `Customer` object before the form is shown to the user - and that requires a bit of code.

Fortunately, this environment makes this reasonably easy. All we need to do is create a small test subroutine to create the `Customer` object, set the `Component` property and show the form.

Add another code module by choosing the Insert | Module menu option. The result should be an empty code window named Book1.xls – Module2 (code).

Now we can add our test routine by typing the following code.

```
Option Explicit

Public Sub Test()

    Dim objCustomer As Customer
    Dim frmCustomer As CustomerEdit

    Set objCustomer = New Customer
    Set frmCustomer = New CustomerEdit

    frmCustomer.Component objCustomer
    frmCustomer.Show

End Sub
```

The code in the `Test` subroutine should look pretty familiar, since it's the same as the code in the File | Customers | New Customer menu option from Chapter 7:

```
Private Sub mnuFileCustNew_Click()

    Dim objCustomer As Customer
    Dim frmCustomer As CustomerEdit
```

```
Set objCustomer = New Customer
Set frmCustomer = New CustomerEdit

frmCustomer.Component objCustomer
frmCustomer.Show

End Sub
```

### Running the Test Routine

If you look at the toolbar in the VBA Editor window you'll see the standard Run, Pause and Stop buttons for debugging, just like in the Visual Basic 6.0 IDE. My first assumption upon seeing them was that they'd work just like the ones in Visual Basic.

Actually, they work similarly, but with an important difference. When you click the Run button, or press *F5*, the editor will run the code for the routine where the cursor is located.

This means that we can simply click anywhere in the code for the Test routine, as long as the cursor is located somewhere in that code, and press *F5*. The VBA Editor will run the Test routine, creating a Customer object and a CustomerEdit form. The form's Component property will be set, and the form will be displayed.

We should now be able to use the form to add a customer - just like the interface we created in Chapter 7. Notice how the State field is automatically made uppercase, and the ZipCode field gets automatically formatted, just like in the Visual Basic forms interface.

> **The rules within the business object are enforced within this interface just as thoroughly as with the Visual Basic forms interface. This is because we are using the same underlying business logic contained within the** VideoObjects **component.**

Once you've added a customer or two using this interface, switch back to the VideoUI program we created in Chapter 7. You should be able to bring up these new customers to view and edit them there. There's no difference between customers added in Excel or within Visual Basic, since both interfaces utilize the same underlying business objects.

Perhaps even more importantly, neither interface has any idea about how the data is actually stored in the database. Both of them rely entirely on the objects to manage those details, making it possible to entirely rewrite or change the database access with no impact on the UI at all.

## Adding a Button to a Spreadsheet

OK, so now we know we've got a working form within Excel. All that remains is to make the form available to the user. As I've indicated, we'll do this by simply adding a button to a spreadsheet, or as Excel calls them, a worksheet.

### Adding a Button to a Worksheet

There are a couple different ways to add controls to a worksheet. We can add a button as a control, or as an element of an Excel Form. In this case, we'll add the button as an element of an Excel Form, since that will make it easy to tie right into the work we've done so far.

To add the button, choose the View | Toolbars | Forms menu option in Excel. This will bring up the Forms palette:

Now we can use this palette to add a button to the worksheet - just as we would add a button to a Visual Basic form. Click on the button icon in the palette, then click and drag within the worksheet to create and size the control.

As soon as you release the mouse after drawing the button on the worksheet, Excel will bring up the Assign Macro dialog so we can associate a macro with the button:

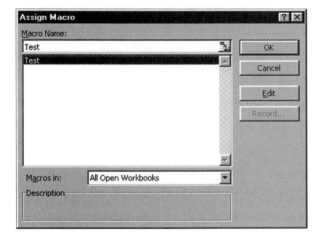

Fortunately, for us, macros in Microsoft Office 97 are simply Visual Basic subroutines that are located in code modules. They do have to be declared as Public subroutines, however, just like we did with the Test subroutine earlier.

In fact, we can see that Test is listed as a valid macro within the workbook. Just click the Test option from the list and then click OK. This will associate the button with the Test subroutine that we built earlier.

### Setting the Button's Caption

The button's caption probably reads Button 1, so we'll want to change that. If we move the mouse over the text in the control the cursor should change to the standard I-beam for text editing. Just click to get an edit cursor within the control and we can then change the caption text to read Add customer:

Now you can click the close box in the upper-right corner of the Form palette. This will switch Excel back to a normal user mode from the form editing mode we've been in so far.

### Trying the Button

Now, when we move the mouse over the Add customer button, the cursor should change to a pointing finger. If you click the button, it will run the associated macro; in this case, that macro is our `Test` routine.

Of course, the `Test` routine creates a `Customer` object and a `CustomerEdit` form, sets the `CustomerEdit` form's `Component` property, and shows the form. This means that any time the button is clicked our form will appear, allowing the user to add a `Customer` object.

Excel always shows forms modally, so we don't need to worry about the user opening dozens of copies at the same time. If the user clicks anywhere else within Excel when the `CustomerEdit` form is displayed, they'll just get a beep: the rest of the application is locked out.

# Using a Document to View Objects

In the first section of this chapter, we looked at how easily Visual Basic forms can be translated into forms within Microsoft Office. Now we'll move on to see how information can be pulled from objects for display within other applications.

This second approach is much more closely allied to whichever Office application we happen to be working on. Our previous example used a type of form that was consistent across all the Office applications; that form could therefore be moved from Excel to Word with relative ease.

In this second example, however, we'll be creating a report using Excel's abilities to display information. To move this report from Excel to Word, for example, would require substantial changes to the interface code we're about to write. In many ways, though, this second approach is more powerful, since it allows us to tap into the strengths of each Office application.

The objects we designed in Chapters 5 and 6 were focused on providing editing and transaction capabilities for our system. We didn't put a lot of thought into making it easy to display information about our objects. Even so, it should be possible to develop a spreadsheet that lists all the video tapes in our inventory and shows their current status. We'll then have a basic report that shows which tapes are available and when the others are due back from the customers.

If this type of display is a requirement for any of our applications, we can choose to design specific read-only objects to provide the necessary information. This is especially true if we're dealing with a three-tier architecture, since we'd then want to optimize the data retrieval process so that all the data we wanted to display was pulled back in one shot.

The way our objects are implemented currently, each object will retrieve its own data. This means the data will come back in small chunks, one object at a time - very slow in a distributed setting.

## Building the Report

Since we've already got Excel up and running, and our workbook has a reference to the `VideoObjects` component, we'll continue to use the same workbook that we used in our earlier example.

Like the previous example, we'll rely on our business objects to do most of the work, but in this case we'll just use a regular Excel workbook for the interface. We won't be developing any forms or using any controls except the button to launch our report.

Also as with the previous example, we'll be writing an Excel macro using VBA to generate the report. The code will therefore look very familiar to any VB programmer.

The first thing we need to do is get back to the VBA Editor within Excel. If you still have it running, then just switch to it; otherwise, choose the Tools | Macro | Visual Basic Editor menu option to bring it up.

Earlier in the chapter, we added a code module, Module1. This module should contain our Test macro that brings up the CustomerEdit form. We'll just add the report code to this code module, since it's already set up and ready to go.

Bring up the Module1 code window by double-clicking the Module1 entry in the Project window. Now let's add a macro subroutine named VideoList.

```
Public Sub VideoList()

End Sub
```

## Printing Column Titles

To make our report readable, we need to add column headers or titles. This is also an excellent opportunity to look at some simple code that puts text into a worksheet:

```
Public Sub VideoList()

    Columns("A:D").Select
    Selection.ClearContents

    Range("A1:D1").Select
    Selection.Font.Bold = True

    Range("A1").Select
    ActiveCell.FormulaR1C1 = "Video title"
    Range("C1").Select
    ActiveCell.FormulaR1C1 = "Acquired"
    Range("D1").Select
    ActiveCell.FormulaR1C1 = "Status"
    Range("A1").Select

End Sub
```

### Clearing the Columns

The first couple of lines are there to make sure the columns where we're going to put in the report don't already have text in them. The first line selects all of columns from A through to D:

```
Columns("A:D").Select
```

The other line clears the contents of those columns, leaving them empty and ready for our report:

```
Selection.ClearContents
```

### Adding the Titles

The rest of the code is quite repetitive. For each column title, we move the current selection to the cell that should contain the text:

```
Range("A1").Select
```

Once the correct cell is selected, the text is inserted. What we're really inserting is an Excel formula, but simple text is just displayed without any processing by Excel:

```
ActiveCell.FormulaR1C1 = "Video title"
```

Finally, to set the column titles apart from the rest of the text, the current cell's contents are set to a bold font:

```
ActiveCell.Font.Bold = True
```

The last line in the routine, so far, just sets the current cell back to the far upper left, A1. This gives us a nice consistent starting point for the code we'll add next.

By this point, you can probably see that programming inside Excel is really no different from programming in Visual Basic with any other object. Excel and all its parts are just a group of objects that are available for your use as a programmer. Of course, to program effectively inside Excel, we need to learn what all the objects are and what they can do. That's pretty much equivalent to learning a whole new language!

*The easiest way to figure out how to use Excel's object is to use the macro recorder to record a macro while you manually walk through the steps you need to do. Then you can go back and read the VBA code contained in the macro to figure out how it works.*

## Adding a Button

Now that we've got a start on our macro, let's add a button to the worksheet so we can try it out. Again, we'll add a button by using the Forms palette and just make it run our VideoList macro routine.

Switch to Excel and bring up the Forms palette by choosing the View | Toolbars | Forms menu option. Choose the Button option and click and drag to put a button on the Sheet1 worksheet.

When you release the mouse button, the Assign Macro dialog should appear:

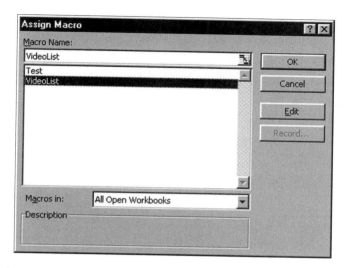

Choose the `VideoList` macro and click OK. Now the button is connected to the macro, so all that remains is to set the button's caption. Change the button's caption to read List video titles.

Now, if we click the button we can watch as Excel clears out columns A through D and puts our column headers across the top. As we continue to build our report, we'll be able to click the button to see the results of the changes as we make them.

## Listing the Video Titles

The first thing we need to do is get a list of all the video titles in the inventory. Fortunately, we created a `Videos` object that can do just that; all we need to do is call its `Load` method with no parameters and it will return a list of all the video titles in the system:

```
Public Sub VideoList()

    Dim objVideos As Videos
    Dim objDisplay As VideoDisplay

    Columns("A:D").Select
    Selection.ClearContents

    Range("A1:D1").Select
    Selection.Font.Bold = True

    Range("A1").Select
    ActiveCell.FormulaR1C1 = "Video title"
    Range("C1").Select
    ActiveCell.FormulaR1C1 = "Acquired"
    Range("D1").Select
    ActiveCell.FormulaR1C1 = "Status"
    Range("A1").Select

    Set objVideos = New Videos
    objVideos.Load
```

```
      For Each objDisplay In objVideos
        With objDisplay
           ActiveCell.Offset(1,0).Range("A1").Select
           ActiveCell.FormulaR1C1 = .Title
        End With
      Next

    End Sub
```

The `Videos` object is a `Collection` object whose items are objects of type `VideoDisplay`. The first thing we need to do is create the `Videos` object and get it loaded with data from the database:

```
    Set objVideos = New Videos
    objVideos.Load
```

Then we can loop through the collection and print the `Title` property for each `VideoDisplay` object it contains. To do this, we use a `For Each...Next` syntax to loop through the collection and retrieve each `VideoDisplay` object:

```
    For Each objDisplay In objVideos
      With objDisplay
        ActiveCell.Offset(1,0).Range("A1").Select
        ActiveCell.FormulaR1C1 = .Title
      End With
    Next
```

The line that sets the current cell is a bit different from anything that we've seen so far. Instead of using an absolute reference, such as A2, this code uses a relative reference. It indicates an offset from the current cell, specifying how far down, then across, to move the current cell:

```
    ActiveCell.Offset(1, 0).Range("A1").Select
```

If you click the List video titles button at this point, you should get a list of video titles from your database. Here's what the display looks like with my sample data:

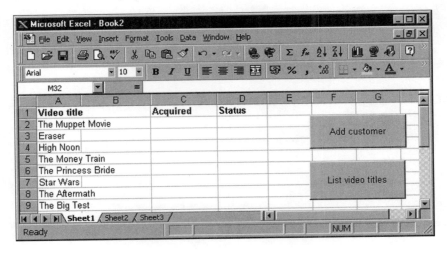

## Listing the Tapes and their Status

Now that we have a list of video titles we just need to add code to list all the tapes for each title and show their status. Fortunately, one of the properties of the `VideoDisplay` object is the `VideoID`.

We can use this property as a parameter to the `Load` method of a `Video` object. Once we have a `Video` object, we can use its `Tapes` property to list all the child `Tape` objects for that `Video`, including their status based on the `CheckedIn` property of the `Tape` object:

```
Public Sub VideoList()

    Dim objVideos As Videos
    Dim objDisplay As VideoDisplay
    Dim objVideo As Video
    Dim objTape As Tape

    Columns("A:D").Select
    Selection.ClearContents

    Range("A1:D1").Select
    Selection.Font.Bold = True

    Range("A1").Select
    ActiveCell.FormulaR1C1 = "Video title"
    Range("C1").Select
    ActiveCell.FormulaR1C1 = "Acquired"
    Range("D1").Select
    ActiveCell.FormulaR1C1 = "Status"
    Range("A1").Select

    Set objVideos = New Videos
    objVideos.Load
    For Each objDisplay In objVideos
      Set objVideo = New Video
      objVideo.Load objDisplay.VideoID

      With objVideo
        ActiveCell.Offset(1,0).Range("A1").Select
        ActiveCell.FormulaR1C1 = .Title
        ActiveCell.Offset(1,2).Range("A1").Select

        For Each objTape In .Tapes
          With objTape
            ActiveCell.FormulaR1C1 = .DateAcquired
            ActiveCell.Offset(0, 1).Range("A1").Select

            If .CheckedOut Then
              ActiveCell.FormulaR1C1 = "Due back " & _
                Format$(.DateDue, "Short date")

            Else
              ActiveCell.FormulaR1C1 ="Available"

            End If

          End With

          ActiveCell.Offset(1, -1).Range("A1").Select
      Next
```

```
        End With
        ActiveCell.Offset(0, -2).Range("A1").Select
     Next

   End Sub
```

Now, for each `VideoDisplay` object, we can turn right around and create an actual `Video` object:

```
   Set objVideo = New Video
   objVideo.Load objDisplay.VideoID
   With objVideo
```

The `Title` property that we display can come from the `Video` object itself rather than from the `VideoDisplay` object at this point, though the line of code to display the value doesn't change.

Because we need to indent the list of tape information to column C, we have a line of code to move the current cell to the right by 2:

```
   ActiveCell.Offset(1,2).Range("A1").Select
```

Then, we can just loop through all the `Tape` objects contained in the `Video` object's `Tapes` collection:

```
   For Each objTape In .Tapes
   With objTape
```

The first thing we display for each tape is the date it was acquired. We've already moved the current cell to the right spot, so we can just display the value and move the cell to the right by one in preparation for displaying the tape's status:

```
   ActiveCell.FormulaR1C1 =.DateAcquired
   ActiveCell.Offset(0,1).Range("A1").Select
```

To make the display more useful, we've also added some code to print the due date for any tape that is currently rented, or the word "Available" for those that aren't rented out:

```
   If .CheckedOut Then
     ActiveCell.FormulaR1C1 = "Due back " & _
       Format$(.DateDue, "Short date")

   Else
     ActiveCell.FormulaR1C1 ="Available"

   End If
```

Of course, we need to move the current cell down one and to the left, so things are positioned properly for the next tape's acquired date:

```
   ActiveCell.Offset(1, -1).Range("A1").Select
```

Once all the `Tape` objects have been displayed, we need to exit the loop and move the current cell to the left by 2. That should return it to column A, where it needs to be in order to display the next `Video` object's `Title` property:

```
ActiveCell.Offset(0, -2).Range("A1").Select
```

## The VideoList Report

Now, if we click the List video titles button, we'll get the full report, including the column headers, the video titles, and the status of each tape:

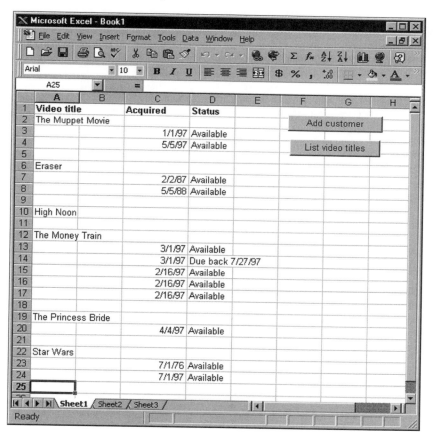

# Summary

In this chapter, we implemented a second interface to our business objects, one that easily coexists with the Visual Basic forms interface that we created in Chapter 7. The new interface was created using Microsoft Excel, but could have been implemented with Word, PowerPoint, Access or Project, with as much ease.

The key concept when thinking about Microsoft Office 97 is that all the applications in the suite use VBA (Visual Basic for Applications) as their macro language. VBA is, literally, the same language supported by Visual Basic 6.0, and so it's easy to translate a Visual Basic UI into forms within Office.

As we saw in our second example, we can also implement an interface using the unique capabilities of each particular Office application. We still use VBA to write the interface code, but the abilities, strengths, and weaknesses of each application are different and will impact the nature of the interface in each case.

This chapter has illustrated not only how easily we can create user-interfaces using Microsoft Office, but also how powerful the concept of component-oriented design really is. By developing our applications as a collection of business objects in one or more components, we make it very easy to add new, specialized user-interfaces without any danger of breaking existing interfaces.

Client software, such as a Visual Basic form, Excel, or any other application, need not know the details of data access or business logic. They only need to deal with each object's properties and methods. Using these, they can be used to easily and safely create whatever user interfaces are required.

Additionally, we can take these new and varied types of user interfaces into account when we design our objects. For example, we might want to allow an Excel user to perform some trend analysis of usage patterns of our videos. To support this capability we may need to enhance or add to our business object model to make this easy to implement. Adding such functionality just improves the robustness of our object model, allowing user interface developers to make broader use of the objects over time.

# 10

# Data-Centric Business Objects

## Overview

Now we're ready to have some serious fun. We have a fully functional program with persistent business objects and two user interfaces, but it's designed as a single-, or at most two-, tier application.

In this chapter we'll move the persistence code from the business objects into a separate ActiveX EXE. We can then put this program on a central application server machine to be used by client workstations, with, possibly, the database server on yet another machine - thus achieving a physical three-tier implementation.

We'll look at the issues involved in actually running our new ActiveX EXE on another machine in Chapter 12. In this chapter we'll keep the focus on splitting the UI-centric and data-centric behaviors of each object to create our new out-of-process server.

In Chapter 4 we covered a number of different techniques that we can use to make objects persistent. Then, in Chapter 8, we took the simplest of those techniques and enhanced our objects to save and restore themselves from the database directly.

In Chapter 4 we looked at a number of ways to serialize an object's data so we can pass an entire object's set of state data as a single parameter to a method.

In that chapter we examined `SetState` and `GetState` methods based on the use of the `LSet` command to convert a user-defined type variable into a simple `String` variable. The ability to move an object's state around as a single entity, in this case a string variable, is very important since it means we can send an entire object across a network in a single call.

Each COM call has a substantial performance penalty associated with it, and, when these calls are handled through DCOM, the penalty is even worse. When designing an application where an object's data must be sent to another program through DCOM, it's very important to minimize the number of properties and methods called on each object.

In general, each of the techniques we examined in Chapter 4 provide us with the functionality we require. Of all of them, the `LSet` technique provides the best performance and moves the smallest amount of data across the network. The other techniques each provide a different set of strengths and weaknesses and may provide appropriate functionality where performance is not the highest concern.

In this chapter we'll continue using the `LSet` technique in order to create an application with the best performance.

# Splitting Out Behaviors

If we look at a simple business object, say the `Customer` object from Chapter 5, it's composed of an interface, internal data and behaviors, as the following diagram shows:

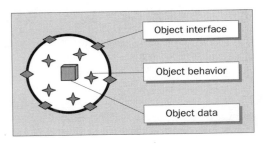

Let's now look more closely at the behaviors of our business objects, and in particular, at those we implemented in Chapter 8.

## Separate UI from Persistence

We can really divide the behaviors of those objects into two distinct parts. There are behaviors that service the UI, and those that exist to manage the object's persistence. What we're talking about here is splitting the object's business rules into two parts and putting the rules that provide a rich user interface close to the client and those that provide data support close to the data source.

The behaviors that manage the object's persistence are contained primarily in the `Fetch`, `Save` and `DeleteObject` methods within the object. Virtually all the other code exists to allow the object to support a rich UI for the user.

What we really want to do is take our single object and break it into two objects, both with the same internal data, but each with specific interface elements and behaviors:

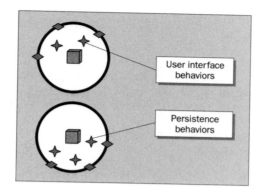

We discussed this concept back in Chapter 2, referring to one half of the object as a UI-centric business object and the other half of the object as a data-centric business object.

The UI-centric business object provides the UI support, containing the properties and methods of our current object along with many of the behaviors.

The data-centric business object implements the behaviors needed to support persistence.

By splitting each business object in two, we can keep the bulk of our business processing close to where it's needed. The UI-centric business object can reside near the UI itself, providing good performance and allowing us to create a rich, interactive user interface. The data-centric business object can reside closer to the data source, again providing for good performance and allowing us to implement powerful data access algorithms with minimal network overhead.

### Splitting the Object's Behavior

Given this approach, we need some way to easily split each business object into two parts. Separating the behaviors themselves is not terribly difficult. All we need to do is create a new object to contain the data-centric processing and move the data-oriented routines from our original business object into the new object.

The major challenge in splitting the objects is managing the shared data. When both halves of the object are contained in a single class module we can share state variables. However, by splitting the object into two parts we need to communicate the relevant state data between the new objects

For instance, if we consider the `Customer` object from Chapter 8, it contains both UI-centric and data-centric routines. We can create a new object, `CustomerPersist`, and move the `Save`, `Fetch` and `DeleteObject` routines to this new object. We'll look at exactly how to do this as we go through this chapter.

By doing this, we make it so our `Customer` object only contains UI-centric behaviors and business rules; that is, all the data-centric routines have been removed. At the same time, our new `CustomerPersist` object gets all the data-centric behaviors and business rules, but none of the UI-centric routines.

This effectively gives us two objects that work together to provide the functionality that we had in the original `Customer` object from Chapter 8. Of course each object will need access to the same set of state data in order to work.

### Moving the Object's State

The question then, is how do we easily move the object's internal data, or state, between the UI-centric and data-centric business objects? Given that we'll be sending this data over a network, our primary constraint is performance and so it's important to move the data very efficiently.

This is where the `GetState` and `SetState` methods come into play. As we saw in Chapter 4, by using the `LSet` statement to implement these methods we can create very efficient routines to convert data from the detailed user defined types that contain the object's data into a simple string variable.

If we add `GetState` and `LetState` methods to *both* of these objects, we can move their data back and forth with ease:

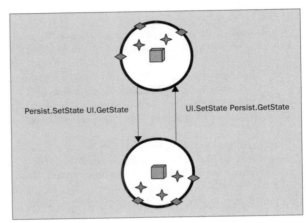

Persist.SetState UI.GetState  UI.SetState Persist.GetState

For instance, to copy the objects state from the UI down to the persistence object we can just write:

```
PersistenceObject.SetState UIObject.GetState
```

The reverse is as simple. To copy the state from the persistence object back to the UI object we can write:

```
UIObject.SetState PersistenceObject.GetState
```

Remember that the UI-centric and data-centric objects here are conceptually two halves of the same object. By implementing `SetState` and `GetState` on both the UI-centric and data-centric objects we make it very easy to move the object's data back and forth between the two halves.

It is also worth considering that the UI-centric and data-centric objects may not share *all* their data. We may have data that is only pertinent to the UI or data-centric object that doesn't need to be transferred via the `SetState` and `GetState` methods.

Equally important is the distinction between data stored in a *database* and data transferred between the UI-centric and data-centric objects. For our two objects to interact properly we may very well transfer data that is never stored in the database. Likewise, our data-centric object may deal with data from the database that is never provided to the UI-centric object at all.

### Client Calling Server

By using the `GetState` and `SetState` methods to copy the data as shown, it doesn't appear to matter whether the method calls are in the UI object, the persistence object or some other part of the program. For instance, if we want to move the object's state data from the data-centric object to the UI-centric object we'd use the following code:

```
UIObject.SetState PersistenceObject.GetState
```

We might write this line of code in the UI-centric object, the data-centric object or some code outside of either object. In a sense it doesn't matter, since the line of code would be the same in all three cases.

In reality however, it does matter where we put the code to move the object's state data back and forth. We are creating a client/server system here, and we need to establish the roles each object will play. As we discussed in Chapter 4, our Component-based Scalable Logical architecture puts the UI-centric objects on the client workstation and the data-centric objects on an application server machine:

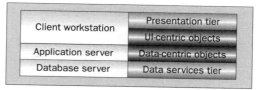

With this architecture it seems clear that our UI-centric business objects are clients of the data-centric business objects. This means that the UI-centric objects are the active objects; they initiate all activity, asking the data-centric objects for services when needed.

Following this model, we'll put the code to move the state data between the two objects into the UI-centric objects. This way they can send the data to the data-centric object before calling any methods that need the data and retrieve the state data from the data-centric objects after each method is called.

# Setting up a Server Project

We will need a place to put the new objects we'll be creating to hold the persistence behaviors. Since this program will be running on an application server machine, let's call the program `VideoServer`.

> In Chapter 12 we'll make the data-centric objects on our application server machine available to other machines on the network via DCOM. To make this easy, we'll put them in an ActiveX EXE.

We'll be dealing with scalability and multi-user issues when we discuss Microsoft Transaction Server in Chapter 12. For now we'll just focus on creating a server program that can be used by a single client workstation. This way we'll be able to keep the examples simpler and better demonstrate the concepts we need to cover regarding distributing objects. At the end of this chapter we'll have a distributed three-tier application, but there will still be quite a lot of work left to do before it's ready for use in a 'real' setting.

To get started, we need to bring up Visual Basic and create a new ActiveX EXE project. Name the project `VideoServer`.

### Using ADO in VideoServer

Since all the code to handle persistence will be in this new project, it's only sensible that we'll need to take appropriate steps to give the project access to our database.

We'll leave the database in Microsoft Access and use ADO to reach it for this chapter. To do a real n-tier implementation we'd need to modify the code to work with SQL Server, Oracle or another database. In Chapter 12 we'll change the code to work with SQL Server to get the full impact of using MTS in an n-tier setting.

To use ADO within this project we need to bring up the project's references dialog and check the Microsoft ActiveX Data Objects 2.0 Library entry from the list.

### Opening the Database

Now we need to add some code to open a connection to the database when the server is started up. This code will be the same as we used in Chapter 8 within the `VideoObjects` project, since we'll be opening the same database. As with the `VideoObjects` project, this code needs to be placed in a code module within the project. Name this module `VOmain` and add the following code:

```
Option Explicit

Public cnVideo As Connection

Public Sub Main()

    Set cnVideo = New Connection
    cnVideo.Provider = "Microsoft.Jet.OLEDB.3.51"
    cnVideo.Mode = adModeReadWrite
    cnVideo.Open "C:\Wrox\VB6 Pro Objects\Video.mdb"

End Sub
```

*You may need to set the database's path to where you have stored it locally.*

We need to make sure that `Sub Main` is the `VideoServer` project's startup option as well. To do this, bring up the project's properties window and change the <u>S</u>tartup Object property to `Sub Main`.

# Making Simple Objects Persistent

# Customer Object

With an understanding of the basic theory of breaking our object into two parts, let's apply it to the `Customer` object to see how it works.

What we'll do here is add `Private GetState` and `SetState` methods to both the UI-centric `Customer` object and the data-centric `CustomerPersist` object. We can use these methods to quickly and easily serialize each object's data into a `String` variable.

Then we'll move the `Fetch`, `Save` and `DeleteObject` subroutines out of the `Customer` object itself and put them into the new `CustomerPersist` object. Once that's done, we can alter the `Fetch` and `Save` methods to return the object's data from `GetState` and the `Save` method to accept the object's data as a parameter so it can call the `SetState` method to load the object's data. Finally we can change the `Customer` object to call the methods on our new object.

This is a variation on our discussion from earlier in the chapter. The idea is that we can't only move the object's data by using `SetState` and `GetState`, but we can combine this with our calls to the `Fetch` and `Save` methods:

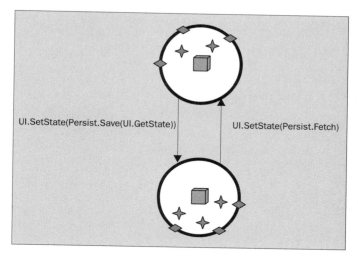

UI.SetState(Persist.Save(UI.GetState))     UI.SetState(Persist.Fetch)

Within the data-centric object we'll implement the `Save` method to call `SetState` using the parameter passed from the UI-centric object. We'll also modify the `Fetch` and `Save` methods to call `GetState` and return that value as a result of the function, allowing the UI-centric object to pass the result to its own `SetState` method.

> *Notice how the* `Save` *method not only accepts the UI object's current state, but also returns the state back from the data-centric object. This is often very important, as the object's data may be changed while it's being processed by the data-centric object. The most common scenario for this is where a value (such as an invoice number) is generated by the database as an object is being saved. This new value needs to be made available to the UI-centric object, so we need to send the data back from the data-centric object to the UI-centric object once the database activity is complete.*

## Adding GetState and SetState to Customer

We've already looked at some basic `GetState` and `SetState` methods back in Chapter 4. These will follow right along the same lines, but with some slight differences.

### Moving the UDT

Open up the `VideoObjects` project in Visual Basic and bring up the `Customer` class module. At the top we have a UDT to hold the object's state. We'll need this UDT both here and in the `CustomerPersist` object we'll be creating shortly.

*The easiest way to work with the examples in this chapter is to open Visual Basic twice, with our* Video *project group from Chapters 7 and 8 in one instance and the new* VideoServer *project in the other. Unfortunately it is not very practical to have more than one EXE type project within a single project group, since only one of them can be set as the startup project. Any other EXE projects would be ignored by Visual Basic were we to run the project in the IDE.*

While we could duplicate the code by declaring it as a Private type in each class, it is much easier to move the UDT to a central BAS module that can be shared between the VideoObjects and VideoServer projects. By storing the UDT in one file, we have a greater level of confidence that both projects will be using the same definition.

Add a new code module to the project and name it VideoTypes. Then move the UDT from the Customer class module into the new module and change it to a Public type:

```
Option Explicit

Public Type CustomerProps
    CustomerID As Long
    Name As String * 50
    Phone As String * 25
    Address1 As String * 30
    Address2 As String * 30
    City As String * 20
    State As String * 2
    ZipCode As String * 10
End Type
```

Once we've saved this new code module to disk we can bring up the VideoServer project and use the Project | Add File menu option to add this very same file to that project as well. This way both our VideoObjects and VideoServer projects will have the same file, so we know they'll have the same UDTs.

### Adding IsNew, IsDeleted and IsDirty

As it stands, the UDT contains all the object's basic data. However, our object also keeps track of whether it is new, changed or deleted. It's important information that should be available to the code that translates our object to and from a database.

For instance, in the Fetch routine in Customer we use the mflgNew variable to know whether to add or update the record. Since we're moving the Fetch routine to another object, we need to make sure we make the value of mflgNew available to that object.

This can be easily accomplished by adding three variables to the UDT to hold these values.

```
Option Explicit

Public Type CustomerProps
    CustomerID As Long
    Name As String * 50
    Phone As String * 25
    Address1 As String * 30
    Address2 As String * 30
    City As String * 20
```

```
        State As String * 2
        ZipCode As String * 10
        IsNew As Boolean
        IsDeleted As Boolean
        IsDirty As Boolean
    End Type
```

We'll add code to maintain these variables when we implement the GetState and SetState methods in a later section.

### Creating the CustomerData Type

In our new GetState and SetState methods we'll be using the LSet command to copy data from our CustomerProps UDT variable into another variable based on a UDT that just contains a string buffer. This new UDT will be called CustomerData, and its string variable needs to have the same length as the CustomerProps UDT. We covered this in detail in Chapter 4, so we won't repeat the discussion here.

Declare CustomerData as follows:

```
    Public Type CustomerData
        Buffer As String * 180
    End Type
```

### The GetState Method

As we implemented it in Chapter 5, our Customer object stores all of its state data in a variable named mudtProps. This variable is based on the UDT, CustomerProps.

The GetState method is a String function that translates the data in mudtProps into a single buffer and returns it as a result. In its simplest form, our GetState method is basically a call to the LSet command, as in Chapter 4. Add this code to the Customer object:

```
    Private Function GetState() As String

      Dim udtData As CustomerData

      LSet udtData = mudtProps
      GetState = udtData.Buffer

    End Function
```

However, we've added the IsNew, IsDeleted and IsDirty variables to the CustomerProps UDT and we need to load their values based on the values of mflgNew, mflgDeleted and mflgDirty. So we need to make the following changes to the code in Customer:

```
    Private Function GetState() As String

      Dim udtData As CustomerData

      With mudtProps
        .IsDeleted = mflgDeleted
```

```
        .IsNew = mflgNew
        .IsDirty = mflgDirty
    End With

    LSet udtData = mudtProps
    GetState = udtData.Buffer

End Function
```

Note that here in the Customer object, GetState is a Private method. The UI developer doesn't need to have any access directly to an object's internal data, in fact providing such access eliminates the benefits of encapsulation.

The GetState and SetState methods will only be used to copy the object's data to and from the persistence object. All the calls to the persistence object will be handled within the Customer object's code and so the only place from which we're able to call these methods is from within the Customer object itself.

### The SetState Method

Like the GetState method, SetState makes use of the LSet command to copy data from one UDT variable to another. In this case we'll be copying a string buffer into our detailed mudtProps variable. Add this SetState method to the Customer object:

```
Private Sub SetState(Buffer As String)

  Dim udtData As CustomerData

  udtData.Buffer = Buffer
  LSet mudtProps = udtData

End Sub
```

Unlike the GetState method, this method doesn't need to deal with the IsNew, IsDeleted and IsDirty variables. Those values are needed by the persistence object, but they are really copies of the Customer object's mflgNew, mflgDeleted and mflgDirty variables. These variables are owned and maintained by the Customer object and so we don't want them to change because of the persistence object. Effectively, we are providing them as read-only values to the persistence object for its use.

## Creating the CustomerPersist Object

Now that we've got the Customer object itself all ready to go, we can move on to create the new data-centric business object, CustomerPersist.

As we discussed earlier in the chapter, CustomerPersist will also have GetState and SetState methods. Since it will need to store the state data as it retrieves and stores it in the database, it will have its own mudtProps variable, also based on the CustomerProps UDT.

We'll also move the Fetch, Save and DeleteObject methods from the Customer class into this new class.

### Adding the CustomerPersist Class

To create the class module, open the `VideoServer` project and select the `Class1` module that was added to the project by default. Set its **Name** property to `CustomerPersist` and make sure its **Instancing** is set to 5-Multiuse.

### Declaring mudtProps in CustomerPersist

Like the `Customer` object, the `CustomerPersist` object will need access to the values from the `CustomerProps` UDT. To be consistent, we'll just declare a `mudtProps` variable within this class like that within `Customer`:

```
Option Explicit

Private mudtProps As CustomerProps
```

The `CustomerProps` UDT is declared in our `VideoTypes` code module that we've included in both this project and the `VideoObjects` project.

### Adding GetState to CustomerPersist

To get data out of `mudtProps`, so it can be returned to the `Customer` object as a result of the `Fetch` function, we'll provide a `GetState` method within `CustomerPersist`:

```
Private Function GetState() As String

  Dim udtData As CustomerData

  LSet udtData = mudtProps
  GetState = udtData.Buffer

End Function
```

This is just a basic `LSet` of the values in `mudtProps` into the string buffer defined by the `CustomerData` UDT. This is a `Private` procedure, since we'll be calling it only from within the `CustomerPersist` object itself – in particular from within the `Fetch` function that we'll alter later in this chapter.

### Adding SetState to CustomerPersist

Likewise, we need a `SetState` method so we can deserialize the `String` variable passed to the `Save` method from the `Customer` object. This buffer needs to be copied into the `mudtProps` variable so that the detailed values are available for use within the `Save` method:

```
Private Sub SetState(Buffer As String)

  Dim udtData As CustomerData

  udtData.Buffer = Buffer
  LSet mudtProps = udtData

End Sub
```

We are now ready to move the `Fetch`, `Save` and `DeleteObject` subroutines from the `Customer` object over to the new `CustomerPersist` class.

In the `Customer` class our three persistence methods were `Private`, but we need to make them available for use by the `Customer` object now that they are in the `CustomerPersist` class. To make this possible, we'll change all three to `Public` methods in the class as we move the code.

### Moving Save to CustomerPersist

The `Save` routine needs a bit of work. The most obvious change is that our new `Save` method needs to accept a parameter and return a value upon completion. We'll be passing the object's state data in a `String` variable from the `Customer` object down to the `CustomerPersist` object by using this parameter:

```
Public Function Save(ByVal Buffer As String) As String
```

The parameter, `Buffer`, is declared using the `ByVal` keyword. This is an important performance consideration when implementing out-of-process ActiveX servers and even more important when using DCOM. In a call to a normal Visual Basic subroutine, parameters are passed by reference, meaning that changes to the parameter value in the subroutine affect the original variable that was passed as a parameter.

When a parameter is passed to an object's method through COM or DCOM a simple reference can't be sent, so COM copies the variable's data to the ActiveX server and provides it as a parameter. Microsoft wanted to make COM transparent to the programmer however, so even though the value was not passed by reference they wanted to simulate the effect. To do this, the parameter is copied *back* from the ActiveX server to the client once the method call is complete. This means in the default case, where parameters are passed by reference, they are copied both *to* and *from* the ActiveX server on each method call.

> Using the `ByVal` keyword in the parameter's declaration indicates to COM that the parameter value doesn't need to be copied back from the ActiveX server to the client program. When we are dealing with large string buffers this is a very important consideration and so we should pretty much always use `ByVal` when declaring parameters on `Public` methods of ActiveX EXE projects.

Once we've received the `Buffer` parameter, we'll need to call the `CustomerPersist` object's `SetState` method to copy the data into our local UDT.

```
Public Function Save(ByVal Buffer As String) As String

    Dim rsCustomer As Recordset
    Dim strSQL As String

    SetState Buffer
```

Now we have full access to the `Customer` object's data, just like our code was actually part of the `Customer` object itself. There are a few more changes we need to make before the `Save` method is ready to work.

The original `Save` method has a reference to `mflgNew`, the variable that indicates if the object is new or not. We need to change the references to this variable so they refer instead to `mudtProps.IsNew`. The `GetState` method in the `Customer` class makes sure this value is correct before it is sent over to the `CustomerPersist` object.

We'll also need to change the way the SELECT statement is generated. When we built this code back in Chapter 8, we used the CustomerID property from the object in the statement:

```
strSQL = "SELECT * FROM CUSTOMER WHERE CUSTOMERID=" & _
    CustomerID
```

That property isn't available over in the CustomerPersist object and so we need to change the code to use the CustomerID value from mudtProps, as shown below:

```
Public Function Save(ByVal Buffer As String) As String

    Dim rsCustomer As Recordset
    Dim strSQL As String

    SetState Buffer

    Set rsCustomer = New Recordset
    strSQL = "SELECT * FROM CUSTOMER WHERE CUSTOMERID=" & _
        mudtProps.CustomerID
    rsCustomer.Open strSQL, cnVideo, , adLockOptimistic
    If mudtProps.IsNew Then rsCustomer.AddNew

    With rsCustomer
      .Fields("Name") = mudtProps.Name
      .Fields("Address1") = mudtProps.Address1
      .Fields("Address2") = mudtProps.Address2
      .Fields("City") = mudtProps.City
      .Fields("State") = mudtProps.State
      .Fields("ZipCode") = mudtProps.ZipCode
      .Fields("Phone") = mudtProps.Phone
      .Update
      If mudtProps.IsNew Then mudtProps.CustomerID = .Fields("CustomerID")
      .Close
    End With

    Set rsCustomer = Nothing

End Function
```

The same is true for the IsNew flag, since that value is now in mudtProps.IsNew rather than being stored in a Private variable.

All that remains is to return the updated value of the object's state as a result of the function. In this case, if we've just added the customer then the CustomerID field has a new value. We need to make sure to get this value back to the UI-centric Customer object once the add operation is complete. We've already declared our Save method as a Function, so we can simply return the object's state as the function's result. We'll use the GetState method to retrieve the state as a string value:

```
    Set rsCustomer = Nothing
    Save = GetState

End Function
```

*We've implemented the Save method as a **stateless, atomic** operation. This means the method does everything it needs to in a single call – no need to set properties or make other method calls. This is a very important design from a performance and scalability perspective. We'll discuss this in much more detail when we move our persistence objects into MTS in Chapter 12.*

## Moving the DeleteObject Method

The DeleteObject method was simple to begin with, and so the only change we need is making it Public rather than Private and change how CustomerID is passed:

```
Public Sub DeleteObject(ByVal CustomerID As Long)

    cnVideo.Execute "DELETE FROM CUSTOMER WHERE CUSTOMERID=" & _
        CustomerID

End Sub
```

## Moving the Fetch Method

The Fetch routine will require some changes. The biggest change we need to make is to change the procedure into a Function so it can return the object's state data as a result:

```
Public Function Fetch(ByVal CustomerID As Long) As String
```

We'll need to add a line at the end of the procedure to call the GetState method and return the value as a result of the Fetch function:

```
    Fetch = GetState

End Function
```

Like the Save method, this routine contains some code that assumes it's running inside the Customer object itself. In particular, we have included calls to the mobjValid object to check whether or not our object's rules are broken.

The mobjValid object is private to the Customer object itself and isn't available in the CustomerPersist object. We need to remove those lines from the Fetch routine and move them back into the Customer object. Here's the code for the CustomerPersist object's Fetch method:

```
Public Function Fetch(ByVal CustomerID As Long) As String

    Dim rsCustomer As Recordset
    Dim strSQL As String

    strSQL = "SELECT * FROM CUSTOMER WHERE CUSTOMERID=" & _
        CustomerID
    Set rsCustomer = New Recordset
    rsCustomer.Open strSQL, cnVideo

    With rsCustomer
        mudtProps.CustomerID = .Fields("CustomerID")
        mudtProps.Name = .Fields("Name")
        mudtProps.Address1 = .Fields("Address1")
        mudtProps.Address2 = .Fields("Address2")
```

```
        mudtProps.City = .Fields("City")
        mudtProps.State = .Fields("State")
        mudtProps.ZipCode = .Fields("ZipCode")
        mudtProps.Phone = .Fields("Phone")
        .Close
    End With

    Set rsCustomer = Nothing
    Fetch = GetState

End Function
```

We originally called the `Fetch` subroutine in the `Customer` object's `Load` method. This is where we now need to move the calls to `mobjValid`. Here's the code for the `Customer` object's `Load` method back in the `VideoObjects` project:

```
Public Sub Load(CustomerID As Long)

    If mflgEditing Then Err.Raise 445
    If Not mflgNew Then Err.Raise 445

    Fetch CustomerID

    mobjValid.RuleBroken "Name", False
    mobjValid.RuleBroken "Phone", False

    mflgNew = False

End Sub
```

# Calling CustomerPersist from Customer

At this point we have a `CustomerPersist` object that can be used to retrieve, save and delete a `Customer` object's data within the database.

All that remains is to go through the `Customer` object itself and change any calls to the `Fetch`, `Save` and `DeleteObject` subroutines so the methods of `CustomerPersist` are used instead. Fortunately, we only need to change two methods in `Customer` - `ApplyEdit` and `Load`.

## Using CreateObject

The `CreateObject` method is used to create objects, very much the way the `New` keyword works within Visual Basic. However, `CreateObject` provides us with more powerful capabilities than the `New` keyword – especially when creating objects that might be running on remote machines (as our `VideoServer` objects will be in Chapter 11).

Visual Basic 6.0 introduces a new optional parameter to the `CreateObject` method. This new parameter allows us to specify the machine name on which the object should be created. Instead of creating an object using the `New` keyword:

```
Set objPersist = New CustomerPersist
```

We can use the `CreateObject` method and also indicate the machine that should run this object:

```
Set objPersist = CreateObject("VideoServer.CustomerPersist", "MYSERVER")
```

All we need to provide is the full object name including both the ActiveX server name and the class name: `VideoServer.CustomerPersist`. Then we can optionally provide a machine name, in this case `MYSERVER`, on which to run the object.

We'll use this technique in our code, as it makes it very easy to switch which machine is running the server application – ideal for testing where we might want to switch from a test machine to production and back again.

Open up the code window for the `VOmain BAS` module in our `VideoObjects` project and add a constant for the server name:

```
Option Explicit

Public Const PERSIST_SERVER = "MYSERVER"
Public cnVideo As Connection
```

*You'll need to replace `MYSERVER` with the name of the server appropriate for your environment. It may be appropriate to retrieve this value from the system registry or a central data source so an administrator can easily change the server name without having to alter the application.*

### Calling DeleteObject from ApplyEdit

All adding, updating and deleting of an object's data is handled through the `ApplyEdit` method. It's in this method that we called the `DeleteObject` and `Save` subroutines. All we need to do is change this code to create a `CustomerPersist` object and call the appropriate method on that object instead.

In the `Customer` object's `ApplyEdit` method we need to change the call to `DeleteObject`:

```
Public Sub ApplyEdit()

  Dim objPersist As CustomerPersist

  If Not mflgEditing Then Err.Raise 445

  Set objPersist = CreateObject("VideoServer.CustomerPersist", PERSIST_SERVER)

  If mflgDeleted Then
    ' code to delete the object's data goes here
    objPersist.DeleteObject mudtProps.CustomerID
    mflgNew = True
    mflgDeleted = False

  ElseIf mflgDirty Or mflgNew Then
    If Not IsValid Then Err.Raise 445
    ' save object to database if appropriate
    Save
    ' save object state
    LSet mudtSave = mudtProps
    mflgNew = False

  End If
```

```
        Set objPersist = Nothing
      mflgDirty = False
      mflgEditing = False

   End Sub
```

This change is pretty easy. We declare `objPersist` and create an instance of a `CustomerPersist` object. Then, instead of calling a private `DeleteObject` subroutine, we just make a simple change to call the `objPersist.DeleteObject` method.

### Calling Save from ApplyEdit

Of course, the `DeleteObject` method is pretty simple. It doesn't require any values from `mudtProps`, only the ID value passed as a parameter. The call to the `Save` method, though, is a different story. Make the following changes to the `ApplyEdit` method in the `Customer` object:

```
   ElseIf mflgDirty Or mflgNew Then
     If Not IsValid Then Err.Raise 445
     ' save object to database if appropriate
     SetState objPersist.Save(GetState)
     ' save object state
     LSet mudtSave = mudtProps
     mflgNew = False

   End If
```

When we implemented the new `Save` method earlier, we designed it to accept the object's current state as a parameter and to return the new or updated state as a result of the function. Passing the current state as a parameter is easy, since we can simply call the `GetState` method to retrieve the current state. We can then use the `SetState` method to update the `Customer` object's state by using the value returned by the `Save` method when it is complete.

Using `SetState` to update the `Customer` object based on the result of the `Save` method is important. Our object's `CustomerID` field doesn't actually contain a meaningful value until after the object has been saved to the database. We are relying on the database to assign the ID value during the add process, and then the code in the `Save` method retrieves the newly assigned value:

```
   If mudtProps.IsNew Then mudtProps.CustomerID = .Fields("CustomerID")
```

Of course the `mudtProps` where this value just got stored is inside the `CustomerPersist` object, not the `Customer` object. Thus, if the object is new when the `Save` method is called it is very important to pull the state back from `CustomerPersist`.

### Calling Fetch from Load

The changes to the `Customer` object's `Load` method are very comparable. We just need to create an instance of the `CustomerPersist` class, call its `Fetch` method and retrieve the state data using the `GetState` method:

```
   Public Sub Load(CustomerID As Long)

     Dim objPersist As CustomerPersist
```

```
        If mflgEditing Then Err.Raise 445
        If Not mflgNew Then Err.Raise 445

        Set objPersist = CreateObject("VideoServer.CustomerPersist", PERSIST_SERVER)
        SetState objPersist.Fetch(CustomerID)
        Set objPersist = Nothing

        mobjValid.RuleBroken "Name", False
        mobjValid.RuleBroken "Phone", False

        mflgNew = False

      End Sub
```

As with the Save method, the Fetch method is virtually the same code we implemented in Chapter 8, so we are loading the object's data the same way we were before, just in a different object. By copying the object's data from the persistence object back to the Customer object we've accomplished the same functionality, but now we can put the data access code on a different computer.

# Making List Objects Persistent

The Customer object provided a good example of making a simple, singular object persistent by using a separate persistence object. The techniques we used are pretty straightforward in that case, but what if we have an entire list or collection of data that we need to persist?

We have a number of examples, including the TextList object, the Customers and Videos objects. The Tapes and InvoiceItems objects probably also fit this category, but since they are child objects, they have their own twist as well.

What we'll focus on now are the read-only list objects. Later on, we'll discuss child objects and use the same techniques. However, child objects bring a lot of additional complexity, and so we'll tackle the easy objects first.

The challenge with objects that are lists of other objects, or that are collections of data, is that we can't afford to pull back each individual object or element across the network. Each DCOM call has a lot of overhead, and if we make a call for each element in the list we could be in trouble. Imagine if the list contains dozens, hundreds or even thousands of elements.

> *Let's look at some statistics in support of this assertion. Don Box quotes inproc object method calls as being 28,000 times faster than a remote object on the same LAN (Source: MSJ vol. 12 no. 5). And in Richard Grimes' Professional DCOM, he tests multiple method calls (e.g. ten calls to send ten strings) against to a single big method call (that is send all ten strings with one call). The total time for the multiple calls was five to ten times longer than the single big method call.*

Instead we need to find a way to bring across all the elements in a single DCOM call. The problem is that with list objects, each object's state is not fixed. With the Customer object we know exactly how big the object's state will be and so we can easily convert it to a buffer. With a list of elements we don't know how many elements there might be and so it becomes much harder.

# The Buffer Object

To help deal with this problem, we can use a utility object that efficiently collects all the elements from a list into a single `String` buffer. If we put the `String` buffer back into this object it can efficiently unpack the buffer, providing easy access to each element in the list. We'll call this the `Buffer` object.

## *Designing the Object*

The `Buffer` object makes some assumptions. The most notable assumption is that each element will have a state or some data that's in a `String` variable. We'll also assume that each element's data is the same length as all the other elements. This works well when dealing with most database information, since the data is basically fixed length in any case.

The object also assumes that the developer has some rough idea of the number of elements that will be added to the buffer. The exact number isn't required, just a rough idea.

### *Focus on Performance*

It's very important to realize why we are building this object in the first place – performance. Most programs retrieve lists of data to be displayed to the user. We populate `ComboBox` and `ListBox` controls in almost every program. Having lots of lists can dramatically slow down a conventional Visual Basic form's load-time; and pulling the data across DCOM and into an object is even worse. The challenge behind designing this object is to come up with a solution that is fast but still effective.

Because of this constraint, there's no error trapping in the object. The focus is entirely on performance and so we're assuming that the client code will use it as intended.

> *If you use this class in your applications you can feel free to add error trapping, but be aware of the ramifications on performance!*

### *String Handling in Visual Basic*

One question to consider is whether we need to go through the work of building a class to handle the buffer. After all, it would be a simple matter to just declare a dynamic string variable and append each element's data into that variable. If they are fixed length elements, it's easy enough to pull them back out on the other end.

Actually this is basically what the `Buffer` object will do, but there is a serious trick involved to get good performance.

> **Visual Basic's string handling is incredibly slow, and string concatenation ranks right at the top of the list when it comes to performance problems.**

To get any measure of performance at all, we need to avoid string concatenations while building the buffer. Fortunately, Visual Basic provides an excellent mechanism we can use to add elements to a buffer with no concatenation.

Most people are familiar with the `Mid$()` function. They use it to return a portion of a string variable like this:

```
strNew = Mid$(strOld, 4, 3)
```

What many people don't know is that `Mid$()` can also be used to put text *into* a string in a specific location:

```
Mid$(strOld, 4, 3) = "ABC"
```

This technique does require that the target string variable is already long enough to hold the data. In this example, `strOld` would need to be at least seven characters long before this statement or the text wouldn't be put into the variable. The easiest way to get a pre-sized string is to use the `Space$()` command:

```
strOld = Space$(7)
```

This is why we want a class. The class needs to pre-size a buffer, then use `Mid$()` to insert each element into the string. Along the way it needs to keep track of the current position in the buffer and possibly resize the buffer if we try to add more elements than will fit in the current buffer.

## Creating the Buffer Class

We'll want to use the `Buffer` class in both the `VideoObjects` and `VideoServer` projects. If we use it in `VideoServer` to pack together a list of elements, we can then create a `Buffer` object in `VideoObjects` to unpack those elements from the buffer.

A good approach is to use the same technique we are using with the `VideoTypes` BAS module. Create a single `Buffer.cls` file and include it in both projects. This way we only have one source file to maintain, and both projects are kept in sync.

In the `VideoServer` project add a new class module. Set its **Name** property to `Buffer` and its **Instancing** property to 1-Private. While we'll be sending the `String` buffer created by this object across the network, the `Buffer` object itself will only be used within this project.

## Initializing the Buffer Object

As we mentioned earlier, the `Buffer` object needs to make some assumptions about the data it is being given. The first assumption is that all the element data will be the same length. That is, each element's data will have a fixed length that is the same as all the other elements. The `Buffer` object also requires that the user provide an estimated count of the number of elements that will be added to the list.

### Declaring Variables

To store these values we'll use - what else? - a UDT:

```
Option Explicit

Private Type BufferProps
  Length As Integer
  EstCount As Long
  MaxCount As Long
  Count As Long
End Type

Private Type BufferData
  Buffer As String * 8
End Type
```

The UDT also includes the current maximum number of elements that will fit in the buffer and a count of the number of elements currently in the buffer.

We've included an overlay, `BufferData`, for use with the `LSet` command later. This will be used in the object's `GetState` method.

We'll also declare a constant to be one longer than the length of `BufferData`:

```
Private Const BUFFER_START = 9
```

We can use this constant to mark the start of the data in our buffer. This way, the first eight characters of our string are reserved to hold the UDT we just defined, and the rest of the buffer can be used to hold the elements of the list.

Of course, we need to declare a variable to act as the buffer:

```
Private mstrBuffer As String
```

And we need a variable to hold the object's data, based on the UDT:

```
Private mudtProps As BufferProps
```

Finally, we need a variable to store the current location in the buffer.

```
Private mlngPos As Long
```

As we add each element to the buffer we need to increment this value to point to the next empty slot where we'll add the next element.

### The Initialize Method

Once the client code has created an instance of the `Buffer` object to add elements, the first thing they need to do is tell the object the length of each element and the estimated number of elements that will be added. To support this, we'll implement an `Initialize` method that takes these values as parameters:

```
Public Sub Initialize(Length As Integer, EstimatedCount As Long)

  With mudtProps
    .Length = Length
    .EstCount = EstimatedCount
    .MaxCount = EstimatedCount
    .Count = 0
    mstrBuffer = Space$(BUFFER_START + .MaxCount * .Length)
    mlngPos = BUFFER_START
  End With

End Sub
```

The routine stores the length and estimated count parameters in `mudtProps`. It also sets `MaxCount` to the estimated count and sets `Count` to zero since we know there is nothing in the buffer.

The next line uses the `Space$()` command to pre-size the buffer. The buffer needs to be big enough to hold the estimated number of elements based on the supplied size. We also need to add room at the beginning of the buffer to fit the data in `mudtProps`:

```
mstrBuffer = Space$(BUFFER_START + .MaxCount * .Length)
```

Finally we need to set `mlngPos` so it points at the first character in the buffer where we can add data. The `BUFFER_START` constant is used to make sure we leave enough room at the beginning of the string to fit the `BufferProps` UDT.

## Adding Elements

Though this class isn't based on a native Visual Basic collection object, it's very much like a collection in many ways. Because of this, we'll emulate the interface from the `Collection` object.

### The Add Method

To add an element to the buffer the client code can use the `Add` method. This method accepts a `String` parameter that contains the element's data. Note that there is no checking of the assumption that the data supplied is of a fixed length that matches the length from the `Initialize` method call.

If the supplied data is too short it will be inserted, with spaces filling in the remaining space. If the data is too long it will be automatically truncated by the call to `Mid$()`.

```
Public Sub Add(Data As String)

  With mudtProps
    Mid$(mstrBuffer, mlngPos, .Length) = Data
    mlngPos = mlngPos + .Length
    .Count = .Count + 1
  End With

End Sub
```

The `Mid$()` command is used to insert the data into the appropriate location in `mstrBuffer`. Then `mlngPos` is incremented by the length indicated in the `Initialize` method call, so we are all set to add the next element. And of course the `Count` value is incremented by one to indicate that we've added an element.

### Extending the Buffer

As shown, the `Add` method will work great - assuming that the estimated count provided in the `Initialize` method was correct. It will even work if the estimate is too big, since the buffer will have extra room. Where it won't work is if the estimate is too small and the buffer runs out of room. Subsequent attempts to add data to the buffer will fail, resulting in lost data. The answer is to extend the buffer as needed:

```
Public Sub Add(Data As String)

  With mudtProps
    If .Count = .MaxCount Then
      mstrBuffer = mstrBuffer & _
        Space$(mudtProps.EstCount / 2 * mudtProps.Length)
      .MaxCount = .MaxCount + mudtProps.EstCount / 2
    End If
```

```
      Mid$(mstrBuffer, mlngPos, .Length) = Data
      mlngPos = mlngPos + .Length
      .Count = .Count + 1
   End With

   End Sub
```

As shown, we've set it up so the buffer is extended by half the original length, assuming that the estimated count isn't off by more than 50%. Even if it were off by more than that amount, the buffer would just extend again.

After all the talk about avoiding concatenation, we've used it here. This isn't a problem, though, since, if we are provided with a reasonable estimated count, the buffer probably won't need to be extended. Even if it does, it probably won't extend many times, certainly far less than if we concatenated each element into the buffer individually.

## GetState and SetState Methods

Now that we've got the object set up to build the buffer, we need to provide a mechanism to copy that buffer across the network. As with our other objects, this one will have GetState and SetState methods. In this case, however, the same class will exist in both projects and so we'll be effectively cloning the object entirely from one machine onto another machine using this technique.

*Of course, this assumes we've remembered to include the* Buffer *class module into both the* VideoObjects *and* VideoServer *projects.*

### GetState Method

The GetState method basically returns the value in mstrBuffer. However, we want to send the data in mudtProps as well, and so the first thing we need to do is use LSet to copy that value into a string buffer. Then we can use Mid$() to put that buffer in the first few characters of mstrBuffer. Remember that we saved room at the start of the buffer for just this data.

```
Public Function GetState() As String

  Dim udtData As BufferData

  LSet udtData = mudtProps
  Mid$(mstrBuffer, 1, Len(udtData.Buffer)) = udtData.Buffer
  GetState = Left$(mstrBuffer, mlngPos)

End Function
```

We're using the Left$() function to only return the portion of mstrBuffer that actually contains data. This way, if the estimated count of elements was way too big, or if we extended the buffer and didn't use all the space, we don't return blank space. Remember that the result of the GetState method will probably be sent across the network via DCOM and so we don't want to send any more data than is absolutely necessary.

### SetState Method

The SetState method can just do the reverse. It gets a buffer as a parameter, pulls the first few characters out and uses LSet to put them into mudtProps:

```
Public Sub SetState(Buffer As String)

  Dim udtData As BufferData

  udtData.Buffer = Mid$(Buffer, 1, Len(udtData.Buffer))
  LSet mudtProps = udtData
  mstrBuffer = Buffer

End Sub
```

Using these two routines, we can copy a buffer containing an entire list of elements from one machine to another as a single String variable:

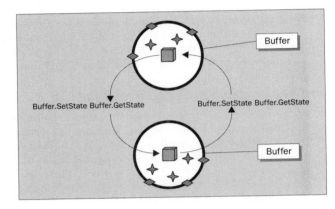

## Retrieving Elements

Once we've copied the String buffer across the network we can use the SetState method to put it back into a Buffer object. This effectively creates a clone of the original Buffer object, with all the data and internal values set and ready to go.

Now we need to implement some mechanism for the client code to pull the elements of the list back out of the buffer. Again we'll emulate the Visual Basic Collection object's interface by implementing similar properties.

### Item Property

To retrieve a single element from the buffer we'll implement an Item property. This property will accept a numeric index to indicate which element to retrieve:

```
Public Property Get Item(Index As Long) As String

  Item = Mid$(mstrBuffer, BUFFER_START + (Index - 1) * _
    mudtProps.Length, mudtProps.Length)

End Property
```

Since all we need to do is return the original string value that we were given through the Add method, we can just use Mid$() to pull out that section of mstrBuffer and return it.

### Informational Properties

The Buffer object provides some basic informational properties. These are read-only, but are important to the code that is using the object to retrieve data.

It's important to know how many elements exist in the buffer. The Count property provides that value:

```
Public Function Count() As Long

    Count = mudtProps.Count

End Function
```

As a convenience, we'll provide the Length value:

```
Public Function Length() As Long

    Length = mudtProps.Length

End Function
```

There are cases where the client code may not know the length of each element and this property can provide that information easily.

### Updating Elements

The final bit of functionality that we'll add to the object is the ability to update an individual element in the buffer. The reason this is important will become clear when we get to discuss child objects later in the chapter. For now, let's just look at how the update capability is implemented.

We already have a Property Get Item routine to retrieve an element's data from the buffer. To keep some level of symmetry, let's create a Property Let Item routine to handle the update process.

```
Public Property Let Item(Index As Long, Buffer As String)

    Mid$(mstrBuffer, BUFFER_START + (Index - 1) * _
        mudtProps.Length, mudtProps.Length) = Buffer

End Property
```

This is basically just the reverse of the Property Get, using Mid$() to put data into mstrBuffer in the right spot rather than pulling it out.

# TextList Object

The Buffer object isn't too complex, but it provides a very nice mechanism by which we can copy an entire list of elements from one object to another. Let's try it out as we update the TextList object to retrieve its data through a persistence object.

In concept we'll be doing the same thing here that we did with the Customer object earlier. We'll create a TextListPersist object in the VideoServer project, then move the TextList object's Fetch routine to the new object.

Of course we'll have to do a bit of extra work, since the Fetch method will now need to load its results into a Buffer object and then the TextList object will need to receive that Buffer object's state data and unpack it.

## Creating *TextListPersist*

Open up the VideoServer project in Visual Basic and add a new class module to the project. Change its Name property to TextListPersist and make sure its Instancing property is 5-Multiuse.

Most of our simple business objects use a UDT to hold their state data. However, list objects typically hold an entire list of information and so they are a bit more complex.

Rather than a UDT, we'll store the object's state in a Buffer object. Let's declare that in the class module.

```
Option Explicit

Private mobjBuffer As Buffer
```

### Adding a UDT for the TextList Data

Because of the way we implemented it, the Buffer object expects that each individual element's data will be the same length. The easiest way to handle this is to put each element in a UDT, use LSet to copy that data into a string and then add that string to the Buffer object.

Bring up the VideoTypes BAS module. We'll need this UDT in both the VideoServer and VideoObjects projects, since we'll use it to unpack the data in the Buffer object when we get to the TextList object's SetState method. Enter both the detailed UDT and the matching string buffer UDT:

```
Public Type TextListProps
   Key As String * 30
   Item As String * 255
End Type

Public Type TextListData
   Buffer As String * 285
End Type
```

We've put some arbitrary, but reasonably large, lengths on both the Key and the Item fields. As we move this code to other applications we may be able to reevaluate the sizes to make them fit the specific data better.

### Moving the Fetch Routine to TextListPersist

Because the TextList object is read-only, the only data access routine it contains is Fetch. It has no Save or DeleteObject since they aren't needed in a read-only setting. This makes our job easier, since we only need to worry about moving that one routine.

Move the Fetch subroutine code from the TextList object over to the new TextListPersist object. The code needs some changes as shown here:

```
Public Function Fetch(ByVal ListName As String) As String

    Dim strSQL As String
    Dim rsList As Recordset
    Dim udtProps As TextListProps
    Dim udtData As TextListData

    Set mobjBuffer = New Buffer
    mobjBuffer.Initialize Len(udtData), 50
    Set rsList = New Recordset
    rsList.Open ListName, cnVideo

    Do While Not rsList.EOF
      With udtProps
        .Item = rsList(1)
        .Key = rsList(0)
      End With

      LSet udtData = udtProps
      mobjBuffer.Add udtData.Buffer
      rsList.MoveNext
    Loop

    rsList.Close
    Set rsList = Nothing
    Fetch = mobjBuffer.GetState

End Function
```

Let's review the changes to the code to see what we've done. First, the `Fetch` routine was a `Private` subroutine, but now it will need to be available to the `TextList` object via DCOM and so it needs to be a `Public Function`. As with the `CustomerPersist` object's `Fetch` method, we'll make this one return the object's state data as a result of the method call:

```
Public Function Fetch(ByVal ListName As String) As String
```

In the original `Fetch` subroutine, we took the results of the recordset and stored them directly in a `Collection` object for later use. Now we need to put each element in the `TextListProps` UDT and then store that in our `Buffer` object. This means we need variables for both `TextListProps` and `TextListData`:

```
Dim udtProps As TextListProps
Dim udtData As TextListData
```

We've already declared `mobjBuffer` as type `Buffer`, but we do need to create an actual instance of the object:

```
Set mobjBuffer = New Buffer
mobjBuffer.Initialize Len(udtData), 50
```

We've also called the `Initialize` method on the `Buffer` object, providing it with the length of the UDT that we'll be using for each element and an estimated count of the number of items. Fifty items is probably way too high, but it's better to make this value a bit too big than too small.

Now we're ready to build the recordset and start looping through each item that is returned from the database. We'll take each item and copy the key and item values into the udtProps variable, then use LSet to copy that into a single string variable:

```
Set rsList = New Recordset
rsList.Open ListName, cnVideo

Do While Not rsList.EOF
  With udtProps
    .Item = rsList(1)
    .Key = rsList(0)
  End With

  LSet udtData = udtProps
```

Once the element's data is in a single string, we can just use mobjBuffer's Add method to add the data to the Buffer object. Then we can loop to the next row in the recordset and do the same thing:

```
    mobjBuffer.Add udtData.Buffer
    rsList.MoveNext
Loop

rsList.Close
Set rsList = Nothing
```

In the end, our Buffer object contains the data from the entire recordset. Once that's done, we can simply use the GetState method on the Buffer object to retrieve the entire set of state data and return it as a result of the function:

```
Fetch = mobjBuffer.GetState
```

Now we can move on to update the TextList object itself.

## Updating TextList

As with the Customer object earlier in the chapter, we need to make some changes to TextList so it calls the Fetch method on the TextListPersist object instead of calling a local Fetch subroutine. We also need to do a bit more work in this case, since we need to copy the resulting data into our internal Collection object.

### Load Method in TextList

The original Load method simply called the Fetch subroutine and left it at that. Our new Load routine will have a bit more code, since it needs to create an instance of TextListPersist, call its Fetch method and then use its GetState method to retrieve the resulting data.

```
Friend Sub Load(ListName As String)

    Dim objPersist As TextListPersist

    Set objPersist = CreateObject("VideoServer.TextListPersist", PERSIST_SERVER)
    SetState objPersist.Fetch(ListName)
    Set objPersist = Nothing

End Sub
```

### SetState Subroutine

The real work comes in the `SetState` routine however, since it is this routine that needs to unpack the resulting data. The string that we are passed as a parameter is actually the state string from the `Buffer` object in `TextListPersist`.

```
Private Sub SetState(Buffer As String)

    Dim objBuffer As Buffer
    Dim lngIndex As Long
    Dim udtProps As TextListProps
    Dim udtData As TextListData

    Set objBuffer = New Buffer
    objBuffer.SetState Buffer

    With objBuffer
      For lngIndex = 1 To objBuffer.Count
        udtData.Buffer = objBuffer.Item(lngIndex)
        LSet udtProps = udtData

        With udtProps
          mcolList.Add Format$(.Item), Format$(.Key)
          mcolKeys.Add Format$(.Key), Format$(.Item)
        End With

      Next

    End With

End Sub
```

The way we designed the `Buffer` object was to be able to accept such a state string and effectively become a clone of the original `Buffer` object, so to start with we've declared a `Buffer` variable:

```
Dim objBuffer As Buffer
```

Since we're looping through each element, we need an index variable as well. For each element we pull out of the `Buffer` object we need to unpack it by using the `TextListProps` and `TextListData` UDTs that we added to the `VideoTypes` BAS module earlier.

To create a 'clone' of the original `Buffer` object, we just need to create an instance of a `Buffer` object, then use its `SetState` method to pass it the string buffer that we were given as a parameter:

```
Set objBuffer = New Buffer
objBuffer.SetState Buffer
```

The `Buffer` object itself has code in the `SetState` method to pull out the object's data, including the length and number of elements in the list.

Now we can just loop through all the elements in the `Buffer` object. Each element will be put into the `udtProps` variable using `LSet` and then those values can be used to populate our two `Collection` objects. The `TextList` object stores everything twice, once for a normal lookup of an item by its key and then again so we can look up a key based on the item's value.

```
With objBuffer
   For lngIndex = 1 To objBuffer.Count
      udtData.Buffer = objBuffer.Item(lngIndex)
      LSet udtProps = udtData

      With udtProps
         mcolList.Add Format$(.Item), Format$(.Key)
         mcolKeys.Add Format$(.Key), Format$(.Item)
      End With

   Next

End With
```

That clinches it. The TextListPersist object loads the information from the database into a Buffer object. The TextList object takes the Buffer object's state and uses it to create a clone of the original Buffer object. From there, it just loops through the elements in the Buffer object, loading them into its internal data store just like the original Fetch subroutine of Chapter 8.

# Display Lists

Our application has two other read-only list objects - Customers and Videos. Like TextList, these objects have a Fetch subroutine that retrieves data from the database and copies it into a collection. There is a difference, however, in that the collection actually contains simple child objects instead of the simple key-value pairs of the TextList object.

The changes to both objects will be virtually identical, so we'll only walk through the Customers object's code. The Videos object can be modified by following the same steps. If you want to check your code see Appendix C.

## CustomersPersist Object

As usual, we need to create a new object in the VideoServer project to hold the data access code. We'll call this one CustomersPersist, make sure its Instancing property is set to 5-Multiuse so the Customers object can create it when needed.

### Create a UDT for each Element

As with the TextList object, we'll need to create a couple of UDTs to store each element's data and to support the LSet copy of the data into a buffer. Of course, each element will be copied into a Buffer object, but we'll get to that in a bit.

```
Public Type CustDisplayProps
   CustomerID As Long
   Name As String * 50
   Phone As String * 25
End Type

Public Type CustDisplayData
   Buffer As String * 77
End Type
```

This declaration goes into the VideoTypes BAS module so it's available to both the VideoServer and VideoObjects projects. The VideoServer project will use it to load the Buffer object, while VideoObjects will use it to pull the data back out of the Buffer object and use it as needed.

The `CustomersPersist` object, like the `TextListPersist` object, will store its state data in a `Buffer` object, so we'll need to declare that in that `CustomersPersist` class module.

```
Option Explicit

Private mobjBuffer As Buffer
```

### The Fetch Routine

Next we need to move the `Fetch` subroutine from the `Customers` object into the `CustomersPersist` object and convert it into a `Public` method for use by the `Customers` object.

Like the `TextList`'s `Fetch` method, the `Customers` object's routine directly loads its internal data from the recordset. We'll need to modify this code to load the recordset data into our `Buffer` object instead, then return the total state from the `Buffer` object as a result of our `Fetch` function.

```
Public Function Fetch(ByVal Name As String, ByVal Phone As String) As String

    Dim rsCustomer As Recordset
    Dim strSQL As String
    Dim strWHERE As String
  ' Dim objDisplay As CustomerDisplay
    Dim udtData As CustDisplayData
    Dim udtProps As CustDisplayProps

    strSQL = "SELECT CUSTOMERID, NAME, PHONE FROM CUSTOMER"
    If Len(Name) > 0 Then _
      strWHERE = "NAME LIKE '" & Name & "%' "

    If Len(Phone) > 0 Then
      If Len(strWHERE) > 0 Then
        strWHERE = strWHERE & " AND PHONE LIKE '" & Phone & "%'"

      Else
        strWHERE = "PHONE LIKE '" & Phone & "%'"
      End If

    End If

    If Len(strWHERE) > 0 Then _
      strSQL = strSQL & " WHERE " & strWHERE
    Set rsCustomer = New Recordset
    rsCustomer.Open strSQL, cnVideo
    Set mobjBuffer = New Buffer
    mobjBuffer.Initialize Len(udtData.Buffer), 100

    Do While Not rsCustomer.EOF
      With udtProps
        .CustomerID = rsCustomer("CustomerID")
        .Name = rsCustomer("Name")
        .Phone = rsCustomer("Phone")
      End With
      LSet udtData = udtProps
      mobjBuffer.Add udtData.Buffer
      rsCustomer.MoveNext
    Loop
```

```
        rsCustomer.Close
        Set rsCustomer = Nothing
        Fetch = mobjBuffer.GetState
```

```
    End Function
```

The original code created a `CustomerDisplay` object for each row in the recordset, then copied the data into that object and added it to a private collection object. The changes we've made here just copy each row's data into `udtProps`, `LSet` that into `udtData` and then add the data to `mobjBuffer`, the `Buffer` object.

Once the `Buffer` object has all the object data, we simply return that data as the result of the `Fetch` method by calling the `Buffer` object's `GetState` method.

## Customers Object

The `Customers` object itself needs to be changed a bit as well. Of course, its `Load` method was used to call a local `Fetch` subroutine and so we'll need to modify that routine. Also we need to add a `SetState` method. This method will accept the result from `CustomersPersist` and will unpack it into a collection of `CustomerDisplay` objects, just like the original `Fetch` routine did with the recordset results.

### Declarations

In the declarations section of the `CustomerDisplay` module we declare the `mudtProps` variable. Prior to this point we've declared it as type `DisplayProps`. However, we've renamed our UDT to `CustDisplayProps` and so we'll need to update this declaration as well:

```
    Private mudtProps As CustDisplayProps
```

### Load Method

The `Load` method needs to create an instance of `CustomersPersist`, then call its `Fetch` method. Once that is done, we can use the `GetState` method on `CustomersPersist` to retrieve the resulting data and put it into the `SetState` method of the `Customers` object itself:

```
    Public Sub Load(Optional Name As String, Optional Phone As String)

        Dim objPersist As CustomersPersist

        Set objPersist = CreateObject("VideoServer.CustomersPersist", PERSIST_SERVER)
        SetState objPersist.Fetch(Name, Phone)
        Set objPersist = Nothing

    End Sub
```

The changes to this routine are just like the changes we made to the `Load` method of the `TextList` object.

### SetState Routine

As with the `TextList` object, the bulk of the work occurs in the `SetState` method. It's here that we unpack the `Buffer` object, using `LSet` to copy each element's data into `udtProps` and from there into a `CustomerDisplay` object:

```
Private Sub SetState(Buffer As String)

  Dim objBuffer As Buffer
  Dim objDisplay As CustomerDisplay
  Dim lngIndex As Long
  Dim udtData As CustDisplayData
  Dim udtProps As CustDisplayProps

  Set objBuffer = New Buffer
  With objBuffer
    .SetState Buffer
    For lngIndex = 1 To .Count
      Set objDisplay = New CustomerDisplay
      udtData.Buffer = .Item(lngIndex)
      LSet udtProps = udtData

      With objDisplay
        .CustomerID = udtProps.CustomerID
        .Name = Trim$(udtProps.Name)
        .Phone = Trim$(udtProps.Phone)
        mcolDisplay.Add objDisplay
        Set objDisplay = Nothing
      End With

    Next

  End With

  Set objBuffer = Nothing

End Sub
```

We should be able to make similar changes to the `Videos` object, creating a matching `VideosPersist` object. Since all these objects are read-only, they are pretty easy to deal with. We don't need to worry about updating data or deleting records, just pulling back the information in the most efficient manner possible.

# Making Child Objects Persistent

At this point we've basically adopted the following sequence of events:

- ❑   Pull out the data access code
- ❑   Put it into another object in another project
- ❑   Modify the original object to call methods on the new persistence object

It's basically the same regardless of whether the object is read-write, read-only or even when it's just a list of data.

Now let's get into the complicated stuff - child objects. This is where things get very interesting and more than a little tricky.

On one level we can view child objects as being very much like the `CustomerDisplay` objects we just loaded in the previous section. The persistence object can just load them into a `Buffer` object and send them across the network. But then who unpacks the buffer? The parent object? Or, perhaps, our custom collection object?

Who packs up the child objects to send them back to the persistence object when the user clicks OK or Apply? Worse still, suppose the child object's data is updated during the update process, how do we get the resulting changes back into the objects?

Our implementation in Chapter 8 was painfully simplistic. When each object saves itself to the database it's very easy for the object to update any changed data or do any other database work required. That's good, but for performance reasons we can't allow each child object to save itself to the database individually. Suppose there are hundreds of child objects? - that would translate into an awful lot of calls across DCOM, bogging down performance and leading to some very unhappy users.

Instead, we need to load all the objects into a `Buffer` object and move them back and forth as a unit. At first glance this doesn't seem too complex. However, it can get tricky when it comes to handling real-world objects.

For example, after we've added a child `Tape` object we need to retrieve that object's state to get the `TapeID` value assigned by the database. If we've packaged *all* our child objects into a single buffer we don't necessarily want to retrieve the data for `Tape` objects that already existed, only for those that are newly added.

In our application we have a couple of parent-child relationships. The `Video` and `Tape` objects have that relationship, as do the `Invoice` and `InvoiceItem` objects. The concepts and techniques that we'll employ here work in both cases, so we'll just go through the `Video` and `Tape` objects. The implementation of the `Invoice` object and its children can be extrapolated from there.

# Making the Video Object Persistent

The `Video` object is the parent of our `Tape` objects. However, we can basically think of it as a simple business object like `Customer`. The hard work comes in when we make the collection of `Tape` objects persistent, but we'll get through the easy part first.

## Global UDTs

Since we'll be moving the `Video` object's data back and forth between the `VideoObjects` and `VideoServer` projects, we need to provide a global UDT to hold that data. This means taking the `VideoProps` UDT from the `Video` class module and putting it into the `VideoTypes` BAS module.

### Moving the VideoProps UDT

Don't forget to add variables to store the values of `mflgNew`, `mflgDeleted` and `mflgDirty`. We'll use these when we build the `VideoServer` object and in the `GetState` method of the `Video` object:

```
Public Type VideoProps
    VideoID As Long
    Title As String * 30
    ReleaseDate As Date
    Studio As String * 30
```

```
        Category As String * 20
        Rating As String * 5
      IsNew As Boolean
      IsDeleted As Boolean
      IsDirty As Boolean
    End Type
```

Notice that we've also changed the data type of the ReleaseDate member to Date (from Variant). This is required because the LSet command won't work if there is a Variant member in our UDT. This is because a Variant doesn't necessarily contain actual data – instead many Variant variables are pointers to data that is stored somewhere else in memory. This precludes LSet from simply doing a memory copy of the data and so Visual Basic raises an error if we attempt such a thing.

### Modifying the Property Get for ReleaseDate

As we were forced to change the ReleaseDate to a Date in VideoProps we need to do an extra bit of work in the Property Get routine of Video:

```
Public Property Get ReleaseDate() As Variant

  With mudtProps
    ReleaseDate = IIf(.ReleaseDate = 0, "", .ReleaseDate)
  End With

End Property
```

This change is required due to the way Visual Basic converts the Date data type to a Variant. Since our Property Get returns a Variant, Visual Basic will convert our variable from a Date to a Variant. Unfortunately, Visual Basic has no concept of an 'empty' Date - instead translating it to 12:00 AM. What we really want to happen with an empty date is to return a blank.

By checking to see if the value of the variable is a numeric 0, we are able to determine if it's 'empty' or blank. If it's 0 then we can simply return an empty string, otherwise we'll return the variable itself since we know it has a valid value.

### Adding a VideoData UDT

We also need to create a VideoData UDT so we can use LSet to copy the detailed data from VideoProps into a single String buffer:

```
Public Type VideoData
  Buffer As String * 94
End Type
```

## The VideoPersist Object

As with the Customer object, we'll need to split out the persistence code into a new object. In the VideoServer project create a new class module named VideoPersist and set its Instancing to 5-Multiuse.

The process to support making the Video object persistent is the same as we used for the Customer object earlier on in the chapter. All we'll do is move the Fetch, Save and DeleteObject methods from Video to VideoPersist and make them Public in scope. Of course, we'll add GetState and SetState methods as well.

```vb
Option Explicit

Private mudtProps As VideoProps

Public Function Save(ByVal Buffer As String) As String

    Dim rsVideo As Recordset
    Dim strSQL As String

    SetState Buffer

    Set rsVideo = New Recordset
    strSQL = "SELECT * FROM Video WHERE VideoID=" & mudtProps.VideoID
    rsVideo.Open strSQL, cnVideo, , adLockOptimistic
    If mudtProps.IsNew Then rsVideo.AddNew

    With rsVideo
      .Fields("Title") = mudtProps.Title
      .Fields("ReleaseDate") = mudtProps.ReleaseDate
      .Fields("Studio") = mudtProps.Studio
      .Fields("Rating") = mudtProps.Rating
      .Fields("Category") = mudtProps.Category
      .Update
      If mudtProps.IsNew Then mudtProps.VideoID = .Fields("VideoID")
      .Close
    End With

    Set rsVideo = Nothing
    Save = GetState

End Function

Public Sub DeleteObject(ByVal VideoID As Long)

    cnVideo.Execute "DELETE FROM Video WHERE VideoID=" & VideoID

End Sub

Public Function Fetch(ByVal VideoID As Long) As String

    Dim rsVideo As Recordset
    Dim strSQL As String

    strSQL = "SELECT * FROM Video WHERE VideoID=" & VideoID
    Set rsVideo = New Recordset
    rsVideo.Open strSQL, cnVideo

    With rsVideo
      mudtProps.VideoID = .Fields("VideoID")
      mudtProps.Title = .Fields("Title")
      mudtProps.ReleaseDate = IIf(IsNull(.Fields("ReleaseDate")), 0, _
        .Fields("ReleaseDate"))
      mudtProps.Studio = .Fields("Studio")
      mudtProps.Rating = .Fields("Rating")
      mudtProps.Category = .Fields("Category")
      rsVideo.Close
    End With

    Set rsVideo = Nothing
    Fetch = GetState
```

```
End Function

Private Sub SetState(Buffer As String)

  Dim udtData As VideoData

  udtData.Buffer = Buffer
  LSet mudtProps = udtData

End Sub

Private Function GetState() As String

  Dim udtData As VideoData

  LSet udtData = mudtProps
  GetState = udtData.Buffer

End Function
```

Since we changed our `ReleaseDate` variable from a `Variant` to a `Date` we need to be a bit more careful with copying values from the database into the variable within the `Fetch` method. We now need to use the `IsNull` method to ensure that we don't try to copy a null value into our variable or we'll get an error.

## The Video Object

The `Video` object itself needs to be updated as well. In particular, we need to change the `ApplyEdit` and `Load` methods to use the `VideoPersist` object's methods instead of private subroutines. We also need to add `GetState` and `SetState` methods as we did with the `Customer` object.

### Updating ApplyEdit in Video

The changes to the `ApplyEdit` method are basically the same ones we made to the `Customer` object's `ApplyEdit` method.

```
Public Sub ApplyEdit()

  Dim objPersist As VideoPersist

  If Not mflgEditing Then Err.Raise 445

  Set objPersist = CreateObject("VideoServer.VideoPersist", PERSIST_SERVER)

  If mflgDeleted And Not mflgNew Then
    ' code to delete the object's data goes here
    objPersist.DeleteObject mudtProps.VideoID
    mflgNew = True
    mflgDeleted = False

  Else
    If Not IsValid Then Err.Raise 445
    ' save object to database if appropriate
    SetState objPersist.Save(GetState)
    ' save object state
    LSet mudtSave = mudtProps
    mflgNew = False
```

```
        End If

        mobjTapes.ApplyEdit mudtProps.VideoID
        Set objPersist = Nothing
        mflgDirty = False
        mflgEditing = False

    End Sub
```

### Updating Load in Video

Likewise, the `Load` method just needs simple enhancement.

```
    Public Sub Load(VideoID As Long)

      Dim objPersist As VideoPersist

      If mflgEditing Then Err.Raise 445
      If Not mflgNew Then Err.Raise 445

      ' code to load the object goes here
      Set objPersist = CreateObject("VideoServer.VideoPersist", PERSIST_SERVER)
      SetState objPersist.Fetch(VideoID)
      Set objPersist = Nothing

      mobjValid.RuleBroken "Title", False

      mobjTapes.Load mudtProps.VideoID
      mflgNew = False

    End Sub
```

The call to the `RuleBroken` method of `mobjValid` shown here was originally in the `Fetch` subroutine. When that routine was moved out of the `Video` object the reference to `mobjValid` became useless and so this line had to move to the `Load` routine:

```
    mobjValid.RuleBroken "Title", False
```

### Adding GetState to Video

The `GetState` method copies the values of `mflgNew`, `mflgDeleted` and `mflgDirty` into `mudtProps`, then uses `LSet` to copy the object's state into a single `String` buffer:

```
    Private Function GetState() As String

      Dim udtData As VideoData

      With mudtProps
        .IsDeleted = mflgDeleted
        .IsNew = mflgNew
        .IsDirty = mflgDirty
      End With

      LSet udtData = mudtProps
      GetState = udtData.Buffer

    End Function
```

### Adding SetState to Video

As with `Customer`, the `SetState` method is even simpler. All it does is copy the buffer into `mudtProps` using the `LSet` command:

```
Private Sub SetState(Buffer As String)

  Dim udtData As VideoData

  udtData.Buffer = Buffer
  LSet mudtProps = udtData

End Sub
```

# Serializing the Tape Objects

So now we're down to brass tacks. The parent object is all set and ready to go, we just need to figure out how to manage the child objects. The key word in that sentence is *manage*. In Chapter 6 we built an object specifically to manage the child objects, the `Tapes` object. What we're about to do here is just an extension to the management job already provided by the `Tapes` object.

Our `Tape` objects provide both child behaviors and regular business object behaviors. For the most part a `Tape` object is a child of the `Video` object. However, we also allow the UI to bring up a `Tape` object by itself for the purpose of calling the `CheckIn` method. This way we can create a UI that prompts the user for a tape's ID number to directly check in the tape.

Right now we'll focus exclusively on the child object behaviors so it's clear exactly how to handle child objects. Later on we'll go back through and add in the code to allow the `Tape` object to retrieve and update its data directly so the UI can use the `CheckIn` method.

As we discussed earlier, the driving force behind this whole endeavor is performance. We need to come up with some mechanism by which all the `Tape` objects can be sent through DCOM in a single method call. If each `Tape` object makes its own calls via DCOM our application's performance will be terrible.

Instead of each child object making the calls, we'll put this code into the `Tapes` object. It can collect all the child object's state data together into a `Buffer` object and send that across the network to a `TapesPersist` object. The `TapesPersist` object can then break the `Buffer` object apart and get each object updated in the database.

What we are doing here is an example of *marshalling* the data, or *serializing* all our `Tape` objects into a single stream of data. We are choosing to marshal all the data from the child objects together into a single unit that we can send over the network. The work of marshalling will be handled by the `Tapes` object, though each individual `Tape` object will have to provide and update its own state data.

## Updating the Tape Object

### Adding GetState to Tape

The first thing we need to do is provide a way to get each individual `Tape` object's state data into and out of the object. As with our other objects, we'll do this by implementing `GetState` and `SetState` methods in the object.

We need to move the `TapeProps` UDT into the `VideoTypes` BAS module and create a `TapeData` UDT so we can convert the detailed properties into a single `String` buffer:

```
Public Type TapeProps
   TapeID As Long
   VideoID As Long
   Title As String * 30
   CheckedOut As Boolean
   DateAcquired As Date
   DateDue As Date
   LateFee As Boolean
   InvoiceID As Long
   IsNew As Boolean
   IsDeleted As Boolean
   IsDirty As Boolean
End Type

Public Type TapeData
   Buffer As String * 52
End Type
```

As with the `ReleaseDate` member in the `VideoProps` UDT, we need to change the `Variant` data type of `DateAcquired` and `DateDue` to `Date`. If we don't do this then the `LSet` command will be unable to copy the data from our detailed UDT variable to the one declared with the `TapeData` UDT.

This also means we have to modify our `Property Get` for `DateAcquired` just like we did for `ReleaseDate`:

```
Public Property Get DateAcquired() As Variant

   With mudtProps
      DateAcquired = IIf(.DateAcquired = 0, "", .DateAcquired)
   End With

End Property
```

The `GetState` method in our `Tape` object is the same as the methods we've implemented in the `Customer` and `Video` objects. The only significant difference is that the method is declared as `Friend` rather than `Private`. This is because the `Tapes` object will be getting and setting each `Tape` object's state and so will need access to the method:

```
Friend Function GetState() As String

   Dim udtData As TapeData

   With mudtProps
      .IsNew = mflgNew
      .IsDeleted = mflgDeleted
      .IsDirty = mflgDirty
   End With

   LSet udtData = mudtProps
   GetState = udtData.Buffer
   mflgNew = False
End Function
```

### Adding SetState to Tape

The SetState is also declared as Friend, but is otherwise quite familiar:

```
Friend Sub SetState(Buffer As String)

  Dim udtData As TapeData

  udtData.Buffer = Buffer
  LSet mudtProps = udtData
  mflgNew = False
  mobjValid.RuleBroken "DateAcquired", False

End Sub
```

Since the SetState will only be called when data is being provided from the database to the object, we've included code to mark any data-oriented rules as unbroken:

```
  mobjValid.RuleBroken "DateAcquired", False
```

This code was in the Fetch subroutine, but as with our previous objects, the Fetch subroutine will be moved to the persistence object and so this code needs to be moved. In the Customer and Video objects we moved it to the Load method, but since Tape is a child object, the Load method isn't going to be used.

The SetState method is therefore the ideal location to indicate that the rule is unbroken, since we know the data supplied is valid because it has just come from the database.

*The assumption is that the data coming from the database is valid if we are certain that there are no other applications working with the data. If there is any form of data access other than through our business objects we might need to add extra data validation in either our UI-centric object's SetState method or in the data-centric object's Fetch method.*

## Updating the Tapes Collection Object

### Adding GetState to Tapes

The Tapes object itself will need GetState and SetState methods as well. These will be a bit different, since the 'state' of the Tapes object is really the collected states of all the Tape objects.

Let's look at the GetState method first:

```
Private Function GetState() As String

  Dim objBuffer As Buffer
  Dim objTape As Tape

  Set objBuffer = New Buffer
  Set objTape = New Tape
  objBuffer.Initialize Len(objTape.GetState), 20

  For Each objTape In mcolTapes
    objBuffer.Add objTape.GetState
```

```
      Next

      GetState = objBuffer.GetState
      Set objBuffer = Nothing

   End Function
```

To start off we need to create a `Buffer` object, `objBuffer`. The hard part in this case is to initialize the new object. We need to know the length of the elements we'll be adding to the `Buffer`. There are many ways to get this length. Here we've simply created a new `Tape` object and taken the length of its `GetState` method's result.

Next we just need to loop through the `Tape` objects and add each one's state to the `Buffer` object:

```
   For Each objTape In mcolTapes
      objBuffer.Add objTape.GetState
   Next
```

After having added all the individual `Tape` object's states to the `Buffer` object, we can simply return the `Buffer` object's state as the result of this `GetState` method:

```
   GetState = objBuffer.GetState
   Set objBuffer = Nothing
```

## Adding SetState to Tapes

The `SetState` method is also a bit unusual when compared to the others we've seen. A while ago we discussed how bi-directional updates of the child objects were tricky. Here we come face-to-face with the issue.

When we go to save a group of `Tape` objects we send them all to the persistence object as a group. The problem is that each item's data may change while it's interacting with the database. For instance, a new `Tape` object gets an ID value as it's being saved. How does that new ID value get back into the `Tape` object itself?

All the child object states come back from the persistence object in a single `Buffer` object. In fact, that `Buffer` object is what we use in this `SetState` routine. The challenge is to figure out which child object needs to be updated from each element in the `Buffer`.

In this case we'll take the easy way out. Rather than trying to identify and update individual `Tape` objects, we'll just drop the reference to all the child objects, effectively destroying them all. Then the `SetState` code can just recreate the collection of child objects based on the current content of the `Buffer` object:

```
   Private Sub SetState(Buffer As String)

      Dim lngIndex As Long
      Dim objTape As Tape
      Dim objBuffer As Buffer

      Set mcolTapes = Nothing
      Set mcolTapes = New Collection
```

These last couple lines create new `Collection` objects for `mcolTapes`. This means that we no longer have a reference to the old objects and so they will terminate. Since those `Collection` objects are the only things with references to the child `Tape` objects, all of those objects will terminate as well.

Using these new and empty `Collection` objects, we can loop through the elements in the `Buffer` object, creating a new `Tape` object for each item:

```
Set objBuffer = New Buffer
objBuffer.SetState Buffer

For lngIndex = 1 To objBuffer.Count
  Set objTape = New Tape
  With objTape
    .SetState objBuffer.Item(lngIndex)
    .SetAsChild Me
  End With
  mcolTapes.Add Item:=objTape
Next

End Sub
```

In the end we've fully rebuilt the collection of child `Tape` objects based on the `Buffer` object's data. This means that the `Tape` objects are all populated with current and correct data from the database, including any new or updated data that might have come into play during the process of adding or updating the objects into the database.

# Creating the Data-Centric Tape Objects

What we've done so far should enable us to take all the data from all the `Tape` objects and marshal it into a single `String` buffer that we can send over the network. The process also works in reverse, in that we can accept a `String` buffer and rebuild all the child `Tape` objects based on the data provided.

As with our other business objects, we also need to create data-centric business objects in the `VideoServer` project to restore, save and delete the child objects' data. Since we've got all the child object data into a single `String` buffer, we'll design our data-centric objects to work with the same `String` buffer, making it easy to transfer our objects' data back and forth between the UI-centric and data-centric objects.

We need a data-centric object for the `Tapes` object to work with, one that can accept and provide a buffer containing all the child objects' data. We also need an object that knows how to save and restore the `Tape` objects themselves. While it would certainly be possible to combine these functions into a single object, it's much more maintainable and readable to keep them separate.

## *The TapesPersist Object*

The `Tapes` object needs a corresponding object in the `VideoServer` project that can accept the `String` buffer, unpack it and save each element's data. This object also needs to have a `Fetch` method to retrieve all the child objects' data, pack it into a buffer and provide it to the `Tapes` object upon request.

# Visual Basic 6 Business Objects

In many ways this object will be very much like the `TextListPersist` and `CustomersPersist` objects that retrieved lists of data earlier in the chapter. The big difference is that this object will also need to be able to write data back out to the database. Also, the actual database code will not be contained in this object, but rather will be contained in a `TapePersist` object that we'll get to later.

## Setting up TapesPersist

Add a new class module to the `VideoServer` project and name it `TapesPersist`. Make sure its Instancing is set to 5-Multiuse, since the `Tapes` object will be creating and working with this object.

## Adding a Fetch Method to TapesPersist

Our existing `Tapes` object's `Load` method contains code to retrieve the list of `TapeID` values from the database for all the records that have the appropriate `VideoID`. This routine will provide the basis for the `TapesPersist` object's `Fetch` method.

Like the original routine, this new routine will create a recordset containing all the valid `TapeID` values from the database. It will then loop through all those ID values, invoking a `Fetch` method to load each `Tape` object's data:

```
Public Function Fetch(ByVal VideoID As Long) As String

  Dim strSQL As String
  Dim rsTape As Recordset
  Dim objBuffer As Buffer
  Dim objPersist As TapePersist
  Dim udtProps As TapeProps

  Set objBuffer = New Buffer
  strSQL = "SELECT TapeID FROM Tape WHERE VideoID=" & VideoID
  Set rsTape = New Recordset
  rsTape.Open strSQL, cnVideo
  Set objPersist = New TapePersist

  With objPersist
    objBuffer.Initialize Len(udtProps), 20

    Do While Not rsTape.EOF
      objBuffer.Add .Fetch(rsTape("TapeID"))
      rsTape.MoveNext
    Loop

  End With

  Set objPersist = Nothing
  rsTape.Close
  Set rsTape = Nothing
  Fetch = objBuffer.GetState

End Function
```

The big difference is that instead of creating a `Tape` object and calling its `Fetch` method, we are now creating a `TapePersist` object and using its `Fetch` method. Once we've called the `Fetch` method we can use the `TapePersist` object's `GetState` method to retrieve that item's state data and add it to `objBuffer`.

### Adding a Save Method to TapesPersist

The `Save` method is a bit more interesting, especially when compared to our earlier methods of this type.

We need to rebuild the `Buffer` object so it contains any changes to each `Tape` object's data. Along the way we want to remove the deleted objects from the buffer since there's no reason to keep them once the data has been removed from the database.

Rather than trying to update the existing `Buffer` object, `objBuffer`, we'll create a new empty `Buffer` object. Elements that are deleted aren't copied into the new buffer, while those that have been added or updated are copied into the buffer once the database activity is complete.

When we're done, the new `Buffer` object contains only data from valid `Tape` objects. The deleted elements are not present, and all the data for the individual elements will include any changes made during the add, or update, process. Now when the `Tapes` object retrieves the `Buffer` object it will actually get the revised and correct data for the `Tape` objects.

The following code creates a `TapePersist` object, which we'll use to save each `Tape` object's data as we loop through the list from the `Buffer` object. It also creates and initializes this new `Buffer` object into which we'll be copying all the updated elements:

```
Public Function Save(ByVal VideoID As Long, ByVal Buffer As String) As String

    Dim objPersist As TapePersist
    Dim objBuffer As Buffer
    Dim objUpdatedTapes As Buffer
    Dim lngIndex As Long
    Dim strBuffer As String

    Set objBuffer = New Buffer
    objBuffer.SetState Buffer
    Set objUpdatedTapes = New Buffer
    objUpdatedTapes.Initialize objBuffer.Length, objBuffer.Count
    Set objPersist = New TapePersist

    For lngIndex = 1 To objBuffer.Count
      With objPersist
        strBuffer = .SaveChild(VideoID, objBuffer.Item(lngIndex))
        If Len(strBuffer) > 0 Then _
          objUpdatedTapes.Add strBuffer
      End With

    Next

    Set objPersist = Nothing
    Save = objUpdatedTapes.GetState

  End Function
```

Now we're ready to work with the `Tape` object data itself. But remember back to where we loaded the elements in the `Buffer` object. We included those that need to be added and updated to the database as well as those that are to be deleted. In our previous `Save` methods we only had to worry about elements being saved, but now we've got to handle those being deleted as well.

The problem is that we have no easy access to the detailed values for each element. To get at the detailed fields we'd have to use `LSet` to copy the buffer into the `TapeProps` UDT. This is an expensive operation just to get at the `IsDeleted` flag, and so we've taken another approach.

Instead of making this routine more complex, we've left it up to the `TapePersist` object to handle the messy details. Rather than calling either `Save` or `DeleteObject` methods on `TapePersist`, we're calling a new method named `SaveChild`. This routine will need to make the determination as to whether the object should be saved or deleted. Like our other `Save` methods, it will accept the object's state as a parameter and will return the new state as a result:

```
strBuffer = .SaveChild(VideoID, objBuffer.Item(lngIndex))
```

The `SaveChild` method also requires the `VideoID` as a parameter. This is important, since each child object needs to know the ID value of the parent `Video` object. This value will end up in the database as a foreign key.

Once each element has been updated into the database we need to copy its state data into our new `Buffer` object, `objUpdatedTapes`. Deleted objects should not be copied into this object - after all, the goal is to have `objUpdatedTapes` contain updated state data for objects that continue to be valid.

To handle this, we'll temporarily store the return value in a `String` variable. If the item has been deleted, the value returned from `SaveChild` will be a zero length string, and we can use that indicator to decide whether to add the state to our `objUpdatedTapes` object.

The final step is to return the updated states for all the `Tape` objects. These are stored in our new `objUpdatedTapes` object, so we can simply return the value from that object's `GetState` method as the result of our `Save` method:

```
Save = objUpdatedTapes.GetState
```

## The TapePersist Object

Of course the code we just implemented needs a `TapePersist` object in order to work. This object will contain the code that actually loads and updates the `Tape` object's data into the database, along with our new `SaveChild` method and `IsDeleted` property.

### Setting up TapePersist

Add a new class module to the `VideoServer` project and name it `TapePersist`. Set its Instancing property to 1-Private. This object is created and used by the `TapesPersist` object, so we don't need to expose it to the outside world.

> *Admittedly we'll need to expose it later, to make the* Tape *object itself able to use the methods implemented here. For right now I want to keep focused on the process of saving child objects.*

Like the single object persistence objects we've built so far, this one's state is composed of a UDT containing the `Tape` object's data. We've already moved the `TapeProps` and `TapeData` UDTs to the `VideoTypes` BAS module, so we're all set to use them in `TapePersist`:

```
Option Explicit

Private mudtProps As TapeProps
```

## Adding SetState and GetState to TapePersist

We also need to implement `GetState` and `SetState` methods to retrieve and set the object's data into the UDT variable:

```
Private Sub SetState(Buffer As String)

  Dim udtData As TapeData

  udtData.Buffer = Buffer
  LSet mudtProps = udtData

End Sub
```

```
Private Function GetState() As String

  Dim udtData As TapeData

  LSet udtData = mudtProps
  GetState = udtData.Buffer

End Function
```

## Moving Fetch to TapePersist

Next, move the `Fetch`, `Save` and `DeleteObject` methods from `Tape` into this object. We'll handle these a bit differently than before. The `Fetch` method will need to be `Friend`, since it is directly called from the `TapesPersist` object:

```
Friend Function Fetch(TapeID As Long) As String

  Dim rsTape As Recordset
  Dim strSQL As String

  strSQL = "SELECT Tape.*,Video.Title " & _
    "FROM Tape INNER JOIN Video ON " & _
    "Tape.VideoID = Video.VideoID " & _
    "WHERE TapeID=" & TapeID
  Set rsTape = New Recordset
  rsTape.Open strSQL, cnVideo

  With rsTape
    mudtProps.TapeID = .Fields("TapeID")
    mudtProps.VideoID = .Fields("VideoID")
    mudtProps.Title = .Fields("Title")
    mudtProps.CheckedOut = .Fields("CheckedOut")
    mudtProps.DateAcquired = IIf(IsNull(.Fields("DateAcquired")), _
      0, .Fields("DateAcquired"))
    mudtProps.DateDue = IIf(IsNull(.Fields("DateDue")), 0, .Fields("DateDue"))
    mudtProps.InvoiceID = .Fields("InvoiceID")
    rsTape.Close
  End With
```

```
    Set rsTape = Nothing
    Fetch = GetState

End Function
```

The changes to the `Fetch` method are simple, change the scope to `Friend` so it can be called from `TapesPersist` and make it a `Function` so it can return the object's state when it is complete. As we've done before, we simply call the `GetState` method to return that state value.

We also need to remove the `RuleBroken` call from `Fetch`, and put it in the `Tape` object's `SetState` method instead:

```
mobjValid.RuleBroken "DateAcquired", False
```

We'll take a closer look at this later in the chapter.

> Throughout the code for this object, no parameters use the `ByVal` keyword, even though the methods may be `Public`. This is because the object itself is `Private`, (since we set its **Instancing** property to **1-Private**) so even the `Public` methods can't be called by code outside the immediate Visual Basic project. Using `ByVal` in this case would be a detriment to performance rather than providing the benefits we see when passing parameters across process boundaries or network connections.

### Moving Save to TapePersist

The `Save` method can remain `Private` in scope. We'll be calling it from the `SaveChild` method rather than directly from the `TapesPersist` object, so it doesn't need to be available outside this class. We do need to change the method to accept the `Buffer` string:

```
Private Function Save(Buffer As String) As String

Dim rsTape As Recordset
Dim rsVideo As Recordset
Dim strSQL As String

SetState Buffer
strSQL = "SELECT * FROM Tape WHERE TapeID=" & mudtProps.TapeID
Set rsTape = New Recordset
rsTape.Open strSQL, cnVideo, , adLockOptimistic
If mudtprops.IsNew Then rsTape.AddNew

With rsTape
  .Fields("VideoID") = mudtprops.VideoID
  .Fields("CheckedOut") = mudtprops.CheckedOut
  .Fields("DateAcquired") = mudtprops.DateAcquired
  .Fields("DateDue") = mudtprops.DateDue
  .Fields("InvoiceID") = mudtprops.InvoiceID
  .Update
  If mudtProps.IsNew Then mudtprops.TapeID = .Fields("TapeID")
  .Close
End With
```

```
      Set rsTape = Nothing
      If mudtProps.IsNew Then
        strSQL = "SELECT TITLE FROM Video WHERE VideoID=" & _
          mudtProps.VideoID
        Set rsVideo = New Recordset
        rsVideo.Open strSQL, cnVideo
        mudtProps.Title = rsVideo("Title")
        rsVideo.Close
        Set rsVideo = Nothing
      End If
      Save = GetState


      If mudtProps.LateFee Then
        ' add the late fee to the customer
        SaveLateFee
      End If

    End Function
```

The first couple of changes in this routine are the same old thing we've done with the others, returning the object's state as a result of the function and replacing `mflgNew` with `mudtProps.IsNew`. This last change is quite different however.

In the original `Tape` object, we had code in the `ApplyEdit` method to call the `SaveLateFee` subroutine if a late fee was indicated by the `mudtProps.LateFee` variable.

```
    If mudtProps.LateFee Then
      ' add the late fee to the customer
      SaveLateFee
    End If
```

### Moving SaveLateFee to TapePersist

The `SaveLateFee` routine actually goes out to the database and adds a record to the `LateFee` table. Since we're moving all the code that works with the database out of the `VideoObjects` project, the `SaveLateFee` subroutine needs to be moved as well, and so does the code that calls it.

The `SaveLateFee` routine can be moved from the `Tape` object to the `TapePersist` object directly and without change. We may change where we've called it from, but it still needs to do the exact same thing it was doing before.

```
    Private Sub SaveLateFee()

      Dim rsLateFee As Recordset
      Dim rsInvoice As Recordset
      Dim strSQL As String

      strSQL = "SELECT CUSTOMERID FROM INVOICE WHERE INVOICEID=" & _
        mudtprops.InvoiceID
      Set rsInvoice = New Recordset
      rsInvoice.Open strSQL, cnVideo
      strSQL = "LateFee"
      Set rsLateFee = New Recordset
      rsLateFee.Open strSQL, cnVideo, , adLockOptimistic
      rsLateFee.AddNew
```

```
    With rsLateFee
       .Fields("CustomerID") = rsInvoice("CustomerID")
       .Fields("TapeID") = mudtprops.TapeID
       .Fields("FeeDate") = Now
       .Fields("DaysOver") = DateDiff("d", mudtprops.DateDue, Now)
       .Fields("Paid") = False
       .Update
       .Close
    End With

    rsInvoice.Close
    Set rsInvoice = Nothing
    Set rsLateFee = Nothing

  End Sub
```

### Moving DeleteObject to TapePersist

Like the SaveLateFee routine, the DeleteObject routine can be moved from Tape to
TapePersist unchanged.

```
  Private Sub DeleteObject(TapeID As Long)

    cnVideo.Execute "DELETE FROM Tape WHERE TapeID=" & TapeID

  End Sub
```

### Adding SaveChild to TapePersist

The SaveChild method isn't all that complex either. Back in the Save method of the
TapesPersist object we called this method instead of the Save or DeleteObject methods
because the TapesPersist object had no easy way of knowing whether this particular Tape object
needed to be saved or deleted.

Now that we're inside the TapePersist object and the object's state is contained in the mudtProps
variable this is trivial. We can directly examine the IsDeleted value and make a determination as
to whether we need to delete the object or call the Save subroutine.

```
  Friend Function SaveChild(VideoID As Long, Buffer As String) As String

    SetState Buffer

    With mudtProps
      If .IsDeleted Then
        DeleteObject .TapeID
        SaveChild = ""

      ElseIf .IsDirty Or .IsNew Then
        .VideoID = VideoID
        SaveChild = Save(GetState)

      Else
        SaveChild = Buffer

      End If

    End With

  End Function
```

We also need to cover the case where the item is neither deleted nor dirty. In such a case we still need to return the object's state data as a result of the function so it can be sent back to the Tapes object as a valid Tape object.

# Updating the Tapes and Tape Objects

At this point the objects in VideoServer are ready to roll. The TapesPersist object will accept all the data for the Tape objects and will use the TapePersist object to retrieve or update them as appropriate.

We've already incorporated GetState and SetState methods into both the Tapes and Tape objects, but there are some other changes we need to make before we're all done.

## The Tapes Object

In the Tapes object we just need to make a couple of changes. In particular, we need to add code so the TapesPersist object's methods are called when needed.

### Updating ApplyEdit in Tapes

In the ApplyEdit method we used to just loop through all the child Tape objects and tell each one to do its own ApplyEdit operation. Now we need to add some code to collect all the child object's state data by using the GetState method we wrote earlier. Then we need to send this data down to the TapesPersist object and let it get everything updated.

```
Public Sub ApplyEdit(VideoID As Long)

    Dim objPersist As TapesPersist

    If Not mflgEditing Then Err.Raise 445

    Set objPersist = CreateObject("VideoServer.TapesPersist", PERSIST_SERVER)
    SetState objPersist.Save(VideoID, GetState)
    Set objPersist = Nothing

    mflgEditing = False

End Sub
```

This is a far cry from the code we had in here before. In fact this is a whole lot simpler. The reason is largely that we are rebuilding all the child Tape objects when the data is retrieved from the TapesPersist object.

Our SetState method drops all references to the child objects, thus terminating them. It then loops through the results from the TapesPersist object and builds new Tape objects with the updated data. This implicitly produces updated child objects as well as removing any deleted objects from memory.

### Updating Load in Tapes

Likewise, the Load method becomes much simpler. Where it used to access the database to retrieve a list of ID values for the child objects, it now simply calls the TapesPersist object's Fetch method and lets that object deal with all the details.

```
Friend Sub Load(VideoID As Long)

    Dim objPersist As TapesPersist

    Set objPersist = CreateObject("VideoServer.TapesPersist", PERSIST_SERVER)
    SetState objPersist.Fetch(VideoID)
    Set objPersist = Nothing

End Sub
```

## The Tape Object

The changes to the Tape object are very easy to implement. In reviewing what we've done to the ApplyEdit and Load methods of the Tapes object, we can see that they no longer call ChildApplyEdit or ChildLoad on each Tape object. Instead they rely on the SetState method to get data into or out of each child object.

### The ChildApplyEdit method

While the SetState method we've written works great in most cases, we have dramatically changed how our child Tape objects are being handled. Up to now, they've been largely responsible for managing their own status – in particular they've kept track of whether they were being edited as a child or not. This has been done, until now, through the ChildBeginEdit, ChildCancelEdit and ChildAppyEdit methods.

Now we've consolidated the functionality of the ChildApplyEdit into the Tapes object's ApplyEdit and the Tape object's SetState methods. However, there's a hole in our logic. Up to now, when the Video object's ApplyEdit was called, we knew it would cascade that call down to the Tapes object and from there to the ChildApplyEdit methods of each child Tape object.

That is no longer true. Now much of the work is done in the Tapes object's ApplyEdit method, and we don't cascade the call down to the child Tape objects. This isn't necessarily a problem - our program will work fine. However, suppose the user only changes some data in the Video object, but not in the child objects at all? It seems like a waste of effort to save all the child objects if none of them have changed – a lot of work for nothing.

Ideally we'd avoid all the network and database overhead involved in saving a bunch of unchanged child Tape objects. Fortunately this isn't too difficult to implement.

The first thing to do is simplify the Tape object's ChildApplyEdit method:

```
Friend Sub ChildApplyEdit(VideoID As Long)

    If Not mflgChildEditing Then Err.Raise 445
    If Not IsValid Then Err.Raise 445

    mflgChildEditing = False

End Sub
```

Since we know that the SetState method will be used if even one Tape object is deleted or dirty, we can be comfortable in the knowledge that the ChildApplyEdit method will only be called to end an editing session when nothing has been changed. All we really need to do in that case is reset the mflgChildEditing flag.

Now we need to move back up the chain and make sure this routine is called when appropriate. Open the `Tapes` object's code window and move to the `ApplyEdit` method. We've changed this method so it merely calls the `TapesPersist` object to do all the work. However, if none of the child objects have been deleted or changed, there is no reason to go through this effort. Let's add a check for this case, and if nothing has changed we'll just run through the child `Tape` objects and call our newly updated `ChildApplyEdit` method:

```
Public Sub ApplyEdit(VideoID As Long)

    Dim objPersist As TapesPersist
    Dim objTape As Tape

    If Not flgEditing Then Err.Raise 445

    If IsDirty Then
      Set objPersist = CreateObject("VideoServer.TapesPersist", PERSIST_SERVER)
      SetState objPersist.Save(VideoID, GetState)
      Set objPersist = Nothing

    Else
      For Each objTape in mcolTapes
        objTape.ChildApplyEdit(VideoID)
      Next

    End If

    mflgEditing = False

End Sub
```

Now we'll only save the child `Tape` objects if one or more of them are dirty or deleted – potentially saving ourselves a lot of network and database traffic.

### The ChildLoad method

Unlike the `ChildApplyEdit` method, the `ChildLoad` method in our `Tape` object really won't be used any longer. We've removed all calls to this method, so now we can just open up the code window for the `Tape` object and remove this routine.

# Making the Tape Object Make Itself Persistent

If we try to recompile the project at this point we'll get some errors in the `Tape` class module. It still has some references to the `Fetch`, `Save` and `DeleteObject` subroutines that we've moved to the `TapePersist` object.

That's because we've focused entirely on the concept of making child objects persistent. Our `Tape` object is more than just a child object however. It's a kind of hybrid, able to fetch and update its data directly as well as through the child mechanism that we've just implemented.

Now that we've got all the parent-child persistence out of the way, let's go back through the `Tape` and `TapePersist` objects and make the final changes.

## Make TapePersist Public

First off, because the Tape object is a hybrid, it will need direct access to the TapePersist object. Simple child objects wouldn't have this access, but in this case it's required.

### Updating the Scope of TapePersist

Bring up the VideoServer project and select the TapePersist class module in the Project window. Change the Instancing property of the class to 5-Multiuse. This will allow the Tape object to directly create instances of the class as needed.

### Updating the Scope of the TapePersist Methods

Now we need to run through the existing methods on the TapePersist object and make sure their scope is still in line with what we need. We need to make sure that the methods we'll be calling from the Tape object are Public and that all the others are either Private or Friend.

| Method | Old scope | New scope |
| --- | --- | --- |
| SaveChild | Friend | Friend |
| Save | Private | Public |
| DeleteObject | Private | Public |
| Fetch | Friend | Public |
| SaveLateFee | Private | Private |
| SetState | Private | Private |
| GetState | Private | Private |

We'll also need to change the parameters for Save, DeleteObject and Fetch to be declared using the ByVal keyword. This is an important performance consideration, as we want to make sure as little data as possible is copied across the network when a Tape object interacts with the TapePersist object.

### Updating ApplyEdit in Tape

Now that we know the Tape object has access to the methods it will need from TapePersist we can simply alter the code that called the Fetch, Save and DeleteObject subroutines. Instead of calling local subroutines we'll change the code to create a TapePersist and use the methods on that object instead.

The ApplyEdit method of the Tape object needs to be modified in the following manner:

```
Public Sub ApplyEdit()

    Dim objPersist As TapePersist

    If mflgChild Then If Not mflgChildEditing Then Err.Raise 445
    If Not mflgChild And flgNew Then Err.Raise 445
    If Not mflgEditing Then Err.Raise 445

    Set objPersist = CreateObject("VideoServer.TapePersist", PERSIST_SERVER)
```

```
         If Not mflgChild Then
            If mflgDeleted And Not mflgNew Then
              ' code to delete the object's data goes here
              objPersist.DeleteObject mudtProps.TapeID
              mflgNew = True
              mflgDeleted = False

            ElseIf mflgDirty Or mflgNew Then
              If Not IsValid Then Err.Raise 445
              ' save object to database if appropriate
              SetState objPersist.Save(GetState)
              ' save object state
              LSet mudtSave = mudtProps
              mflgNew = False
            End If
            mflgDirty = False

          Else
            If Not mobjParent Is Nothing Then
              mobjParent.AddChild Me
              Set mobjParent = Nothing
            End If

          End If

          Set objPersist = Nothing
          mflgEditing = False

       End Sub
```

We also need to remove the call to the SaveLateFee method. We moved that method from the
Tape object to the data-centric TapePersist object earlier in the chapter, so we no longer want to
try and call it from the ApplyEdit method.

```
       If mudtProps.LateFee Then
         ' add the late fee to the customer
         SaveLateFee
       End If
```

### Updating Load in Tape

Likewise, the Load method needs to be changed:

```
       Public Sub Load(TapeID As Long)

          Dim objPersist As TapePersist

          If mflgChild Then Err.Raise 445
          If mflgEditing Then Err.Raise 445
          If Not mflgNew Then Err.Raise 445

          ' code to load the object goes here
          Set objPersist = CreateObject("VideoServer.TapePersist", PERSIST_SERVER)
          SetState objPersist.Fetch(TapeID)
          Set objPersist = Nothing

          mflgNew = False

       End Sub
```

# Updating the Invoice Related objects

The changes required to the `Invoice` object and its various children are very similar to those we performed on the `Video` object and its child `Tape` objects. Due to the similarity we won't walk through the code. At the same time there are a few notable differences in implementation, so I'll quickly run through them at a high level here.

The changes to the `InvoiceItems` object are very similar to what we've just done with the `Tapes` object. However, in the case of `InvoiceItems` we have two different types of child object and so things are a bit more complex.

Instead of a single `GetState` and `SetState` within the `InvoiceTapes` object, we'll need to implement `GetFees` and `SetFees` as well as `GetTapes` and `SetTapes` to support each type of child object. The concept is very similar, but we'll end up with a serialized set of data for all the late fee objects and another for all the `InvoiceTape` objects.

Once we've got both types of child object serialized into single `String` variables we can pass them to the `InvoiceTapesPersist` object in a manner very similar to how we called the `TapesPersist` object earlier. However, instead of single `Fetch` and `Save` methods, `InvoiceTapesPersist` will have `FetchFees`, `FetchTapes`, `SaveFees` and `SaveTapes` methods.

Alternately, we could implement `Fetch` and `Save` methods that accept two read-write parameters, one for fees and one for tapes. Instead of returning values as a result of the method, this type of method would alter the parameter values themselves, using that as a mechanism for returning the updated values. While this approach has some merit, it is typically best to avoid creating methods that have 'side effects' – meaning methods that alter parameter values as an integral part of their operation.

*If you want to check the code you should have created for these class' take a look at Appendix C.*

# Removing Data Access from VideoObjects

With these changes, our objects can now work together to directly retrieve and update data from the database. At this point we should have the same functionality as we had in Chapter 8, but all the data access is handled by the `VideoServer` ActiveX server rather than by the `VideoObjects` DLL itself.

Also at this point, none of the objects in the `VideoObjects` project will contain any data access code at all. This means that we can open the `VOmain` BAS module and remove the code that declares `cnVideo` and that opens a connection to the database. We no longer need any access to the database in this project.

We can also remove the reference to the ADO library from the project. Choose the Project | References... menu option and uncheck the Microsoft ActiveX Data Objects 2.0 Library item in the References list:

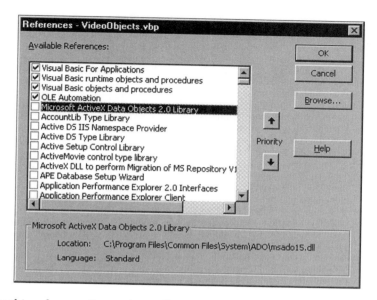

If we don't remove this reference the project will continue to require the ADO libraries to be present and loaded when the program is running. This consumes unneeded resources on the client workstation and would generally be sloppy programming in any case.

# Summary

Here, at the end of the chapter, we should be able to run the VideoUI client, or the Excel client we created in Chapter 9 for that matter. For this to work we will need to make sure the value of the PERSIST_SERVER constant is changed from MYSERVER to the name of our development workstation. The clients will work with the business objects in VideoObjects.dll as always, without change.

Of course the business objects themselves will now be communicating through COM to the VideoServer server application. At this point that application will be running on our client workstation along with our UI application, but we've effectively separated our UI-centric objects from our data-centric objects nonetheless.

In Chapter 11 we'll take the VideoServer server and run it on a separate application server machine, using DCOM to allow communication between the client workstation and the application server. Then in Chapter 12 we'll convert it to run inside Microsoft Transaction Server. This will provide our application with much greater scalability, as well as providing transaction support for our database activity.

Finally we'll wrap up with three chapters on web development. In Chapter 13 we'll look at implementing a Web interface to our business objects by using Active Server Pages. In Chapter 14 we'll create an interface using the new IIS Application capability of Visual Basic 6.0, and in Chapter 15 we'll build a DHTML Application – another new type of application in Visual Basic 6.0.

# 11

# Distributing Objects using DCOM

## Overview

In Chapter 10 we took the video rental business objects we created in Chapter 8 and split the data persistence routines into separate data-centric business objects. We put these data-centric objects into an ActiveX EXE server named `VideoServer`. By having each of our business objects split into two parts, a UI-centric object and a data-centric object, we have changed our video rental application to follow the CSLA architecture we established in Chapter 2.

As we left it in Chapter 10, however, our data-centric objects remain on the client workstation, so we are still running in, at most, a two-tier physical environment as shown in the following figure:

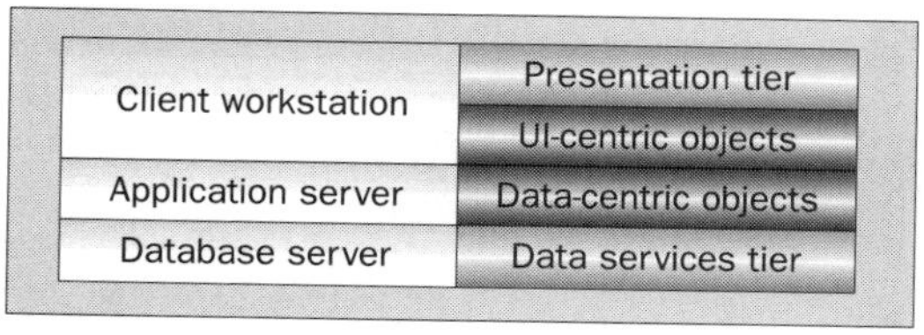

| Client workstation | Presentation tier |
| | UI-centric objects |
| Database server | Data-centric objects |
| | Data services tier |

In this chapter we'll move closer to a three-tier physical architecture, by seeing how we can run our `VideoServer` program on an application server. This will move the data-centric business objects off the client workstation and onto a separate machine. If we were to have the database running on a third machine we'd have a full three-tier physical implementation.

| Client workstation | Presentation tier |
| | UI-centric objects |
| Application server | Data-centric objects |
| Database server | Data services tier |

We won't worry about setting up an actual database server until Chapter 12, since in this chapter we'll focus on running the `VideoServer` program on the application server machine. This means is that we'll need to have a machine separate from our client workstations that is accessible through a network. This machine will act as our application server.

# Application Server Issues

Of course, effectively running our objects on an application server is no small feat. An application server needs to support many concurrent client workstations within the limitations of the CPU, memory and database connections. Usually this involves creation of a pool manager, database-connection management, data caching and record-locking management.

A pool manager is a type of application that runs on a server machine and manages the creation and usage of objects on that server. In this chapter we'll see how the objects contained in our `VideoServer` program can be used by a client workstation across the network. While this is useful, it can swiftly become a problem if we have a lot of client workstations all competing for our `VideoServer` program on the same server. This is where a pool manager comes into play – managing the objects on the server so it's possible to support many client workstations all at the same time.

Distributing an application's processing across multiple machines is complex. There are many issues involved, including performance and support for many concurrent users. The topic is complicated enough for me to devote two chapters to covering the basics alone.

In Chapter 10, we made changes to the code so that the `VideoServer` project handles all the data access. Our UI-centric business objects remain in the `VideoObjects` in-process server, but they rely on the data-centric objects in `VideoServer` to communicate with the database. We can now look at running the `VideoServer` program on an application server machine. The `VideoObjects` and `VideoServer` ActiveX servers will communicate with each other using DCOM.

Since our `VideoServer` program uses a database connection we have to worry about multiple users using the same connection, or each user establishing multiple connections. Also, we still haven't addressed any database transaction issues. Even in our implementation from Chapter 10, when a `Video` object is saved and one of its `Tape` objects fails to save then nothing should be saved. Our current code would leave some data saved and some not.

> *Many of these issues are typically addressed by developing a pool manager to coordinate and control the use of the server's objects. On the Visual Basic CD there is a sample pool manager project, PoolMngr, that we can use to start developing our own pool manager. The PoolMngr project is very complex, and if we look at it, we can swiftly see why we'd want to think twice before implementing our own pool manager.*

> *Fortunately, Microsoft provides the Microsoft Transaction Server (MTS) product to take care of many of these details, as these issues should really form part of the operating system. In Chapter 12 we'll deal with pool management and other application server issues by putting our data-centric objects into an ActiveX DLL that can be used within MTS.*

Rather than pursuing a homemade pool manager in this chapter, we're just going to look at how to use DCOM to distribute the `VideoServer` program to another machine. In Chapter 12 we'll use MTS (Microsoft Transaction Server) to address many of the application server issues we just mentioned.

# Building the VideoServer Project

In Chapter 10 we developed the `VideoServer` project on the same machine as the `VideoObjects` and `VideoUI` projects. This is an easy approach, as we can test everything on one machine without having to worry about remote registration and other DCOM concerns.

Now, however, we need to go through the process of moving the `VideoServer` program to another machine. The first thing we need to do is make some changes to the `VideoServer` project itself.

Bring up the `VideoServer` project in Visual Basic. The changes we need to make are all within the Project Properties dialog, so choose the Project | VideoServer Properties... menu option.

## Unattended Execution

On the General tab, check the Unattended Execution option. This option is important for any server program:

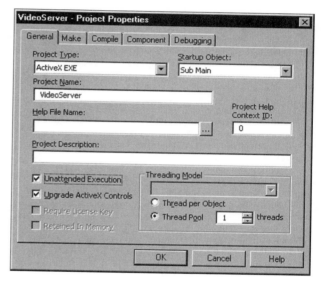

This option prevents Visual Basic from displaying any message boxes from the program and it makes sure you haven't included any forms or controls in your project. This is important because message boxes or other display elements will cause the program to expect user input. Of course the program is running on a server, not on the user's workstation and so there'd be no one there to provide the input, and typically this would hang the server program.

## Multi-threading

Visual Basic allows us to create programs that run in multiple threads of execution. This means that we can have a single program running in a single process, but that program may have multiple threads running at the same time.

Visual Basic uses apartment-model threading, which means that each thread lives in its own 'apartment'. To our code, an apartment seems like a separate process from any other apartment – there's no shared memory, no global variables between threads, and so on. In reality all the threads are running inside the same process, but to each thread that's not how it appears.

*Multi-threading is mostly important if we intend to run our* VideoServer *program on a computer with more than one CPU. On a computer with only one CPU, only one thread can run at a time, whereas with multiple CPUs it is possible for each CPU to be running a different thread - all at the same time.*

*Even with one CPU multi-threading is powerful. While one thread is waiting for a resource, perhaps waiting for the disk to retrieve data, other threads are allowed to utilize the CPU. This provides the illusion that the computer is doing more than one thing at a time, but more importantly allows multiple threads to be productive by sharing the CPU.*

## Fixed Thread Pool

By default, Visual Basic selects this option, so our program runs in a thread pool composed of a single thread. What this means is that the program will then run as it normally would, since all programs get a single thread of operation whether they are unattended or not.

We can raise the number of threads in the pool if we'd like. By doing this we are allowing Visual Basic to create more than one thread within the program's process. If we increase the thread pool count, the program's objects will be created in different threads as time goes on. There is no way to predict which of the objects will be created in which thread, Visual Basic assigns them to threads using a round-robin algorithm.

The key thing is that each thread acts like a process. This means each thread gets its own global cnVideo variable and Sub Main runs once when the thread starts up.

In our case this is less than ideal. Since many objects may run inside a single thread, but each thread has its own cnVideo we'll have many objects sharing a single database connection. This can lead to conflicts between clients, since different clients may own different objects. Especially if we add BeginTrans and CommitTrans statements to our data access code we'll find that our objects start committing transactions from other clients, and all sorts of messiness will follow.

## Thread per Object

The other option we are given is to have one thread for each object running in the server process. More accurately, there will be one thread for each *externally created* object. The TapesPersist object will get its own thread, but when it creates a TapePersist object, that object will run inside the same thread since it wasn't created by an external entity.

The threads we're talking about here work the same as with a thread pool. Each thread gets its own global cnVideo variable and runs Sub Main when it starts up.

The big difference here is that, when a client creates an object, that object runs in its own memory space, with its own database connection. Obviously this isn't ideal for large numbers of clients, since we could end up with a very large number of database connections.

However, we'll use this approach here since it is the simple way to support a number of clients without the complexity of creating a pool manager. Since each thread gets its own database connection, we don't need to worry about two clients trying to use our server at the same time and ending up using the same database connection. With this approach, each client will create its own object, and that object will automatically get its own thread - and thus its own memory and database connection.

Click the Thread per object option as shown in the screenshot:

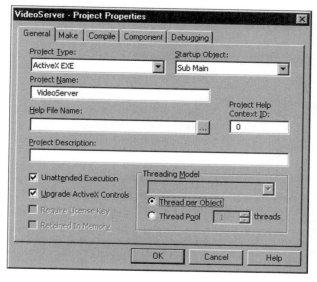

While this is the setting we'll use in this chapter, it's still not the ideal solution. With this setting, each object created by the client workstation will end up running within its own thread – each thinking it has its own process. This means that each object will have its own connection to the database, thus quickly consuming a lot of database resources and also precluding any form of transactional support for our data access.

# Creating Remote Server Files

If we're going to run this program on a remote server we need some way of making each client aware of what the server can do and where to find it on the network. This is handled by a couple of key files that Visual Basic will create for us.

Choose the Component tab in the Project Properties dialog and click on the Remote Server Files option:

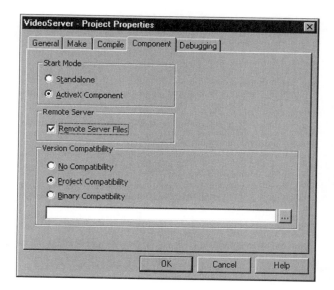

With this selected, Visual Basic will create the appropriate files next time we compile this project.

## TLB File

Our clients will need to know what the ActiveX server can do. What this really means is that the client program needs to know the interface definition of the server, basically a list of its classes and their properties and methods.

This is less a Visual Basic issue than a COM issue, because all COM servers should make this information available regardless of what language was used to develop them. They don't have to do this, but it makes the server much easier to work with when it comes to writing client programs. To make the information available, most COM servers provide a **type library** file, usually with a TLB extension.

This type library contains the definitions for all the classes and their interfaces. Using the information in this file, a developer can find out the names and data types of all the parameters, return values and anything else that is important when developing a client program.

With the Remote Server Files option checked in a project's properties, Visual Basic will create a TLB file for us that contains all this information for our program. This file is created each time the project is compiled.

## VBR File

The other file that is created with the Remote Server Files option is a VBR file. This file is specific to Visual Basic, and provides the mechanism by which the client workstation can register the ActiveX server in its registry.

When the program is running on a server machine it needs to be registered on the server. The thing is, it also needs to be registered on each client workstation along with some extra information about network connections to the server and so forth.

We'll talk about setting up a client shortly, and this VBR file will be a key piece of that discussion.

# Binary Compatibility

The last item we need to change is also on the Component tab of the Project Properties dialog. In Chapter 7 we discussed how the Version Compatibility options work and what they do in general terms.

So far we've been using either Project Compatibility or Binary Compatibility during development of our programs. This is the Visual Basic default and typically works great – during development.

When we start putting components on different machines things get more complex. While it is certainly possible to stick with Project Compatibility and still use DCOM to access your ActiveX server, it's much easier to get everything working by using Binary Compatibility.

As we discussed in Chapter 7, Binary Compatibility effectively freezes the GUID values for the program itself, along with all its classes. Project Compatibility freezes the program's GUID along with its class GUIDs, or CLSIDs, but not everything that is required to consistently connect our client applications to the server program. As we register the VideoServer program on the server and then on multiple clients, everything will be much simpler if none of the GUID values for the program are changing.

We'll need to have compiled the program at least once before we can switch to Binary Compatibility. After we've compiled it, we need to make a copy of the EXE file. Once we've done that we can return to the Project Properties window and click the <u>B</u>inary Compatibility option.

Then set the filename of the compatible server to the copy of the original EXE. In this example we've simply used the copy and paste options in Explorer to create a copy. It is important to use a copy of the server for compatibility rather than the server itself because our actual server EXE is recreated each time we compile the program. It is possible for Visual Basic to get confused and lose the server's GUID values if we make our server's EXE also be the compatible server.

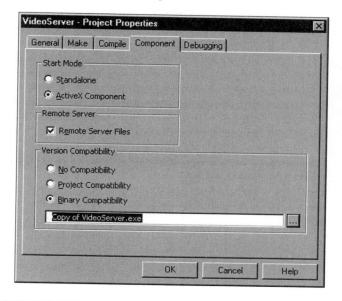

Make sure to save the project after making all these changes. We'll also want to make sure to recompile the project at least once after we've changed the **Unatt<u>e</u>nded Execution** and **R<u>e</u>mote Server File** options so they take effect.

## Check the Database Location

Keep in mind that we're going to be installing the server program on an application server somewhere on our network. For our ADO code to continue to work we need to double-check the code in Sub Main to make sure the database location is correct on the application server machine.

The dangerous part about putting code in an ActiveX server's Sub Main is that if it fails we won't get any meaningful error messages from Visual Basic. All we'll get is a generic OLE Automation error telling us that our object couldn't be created.

In this case, if the database fails to open an error will be raised, but all we'll see is a generic and unenlightening error message on the client. This type of problem can lead to hours of searching for solutions only to find that the problem was as simple as an error in Sub Main.

A good solution to this is to trap any errors in Sub Main and write them to a log file.

```
    Public Sub Main()

        On Error GoTo ErrHandler
        Set cnVideo = New Connection
```

```
    cnVideo.Provider = "Microsoft.Jet.OLEDB.3.51"
    cnVideo.Mode = adModeReadWrite
    cnVideo.Open "C:\Wrox\VB6 Pro Objects\Video.mdb"
    Exit Sub

ErrHandler:
    App.LogEvent Err.Description & " (" & Err.Number & ")", _
        vbLogEventTypeWarning

End Sub
```

In the code shown here, we are using Visual Basic's App object's LogEvent method to write the message to the Windows NT application event log. If we have this program running under Windows 95 or 98 the message will be written to a log file in the Windows system directory.

# Installing VideoServer on the Server

Now that we've got the VideoServer ActiveX server project ready to roll we can proceed to installing it on the server machine.

> *If you are using something other than NT on your application server the overall process to get everything set up will be similar. However, only NT will provide you with the full range of network protocols for your clients to connect through, and NT is substantially more stable and scalable than other versions of Windows. These are important considerations when setting up an application server.*

It's possible we've been developing the software right on the application server machine. Typically this isn't a good practice, but it certainly simplifies things. We'll be going through the process of moving the program to the server machine and getting it registered. If we've developed the program on the server machine then it is already there and it is already registered, and we can skip past the next section.

## Installing VideoServer

Before we can make the server program available to client workstations we need to install it on the application server computer. Assuming we didn't develop the program on that computer and that we don't have Visual Basic itself installed on the server computer, we'll need to install a number of files onto that machine.

Things can be simpler if we've got Visual Basic itself, or possibly other Visual Basic applications, already installed on the server machine. In this case all the supporting files for Visual Basic and probably for ADO will already be installed and all we need to do is install and register the VideoServer server.

In fact, it can be very confusing to do our development on either the server machine or a client machine. When we compile the applications Visual Basic writes entries into the registry. When we install programs through a Setup program it writes entries into the registry. These entries are almost guaranteed to get messed up and leave us unable to do anything productive at all.

Ideally we'd develop your components on one or more development machines and then use a Setup program to get them placed onto your server and client workstations.

## Using the Package and Deployment Wizard

If we don't know that all the required files exist on the application server computer we'll need to use the Package and Deployment Wizard or some equivalent tool to install all the Visual Basic and ADO support files along with our program file on the machine.

*The Package and Deployment Wizard is the replacement for what was the Setup Wizard in previous versions of Visual Basic.*

We're not going to go through the process of using the Package and Deployment Wizard in detail. There's really only one panel in the wizard that is important for our needs, though the wizard will prompt us with a potentially confusing dialog that we need to discuss as well.

*The Package and Deployment Wizard may not be available in the Add-Ins menu right from the start. If it is not listed there, we'll need to use the Add-In Manager menu option to load the wizard into our environment.*

### Remote Automation

As we go through the wizard to create our setup program, we'll be asked if our application will be used as a Remote Automation (RA) server. This can be confusing, as basically the question is whether the server will be accessed using Remote Automation as in Visual Basic 4.0. The only time you'd answer Yes would be if you plan to get at this program via Remote Automation, otherwise answer No.

*Remote Automation is useful in two areas. The most typical use is for 16-bit client workstations, which have no support for DCOM. The other use is for Windows 95 workstations that don't have a TCP/IP connection to our application server. DCOM for Windows 95 only supports the TCP/IP network protocol, so if we're not using that protocol on our network we'll need to use Remote Automation.*

In this chapter we'll assume we're using DCOM, not Remote Automation, and so No is appropriate.

### Shared Files

Launch the wizard and go through all the panels until we reach the Shared Files panel:

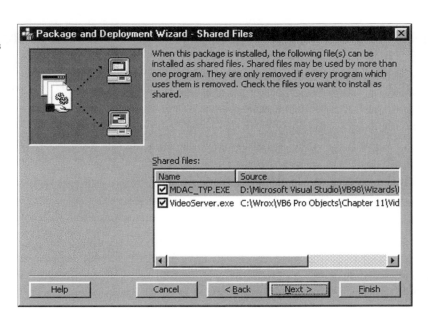

We need to make sure to check the box by our application on this panel. This option is appropriate for a shared server like `VideoServer`. If we end up with various applications that make use of our server we want to make sure that the server isn't uninstalled until all the client applications are removed.

### Completing the Install

Once we've completed the process of running the Package and Deployment Wizard, just take the resulting installation files and install the program on the application server. This will put all the required files in the correct directories and get them registered as needed.

That's not the last step, because the component still needs to be set up to work with DCOM. We'll get to that shortly.

> **It's wise not to install a new version of an ActiveX component on a machine where one is already installed. First uninstall the component by using its uninstall program. Worse, though, is deleting a registered server. When Explorer tells you that the server is registered and you say Yes to moving it to the Recycle Bin, it will helpfully change the `LocalServer32` path to point to the Recycle Bin. Now when you empty the bin, the registry will be wrong.**

## Manual Registration

For subsequent installations or upgrades to an ActiveX component we can handle the register and unregister process manually. If all the required support files are in place and properly registered we can just unregister the old program, copy in the new version and register it.

### Unregister the Previous Version

To unregister a previous installation of `VideoServer`, go to the Windows Start menu and choose the Run option. Then run the `VideoServer` program itself using the `/unregserver` switch on the command line:

### Copy and Register the New Version

Once we're sure that the program is no longer registered, we can copy the upgraded version into place and register it using a similar technique.

Choose the Run option from the Windows Start menu and run the program using the `/regserver` switch on the command line. This will register the program in the Windows registry:

# DCOM Configuration

Once the appropriate version of the VideoServer ActiveX server is installed and registered on the application server machine all we need to do is get it set up for DCOM. This isn't a difficult thing to do; in fact it is pretty much all set to go by default. The only thing we typically need to do is set the security permissions on the VideoServer server so clients can create and use its objects.

DCOM provides a program, Dcomcnfg.exe, that we can use to set the permissions on our server program. By default there is no icon or shortcut to this program. To run it, choose the Run option from the Windows Start menu and enter dcomcnfg:

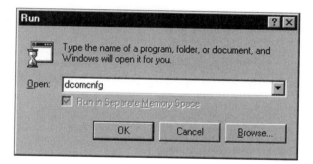

## *Enabling DCOM*

The program provides three tabs. The first thing we need to do is make sure that DCOM is actually enabled on this computer. It is by default, but it is well worth checking to make sure someone hasn't disabled it, as we may think that our program doesn't compile, when, in reality, DCOM just isn't enabled.

Choose the Default Properties tab and check to make sure the Enable Distributed COM on this computer option is checked:

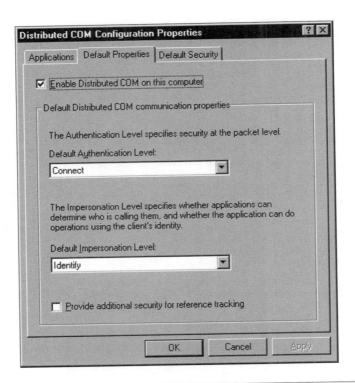

The other options on this panel are important, but should be set to workable values by default. For more details about these options you can refer to *Professional DCOM Programming* (ISBN 1-816000-60X) from Wrox Press.

## Setting VideoServer Permissions

Once we're sure that DCOM is enabled on this computer we can move on to setting the permissions on the `VideoServer` ActiveX server. The default security settings don't allow remote users to start up or use objects within a server. This is typically a good thing, since we probably don't want people starting up any old server and using its objects.

### Selecting the VideoServer Application

We need to switch back to the Applications tab and select the `VideoServer` server from the list displayed there:

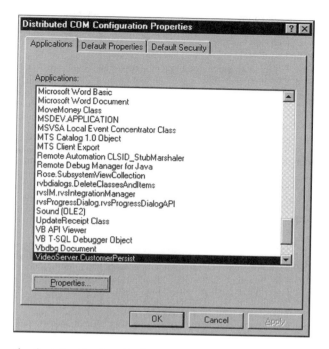

Don't be confused by the fact that it also displays a class name, in this case `CustomerPersist`. Even though the program displays one of the server's classes in the list, we are really operating on the server itself rather than any specific class inside the server.

Once we've chosen the server, click on the Properties... button to bring up the properties for `VideoServer`:

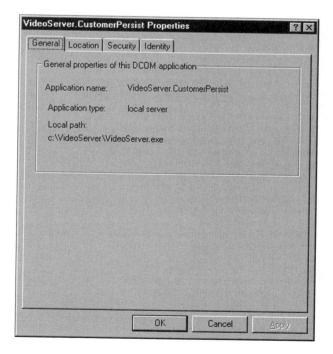

The General tab displays information about the ActiveX server, including its name, whether it is running 'local' or 'remote' and the path to the component itself. The path can be quite useful during debugging, as we can use this to make sure that DCOM is running the program we think it is running.

For instance, things can get very complex if we don't uninstall the program before reinstalling or recompiling it. We can end up with duplicate entries for the server in the registry and it can be difficult to know which one is which without referring back to the path.

### Setting VideoServer Permissions

For our purposes at the moment, however, we are interested in the Security tab. The default security won't allow client workstations to use the VideoServer server, so we need to switch the options on this server to use custom permissions. This is true for both accessing and launching the server application as shown in the screenshot:

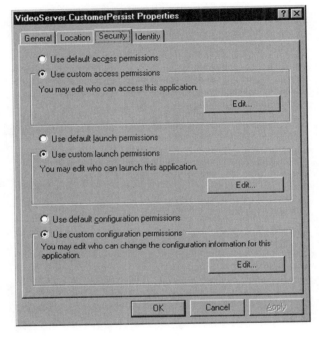

For both the access and launch permissions we need to click on the Edit... button and customize the permissions. The changes are the same for both permissions, so we'll just walk through the steps, then they need to be repeated for both cases.

Click the Edit... button to bring up the Registry Value Permissions dialog.

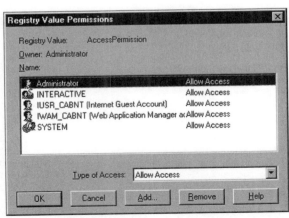

By default, the only users that have any access are ones local to this machine. We can set the permissions as required by the specific environment, but the easiest approach is to add the Everyone group to this list. Keep in mind that this opens up the server machine for anyone to start our object – something that might not be desirable for anything beyond testing.

To do this, click the <u>A</u>dd... button to bring up the Add Users and Groups dialog.

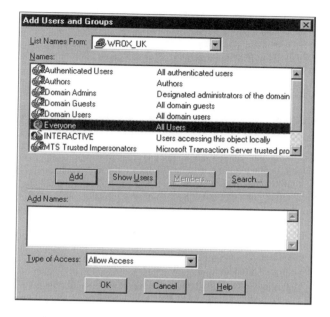

Then double-click the Everyone entry on the list and click OK. The result should be that the Everyone group is added to the list of people who can either access or launch the `VideoServer` server application:

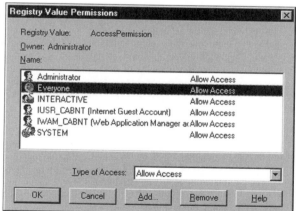

Click OK on this dialog and repeat the process for the launch permissions.

### Set the Identity Account

There is one last thing we need to change. On the main properties screen, switch to the Identity tab. By default the user account is set to The <u>l</u>aunching user. This option means that our server application will be run under the user account of the user logged into the client workstation.

If that user has no account on our NT server, they won't be able to run our server application – thus they won't be able to get at our objects.

This setting can also cause performance issues, since DCOM will start up a separate process for each user account that accesses our server. This happens regardless of the threading model or instancing settings that we have set up in our project or its objects.

The best thing to do is to choose to run the server under a specific user account, supplying the user and password information on this tab:

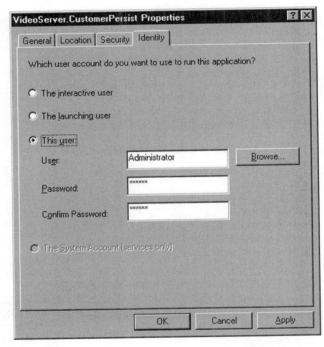

This way, DCOM will run our server program under this user account, regardless of who each client might be. Also, all client users will have their objects running within the same process – subject to the threading and object instancing settings we chose when developing our out-of-process server.

# Building the VideoObjects Project

Throughout the last chapter, we've been developing the `VideoObjects` project with a reference to either the `VideoServer` project itself, or the `VideoServer` EXE file. At this point we need to change this reference to use the `VideoServer` project's TLB, or type library, file.

### Using the TLB File from VideoServer

The TLB file is the final authority on the `VideoServer` server's public interface and GUID values for identification. This is the file that will be defining the `VideoServer` server on each client workstation where your program will be running. Thus it is very important that our client project, `VideoObjects`, also use the TLB file to get its information.

Before going any further, we'll need access to the most recent TLB file for `VideoServer`. If it's not already on our development machine, we'll want to copy it to the Windows 98 `\System` directory or the Windows NT `\System32` directory as appropriate. This is the location that the TLB file will end up being installed by the setup program we'll be creating shortly and so we might as well put it there as well.

### Changing the VideoObjects Server's Reference

To make this change, bring up the `VideoObjects` project in Visual Basic and open its Project References dialog. Deselect the `VideoServer` entry from the list. By looking at the Location field at the bottom of the panel we can tell whether it's using the VBP or EXE file to gets its information.

> *Before switching the reference, we need to make sure that* `VideoServer` *is not registered on our development machine. If we're developing* `VideoObjects` *on a different machine than* `VideoServer` *we probably don't have a problem, but if we've been developing on the same machine then* `VideoServer` *will be registered. Before trying to add a reference to our TLB file we need to dereference* `VideoServer` *using by running* `VideoServer.exe` *with the* `/unregserver` *command-line switch.*

Next, click the Browse button and select the `VideoServer.TLB` file. An entry will be added to the list of available references so we can check it and we're all set.

The Location field near the bottom of the dialog shows that the reference is now using a TLB file to get its information:

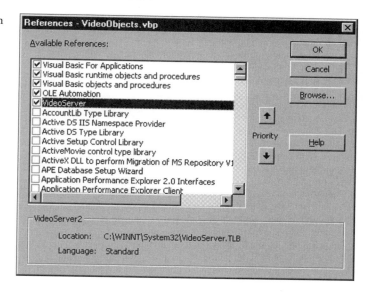

# Setting up the Client

Though `VideoServer` is installed and configured on the application server machine, we still need to make it available to every client machine that needs to use it. This means that we need to register `VideoServer` on each client in a special way so that the client workstation knows to find the server's objects via DCOM.

There are two ways we can do this, either by using a setup tool such as the Visual Basic Package and Deployment Wizard or manually using a program supplied with Visual Basic called `Clireg32.exe`.

# Using the Package and Deployment Wizard

In previous versions of Visual Basic, the Setup Wizard has been pretty inflexible and undependable. The new Package and Deployment Wizard wizard is much more powerful and provides us with the capabilities we need to deploy our application. The wizard makes it very easy to create setup and deployment packages for our `VideoUI` application. Before we can create that setup program however, we need to create a **dependency file** for our `VideoObjects` DLL so the wizard knows how to not only install the DLL, but also to connect it to our `VideoServer` application on the server machine.

## *Creating a Dependency File for VideoObjects*

We'll be creating a setup program to install the client program, `VideoUI`. However, `VideoUI` requires the `VideoObjects` DLL in order to run and so this file will be included automatically by the wizard in the `VideoUI` setup program. The trick is that our `VideoObjects` DLL itself has a requirement for the `VideoServer` application and needs to know where it is and how to connect to it.

Visual Basic 6.0's Package and Deployment Wizard uses a DEP file, or dependency file, to make sure it has any required support files for each ActiveX component that is included for setup. This means that the wizard will expect a DEP file to exist for the `VideoObjects` ActiveX component so it can make sure it gets any support files required by the DLL.

Let's walk through the process of creating the DEP file for our `VideoObjects` DLL.

### *Copy the VideoServer TLB File*

To start off, we need to make sure that the development machine has access to the required files from `VideoServer`. Both the current TLB and VBR files should be copied to the Windows 95 `\System` directory or the Windows NT `\System32` directory. These files will be used by the setup wizard to define the `VideoServer` server's requirements for the dependency file.

Creating a dependency file is basically the same as creating a regular setup program. Open the `VideoObjects` project and run the **Package and Deployment Wizard** from the **Add-Ins** menu:

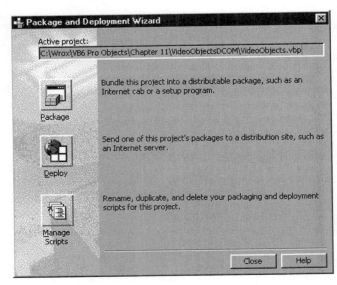

Choose the <u>P</u>ackage option from this dialog, as we'll be creating a form of setup package for our DLL. At this point the wizard will scan our application looking for dependencies and to make sure all our files are current. The wizard may offer to recompile our DLL if any source files are newer than the currently compiled version of the DLL.

### Generate Dependency File

At the next dialog we have an option to create either a regular setup program, an Internet setup program or a dependency file. We'll want to choose the dependency file option:

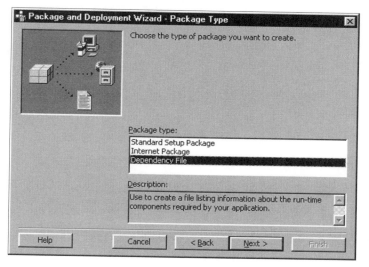

The next dialog simply asks us where we'd like to create the DEP file. It isn't clear why this question is even asked, since the DEP file *must* reside in the same directory as our DLL. We'll need to make sure to choose the same directory where we have the DLL.

### Handling dependencies for VideoServer.exe

At this point the wizard will come up with a warning dialog to inform us that it doesn't have any dependency information for our `VideoServer` application.

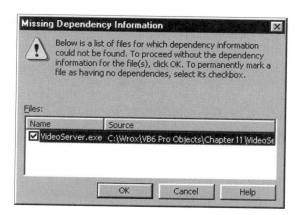

This is true, since we've never run the wizard against the `VideoServer` project to create a DEP file for it. That's OK though, since we really don't want to install the server application itself on the client workstations. Instead we'll want to establish a connection between the client machine and the server on which our `VideoServer` application will be running. Since we don't need any dependency information from `VideoServer`, we can simply check the box on this dialog and proceed – then we won't be asked this question in the future either.

### Adding the correct list of dependency files

This next dialog is where the real fun happens:

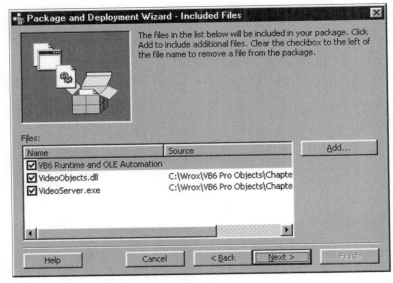

The dialog lists those files which are required for our `VideoObjects` DLL to function. Notice that the wizard has identified both the VB6 runtime and our `VideoServer.exe` as being required. Of course we know we don't want the `VideoServer.exe` file itself installed on the client workstations. Instead, we'll want to change that reference from the EXE to the `VideoServer` project's VBR file.

As we discussed earlier in this chapter, the VBR file contains the information required by a client to register and work with a remote ActiveX server, such as our `VideoServer` application.

Simply uncheck the box for `VideoServer.exe` and then click the **Add** button to add a new file to our dependency list. Use the subsequent dialog to select the `VideoServer.VBR` file and click OK.

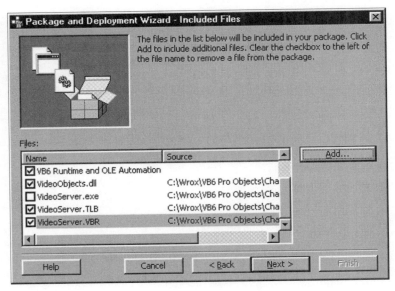

The wizard is pretty intelligent regarding VBR files. It not only adds a reference to the VBR file itself, but also brings in entries for the TLB file and a couple other files that are required for deployment: AUTPRX32.DLL and CLIREG32.EXE. We'll discuss CLIREG32.EXE later in the chapter, but for now all we need to know is that these files are required for our VideoObjects DLL to connect to the VideoServer EXE on another machine.

### Completing the Package and Deployment Wizard

The rest of the wizard is just like creating a setup program, except that instead of a setup program we'll get a DEP file for the VideoObjects ActiveX component. The file will be named VideoObjects.DEP, using the same name as the DLL file.

## Setup for VideoUI

Now we're ready to create an actual setup program for the VideoUI client program. We'll make use of the dependency file that we just created for VideoObjects in this process.

Open the VideoUI project and start the Package and Deployment Wizard from the Add-Ins menu. Simply create a standard setup package, just like for any other program we'd like to install. The wizard will run through the steps to create a setup program as usual.

### Listing the Included Files

When we get to the Included Files panel of the wizard, it will automatically identify the requirement for VideoObjects.DLL. Then using the DEP file we created earlier, it will not only include our DLL, but also all the files required for connecting to our VideoServer application:

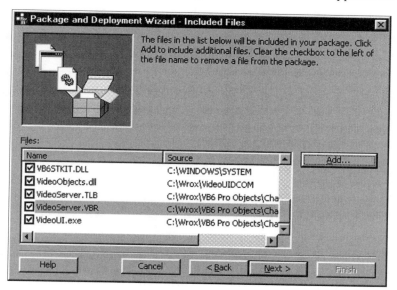

### Setting up Remote Servers

VideoUI requires our VideoObjects and it, in turn, requires access to a remote ActiveX server, VideoServer. The wizard detects this and brings up a new dialog to help us set up the connection from the client to our ActiveX server:

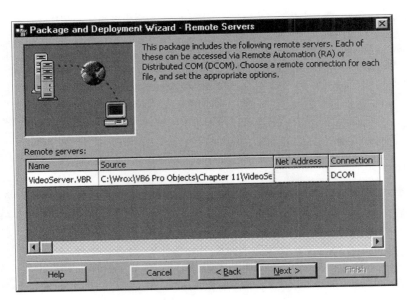

Each VBR file indicates a connection to a remote ActiveX server. The wizard displays a list of the VBR files required by our application and allows us to specify the network address or machine name where that server will be found. It also allows us to choose between using DCOM or Remote Automation for connecting to that server.

*As we mentioned earlier, Remote Automation is generally only useful for 16-bit clients or Windows 95 clients that don't have TCP/IP access to the server that will be running our server application.*

We'll want to click in the Net Address column and enter the machine name or IP address of the machine where we'll be running our VideoServer application. Then simply click the Next button to proceed. Our final setup program will contain the information about where our ActiveX server will be run so it can properly register it on the client workstation.

### Completing the Client Install

Once the wizard is complete we should have a setup program that we can run on our clients. This setup program will install the VideoUI client program and the VideoObjects DLL. It will also add the required entries in the system's registry so the VideoServer server will be available through DCOM.

It's also worth noting that the VideoServer.TLB and VideoServer.VBR files will be installed into the Windows 95\98 \System or Windows NT \System32 directory on each client workstation.

# Using CLIREG32

If we change and recompile the `VideoServer` project, Visual Basic will create new VBR and TLB files. There may be cases where we change a server like this, but where we don't need to change and redistribute the `VideoObjects.dll` file. For instance, perhaps we've added functionality to `VideoServer` for some other client DLL and `VideoObjects.dll` wasn't affected.

In a case like this we may choose to manually update the client machine's registries with the new `VideoServer` server information rather than using the **Package and Deployment Wizard** to create a setup program to handle it.

## *Unregister VideoServer*

If we've already got the remote `VideoServer` server registered on this client it's important to unregister it before proceeding. Just like any other registry activity, if we register an already-registered program and the UUIDs (CLSID, TypeLibID, IID and AppID) are different from the previous version, we are asking for double entries in the registry and all sorts of confusion.

In the `\Clisvr` directory under your Visual Basic installation there is a program named `Clireg32.exe`. This program will register and unregister a remote server by using its VBR and TLB files. This program should have been installed on the client workstation when we installed our `VideoUI` application, since it is automatically included by the **Package and Deployment Wizard**.

It's easiest to run this program from the DOS prompt, though we can use the Run option from the Windows Start menu as well.

The command to unregister the server is:

```
CLIREG32.EXE C:\WINNT\SYSTEM32\VIDEOSERVER.VBR -u
```

## *Copy VideoServer's TLB and VBR Files to \System32*

After we've unregistered the remote server, we can proceed to update the VBR and TLB files in the Windows system directory. To do this, just copy the updated `VideoServer.TLB` and `VideoServer.VBR` files into the client workstation's Windows system directory. This will be `\System` for Windows 95 or `\System32` for Windows NT.

Most likely we'll be replacing existing files with the new ones, though we can certainly use this technique to register a remote server for the first time as well. If this is a first time installation we won't have to unregister the server of course.

## *Register VideoServer.VBR*

Once the TLB and VBR files are in place we are ready to register the remote server on the client.

The command to register a remote server is:

```
CLIREG32.EXE C:\WINNT\SYSTEM32\VIDEOSERVER.VBR
```

The program will display a copyright dialog, then move on to the dialog shown in the screenshot:

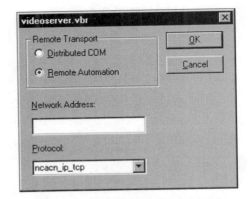

In our case we'll want to switch the Remote Transport to Distributed COM and enter the Network Address of our application server machine:

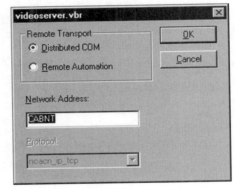

The end result here is the same as if we'd run our earlier setup program on this client workstation. The VideoServer ActiveX server is registered as a remote client, with DCOM knowing how to find and invoke the server when needed.

# Summary

Here, at the end of the chapter, we should be able to run the `VideoUI` client, or the Excel client we created in Chapter 9 for that matter. The clients will work with the business objects in `VideoObjects.dll` as always, without change.

Of course the UI-centric business objects themselves will now be communicating through DCOM to the `VideoServer` server application that is running on our application server machine.

Due the highly-efficient marshalling we implemented in Chapter 10 to transfer data to and from the application server, we should find that performance is barely degraded when compared to running the `VideoServer` server on the same machine as the client. Obviously this will vary greatly depending on the network configuration and load.

In Chapter 12 we'll take the `VideoServer` server and convert it to run inside Microsoft Transaction Server. This will provide our application with much greater scalability, as well as providing transaction support for our database activity.

Then in Chapter 13 we'll look at implementing a web interface to our business objects by using Active Server Pages.

# 12

# Running Server Components in MTS

## Overview

In Chapters 10 and 11, we converted our video rental store application from a one or two-tier implementation into a three-tier implementation. We used DCOM between the client and application server, and arranged for the application server to access the database.

*Technically, our implementation, though a three-tier logical architecture, was physically two-tier, since the application server used a JET database. It's easy to change the code to talk to a SQL database, such as Oracle or Microsoft SQL Server, something we're going to do in this chapter, then we can count it as a physical three-tier implementation.*

Our focus was clearly on the important issues surrounding how the client objects communicate with the application server. Without a solid foundation for this communication, our application would have suffered from serious performance problems as a result of networking and DCOM overhead.

To sustain that focus, we intentionally ignored some important issues:

❑ Scalability of an application for a large number of clients
❑ Multi-user support
❑ Database transactions - atomic units of work where a set of database updates are either all completed successfully (committed) or completely undone (rolled back)

Now that we've gone through the basic principles of communication between client and server machines, we're ready to properly consider these issues.

In this chapter, we'll use Microsoft Transaction Server (MTS) on our application server machine to address these issues. This will require some modification to the `VideoServer` project, but there'll be no impact on our client-side business objects or UI code, which illustrates one of the main benefits of our distributed architecture.

> **Throughout this chapter, we'll be using Microsoft Transaction Server version 2.0. This is the version of MTS that is distributed along with Visual Studio 6.0 Enterprise Edition and the Windows NT 4.0 Option Pack.**

We'll start off by taking a good look at the issues of scalability, multi-user support and database transactions. We'll then move on to consider the some of the philosophy and practical implications of MTS objects, before we get down to the really interesting task of getting our `VideoServer` server running on MTS.

# Supporting Multiple Clients

Until fairly recently, we'd have had to provide scalable multi-user support by implementing a pool or queue manager of some sort. This manager would create and maintain our server-side objects, making them available to clients on request, but with a level of control on the server - for example, for user access and resource allocation.

This manager would also need to provide some form of database-connection pooling. Opening a database connection can be a time consuming process. If a new connection needs to be opened each time a client tries to use an object, our performance will suffer greatly. To avoid this, some entity on the server (usually the pool manager) keeps a pool of open database connections for general use by server-side objects.

## *Keeping Objects Alive*

From a performance standpoint, it's very important that the `VideoServer` objects don't disappear every time a client is done with them. There's a fair amount of overhead in starting a new process under Windows. If the `VideoServer` server is not running when a client makes a request, Windows needs to run this server to start a new process. As soon as no clients are talking to the server the process would shut down, putting us back at having to start a new process for the next client.

On the other side of the coin, the application server machine has only so much memory, and the CPU can handle only so many threads before performance degrades. If we keep all our server programs and their objects loaded all the time, such that there are enough for all our clients, the server machine will probably run out of memory (causing excessive paging of memory to disk), or CPU bandwidth, or both. These performance problems will get worse as we scale up the application across the enterprise, or the Internet.

Microsoft recognized that this was a universal problem for designers of distributed systems. The result is MTS, which provides us with a solution to the problem of managing the demands of multiple clients for our objects. Microsoft has recognized the importance of these services and so they intend to incorporate MTS directly into the NT operating system.

MTS has been described as a *transactional ORB*. We'll talk about the transactional part later, but the ORB description directly applies to what we're talking about here. ORB stands for **object request broker**, which is basically a piece of software that manages objects on a server machine and provides a standard way to access them from clients. MTS may or may not qualify as an ORB, but it certainly provides us with a way to manage our server-side objects - without having to write our own object-management software.

### Keeping the DLL Loaded

The basic functionality of keeping our ActiveX server loaded in memory for a few minutes is totally transparent, that is we don't perform any special coding for our program to take advantage of this feature!

Of course, the server DLLs aren't kept around forever. If MTS did that, the server machine would run out of memory. Instead, MTS can be set to keep inactive DLLs around for a certain number of minutes; then they are released.

> *The default setting is three minutes of inactivity before an ActiveX server DLL is unloaded from memory.*

### Keeping Objects Loaded

The object pooling capability of MTS appears to be a powerful feature that we'd want to take advantage of. Object pooling is the idea that an object, or instance of a class, would be kept loaded in memory by MTS – even after the client program has released the object. This same object could then be used by subsequent clients who request a reference to another object of the same class. After all, if we can keep objects instantiated and loaded in memory we should expect to see some performance benefits as opposed to creating an object each time we need it.

While there are certainly some potential performance benefits to be gained from object pooling, they aren't as great as we might at first expect. Certainly there is some overhead involved in simply creating and terminating an object, but the real benefit would be gained by not having to run any intensive initialisation code that our object's perform as they are instantiated.

The objects in our `VideoServer` server don't have `Class_Initialize` routines. Thus, they don't have any substantial processing that occurs as each object is created. We do have a `Sub Main` procedure that opens our database connection, but virtually all the overhead of that activity will be handled by how MTS manages database connection pooling as we'll discuss later.

This is all very fortunate for us, since MTS 2.0 doesn't support object pooling .

> **MTS 2.0 does not support object pooling.**

In our case, our objects don't do any extra processing as they are instantiated. The biggest performance boost we'll gain by placing our components in MTS is from the fact that the DLL itself will remain loaded in memory, making object creation a very fast and efficient process.

### Limiting the Number of Objects

Many pool managers provide a way to limit the number of objects created on the application server. MTS, on the other hand, provides no mechanism to limit the number of objects that can exist at any given time.

If two clients request the same object at the same time, MTS will create two instances of the object so that each client can have one. A new object is created every time a client requests an instance and there isn't one already available. This means that if a couple of hundred clients request the same object, MTS might try to create a couple of hundred instances of the object!

> *This may seem like an unlikely scenario, but consider an object that verifies a user's identity.*
> *This object could be used as users log into an application, and at the beginning of the workday*
> *there may be hundreds of users trying to log in within a very small span of time.*

The long term answer for MTS appears to be in future versions of Windows NT, where MTS can spread the objects across several NT machines in a cluster. This would be transparent to the client applications, but would allow a form of load balancing across several machines - hopefully allowing MTS to create enough objects to handle the peak load.

## Database Connections

The other major performance concern deals with database connections. Opening a connection to a database can take quite a bit of time - often enough time to be a performance problem for our end users.

MTS provides a solution to this problem as well, in the form of database connection pooling. This means that when an object opens a connection to the database, and then closes it when it's done, the database connection resource manager within MTS steps in and actually keeps the connection open. The next time an object needs a connection to the database, MTS transparently provides one of the pre-opened connections when the object makes its call to ODBC to get a connection.

The database connection resource manager isn't really part of MTS at all. The OLE DB provider for SQL Server is one such resource manager, and ODBC 3.5 is also a resource manager. By providing database connection pooling through resource managers in this fashion, MTS can support connection pooling for any sufficiently advanced data access technology.

Note that we've only listed OLE DB for SQL Server and ODBC. Not every database provider supports connection pooling through MTS. For instance, database connection pooling isn't available to a program that's using an ISAM database such as JET.

Assuming that our program is using a supported OLE DB provider (such as SQL Server or Oracle) or an ODBC 3.5 or higher connection to the database then database connection pooling is directly available to us.

There are a couple rules to be aware of regarding this pooling however. Connections are reused based on the `Connect` string used when opening the connection. If a connection is opened with one Connect string, it will only be reused by subsequent programs that use the exact same `Connect` string.

The biggest impact here is that the `Connect` string includes the user id and password being used to connect to the database. This means that database connections are pooled *by user* for each database. To make the most effective use of connection pooling we'll want to connect to the database using the same user id and password as much as possible.

> Often this means that we'll create a user id for our *application* rather than for each actual user that might connect.

# Database Transactions

Our application in Chapter 10 provided no support for database transactions. For instance, when we saved a `Video` object and all its `Tape` objects, it was possible for one of the `Tape` objects to fail to save. If this were to happen, we could end up with some objects saved and others not, and our database would contain inaccurate and incomplete data.

Ideally, we'd start a database transaction before saving the `Video` object, then commit it once all the `Tape` objects were saved. If any problems occurred during the save process, we could then roll back the entire transaction, resulting in nothing being saved. While we could certainly handle this by adding a bit of code to our `VideoServer` server to support transactions, we intentionally left this out of the picture until now so we could see how MTS handles the problem.

Earlier, we noted that MTS is sometimes described as a *transactional ORB*. We've already discussed the ORB part of the description, so let's look at its transactional support.

Just as MTS provides database connection pooling, it also provides database transactions on our behalf. Behind the scenes, things are a bit more complex. MTS actually uses Microsoft's Distributed Transaction Coordinator (DTC) to handle the transactions; but for our purposes, it's enough to know that we can tell MTS which objects require or support transactions and modify each object to indicate whether it completed successfully. MTS will handle the details from there.

If any of our data access doesn't go through a data source supported by DTC, then we can't rely on MTS to provide transaction support for that data access. For instance, if one of our objects writes to a simple text file, then MTS does nothing to help us roll back our changes or even know that we need to roll them back ourselves.

To implement this feature, we're required to make some changes to our application: both in the `VideoServer` and the `VideoObjects` projects. MTS needs to know which objects perform actions as a result of other objects, so they can all be coordinated as a transaction. We'll get into the specific details later in this chapter.

# Stateless Objects

MTS was designed with a certain philosophy of how an application server should be constructed. To make objects fit seamlessly into the MTS environment, it's easiest to adopt and follow that philosophy in our object design.

In Chapter 10, when we separated our business objects into UI-centric and data-centric objects, we also separated the management of state between the objects. Our UI-centric objects in the `VideoObjects.dll` retain state – they maintain consistent information across many property or method calls. Our data-centric objects in `VideoServer.exe`, on the other hand, are stateless – they don't retain any meaningful information from one method call to the next.

The basic philosophy of MTS indicates that objects should not retain state. Instead, objects should provide methods that accept parameters with all the data they'll need to function. Then, when the method is complete, the object should retain no information: instead relying on the calling code to provide any required data as parameters for subsequent method calls.

While the concept of stateless objects is very important, it can reduce our objects to nothing more than a collection of self-contained procedures. This means that the objects running inside of MTS don't meet the normal definition of an object, being composed of an interface, behaviors and, of course, state.

There is a tradeoff here. Objects with state are much more powerful and flexible, and are able to provide more functionality on the application server. On the other hand, stateless objects fit better into a transactional scheme, where the goal is to get in, call a function, and get out as fast as possible.

> **Basically, it boils down to stateful objects having more capabilities, with stateless objects providing better performance.**

This is where CLSA comes in handy. With this architecture we are able to take advantage of the best of both worlds. Our UI-centric objects are stateful, and so we can take advantage of the power and flexibility they provide. At the same time, our data-centric objects are stateless. Since they are running on a central server being shared by many users, this is important as we gain all the performance and scalability benefits provided by stateless objects.

# ActiveX DLL Servers

Objects that are to run in MTS must be contained in an ActiveX DLL. By default, MTS will create instances of the objects from within the DLL such that they run in a process controlled by MTS itself, though it can create instances of objects that are running in another process, such as IIS. By residing in a DLL, our objects allow MTS to handle issues such as creation, termination and threading.

Our `VideoServer` server is an ActiveX EXE. Since DCOM can only create instances of objects from an EXE server, that was our only choice. MTS 'tricks' DCOM - making DCOM believe that it can create instances of objects from a DLL. Of course, DCOM ends up talking to MTS, and it is MTS that creates the objects from the DLL.

If we're going to move our server-side objects into MTS, we'll need to convert the `VideoServer` project to an ActiveX DLL. Fortunately, this is a very simple change, and we'll get into the details later in the chapter.

# Context

One of the more advanced, but very important concepts for objects running in the MTS environment is that of **context**. When MTS provides a reference to an object, it also creates another object behind the scenes. This other object exists to maintain the context in which our object will run.

Every object that's running in the MTS environment has one of these `ObjectContext` objects associated with it. This object allows MTS to provide both database transaction support and security features to our objects.

## Transactions

The ObjectContext includes information about any current transaction that is taking place. We already discussed transactional support and what it can do for us. This Context object is a key part of how MTS implements transactions.

The Context object waits for each object that is part of the transaction to indicate whether it succeeded or failed. If it succeeded, our object will call the SetComplete method on the Context object; if it failed, it will call the SetAbort method. Either way, the Context object ends up knowing whether or not all the objects involved in the transaction succeeded. If they did not, MTS uses DTC to roll back any database changes performed by any of the objects.

Later in the chapter, we'll see how we can use the Context object to provide transactional support for our Video object and its children. We'll make some changes to the objects in both the VideoServer and VideoObjects servers so they take advantage of the MTS context object to run within a transaction.

## Security

Another function of the Context object is that of security. MTS implements security on two levels. With MTS, we can restrict which users can access specific interfaces or specific objects. We can also add code to our objects to restrict their behavior - based on the role of the client that's working with the object.

MTS security is handled through a concept of **roles**. A role can have a list of Windows NT users or user groups assigned to it. Then we can set MTS to allow only certain roles to have access to our objects or object interfaces. Within our object's code, we can also check the current client's role by calling the IsCallerInRole method of the MTS Context object.

> *We won't get into MTS security in this chapter. It can be a very complex and involved topic, and it's best addressed by a book specifically about implementing components in MTS. Try Professional MTS Programming also by Wrox Press (ISBN: 1861002440)*

# Object Creation and References

Another area where MTS imposes some constraints is when we're creating objects or passing references to objects as parameters or return values of methods. When an object is created within the MTS environment, MTS needs to know about that object so it can create a Context object for it - and so it can manage it appropriately.

In this section, we're only going to discuss objects created by other objects that are running in the MTS environment. What we're concerned with here are objects created by other MTS objects, and references to MTS objects, that might be passed back to the client.

## Object Lifetimes in MTS

Visual Basic objects within the MTS environment have different lifetimes than other objects. In particular, MTS may destroy an object even though our client application still thinks it retains a reference to that object.

If the object has called the SetComplete or SetAbort methods of the ObjectContext object, then MTS will instantly deactivate and destroy that object – leaving the client thinking it still has a reference to the object. This is not a problem! If the client tries to use its reference to the object, MTS will actually create a new instance of the object behind the scenes.

This means that our client programs can be written to hold references to objects in MTS without worrying about consuming large amounts of memory or other resources on the server machine. MTS will destroy and recreate objects transparently to the client, meaning that objects will only exist as long as they are physically needed.

## Creating MTS Objects with Visual Basic

To make all these capabilities possible, it's important that MTS be aware of what objects are created and which clients hold references to them. Visual Basic provides two ways to create objects: the New keyword and the CreateObject method. MTS works with each of these differently, and also provides a third method for creating an object: CreateInstance. Let's take a look at these three methods now.

### The New Keyword

The New keyword acts just like CreateObject when creating an object from another ActiveX server, but it actually bypasses some COM processing when it creates an instance of a class that's within the same ActiveX server.

The New keyword *must* be used to create objects from classes with Instancing properties of 1-Private or 2-PublicNotCreateable. If we try to use CreateObject to create instances of these classes, it's treated as though an external client were trying to create the object - and since they can't be created by external clients, we'll get an error.

For classes that can be publicly created, the exact opposite is true. Because the New keyword sometimes bypasses COM, we should *never* use it to create objects with Instancing properties of 3 or higher.

If we create an object with the New keyword, that object will be created without MTS support. It will run inside the same thread and context as our current object, but MTS doesn't know it's there, and in fact it doesn't care. The object will function as regular code, like that found in a BAS module within the component.

Any attempt to pass a reference to an object created with the New keyword will fail, regardless of the Instancing property set on the class. And as soon as we try to provide a reference to this object - to a client or other MTS object - MTS will notice that we're attempting to provide a reference to something it doesn't know about, and it will prevent the reference from working.

### The CreateObject Method

Another way we can create objects using Visual Basic is the CreateObject method. CreateObject *always* uses COM to create instances of a class, regardless of whether that class is in the current ActiveX server or in a different server. CreateObject is always acceptable within the MTS environment, although it doesn't offer all the capabilities that we might want.

When an object is created using CreateObject, it's as if that object were created by a client, even though it may actually have been created by another object inside MTS. This is perfectly acceptable from the viewpoint of our objects and also MTS.

The caveat with using CreateObject is that the object reference returned should not be passed back to a client. The creating object can use the reference all it wants, without any problem; but that reference should not be provided to any other objects or clients as a parameter or the result of a function.

### The CreateInstance Method

CreateObject references not only shouldn't be passed back to clients, but objects created this way don't provide MTS security or transaction support. In these cases, we want to create each new object such that it will inherit the current object's context information about security and transactions.

This is where the `ObjectContext` object's `CreateInstance` method comes into play. `CreateInstance` is called just like `CreateObject`, but behind the scenes it does some extra work.

When a new object is created with `CreateInstance`, MTS copies the creating object's context information to the new object's `ObjectContext` object. This means that the new object's context has the same security and transaction environment as the creating object.

As we'll see when we implement the `VideoPersist` and `TapePersist` objects with transactional support, the use of `CreateInstance` is an integral part of the process.

References to objects created using `CreateInstance` can be safely passed back to clients or to other MTS objects. Since MTS itself was part of the creation process for these objects, everything is all set for MTS to manage any client references created through `CreateInstance`.

## Error Handling

In our `VideoServer` project, we didn't take any steps to handle errors that might be encountered while accessing the database. This was intentional, since any errors that might occur would automatically be raised back through DCOM to the client. Then the client would be able to trap and deal with the error as desired.

MTS 2.0 handles errors the same way, allowing us to have our `VideoServer` application simply raise any error and it will be returned back to the client just like normal.

The only caveat to this comes when we start implementing transactional support within our data-centric objects. As we've discussed, we need to either call `SetComplete` or `SetAbort` within our components to tell MTS whether the method call was successful or not. If we encounter an error within a method call we'll need to make sure to call the `SetAbort` method on our `ObjectContext` object.

To handle this, we'll add code to trap errors so we can call `SetAbort` in the case of an error. We'll also want to let the client know that an error occurred so it can react to it as desired. To provide this functionality we'll simply re-raise the same error from within our error handling code.

# Getting VideoServer Ready for MTS

Now that we've got the basics of MTS down, let's move on to get our `VideoServer` ActiveX server running in the MTS environment.

To keep things simple, it's best to make a copy of the `VideoServer` server code into a new directory. We'll be making a number of changes to this program, not the least of which is changing it from an ActiveX EXE to an ActiveX DLL. While we could certainly just change the current program over, this approach will give us an opportunity to illustrate how little impact MTS will have on the client code - so we'll make both the `VideoServer` EXE and the new DLL available at the same time.

## VideoServer Properties

Bring up the copy of `VideoServer` project in Visual Basic. We'll actually make a couple of changes to the project at this point, both in the Project Properties dialog.

## *Changing to an ActiveX DLL*

Choose the Project | VideoServer
Properties... menu option to bring up the
Project Properties dialog. On this screen,
we'll change the Project Type field to
ActiveX DLL, as shown here:

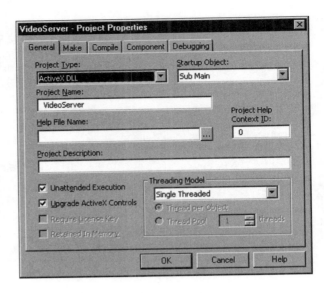

## *Changing the Project Name*

Now change the Project Name field to VideoServerMTS. This way, the new DLL version of our
server will have a different name than the original EXE server, and they can both be registered on
our clients at the same time without conflicting.

> Instead of modifying the existing VideoServer server, we're basically
> creating a brand new server, VideoServerMTS that provides the same
> functionality.

## *Unattended Execution and Threading Model*

In Chapter 11 we selected the Unattended Execution option in the VideoServer server. This
option makes sure that our server has no forms or controls and redirects any calls to the MsgBox
method so they're written to a log file.

We still want this behavior within MTS, since the VideoServerMTS server will be running on a
server machine, not the user's machine. So we'll leave this option turned on in this new ActiveX
server project.

We need to change the Threading Model property for our new VideoServerMTS server. The
Threading Model for VideoServer was set so we got a different thread for each object that was
created by a client. Now we're going to be running our server within MTS and allowing it to manage
the threads for our server program.

Visual Basic provides us with different options for threading a DLL server than for an EXE server. Since `VideoServerMTS` is a DLL, we will have the **Apartment Threaded** option available. This setting indicates that our DLL supports multiple threads, with each thread simulating a separate process for all the objects running within it. This is the preferred setting for MTS, since it allows MTS to create multiple threads for our DLL.

> *With support for apartment threading, MTS is able to efficiently run a large number of our server's objects in various threads. The ability to run many objects in a single process, but with multiple threads, is a significant performance benefit.*

At this point, we've got the project switched over to a DLL with a new server name, so click the OK button and save the project.

## Compatible Server

Since we're creating a new server, we need to switch our project's compatible server from the old EXE to our DLL.

First, bring up the project's properties dialog and make sure the **Version Compatibility** setting is changed to **No** Compatibility. We discussed compatibility settings in some detail back in Chapter 7.

Our `VideoServer` DLL currently has a GUID that identifies the server to any clients. Since we are trying to create a new server, `VideoServerMTS`, we need to make sure it gets assigned a different GUID, otherwise our client programs will get our two servers, each with the same GUID, confused.

By setting the **Version Compatibility** to **No Compatibility** and recompiling the program we'll cause Visual Basic to assign a new GUID to our `VideoServerMTS` DLL.

> **This is important, because we need to compile our DLL, just the one time, without compatibility - so it creates new GUID values for the MTS-based server, the classes and the interfaces.**

The next step in this process is to compile our project to create `VideoServerMTS.DLL`. Just choose the **File** | **Make** VideoServerMTS.dll menu option and go from there.

As we did in Chapter 11 with the `VideoServer` DLL, use the Windows Explorer to make a copy of this new DLL, so we can use the copy for our compatible server. Once that's complete, bring up the project's properties dialog again, and change the **Version Compatibility** setting back to **Binary Compatibility**. Select the copy of our new DLL to be the compatible server.

Make sure to save the project once we've made this change. This will ensure that subsequent compiles of the project will retain the GUID values for the ActiveX server, its classes and their public interfaces.

> **As we discussed in Chapter 11 with the `VideoServer` ActiveX EXE server, it's very important to use Binary Compatibility to keep these GUID values constant. Any time the values change, we'll need to reregister the ActiveX server on all our client workstations - or our application will cease functioning.**

# Object Creation and References

Visual Basic provides us with two ways to create objects:

- ❑ The New keyword
- ❑ The CreateObject method

Normally we can choose to use either of these techniques to create our objects. Once we have a reference to an object we can use it as we wish, including passing the reference as a parameter to other objects or routines within our application. In Chapter 10 we implemented our objects in the VideoObjects DLL to use the CreateObject method to create any objects from the VideoServer application so we could easily specify on which machine those objects should be run. However, within our VideoServer application itself we are using the New keyword exclusively.

When using MTS, there are some constraints placed on how we can create objects and work with our object references. We discussed the basics of these constraints earlier, so now let's see how they impact our project.

We're fortunate in that the VideoServerMTS project contains no objects that return references to other objects, or that pass such references as parameters. This simplifies our task somewhat, since we don't need to worry about making sure those references are appropriate for use by clients.

## Using CreateObject Instead of New

What we do need to change within the VideoServerMTS project are all the cases where the New keyword is used to create objects that are to be used by other objects within MTS. Objects created using the New keyword are not properly controlled by MTS, so the recommendation is quite definitely not to use it. Instead, we should use the CreateObject method to create these objects.

### Using CreateObject

For instance, the TapesPersist object's Fetch method contains code that creates a TapePersist object:

```
Set objPersist = New TapePersist
```

The TapePersist class has an Instancing property of 5-Multiuse, so we can't continue to use the New keyword to create the object. Therefore, we'll change this line of code to use the CreateObject method:

```
Set objPersist = CreateObject("VideoServerMTS.TapePersist")
```

*While this is technically correct, and this change is recommended, it's possible to continue to use the New keyword. If we leave the TapesPersist routine alone, allowing the TapePersist object to be created with the New keyword, the program will continue to run just fine. However, if we watch the activity on the server, using the MTS Explorer we'll cover later, we find that it appears as though no TapePersist object was ever created. This is because objects created with the New keyword aren't noticed by MTS.*

### Calling Friend Properties and Methods

There's an important caveat to making this change to CreateObject. Any interface elements declared using Friend scope will no longer be available for use in any objects created using CreateObject.

> Friend *scope implies that properties and methods are only available to other code running in the same ActiveX component as the object.*

Normally, CreateObject would create an object such that Friend elements continue to work just fine. In the MTS environment, however, when we use CreateObject the new object will be created in such a manner that any attempt to call a Friend property or method will result in an error.

This comes into play in the VideoServerMTS project as well. For instance, in the TapesPersist.Save method, we create an instance of TapePersist. This was done with the New keyword, but now it should be done with CreateObject:

```
Set objPersist = CreateObject("VideoServerMTS.TapePersist")
```

However, this routine also makes a call to a method on the TapePersist object that has Friend scope:

```
For lngIndex = 1 To objBuffer.Count
  With objPersist
    strBuffer = .SaveChild(VideoID, objBuffer.Item(lngIndex))
    If Len(strBuffer) > 0 Then _
      objUpdatedTapes.Add strBuffer
  End With

Next
```

This method is declared as Friend because we didn't want to expose it for use by the Tape object itself: that is, it's only appropriate for calling from the TapesPersist object. Unfortunately, the only solution to our dilemma is to change its scope to Public within the TapePersist class. We'll just have to live with the fact that the method has a broader scope than we'd prefer:

```
Public Function SaveChild(VideoID As Long, Buffer As String) As String
```

Our object contains a number of properties and methods declared with Friend scope. When we create an object with CreateObject we are using late binding, and that means we can't call anything that's not Public in scope. This means that we don't need to change *all* our properties and methods from Friend to Public, only those that are called using late binding. And this includes any method call where an object is created using CreateObject.

## Using the New Keyword

As we noted earlier, we do need to continue using the New keyword to create Private objects. The TapesPersist object's Fetch method also creates a new Buffer object using the New keyword:

```
Set objBuffer = New Buffer
```

We should leave this code alone. If we try to create the `Buffer` object using `CreateObject`, or the `ObjectContext` object's `CreateInstance` method, we'll get an error. Either of these approaches will attempt to create the object as if from an external client, and the `Buffer` class has an Instancing property of 1-Private, so external clients can't create or reference it.

With the `New` keyword, the `Buffer` object will be running in the same environment and with the same context object as the `TapesPersist` object itself. From the viewpoint of MTS, our `Buffer` object is just some code that's being used by `TapesPersist`, and not an actual object at all.

# SQL Data Sources

At this point, our new project is technically able to run in the MTS environment. However, as it stands it wouldn't take advantage of the database-connection pooling provided by MTS, because we're still using a JET database – a type of database not supported by MTS for connection pooling.

## Three-tier Architecture

Obviously, this is a very desirable feature, and one that we want to make use of in our program. Besides, if we switch from a JET database to Microsoft SQL Server, we'll have a more scalable implementation with potential for client workstations, an application server running MTS and a database server running SQL Server.

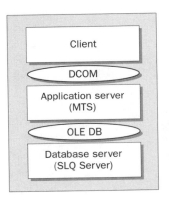

Fortunately for us, ADO makes the transition virtually seamless. We are already using ADO to talk to the OLE DB provider for JET databases, so all we really need to do is switch our data source to use the OLE DB provider for SQL Server. The remainder of our data access code will continue to function as we intended.

## Switching from JET to SQL Server

Before we get into the details of our Visual Basic code changes, we need to do bit of groundwork.

For this chapter, we'll move our JET database into a Microsoft SQL Server database by using the Access 97 Upsizing Wizard. This wizard is freely available from Microsoft - it will quickly move our entire database, including tables, indexes, relationships and data, from an Access 97 database into a SQL Server database.

> There is a caveat with the move from Access to SQL Server. One of our tables, `Tape`, is a reserved word within SQL Server, so the wizard automatically renames the table to `Tape_`. While this is not a big problem, it does mean that our program's SQL statements that reference the `Tape` table will need to be slightly altered to reference `Tape_` instead.

The `Execute` command itself remains unchanged, we just need to create a `Connection` object within the routine itself. This change needs to be made for each `DeleteObject` method in the `VideoServerMTS` project.

### Updating the Fetch Methods

As with the `DeleteObject` methods, all the `Fetch` methods will need to be changed. All we need to do is change our call to the `Recordset` object's `Open` method. Instead of using `cnVideo` as a `Connection` object, we'll provide our `DB_CONNECT` constant.

A database connection is still opened using this approach, but it is done automatically by the `Recordset` object as it opens. This is basically a shortcut – rather than opening a `Connection` object and then a `Recordset` object, we are allowing ADO to do that work for us.

For instance, the `VideosPersist` object's `Fetch` method will be changed as follows:

```
Set rsVideo = New Recordset
rsVideo.Open strSQL, DB_CONNECT
```

The remainder of the code in the procedure will remain untouched. We'll need to make this change to the `Fetch` methods throughout the `VideoServerMTS` project.

### Updating the Save Methods

As with the `Fetch` methods, our `Save` methods already make use of a `Recordset` object. However, we'll need to do a bit more work in our `Save` methods than we did for the `Fetch` methods.

The most obvious change is to modify the `Open` method call to use `DB_CONNECT` instead of our `cnVideo` object.

However, we also will need to change the cursor type we're creating for our `Recordset` object. By default, the cursor type is a forward-only cursor. While this worked fine in our JET database, it won't be so ideal with SQL Server. The reason will be apparent when we look at the other change we'll need to make to our `Save` methods.

For now run through the `Save` methods and change the `Open` statements to use `DB_CONNECT` and to specify a cursor type of `adOpenKeyset`. For instance, the `TapePersist` object's `Save` method contains the following code:

```
Set rsTape = New Recordset
rsTape.Open strSQL, DB_CONNECT, adOpenKeyset, adLockOptimistic
If mudtProps.IsNew Then rsTape.AddNew
```

The same changes need to be made to the `Open` method calls in each `Save` method within the `VideoServerMTS` project. Any other routines that access the database will likewise need to be changed – the `SaveLateFee` method of the `TapePersist` object is one example.

We need to make one other change to our `Save` methods. With the OLE DB provider for JET, we were able to add a new record to a table and have the OLE DB provider automatically update our `Recordset` object with any new values from the table – specifically values generated using the `Autonumber` column type in Access. With the OLE DB provider for SQL Server however, this functionality isn't supported.

Where our `TapePersist` object's `Save` method had a line such as:

```
If mudtProps.IsNew Then mudtProps.TapeID = .Fields("TapeID")
```

This simply retrieved the updated value from the table. With SQL Server however, the value is not automatically updated into our `Recordset` object, so we need to force the issue. Since we've switch the `Recordset` object's cursor type to `adOpenKeyset`, we can use the `Bookmark` property of the `Recordset` object to reset the cursor position to the current record – causing the values from the table itself to be refreshed into our `Recordset` object.

Replace the line above with the following:

```
If mudtProps.IsNew Then
   .Bookmark = .Bookmark
   mudtProps.TapeID = .Fields("TapeID")
End If
```

We'll need to go through all the `Save` methods in the project and make the same change.

The only remaining thing to do is make sure that all the classes are MultiUse otherwise when we add the class' to an MTS package they won't be visible to the client.

With these changes, the `VideoServerMTS` server is now completely converted to use the OLE DB provider for SQL Server. We'll now automatically get the benefit of MTS database connection pooling.

# Running VideoServerMTS in MTS

Once we've implemented the changes from the previous section, we're all ready to put our server into the MTS environment.

Later in this chapter, we'll see how we can use `ObjectContext` to implement transactional support for saving the `Video` object and its child objects; but for now, we can just put the `VideoServerMTS` server into MTS and immediately gain the benefits of object and database connection pooling.

## Installing the Server in MTS

Moving an ActiveX server into the MTS environment is literally as simple as drag-and-drop. It is an amazingly simple process. Let's go through the steps.

> Before moving the DLL into MTS, it is often very valuable to make sure the program runs with the `VideoServerMTS` server *outside* of MTS. This allows us to run `VideoServerMTS` in Visual Basic's debug mode and make sure it is working properly. Once that's done, it is much easier to copy it into MTS and go from there.

## Copy the DLL to the Server machine

First off, we need to make the `VideoServerMTS.dll` file available to the application server machine that is running MTS. We can do this by copying the DLL to the application server machine's hard drive. There is no need to manually register the DLL on the application server, we'll let MTS register it for us, as we'll see shortly.

*In fact, the easiest way to work with MTS is to have Visual Basic 6.0 installed on the MTS server machine. MTS provides a Visual Basic add-in that automatically updates the appropriate registry entries when the DLL is recompiled. If we're doing our development on a separate machine, we'll need to manually refresh the component on the server each time we recompile the DLL, and recopy it to the MTS server machine.*

## Using the Transaction Server Explorer

Once the DLL is available to the MTS server machine, bring up the Transaction Server Explorer using the Windows Start menu. The MTS explorer is actually a plug-in module for the Microsoft Management Console, so don't be surprised when the MMC splash screen shows up.

In the left pane, open up the My Computer entry and select the Packages Installed entry from the list. MTS comes with a couple of pre-built packages, as shown in the screenshot:

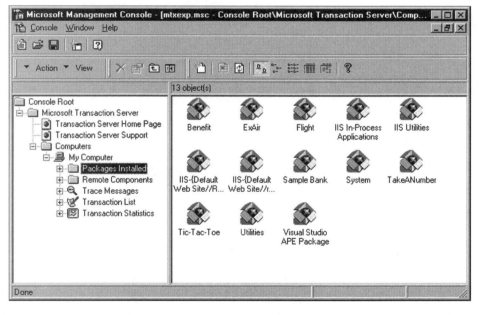

In MTS, a **package** is a way of containing related components. Microsoft has indicated that at some point MTS may allow packages to contain selected objects from within an ActiveX DLL, but, at this time, packages must contain all the objects from any DLL included in the package.

## Adding a New Package

We need to add a new package for our server, so choose the Action | New | Package option from the toolbar. MTS will bring up a wizard to guide us through the process of adding the package. On the first panel, we need to indicate whether we're importing an existing package or creating a new one. Since our `VideoServerMTS` server has never been placed in MTS before, we need to create an empty package to hold it:

Next, we need to supply a name for the package. In this case, let's enter the name as `VideoServerMTS`, just like the name of our DLL. There's no requirement that the names match, but here it makes sense:

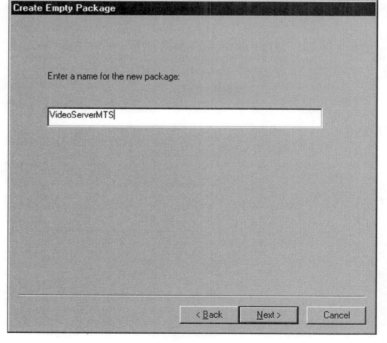

On the next panel, we need to provide MTS with information about the NT user under which the component will be running. We can then supply a specific user and password, or allow MTS to install the component to run under the currently logged-on user. We'll typically want to choose the second option and enter a username under which the component can be run. In this case we'll run it under the `Administrator` account:

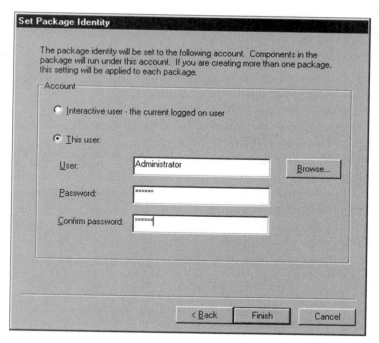

When we click Finish, MTS will add a new package to the list of packages shown in the explorer window:

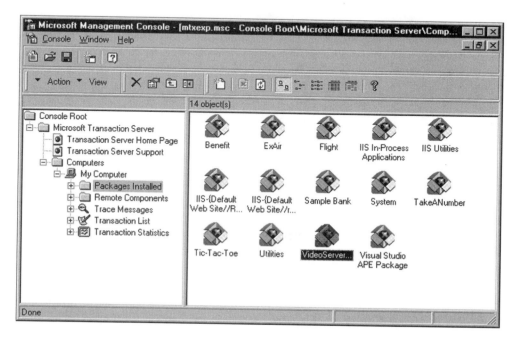

### *Copying the DLL into the Package*

Now comes the drag-and-drop part of the process. In the left pane, expand the Packages Installed item and then expand the VideoServerMTS item. We'll see entries for both the Components and Roles that belong to this package.

The Roles entry is where we'd set up security for this package. In this case we'll just accept the default security settings.

What we are concerned about is the Components item, since this is where we need to install our objects. Select the Components item in the left pane, then simply drag the VideoServerMTS.dll file from the Windows NT Explorer into the right pane of the Transaction Server Explorer. The result will be a listing of all the classes contained in our DLL, shown as components of this package in MTS:

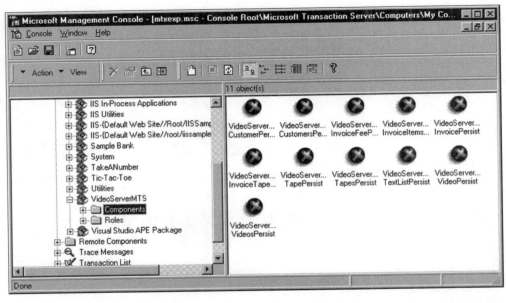

With these few steps, we've installed our server program into MTS. Now all we need to do is get the server registered on our client machine and switch our VideoObjects project to reference our MTS server rather than the VideoServer EXE server from Chapter 10.

# Creating the Client Setup

In Chapter 11, we created a client setup program using Visual Basic's Package and Deployment Wizard and that is still most likely the simplest way to install our applications on client workstations. From the perspective of our client application there is no difference between creating objects from an ActiveX EXE server and an ActiveX DLL server running within MTS. Either way, we simply need to indicate the dependency on a VBR file and specify the server name where the objects will be run.

MTS does provide its own mechanism for installing references to a package. This process is tied into the same process MTS uses to take a package that's installed on one server and move it to another MTS server. Along with the information needed to copy the package to another server, MTS also creates a client install program. This may be useful in some cases where we simply want to install a reference to our MTS package without installing an actual Visual Basic application on the client.

If we select the VideoServerMTS
package in the left pane of the
Transaction Server Explorer, we can
then select the Action | Export option
from the toolbar. This will bring up a
dialog to prompt us where the
package information is to be exported:

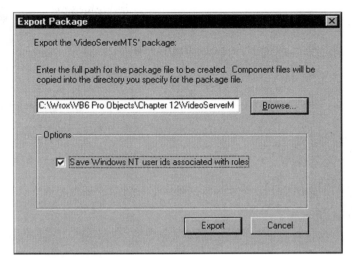

When we click the Export button, MTS will create the PAK file in the directory we've indicated. The
PAK file can be used to import our package into another installation of MTS. In addition, MTS will
also create a `clients` subdirectory beneath the directory where the PAK file is placed, for the client
install program.

The client install program will have the same name as the PAK file, but it will be an executable
program. Everything needed to install and register the required software on the client will be
included in this self-installing EXE file. All we need to do is get the program to the client workstation
and run it.

*With Visual Basic components, the client installation will not only register the server on the*
*client, but it will also copy the `VideoServerMTS.dll` file itself on to the client's hard drive.*

Once the installation program has been run on the client, our `VideoServerMTS` server will appear
as a valid option for use by ActiveX client programs. DCOM will transparently route any calls to the
server across the network to our MTS server machine. From there, they'll be routed to the
appropriate object in our server.

# Making VideoObjects Use the New Server

With `VideoServerMTS` registered on our client workstations, all that remains is to change our
`VideoObjects` project so that it references `VideoServerMTS` rather than `VideoServer`.

Since both servers provide the same classes, with the same properties and methods, we don't need to
make any code changes to the `VideoObjects` project at all. Of course, the `VideoUI` project doesn't
even know about the `VideoServer` project in the first place, so it won't need any changes either.

Bring up the `VideoObjects` project in Visual Basic. Then open up the project's references dialog
and deselect the `VideoServer` option. We no longer need to use our ActiveX EXE server via
DCOM, since we'll now be using our new MTS-based server.

Page down through the list to find the `VideoServerMTS` option, and select it. This will cause our `VideoObjects` project to reference the new server running in MTS:

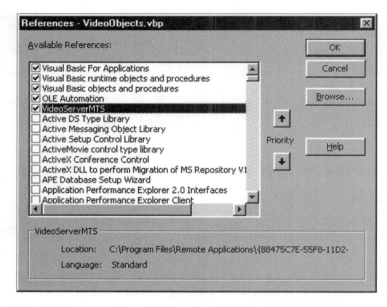

With the correct server application referenced, all that remains is to change all our `CreateObject` method calls to specify the right server name. For instance, our `Customer` object uses a `CreateObject` call such as:

```
Set objPersist = CreateObject("VideoServer.CustomerPersist", PERSIST_SERVER)
```

We simply need to change the server name portion of this line to reflect our new server name:

```
Set objPersist = CreateObject("VideoServerMTS.CustomerPersist", PERSIST_SERVER)
```

This change can most easily be made by doing a mass search-and-replace throughout the entire `VideoObjects` project to change `CreateObject("VideoServer.` to `CreateObject("VideoServerMTS.` and we'll be all set.

Now save and recompile this project. At this point, we should be able to run the `VideoUI` client program, and everything should work.

*There will be a noticeable pause the first time we choose a menu option that retrieves or saves data, since MTS will need to start up our server. After that, however, we should find that the application is quite responsive.*

*By default, if we let the server sit idle for three minutes, MTS will release our server. The next user trying to retrieve or save data from the database will incur the same pause while MTS reloads our server into memory again.*

# MTS Transactions

What we've achieved so far, in this chapter, works well for non-transactional objects such as `CustomerPersist`. Each method in `CustomerPersist` only performs a single database operation: retrieving, updating or deleting a single record in the database. There's no need to worry about database transactions when we're working with a single record.

But this is not the case with the `Video` object and its child `Tape` objects (or the `Invoice` object and its child objects). When we save a `Video` object through the `VideoPersist` object, it not only updates a single record; but the overall transaction also includes the corresponding updates to all of its child `Tape` objects. Each `Tape` object is saved through a `TapePersist` object, which updates another record.

We'll implement a solution that is ideal from an MTS perspective in terms of dealing with our parent `Video` and child `Tape` objects. This will require some changes to both the `VideoServerMTS` and the `VideoObjects` projects. Even with these changes, we still won't need to change our `VideoUI` project in any way, as we've done a good job of insulating our UI from any business functionality.

Before we dive into those changes however, we need to get a good understanding of how MTS handles each object's context and how we can use that context to implement transactions.

# ObjectContext Objects

MTS provides a mechanism by which we can implement a transaction to protect any updates to the `Video` object and its child objects. The best way to view transactions in MTS is to consider that one of the objects is the 'parent' object that owns the transaction. All other objects are subordinate to that object. The parent object is the one that is created by the base client; in this case, our `VideoObjects` code.

## Getting an ObjectContext Reference

Earlier in the chapter, we discussed how MTS transparently creates a Context object for each one of our objects it creates. This means that it automatically creates a Context object for our `VideoPersist` object, and another for each `TapePersist` object we might create.

We can easily get access to this Context object from within our objects. Open the `VideoServerMTS` project in Visual Basic, and bring up its **References** dialog. MTS provides a DLL we can reference from within our project to provide us with access to the `ObjectContext` object and its interface. Scroll through the list of servers to find and select the **Microsoft Transaction Server Type Library** entry.

With this reference, we can add code in any one of our methods to get a reference to the `ObjectContext` associated with our persistence object:

```
Dim objContext As ObjectContext
```

Along with the `ObjectContext` class, the reference to `Mtxas.dll` provides us with a method, `GetObjectContext`. This method will return a reference to the current object's context object:

```
Set objContext = GetObjectContext
```

In the next section, we'll see how we can get a reference to the context object each time our object is activated. Using this technique, we can have access to the `objContext` variable at all times within our object's code.

## Linking Context Objects

As we discussed earlier in this chapter, Context objects provide us with access to both the security and transaction features of MTS. Our transaction effectively spans the `VideoPersist`, `TapesPersist` and `TapePersist` objects. In order for MTS to provide transactional support, the Context objects behind each of our persistence objects need to be aware of each other.

This is where things get interesting, since the only way the Context objects can know about each other is if the client only creates the first persistence object. Each time the client program creates an object in MTS, we get a new – totally separate – context for our object.

If, on the other hand, an object running within MTS creates another object, we can link the new object's context to the original object. This is shown in the following figure:

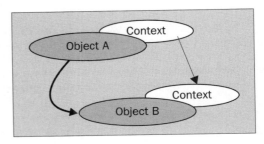

In this figure, object **A** creates object **B**. Since both objects are running within MTS, a link is established between object **A**'s context and the context of object **B**. This link between context objects is what allows MTS to make sure all our objects properly work together to complete the transaction.

> To support transactions, all subsequent server-side objects involved in the transaction must be created by one server-side object.

### Creating Objects from the Client

As it stands in our application right now, the client code in `VideoObjects` directly creates and uses the `VideoPersist` and `TapesPersist` objects. Both objects are created using the `CreateObject` method within the `VideoObjects` project, and then the code uses various methods of both objects.

The problem with this is that we'll get two context objects, one for `VideoPersist` and another for `TapesPersist`, that know nothing about each other. From the MTS perspective, it's as though two different clients were using objects within the server, so there's no way for it to link these two context objects or support any form of transaction.

We'll cover a solution to this problem later in the chapter, but for now let's focus on getting the `TapesPersist` and `TapePersist` objects working together.

In the final analysis, the base client (in this case our `VideoObjects` code) can only *create* a single MTS object. From that point forward, all other MTS objects must be created by other MTS objects using the `CreateInstance` method.

References to these objects may be returned to the base client and used. Since they were created by other objects with `CreateInstance`, they already have a properly-configured context object, so it doesn't matter what code calls their methods.

### Using CreateInstance

As we discussed, all the objects in a transaction must be created by other objects on the MTS server. We can't use the `New` keyword or the `CreateObject` command to create these objects, as those techniques won't link the context object of the new object back to that of the creating object. Instead, we need to use the `CreateInstance` method on our Context object to create each subsequent object.

For instance, in the `TapesPersist` object, both the `Fetch` and `Save` methods create `TapePersist` objects using the `CreateObject` method. These routines need to be changed to use `CreateInstance`, as shown here:

```
Set objPersist = objContext.CreateInstance("VideoServerMTS.TapePersist")
```

With this change, the `TapePersist` objects are created with a context object that is linked to the `TapesPersist` object's context. This means that the `TapePersist` objects will share security and transaction information with the `TapesPersist` object.

Now let's take a closer look at how we can get a reference to those Context objects within our own objects.

# The ObjectControl interface

Objects running in MTS can implement a special interface which provides a mechanism by which MTS can interact with the objects. This is called the `ObjectControl` interface and we can implement in our objects by using the `Implements` keyword – we'll get into the details momentarily.

Objects wishing to support pooling (when MTS itself provides it) will need to implement the `ObjectControl` interface. Additionally, MTS uses this interface to tell our object when a client has started using the object and when the client is done using it.

Through this interface, our object will implement three methods: `Activate`, `Deactivate` and `CanBePooled`. Pooling uses the `CanBePooled` method, but we can also make very good use of the `Activate` and `Deactivate` methods to support transactions.

> **We'll need to make these changes to all three objects. We'll go through the steps with the** `VideoPersist` **object, and you can follow suit on the** `TapesPersist` **and** `TapePersist` **objects.**

As we discussed earlier, the first thing to do is make sure that `Mtxas.dll` has been added to the `VideoServerMTS` project's references.

We need to use the `Implements` keyword at the top of the class to indicate that we want to implement a new interface:

```
Option Explicit

Implements ObjectControl

Private mobjContext As ObjectContext
Private mudtProps As VideoProps
```

We've also added the declaration of a variable to store a reference to our Context object. We'll set this value shortly.

Once the `Implements ObjectControl` statement has been added, Visual Basic will expect us to add implementations for all elements of that interface. In this case, we need to add three methods. We'll look at these methods now.

## ObjectControl_CanBePooled

The `CanBePooled` method simply returns a `Boolean` value to indicate whether our object is set up for pooling. Since MTS doesn't currently support object pooling – and because we can't predict exactly what might be required when MTS *does* support it - let's return `False` just to be on the safe side:

```
Private Function ObjectControl_CanBePooled() As Boolean

   ObjectControl_CanBePooled = False

End Function
```

## ObjectControl_Activate

The `Activate` method is more important to our transaction. This method is called by MTS each time our object is about to be used by a new client. Since we've indicated our object is not to be pooled, this will only get called when our object is created. If we were using pooling, it would be called right before a new client began using our object.

In any case, we'll want to use this method to initialize anything our object will need each time it is used:

```
Private Sub ObjectControl_Activate()

   Set mobjContext = GetObjectContext

End Sub
```

The `Activate` method call is the first time that we can access our object's context object - as we can't gain access to the context object within the `Class_Initialize` event.

We'll need the Context object in a few places within our code, and so this is an ideal spot to get a reference to the context object and keep it until we are deactivated.

The code here simply gets a reference to our Context object using the `GetObjectContext` method, supplied by referencing the MTS type library. We've stored the reference in `mobjContext`, the variable we declared at the top of the class module.

### ObjectControl_Deactivate

MTS will call our `Deactivate` method when the object is done with its work. If we were creating an object to support pooling, this would be the routine where we'd reset all module-level variables to the state they were in when the object was first created.

In our case, we'll use this opportunity to release the reference to our Context object:

```
Private Sub ObjectControl_Deactivate()

    Set mobjContext = Nothing

End Sub
```

The object may or may not ever be reactivated, and so it isn't appropriate to retain a reference to the Context object beyond the call to `Deactivate`. In fact, `Deactivate` is the last point at which our reference to the Context object continues to be valid. If our object is now terminated, the Context object reference won't be valid in the `Class_Terminate` event, regardless of whether we drop the reference here.

# Recordset Cursor types

Transactions impose certain extra restrictions on how we work with databases. As we've discussed, MTS uses the Distributed Transaction Coordinator (DTC) to manage its transactions. Not all types of database cursor can be used when we are working with transactions through DTC – unfortunately this includes the default cursor type used by ADO.

By default, ADO `Recordset` objects use forward-only cursors. For many purposes this type of cursor is very fast and efficient – a good choice. However, this type of cursor can't be updated or changed as part of a transaction.

Since we're changing all of our objects to provide transactional support by calling `SetComplete` and `SetAbort`, we also will need to change all of the methods that update data in `Recordset` objects to use a different type of cursor.

ADO provides four types of cursor:

| | |
|---|---|
| `adOpenForwardOnly` | The default cursor type – provides a recordset that can only be scrolled through in a forward direction |
| `adOpenKeyset` | Provides a recordset that reflects data changed by other users, but doesn't know about records other users may have added |
| `adOpenDynamic` | Provides a recordset that reflects records that are added, deleted or changed by other users |
| `adOpenOpenStatic` | Provides a recordset that doesn't reflect any changes to the data that might be made by other users |

Of these cursor types, the forward-only cursor tends to be the most efficient for performance. However, the next most efficient type of cursor is typically the Keyset cursor. Fortunately for us, the Keyset cursor *does* allow us to change data within MTS transactions.

Since we already went through all our `Save` methods as we converted from JET to SQL Server and made sure our cursor type was set to `adOpenKeyset`, we already have this issue covered. However, it's worth noting that the default cursor type for ADO `Recordset` objects does preclude altering data within the context of a transaction.

# A Hierarchical View of Transactions

We already have a hierarchy with our objects on the `VideoObjects` side:

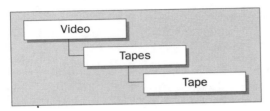

If we follow the same scheme on the MTS side, our parent object would be the `VideoPersist` object, and it would be responsible for creating the `TapesPersist` object.

As it stands now, our `TapePersist` object is created by the `TapesPersist` object. Unfortunately, our `TapesPersist` object is not created by the `VideoPersist` object – instead it is created directly from the `Tapes` object on the client.

What we really need to do is consider the `Tape` objects to be *part of* the `Video` object. This means that the process of saving the `Tape` objects should be included right into the process of saving the parent `Video` object. The easiest way to do this is to change the `VideoPersist` object's `Save` method to accept not only the `Video` object's state data, but also that of the `Tape` child objects.

If we make that change, then the `Tapes` object wouldn't need to interact directly with the `VideoServer` application at all – instead, the `VideoPersist` object would create the `TapesPersist` object and call its `Save` method. This is ideal, since the entire process of saving the `Video` and all the subordinate `Tape` objects can be accomplished in a single method call from the client workstation to the server.

> *Also remember that we have a similar hierarchy with the Invoice related objects so comparable changes to those I am about to make will also need to be applied to those objects. See Appendix C for a listing of the code you should also be creating for the Invoice objects.*

## Changing the VideoPersist Save method

First off, we'll change the `VideoPersist` object's `Save` method to accept the state data for not only the `Video` object itself, but also the `Video` object's child `Tape` objects. Open the `VideoServerMTS` project and bring up the `VideoPersist` object's code window.

The changes we need to make here are not terribly complex. We'll change the routine to accept another parameter for the `Tapes` object's state data:

```
Public Function Save(ByVal Buffer As String, TapesBuffer As String) As String
```

Note that the `TapesBuffer` parameter is read-write – we aren't using the `ByVal` keyword. This is intentional, since we need some way to return the updated list of `Tape` object's to the client. Prior to making these changes, our `Tapes` object has been directly calling the `TapesPersist` object and not only updating data, but getting back a set of updated data. We need to preserve that functionality with our new solution as well.

The only other change we need to make to the `Save` method is to add code to create an instance of the `TapesPersist` object and call its `Save` method:

```
Public Function Save(ByVal Buffer As String, TapesBuffer As String) As String

    Dim rsVideo As Recordset
    Dim strSQL As String
    Dim objPersist As TapesPersist

    SetState Buffer
    Set rsVideo = New Recordset
    strSQL = "SELECT * FROM Video WHERE VideoID=" & mudtProps.VideoID
    rsVideo.Open strSQL, DB_CONNECT, adOpenKeyset, adLockOptimistic
    If mudtProps.IsNew Then rsVideo.AddNew

    With rsVideo
      .Fields("Title") = mudtProps.Title
      .Fields("ReleaseDate") = mudtProps.ReleaseDate
      .Fields("Studio") = mudtProps.Studio
      .Fields("Rating") = mudtProps.Rating
      .Fields("Category") = mudtProps.Category
      .Update
      If mudtProps.IsNew Then
        .Bookmark = .Bookmark
        mudtProps.VideoID = .Fields("VideoID")
      End If
      .Close
    End With

    Set rsVideo = Nothing
    Save = GetState
    Set objPersist = mobjContext.CreateInstance("VideoServerMTS.TapesPersist")
    TapesBuffer = objPersist.Save(mudtProps.VideoID, TapesBuffer)
    Set objPersist = Nothing

End Function
```

The `TapesPersist` object already implements the `Save` method to accept a state string as a parameter and return an updated state string as the result of the method. Rather than calling this method from the `Tapes` object itself, we can simply call it here from the `VideoPersist` object.

We've already updated the `TapesPersist` object to use the `CreateInstance` method from the context object when creating the `TapePersist` objects, so they are already using linked context objects. In this code we again use the `CreateInstance` method to create the `TapesPersist` object itself, thus linking its context to the context of our `VideoPersist` object. This means that all three types of object (`VideoPersist`, `TapesPersist` and `TapePersist`) are set up to share their context – meaning they are all ready to support transactions.

At this point we'll want to save
and recompile the
`VideoServerMTS` project.
We'll get warnings regarding
incompatibility – after all we
did just change the server's
public interface. In this case
we'll have Visual Basic
preserve compatibility with our
existing server:

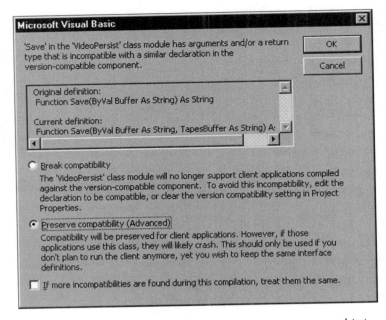

We know we're going to head right over and update the `VideoObjects` project anyway, so this is
the simplest choice.

## Updating the Tapes object

With the `Save` method of our `VideoPersist` object updated, we're ready to move back to the
`VideoObjects` project and change how our `Video` object interacts with the `VideoPersist` object.
Bring up the `VideoObjects` project in Visual Basic.

The `VideoPersist` object's `Save` method is called from within the `ApplyEdit` method in `Video`.
We'll need to change that call to pass the entire state from the `Tapes` object to `VideoPersist`,
retrieve it and then pass it back into the `Tapes` object. Before we can do this however, we need to
make some changes to our `Tapes` object itself.

The most obvious change we need to make is to change the `Tapes` object's `ApplyEdit` method so it
no longer directly interacts with the `TapesPersist` object:

```
Public Sub ApplyEdit(VideoID As Long)

'   Dim objPersist As TapesPersist
    Dim objTape As Tape

    If Not mflgEditing Then Err.Raise 445

'   If IsDirty Then
'       Set objPersist = CreateObject("VideoServer.TapesPersist", PERSIST_SERVER)
'       SetState objPersist.Save(VideoID, GetState)
'       Set objPersist = Nothing
'   Else
    For Each objTape In mcolTapes
```

```
                objTape.ChildApplyEdit
        Next
'    End If

        mflgEditing = False

    End Sub
```

In this case we've simply commented out the lines that interact with the server-side object.

Now we need to figure out how the `Video` object is going to retrieve and set the state of our `Tapes` object. The most direct approach is to allow the `Video` object to call our `Tapes` object's `SetState` and `GetState` methods. These methods already implement the functionality that we need, so that choice involves very little work. We can simply change the scope of these two methods from `Private` to `Friend` and we're all set.

```
    Friend Sub SetState(ByVal Buffer As String)

        Dim lngIndex As Long
        Dim objTape As Tape
        Dim objBuffer As Buffer

        Set mcolTapes = Nothing
        Set mcolTapes = New Collection
        Set objBuffer = New Buffer
        objBuffer.SetState Buffer

        For lngIndex = 1 To objBuffer.Count
          Set objTape = New Tape

          With objTape
            .SetAsChild
            .SetState objBuffer.Item(lngIndex)
            If mflgEditing Then .ChildBeginEdit
          End With

          mcolTapes.Add Item:=objTape

        Next

    End Sub
```

Only one thing remains, and it probably isn't something that we'd think of right off. In the `Video` object's `ApplyEdit` method we only call the `VideoPersist` object's `Save` method if the `Video` object is new or has been changed. However, to this point we've been always calling the `Tapes` object and allowing it to determine if any child objects are new or dirty. Since we want to combine the process of saving the `Video` with that of saving the `Tapes` object we need some way of knowing if the `Tapes` object is 'dirty' or not.

To handle this, we'll simply implement a new `IsDirty` property on the `Tapes` object. This property can scan through all the child `Tape` objects to find if any of them are new or have been changed.

```
    Friend Property Get IsDirty() As Boolean

        Dim objTape As Tape
```

```
     IsDirty = False

     For Each objTape In mcolTapes
       If objTape.IsDirty Then
         IsDirty = True
         Exit For
       End If

     Next

   End Property
```

Now our `Tapes` object is ready to support everything we need for the `Video` object to save its state.

## Updating the Video object

Open the code window for the `Video` class module. The only routine needing to be changed here is the `ApplyEdit` method where we want to update the call to the `VideoPersist` object's `Save` method.

```
Public Sub ApplyEdit()

   Dim objPersist As VideoPersist
   Dim strTapes As String

   If Not mflgEditing Then Err.Raise 445

   Set objPersist = CreateObject("VideoServerMTS.VideoPersist", PERSIST_SERVER)

   If mflgDeleted And Not mflgNew Then
     ' code to delete the object's data goes here
     objPersist.DeleteObject mudtProps.VideoID
     mflgNew = True
     mflgDeleted = False

   ElseIf mflgDirty Or mobjTapes.IsDirty Or mflgNew Then
     If Not IsValid Then Err.Raise 445
     ' save object to database if appropriate
     strTapes = mobjTapes.GetState
     SetState objPersist.Save(GetState, strTapes)
     mobjTapes.SetState strTapes
     ' save object state
     LSet mudtSave = mudtProps
     mflgNew = False

   End If

   mobjTapes.ApplyEdit mudtProps.VideoID
   Set objPersist = Nothing
   mflgDirty = False
   mflgEditing = False

End Sub
```

The first real change to the code is that we can no longer simply rely on checking `mflgDirty` to see if our object has changed. We also need to call the `IsDirty` property from the `Tapes` object to find out if any of the child objects have been changed. This is the `IsDirty` property that we just implemented in the `Tapes` object:

```
ElseIf mflgDirty Or mobjTapes.IsDirty Or mflgNew Then
```

Then we need to change our call to the `Save` method to pass the state string from the `Tapes` object as a parameter. To make things a bit more complex however, we also need to accept that parameter back and use it in a call to the `Tapes` object's `SetState` method. To support this, we've used a `String` variable to receive the `Tapes` object's state data from the `GetState` method, act as the parameter and then be sent back to the `SetState` method:

```
strTapes = mobjTapes.GetState
SetState objPersist.Save(GetState, strTapes)
mobjTapes.SetState strTapes
```

At this point we've updated our objects in `VideoObjects` so only the `Video` object interacts with the objects in the `VideoServerMTS` ActiveX server. When we save a `Video` object we are also saving all its child `Tape` objects with the same method call to the server.

We're now ready to change our `VideoServerMTS` objects to support transactions.

# Indicating Transaction Status

Let's take some time out for a bit of theory. We've already discussed some of the philosophy followed by MTS and how ideal objects should function. An ideal MTS object is totally stateless, with each method being totally atomic - meaning nothing is retained between calls to the object. This means that it won't matter if a client calls a method on one object and another method on a different object of the same class.

Our objects meet these requirements, as they are stateless and our methods atomic. From method-call to method-call, our objects don't retain any meaningful data – the definition of stateless. Moreover, each method stands alone – we don't have any methods that require that another method be called either before or after it to guarantee that the method will work.

Ideally this means we won't use any module level variables or use the `Static` keyword to declare any variables. While we are using a few module level variables in our objects, they do not maintain any meaningful data from method call to method call and so they aren't a problem. When possible, however, it is best to avoid the use of module level variables, since that way there's no chance of accidentally assuming the variable will maintain data across method calls.

## Calling SetComplete and SetAbort

`SetComplete` and `SetAbort` are methods on the `ObjectContext` object. These methods are called by our object to indicate that we've done all our work. `SetComplete` indicates that everything went successfully within this object, while `SetAbort` indicates that something went wrong and that the transaction must be rolled back.

A call to `SetComplete` doesn't guarantee that the transaction will be committed. If any object in the transaction calls `SetAbort`, the entire transaction will be rolled back, including any work done by objects that called `SetComplete`. Only if all the objects call `SetComplete` then MTS will commit the transaction, including all the work done by all objects.

> It's very important to understand that as soon as `SetComplete` or `SetAbort` are called, the object is deactivated. Even though a client might *think* it retains a reference to the object, that object is gone. Subsequent method calls by the client will be routed to a new instance of the object.

Since our objects are stateless, we can simply call `SetComplete` or `SetAbort` within each `Public` method of our objects. We'll call `SetComplete` if we run through without any problems, or `SetAbort` in the case where we run into any errors or other problems.

### SetComplete

Calling `SetComplete` is pretty straightforward. We've already implemented code in each object to get access to the context object and stored that reference in the `mobjContext` variable. Now we can simply call the `SetComplete` method of that object at the bottom of each `Public` method. For instance, in the `VideoPersist` object's `Save` method we'll add a line:

```
Public Function Save(ByVal Buffer As String, TapesBuffer As String) As String

    Dim rsVideo As Recordset
    Dim strSQL As String
    Dim objPersist As TapesPersist

    SetState Buffer
    Set rsVideo = New Recordset
    strSQL = "SELECT * FROM Video WHERE VideoID=" & mudtProps.VideoID
    rsVideo.Open strSQL, DB_CONNECT, adOpenKeyset, adLockOptimistic
    If mudtProps.IsNew Then rsVideo.AddNew

    With rsVideo
      .Fields("Title") = mudtProps.Title
      .Fields("ReleaseDate") = mudtProps.ReleaseDate
      .Fields("Studio") = mudtProps.Studio
      .Fields("Rating") = mudtProps.Rating
      .Fields("Category") = mudtProps.Category
      .Update
      If mudtProps.IsNew Then
        .Bookmark = .Bookmark
        mudtProps.VideoID = .Fields("VideoID")
      End If
      .Close
    End With

    Set rsVideo = Nothing
    Save = GetState
    Set objPersist = mobjContext.CreateInstance("VideoServerMTS.TapesPersist")
    TapesBuffer = objPersist.Save(mudtProps.VideoID, TapesBuffer)
    Set objPersist = Nothing
    mobjContext.SetComplete

End Function
```

We'll need to make a similar change to every `Save` method in the project where we've declared the `mobjContext` variable.

We'll need to add a `SetComplete` call to each `DeleteObject` method as well. For instance, in the `TapePersist` object's `DeleteObject` method we'll make the following change:

```
Public Sub DeleteObject(TapeID As Long)

    Dim cnVideo As Connection

    Set cnVideo = New Connection
    cnVideo.Open DB_CONNECT
    cnVideo.Execute "DELETE FROM Tape_ WHERE TapeID=" & TapeID
    cnVideo.Close
    Set cnVideo = Nothing
    mobjContext.SetComplete

End Sub
```

What might not be so obvious is that the `Fetch` routines will also need calls to `SetComplete`. Once an object is set up as transactional, *every* `Public` method needs to tell MTS when it is complete so that MTS knows when it can be released. In the `Fetch` method of the `TapesPersist` object we'll add a line:

```
Public Function Fetch(ByVal VideoID As Long) As String

    Dim strSQL As String
    Dim rsTape As Recordset
    Dim objBuffer As Buffer
    Dim objPersist As TapePersist
    Dim udtProps As TapeProps

    Set objBuffer = New Buffer
    strSQL = "SELECT TapeID FROM Tape_ WHERE VideoID=" & VideoID
    Set rsTape = New Recordset
    rsTape.Open strSQL, DB_CONNECT
    Set objPersist = mobjContext.CreateInstance("VideoServerMTS.TapePersist")

    With objPersist
      objBuffer.Initialize Len(udtProps), 20

      Do While Not rsTape.EOF
        objBuffer.Add .Fetch(rsTape("TapeID"))
        rsTape.MoveNext
      Loop

    End With

    Set objPersist = Nothing
    rsTape.Close
    Set rsTape = Nothing
    Fetch = objBuffer.GetState
    mobjContext.SetComplete

End Function
```

Without this call, MTS wouldn't know when the `Fetch` method was actually complete, so it might not release the object as appropriate. We'll need to make a similar change to all the `Fetch` methods in our project where we've declared `mobjContext`.

We have a couple other `Public` methods that will need calls to `SetComplete` as well. The `TapePersist` object has a `SaveChild` method that is used to call the `Save` and `DeleteObject` methods. We've already placed `SetComplete` calls in both of those routines, but there is a third option within `SaveChild` – where the object is neither deleted nor dirty:

```
Public Function SaveChild(VideoID As Long, Buffer As String) As String

  SetState Buffer

  With mudtProps
    If .IsDeleted Then
      DeleteObject .TapeID
      SaveChild = ""

    ElseIf .IsDirty Or .IsNew Then
      .VideoID = VideoID
      SaveChild = Save(GetState)

    Else
      SaveChild = Buffer
      mobjContext.SetComplete

    End If

  End With

End Function
```

Even though this option doesn't even interact with the database we still need to call `SetComplete` so MTS knows that the operation has completed successfully.

The `TapePersist` object also has a `CheckOut` method that is called during the process of saving an `Invoice` object. This method was implemented back in Chapter 6 in the `VideoObjects` project, but since it interacts with the database it obviously had to move here to the `TapePersist` object. Since it is called from another object, this method needs to call `SetComplete` as well:

```
Public Sub CheckOut(ByVal TapeID As Long, ByVal InvoiceID As Long)

  Dim rsTape As Recordset
  Dim strSQL As String

  strSQL = "SELECT * FROM Tape_ WHERE TapeID=" & TapeID
  Set rsTape = New Recordset
  rsTape.Open strSQL, DB_CONNECT, adOpenKeyset, adLockOptimistic

  With rsTape
    .Fields("CheckedOut") = True
    .Fields("DateDue") = DateAdd("d", 2, Now)
    .Fields("InvoiceID") = InvoiceID
    .Update
    .Close
  End With

  Set rsTape = Nothing
  mobjContext.SetComplete

End Sub
```

Similar changes will need to be made to the `InvoicePersist` object, the `InvoiceItemsPersist` object and its `InvoiceTapePersist` and `InvoiceFeePersist` child objects.

Whether we choose to call `SetComplete` within non-transactional objects is optional. Our `CustomerPersist` object, for instance, only retrieves or updates a single record in the database, so transactional support is hardly needed. However, it doesn't hurt to call `SetComplete` at the end of each method in the object regardless.

In general, its a good idea to add calls to `SetComplete` even when objects aren't transactional. After all, we never know when our business requirements might change and our object could end up being used in a transaction that we didn't anticipate. By coding all our objects to support transactions, we might make our lives easier down the road.

### SetAbort

Adding the calls `SetComplete` was pretty straightforward. `SetAbort` is a bit more complex, since we don't always know what might make one of our method calls fail. If our object fails, at any point, then we need to call `SetAbort` to indicate to MTS that something went wrong. The most comprehensive solution is to add error handlers to all the routines where we also implemented `SetComplete`. Then we can simply add a call to `SetAbort` to each error handler.

The error handler doesn't need to be complex. For instance, we can implement an error handler in the `VideoPersist` object's `DeleteObject` method as shown here:

```
Public Sub DeleteObject(VideoID As Long)

   Dim cnVideo As Connection

   On Error GoTo errh
   Set cnVideo = New Connection
   cnVideo.Open DB_CONNECT
   cnVideo.Execute "DELETE FROM Video WHERE VideoID=" & VideoID
   cnVideo.Close
   Set cnVideo = Nothing
   mobjContext.SetComplete
   Exit Sub

errh:
   mobjContext.SetAbort
   With Err
      .Raise .Number, .Source, .Description
   End With

End Sub
```

This error handler simply calls the `SetAbort` method on our Context object, then re-raises the error so it's sent back to the client as usual. By calling `SetAbort`, we are telling MTS to roll back any transaction that might be in progress.

We'll need to go through every method where we implemented `SetComplete` and add this error handling code to each one. Then, any time we run into any problem we're sure that we'll have called `SetAbort` so MTS knows to abort any current transaction.

# Establishing a Transaction

We have changed the `VideoServerMTS` project and its classes so they follow the rules for transaction processing and object reference passing. We've changed the `VideoObjects` code (in the case of the `Video` and `Tapes` objects) to behave as required by creating a single MTS object and letting that object create any other objects it needs in order to complete its work.

All that work got our program ready to support transactions. Now all that remains is to flip the final switch so MTS knows to use our objects in a transactional context. Visual Basic 6.0 makes this very easy to do: we just need to set some properties on our objects with the IDE and recompile our DLL.

Each `Public` class in our `VideoServerMTS` project has a `MTSTransactionMode` property that is used by MTS to determine how the object handles transactions. The property can have the following values:

| Option | Description |
|---|---|
| 0-NotAnMTSObject | This is the default option and indicates that the object not only doesn't contain the code needed to support transactions, but it is totally unaware of MTS. Objects that were not written for MTS fall into this category. |
| 1-NoTransactions | This option tells MTS that, while the object may be aware of MTS, it's never to be run as part of a transaction. |
| 2-RequiresTransaction | This means that the object must run within a transaction. If one is already started, it will join it; but if the object is created outside the context of an existing transaction then a new transaction will be started. |
| 3-UsesTransaction | This option indicates that the object is programmed to support transactions but does not require one. If this object is created by another object within a transaction then it will participate in that transaction. If it's created outside of any transaction then it will run with no problem, just without any transactional support. |
| 4-RequiresNewTransaction | With this option, any time an instance of this object is created, it will start a new transaction. This will happen regardless of whether it was created by an object within an existing transaction or not. |

All of our objects are now MTS-aware and make appropriate calls to `SetComplete` and `SetAbort`. This means that all of our objects can at least be marked as 3-UsesTransaction. The objects we should set to this value are:

```
CustomerPersist        CustomersPersist
TextListPersist        VideosPersist
```

We have designed the `VideoPersist` object to be the parent object of a transaction. This means that it requires a transaction any time it is used. We should set its MTSTransactionMode property to 2-RequiresTransaction.

Likewise, the `TapesPersist` object is set up with the assumption that it's part of a transaction and should have its value set to 2-RequiresTransaction.

The `TapePersist` object isn't quite so clear. It may be called from the `TapesPersist` object, or from the `InvoiceTapePersist` object. However, it might also be called directly from the `Tape` object in the `VideoObjects` DLL in the case of the `CheckIn` method. In this last case there is no need for transactional support, since it is a singular, atomic operation. The calls from both `TapesPersist` and `InvoiceTapePersist` are definitely transactional however. If we set the `MTSTransactionMode` property to 3-UsesTransaction then the object will partake of any transaction in process and yet won't start one if it is called directly from the `VideoObjects` DLL.

The `Invoice` related objects should all be set to 2-RequiresTransaction, since they are all part of a larger transaction whenever an `Invoice` object is being saved.

Once these properties have been set on our class modules, we need to save and recompile the project. After it has been recompiled we'll want to update MTS with the new information. This requires us to remove the components from MTS and re-add our DLL to the package as we did earlier in this chapter. Once that's complete we should find that all our objects have the correct transactional settings.

For instance, select the `VideoServerMTS.VideoPersist` item from the MTS explorer, right-click on it and choose the Properties menu. Then select the Transaction tab on the dialog:

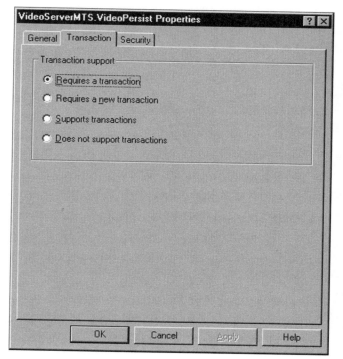

The actual terminology used within MTS is a bit different than that within Visual Basic, but we can clearly see that MTS has picked up on the fact that our `VideoPersist` object is set to require a transaction when it runs.

# Distributed Transaction Coordinator

The last area we're going to cover is the DTC (Distributed Transaction Coordinator). This is a service that was originally released as part of Microsoft SQL Server 6.0, but is now considered part of MTS.

DTC is used to handle transactions over multiple or distributed databases. It's also what really provides support for transactions within MTS. Of course, as object programmers, we never see DTC - since MTS takes care of those details behind the scenes. Still, it's important to know it's there and being used.

The one time that we might need to worry about DTC is when it isn't started on our MTS server machine, and that's what we'll cover in this section. If the DTC isn't running, we will be unable to create instances of any MTS objects marked as requiring a transaction. In our case, this includes both the `VideoPersist` and `TapesPersist` objects.

*DTC may be set to automatically start when NT boots up on the server, and if so then we won't need to worry about this issue at all.*

## Manually Starting the DTC

To start the DTC, we can use a couple different tools.

### SQL Service Manager

If we have SQL Server installed on our server machine, we can use the SQL Service Manager to start the service. We can run this application from the Windows Start menu:

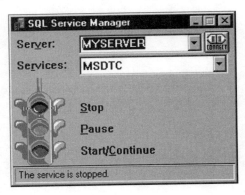

SQL Server 6.5

SQL Server 7

This figure shows the DTC service as being stopped, indicated by the red box on the left (or red light in the stoplight)

To start the service, simply click on the green arrow or double-click on the green light. The status bar at the bottom will indicate first that the service is starting, and then that it's running:

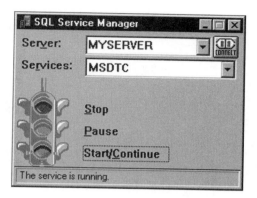

SQL Server 6.5

SQL Server 7

### Transaction Server Explorer

If we don't have SQL Server installed on our machine, we can use the Transaction Server Explorer to start and stop the DTC service. To do this simply select the My Computer item from the left-hand panel of the explorer, right-click on it and choose the Start MS DTC menu item:

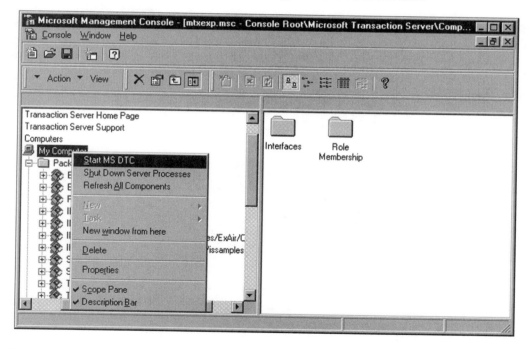

*The same menu provides options to pause or stop the service if necessary.*

## Starting DTC as NT Boots

If we're planning to support transactions on a regular basis, we'll probably want to make sure that the DTC service starts automatically each time Windows NT is booted. This is done using the Services applet from our computer's Control Panel.

If we run the Services applet, we should be able to find the DTC entry in the list of services:

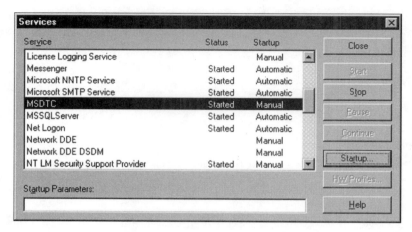

As shown in this figure, MSDTC is currently set up for manual startup. To change this setting, highlight the MSDTC item in the list and click the Startup button to the right. We can then select the Automatic option in the window so the DTC service will be started whenever Windows NT is booted:

# Summary

At this point in the book, we've realized our goal of creating a full three-tier physical client/server system. Better still, we've used distributed object technology to accomplish the goal, with our business objects doing some work on the client and some on the application server within MTS. All this without changing any of our UI code within the VideoUI project or even within our Excel application.

In this chapter, we moved our persistence server, VideoServer, into Microsoft Transaction Server. This provides us with some significant benefits today, including:

- ❑ Database connection pooling
- ❑ Transaction support
- ❑ Limited object pool management

As MTS matures, we can look forward to better object pooling. We'll also see fault tolerance and load balancing as MTS becomes integrated with Windows NT clustering. Microsoft has indicated that they consider MTS to be a vital piece of their COM strategy.

Microsoft Transaction Server enables Visual Basic and other COM-compliant languages to tackle large, mission critical systems.

Now that we've got a full-blown three tier client/server system running, we'll move on to explore some other types of application architectures that we can build on this foundation. In Chapter 13 we'll replace our forms-based user interface with an HTML interface generated using Active Server Pages – leveraging all the UI-centric and data-centric objects we've built. In Chapter 14 we'll build yet another HTML interface, but this time using the new IIS Application in Visual Basic 6.0. Finally we'll wrap up by building another new type of application in Visual Basic 6.0: a DHTML Application.

# 13

# An Active Server Pages Interface

## Overview

From the very beginning of the book, we've been exploring how we can develop our applications so that the user interface is separate from the application itself. In Chapter 7, we implemented a traditional Visual Basic interface to our application. Then, in Chapter 9, we implemented an interface using Excel - without changing the application itself.

Extending that concept, we also separated the application's business logic into two parts - the data-centric and the UI-centric processing. We've done this in two ways, using DCOM directly in Chapters 10 and 11, and most recently using Microsoft Transaction Server in Chapter 12.

Back in Chapter 2, I proposed an architecture where an application is composed of four basic parts:

- ❑ Presentation tier
- ❑ UI-centric business objects
- ❑ Data-centric object services
- ❑ Data services tier

In Chapter 4 we proposed an Internet development architecture based on Visual Basic 6.0's new IIS Application (which we'll examine in Chapter 14). Active Server Pages fill the same niche as IIS Applications, as shown in the following diagram:

| Web browser | Presentation tier |
|---|---|
| Web server | ASP interface |
| | UI-centric objects |
| | Data-centric objects |
| Database server | Data services tier |

Hopefully, by now, the benefits of partitioning our application in this manner are clear. With very little effort we've built two different user interfaces and switched from one type of database to another. In a traditional Visual Basic application either change would have most likely meant a significant rewrite of the code. With the techniques we've employed in this book, neither change was particularly difficult.

# An HTML User Interface

In this chapter I want to further illustrate just how easy it is to add radically different user interfaces. I think that most people would agree that a traditional Visual Basic user interface, or even one from Microsoft Office, is very different to what a user would experience using a web browser.

Where the Visual Basic or Office interface is likely to be highly interactive, a browser interface is typically batch-oriented. The user enters a screen's worth of information, clicks a button and the entire screen is processed as a unit. Plus, the user is also provided with useful hyperlinks and friendly navigational capabilities that are often unavailable in a traditional UI.

> *HTML has recently developed into Dynamic HTML (DHTML), available in IE4 and Netscape Communicator 4. The flexibility of traditional UI coding is now available within the browser window, in addition to the excellent text and image handling capabilities found in ordinary HTML. The use of DHTML UIs in 'hybrid' applications is now a real possibility. For more information, I suggest you look at the Microsoft web site and at* Professional IE4 Programming *(ISBN 1-861000-70-7) from Wrox Press.*

To implement this interface we'll use Active Server Pages (ASP). ASP provides us with a *server-side* scripting environment where we can interact with objects on our Web server machine, using them to get information to dynamically build web pages in HTML for our clients.

# Designing for the Internet

Following our video rental store scenario, we'll provide an interface that may be available via the Internet. This means that our end users may be using any number of different browsers running under a wide variety of operating systems.

In today's world there is no truly universal client-side scripting tool. Neither JavaScript nor VBScript are guaranteed to run properly across all operating systems and all browsers. This means we can't use any client-side scripting if we want to make sure our user interface will be available to as many of our fictitious store's customers as possible.

*VBScript is the common name for Visual Basic Scripting Edition, and is a scripting language based on a subset of Visual Basic.*

The same is true for controls or components. ActiveX controls are very powerful, but they also have a limited audience. In the grand scheme of things, few browsers or operating systems support ActiveX controls, and so again we need to avoid using them.

> Of course, if we're working on an intranet, we can enforce a standard browser type, and, with the right choice of browser, expand the range of technologies available to us. However, to utilize the widest possible client-side applicability, we're going to stick with standard HTML.

## Architecture of the UI

As I'll illustrate later, we can use ASP to construct a user interface where the client workstation sends or receives standard HTML. The user sees displays constructed with HTML and provides information back to the web server using HTML forms or other valid HTML information-passing techniques.

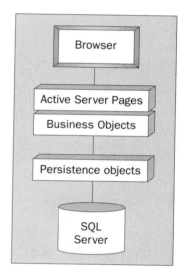

Our ASP scripts are responsible for using the user's input to interact with our business objects in order to generate the HTML to be sent back to the browser. Used this way, our ASP code will be interacting with the business objects in much the same way as the code behind our forms in a traditional Visual Basic application.

In our traditional Visual Basic UI we added code to allow the controls on the form to interact with the business objects. The ASP scripts are no different. They allow the HTML forms to interact with the business objects and provide HTML back to the browser in response to any activity.

The business objects themselves will remain effectively unchanged. We've already implemented the objects to communicate through DCOM with the persistence objects running within an MTS environment. This communication is unaffected by the UI, so it doesn't matter whether the business objects are being used by a Visual Basic interface, Excel or an Active Server Pages script. In each case, the business objects interact with the objects in MTS in exactly the same way.

# Active Server Pages

Web developers have been using various techniques to create software on the web server since the very early days of the technology. One of the earliest techniques involved having the web server recognize certain file extensions as being scripts. The server would run this script, providing any arguments from the URL to the script and sending any output from the script back to the user's browser. This was made into a standard called the Common Gateway Interface, or CGI.

While effective, CGI required the use of tools that supported C style input and output and so the development tool set was quite limited. For the most part, only programs that worked on a command line could operate with CGI.

Various workarounds to the limitations of communicating through CGI then started to appear. Microsoft backed ISAPI, which is very similar in concept to CGI, but runs the called programs within the server process for extra performance. It also introduced the notion of an ISAPI filter, a DLL which intercepts each browser request and can decide what content to return.

While ISAPI broadened the number of development tools that could be used for server-side development in Windows, it also suffered from some of the same limitations as CGI; i.e. it was difficult to develop to. Neither technique provides any real environment for scripts.

ASP is one of a number of development environments that attempts to address these shortcomings. ASP uses ISAPI to communicate with the web server itself, but it goes far beyond ISAPI in what it provides to the scripts that run inside its environment.

> *One point to note is that ASP 2.0 supports transactions on MTS 2.0 within the scripting page. This is interesting, but not very relevant here, as the* `VideoObjects` *DLL has transactional support built right into its objects. If we depended on the ASP script to maintain an overall transactional view of the components executing on the page, and roll back or commit based on the success of all the components, we would have reduced the flexibility of our business objects for use in a variety of UIs.*

# A Simple ASP Script

Before we get too far into the ASP environment, let's take a quick look at what a script looks like and how it might work. The traditional thing to do is to create a simple 'Hello world' program, and I'd hate to break with tradition.

> *ASP scripts are simple text. You can create them using Visual Interdev, Microsoft FrontPage or any number of other web-authoring tools. Throughout this chapter however, I'll use Notepad to keep things simple and to illustrate that ASP programming doesn't necessarily require complex tools.*

## Set up the Script Directory

In order for your web server to realize that files with an ASP extension are programs and not simple HTML we need to set the web directory to have Execute permissions. This is done differently depending on whether you are using Microsoft Internet Information Server (IIS) or Personal Web Server. Since any serious business application should be running under Windows NT, I'll stick to IIS for this demonstration.

### Creating a Directory for the Files

Before we get started with IIS itself, we need to make sure we have a physical directory on the disk in which to store our files. I won't go through the details of using the Windows Explorer, suffice it to say we need to create a folder to hold our scripts.

On your web server machine you should (by default) have an `Inetpub\wwwroot` directory where IIS prefers to have all the web files located. On my server this is `d:\Inetpub\wwwroot` and so it is under this directory that I will create a `helloworld` directory, `d:\Inetpub\wwwroot\helloworld`.

> *If this directory is on an NTFS drive you may need to change its permissions so the relevant files are accessible to IUSER_servername for Read and Execute. I'll leave those details up to you.*

### Microsoft Internet Service Manager

The tool we need to use to manage our web site is the Internet Service Manager. As with the MTS Service Manager we used in Chapter 12, this tool runs as a plug-in within the Microsoft Management Console (MMC). This program will display all the Internet services that are running on our NT machine, or other NT machines that we are allowed to manage.

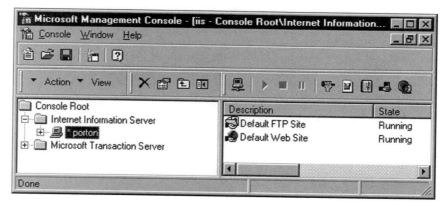

If we right-click on the **Default Web Site** option in the right-hand panel we'll get a menu. Click on the option for **New | Virtual Directory**. This will bring up the **New Virtual Directory Wizard** which will guide us through the process of setting up our directory.

The first step is to give our new directory a name, so we'll stick with the theme of `helloworld`:

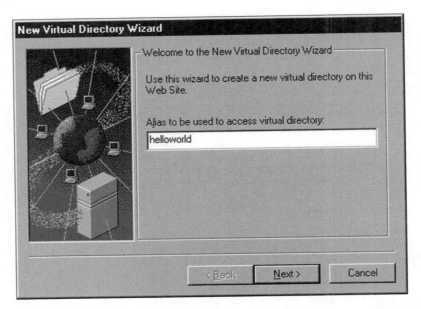

The next step is to identify the directory where our files will be located. We've already created a helloworld directory under wwwroot, so we can simply enter that path into the dialog:

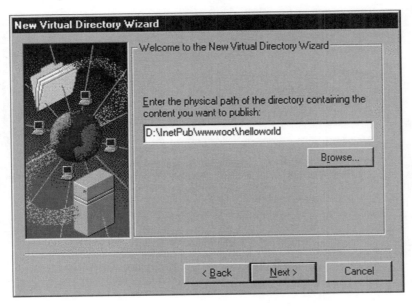

The next panel is important, as it is here that we need to make sure to indicate our directory needs execute access:

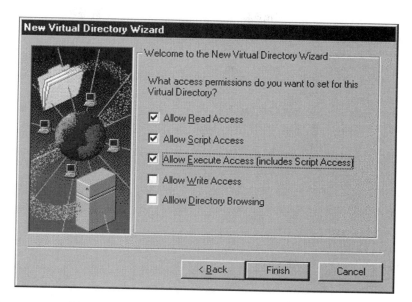

By checking the option to Allow Execute Access (includes Script Access), we are indicating to IIS that this directory will contain script files that are to be run on the server when the user attempts to access them.

When we click the Finish button the wizard will create our virtual directory. When it is complete, our new directory will be displayed in the left-hand panel:

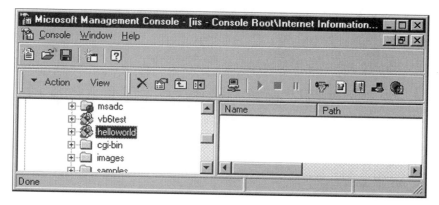

Now our directory is ready for use. With execute access set on the directory, IIS will automatically execute any script files that we place in the `helloworld` directory.

> **With a virtual directory name of** `helloworld` **and my server's name of** `porton`, **the URL to our files will be**
> `http://porton/helloworld/filename`.

## *Create the Script*

ASP scripts are stored in files with an ASP extension, for example `hello.asp`. They are a mix of HTML and the scripting language of your choice. The default scripting language for ASP is VBScript, which will work great for us.

### *Simple HTML*

The first thing I want to do is demonstrate how HTML can be used in an ASP script. Consider the following:

```
<HTML>
<BODY>
<P>Hello world</P>
</BODY>
</HTML>
```

This bit of code is HTML to print Hello world in the browser's display. You might find this code in a file with a `.htm` or `.html` extension. You might also find it in a file with a `.asp` extension, since ASP scripts can contain regular HTML.

Bring up Notepad and enter the code from above. Save the file in your `helloworld` directory as `hello.asp`. Now bring up your browser and enter a URL to get at the new file. For example, with my server's name of `porton`, the URL is:

        http://porton/helloworld/hello.asp

The browser should come up with the words Hello world on an otherwise blank page.

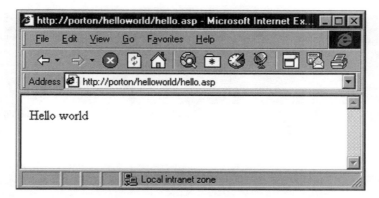

### *Adding Code*

Other than illustrating how we can have HTML in our scripts, that was not terribly interesting. Now let's extend our script to include some code.

We need to indicate to ASP what sections of our file contain code and what sections contain HTML. This is done by enclosing the code within a set of brackets `<%` and `%>`. These brackets might enclose a single statement or an entire block of code spanning many lines. Either way works just fine as far as ASP is concerned.

Change the text in Notepad as shown.

```
<HTML>
<BODY>
<% For Index = 1 to 5 %>
<P>Hello world</P>
<% Next %>
</BODY>
</HTML>
```

Now save the file and refresh your browser. You should see that we get Hello world displayed five times instead of just once.

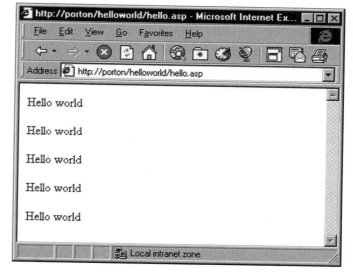

ASP interpreted our `For...Next` loop as you'd expect of any such loop in Visual Basic. What might not have been obvious until running the script is that all the HTML within the `For...Next` loop is repeated as though it were part of the code.

### Mixing Code and HTML

As a final example, let's incorporate some script code on the same line as our HTML. Change the script as shown here:

```
<HTML>
<BODY>
<% For Index = 1 to 5 %>
<P>Hello world <% =Index %></P>
<% Next %>
</BODY>
</HTML>
```

If you now save and run this script you should see something like the result shown in this figure here:

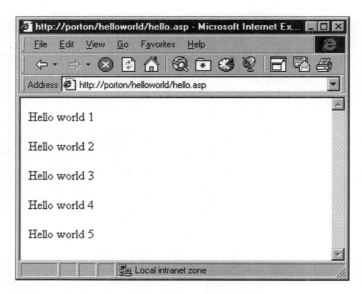

What we've done is mixed some HTML and some script code together on the same line.

```
<P>Hello world <% =Index %></P>
```

As before, the code is enclosed within the `<%` and `%>` brackets. In this case we are just printing the value of `Index` into the output that goes back to the browser. The syntax `=variable` is a shorthand for printing any value into the output stream being sent to the browser.

Just to show that ASP has done what it should; if you view the source of the displayed page, you'll get the following, HTML-only code:

```
<HTML>
<BODY>

<P>Hello world 1</P>

<P>Hello world 2</P>

<P>Hello world 3</P>

<P>Hello world 4</P>

<P>Hello world 5</P>

</BODY>
</HTML>
```

# The ASP Environment

Scripts running in the ASP environment may be authored using either JavaScript or VBScript. ASP provides developers in either language with a powerful, standard environment with which to create software.

ASP provides support for security, as well as the concept of a *session*, which spans multiple interactions with a single user and the friendly parsing of user input or other arguments on the URL. In fact, ASP supplies five main objects to every script, and these objects provide the scripts with properties and methods to support these advanced concepts:

- ❑   Application
- ❑   Request
- ❑   Response
- ❑   Server
- ❑   Session

*I am not going to go through the details of all these objects. ASP development is a topic for whole books, like* Professional Active Server Pages 2.0 *(ISBN 1-861001-26-6) from Wrox Press. Sample code for the book is available at* http://rapid.wrox.co.uk. *I recommend you explore that and the ASP documentation from Microsoft for more detailed information. Within this chapter we'll see how we can latch a simple ASP script into our business object code.*

I will cover selected methods of the Request, Response and Server objects, since we'll be using them to develop our new UI. Request and Response are the most basic of the objects, providing each ASP script with the ability to receive information from the user and to provide dynamic information back for display in the browser. The Server object allows our script to gain access to services provided by the web server itself.

## The Request Object

One of the biggest limitations of CGI and ISAPI is that they provide no standard or easy way for the script to get at the information supplied by the user or provided as arguments on the URL. ASP's Request object is the answer to this problem.

Script code can use the Request object's methods to easily get at any data provided by the user, be it from an HTML form or the URL itself. In our UI we'll use both of these techniques to provide input to the script, so let's look at how this is done.

### Request.QueryString

One way to send information to an ASP script is to send it as a parameter on the URL. The syntax for this type of URL is like this:

```
http://server/directory/page.asp?key=value
```

For instance, if we wanted to send a parameter to our hello.asp script we might use a URL like:

```
http://porton/helloworld/hello.asp?count=5
```

Were we to do this, we could alter our ASP script to take advantage of the parameter value to vary the number of times we go through our For...Next loop.

```
<HTML>
<BODY>
<% For Index = 1 to Request.QueryString("count") %>
<P>Hello world <% =Index %></P>
<% Next %>
</BODY>
</HTML>
```

As you can see, `QueryString` requires that you indicate the name of the parameter for which you are looking. Alternatively, you can use a numeric value to indicate the parameter by position. For instance, to get the third parameter you could use `Request.QueryString(3)`.

You might have also noted that I didn't make any allowances for the data type of the value returned. This is because all values of any variable in ASP are `Variant`. ASP has no concept of data types, so everything is always a `Variant`. As you'll see later in the chapter, we'll need to take some steps to overcome this when we are talking to our objects.

### Request.Form

HTML forms are very old, at least in terms of Internet chronology. These forms allow us to create input forms so that the user can enter values into text boxes, select from lists, radio buttons or check boxes and work with combo boxes.

The `Request` object makes it very easy for us to retrieve the values entered by the user into each of the controls in our HTML forms. The `Form` collection of the `Request` object is very similar to `QueryString`, requiring us to indicate which field's data we want to get and returning the corresponding value.

For instance, suppose we have an HTML form with a text box named `txtName`. In our ASP script we can use the value entered by the user as shown:

```
<HTML>
<BODY>
<% For Index = 1 to Request.QueryString("count") %>
<P><% =Request.Form("txtName") %></P>
<% Next %>
</BODY>
</HTML>
```

Again I am using the `=value` shortcut to include the value returned by `Request.Form` directly into the HTML that is sent back to the browser. The example itself simply prints the contents of the textbox `count` number of times on the returned page.

## The Response Object

The `Response` object is the opposite of the `Request` object. Instead of collecting information from the user, the `Response` object is what we use to send information back to the browser.

We've already used the `Response` object by using the `=value` shortcut to send the value of a variable back to the browser as HTML. This is really a shortcut for the `Write` method of the `Response` object.

To see how this can work, let's rewrite our `hello.asp` file so it contains no HTML, only code. Needless to say, this is deliberate overkill - we're just proving a point:

```
<%
Response.Write "<HTML>"
Response.Write "<BODY>"
For Index = 1 to 5
  Response.Write "<P>Hello world " & Index & "</P>"
Next
Response.Write "</BODY>"
Response.Write "</HTML>"
%>
```

Rather than mixing HTML and code, this new script is all code. Of course, we want the resulting output to be HTML, and so I am using `Response.Write` to send all the same HTML code to the output stream.

If you run this script, you should get the same result as we had earlier. From the browser's perspective, this is no different from our very first page.

## The Server Object

Our intent is to use ASP scripting code to create a user interface for our business objects. This implies that our scripts will have access to the business objects so our ASP code can interact with the objects' properties and methods.

One of the `Server` object's methods is `CreateObject`, and it pretty much does what you'd expect. Just like the `CreateObject` method within Visual Basic, you merely send it the ActiveX server name and class name and it returns a reference to the object.

```
Set objVideo = Server.CreateObject("VideoObjects.Video")
```

There are some differences. By default, ASP will only allow you to create objects from an in-process server, not from any out-of-process or remote servers. Fortunately for us, our business objects are contained within a DLL and so we don't need to worry.

However, the fact that our business objects turn right around and create objects on a remote machine is not problematic for ASP. Basically ASP prevents us from *directly* creating out of process server objects, but we can do pretty much whatever we want within the objects in our DLLs.

# Updating our ActiveX Servers

Now that we've got the basics of using ASP, let's look at how this new user interface will change our existing ActiveX servers, `VideoObjects` and `VideoServerMTS`.

As far as code changes go, we need to change absolutely *nothing*. Since we've designed our business objects to support a robust and interactive UI, we already have everything we need to support this new UI. Remember that a web-based UI is going to be batch oriented, and for our business objects that means simpler.

We don't have to worry about Cancel or Apply buttons. The only time data will be sent back to the server is if the user clicks an OK button, and so we only need to worry about the case where the user wants to save data or run a search. Our objects already provide access to the properties that can either be displayed in the browser, or set based on data entered by the user.

# ASP and Threading Models

Where we do need to make a change is in the Properties dialog of the `VideoObjects` DLL.

The change we need to make is pretty simple. Our DLL will be running within IIS on a server machine – probably far away from any actual users. Due to this we want to make sure that the DLL doesn't bring up any dialog boxes or other user interface elements – even by accident. To make sure this is the case, we'll simply check the box for Unattended Execution and recompile the DLL.

Bring up the `VideoObjects` project in Visual Basic. Choose the Project | VideoObjects Properties... menu option.

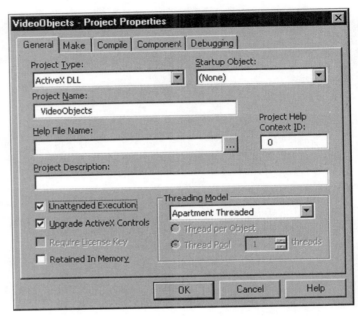

Check the Unattended Execution option as shown in the figure.

Don't forget to save these changes and recompile the DLL for this change to take effect.

With this one simple change we've upgraded our entire application to be ready for use by ASP. Now we need to make sure our DLL is available for use by ASP.

# Installing the VideoObjects DLL

For our ASP scripts to use the business objects in our DLL we need to make the DLL available to ASP. This means installing the DLL on our web server machine. It also means we need to run the client install program to register the `VideoPersistMTS` objects on the web server machine.

If your web server machine doesn't have Visual Basic, or any Visual Basic programs installed you'll need to use the Package and Deployment Wizard (as we did in Chapter 11) to create an installation set for the `VideoObjects` DLL. This will install not only the DLL, but all the required Visual Basic support files with which it needs to operate.

### Loading the Video Object

Now that we have a reference to a `Video` object we can call its `Load` method to tell it to retrieve values from the database. As you may recall, the `Load` method accepts the `VideoID` value as its single parameter. In this case we'll use the ASP `Request` object's `QueryString` method to get the ID value from the URL.

```
myVideo.Load CLng(Request.QueryString("id"))
%>
```

By using the `QueryString` method we have set up our script so we can pass a `Video` object's ID value on the URL. For example:

```
http://porton/wroxvideo/getvideo.asp?id=3
```

The `QueryString` method is used to retrieve the value of the id parameter from the URL. Here's where we need to watch what we're doing, though, because the value returned by `QueryString` is a `Variant` just like everything else in VBScript, but our `Load` method expects a `Long`.

Were we using early binding in the Visual Basic environment the `Variant` value would automatically be converted to a `Long` and we'd have to do no work. VBScript provides no support for early binding, so our objects will always be late bound. This means that VBScript has no way of knowing that the parameter is supposed to be a `Long`, and thus it doesn't perform type conversion.

To solve this problem we need to manually convert the variable to the correct type. In this case we need to use the `CLng()` function to convert the `Variant` to a `Long`.

## Setting the Document Title

At this point we've got a fully loaded `Video` object. Now we can move on to create HTML, along with some code, to display pertinent information about the video title to the user.

The first thing we'll do is indicate the title of our web page. This is done in the `<HEAD>` section of the document by using the `<TITLE>` tag.

```
<HTML>
<HEAD>
<TITLE><% Response.Write myVideo.Title %></TITLE>
</HEAD>
```

What I've done here is mix a bit of HTML with a bit of code. Rather than providing a static title for the document we are using the `Video` object's `Title` property as the title using the `Write` method of the `Response` object. The VBScript code, as usual, is wrapped within the `<%` and `%>` tags.

## The Document Body

With the object loaded, and the document's title set, we are ready to create the body of the document. This is started with the `<BODY>` tag, and I've also inserted a couple of blank paragraphs to leave a bit of space at the top, one in HTML and the second through code.

```
<BODY>
<P>
<%
Response.Write "</P>"
```

*The rest of the body of our document will be created from code. Obviously in any real application you'd want a much more complex document, with various graphics, fonts, colors and all the other exciting bells and whistles that come with web documents. In this example I'm avoiding all those things so we can focus directly on the code that generates the dynamic text for the display.*

## Displaying the Studio and Title

Our first line of output will display the studio where the video was produced along with the video's title.

```
Response.Write "<P>" & myVideo.Studio & " Presents "
Response.Write Chr(34) & myVideo.Title & Chr(34) & "</P>"
```

There are a couple interesting things here. These two lines of code actually create only one line in the display. HTML only breaks lines when we tell it to by using a tag (in this case </P>), and the first line here has no tag to break the line.

Both lines use the & character for string concatenation, just like Visual Basic itself. I have set this up so the video's title is placed within double quotes. To do this I am using the Chr() function, passing the value 34 which is the ASCII value for the double quote character.

## Displaying the Rating

In this next bit of code, we'll display the video's rating, along with descriptive text indicating the meaning of the rating. Ideally we might have our business object provide this information, but since it wasn't required for our other interfaces it was not included in the object. Instead we'll use a Select...Case statement to display the appropriate text.

We'll now copy the Rating property from our Video object into a variable. I've prefixed the variable with str to indicate it contains a string value. Even though VBScript variables are all Variants, it doesn't hurt to indicate the data type we believe the variable holds to increase our program's readability.

```
strRating = Trim(myVideo.Rating)
Response.Write "<P>This movie is rated '" & strRating & "', "
Select Case strRating
Case "G"
   Response.Write "suitable for general audiences"
Case "PG"
   Response.Write "parental guidance suggested"
Case "PG-13"
   Response.Write "not suitable for children under age 13"
Case "R"
   Response.Write "children under 17 not admitted without parent"
Case "NR"
   Response.Write "not rated - for mature audiences"
End Select
Response.Write "</P>"
```

Again, all this code generates a single line in the display. Only the last line written to the output stream, </P>, causes the browser to break to a new paragraph.

### Counting the Number of Tapes

By this point you've probably had enough of simply displaying text. The only other piece of critical information our video store's customers will probably want is whether there are any tapes available for rental. Fortunately for us, by loading the Video object we have also loaded all its child Tape objects.

This provides us with the opportunity to take advantage of one of the biggest advantages of business objects: they are evolutionary. This means we can easily add capabilities to our objects as the need arises over time, making them more and more powerful as they grow.

In this case, we'll just add a new property to our Tapes object to provide the count of available tapes for the current video title. We'll call this property AvailableCount. To add this property, open the VideoObjects project and bring up the code window for the Tapes object. Add the following code:

```
Public Property Get AvailableCount() As Long

    Dim objTape As Tape
    Dim lngAvailable As Long

    For Each objTape In mcolTapes
      If Not objTape.CheckedOut Then _
        lngAvailable = lngAvailable + 1
    Next
    AvailableCount = lngAvailable

End Property
```

All we're really doing here is running through the colTapes collection to scan through all the Tape objects and find out which ones have been rented and which are available. Make sure to recompile the VideoObjects project to make this new property available to our client code.

With the number of available tapes so easily available we can use an If...ElseIf structure to provide a user-friendly display of the number of tapes.

```
intAvail = myVideo.Tapes.AvailableCount

Response.Write "<P>We have "
If intAvail = 0 Then
  Response.Write "no tapes "
ElseIf intAvail = 1 Then
  Response.Write "1 tape "
Else
  Response.Write intAvail & " tapes "
End If
Response.Write "available for rental</P>"
```

## Wrapping up the Document

With that, we've created the body of our document. All we need to do now is set our object variable to Nothing to release the object and provide the HTML to indicate the document is done.

```
Set myVideo = Nothing
%>
</BODY>
</HTML>
```

Save this file as `getvideo.asp` into the directory where you are storing our new UI. As I mentioned, I am using a directory named `wroxvideo`. Make sure the directory's **Execute** attribute is checked on, using the Internet Services Manager application.

# Running the Script

Running our program is easy. All we need to do is bring up our browser, pretty much any browser will do, and enter the URL to our script file. We do need to pass the ID parameter on the URL line after the ? symbol. For example:

```
http://porton/wroxvideo/getvideo.asp?id=3
```

This will cause IIS to invoke ASP. ASP in turn will run our script, executing the code we've included and producing a web page that displays the details about the video with a `VideoID` of 3.

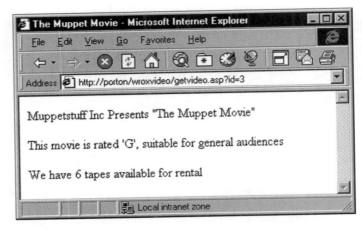

Notice how the title bar of the browser indicates our video's title, while the body of the text in the browser is assembled, as we'd expect from the code we just implemented.

While this is a very useful display of information, it is pretty limited in its use. To get any information the user needs to supply the video's ID number. Obviously we can't expect our video store's customers to know the ID value for every video title, so we need to come up with a solution to this problem.

# Getting a List of Video Titles

In the UI we created using Visual Basic we included a screen where the user could enter part or all of a video's title or studio and get a list of matching values from the database. This result set was returned through the `Videos` object as a collection of `VideoDisplay` objects.

We can provide the same functionality through our web interface. First we can show the user a form, allowing them to enter part or all of the video's title and studio. Based on the values entered we can load a `Videos` object and display the results for the user.

Better still, we can set up each video title to be a hyperlink back to our `getvideo.asp` script so the user can click on a video title to get details about that specific video. I realize that from a user's perspective I'm presenting these two scripts in reverse order, but I wanted to get the easy one out of the way first and then tackle this one.

# A Recursive HTML Form

Using ASP, we can create scripts that present the user with a form, and then send the user's input values back to the *same* script. This can be a very elegant way to package all the code for an HTML form into the same file, making it easy to develop and maintain.

## The HTML Form

The first thing we need to look at is the HTML form code itself. I'm not going to get into the details of the HTML in `VideoSearch.html` - suffice it to say that the following HTML code will display a form with two text-input boxes, an Enter button and a Cancel button.

```
<HTML>
<HEAD>
<TITLE>Get Video Criteria</TITLE>
</HEAD>
<BODY>
<FORM ACTION="getvideos.asp" METHOD="POST">
  Title:<BR>
  <INPUT TYPE=TEXT NAME="txtTitle"><P>
  Studio:<BR>
  <INPUT TYPE=TEXT NAME="txtStudio"><P>
  <INPUT TYPE=SUBMIT VALUE="Enter">
  <INPUT TYPE=RESET VALUE="Cancel">
</FORM>
</BODY>
</HTML>
```

If the user clicks the Cancel button the form is simply reset by the browser; nothing is sent back to the web server. When the user clicks Enter however, the form is posted back to the web server. The results are sent to the URL indicated by the `ACTION` attribute of the `<FORM>` tag.

```
<FORM ACTION="getvideos.asp" METHOD="POST">
```

We'll be naming our script `getvideos.asp`, so this line of code indicates that the contents of the controls on the form are to be sent back to our script file.

## Handling the Recursion

Obviously when the user clicks the Enter button they won't be expecting to see the form simply redisplayed. Yet this is what would happen if we don't take some extra steps in our code to see if the script is being run as a result of the Enter button being clicked.

We could add VBScript code to see if the user entered a value in either the Title or Studio fields and use that to branch off to different code. However it is possible the user might not enter a value in either field, and yet we still want to react to the fact that the Enter button was clicked.

The answer lies in the ability of an HTML form to have a hidden 'control', for example:

```
<INPUT TYPE=HIDDEN NAME="hdnAction" VALUE="0">
```

These controls can have a value assigned to them, but they aren't visible to the user. When the Enter button is clicked, the values of all controls on the form are sent back to our script. On the other hand, when a script is run directly, for instance by the user moving to that URL, no control information is provided to the script at all.

If we add code at the top of our script to check for the presence of the hidden control then we can easily know whether our script was invoked through a URL directly, or by the user clicking the Enter button on our form.

```
<%
If Request.Form("hdnAction") = Empty Then
%>
  <HTML>
  <HEAD>
  <TITLE>Get Video Criteria</TITLE>
  </HEAD>
  <BODY>
  <FORM ACTION="getvideos.asp" METHOD="POST">
    <INPUT TYPE=HIDDEN NAME="hdnAction" VALUE="0">
    Title:<BR>
    <INPUT TYPE=TEXT NAME="txtTitle"><P>
    Studio:<BR>
    <INPUT TYPE=TEXT NAME="txtStudio"><P>
    <INPUT TYPE=SUBMIT VALUE="Enter">
    <INPUT TYPE=RESET VALUE="Cancel">
  </FORM>
  </BODY>
  </HTML>
<%
Else
%>
  ... Code or HTML goes here ...
<%
End If
%>
```

At the top we have an `If...Then` statement that checks to see if the hidden control, `hdnAction`, exists. If we got here by the user clicking on the Enter button the control won't be empty since it will contain the value 0. In this case VBScript will branch down to the `Else` statement and execute any code found there.

Basically we've created two entire documents within a single file. If the script is run directly from a URL the document will consist of everything from the `If...Then` down to the `Else` statement. On the other hand, if the script is run via the Enter key being pressed then the document will consist of everything between the `Else` and `End If` statements.

What we have is the definition of our HTML form at the top and all the code to process the results at the bottom. This structure makes for contained and maintainable HTML forms.

# Displaying the List of Videos

Now that we've got the basics of our recursive HTML form put together we need to add the code to process the data entered by the user. To make the results readable we'll present them to the user in an HTML table, displaying both the video's title and its release date.

## *Creating the Videos Object*

As with the `Video` object earlier, we need to use the ASP `Server` object's `CreateObject` method to create an instance of our `Videos` object.

```
<%
Else
    Set myVideos = Server.CreateObject("VideoObjects.Videos")
```

### *Loading the Object*

Once we have a reference to our new object we can call its `Load` method, using the title and studio values entered by the user as criteria. For readability I have included code here to copy the user-supplied values into the variables - `strTitle` and `strStudio`. To get the values from the form's controls we are using the ASP `Request` object's `Form` collection as discussed earlier in the chapter.

```
        strTitle = Request.Form("txtTitle")
        strStudio = Request.Form("txtStudio")
        myVideos.Load CStr(strTitle), CStr(strStudio)
        %>
```

The `Load` method expects that its parameters will be of the `String` data type. Just like the `Load` method of the `Video` object, we need to manually convert our variables to the appropriate type to avoid a type mismatch error from VBScript. In this case we'll use the `CStr()` function to convert the `Variant` variables to the `String` data type.

## *Setting up the Document*

With our object loaded and ready to go, we can start creating the HTML document itself. The first thing we need to do is set the document's title. We'll also indicate that we're starting the document's body and add a line of text indicating what type of information is being displayed.

```
        myVideos.Load CStr(strTitle), CStr(strStudio)
        %>
        <HTML>
        <HEAD>
        <TITLE>Video List</TITLE>
        </HEAD>
        <BODY>
        <P>Here is a list of video titles from our wide selection:</P>
```

## *Building the Table*

Onto the table itself. The first thing to do is to use the `<TABLE>` tag to indicate we are building a table. Then we'll add column headers to indicate the contents of each column in the table.

```
<TABLE BORDER=1>
<TR>
<TD>Title</TD>
<TD>Release date</TD>
</TR>
```

Once the table is set up we can use a `For...Each` loop to go through each element in the `Videos` object and display its data. The elements of the `Videos` object are individual `VideoDisplay` objects, each with `VideoID`, `Title` and `ReleaseDate` properties.

```
<%
For Each Video In myVideos
  Response.Write "<TR>"
```

The `<TR>` tag indicates we are starting a new row in the table. We'll want a new row for each element in our `Videos` object.

### Adding a Hyperlinked Field

The next few lines are interesting because they are a mix of HTML and VBScript, all jumbled together. In the end they combine to display the video's title in the first column of our new row, with the title itself being a hyperlink back to our `getvideo.asp` script.

```
%>
<TD><A href="getvideo.asp?id=<% =Video.VideoID %>">
  <%= Video.Title %></A></TD>
<%
```

The second line shown here creates the URL reference to the `getvideo.asp` file. It also appends the `id` parameter, passing the `VideoID` value from the current `VideoDisplay` object. Earlier in the chapter we created the `getvideo.asp` script to look for the ID parameter and use its value as the key when loading the details about the specific video. So by passing the `VideoID` property as that parameter here, we provide the user with a friendly way to get at the `getvideo.asp` script's functionality.

The next line puts the `Title` property of our `VideoDisplay` object into the output stream so it is displayed for the user. Since this value is enclosed within the `<A>` and `</A>` tags it is considered to be a hyperlink and so it will be displayed appropriately in the browser.

### Displaying the ReleaseDate Property

The other column of information we'll display to the user is the video's release date from the object's `ReleaseDate` property. The HTML to include this column in the table is quite straightforward.

Once the date is added to the table we need to use the `</TR>` tag to indicate that this row of the table is complete:

```
Response.Write "<TD>" & Video.ReleaseDate & "</TD>"
Response.Write "</TR>"
Next
```

Now that we've added this particular VideoDisplay object's data to the table, we can just continue looping through the rest of the elements in the Videos object, displaying each one in turn.

### Wrapping up the Document

With the table complete, all that remains is to close out both our object and the HTML. As usual, we need to set our object variable to Nothing to release our reference to the object. Then we can add the HTML to close out the table, the body of the document and the document itself.

```
    Set myVideos = Nothing
    %>
    </TABLE>
    </BODY>
    </HTML>
<%
End If
%>
```

Now save this file in your script directory as getvideos.asp. In my case I'm saving it into the wroxvideo directory along with the getvideo.asp file. It is important that these two files be located in the same directory, since we've implemented hyperlinks from the getvideos.asp script back to the getvideo.asp script we created earlier.

# Running the Script

We can run this script pretty much the same way we ran getvideo.asp. Simply enter the URL to getvideos.asp as your browser's address. In my case the URL will be

```
http://porton/wroxvideo/getvideos.asp
```

The browser should come up and display our HTML form, allowing us to enter values for the title and studio, along with options to click the Enter or Cancel button.

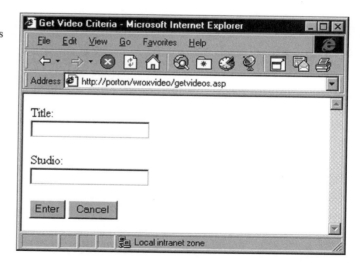

If we now enter values into the Title and Studio fields and click the Cancel button you'll see that the browser resets the fields to be blank. There is no network traffic here; the Cancel button is entirely handled by the browser itself.

If, on the other hand, you click the Enter button, with or without criteria, the browser will send the results of the form back to the `getvideos.asp` script. Since the form also includes our hidden control, `hdnAction`, our VBScript code will branch down to the `Else` clause where we can process the values in the Title and Studio fields.

The result will be the display of a table of video titles along with their release dates.

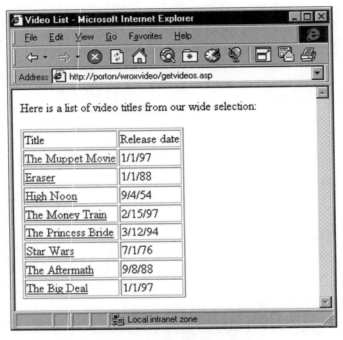

As you can see, all the video titles are hyperlinks. In the figure above, the status bar can show the URL that will be invoked if we click on the first item in the table. This should look familiar, as it is the same URL I entered manually when we were testing the `getvideo.asp` script earlier in the chapter.

If we now click on the first item in the table the browser will send that URL to the web server. This will run our `getvideo.asp` script and should produce the same result we got in our earlier tests.

# Summary

In this chapter we've taken a full n-tier client server application and added an entirely new and different user interface with almost no effort. By extending the examples I've shown in this chapter you could easily create a browser-based UI that provides all the capabilities of the Visual Basic interface we created in Chapter 7.

While the ability to use Active Server Pages to create a browser-based user interface is very powerful, Visual Basic 6.0 provides even more capabilities for building browser-based applications. In Chapter 14 we'll take a look at one of these new features: IIS Applications.

# 14

# An IIS Application Interface

## Overview

In Chapter 13 we created a browser-based user interface by making use of Active Server Pages (ASP). While ASP is very powerful, Visual Basic 6.0 provides us with a new, and in many ways more powerful, approach for creating this type of user interface application: IIS Applications.

An IIS Application is very similar to an ASP application, but instead of being written as a mix of HTML and VBScript, an IIS Application is written totally within Visual Basic 6.0, with separate HTML files used as templates for generating the user interface.

As with the other user interfaces we've designed in this book, including the Visual Basic forms interface, the interface in Microsoft Excel and the browser-based interface in ASP, implementing this interface will require no modifications to our UI-centric or data-centric objects. VideoObjects.dll and VideoServerMTS.dll will remain entirely unchanged.

In this chapter we'll implement a new user interface just like the one we created in Chapter 13. The interface itself will still be entirely browser-based, but the technology we use to create it will be quite different in many ways from Active Server Pages.

# IIS Applications

Internet Information Server (IIS) Applications are a new feature of Visual Basic 6.0. They provide Visual Basic developers with the ability to create applications that fill the same niche as Active Server Pages (ASP) when building browser-based applications.

The following diagram demonstrates how IIS Applications fit into the application architecture we used in Chapter 13:

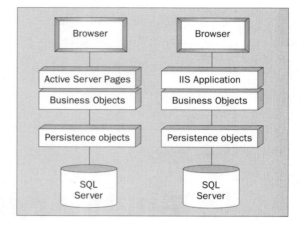

As shown in the diagram, both ASP and IIS Applications interact with our UI-centric business objects in our `VideoObjects` DLL and provide HTML to the browser in order to interact with the user.

ASP provides a *page-based* approach to application development, where the application is composed of text files containing a mix of HTML and VBScript or JavaScript. Before each of these text files is sent from IIS out to the user's browser they are interpreted and any scripting code contained in the file is run on the server, thus altering the HTML that is finally sent to the browser.

IIS Applications take a different approach, separating the HTML from the code. With an IIS Application, the code is written in Visual Basic and is compiled into one or more `WebClass` objects. Any HTML (or other files) that might need to be sent from IIS to the browser are compiled into the application as `WebItem` objects. Each `WebClass` typically has one or more `WebItem` objects that it uses to generate the interface displayed to the user.

I won't go into great depth regarding IIS Applications. They are a very complex type of application, with many nuances that are outside the scope of creating a user interface similar to that which we created with ASP in Chapter 13. However, there are a number of key concepts that we need to explore before we can move on to creating that user interface.

## ASP Object Model

The ASP environment is very powerful. As we discussed in Chapter 13, ASP provides us with a set of objects that allow us to interact with the user's browser and the IIS server itself. These objects are:

- ❑ Request
- ❑ Response
- ❑ Session

 ❑ Application
 ❑ Server

We discussed each of these to some degree in Chapter 13, so I won't revisit the details here.

The key point here is that these objects are also available within our IIS Application. This means that we can receive input from the browser by using the Request object and send information back to the browser using the Response object. These objects work no differently from within Visual Basic than they do within an ASP page, so if you are familiar with ASP programming the availability of these objects makes for a nice transition to IIS Application programming.

# WebClass Objects

An IIS Application contains at least one WebClass module. A WebClass can be thought of as the interface point between the browser and the IIS Application itself.

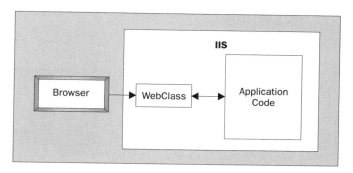

To the outside world (read browser), the WebClass appears as a simple ASP page. For instance, a WebClass module named WebClass1 would appear to a client's browser as WebClass1.asp. In reality however, any requests sent from the browser to this 'ASP' page are really routed to the WebClass1 object within our Visual Basic application.

> *Behind the scenes Visual Basic really does create an ASP page as I just described. This ASP page is a very short, standard bit of code that simply relays any client requests through an IIS Application runtime DLL and into our WebClass object. None of this matters much to us as developers, since we simply see the client request come into our object as a method call – nothing complex about that.*

WebClass objects have a set of special properties and methods that allow them to function effectively within the web server environment. We won't cover all of them here, just some key ones that will be important as we create our application.

| | |
|---|---|
| NameInURL property | This property allows us to specify the URL name that will be used by the client's browser to access our WebClass. This is the name of the 'ASP page' that the client will access when they connect to our object. |
| WebClass_Start event | This event occurs within our WebClass as soon as the object has been fully loaded. This is analogous to the Form_Load event in a regular Visual Basic form. |

A number of other events occur during the lifetime of a WebClass object, including
`WebClass_Initialize` and `WebClass_Terminate`, which operate just like the `Initialize`
and `Terminate` events of any other class module.

## Hello World Example

Let's create a simple 'Hello world' application using a WebClass to get the basic concept down.

Open up Visual Basic and create a new
IIS Application project.

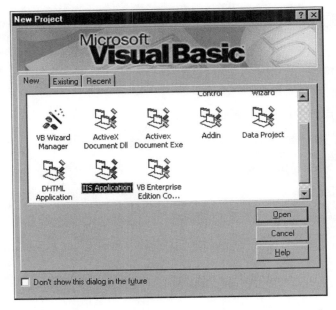

Visual Basic will automatically add a WebClass to our project. WebClasses are edited using a specific
WebClass designer. The WebClass appears under the Designers entry in the Project window within
the IDE.

> *Designers are one of the ways in which Visual Basic can be extended. Every type of module we
> work with in Visual Basic is actually edited or manipulated by a designer. The common types of
> modules, Form, Class and Module are all supported by built-in designers, but others can be
> added. Visual Basic 6.0 makes heavy use of designers to support new application concepts such as
> WebClasses.*

Double-click on the WebClass1
entry to bring up the designer
within the IDE.

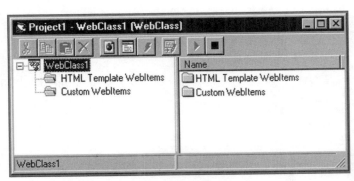

As we discussed earlier, the `WebClass_Start` event fires as our WebClass object is instantiated by a request from the client. To create a simple 'Hello world' application we can simply add code to this event procedure to send the appropriate HTML back to the client's browser.

To open a code window for our WebClass, simply double-click on the **WebClass1** item in the left-hand pane of the designer window. Visual Basic starts us with some basic template code in the `WebClass_Start` procedure:

```
Private Sub WebClass_Start()

    'Write a reply to the user
    With Response
        .Write "<html>"
        .Write "<body>"
        .Write "<h1><font face=""Arial"">WebClass1's Starting Page</font></h1>"
        .Write "<p>This response was created in the Start event of WebClass1.</p>"
        .Write "</body>"
        .Write "</html>"
    End With

End Sub
```

As we discussed earlier in the chapter, the ASP `Response` object is directly available from within our IIS Application. This code simply uses the `Response` object's `Write` method to send some simple HTML back to the client. We'll just alter this HTML to display our new message:

```
Private Sub WebClass_Start()

    'Write a reply to the user
    With Response
        .Write "<html>"
        .Write "<body>"
        .Write "<h1><font face=""Arial"">Hello world!</font></h1>"
        .Write "<p>This is our simple Hello world application.</p>"
        .Write "</body>"
        .Write "</html>"
    End With

End Sub
```

That's all there is to it. We can now press **F5** to run our application. Visual Basic will prompt us as to how it should run the program.

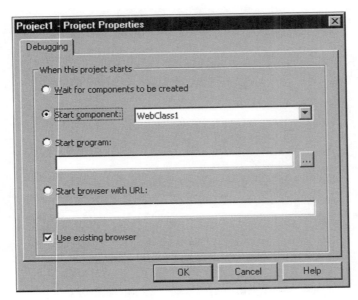

We can simply accept the default, since in this case we want to run the WebClass1 component from within our application, thus causing our WebClass_Start event to be run as it starts up.

It is also likely that our development machine is set up to preclude the ASP objects from launching out-of-process ActiveX servers. This is the default setting when IIS is installed, though virtually all development products based on IIS or ASP change the setting to allow debugging. Visual Basic 6.0 is no exception – in order to run our application in debug mode, there is a registry setting that must be changed. Fortunately this process is automated by Visual Basic, so we'll simply see the following dialog:

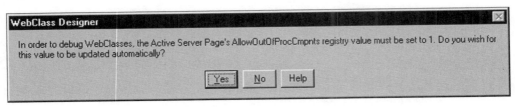

Just click Yes to change the setting and move on.

Since this is a web server application, Visual Basic will automatically create a virtual root directory for our application. This is basically the same concept as the virtual root we created for our helloworld application in Chapter 13, but Visual Basic automates the process almost entirely. As we are running the application directly from within the IDE (and since we didn't save the application to a directory yet), Visual Basic will simply create a virtual directory for our system's temp directory.

We'll be prompted by Visual Basic to confirm that we do want to create this virtual root, so click OK to create it:

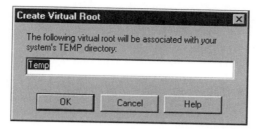

If we click OK here, Visual Basic will create the virtual directory and then run our application.

Notice that the URL for this page is using the new virtual directory Temp. More importantly however, the name of the file being accessed is WebClass1.ASP – just as we'd predict for an IIS Application.

When the browser requested that WebClass1.ASP be displayed, IIS retrieved the automatically generated stub ASP file and ran it in the ASP environment. Of course the stub file simply routed the browser's request to our IIS Application which instantiated our WebClass object. This, in turn, caused the WebClass object's WebClass_Start event to fire, running our code and producing the display we see in the browser.

Keep this project open, since we'll build on it as we discuss WebItems.

## WebItem Objects

Each WebClass object acts as a gateway between the client's browser and our application. As we've seen, the code in our WebClass object can directly generate HTML and send it to the browser using the Response object. However, this doesn't help us separate the user interface from our code in any way.

Instead, we can store the HTML that makes up our user interface in template files that are imported into our application at design time. Within our project, these templates appear as WebItem objects that can be manipulated by our application's code.

WebItems are a key part of any IIS Application. We can think of them as being somewhat analogous to a traditional Visual Basic form, in that they provide the interface that we send to the browser to be displayed for the user.

This is very different from ASP, where the HTML is mixed right in with our application's code. With IIS Applications, the HTML is stored in these separate WebItem objects, while our code is compiled into the WebClass object that owns the WebItem. When we need to display something in the user's browser, we can simply call the `WriteTemplate` method of a WebItem object to send it to the browser.

WebItems can be virtually any type of file, though they are typically HTML or DHTML text files that are imported into our application. If we choose to however, we can use WebItems to store graphic images, sounds or anything else that we may want to send to the browser as our application is running.

To see how WebItems work, let's alter the 'Hello world' program we just created to use an HTML template instead of directly generating the HTML using the `Response` object.

## Hello World Example

The first thing we'll need to do is create our HTML template file. Visual Basic doesn't provide us with any way to create WebItems from directly within the IDE. Instead, we need to use some other tool to author our HTML files, save them to disk and them import them into our project. Once they are in the project Visual Basic allows us to edit them by launching our editor from the IDE.

To create our template I'll just use Notepad. For more complex page creation we'd probably want to use something like Visual Interdev or Microsoft Frontpage, but for this simple example Notepad will work fine.

Open up Notepad and enter the following text:

```
<html>
<body>
<h1><font face=""Arial"">Hello world!</font></h1>
<p>Saying hello from our HTML template.</p>
</body>
</html>
```

Then save the file anywhere you choose on your machine. I'm going to save it as `d:\hello.htm`.

> *Make sure to change the* Save as type *option to* All files, *or Notepad will automatically append* `.txt` *to the end of our filename – and that can be confusing.*

The next thing we need to do is save our IIS Application to disk. It doesn't matter a lot where we save the application, but we should be aware that next time we run our application Visual Basic will automatically create a virtual directory pointed to where ever we save it.

> **Visual Basic won't allow us to add WebItems to an IIS Application project until that project has been saved to disk.**

Now that we've created a template HTML file and we've saved our IIS Application project, we are ready to move on and add a WebItem for the template to our project. To do this, bring up the designer window for `WebClass1`. In the left-hand pane of the window is an entry for **HTML Template WebItems**. Right-click on this entry and choose the **Add HTML template** menu option.

Using the file dialog that comes up, find and open the HTML template file we created with Notepad. We'll be returned to the WebClass designer, with a new WebItem template added to the tree in the left-hand pane. We are given an opportunity to change the name of the new template, so let's change it to `Hello`.

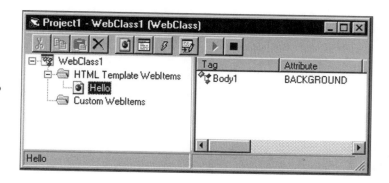

*Notice that in the right-hand pane of the designer there is an entry for `Body1`. This is the only HTML element in our template file, but if we had a more complex template then all the various HTML elements in our template would be listed in the right-hand pane. Items listed in this pane can be programmed to respond to various user actions. We won't need to use this capability for our 'Hello world' program however.*

All that remains is to change our `WebClass_Start` procedure to display our template instead of sending raw HTML via the `Response` object. Open up the code window and change the `WebClass_Start` procedure as shown here:

```
Private Sub WebClass_Start()

    'Write a reply to the user
    Hello.WriteTemplate

End Sub
```

As you press the '.' after `Hello`, notice that Visual Basic drops down a list of the methods valid for the `Hello` WebItem – thus illustrating that our `Hello` template is now a full-blown object within our project.

The `WriteTemplate` method on a WebItem simply sends the WebItem to the client's browser. On the surface this is very simple, but in reality it is a powerful capability. For instance, we can send a series of WebItems to the client by calling each WebItem's `WriteTemplate` method in turn, thus possibly building an HTML display by concatenating various parts of the page from different templates. For instance, we might do something like this:

```
StandardHeader.WriteTemplate
ThisPage.WriteTemplate
Footer2.WriteTemplate
```

Now we've got our application set up so when the WebClass is accessed it simply sends our new WebItem to the browser. Press *F5* and see how it runs.

*Remember that the first time we run the program now, since we've saved it to a directory, Visual Basic will create a new virtual directory – named by using our Visual Basic project name.*

The display in the browser is very similar to that from our first 'Hello world' program, but now we're obviously displaying the text from our WebItem – sent to the client using just a single line of code.

## Tag Substitution

In the previous example we saw how an HTML template can be simply sent to the browser unchanged. While this is useful, it could be quite limiting. In many cases we'll need to populate the template with data from objects or databases before it is sent to the browser. Ideally we'd be able to create an HTML template with simple placeholders wherever we'd like the real data to be displayed – exactly the functionality provided by Visual Basic.

WebClass objects provide us with a very powerful and yet easy to use mechanism for altering HTML templates as they are sent to the browser. The technique is called **tag substitution**, and is simply the process of replacing specific tags (text) within the HTML template with whatever text we actually want to send to the browser.

In the left-hand pane of the designer window, click on the Hello WebItem entry. Notice in the Properties window that there is a TagPrefix property displayed. It should read 'WC@' by default. This is the special tag we can insert into our HTML to indicate an area where text should be supplied by our WebItem object. For instance, we might create a tag as follows:

```
<WC@Video>Title</WC@Video>
```

As the WebItem is being sent to the browser as a result of the WriteTemplate method call, Visual Basic scans the HTML looking for this tag. Each time it finds this tag in the template, a ProcessTag event is raised within our WebItem. The text immediately following the tag prefix ('Video' in our example) is passed as a parameter, as is the text between the opening and closing tag ('Title' in the example).

We can add code to this event procedure to supply whatever text we feel is appropriate. For instance, in response to the example shown above we might write the following code:

```
Private Sub Hello_ProcessTag(ByVal TagName As String, TagContents As String, _
    SendTags As Boolean)
  TagContents = "<P>The tag name is " & TagName & "</P>" & _
    "<P>The tag text is " & TagContents & "</P>"
End Sub
```

Notice that the event name is `Hello_ProcessTag`. The WebItem name is used to prefix the event name itself, allowing us to have different event handlers for each WebItem in our project.

The text we want placed into the HTML being sent to the browser must be placed into the `TagContents` parameter. However, the `TagContents` parameter initially contains whatever text was between the opening and closing tag in the template. In this simple example, we're replacing the text with two lines of text for display in the browser – the first displays the name of the tag ('Video') and the second displays the initial text between the tags ('Title').

## Tag Substitution Example

Using our 'Hello world' example from above, let's try out tag substitution. Right-click on the Hello item in the designer and choose the Edit HTML template menu option. By default this will bring up Notepad to allow us to edit the HTML in our template.

*You may have changed the HTML editor on your development machine, in which case Visual Basic will launch your HTML editor of choice instead of Notepad.*

Change the template as shown:

```
<html>
<body>
<h1><font face="" Arial"">Hello world!</font></h1>
<p><WC@SomeTag>Some text</WC@SomeTag></p>
</body>
</html>
```

Close Notepad, saving the changes to the file. Visual Basic will inform us that the template has been changed and will ask if it should update its copy to reflect the changes:

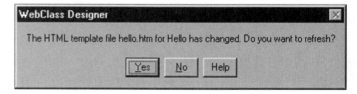

Choose Yes, as we do want our changes to be updated into the project.

Now we can move on to creating the `ProcessTag` event procedure so we can write code to respond to the tag we just added as the template is being sent to the browser. Open up the code window by double-clicking on the Hello entry in the left-hand pane of the designer. Then choose the `ProcessTag` item from the procedure list in the upper-right of the code window. Now add the following code:

```
Private Sub Hello_ProcessTag(ByVal TagName As String, TagContents As String, _
    SendTags As Boolean)
  TagContents = "Substituting some text in our template"
End Sub
```

If we now press *F5* to run the application, we'll be presented with a browser window displaying our 'Hello world' message, but with the text from the `ProcessTag` procedure rather than the text that is actually in our template:

This is a very powerful technique, since we can use `Select..Case` or `If..Else` code to provide the appropriate text based on the values of the `TagName` and `TagContents` parameter values within the `ProcessTag` procedure. We'll explore this in more detail as we build our Video store interface.

# Displaying Details of a Video

We've seen how to create simple programs by using IIS Applications – both using the ASP objects such as `Response`, and using the concept of WebItems. Now we're ready to move on and create a new project that interacts with our Video store business objects. We'll create the same functionality that we did in Chapter 13, thus illustrating both the similarities and differences between building browser-based applications using ASP and IIS Applications.

As in Chapter 13, the first thing we'll do is create a simple script to display the details about a video title. Before we get into our new code however, we need to make sure our Video application objects are available to our development machine.

# Installing the VideoObjects DLL

As with our other user interfaces, we need to make our `VideoObjects` DLL available to the code that is building the interface itself. With ASP we needed to install the `VideoObjects` DLL on the web server machine. The same is true with IIS Applications, since they also run on our IIS web server.

For development purposes however, we simply need to make sure that the `VideoObjects` DLL is installed and registered on our development machine. We also need to make sure we have our `VideoServerMTS` objects registered on our development machine – and on the web server once we deploy the application.

At this point we have our web server machine all set up as a client workstation, with `VideoObjects` and `VideoServerMTS` both registered. Were we to install our `VideoUI` client program on the web server it should be able to run just like it does on any other client workstation. We are now ready to move on to create our web-based user interface.

# Designing the Application

Now we need to give some thought to the structure of our application. From the perspective of a client, each of our WebClass objects will appear as a separate ASP file. One approach to designing our application would be to create a different WebClass for each display we want to send to the browser – thus providing the browser with an entire set of 'ASP pages' with which to interact.

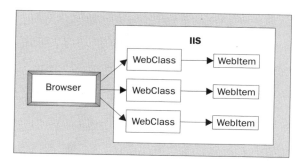

This would be pretty analogous to how we'd implement the application using ASP itself, but isn't necessarily the best design approach for an IIS Application.

With an IIS Application, it makes much more sense to have a WebClass that encapsulates an entire group of related functionality. We can then use multiple WebItems to display the appropriate user interfaces, all being used to support the related functionality encapsulated by our WebClass.

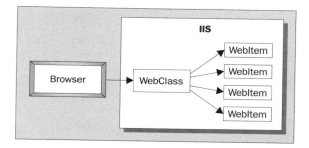

This approach keeps all of our related application code together, while leveraging our ability to show the appropriate display to the user based on our business logic.

That's not to say that we won't have multiple WebClass objects in some projects, just that each WebClass will probably encapsulate a group of related functionality rather than merely representing a single page for display in the browser. We'll follow this scheme as we develop our application to search for video information and to display details about each video selected by the user.

# Creating our IIS Application

We'll create our user interface in a new IIS Application, so bring up Visual Basic and open a new IIS Application. Using the Project | Properties menu option, bring up the dialog and change the project's name to `VideoIIS`. The rest of the properties for our project are already set up correctly, including the threading model, the unattended execution setting, etc.

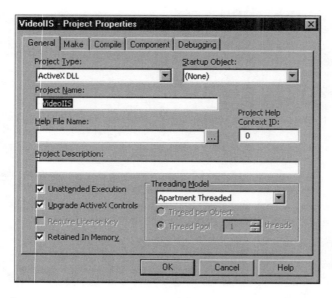

Change the name of WebClass1 to GetVideos by using its Properties window. This is very similar to changing the **Name** property of a regular Form or Class module. Also change the NameInURL property to getvideos.

Now we need to save our project. The next thing we'll be doing is adding WebItems to the project, and Visual Basic won't allow us to do that until after we've saved the project. In my case I'm saving the project to a directory named d:\vb6\VideoIIS. You can save it as appropriate on your development machine, keeping in mind that Visual Basic will create a virtual directory for our application the first time we run it.

## The SearchForm WebItem

We'll emulate the functionality provided by our Visual Basic forms-based application in regards to finding information about Video objects. This will also be virtually identical to the functionality we created using ASP in Chapter 13. The first step for the user is to be able to enter criteria for the Video object's title and studio.

Since our user interface itself is browser-based, the technologies we have at our disposal on the client are identical to those for an ASP application.

> **Virtually all of the browser-based design concerns we discussed in Chapter 13 apply here. IIS Applications provide no more or less functionality to the user's browser than do Active Server Pages. The only thing different is how we develop the code on the web server.**

This means that, as with our ASP application, we'll use an HTML form to allow the user to enter search criteria. When the user clicks on the HTML submit button the form's contents will be transmitted back to the web server – in this case to our WebClass object. This will cause the object's WebClass_Response event to be fired, allowing us to write Visual Basic code to react to the user's request.

### Creating the Template

We can develop the HTML form using any HTML authoring tool that supports forms. I'm just using Notepad since the form will be nothing more than a small text file. Enter the following code:

```
<HTML>
<HEAD>
<TITLE>Get Video Criteria</TITLE>
</HEAD>
<BODY>
<FORM ACTION="getvideos.asp" METHOD="post">
  Title:<BR>
  <INPUT NAME="txtTitle" ><P>
  Studio:<BR>
  <INPUT NAME="txtStudio" ><P>
  <INPUT TYPE=submit VALUE="Enter">
  <INPUT TYPE=reset VALUE="Cancel">
  </FORM></P>
</BODY>
</HTML>
```

Comparing this code to the HTML that we used to create the form in Chapter 13 you'll see that it is virtually identical. The biggest difference is that this form contains no hidden field:

```
<INPUT TYPE=HIDDEN NAME="hdnAction" VALUE="1">
```

This is because we'll be using a different technique to determine when the user has clicked the submit button and requested that we provide a display of Video objects. We'll explore that shortly.

For now, we'll want to save this file to disk. In my case I'm saving it to d:\searchform.htm. Once the file is saved to disk we are in a position to add it to our project as a WebItem.

In the GetVideos WebClass designer, right-click on the GetVideos entry and choose **Add HTML template** from the menu, then select our HTML template file and add it to the project. Once the template has been added we are provided with an opportunity to change its name, so we'll change it to **SearchForm** – thus creating a SearchForm WebItem object within our project.

### Updating WebClass_Start

With that done, we can add code to display this form when our GetVideos WebClass is accessed by simply adding a line to the WebClass_Start event procedure. Open up the code window from the designer and change the WebClass_Start procedure as shown:

```
Private Sub WebClass_Start()
   SearchForm.WriteTemplate
End Sub
```

### Running the Application

At this point we can press *F5* to run the application. Visual Basic will create a virtual directory the first time we do this, and will then bring up a browser window to display our form:

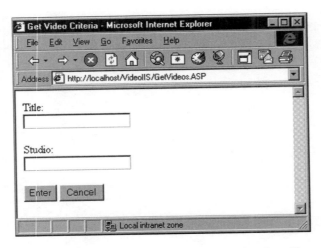

Not surprisingly, this form appears identical to the one we created in Chapter 13. Of course nothing really happens when we click the Enter button yet – we need to add code to our WebClass object to recognise that the user clicked the button and respond appropriately.

## The ListVideos WebItem

Now that we've got a form into which the user can enter search criteria, we need to enhance our WebClass to respond to whatever the user might enter. Before we add code to respond to the user however, let's create another HTML template that we can use to display the search results.

Again, we'll design the display around the same idea we used in Chapter 13 – a simple HTML table displaying the search results, with each Video object's Title being used as a hyperlink to a more detailed display.

To dynamically insert our search results into an HTML template, we'll use tag substitution – just like we did with our 'Hello world' application earlier in the chapter.

### Creating the Template

Again we need to create an HTML template file and save it somewhere on disk. The template will contain the HTML to draw our table. The basic table will be drawn with the following HTML:

```
<HTML>
  <HEAD>
  <TITLE>Video List</TITLE>
  </HEAD>
  <BODY>
  <P>Here is a list of video titles from our wide selection:</P>
  <TABLE BORDER=1>
  <TR>
  <TD>Title</TD>
  <TD>Release date</TD>
  </TR>
  </TABLE>
  </BODY>
</HTML>
```

This HTML will display a table with a single row to display our column headers: Title and Release date. However, at this point there is nothing to indicate where or how our actual data should be inserted into the table. Not only that, but we need to display not merely a single piece of information, but rather we need to generate an entire table of data dynamically – based on the results of our query.

Our challenge lies in that the template is a static bit of HTML. Since we don't know the number of rows of data we might need to display, it isn't very practical to set up a series of rows in the table and then do simple tag substitution. Such an implementation might look like this:

```
<HTML>
  <HEAD>
  <TITLE>Video List</TITLE>
  </HEAD>
  <BODY>
  <P>Here is a list of video titles from our wide selection:</P>
  <TABLE BORDER=1>
  <TR>
  <TD>Title</TD>
  <TD>Release date</TD>
  </TR>
  <TR>
  <TD><WC@Videos>Title1</WC@Videos></TD>
  <TD><WC@Videos>ReleaseDate1</WC@Videos></TD>
  </TR>
  <TR>
  <TD><WC@Videos>Title2</WC@Videos></TD>
  <TD><WC@Videos>ReleaseDate2</WC@Videos></TD>
  </TR>
  </TABLE>
  </BODY>
</HTML>
```

The problem here is that we've only allowed for two rows of data to be displayed. There's no way for our application to add more rows if needed. Of course we could create the template with as many rows as we might ever get, but then we'd typically have a lot of empty rows of data in our display.

Instead, it is better to dynamically generate all the HTML for the rows of the table from within our Visual Basic code. Taking this approach, our template can simply provide a 'WC@' tag to indicate where in the template our program should insert the rows. Since this is the approach we'll take, change our template to read as follows:

```
<HTML>
  <HEAD>
  <TITLE>Video List</TITLE>
  </HEAD>
  <BODY>
  <P>Here is a list of video titles from our wide selection:</P>
  <TABLE BORDER=1>
  <TR>
  <TD>Title</TD>
  <TD>Release date</TD>
  </TR>
<WC@Videos>Table</WC@Videos>
  </TABLE>
  </BODY>
</HTML>
```

The tag in this template is right after we've added the column header row, but before we've closed the table with the `</TABLE>` tag. Our Visual Basic code just needs to add one or more properly formed HTML table rows and we're all set.

Save the template file, then right-click on the **GetVideos** entry in the WebClass designer and add the template to our project. Change the WebItem's name to `ListVideos`, thus setting up a `ListVideos` object for our use within our code.

### Updating WebClass_Start

Now we can enhance our Visual Basic code to receive the criteria entered by the user into our `SearchForm` HTML form. Using that criteria, we'll instantiate a `Videos` object and then use the `WriteTemplate` method of our new `ListVideos` WebItem to send the table display back to the user's browser. As `ListVideos` is being sent to the browser, the `ListVideos_ProcessTag` event will be fired since we included a 'WC@' tag in the template.

Open the code window for the `GetVideos` WebClass. In the `WebClass_Start` procedure we already have a line of code to send the `SearchForm` WebItem to the browser.

```
Private Sub WebClass_Start()
   SearchForm.WriteTemplate
End Sub
```

That is a great start, but we need to enhance this procedure to some degree. When the user clicks the **Enter** button in their browser, the form's results will be sent back to the web server, causing it to create an instance of our `GetVideos` WebClass object. Of course this, in turn, will cause the `Start` event to fire – just like when the user accessed `GetVideos` in the first place.

We need a way to determine whether the user has come to our `GetVideos` WebClass on their own, or whether they've come here from our `SearchForm` HTML form and are actually wishing to see the results of a search. To do this, we'll use the `Request` object from ASP. The `Request` object has a `Form` property, providing us with a reference to an object that represents all the elements contained on the HTML form (if any) that were on the page when the user clicked **Enter**.

The `Form` object has a `Count` property to indicate the number of fields on the HTML form. If the user came to our `GetVideos` object by simply entering the URL into their browser, then they didn't come from an HTML form at all and this `Count` will be zero. However, when they get here by clicking **Enter** on our `SearchForm`, `Count` will be two – since we have two entry fields on our form.

We can use this `Count` property to decide whether to display the `SearchForm` WebItem (in case the user simply entered our URL), or to display the `ListVideos` WebItem to show the results of our search:

```
Private Sub WebClass_Start()
   If Request.Form.Count = 0 Then
      SearchForm.WriteTemplate
   Else
      ListVideos.WriteTemplate
   End If
End Sub
```

### Loading the Videos Object

Before we actually send the ListVideos WebItem, we'll probably want to use the criteria entered by the user on the form to create and populate a Videos object. Again we'll use the ASP Request object to get at the form's fields via the Form object.

To start with, declare a variable, objVideos, of type Videos as a module-level variable.

```
Option Explicit

Private objVideos As Videos
```

This needs to be a module-level variable because we'll be creating and loading it here in the WebClass_Start procedure, but we'll actually be using the Videos object's data in the ListVideos_ProcessTag procedure in order to build the rows of our HTML table.

Now we can change the code in our WebClass_Start procedure to use the fields from the HTML form as parameters for the Videos object's Load method:

```
Private Sub WebClass_Start()
   With Request.Form
      If .Count = 0 Then
         SearchForm.WriteTemplate
      Else
         Set objVideos = New Videos
         objVideos.Load .Item("txtTitle"), .Item("txtStudio")
         ListVideos.WriteTemplate
      End If
   End With
End Sub
```

We've retained the check to see if the Count property is zero. If it is not zero, then we know we've come from the SearchForm and need to load our Videos object. This is as simple as creating a new Videos object and then calling its Load method – using the two fields from our HTML form as parameters. Once we've loaded our UI-centric business object, we can simply call the WriteTemplate method of our ListVideos WebItem to send the results back to the browser.

> *Notice how similar this code is to the code we created using ASP in Chapter 13. The biggest difference between the two is that with our new IIS Application the Visual Basic code is separated from the HTML itself – making our application much easier to read and maintain. We can change the HTML templates fairly radically with no impact on our Visual Basic code whatsoever.*

### Building the HTML Table

As the ListVideos HTML template object is being sent to the browser, Visual Basic will scan through the HTML looking for any tags that need substitution. We've included a 'WC@' tag in our template, so Visual Basic will find it and will then raise the ListVideos_ProcessTag event to allow us to provide the text that is to be substituted for that tag. In this case, we're going to replace the tag with one or more rows of data. Each row will be created using the syntax for an HTML row, so it will fit seamlessly into our template for display.

The code to build the rows of the table will be quite similar to the code we used for this purpose in Chapter 13. We'll need to declare a VideoDisplay object, then simply use a For..Each loop to run through all the items in our Videos object – creating an HTML table row for each one.

```
Private Sub ListVideos_ProcessTag(ByVal TagName As String, _
    TagContents As String, SendTags As Boolean)
  Dim strResponse As String
  Dim objItem As VideoDisplay

  For Each objItem In objVideos
    strResponse = strResponse & "<TR>"

    strResponse = strResponse & "<TD>" & objItem.Title & "</TD>"
    strResponse = strResponse & "<TD>" & objItem.ReleaseDate
    strResponse = strResponse & "</TD>"

    strResponse = strResponse & "</TR>"
  Next
  Set objVideos = Nothing
  TagContents = strResponse
End Sub
```

This code is pretty straightforward. For each VideoDisplay object we simply add a <TR> tag, then add our two data fields, Title and ReleaseDate, bracketed by the <TD> tag to indicate they are table data. Finally we close with the </TR> tag to indicate we've completed the row in our HTML table. All of this is concatenated together into a variable, strResponse, which in the end is returned as our result via the TagContents parameter.

> *The HTML in this chapter is very simple but if you want to learn more about it, take a look at Instant HTML Programmer's Reference, HTML 4.0 Edition (ISBN 1-861001-56-8).*

Once we've looped through all the items in objVideos, we set it to Nothing, releasing the reference to that object. After all, we've built the display for the user's browser, so we no longer have any use for that object.

> *If our application was more complex we might need to keep the reference for subsequent tag substitutions, but in this case we know we're all done.*

## Running the Application

At this point we can run our application. We can enter criteria into the initial form that comes up, and when we click the Enter button we'll be presented with a second display that shows the list of Video objects matching our criteria.

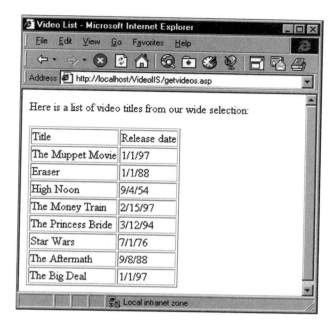

So far we've seen how to create and respond to HTML forms and how to use tag substitution to create a table to display a set of result data. Now let's wrap up by creating a detailed display form for a specific video.

## The DisplayVideo WebItem

The final piece of our new user interface will be a detailed display of a Video object in the user's browser – just like the one we created in Chapter 13 using ASP. During this process we'll get to use some other features of IIS Applications. In particular, we'll see how we can make a hyperlink on one page call back into our application to display data on a second page. The URL linking to the second page will effectively raise an event within our application to indicate what should be displayed.

### Creating the Template

We'll need to create an HTML template for our new display. To do this we can use Notepad to enter the HTML, save it as a file and add it to our project just like we've done with the other templates so far this chapter. Here's the HTML for our template:

```
<HTML>
<HEAD>
<TITLE><WC@Video>Title</WC@Video></TITLE>
</HEAD>
<BODY>
<P>
<P>
<H1><WC@VIDEO>Studio</WC@VIDEO>
Presents <WC@VIDEO>Title</WC@VIDEO></H1>
<P>This movie is rated '<WC@VIDEO>Rating</WC@VIDEO>'
<WC@VIDEO>RatingText</WC@VIDEO>
</P>
<P>We have <WC@VIDEO>TapeCount</WC@VIDEO> available for rental</P>
</BODY>
</HTML>
```

This is essentially the same HTML that we used for our detailed display in Chapter 13. However, here we don't need to mix code in with the HTML, since the code will be contained within our application itself. It is quite simple to read the HTML itself and pick out the 'WC@' tags where we'll be substituting actual data from our `Video` object.

Note the different text that we've placed between each `<WC@VIDEO>` tag. We'll be using the text between the tags to indicate which particular type of information is to be substituted in each case.

Once this template is added to our project, name it **DisplayVideo**, thus creating a `DisplayVideo` object for use within our application.

### Using the URLfor Method

Now that we've got a WebItem to display, let's go back and enhance the HTML in our search results table so each title acts as a hyperlink to our new template. This is done a little differently in an IIS Application than it was using ASP.

Hyperlinks that directly reference WebItems in our application need to be in a specific format that is understood by Visual Basic. When such a URL is sent to our web server, the call is routed to our IIS Application and results in a `Respond` event being raised for the specific WebItem that is being referenced in the URL. For our `DisplayVideo` WebItem, for example, the event raised is named `DisplayVideo_Respond`. We can add code to the event procedure associated with this event and take appropriate actions to fulfil the user's request.

To create the hyperlink itself we'll still use the `<A href=>` style HTML tag, but in order to make sure we've got a valid URL for our WebItem we'll generate the URL being referenced by using a built-in method of IIS Applications called `URLfor`.

`URLfor` is a method that accepts a WebItem object as a parameter and returns a URL that can be used to directly call that WebItem from the browser. The `URLfor` method also accepts a second, optional, parameter which can be used to raise a specific event within the WebItem. We'll be using all these features to create our hyperlinks.

For instance, to create a URL that raises the `Respond` event for our new `DisplayVideo` WebItem, we might use the following:

```
strURL = "<A href=""" & URLFor(DisplayVideo) & """>Jump to page</A>"
```

If the user were to click on such a link it would cause the `DisplayVideo_Respond` event to be fired within our application. We can add code to this event procedure to do whatever we choose in response to the user clicking that hyperlink. Unfortunately, this doesn't give us much information to go on. We don't know where the hyperlink came from or what the user might specifically want us to do.

### Raising Events Using the URLfor Method

In our particular case, simply raising the `Respond` event doesn't provide us with the ID number of the `Video` object to be displayed. We have no way of knowing which Video to display. This is where the second parameter of the `URLfor` method comes into play.

We can pass a second parameter to the URLfor method. This parameter is a String that indicates the name of an event to be raised within our WebItem. If this parameter is provided, the URL will cause the UserEvent event to fire rather than the Respond event. For our DisplayVideo WebItem, this event will be named DisplayVideo_UserEvent. The String value we provided in the URLfor method call is passed as a parameter to the UserEvent procedure, thus allowing us to pass specific values through the URL and into our application code. For instance, we might create the following URL:

```
strURL = "<A href=""" & URLFor(DisplayVideo, "5") & """>Jump to page</A>"
```

If the user clicks on the hyperlink generated by this line of code, the URL sent to our web server will cause the DisplayVideo_UserEvent procedure to be run, passing the value '5' as a parameter to our code. We can then use this value to determine a course of action. In our case, we'll use this value to call a Video object's Load method, using '5' as the parameter in that call.

### Adding Hyperlinks to Our Table

Armed with our knowledge of URLfor, let's revisit the code that builds the table of video information and add hyperlinks to the entries in that table. We can use URLfor to generate a hyperlink to our DisplayVideo WebItem, and pass each VideoDisplay object's VideoID value as the second parameter – thus causing the UserEvent procedure to be run, with the VideoID value provided as a parameter.

```
Private Sub ListVideos_ProcessTag(ByVal TagName As String, _
    TagContents As String, SendTags As Boolean)
  Dim strResponse As String
  Dim objItem As VideoDisplay

  For Each objItem In objVideos
    strResponse = strResponse & "<TR>"

    strResponse = strResponse & "<TD><A href=""" & _
      URLFor(DisplayVideo, Format$(objItem.VideoID)) & """>" & _
      objItem.Title & "</A></TD>"
    strResponse = strResponse & "<TD>" & objItem.ReleaseDate
    strResponse = strResponse & "</TD>"
    strResponse = strResponse & "</TR>"
  Next
  Set objVideos = Nothing
  TagContents = strResponse
End Sub
```

### Implementing the UserEvent Procedure

Now we need to implement the code in DisplayVideo_UserEvent to accept the VideoID value as a parameter and use it to call the Load method on a Video object. Once we have a valid Video object, we can use the WriteTemplate method of our DisplayVideo WebItem to send it to the browser. Of course, it contains a number of 'WC@' tags, so the DisplayVideo_ProcessTag event will fire for each of them, allowing us to replace the tags with data from our Video object.

First though, we need to implement the UserEvent procedure. Since we'll be using a Video object, we need to declare a variable to hold its reference. We'll declare this as a module-level variable, since we'll not only be using it in our UserEvent procedure, but also in the ProcessTag procedure that we'll create next.

```
Option Explicit

Private objVideos As Videos
Private objVideo As Video
```

Next we can move on and create the `DisplayVideo_UserEvent` procedure itself:

```
Private Sub DisplayVideo_UserEvent(ByVal EventName As String)
   Set objVideo = New Video
   objVideo.Load Val(EventName)
   DisplayVideo.WriteTemplate
End Sub
```

The code here is quite straightforward, since all we need to do is create a new `Video` object, call its `Load` method and then send the `DisplayVideo` template out to the browser.

### Implementing the ProcessTag Procedure

As the `DisplayVideo` WebItem is being sent to the browser, Visual Basic will scan the HTML to find any tags in need of replacement. In our template we have several. Each time Visual Basic encounters such a tag, it will fire the `ProcessTag` event, causing the `DisplayVideo_ProcessTag` procedure to be run.

We'll add code to this procedure to send the appropriate replacement text for each tag. The code to produce each bit of replacement text is essentially the same code we wrote in ASP in Chapter 13. Here, however, the code is not VBScript, but is actual Visual Basic – and of course the code isn't mixed in with the HTML in our template, but instead is run in response to a tag substitution event.

```
Private Sub DisplayVideo_ProcessTag(ByVal TagName As String, _
    TagContents As String, SendTags As Boolean)
   Dim intAvail As Integer

   Select Case TagContents
```

To start off, we'll simply declare a couple variables that we'll need. We didn't declare these variables in our ASP code only because ASP treats everything as a `Variant`. Now however, we need to declare them and provide them with actual data types.

We also start off with a `Select..Case` statement based on the `TagContents` parameter. When we created our HTML template, we inserted tags such as `<WC@VIDEO>Title</WC@VIDEO>` wherever we needed to insert dynamic data. The text between the tags, in this case `Title`, is passed to the `ProcessTag` procedure in the `TagContents` parameter. We can use this as our key to indicate which specific tag we're going to replace.

> **This is exceedingly powerful. We, as Visual Basic developers, can create a WebItem's ProcessTag procedure and simply provide the list of tag names in a document to an HTML author. That person can create their HTML page any way they choose, as long as they use the tag names we provided wherever they need dynamic data inserted. This provides almost total separation between the user interface and our business logic in Visual Basic.**

All we need to do now is implement the specific code for each of the tag names we placed in our HTML template. The first three are trivial, simply returning property values from our Video object upon request:

```
    Case "Title"
       TagContents = objVideo.Title
    Case "Studio"
       TagContents = objVideo.Studio
    Case "Rating"
       TagContents = objVideo.Rating
```

The `RatingText` item is a bit more interesting. In this case we're taking the `Video` object's `Rating` property and using it to determine a set of specific text to return. This code is virtually identical to the VBScript we used in Chapter 13.

```
    Case "RatingText"
      Select Case objVideo.Rating
      Case "G"
        TagContents = "suitable for general audiences"
      Case "PG"
        TagContents = "parental guidance suggested"
      Case "PG-13"
        TagContents = "not suitable for children under age 13"
      Case "R"
        TagContents = "children under 17 not admitted without parent"
      Case "NR"
        TagContents = "not rated - for mature audiences"
      End Select
```

The `TapeCount` item is, again, very similar to what we did in Chapter 13. We'll make use of the `AvailableCount` property we added to the `Tapes` object in Chapter 13 and simply return the appropriate text to be displayed.

```
    Case "TapeCount"
      intAvail = objVideo.Tapes.AvailableCount
      If intAvail = 0 Then
        TagContents = "no tapes "
      ElseIf intAvail = 1 Then
        TagContents = "1 tape "
      Else
        TagContents = intAvail & " tapes "
      End If
    End Select
  End Sub
```

It is important to note that our Visual Basic code doesn't know (or care) in which order these tags might be called – or if they'll even be called at all. All those details are entirely up to the HTML template author. We can totally rearrange the HTML template – changing its appearance to the user radically – and still have no impact on our Visual Basic code in any way.

### Running the Application

We can now run our application, using the search form and then clicking on any of the videos listed in our search results table. This will result in our new code being run and the selected video's details being displayed in the browser:

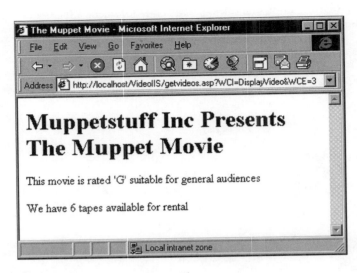

Notice the somewhat cryptic URL used to generate this page.

```
http://localhost/VideoIIS/getvideos.asp?WCI=DisplayVideo&WCE=3
```

This is the URL that was generated with our call to the URLfor method as we built the search results table. The parameters passed after the '?' indicate the WebItem and event name that are to be called within our application:

| | |
|---|---|
| WCI | WebClass Item (or WebItem) to be called. In this case, DisplayVideo. |
| WCE | WebClass event to be called. This value will be passed as a parameter to the UserEvent procedure for the WebItem identified by the WCI parameter. |

# Summary

IIS Applications are a powerful new feature in Visual Basic 6.0. In this chapter we've merely scratched the surface of the capabilities they provide. The interface we've created here is virtually identical to the one we created using ASP in Chapter 13, but it was created entirely within Visual Basic. By extending the examples I've shown in this chapter you could easily create a browser-based UI that provides all the capabilities of the Visual Basic interface we created in Chapter 7.

Even better than the ease with which we were able to add this new interface is the fact that the existing interfaces still function. Since our application's behavior is entirely contained within the business objects themselves we can easily and safely add various user interfaces as the needs of the business change.

Regardless of whether our business object's data persistence code is in the objects themselves, in a DCOM server or running in MTS, we always gain these benefits of the separation of the interface from the business objects. And as we've seen through Chapters 8, 10 and 12, it is very easy to move the data persistence processing out of the objects and onto other machines without affecting the business logic or the UI to any significant degree.

Whether you are developing an application for a single PC or for an enterprise-wide distributed network the logical model I've presented in this book will help you. Smaller applications benefit because they are more easily maintained and extended. Larger applications gain those benefits plus scalability and the ability to exploit the resources of both your client workstations as well as server machines. By keeping the UI processing close to the user and the data processing close to the database these applications minimize network load and maximize performance.

# A DHTML Application Interface

## Overview

We've held to a consistent theme throughout the book – that of separation of the user interface from business logic, and business logic from database access. The CSLA is entirely based around this premise. We've seen how we can create a user interface with traditional Visual Basic forms (in Chapter 7), and using Microsoft Office tools such as Excel (in Chapter 9).

Visual Basic 6.0 introduces a new way to create user interfaces – the DHMTL Application. With the rising popularity of browser-based user interfaces there has been an explosion of Internet-oriented development tools. At the same time, there has been a lot of pressure by developers for vendors to find ways to leverage skill sets and experience by finding ways for existing tools to be used in creating browser-based applications.

> **DHTML Applications are *browser-based*, not necessarily *Internet-based*. They don't require a web server, just a browser.**

DHTML Applications are one possible answer for developers. They allow Visual Basic developers to create browser-based applications by treating forms created in the browser very much like traditional Visual Basic Form objects. With these new applications, we are able to program DHTML forms using the same familiar language and development approach as we have been doing with Visual Basic for years.

Of course there are some differences. Browser technology is still in its infancy and so it is difficult to accomplish certain tasks that we take for granted with traditional form-based development. At the same time, DHTML makes other things much easier to do that ever before. Things that might take many lines of Visual Basic code in a form can be done with a single line of DHTML.

In this chapter we'll implement a user interface based on our video store business objects. As with our Microsoft Office user interface, this new interface will require no changes to our business objects or to our data access code – further illustrating the powerful benefits to be gained by CSLA.

# DHTML Applications

Dynamic HTML (DHTML) Applications are a new feature of Visual Basic 6.0. They provide Visual Basic developers with the ability to leverage their existing knowledge of Visual Basic and Visual Basic's development approach when creating browser-based user interfaces.

The following table illustrates how traditional form-based development compares to how we approach DHTML Applications:

| Form-based | DHTML Application |
| --- | --- |
| Form module | DHTML designer |
| Code-behind-forms | Code-behind-DHTML designer |
| Language: Visual Basic | Language: Visual Basic |
| Standard VB controls | Standard HTML controls |
| Use of ActiveX controls | Use of ActiveX controls |
| Access to COM components | Access to COM components |
| Requires Win32 platform | Requires Win32 platform |

> **DHTML Applications simply use the browser, running DHTML, as an alternate form surface for creation of the user interface.**

Virtually every aspect of development within Visual Basic is the same with a DHTML Application as it is with a regular form-based user interface. We draw the user interface, placing controls where we want them. We then double-click on controls to add Visual Basic code behind the control – responding to the control's events. This is true with traditional forms and also with the new DHTML designer.

It's also important to note that DHTML Applications really are Visual Basic applications – regardless of whether the user interface is in a browser or not. This means that they can only be installed and run on 32-bit Windows operating systems – just like any other Visual Basic 32-bit application.

> **DHTML Applications are only available on Win32 operating systems such as Windows 95, 98 or NT – and they only work with Microsoft Internet Explorer 4 or higher.**

DHTML Applications do have some differences from traditional development. Let's take a look some of the key differences that we'll encounter as we create a new user interface on top of our video store business objects.

# DHTML Application Design Issues

Dynamic HTML is an extension to the Hypertext Markup Language (HTML) that has been popularized by the explosion of browser-based user interfaces. HTML remains the common language understood across virtually all browsers. DHTML, being much newer, is not universally understood – nor is it consistent across those browsers where it is implemented.

## Powerful Display Options

However, DHTML (as implemented in Microsoft Internet Explorer 4.0) provides us with some very powerful capabilities we can use when designing our user interfaces. DHTML makes working with fonts, graphics and sounds a trivial matter. In fact, the DHTML language is specifically geared around these concepts!

While we can work with fonts from within Visual Basic, we might end up writing a lot of code. If we want to create a compelling, colorful display for the user in Visual Basic we'd use a lot of `Form.Print` statements, along with numerous lines of code to change font styles, current X and Y positions on the form and who knows what else. And just think what we might have to do if the user resizes the form!

DHTML is designed around the idea that we'll be placing text all over the place – using various fonts, colors and so forth. Better still, with DHTML the entire display will be automatically resized if the user changes the size of the browser window. No extra code required.

In Visual Basic, to display a picture we'd need to use a control, place it on the form in the right size and position. If any of these might vary then we'd need to write code to adjust the form or the control or both as appropriate. With DHTML, none of these issues ever come up. The picture is displayed directly within the browser, and it takes care of any sizing or positional issues that might come up.

Playing sounds, such as a song when our application loads, is not trivial in Visual Basic. We need to use an ActiveX control or make some API calls to get the music playing. With DHTML, we simply instruct the browser to play the sounds from a file, be they music or simpler sounds, and the browser takes care of the rest. Instead of possibly writing many lines of code, we simply make a single reference to the file containing our sound and away we go.

In general, DHTML makes it very easy for us to create very graphical and compelling user interfaces with little or no code. To do the same in Visual Basic using `Form` modules would involve immense amounts of code and effort in comparison.

Most of these powerful DHTML features are directly available from within current DHTML editing tools such as Microsoft FrontPage or Visual Interdev 6.0. Fortunately, Visual Basic makes it very easy for us to import our DHTML files from outside the IDE, and then to continue to edit the DHTML files using the tool of our choice. This means we can use whatever DHTML editor we like for creating our user interfaces.

## Built-In Objects

Visual Basic provides us with some key built-in objects when we develop DHTML Applications. These objects allow us to write code that taps into the environment where our application is running. If we need to interact with the browser or our current DHTML page we'll use these objects to do it:

| | |
|---|---|
| `BaseWindow` | Represents the browser in which our application is running. Through this object we can get at most of the functions provided by the browser, including navigating to new pages. |
| `Document` | Represents the DHTML page being displayed in the browser. We can use this object to access the Document Object Model (DOM) for the current page. |
| `DHTMLPage` | This is the Visual Basic object that represents the current page. It's most analogous to a `Form` or `Class` in more traditional applications. |

These built-in objects come into play frequently when building DHTML Applications. We'll use the `BaseWindow` object to navigate from page to page. We'll use the `Document` object to dynamically alter the content of our page, and of course we'll use the `DHTMLPage` object to know when our page has been loaded and when it's being shut down.

These objects have many more capabilities as well, but these are perhaps the most common uses we'll have for them.

## Page-Oriented Design

Browser-based applications are centered primarily around the concept of a *page*. A browser can only display a single set of information at a time – and whatever is currently being displayed is considered a page of information. We can think of a browser as a single sheet of paper. We can draw on it all we'd like, but it is never going to be more than one sheet.

DHTML Applications, as they run in the browser, are also centered primarily around this concept of a page. While a traditional Visual Basic application might be made up of many forms, a DHTML Application is made up of many pages. The catch is that we can really only display a single page at a time, as opposed to a traditional program where we may display many forms at once.

With traditional Visual Basic forms we have options of MDI, SDI or even multiple-SDI (like Visual Basic 3.0, etc.). With DHTML Applications we have one option – a single page in the browser.

## Passing Information from Page to Page

With this page-oriented paradigm comes some other interesting challenges. Moving from one form to another in Visual Basic and passing information to the new form along the way is trivial. We might have code in `Form1` such as:

```
Dim frmNew As Form

Set frmNew = New Form2
frmNew.MyData = "Some data"
frmNew.Show
```

In this example we've created an instance of `Form2` while we're still running code in `Form1`. This means we can simply move data from one form to the next by setting properties.

With DHTML Applications things are a bit different. Since only one page can exist at a time, we can't have this overlap where a page gets loaded while the previous one is running. Instead, our current page is gone before the new one is displayed. This means we can't simply write code to set properties on the next page – instead we need to come up with some other mechanism to transfer data from one page to the next.

Visual Basic provides a solution to this problem in the form of a client-side cookie (like a property bag), and `PutProperty` and `GetProperty` methods to get data into and out of that cookie. We'll explore these later in the chapter, but here's a quick example showing how we might move from `DHTMLPage1` to `DHTMLPage2` – along with passing some data:

```
PutProperty BaseWindow.Document, "MyData", "Some data"
BaseWindow.navigate "DHTMLProject1_DHTMLPage2.htm"
```

We start by simply calling the `PutProperty` method (provided in a `BAS` module as part of the DHTML Application's project template) to store a property named `MyData` with the value `"Some data"`. Once we've stored the data, we can use the built-in `BaseWindow` object's `navigate` method to transition from our current page to the new `DHTMLPage2` page.

> While the page we're navigating to here has an `htm` extension, we need to be careful. DHTML Applications are not entirely consistent regarding whether the extension is `htm` or `html`. Throughout this chapter I'm sticking with an `htm` extension, but you will probably find some that need to be `html`.

As `DHTMLPage2` starts up it might contain the following code to retrieve the `MyData` value from the cookie:

```
strData = GetProperty(BaseWindow.Document, "MyData")
```

Notice how in both cases we pass `BaseWindow.Document` as a parameter. This is used by the `PutProperty` and `GetProperty` methods to get at the client-side cookie storing our data. The cookie is directly tied to the current instance of the browser (represented by the `BaseWindow` object), so each instance of the browser has its own cookie. Beyond this, the cookie only lasts as long as the browser is running – as soon as the browser is shut down, the cookie is gone forever.

# A Simple DHTML Application

Before we move into building an interface for our video store objects, let's build a simple DHTML Application just to explore the basic process. We'll just create a single DHTML form and put some Visual Basic code behind it. From there we can move on to build a more complex interface.

Bring up Visual Basic and create a new **DHTML Application** project:

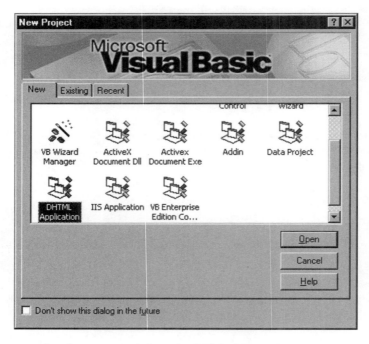

The project will be started with a BAS module and a DHTMLPage designer all ready to go. The BAS module simply contains the PutProperty and GetProperty methods for our use. The DHTMLPage1 designer represents the page we'll be building – just like the default Form1 entry that is automatically added to a **Standard EXE** project.

If we double-click on the DHTMLPage1 entry in the **Project** window we'll be presented with the DHTMLPage designer window:

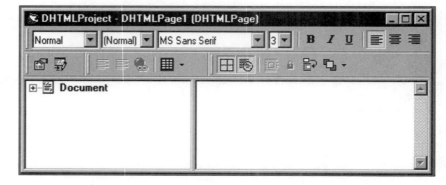

The left-hand pane of this designer represents the objects that are part of our DHTML page, while the right-hand pane is a WYSIWYG display of those objects as they'll appear in the user's browser.

*While we can use this designer to build a user interface (and we will in this chapter), it's much more likely that we'll use Microsoft Visual Interdev 6.0 or some other DHTML editing tool to edit our pages and simply import them into this designer to add Visual Basic code. There are other tools that are much more powerful when it comes to creating DHTML pages and we'll typically want to use them instead of this designer.*

## Building the Page

Now let's build a simple page using the designer. Once that's done we'll add a bit of Visual Basic code just to see how it all works.

### Setting Document Properties

Using the DHTMLPage designer we can set many different properties on our document. For instance, if we click on the Document entry in the left-hand pane we can manipulate its properties using the Visual Basic Properties window – just like with a regular Form object.

In the Properties window, select the bgColor entry, type lightblue and press *Enter*. The text will be replaced with #add8e6 and our document background in the right-hand pane will turn light blue.

### Adding Elements to the Page

Take a look at the Visual Basic toolbox. It has a second tab named HTML that contains all the native HTML controls supported by browsers. The General tab is still available, but if we switch to it we'll see that all the controls are grayed out. This is because the standard Visual Basic controls aren't available for use in a DHTML Application. We can use the standard HTML controls, and we can use ActiveX controls that we might add to our application, but not the standard controls natively available in Visual Basic forms.

Click on the Button option from the HTML tab and then draw the button in the right-hand of the designer. This process is pretty similar to what we'd to when building a standard Visual Basic form. Change this control's value property to Display rather than Button1.

Now click on the TextField option in the toolbox and drag that control on the page as well. Change this control's value property to be blank so it starts with nothing in the display.

We can drag the elements around on the page and position them as we desire. Keep in mind that their real position will be determined by the browser at run-time. The positions will vary based on the size of the browser window and may change dynamically if the user resizes the window while our program is running.

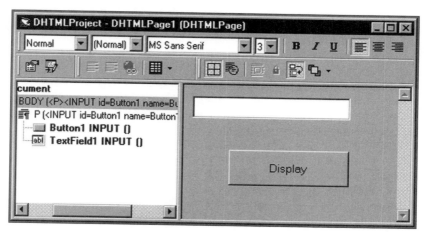

Notice how our controls are not only displayed in the right-hand pane, but are also listed as elements in our document on the left. The left-hand pane gives us a quick overview of all the elements that make up our page, providing easy access to any of those elements for setting properties or accessing the code window.

## Programming the Page

With our page basically set up, let's add some simple code behind the Button control to display the text from the TextField in a simple message box.

Before we get into the code itself however, we need to be aware of a subtle difference between controls in a DHTML page as compared to controls in a regular form. On a regular form, we identify controls by using their Name property. A control with a Name property of X would have a X_Click event procedure for instance.

With DHTML pages, controls are identified by their id property rather than the Name property. They still *have* a Name property - it just isn't used to identify the control. Thus, a control with an id property of X would have a X_onclick event procedure – illustrating another interesting difference, in that most event names are different for HTML controls as opposed to standard Visual Basic controls.

Change the id property of the TextField control to txtText. Also change the id property of the Button control to cmdDisplay. This is very analogous to setting the Name properties on controls within a regular Visual Basic form.

Now we can simply double-click on the Display button to bring up the code window for its onclick event.

```
Option Explicit

Private Function cmdDisplay_onclick() As Boolean

End Function
```

Interestingly enough, the Option Explicit setting in Visual Basic doesn't seem to be honored by this new type of application. As it is vitally important that this setting be enabled, I've added it at the top of the code module.

From here things are pretty much the same as if we were writing a regular Visual Basic program. We can simply call the MsgBox method, using the Value property of our txtText control as a parameter:

```
Private Function cmdDisplay_onclick() As Boolean

    MsgBox txtText.Value

End Function
```

## Running the Program

With our program complete, we can simply press *F5* to run it in debug mode. We'll be prompted as to how we want to run the program:

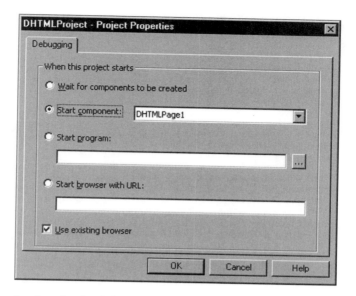

In this case we can simply take the default, since we want to start our new DHTML page to test it.

Visual Basic will launch Internet Explorer and it will bring up our new page. We should be able to enter any text we'd like into our `TextField` control, and when we click on the button our program will display that text in a message box.

There's a trick here though. When we're running a DHTML Application in debug mode (like we are here), any message boxes or other dialogs are raised from Visual Basic itself rather than from the browser. This means that we'll need to click on the Visual Basic IDE in order to see the message box. This won't happen if we compile the program and then run it directly from the browser rather than in debug mode.

This simple demonstration illustrates just how similar the development of a DHTML Application is compared to a traditional forms-based application. We should be ready to move on and create a user interface making use of our video store business objects.

# Editing the Customer Object

To demonstrate how we can create a user interface for our video store business objects, we'll create a page that has the same functionality as the `Customer` form we designed in Chapter 7. Of course we'll also need to provide some way to find the `Customer` object to be edited, so we'll also replicate the functionality of the `CustomerSearch` and `CustomerList` forms using DHTML pages.

## The CustSearch Page

The first DHTML page we'll create will have the same functionality as the `CustomerSearch` form from Chapter 7. This page is pretty straightforward, as it simply allows the user to enter search criteria for the `Name` and `Phone` properties.

When the user clicks OK on our form in Chapter 7 our application brings up the `CustomerList` form to display the results. In our DHTML Application we'll bring up a `CustList` DHTML page instead – but the application flow will remain pretty similar from the user's perspective.

## Setting up the Project

Open a new DHTML Application in Visual Basic. Change the project's Name property to `VideoDHTML` by using the Project | Properties... menu option.

Once that's done, double-click on the `DHTMLPage1` option in the Project window. Change the designer's Name and `id` property to `CustSearch`. This is the name Visual Basic will use as we refer to our DHTML page object within our code.

## Building the Page

Now use the DHTMLPage designer to add text along with `TextField` and `Button` controls to appear as shown in the following diagram.

*It is possible that your display won't match this exactly. In particular, the circular arrow icons represent each control we've placed on the form. The exact location of the circular arrows is relatively unimportant and may vary depending on the exact order in which you added the controls to the form.*

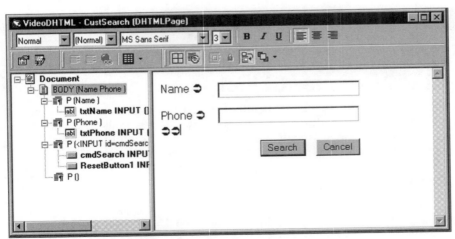

Note that the Search button is a regular Button control, while the Cancel button is a ResetButton control. ResetButton controls automatically blank all the entry fields on a form when clicked – a useful bit of functionality for a page like this. In a regular Visual Basic form we'd have needed to code that functionality ourselves.

Set the id properties for the first TextField control to txtName and the second to txtPhone. Change the id fields of the buttons to cmdSearch and cmdCancel as well.

## Adding the Code

The code for this form is very small – just like the code was for our CustomerSearch form in Chapter 7. However, our approach here is quite a bit different than it was in Chapter 7. In our form-based interface, we simply took the values supplied by the user and then provided them back to our main program via properties on our form.

In this new DHTML application, we'll be moving from the current page to a new page that will display the search results. Instead of providing the user's criteria as properties on a form, we'll need to store it in our client-side cookie so the values can be retrieved by the next page to be displayed. To do this we'll use the PutProperties method as we discussed earlier in the chapter. Then we'll use the BaseWindow object (representing the browser itself) to navigate to the next page.

Double-click on the Search button to bring up the code window for its onclick event procedure and add the following code:

```
Option Explicit

Private Function cmdSearch_onclick() As Boolean

    PutProperty BaseWindow.Document, "SearchName", txtName.Value
    PutProperty BaseWindow.Document, "SearchPhone", txtPhone.Value
    BaseWindow.navigate "VideoDHTML_CustList.htm"


End Function
```

This code uses the PutProperty method for each of the criteria values entered by the user – storing them in our browser's client-side cookie for later use. It then calls the navigate method of the BaseWindow object to move us on to the CustList page – so let's move on and create that page.

> *Notice how the URL is built for navigating to another page within our DHTML Application. First we use the project name* VideoDHTML, *an underscore and then the page name and wrapping up with* '.htm'. *When we compile our application, Visual Basic automatically creates* .htm *files for each DHTML page in our project, using this convention to name them.*

We'll probably want to save our project at this point so we don't lose our changes.

# The CustList Page

At this point our application really won't run very well. In particular because we have code that attempts to navigate to a CustList page that doesn't yet exist. This page needs to accept the criteria entered by the user on the CustSearch page and generate a list of matching customers. Fortunately for us, we have already implemented this basic functionality through our Customers object and its related CustomerDisplay objects. All we need to do is build a form to display these objects.

## Adding the Page

In our existing VideoDHTML project, choose the Project | Add DHTML Page menu option to add a new DHTMLPage designer to the project.

We'll be presented with a dialog as shown here:

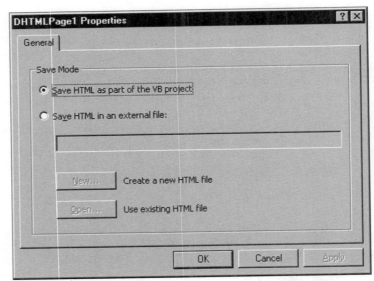

This dialog is powerful, as it allows us to access a number of options about how to manage our HTML. By default, the HTML that defines our display will be stored directly as part of our Visual Basic project. While this is the most convenient option, it may not always be desirable.

If we opt to save the HTML into an external file, we gain some capabilities. This option is required if we want to use an external editor, such as Visual InterDev or Frontpage, to edit our HTML.

Were we to choose to save the HTML as an external file, we'd also have the opportunity at this point to either create a new HTML file, or to import an existing HTML file. If we already have HTML pages designed for our application and we just want to add code, this ability to import existing files is very powerful.

In our case we'll simply select the default and click OK. Once the designer is added, change its Name property to CustList and open up the designer window.

## *Retrieving Values from the Cookie*

In the `CustSearch` page we stored the values entered by the user into a client-side cookie by using the `PutProperty` method. In the `CustList` page, we'll need to retrieve those values so we can use them when calling the `Load` method of our `Customers` object. We can do this using the `GetPropery` method provided for us in the `modDHTML BAS` module.

The first event that fires when a DHTML page is being started is the `DHTMLPage_Load` event. This is very similar to the `Form_Load` event that fires when a regular Visual Basic form is loaded. We'll use this routine to retrieve the values entered by the user and stored in the cookie. Then we'll use those values to load a `Customers` object by calling its `Load` method. You'll need to use the **Project** window to open the code module for `CustList`:

```
Private Sub DHTMLPage_Load()

    Dim strName As String
    Dim strPhone As String
    Dim objCustomers As Customers
    Dim divCustInfo As Object

    strName = GetProperty(BaseWindow.Document, "SearchName")
    strPhone = GetProperty(BaseWindow.Document, "SearchPhone")

    Set objCustomers = New Customers
    objCustomers.Load strName, strPhone

End Sub
```

We'll add code to actually use the `Customers` object as we get further into building our page. For now it is enough that we've moved from one page to the next, passing data values from one to the next and then using those values to load our business object with data.

## *Using ActiveX Controls in a DHTML Page*

Now that we have a fully loaded `Customers` object, we need some way to display the `CustomerDisplay` objects it contains. In the `CustomerList` form from Chapter 7 we used the `ListView` control to display our data. Here we have a dilemma, since there are no standard HTML controls that provide similar functionality.

Fortunately for us, we can use ActiveX controls as easily in DHTML pages as we do within regular Visual Basic forms. Therefore, we'll simply use the `ListView` control here just like we did back in Chapter 7.

Right-click on the toolbox and choose the **Components...** option from the menu. Just as we did in Chapter 7, we'll use the **Components** dialog to add a reference to the **Microsoft Windows Common Controls 6.0**. This will add the controls it contains to the **General** tab of the toolbox.

Now we can click on the `ListView` control from the toolbox and draw an instance of the control in the right-hand pane of our `CustList` page. While we're at it, add two `Button` controls from the **HTML** tab of the toolbox:

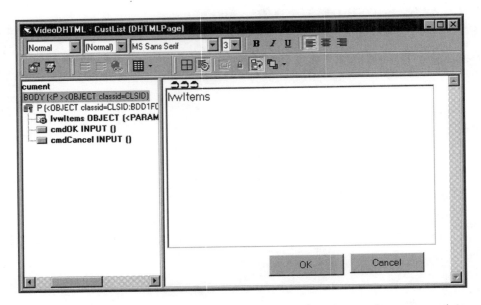

Set the `id` properties of the controls to `lvwItems`, `cmdOK` and `cmdCancel` as appropriate.

At this point, we'd normally use the `ListView` control's properties dialog to set it up with the appropriate columns to display. Unfortunately, properties set in this manner aren't reliably set for our control at run-time. Therefore, we'll do this setup via code before we display our `CustomerDisplay` objects.

## Loading the ListView Control

Now we've got a `Customers` object with data and a `ListView` control to display that data, so let's write a procedure, `ListCustomers`, to handle this task. We'll write it to accept the `Customers` object as a parameter so we can easily call it from our `DHTMLPage_Load` procedure.

Not surprisingly, we can lift most of this code verbatim out of the `CustomerList` form from Chapter 7. After all, we are trying to load data from the same `Customers` object into the same `ListView` ActiveX control:

```
Private Sub ListCustomers(objCustomers As Customers)

  Dim objItem As CustomerDisplay
  Dim itmList As ListItem
  Dim lngIndex As Long

  With lvwItems
    .View = lvwReport
    .FullRowSelect = True
    .LabelEdit = lvwManual
    .ColumnHeaders(1).Text = "Name"
    .ColumnHeaders.Add Text:="Phone"
  End With
```

```
        For lngIndex = 1 To objCustomers.Count
          Set objItem = objCustomers.Item(lngIndex)
          Set itmList = _
            lvwItems.ListItems.Add(Key:= _
            Format$(objItem.CustomerID) & " K")

          With itmList
            .Text = objItem.Name
            .SubItems(1) = objItem.Phone
          End With

        Next

    End Sub
```

Before we actually load the data into the `ListView` control, we need to set it up by changing its `View` property to `lvwReport` and making the other changes we made in Chapter 7 through the use of the control's properties dialog:

```
With lvwItems
  .View = lvwReport
  .FullRowSelect = True
  .LabelEdit = lvwManual
  .ColumnHeaders(1).Text = "Name"
  .ColumnHeaders.Add Text:="Phone"
End With
```

Once that's done the rest of the procedure is the same as we wrote in Chapter 7.

Now we can simply update the code in our `DHTMLPage_Load` procedure to call our new method and load the `ListView` control:

```
Private Sub DHTMLPage_Load()

  Dim strName As String
  Dim strPhone As String
  Dim objCustomers As Customers
  Dim divCustInfo As Object

  strName = GetProperty(BaseWindow.Document, "SearchName")
  strPhone = GetProperty(BaseWindow.Document, "SearchPhone")

  Set objCustomers = New Customers
  objCustomers.Load strName, strPhone

  ListCustomers objCustomers
  Set objCustomers = Nothing

End Sub
```

Once the display has been loaded we don't need the `Customers` object any more, so we'll set its reference to `Nothing`.

## Implementing the Cancel Button

Our page has a Cancel button. Of course, it isn't entirely clear what we would want a Cancel button to do in this case – after all, we're viewing a list of data so there's really nothing to undo or stop.

On the other hand, the data being displayed is derived from the criteria entered by the user on our `CustSearch` page. It might make good sense for the Cancel button to move us back to that page so the user can change the criteria they entered.

Double-click on the Cancel button to bring up its `onclick` event procedure and add the following code:

```
Private Function cmdCancel_onclick() As Boolean

    BaseWindow.navigate "VideoDHTML_CustSearch.htm"

End Function
```

This code just uses the `navigate` method of the `BaseWindow` object to cause the browser to bring up the `CustSearch` page from our application.

## Running the Program

At this point, we've got an application that basically works. We can enter search criteria, view the results and return to change the criteria if we so desire. To run the program we can just press *F5* to run the program.

The first time we do this Visual Basic will prompt us as to how we want to start the application. We'll want to make sure the Start component option is chosen and that the component to be started is `CustSearch`. Once that's set, click OK and Visual Basic will bring up the browser, allowing us to enter some criteria and see the results:

The only thing we haven't done at this point is added the code to move us from this page on to the page where we'll actually edit a `Customer` object - `CustEdit`.

## Implementing the OK Button

Moving from the `CustList` page to a `CustEdit` page is pretty similar to moving from `CustSearch` to `CustList`. We'll simply use the `PutProperty` method to store the `CustomerID` value from the customer selected by the user, then use the `navigate` method of `BaseWindow` to cause the browser to switch to the new page.

> *It is interesting to note that none of these page transitions in any way require a web server. DHTML Applications can be installed and run on a client workstation that has no access to the Internet or an Intranet if we so desire. They are really very much like regular Visual Basic applications except that their display is contained within a browser instead of in a regular window.*
>
> *DHTML Applications are an example of the evolution of client/server technology. They allow us to provide our users with interfaces that are similar in power and capability to traditional forms-based interfaces, but with the display and deployment advantages of browser-based user interfaces.*
>
> *Thin clients solve logistic and deployment issues with the cost of having a less powerful user interface, while thick clients provide robust user interfaces, but can be difficult to deploy. DHTML Applications are a step toward providing us with the best of both these worlds.*

Double-click on the OK button in the DHTML page designer to bring up the code window for the `onclick` event. Enter the following code:

```
Private Function cmdOK_onclick() As Boolean

    PutProperty BaseWindow.Document, "CustomerID", Val(lvwItems.SelectedItem.Key)
    BaseWindow.navigate "VideoDHTML_CustEdit.htm"

End Function
```

The item selected by the user is accessible to us via the `lvwItems.SelectedItem` property. When we loaded the `ListView` control we put the `CustomerID` value into each item's `Key` property.

We'll use the `PutProperty` method to store that value into the client-side cookie. Then we'll just navigate to the `CustEdit` page where we'll be editing the `Customer` object itself.

# The CustEdit page

Now that we've got the ability to search for a customer and select one from a list of results we're finally ready to implement a page that let's us edit a `Customer` object itself. We'll name this last page `CustEdit`. It will provide essentially the same functionality as our `Customer` form from Chapter 7, including OK, Cancel and Apply buttons.

## Setting Up the Page

As with the other pages we've added so far, we'll use the Project | Add DHTML page menu item to add a new DHTMLPage designer. Set its `Name` property to `CustEdit` and add text and standard HTML controls as shown in this figure:

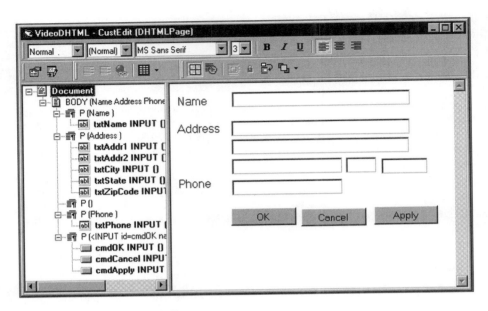

Set the controls' id properties as follows:

| | |
|---|---|
| TextField | txtName |
| TextField | txtAddr1 |
| TextField | txtAddr2 |
| TextField | txtCity |
| TextField | txtState |
| TextField | txtZipCode |
| TextField | txtPhone |
| Button | cmdOK |
| Button | cmdCancel |
| Button | cmdApply |

Once that's done we are ready to move on and add code to the page. In general, we've duplicated the form from Chapter 7, only in this case we've used HTML standard controls and a DHTML page.

## Adding Code to the Page

Much of the code we'll implement here can be lifted from the Customer form in Chapter 7 with only slight changes. There are certain capabilities that are present in Visual Basic standard controls, but aren't available with the HTML controls.

### The onchange Events

For instance, add the txtName_onchange event procedure in the CustEdit code window:

```
Private Function txtName_onchange() As Boolean

  If mflgLoading Then Exit Function
  On Error Resume Next
  mobjCustomer.Name = txtName.Value
  If Err Then
    Beep
    txtName.Value = mobjCustomer.Name
  End If

End Function
```

Compare this to the `txtName_Change` event from Chapter 7:

```
Private Sub txtName_Change()
  Dim intPos As Integer

  If mflgLoading Then Exit Sub
  On Error Resume Next
  mobjCustomer.Name = txtName
  If Err Then
    Beep
    intPos = txtName.SelStart
    txtName = mobjCustomer.Name
    txtName.SelStart = intPos - 1
  End If
End Sub
```

The basic functionality is the same – in both cases we copy the current value from the control into our `Customer` object and check for an error. Where the functionality differs is in our error handling. With Visual Basic controls we can determine the location of the cursor, reset the text in the control and restore the cursor's position. Unfortunately, with the HTML controls there is no way to determine or set the cursor's position within the text. This means we are reduced to simply restoring the object's value back into the control – at least ensuring that the user's display matches the value in our business object.

We'll implement the same changes for the `onchange` events of all the controls:

```
Private Function txtAddr1_onchange() As Boolean

  If mflgLoading Then Exit Function
  On Error Resume Next
  mobjCustomer.Address1 = txtAddr1.Value

  If Err Then
    Beep
    txtAddr1.Value = mobjCustomer.Address1
  End If

End Function

Private Function txtAddr2_onchange() As Boolean

  If mflgLoading Then Exit Function
  On Error Resume Next
  mobjCustomer.Address2 = txtAddr2.Value
```

```
   If Err Then
     Beep
     txtAddr2.Value = mobjCustomer.Address2
   End If

End Function


Private Function txtCity_onchange() As Boolean

   If mflgLoading Then Exit Function
   On Error Resume Next
   mobjCustomer.City = txtCity.Value

   If Err Then
     Beep
     txtCity.Value = mobjCustomer.City
   End If

End Function


Private Function txtState_onchange() As Boolean

   If mflgLoading Then Exit Function
   On Error Resume Next
   mobjCustomer.State = txtState.Value

   If Err Then
     Beep
     txtState.Value = mobjCustomer.State
   End If

End Function


Private Function txtZipCode_onchange() As Boolean

   If mflgLoading Then Exit Function
   On Error Resume Next
   mobjCustomer.ZipCode = txtZipCode.Value

   If Err Then
     Beep
     txtZipCode.Value = mobjCustomer.ZipCode
   End If

End Function


Private Function txtPhone_onchange() As Boolean

   If mflgLoading Then Exit Function
   On Error Resume Next
   mobjCustomer.Phone = txtPhone.Value

   If Err Then
     Beep
     txtPhone.Value = mobjCustomer.Phone
   End If

End Function
```

### LostFocus Functionality

In addition to the Change event, our traditional forms-based user interface in Chapter 7 also made use of the LostFocus event. The equivalent event in a DHTML form is the onblur event. We'll put code in each text box control's onblur event to retrieve the value from the business object and update the display on the form. This is particularly important for those values where the business object alters the value – such as the State property of the Customer object.

Here's the txtState_onblur event procedure:

```
Private Sub txtState_onblur()
   txtState.Value = mobjCustomer.State
End Sub
```

Enter this into the code window. Run through the other text controls on the form and create similar event procedures for them as well.

This gives our DHTML form virtually the same capabilities as our Visual Basic form did in Chapter 7.

### Module-Level Variables

Of course we still need to declare some module-level variables before things will work. In particular, we need to declare mobjCustomer and mflgLoading – just like in Chapter 7:

```
Option Explicit
```

```
Private WithEvents mobjCustomer As Customer
Private mflgLoading As Boolean
```

### Enabling and Disabling OK and Apply

Since we've declared mobjCustomer using the WithEvents keyword we will receive any events raised by that object. We implemented the Customer object to raise an IsValid event to indicate when the OK and Apply buttons should be enabled or disabled.

There is some difference here. Visual Basic's button controls have an Enabled property, but HTML button controls have the reverse – a disabled property:

```
Private Sub mobjCustomer_Valid(IsValid As Boolean)

   cmdOK.disabled = Not IsValid
   cmdApply.disabled = Not IsValid

End Sub
```

Instead of setting the property to the IsValid parameter, we need to use the Not keyword to get the correct functionality.

Along the same lines, we need to reverse the logic in the `EnableOK` method:

```
Private Sub EnableOK(flgValid As Boolean)

  cmdOK.disabled = Not flgValid
  cmdApply.disabled = Not flgValid

End Sub
```

## Loading the Customer Object

As with the `CustList` page, we need to retrieve the value stored in the client-side cookie and use it to load our business object's data. In this case we'll use it as a parameter to the `Load` method of our `Customer` object. We want to do this processing as our page is being loaded, so we'll add the code to the `DHTMLPage_Load` event procedure.

As in our `Customer` form in Chapter 7, we'll also use this procedure to place the object's values in all our `TextField` controls and get the form ready for the user:

```
Private Sub DHTMLPage_Load()

  Dim lngID As Long

  mflgLoading = True
  lngID = GetProperty(BaseWindow.Document, "CustomerID")
  Set mobjCustomer = New Customer
  mobjCustomer.Load lngID

  With mobjCustomer
    EnableOK .IsValid
    If .IsNew Then
      BaseWindow.Document.Title = "Customer [(new)]"

    Else
      BaseWindow.Document.Title = "Customer [" & .Name & "]"

    End If

    txtName.Value = .Name
    txtAddr1.Value = .Address1
    txtAddr2.Value = .Address2
    txtCity.Value = .City
    txtState.Value = .State
    txtZipCode.Value = .ZipCode
    txtPhone.Value = .Phone
    .BeginEdit
  End With

  mflgLoading = False

End Sub
```

Other than a couple minor differences, this code is right out of Chapter 7.

DHTML pages don't have a `Caption` property, instead we need to set the title in the browser's title bar. This is done by setting the `BaseWindow.Document.Title` property – just like we'd set a form's `Caption`, but this affects the browser window instead.

The other difference is where we're copying the data values from the `Customer` object to each field on the page. With Visual Basic controls the `Text` property is the default, so we didn't specify any property while assigning the data:

```
txtName = .Name
```

With the HTML controls however, there are no default properties, so we need to specify the `Value` property explicitly for each control:

```
txtName.Value = .Name
```

Notice how we use the `mflgLoading` variable here just like in a regular Visual Basic form. Either way, we need to have code that prevents the controls from acting on their `onchange` or `Change` events as we are loading data from the object into the page or form.

In almost every way, this DHTML form is coded the same as a regular Visual Basic form.

### Coding the Buttons

We've coded everything except the buttons on the page. The code for the buttons is somewhat different than that from our form in Chapter 7. In particular, both the OK and Cancel buttons can't simply unload a form – rather they need to navigate to some other page. The Apply button does end up being identical to that in a regular form.

Let's look at the Apply button first:

```
Private Function cmdApply_onclick() As Boolean

  mobjCustomer.ApplyEdit
  mobjCustomer.BeginEdit

End Function
```

As in any other user interface, when the user clicks Apply we need to call the business object's `ApplyEdit` method to save any changes and then call `BeginEdit` to resume the editing process.

The OK button also calls `ApplyEdit` to save changes, but then we need to leave the current page. In a form-based user interface we'd simply unload the form, but here we'll need to navigate to another page. Were we implementing a full-blown user interface we'd probably navigate to some menu page, but here we'll simply return to the page where we started: `CustSearch`:

```
Private Function cmdOK_onclick() As Boolean

  mobjCustomer.ApplyEdit
  BaseWindow.navigate "VideoDHTML_CustSearch.htm"

End Function
```

Like the OK button, the Cancel button also navigates to another page. First though, it needs to call the `CancelEdit` method on our business object to make sure that any changes we've made to the object are not saved:

```
Private Function cmdCancel_onclick() As Boolean

  mobjCustomer.CancelEdit
  BaseWindow.navigate "VideoDHTML_CustSearch.htm"

End Function
```

## Running the Program

With those last changes our program is complete. We can now enter search criteria to get a list of customers. We can then select one of the customers and bring up a page to edit the information for the selected Customer object:

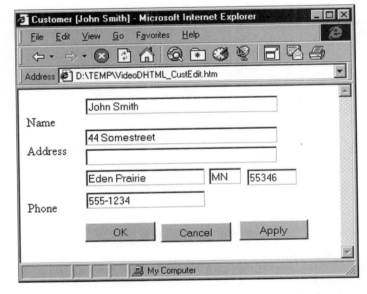

This page provides the same basic functionality as our Customer form from Chapter 7. In this case however, our interface is provided through the browser, allowing us to take advantage of its ability to easily display complex fonts, graphics and sounds if we so desire.

# Summary

DHTML Applications provide a new way for Visual Basic developers to build user interfaces. When compared to traditional forms-based user interfaces they bring their own set of advantages and drawbacks.

In any case, we have seen how CSLA makes it very easy for us to leverage the business logic we implemented in our business objects. We were able to implement an entirely new type of user interface – using an entirely new technology for Visual Basic 6.0 – with absolutely no change to our business objects or their underlying data access code.

Regardless of whether our business object's data persistence code is in the objects themselves, in a DCOM server or running in MTS, we always gain these benefits of the separation of the interface from the business objects. And as we've seen through Chapters 8, 10 and 12, it is very easy to move the data persistence processing out of the objects and onto other machines without affecting the business logic or the UI to any significant degree.

Whether you are developing an application for a single PC or for an enterprise-wide distributed network the logical model I've presented in this book will help you. Smaller applications benefit because they are more easily maintained and extended. Larger applications gain those benefits plus scalability and the ability to exploit the resources of both your client workstations as well as server machines. By keeping the UI processing close to the user and the data processing close to the database these applications minimize network load and maximize performance.

# Conclusion

Here we are at the end of the journey. Or perhaps it's better to say that we are at the beginning. While we've explored a lot of concepts and applied them to build an application, this book really only provides a first glimpse into the full capabilities of business objects and my CSLA architecture.

My motivation in writing this book was to share some of the lessons and techniques I've learned while developing complex client/server applications. Making use of business objects in software development is an important consideration all by itself. However, the challenges involved in not only using objects, but also working in an n-tier client/server environment can be truly daunting. While there are many possible solutions and approaches to these problems, I wanted to at least address those that I have used successfully.

Business objects lie at the core of everything we've discussed in this book. They provide us with a powerful way to examine business problems and to model the related business entities and processes within our applications. Traditional programming approaches tend to focus more on the program and less on the business. Object-oriented design helps encourage us to focus first on the business and the business need, and then deal with the technology as a secondary issue.

In Chapter 3 we saw how closely tied our objects are to the business we're trying to model. Each object, and each object's attributes and behaviors were derived from the business case. By taking this approach, we are able to construct a set of objects that represent the entities and concepts that pertain to our business. Once we have these objects, we can use them to create our application, modeling the business and providing the required functionality.

The really powerful part is that these objects are largely independent of each other. By this I mean that once we have a Customer object, it isn't tied to an Invoice such that we can *only* use it with an Invoice. We can also use it to analyze buying patterns, provide mailing lists and any other business process that involves a customer. This level of reuse is very hard to achieve with non-object approaches, but is a natural outcome of good object-oriented design.

In Chapter 4 we began to bridge the gap between object-oriented programming and client/server programming, following the CSLA architecture laid out in Chapter 2. The challenge we face is not trivial. The object-oriented approach to software design, while inherently based on client/server concepts, doesn't naturally lend itself to high performance in an n-tier environment.

During the object-oriented design process, we are typically very focused on modeling the business and creating objects that accurately reflect business entities. This often leaves us with objects that work very well together when modeling a business process, but may not provide efficient communication between processes or across a network connection – and yet this is exactly what we expect to do in a client/server application.

This is really where the CSLA comes into play – providing us with an architecture and approach that allows us to use object-oriented design and still take advantage of client/server technologies.

The first, and possibly most important, consideration is the separation of business logic from the user interface. By taking care to keep business rules and processing in our business objects we make it very easy to swap out one user interface for another. Even more likely, we'll probably need to implement *multiple* user interfaces for the same set of business objects.

I have noticed a rapidly increasing trend toward providing multiple user interfaces for a single application. Internal users want the powerful user interface provided by traditional Visual Basic forms. At the same time, external users (such as customers or suppliers) often also need some level of access to the application. Because this is becoming such a typical requirement, I've spent a lot of effort creating a variety of user interfaces based on our common set of video store objects. We've created interfaces using Visual Basic forms, Microsoft Excel, Active Server Pages, IIS Applications and DHTML Applications.

What may not be immediately apparent, but is nonetheless very important, is that we can create an application that uses a mix of any or all of these user interface types – *all at the same time*! For instance, the CSLA and our business object approach allow us to create a robust user interface for our internal users, and a totally browser-independent HTML user interface for our external customers. In addition, we might create a Microsoft Office interface to the objects when creating an executive information system or financial analysis system.

All of these interfaces can reuse the same business objects and the same n-tier design – basically they can reuse all the hard parts of the application!

Another major benefit of the CSLA is flexibility of design. I can't even count the number of applications I've seen written in a single or 2-tier approach, to be used by a limited number of users. The next thing we know, the application has either become popular or has grown in functionality and all of a sudden we've got many times the number of original users. Not surprisingly, performance problems start to crop up...

In many applications developed along more traditional lines, moving from one or two tiers to an n-tier architecture means rewriting much of the application. Serious time, serious money.

If our application were originally designed with the CSLA approach however, we'd have an application like the video store in Chapter 8. Moving from that single-tier application to the n-tier application we employ in Chapters 10 and later is fairly mechanical. Certainly there are some significant changes to our objects, but typically not where the business rules and logic are concerned. Instead, the changes deal with inter-object communication, thus minimizing the risk of introducing business-related bugs during the transition.

While not exactly trivial, the process of partitioning an application based on CSLA from one tier to n-tiers is much easier than the same process with many other application architectures.

The final point I want to touch on is scalability. At the end of Chapter 12 we have an application that can handle a very large number of users and do it very well. Not only do we make efficient use of our centralized resources, via MTS and its thread management and database connection pooling, but we also make efficient use of each client workstation.

Much is said these days about 'thin' clients and their benefits. Certainly no one can argue that the thinner the client the easier it is to install and maintain each client workstation. However, most client workstations today are very powerful computers. The Pentium processor sitting on the user's desk today is faster and more powerful than many processors that ran entire companies just a few years ago. To ignore that power is to limit the scalability of our applications.

By breaking our business objects into UI-centric and data-centric parts, we allow ourselves, as designers and developers, to place appropriate logic in the appropriate place. For a robust user interface, we want to put as much UI-oriented business logic as physically close to the user as possible. At the same time, to achieve maximum scalability, we also need to keep as much data-oriented business logic as physically close to the database as possible.

With both UI-centric and data-centric objects, our architecture provides the mechanism by which we can intelligently place our business logic where it works best. This allows us to *choose* how much of the power of each client workstation we want to use or how much we want to centralize the processing on a super-server running MTS.

It is my most sincere hope that, having read this book, you are able to leverage some of the concepts and gain some of the benefits I've seen by employing these techniques. By merging the best ideas from object-oriented design with the powerful capabilities of client/server computing we can create truly impressive applications. Microsoft has provided us with a wonderful tool set in this regard, with COM, MTS, MSMQ, Visual Basic and more.

Code well and have fun!

Rockford Lhotka

# Appendix A: Building Objects and Components with Visual Basic

So far we've looked at business objects, what they are and how we can use them to improve our software development. We've also discussed how they can be used to create binary components to facilitate reuse of our code and to implement complex n-tier client/server architectures.

Now let's look at how to create objects using Visual Basic. We can create them directly, by entering all the code ourselves, or we can use a wizard supplied with Visual Basic. In the first section of this appendix, we'll take a look at both of these techniques as we implement a basic object.

Once we have a solid handle on creating objects, we'll take a look at the various types of binary component we can create with Visual Basic. Since components are based on objects, we'll make use of our ability to create objects as we build our different components.

## Building Objects in Visual Basic

**Class modules** are the centerpiece of Visual Basic's ability to create objects and components. At first sight, a class module seems like just another code module - it's so similar to a form or code module. Looking more closely, though, there are some substantial differences.

Class modules can contain variables and code, including sub routines, functions and properties. Our programs can't directly use any of these variables or code, however, since a class module just provides a template to be used when creating an **object**.

As an example, let's assume we have a class module that contains code to draw a circle. Say this class module is named CircleShape and that it has a Radius property and a Draw method.

It seems pretty straightforward to use the class something like this:

```
CircleShape.Radius = 200
CircleShape.Draw
```

Unfortunately this won't work because we can't interact with a class module directly. Instead, we first need to create a new object based on the CircleShape class:

```
Dim objCircle as CircleShape

Set objCircle = New CircleShape
```

Alternatively, we can combine the statements:

```
Dim objCircle As New CircleShape
```

Then we can use the objCircle *object* to get at the code in the class module:

```
objCircle.Radius = 200
objCircle.Draw
```

Let's look at how to create a class using Visual Basic and its class modules.

# Class Modules from Scratch

Creating a class module is as easy as creating a form or code module. While we can create a class module by hand, Visual Basic also provides a wizard to help us out. We'll look at the wizard later; for now let's see how easy it is to just jump in and directly code a class module.

Since we've already discussed a CircleShape class, let's look at how we might implement such a class in Visual Basic. Then we'll also create a form with some client code so we can create an object and use the code within our new class.

First off, open Visual Basic and choose to create a Standard EXE project from the New Project dialog. Then choose the Project | Add Class Module menu option. From the Add Class Module dialog, choose the Class Module option and click Open.

In the code window that appears, enter the following:

```
Option Explicit

Private sngX As Single
Private sngY As Single
Private sngRadius As Single
Private frmForm As Form
```

```
Public Property Let CurrentX(Value As Single)
   sngX = Value
End Property

Public Property Get CurrentX() As Single
   CurrentX = sngX
End Property

Public Property Let CurrentY(Value As Single)
   sngY = Value
End Property

Public Property Get CurrentY() As Single
   CurrentY = sngY
End Property

Public Property Let Radius(Value As Single)
   sngRadius = Value
End Property

Public Property Get Radius() As Single
   Radius = sngRadius
End Property

Public Property Set Form(Value As Form)
   Set frmForm = Value
End Property

Public Sub Draw()
   frmForm.Circle (sngX, sngY), sngRadius
End Sub
```

This code includes everything a `CircleShape` object will need to know in order to function properly. Each `CircleShape` object we create will get its own copy of the `Private` instance variables:

```
Private sngX As Single
Private sngY As Single
Private sngRadius As Single
Private frmForm As Form
```

These variables are not accessible to any code outside of the class module itself.

We control how these values are accessed by implementing `Property Let`, `Property Get` and `Property Set` routines within our code. For instance, the `sngX` instance variable gets its value when the client code provides a value to our object's `CurrentX` property.

```
Public Property Let CurrentX(Value As Single)
   sngX = Value
End Property
```

The complimentary `Property Get` routine allows a client program to retrieve the value of our `sngX` variable.

```
Public Property Get CurrentX() As Single
  CurrentX = sngX
End Property
```

Our class also implements a `Draw` method with the following code:

```
Public Sub Draw()
  frmForm.Circle (sngX, sngY), sngRadius
End Sub
```

Change the name of the class to `CircleShape` in the class module's properties window.

Let's try our new `CircleShape` class by drawing a circle on a form. Open the code window for `Form1` and enter the following:

```
Option Explicit

Private Sub Form_Click()
  Dim objCircle As New CircleShape

  With objCircle
    Set .Form = Me
    .CurrentX = 500
    .CurrentY = 500
    .Radius = 200
    .Draw
  End With
End Sub
```

Note that `Circle` is a reserved word in Visual Basic, so when you type `Dim objCircle` you will need to enter the line like this:

```
Dim objCircle As New CircleShape
```

Notice how easy it is to work with the `objCircle` object. In fact, working with our new object is no different than working with any of Visual Basic's built in objects, such as the `Printer` object, or even a control such as a `TextBox`. In all of these cases, we are simply setting properties and calling methods just as we have done with our `objCircle` object.

Now we can run the project and click on the form. The circle should appear in the upper-left corner.

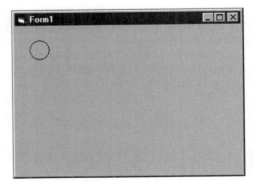

Though this `CircleShape` class is obviously not a business object like a `Customer` or `Product` might be, it does illustrate just how easy it is to create a class within Visual Basic. Creating a `Customer` class is no more difficult than our `CircleShape` class, it just might have more properties and methods and a bit more code in those routines.

We'll be using the `CircleShape` class module in the next section, so we'll want to save the project at this point. Save the project under the name `CircleDemo` in a directory on the hard drive.

# Using the Class Builder

As we've just seen, creating a class from scratch is not terribly difficult. Visual Basic 6.0 also comes with a Class Builder wizard to help create and maintain classes. This wizard provides a structured Windows-style interface that you can use to enter the properties and methods for your classes.

Let's walk through the process of creating our `CircleShape` class using the wizard. We're recreating the same class as above, just using a different approach. Open Visual Basic and choose to create a Standard EXE project from the New Project dialog.

Choose the Project | Add Class Module menu option. From the Add Class Module dialog choose the VB Class Builder option:

The Class Builder window will now appear as shown in the figure.

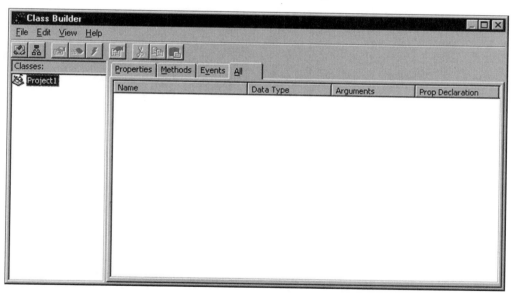

The display on the left shows our project and lists the classes within that project. Of course, the display is pretty empty, since we haven't added any classes. On the right, we have a choice of displays, allowing us to view the properties, methods, and events for the class selected on the left.

Now click the Add New Class button or choose File | New | Class....

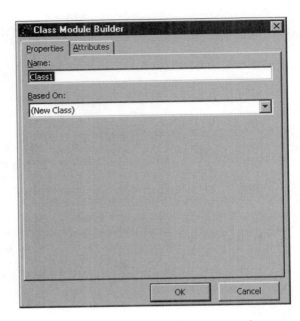

We can use this dialog to set the basic properties of our class. Since this is our first class in this project, it is automatically a top-level class. The options in this dialog will change as we create child classes. Change the name of the class to `CircleShape`.

If we click on the Attributes tab, we can enter a description for your class and set up a help context id.

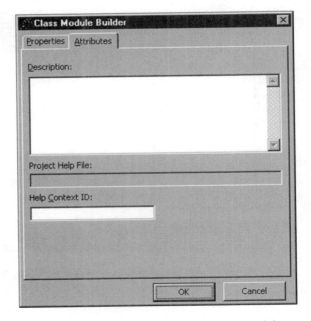

This class description will appear in the Visual Basic object browser, and so it can be very useful - although, for now, we'll leave both these fields blank. Just click OK to return to the Class Builder screen:

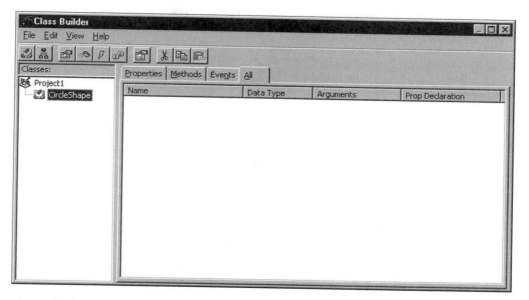

Now that we're back at this screen we can see that there are a number of changes to the options. Our new class is shown on the left, and the buttons to add a new property, method, and event are now enabled.

Click the Add New Property to Current Class button on the left or choose File | New | Property... to bring up the Property Builder dialog:

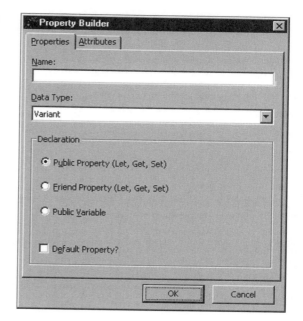

This screen provides all the options we need to set up a property for a class.

Let's name this property `CurrentX` and change the **Data Type** to `Single`. The possible data types are:

| | | |
|---|---|---|
| Byte | Boolean | Integer |
| Long | Single | Double |
| Currency | Date | String |
| Variant | Object | Collection |
| ErrObject | StdFont | StdPicture |
| CircleShape | | |

All these are the normal Visual Basic data types, except for `CircleShape`. As we add classes to our project through the Class Builder the class names will become available in the list. This means that we can easily create properties that accept or return objects based on our classes.

Notice the options in the **Declaration** frame. These options control the scope of our property, meaning they control who can see the property. The concept is the same as declaring a variable using the `Private` or `Public` keywords. By default, our property is part of our class's public interface and it will be declared with the `Public` keyword.

We could choose to declare it using the `Friend` keyword, in which case the property would only be available to code within our project. This really only comes into play if we are creating an ActiveX server, since `Friend` properties aren't available to our server's clients.

The third option is a carryover from Visual Basic 4.0, and is another way to create public properties. In the code, this will appear as a `Public` variable. Behind the scenes, though, Visual Basic 6.0 will actually create `Property Let` and `Property Get` procedures for us.

> *The way Visual Basic 6.0 handles* `Public` *variables in class modules is a substantial improvement over Visual Basic 4.0, in terms of documenting classes, since the hidden* `Property Let` *and* `Property Get` *procedures show up in Visual Basic's object browser. On the other hand, in Visual Basic 4.0,* `Public` *variables offered a speed benefit over regular properties, and that benefit has been lost with Visual Basic 6.0's implementation.*

We can also check the **Default Property** checkbox on one of our properties. This indicates to Visual Basic that the property is to be the default for our class. Most native Visual Basic objects have default properties or methods. For instance, the `TextBox` control's default property is `Text` - so a programmer can just say `MyTextBox = "Hello world"` rather than `MyTextBox.Text = "Hello world"`. Checking this box provides the same feature to our class.

The **Attributes** tab of this screen is identical to the class attributes, allowing us to enter a description for display in the Visual Basic object browser, and a help context id. We'll leave these blank for now, so just click the **OK** button.

Using the same technique, add the following properties:

| Property | Data Type |
|----------|-----------|
| CurrentY | Single |
| Radius | Single |
| Form | Object |

We've encountered a couple of limitations of the Class Builder at this point. First, in the CircleShape class that we built from scratch, the Form property was write-only (with just a Property Set); but the Class Builder doesn't provide this option. Second, we were able to type the Form property As Form before; but with the Class Builder we have to use the more general and less efficient Object data type. We'll fix these problems once we're done with the wizard.

Now all that's left is to add our Draw method - so click on the New Method button or choose File | New | Method... to add a new method.

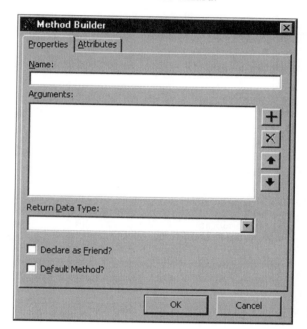

Set the name of the method to Draw.

Our Draw method has no arguments but, as you can see, this dialog allows you to add, remove and order the arguments for each method. We can also put in a Return Data Type. In our case, we'll leave this blank - so as to create a subroutine rather than a function.

The Declare as Friend and Default Method options work similarly to the same options on the Property Builder dialog that we discussed earlier.

Again, the attributes tab is the same as we've seen, and we'll leave it blank for this example.

Click OK and we'll return to the Class Builder.

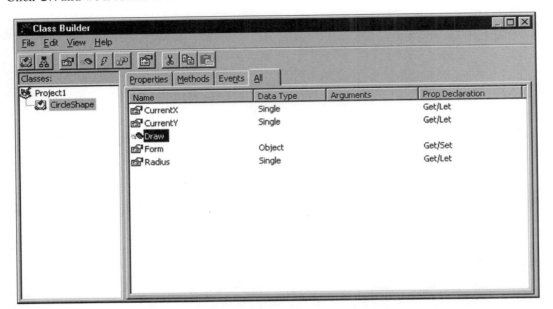

Now just close the Class Builder. The wizard will ask whether we want to update our project, so choose Yes and we'll be on our way. The Class Builder will work a bit at this point and then we should be back in the regular Visual Basic environment, with the code window for our new class displayed.

As we noticed earlier, the Class Builder has some limitations, so we need to clean up some of the code it generated. To start with, it didn't let us make the Form property write-only, so we need to remove the following code:

```
Public Property Get Form() As Object
'used when retrieving value of a property, on the right side of an assignment.
'Syntax: Debug.Print X.Form
    Set Form = mvarForm
End Property
```

The other thing the tool didn't let us do was declare the Form property as type Form; we had to make it type Object. Let's fix that now by finding the following routine:

```
Public Property Set Form(ByVal vData As Object)
'used when assigning an Object to the property, on the left side of a Set
statement.
'Syntax: Set x.Form = Form1
    Set mvarForm = vData
End Property
```

Change the first line so the routine appears like this:

```
Public Property Set Form(ByVal vData As Form)
'used when assigning an Object to the property, on the left side of a Set
statement.
'Syntax: Set x.Form = Form1
    Set mvarForm = vData
End Property
```

And in the declarations section, at the top of the code module, make the following change from `Object` to `Form`:

```
Private mvarForm As Form 'local copy
```

Finally, we need to add the code for the `Draw` method:

```
Public Sub Draw()
    mvarForm.Circle (mvarCurrentX, mvarCurrentY), mvarRadius
End Sub
```

At this point we can test our new `CircleShape` class using the same test code as in our earlier example. Open the code window for `Form1` and enter the following:

```
Option Explicit

Private Sub Form_Click()
  Dim objCircle As New CircleShape

  With objCircle
    Set .Form = Me
    .CurrentX = 500
    .CurrentY = 500
    .Radius = 200
    .Draw
  End With
End Sub
```

Now just run this program to see the results.

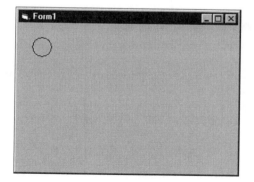

Not surprisingly, this circle looks just like the one from the `CircleShape` class we implemented manually. The wizard merely provides us with another tool for developing a basic class module. In many cases it can be quicker and easier to simply enter the code by hand, though the wizard does provide easy access to advanced features such as property and method descriptions.

# ActiveX Components

Now that we've gone through the basics of creating classes and objects in Visual Basic, let's look at how objects can be packaged inside components. There are three basic types of ActiveX components:

- ❑ Out-of-process (EXE)
- ❑ In-process (DLL)
- ❑ Control (OCX)

The first two of these are created in an almost identical fashion; but the third type, where we put objects into a control, is rather different.

We'll look at each of these component types in turn and see how they are created. Since our components are based on classes we'll need a class to use in building our components. Since we've already got it implemented, we'll use the CircleShape class from the previous section.

There are many issues surrounding when to use each type of component and how they should be designed. We go into those issues throughout the book. Right now, though, let's focus on how each type of component is created.

# ActiveX EXEs

To create an out-of-process ActiveX server with Visual Basic, you need to create an ActiveX EXE project. The result will be an executable program, just like any other, except that the program will allow other programs to use some or all of its objects.

To get started, open up Visual Basic and select the ActiveX EXE from the New Project dialog. Visual Basic will create a new project with a single class module called Class1. This is one of the differences between this project type and a Standard EXE project, where the default starting point is a form.

We won't be using the Class1 code module, so right-click on the module in the Project window and remove it from the project.

## Adding Our Class

We'll start with the code from our original CircleShape class. We saved this file in the CircleDemo project, so we should be able to choose the Project | Add File menu option to bring that the CircleShape class module into our new project.

We need to make some minor changes to our code for it to work in an out-of-process server. In particular, objects of type Form are always private in Visual Basic 6.0. This means that we can't accept a parameter of type Form from another program since the compiler will reject it. Since we are creating an ActiveX server for use by other programs we'll need to avoid this problem.

Our CircleShape class has a Form property that accepts a Form type value. We'll have to change this to accept an Object value instead to dodge this restriction.

```
Public Property Set Form(Value As Object)
   Set frmForm = Value
End Property
```

And, of course, we'll need to change the declarations section at the top of the module:

```
Private frmForm As Object
```

## The Instancing Property

When we are creating an ActiveX server we get to choose how each of our class modules can be used by client programs. This is controlled using the Instancing property for each class module. What we are setting with this property is essentially the scope of our class.

The available instancing properties are:

| Instancing Property | Description |
| --- | --- |
| 1-Private | Used to indicate that the class can only be used within this ActiveX server, and is not available to any other programs or components. |
| 2-PublicNotCreatable | Used to indicate that the class can be used by other programs or components, but that those programs can not create instances of the class. This means that they have to rely on other objects within the server to create this object and return a reference. |
| 3-SingleUse | Used to indicate that the class can be used by other programs or components. Each time they create an object from this class, the object will be created inside a new process; therefore, there is a single use of this class per process. |
| 4-GlobalSingleUse | This is the same as SingleUse except that the client does not create an explicit object from this class, but rather one is created automatically. All the methods and properties of this class are directly available to the programmer as though they were part of the Visual Basic language itself. |
| 5-MultiUse | Used to indicate that the class can be used by other programs and components. All objects created from this class will exist inside the same process, the exact opposite behavior from SingleUse. |
| 6-GlobalMultiUse | Like GlobalSingleUse, this is a way to make the properties and methods of the class appear to be part of the Visual Basic language in the client program. Like MultiUse, though, each client won't load a new process to hold this object: all the clients will get their own object within the same server process. |

For our CircleShape class, we'll want the Instancing property set to 5-Multiuse so it can be created and used by client programs.

At this point, we could add as many other classes as we desired to the project, and they'd all end up inside the same out-of-process server when we were done. Notice that we can use the Instancing property, for each class, to indicate whether it will be available to other programs or just available within our server itself.

## *Setting the Project Properties*

We're done with the code, so we just need to make a couple of adjustments to the project's properties. Choose Project | Project1 Properties... to bring up this dialog:

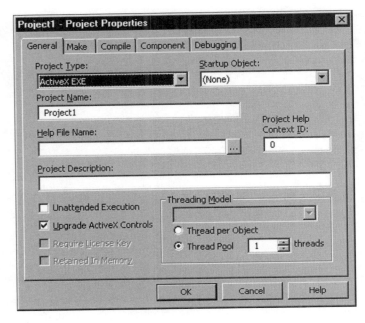

We won't go through this entire dialog in detail. There are just a few fields that are important for an ActiveX server, and they are all on this tab:

❑ Project Type
❑ Project Name
❑ Unattended Execution

### *Project Type*

The Project Type is already set for us, since we picked this type of project when we created it. Still, it is worth noting, since we can change our project's type later on if we need to.

*There are some serious caveats to making such a change, though, so be careful! In particular, switching between ActiveX EXEs and ActiveX DLLs can be tricky. You need to make sure you unregister the existing server before you make the switch. If it was an EXE, run the program using the /UNREGSERVER switch, or if it was a DLL, you'll need to use the Regsvr32.exe utility from the Visual Basic CD with the /U switch.*

### *Project Name*

The Project Name should also be changed. We gave our class the name CircleShape, and that will be the name our client code will use to create objects based on the class. However, our ActiveX server itself needs a name. The Project Name field is how we set that up. In this case, let's change the value to read CircleServer, since our server is just there to make circles.

When a client program or component uses our server, they'll add it to their project's list of references by using our **Project Name**. Alternatively, they might use the `CreateObject` function to create an object from our server. For instance:

```
Set objCircle = CreateObject("CircleServer.CircleShape")
```

This line of code creates an instance of our class. To do this it references both the name of our ActiveX server and of our class module.

### Unattended Execution

The Unattended Execution option is used to indicate to Visual Basic that this program is intended for use where there is no interactive user. This option is primarily intended for our use in creating ActiveX servers just like the one we are creating now, so we'll want to check this box.

By selecting this option we are telling Visual Basic to help us out by preventing the program from making any attempt to directly interact with a user. We'll be prohibited from having any forms in our project, preventing us from 'accidentally' creating a display that requires user input.

Also, Visual Basic will automatically redirect any `MsgBox` function or method calls such that they are written into the system's event log. Under Windows NT this will be the Application Event log and under Windows 95 this will be a log file in the Windows root directory.

### Threading Model

The Threading Model frame lets us tap into Visual Basic 6.0's ability to create multithreaded servers. We discuss multithreading and how it can be useful at various stages in the book where we designing business object servers. For now we'll leave these options alone.

## Compiling the Server

To compile our new ActiveX server choose File | Make CircleServer.exe. This doesn't appear any different than compiling any other Visual Basic program, but there are a lot of differences behind the scenes.

Since this is an ActiveX component, Visual Basic automatically adds entries to the Windows registry for our server and each class it contains. These entries are used by any client programs so they can find the server and its classes.

## Testing Our Server

Let's quickly run through a client program to test our server. We'll essentially be using the same client program from our earlier examples with the `CircleShape` class, but this new program will use the `CircleShape` class from our new ActiveX server.

Start a new copy of Visual Basic and create a **Standard EXE** project.

The first thing we need to do is make our program aware of our server. This is done by referencing our ActiveX server within the client program. To do this choose Project | References to bring up the following dialog:

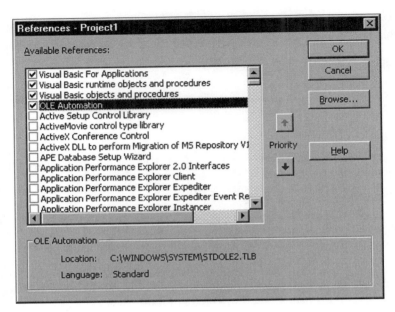

Now scroll down through the list to find the CircleServer entry, click its checkbox on, and click OK.

This will create a reference from our client program to the ActiveX server, making the classes in our server directly available to our client program. To the code in our client it will appear as though all the class modules from the CircleServer program were included directly into the client project – except of course that they'll really be running in our out-of-process server.

Now open the code window for Form1 and enter the following familiar code:

```
Option Explicit

Private Sub Form_Click()
  Dim objCircle As New CircleShape

  With objCircle
    Set .Form = Me
    .CurrentX = 500
    .CurrentY = 500
    .Radius = 200
    .Draw
  End With
End Sub
```

Now we can just run the program and click on the form to see a circle appear as in our previous examples.

Mostly likely we'll see that the circle appears somewhat more slowly than before. This is because Windows has to start up a new process for our ActiveX server before our client program can get the CircleShape object to work with.

# ActiveX DLLs

In-process servers are created in exactly the same way as out-of-process servers, with just a couple of minor exceptions. These servers are ActiveX DLLs that run within the context of the client's process. This means they technically share the client's memory, though Visual Basic prevents our server's code from directly interacting with the client's code – all the interaction occurs through our objects, as with an out-of-process server.

> If you created the `CircleServer` in the previous example, and you are now going to adapt it to be a DLL, don't forget to unregister `CircleServer.exe` before getting started. To do this, simply use the Run command from the Start menu, and type `PATH/circleserver /unregister`.

## *Setting up the Server*

To create an in-process server, we need to choose the ActiveX DLL option from the New Project dialog. Just as when we created a new ActiveX EXE project, we're presented with a brand new class module all ready to go. At this point, we can add classes just like we did for our out-of-process server.

We'll use the same `CircleShape` class as before, so choose the Project | Add File menu option and add the `CircleShape` class module from the **ClassDemo** project.

### The Instancing Property

An important difference in the class module properties is within the Instancing selections. Classes in a DLL are more restricted in their options than those in an EXE. The available options are:

- ❏ 1-Private
- ❏ 2-PublicNotCreatable
- ❏ 5-MultiUse
- ❏ 6-GlobalMultiUse

In particular, the SingleUse and GlobalSingleUse options are missing. This is because in-process servers are literally loaded into the client's process, or memory space. It is not possible to start up a new in-process server to house each object that is created, which is exactly the definition of the single use instancing options.

## *Project Properties*

As with an ActiveX EXE, we'll need to set some properties in the Project Properties dialog for our ActiveX DLL.

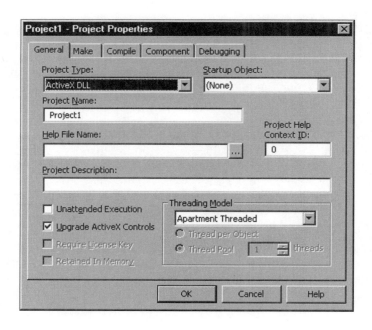

### Project Type

The Project Type is, of course, ActiveX DLL. In fact, we could have chosen to change the Project Type of our original server from ActiveX EXE to ActiveX DLL rather than creating a new project. Either way, we need to unregister the original server before trying to compile our new version.

### Project Name

As with our out-of-process server, we need to set the Project Name value in the Project Properties dialog. This name is used by our client developer to reference our ActiveX server and so we don't want it to read something like `Project1`.

### Unattended Execution

We'll want to check the Unattended Execution option in this project as well. This serves exactly the same purpose as our earlier out-of-process server.

### Threading Model

The Threading Model frame's options are a bit more restricted here than they were with our ActiveX EXE. This is because a DLL always runs in the context of the client program's process and so it makes use of the threads in that process rather than having its own. Because of this it makes no sense to indicate whether threads will be created for each object or as a pool – all that is handled by the process itself.

## Compiling the Server

To compile our new ActiveX server choose File | Make CircleServer.dll. As with our out-of-process server, our DLL is an ActiveX component and so Visual Basic will automatically add entries to the Windows registry for the server and each class it contains.

## Testing the Server

If we build `CircleServer` as a DLL, we can use the exact same client program that we used to test the `CircleServer` EXE. It will work without a single change to its code.

### Re-referencing the Server

The one thing we will need to do before we can run the client program is re-reference the server using the Project | References menu choice. We need to do this because the server's global unique identifier (GUID) has changed.

Anytime we recompile an ActiveX server project without having a compatible server set up the server's GUID will be regenerated. This is certainly true when you change from an out-of-process to an in-process server. Even though on the screen we are referencing our servers by name, Visual Basic actually references them using the server's GUID behind the scenes.

We discuss GUID values, compatible servers and other related issues in Chapters 7 and 11. In any case, it is a good idea to read through the Visual Basic manuals to get a good feel for how this works before launching into any sizable project using ActiveX servers. These can be significant development hurdles to overcome without having a good grasp of how GUIDs work.

### Running the Test

Other than the server reference everything will operate just like it did in the previous example. You may notice that the program runs faster - it is much easier for Windows to load a DLL than to start up a new process for an EXE.

# ActiveX Controls

Out-of-process and in-process ActiveX servers are by far the most common way to package business objects into components. However, Visual Basic 6.0 provides us with the ability to create ActiveX controls, and it is perfectly possible to put business objects in a control.

In general it is a better practice to put our business objects in either in-process or out-of-process servers than in controls. Controls are a specialized form of component, geared towards acting as widgets for use in creating user interfaces. At the same time, there are more mechanisms for distribution of ActiveX controls to our client workstations than exist for either in-process or out-of-process servers and so there are times when placing business objects in a control can be an attractive option.

ActiveX controls also have the restriction that they must be contained within a form. This means that the client program needs to include a form to contain the control. Our in-process and out-of-process servers, on the other hand, can be used by any client regardless of whether they contain a form.

ActiveX controls are quite similar to an in-process server. They are loaded into the client's process, sharing the same memory. There are, however, some significant differences in the interface that you can provide to the client developer when you're implementing an ActiveX control as compared an ActiveX DLL.

## Setting up the Server

Using the now familiar `CircleShape` class, I'll walk through the process of creating an ActiveX control to house business objects. The control itself will be invisible at runtime, since we aren't trying to build a screen widget. In this case we're just trying to create an alternative form of component to house our objects.

Open a new project in Visual Basic and choose the ActiveX Control option. Visual Basic will come up with an ActiveX control 'form' for you to work with, which can be used to define the control's runtime user interface.

### Setting up the Control

For the most part, we'll simply ignore this interface element, since we're trying to create an invisible control. However, there is at least one interface-related duty we should perform to make our control work.

In particular, we need to change the control's `InvisibleAtRuntime` property to `True` using the property window. This means our control will be visible at design time, so a client programmer can work with it; but it won't be visible to the end user at run time. This is the same way that the `Timer` control works, for example.

> *We may also want to resize the control to be substantially smaller, or even set its* `Picture`
> *property to give it a pleasing appearance for the programmer using it at design time. To keep the*
> *focus on the business object aspect, we'll avoid those possibilities in this example. For more*
> *information on ActiveX control development, you can refer to* Instant Visual Basic 5 ActiveX
> Control Creation *(ISBN 1-861000-235) from Wrox Press.*

While we're working with the control itself, let's give it a descriptive name. Change the control's name property to `CircleControl`.

## Adding the CircleShape Class

Now choose Project | Add File menu option and bring in the `CircleShape` class module from the `CircleDemo` project.

As with an ActiveX EXE or DLL, we can add as many classes as we want to this project. An ActiveX control can contain an entire group of business objects simply by adding those classes to the project.

### The Instancing Property

The Instancing options are even more limited than with an ActiveX DLL. The only options available are 1-Private and 2-PublicNotCreatable. This is because the control itself provides the only public interface to this type of component. Client programs can't just reach into a control and work with the classes it contains. This means that we'll have to put methods on the control to provide access to the business objects inside.

The Instancing property of our `CircleShape` class is automatically set for public use, with the value 2-PublicNotCreatable.

## Adding a Method to get an Object

Now we need to add a method to our control's interface so our client program can ask for a `CircleShape` object. To do this, add the following code to the control's code window:

```
Option Explicit

Public Function GetCircle() As CircleShape
   Set GetCircle = New CircleShape
End Function
```

## Testing the Control

All that remains is to test what we've done - so we'll add a project directly into the current Visual Basic session. To do this close down all the edit windows for the control. Don't close Visual Basic itself, just all the code and form design windows inside the Visual Basic session.

Then choose File | Add Project to get the new project dialog and choose the Standard EXE option. You should end up looking at a brand new form in a new project, but still within the same Visual Basic environment where we built the control.

Now simply grab our new control off the toolbox and put it on the form. Since we didn't change the control's icon, it should appear on the toolbox like this:

Once we've added the control, our form won't look much different:

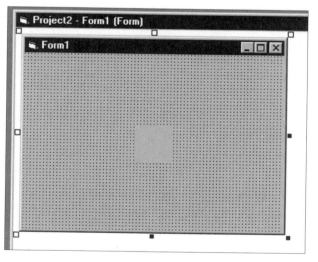

The blank area in the center is our control. Obviously, if we'd been creating a commercial control then we'd want to put a picture in our control for a production setting. For our current purposes, however, we're all set.

All that remains is to add some code to the form's code window:

```
Option Explicit

Private Sub Form_Click()
  Dim objCircle As CircleShape

  Set objCircle = CircleControl1.GetCircle
  With objCircle
    Set .Form = Me
    .CurrentX = 500
    .CurrentY = 500
    .Radius = 200
    .Draw
  End With
End Sub
```

This code is very similar to our previous examples, but we need to look at a couple key points.

First off, notice that we are still able to declare our variable as type `CircleShape`. The `CircleShape` class in the control is public - it is just not directly creatable. Since it is public, we can use it as a data type within any form that contains the control.

```
Dim objCircle As CircleShape
```

We did have to eliminate the `New` keyword of course, since we couldn't directly create a `CircleShape` object out of the control. Instead, we've added a new line of code to create the `CircleShape` object by calling the control's `GetCircle` method:

```
Set objCircle = CircleControl1.GetCircle
```

So, with two small changes, we've converted our client program from working with an ActiveX DLL to working with an ActiveX control.

Now just run the program, and click on the form to see the circle show up.

# Summary

In this appendix we covered the mechanics of creating objects using Visual Basic. We then took those concepts and used them to create binary components.

We looked at all three types of components we can create in Visual Basic:

- ❑ ActiveX EXEs
- ❑ ActiveX DLLs
- ❑ ActiveX controls

# Appendix B: Unified Modeling Language

The Unified Modeling Language (UML) encompasses a number of different notations for different purposes, including the following diagrams:

- ❑ Static class
- ❑ Sequence
- ❑ Use case
- ❑ State transition
- ❑ Activity
- ❑ Component
- ❑ Deployment

This appendix will briefly cover static class diagrams as they are represented in the Unified Modeling Language (UML), since they are the only type of UML diagram used in this book.

*Throughout this book, all UML diagrams have been created using Microsoft Visual Modeler. This tool is available from Microsoft to all Visual Basic Enterprise owners.*

# Static Class Diagram

Static class diagrams are very similar, in many ways, to standard entity relationship (ER) diagrams used in more traditional analysis techniques. They show the static, or constant, relationships between objects.

# Classes

The core of a class diagram is – not surprisingly – the class and its related notation. Let's look at how a class is displayed in UML, then we'll move on to look at how class relationships are displayed.

### Class Display

A class, in UML, is shown as a box with the class name near the top center. For example:

This diagram shows a class named A Class. The two lines below the class name separate the spaces where properties and methods will be displayed.

### Property Display

Most classes have some attributes, or properties. In UML, we display the properties for a class immediately below the class name, after the first line:

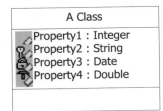

In the diagram we've listed four properties, Property1, Property2, Property3 and Property4. Each property's data type is shown to the right, after a colon.

The icons to the left of each property indicate scope. In the diagram, each property has been assigned a different scope to illustrate all the possible options. The following table describes each one:

| Property | Scope | Description |
|----------|-------|-------------|
| Property1 | Public | Public scope, the same as Visual Basic's Public keyword. |
| Property2 | Protected | Visual Basic has no direct analog to this scope. It can be useful in portraying properties with Friend scope. |
| Property3 | Private | Private scope, the same as Visual Basic's Private keyword. |
| Property4 | Implementation | Visual Basic has no analog to this scope. |

## *Method Display*

The methods for a class are displayed below the properties, after the second line in the class box:

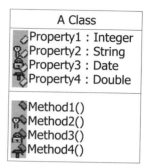

In the diagram we have four methods. The first method, `Method1`, is shown to accept a parameter, `Price`. The other methods do not accept parameters.

As with the properties, the icons to the far left indicate the scope of each method.

# Class Relationships

The primary intent of a static class diagram is to show the relationships between classes. We'll go through the common relationships and show the notations used for each.

## *General Relationship*

General relationships cover a lot of ground, including:

❑ One object using another
❑ One object knowing about another
❑ One object creating another

In UML, a general relationship between classes is expressed using the following notation:

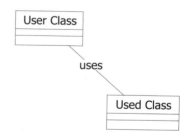

This diagram shows two classes, where the `User Class` is in a relationship where it uses the `Used Class`. Another word could be substituted for `uses` in the diagram to indicate a different type of relationship, for example; `displays`, `owns` or `contains`.

## Aggregation

UML provides a special notation to denote aggregation. This is the case where one object is composed of one or more other objects. The notation looks like:

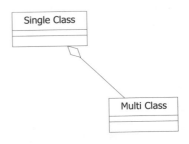

In this case `Class1` is composed of `Class2`. Another way to say this is that `Class2` is aggregated into `Class1`.

## Generalization (Inheritance)

Generalization is an analysis technique by which we identify a general class that can be used to create other, more specialized, classes. In UML we can show this relationship as:

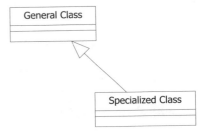

In this diagram the `Specialized Class` is created by inheriting from the `General Class`.

## Multiplicity

One key piece of information required by UML for all relationship types is **multiplicity**. Multiplicity indicates how many objects of each class are involved in the relationship.

For instance, take a look at the following diagram:

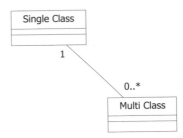

In this diagram, one instance of the `Single Class` has a relationship with zero or more instances of the `Multi Class` class. UML allows us to specify any level of multiplicity, though the common ones include:

| Multiplicity | Meaning |
|---|---|
| 0 | Zero |
| 1 | One |
| 0..* | Zero or more |
| 1..* | One or more |
| n | A particular number |
| x..y | A range |

Technically, UML requires us to indicate multiplicity for each object in a relationship. This is true for all the different types of relationship that we include in a diagram.

# Summary

This has been a highly cursory look at UML, intended simply to explain the class diagrams developed in this book to illustrate the VideoStore application. If you want to learn more, I suggest you look at *Instant UML* (ISBN 1-861000-87-1) also published by Wrox Press.

# Appendix C: Additional Code

In several chapters, notably 10 and 12, I left it up to you to add some of the coding without walking you through each step. Although you will be able to find all this code available for download at the Wrox Press website (www.wrox.com) I have chosen to include a simple listing of all the additional code that you should be creating.

## Chapter 10

### The Videos Objects

```
Option Explicit

Private mcolDisplay As Collection

Private Sub Class_Initialize()

  Set mcolDisplay = New Collection

End Sub

Public Sub Load(Optional Title As String, Optional Studio As String)

  Dim objPersist As VideosPersist

  Set objPersist = CreateObject("VideoServer.VideosPersist", PERSIST_SERVER)
  SetState objPersist.Fetch(Title, Studio)
  Set objPersist = Nothing

End Sub
```

```
Public Function Item(ByVal Index As Variant) As VideoDisplay

   Set Item = mcolDisplay(Index)

End Function
```

```
Public Function Count() As Long

   Count = mcolDisplay.Count

End Function
```

```
' NewEnum must return the IUnknown interface of a
' collection's enumerator.
Public Function NewEnum() As IUnknown

   Set NewEnum = mcolDisplay.[_NewEnum]

End Function
```

```
Private Sub SetState(Buffer As String)

   Dim objBuffer As Buffer
   Dim objDisplay As VideoDisplay
   Dim lngIndex As Long
   Dim udtData As VideoDisplayData
   Dim udtProps As VideoDisplayProps

   Set objBuffer = New Buffer
   With objBuffer
     .SetState Buffer
     For lngIndex = 1 To .Count
       Set objDisplay = New VideoDisplay
       udtData.Buffer = .Item(lngIndex)
       LSet udtProps = udtData

       With objDisplay
         .VideoID = udtProps.VideoID
         .Title = Trim$(udtProps.Title)
         .ReleaseDate = udtProps.ReleaseDate
         mcolDisplay.Add objDisplay
         Set objDisplay = Nothing
       End With

     Next

   End With

   Set objBuffer = Nothing

End Sub
```

## The VideosPersist Object

```
Option Explicit

Private mobjBuffer As Buffer
```

```
Public Function Fetch(ByVal Title As String, ByVal Studio As String) As String

    Dim rsVideo As Recordset
    Dim strSQL As String
    Dim strWHERE As String
'   Dim objDisplay As VideoDisplay
    Dim udtData As VideoDisplayData
    Dim udtProps As VideoDisplayProps

    strSQL = "SELECT VideoID, TITLE,RELEASEDATE FROM Video"
    If Len(Title) > 0 Then _
        strWHERE = "TITLE LIKE '" & Title & "%' "

    If Len(Studio) > 0 Then

        If Len(strWHERE) > 0 Then
            strWHERE = strWHERE & " AND STUDIO LIKE '" & Studio & "%'"

        Else
            strWHERE = "STUDIO LIKE '" & Studio & "%'"

        End If

    End If

    If Len(strWHERE) > 0 Then _
        strSQL = strSQL & " WHERE " & strWHERE
    Set rsVideo = New Recordset
    rsVideo.Open strSQL, cnVideo
    Set mobjBuffer = New Buffer
    mobjBuffer.Initialize Len(udtData.Buffer), 100

    Do While Not rsVideo.EOF
        With udtProps
            .VideoID = rsVideo("VideoID")
            .Title = rsVideo("Title")
            .ReleaseDate = rsVideo("ReleaseDate")
        End With
        LSet udtData = udtProps
        mobjBuffer.Add udtData.Buffer
        rsVideo.MoveNext
    Loop

    rsVideo.Close
    Set rsVideo = Nothing
    Fetch = mobjBuffer.GetState

End Function
```

## The Invoice Object

The Invoice Object no longer has a Save, DeleteObject or Fetch routine plus the
InvoiceProps UDT has been moved to the VideoTypes module. In addition, the following
routines have been modified:

```
Public Sub ApplyEdit()

    Dim objPersist As InvoicePersist
```

```
      If Not mflgEditing Then Err.Raise 445

      Set objPersist = CreateObject("VideoServer.InvoicePersist", PERSIST_SERVER)

      If mflgDeleted And Not mflgNew Then
        ' code to delete the object's data goes here
        objPersist.DeleteObject mudtProps.InvoiceID
        mflgNew = True
        mflgDeleted = False

      ElseIf mflgDirty Or mflgNew Then
        If Not IsValid Then Err.Raise 445
        ' save object to database if appropriate
        SetState objPersist.Save(GetState)
        ' save object state
        LSet mudtSave = mudtProps
        mflgNew = False

      End If

      Set objPersist = Nothing
      mflgDirty = False
      mflgEditing = False
      mobjItems.ApplyEdit mudtProps.InvoiceID

    End Sub

    Public Sub Load(InvoiceID As Long)

      Dim objPersist As VideoPersist

      If mflgEditing Then Err.Raise 445
      If Not mflgNew Then Err.Raise 445

      ' code to load the object goes here
      Set objPersist = CreateObject("VideoServer.VideoPersist", PERSIST_SERVER)
      SetState objPersist.Fetch(InvoiceID)
      Set objPersist = Nothing
      mflgNew = False

      mobjValid.RuleBroken "Customer", False

      mobjItems.Load mudtProps.InvoiceID

    End Sub
```

The following routines have also been added:

```
    Public Function CreateInvoice() As Invoice

      Dim objInvoice As Invoice

      Set objInvoice = New Invoice
      objInvoice.Initialize Me
      Set CreateInvoice = objInvoice
      Set objInvoice = Nothing

    End Function
```

```vb
Private Function GetState() As String

  Dim udtData As InvoiceData

  With mudtProps
    .IsDeleted = mflgDeleted
    .IsNew = mflgNew
    .IsDirty = mflgDirty
    .SubTotal = SubTotal
    .Tax = Tax
    .Total = Total
  End With

  LSet udtData = mudtProps
  GetState = udtData.Buffer

End Function
```

```vb
Private Sub SetState(Buffer As String)

  Dim udtData As InvoiceData

  udtData.Buffer = Buffer
  LSet mudtProps = udtData

End Sub
```

## The InvoicePersist Object

```vb
Option Explicit

Private mudtProps As InvoiceProps

Private Function GetState() As String

  Dim udtData As InvoiceData

  LSet udtData = mudtProps
  GetState = udtData.Buffer

End Function

Private Sub SetState(Buffer As String)

  Dim udtData As InvoiceData

  udtData.Buffer = Buffer
  LSet mudtProps = udtData

End Sub

Public Function Save(ByVal Buffer As String) As String

  Dim rsInvoice As Recordset
  Dim strSQL As String

  SetState Buffer
  strSQL = "SELECT * FROM Invoice WHERE InvoiceID=" & mudtProps.InvoiceID
```

```
    Set rsInvoice = New Recordset
    rsInvoice.Open strSQL, cnVideo, , adLockOptimistic
    If mudtProps.IsNew Then rsInvoice.AddNew

    With rsInvoice
      .Fields("CustomerID") = mudtProps.CustomerID
      .Fields("Subtotal") = mudtProps.SubTotal
      .Fields("Tax") = mudtProps.Tax
      .Fields("Total") = mudtProps.Total
      .Update
      If mudtProps.IsNew Then mudtProps.InvoiceID = .Fields("InvoiceID")
      .Close
    End With

    strSQL = "SELECT NAME,PHONE FROM Customer " & _
      "WHERE CustomerID=" & mudtProps.CustomerID
    rsInvoice.Open strSQL, cnVideo
    mudtProps.CustomerName = rsInvoice("Name")
    mudtProps.CustomerPhone = rsInvoice("Phone")
    rsInvoice.Close
    Set rsInvoice = Nothing
    Save = GetState

End Function
```

```
Public Sub DeleteObject(ByVal InvoiceID As Long)

  cnVideo.Execute "DELETE FROM Invoice WHERE InvoiceID=" & _
    InvoiceID

End Sub
```

```
Public Function Fetch(ByVal InvoiceID As Long) As String

  Dim rsInvoice As Recordset
  Dim strSQL As String

  strSQL = "SELECT Invoice.*,Customer.Name,Customer.Phone " & _
    "FROM Invoice INNER JOIN Customer ON " & _
    "Invoice.CustomerID = Customer.CustomerID " & _
    "WHERE InvoiceID=" & CStr(InvoiceID)
  Set rsInvoice = New Recordset
  rsInvoice.Open strSQL, cnVideo

  With rsInvoice
    mudtProps.InvoiceID = .Fields("InvoiceID")
    mudtProps.CustomerID = .Fields("CustomerID")
    mudtProps.CustomerName = .Fields("Name")
    mudtProps.CustomerPhone = .Fields("Phone")
    .Close
  End With

  Set rsInvoice = Nothing
  Fetch = GetState

End Function
```

## *The InvoiceItems Object*

The following routines have been modified:

```
Public Sub ApplyEdit(InvoiceID As Long)

  Dim objPersist As InvoiceItemsPersist
  Dim strTapes As String
  Dim strFees As String

  If Not mflgEditing Then Err.Raise 445

  Set objPersist = _
      CreateObject("VideoServer.InvoiceItemsPersist", PERSIST_SERVER)
  strTapes = objPersist.SaveTapes(InvoiceID, GetTapes)
  strFees = objPersist.SaveFees(GetFees)
  Set objPersist = Nothing

  Set mcolItems = Nothing
  Set mcolItems = New Collection
  SetTapes strTapes
  SetFees strFees

  mflgEditing = False

End Sub
```

```
Friend Sub Load(InvoiceID As Long)

  Dim objPersist As InvoiceItemsPersist

  If mflgEditing Then Err.Raise 445

  Set objPersist = _
      CreateObject("VideoServer.InvoiceItemsPersist", PERSIST_SERVER)
  SetTapes objPersist.FetchTapes(InvoiceID)
  Set objPersist = Nothing

End Sub
```

```
Friend Sub LoadFees(CustomerID As Long)

  Dim objPersist As InvoiceItemsPersist

  If mflgEditing Then Err.Raise 445

  Set objPersist = _
      CreateObject("VideoServer.InvoiceItemsPersist", PERSIST_SERVER)
  SetFees objPersist.FetchFees(CustomerID)
  Set objPersist = Nothing

End Sub
```

The following routines have been added:

```
Private Function GetTapes() As String

  Dim objBuffer As Buffer
  Dim objItem As InvoiceItem
```

```vb
    Dim objTape As InvoiceTape

    Set objBuffer = New Buffer
    Set objTape = New InvoiceTape
    objBuffer.Initialize Len(objTape.GetState), 20
    Set objTape = Nothing

    For Each objItem In mcolItems
      If objItem.ItemType = ITEM_TAPE Then
        Set objTape = objItem
        objBuffer.Add objTape.GetState
      End If
    Next

    GetTapes = objBuffer.GetState
    Set objBuffer = Nothing

End Function
```

```vb
Private Sub SetTapes(Buffer As String)

    Dim lngIndex As Long
    Dim objTape As InvoiceTape
    Dim objBuffer As Buffer

    Set objBuffer = New Buffer
    objBuffer.SetState Buffer

    For lngIndex = 1 To objBuffer.Count
      Set objTape = New InvoiceTape
      objTape.SetState objBuffer.Item(lngIndex)
      mcolItems.Add Item:=objTape
    Next

End Sub
```

```vb
Private Function GetFees() As String

    Dim objBuffer As Buffer
    Dim objItem As InvoiceItem
    Dim objFee As InvoiceFee

    Set objBuffer = New Buffer
    Set objFee = New InvoiceFee
    objBuffer.Initialize Len(objFee.GetState), 20
    Set objFee = Nothing

    For Each objItem In colItems
      If objItem.ItemType = ITEM_FEE Then
        Set objFee = objItem
        objBuffer.Add objFee.GetState
      End If
    Next

    GetFees = objBuffer.GetState
    Set objBuffer = Nothing

End Function
```

```
      Private Sub SetFees(Buffer As String)

        Dim lngIndex As Long
        Dim objFee As InvoiceFee
        Dim objBuffer As Buffer

        Set objBuffer = New Buffer
        objBuffer.SetState Buffer

        For lngIndex = 1 To objBuffer.Count
          Set objFee = New InvoiceFee
          objFee.SetState objBuffer.Item(lngIndex)
          mcolItems.Add Item:=objFee
        Next

      End Sub
```

## The InvoiceItemsPersist Object

```
      Option Explicit

      Public Function FetchTapes(InvoiceID As Long) As String

        Dim rsItems As Recordset
        Dim strSQL As String
        Dim objBuffer As Buffer
        Dim udtProps As InvoiceTapeProps
        Dim objPersist As InvoiceTapePersist

        strSQL = "SELECT ITEMID FROM INVOICETAPE " & _
          "WHERE INVOICEID=" & InvoiceID
        Set rsItems = New Recordset
        rsItems.Open strSQL, cnVideo
        Set objBuffer = New Buffer
        objBuffer.Initialize Len(udtProps), 10
        Set objPersist = New InvoiceTapePersist

        Do While Not rsItems.EOF
          objBuffer.Add objPersist.Fetch(rsItems("ItemID"))
        Loop

        rsItems.Close
        Set rsItems = Nothing
        FetchTapes = objBuffer.GetState

      End Function


      Public Function FetchFees(CustomerID As Long) As String

        Dim rsItems As Recordset
        Dim strSQL As String
        Dim objBuffer As Buffer
        Dim udtProps As FeeProps
        Dim objPersist As InvoiceFeePersist

        strSQL = "SELECT FEEID FROM LATEFEE " & _
          "WHERE DELETED=FALSE AND PAID=FALSE AND " & _
          "CUSTOMERID=" & CustomerID
        Set rsItems = New Recordset
```

```
    rsItems.Open strSQL, cnVideo
    Set objBuffer = New Buffer
    objBuffer.Initialize Len(udtProps), 10
    Set objPersist = New InvoiceFeePersist

    Do While Not rsItems.EOF
      objBuffer.Add objPersist.Fetch(rsItems("FeeID"))
      rsItems.MoveNext
    Loop

    rsItems.Close
    Set rsItems = Nothing
    FetchFees = objBuffer.GetState

End Function
```

```
Public Function SaveTapes(InvoiceID As Long, Buffer As String) As String

    Dim objBuffer As Buffer
    Dim objUpdatedTapes As Buffer
    Dim objPersist As InvoiceTapePersist
    Dim lngIndex As Long
    Dim strBuffer As String

    Set objBuffer = New Buffer
    Set objUpdatedTapes = New Buffer
    objBuffer.SetState Buffer
    objUpdatedTapes.Initialize objBuffer.Length, objBuffer.Count
    Set objPersist = New InvoiceTapePersist

    For lngIndex = 1 To objBuffer.Count
      With objPersist
        strBuffer = .Save(InvoiceID, objBuffer.Item(lngIndex))
        If Len(strBuffer) > 0 Then _
          objUpdatedTapes.Add strBuffer
      End With
    Next

    Set objPersist = Nothing
    SaveTapes = objUpdatedTapes.GetState

End Function
```

```
Public Function SaveFees(Buffer As String) As String

    Dim objBuffer As Buffer
    Dim objUpdatedFees As Buffer
    Dim objPersist As InvoiceFeePersist
    Dim lngIndex As Long
    Dim strBuffer As String

    Set objBuffer = New Buffer
    Set objUpdatedFees = New Buffer
    objBuffer.SetState Buffer
    objUpdatedFees.Initialize objBuffer.Length, objBuffer.Count
    Set objPersist = New InvoiceFeePersist

    For lngIndex = 1 To objBuffer.Count
      With objPersist
        strBuffer = .Save(objBuffer.Item(lngIndex))
```

```
            If Len(strBuffer) > 0 Then _
                objUpdatedFees.Add strBuffer
        End With
    Next

    Set objPersist = Nothing
    SaveFees = objUpdatedFees.GetState

End Function
```

## The InvoiceFee Object

The `FeeProps` UDT has been move to `VideoTypes.BAS`. The `ChildLoad`, `ChildApplyEdit`, `Fetch`, `DeleteObject` and `Save` routines have been removed. The following have been added:

```
Friend Function GetState() As String

    Dim udtData As FeeData

    With mudtProps
        .IsNew = mflgNew
        .IsDeleted = mflgDeleted
        .IsDirty = mflgDirty
    End With

    LSet udtData = mudtProps
    GetState = udtData.Buffer
    mflgNew = False

End Function
```

```
Friend Sub SetState(Buffer As String)

    Dim udtData As FeeData

    udtData.Buffer = Buffer
    LSet mudtProps = udtData
    mflgNew = False

    Pay

End Sub
```

## The InvoiceFeePersist Object

```
Option Explicit
```

```
Private mudtProps As FeeProps
```

```
Private Sub SetState(Buffer As String)

    Dim udtData As FeeData

    udtData.Buffer = Buffer
    LSet mudtProps = udtData

End Sub
```

```vb
Private Function GetState() As String

  Dim udtData As FeeData

  LSet udtData = mudtProps
  GetState = udtData.Buffer

End Function
```

```vb
Friend Function Fetch(FeeID As Long) As String

  Dim rsLateFee As Recordset
  Dim strSQL As String

  strSQL = "SELECT LateFee.*, Video.Title " & _
    "FROM (LateFee INNER JOIN Tape ON " & _
    "LateFee.TapeID = Tape.TapeID) " & _
    "INNER JOIN Video ON Tape.VideoID = Video.VideoID " & _
    "WHERE LateFee.FeeID=" & Format$(FeeID)
  Set rsLateFee = New Recordset
  rsLateFee.Open strSQL, cnVideo

  With rsLateFee
    mudtProps.FeeID = .Fields("FeeID")
    mudtProps.VideoTitle = .Fields("Title")
    mudtProps.EnteredDate = .Fields("FeeDate")
    mudtProps.DaysOver = .Fields("DaysOver")
    mudtProps.Paid = .Fields("Paid")
    If Not IsNull(.Fields("PaidDate")) Then _
      mudtProps.PaidDate = .Fields("PaidDate")
    .Close
  End With

  Set rsLateFee = Nothing
  Fetch = GetState

End Function
```

```vb
Private Sub DeleteObject(FeeID As Long)

  Dim rsLateFee As Recordset
  Dim strSQL As String

  strSQL = "SELECT DELETED FROM LateFee WHERE FeeID=" & FeeID
  Set rsLateFee = New Recordset
  rsLateFee.Open strSQL, cnVideo

  With rsLateFee
    .Fields("Deleted") = True
    .Update
    .Close
  End With

End Sub
```

```vb
Friend Function Save(Buffer As String) As String

  Dim rsLateFee As Recordset
```

```
    Dim strSQL As String

    SetState Buffer
    If mudtProps.IsDeleted Then
      DeleteObject mudtProps.FeeID
      Exit Function
    End If

    strSQL = "SELECT * FROM LateFee WHERE FeeID=" & _
      mudtProps.FeeID
    Set rsLateFee = New Recordset
    rsLateFee.Open strSQL, cnVideo, , adLockOptimistic
    If mudtProps.IsNew Then rsLateFee.AddNew

    With rsLateFee
      .Fields("Paid") = mudtProps.Paid
      .Fields("PaidDate") = mudtProps.PaidDate
      .Update
      If mudtProps.IsNew Then mudtProps.FeeID = .Fields("FeeID")
      .Close
    End With

    Set rsLateFee = Nothing
    Save = GetState

End Function
```

## The InvoiceTape Object

Similar changes as the `InvoiceFee` object:

```
Friend Function GetState() As String

  Dim udtData As InvoiceTapeData

  With mudtProps
    .IsNew = mflgNew
    .IsDeleted = mflgDeleted
    .IsDirty = mflgDirty
  End With

  LSet udtData = mudtProps
  GetState = udtData.Buffer
  mflgNew = False

End Function
```

```
Friend Sub SetState(Buffer As String)

  Dim udtData As InvoiceTapeData

  udtData.Buffer = Buffer
  LSet mudtProps = udtData
  mflgNew = False

End Sub
```

## The InvoiceTapePersist Object

```vb
Option Explicit

Private mudtProps As InvoiceTapeProps

Private Sub SetState(Buffer As String)

  Dim udtData As InvoiceTapeData

  udtData.Buffer = Buffer
  LSet mudtProps = udtData

End Sub

Private Function GetState() As String

  Dim udtData As InvoiceTapeData

  LSet udtData = mudtProps
  GetState = udtData.Buffer

End Function

Private Sub DeleteObject(ItemID As Long)

  cnVideo.Execute "DELETE FROM InvoiceTape WHERE ItemID=" & _
    CStr(ItemID)

End Sub

Friend Function Fetch(ItemID As Long) As String

  Dim rsInvoiceTape As Recordset
  Dim strSQL As String

  strSQL = "SELECT InvoiceTape.*, Video.Title " & _
    "FROM (InvoiceTape INNER JOIN Tape ON " & _
    "InvoiceTape.TapeID = Tape.TapeID) " & _
    "INNER JOIN Video ON Tape.VideoID = Video.VideoID " & _
    "WHERE InvoiceTape.ItemID=" & ItemID
  Set rsInvoiceTape = New Recordset
  rsInvoiceTape.Open strSQL, cnVideo

  With rsInvoiceTape
    mudtProps.ItemID = .Fields("ItemID")
    mudtProps.TapeID = .Fields("TapeID")
    mudtProps.Title = .Fields("Title")
    mudtProps.Price = .Fields("Price")
    .Close
  End With

  Set rsInvoiceTape = Nothing
  Fetch = GetState

End Function

Friend Function Save(InvoiceID As Long, Buffer As String) As String

  Dim rsInvoiceTape As Recordset
```

```
          Dim strSQL As String
          Dim objPersist As TapePersist

          SetState Buffer
          If mudtProps.IsDeleted Then
            DeleteObject mudtProps.ItemID
            Exit Function
          End If

          strSQL = "SELECT * FROM InvoiceTape WHERE ItemID=" & _
            CStr(mudtProps.ItemID)
          Set rsInvoiceTape = New Recordset
          rsInvoiceTape.Open strSQL, cnVideo, , adLockOptimistic
          If mudtProps.IsNew Then rsInvoiceTape.AddNew

          With rsInvoiceTape
            .Fields("InvoiceID") = InvoiceID
            .Fields("TapeID") = mudtProps.TapeID
            .Fields("Price") = mudtProps.Price
            .Update
            If mudtProps.IsNew Then mudtProps.ItemID = .Fields("ItemID")
            .Close
          End With

          Set objPersist = New TapePersist
          objPersist.CheckOut mudtProps.TapeID, InvoiceID
          Set objPersist = Nothing

          If mudtProps.IsNew Then
            strSQL = "SELECT Video.Title " & _
              "FROM Tape INNER JOIN Video ON " & _
              "Tape.VideoID = Video.VideoID " & _
              "WHERE Tape.TapeID=" & mudtProps.TapeID
            rsInvoiceTape.Open strSQL, cnVideo
            mudtProps.Title = rsInvoiceTape("Title")
            rsInvoiceTape.Close
          End If

          Set rsInvoiceTape = Nothing
          Save = GetState

        End Function
```

## Adding to the VideoTypes.BAS module

```
        Public Type VideoDisplayProps
          VideoID As Long
          Title As String * 30
          ReleaseDate As Date
        End Type


        Public Type VideoDisplayData
          Buffer As String * 36
        End Type


        Public Type InvoiceProps
          InvoiceID As Long
          CustomerID As Long
```

```
        CustomerName As String * 50
        CustomerPhone As String * 25
        SubTotal As Double
        Tax As Double
        Total As Double
        IsNew As Boolean
        IsDeleted As Boolean
        IsDirty As Boolean
    End Type
```

```
    Public Type InvoiceData
        Buffer As String * 96
    End Type
```

```
    Public Type FeeProps
        InvoiceID As Long
        FeeID As Long
        VideoTitle As String * 30
        EnteredDate As Date
        DaysOver As Integer
        Paid As Boolean
        PaidDate As Date
        IsNew As Boolean
        IsDeleted As Boolean
        IsDirty As Boolean
    End Type
```

```
    Public Type FeeData
        Buffer As String * 48
    End Type
```

```
    Public Type InvoiceTapeProps
        InvoiceID As Long
        ItemID As Long
        TapeID As Long
        Title As String * 30
        Price As Double
        IsNew As Boolean
        IsDeleted As Boolean
        IsDirty As Boolean
    End Type
```

```
    Public Type InvoiceTapeData
        Buffer As String * 44
    End Type
```

# Chapter 12

## *The Invoice Object*

The ApplyEdit routine needs modifying slightly:

```
    ElseIf mflgDirty Or mflgNew Then
        If Not IsValid Then Err.Raise 445
        ' save object to database if appropriate
        strTapes = mobjItems.GetTapes
```

```
        strFees = mobjItems.GetFees
        SetState objPersist.Save(GetState, strTapes, strFees)
        mobjItems.SetTapes strTapes
        mobjItems.SetFees strFees
        ' save object state
        LSet mudtSave = mudtProps
        mflgNew = False
```

## The InvoicePersist Object

```
Option Explicit

Implements ObjectControl

Private mobjContext As ObjectContext
Private mudtProps As InvoiceProps

Private Function GetState() As String

  Dim udtData As InvoiceData

  LSet udtData = mudtProps
  GetState = udtData.Buffer

End Function

Private Sub SetState(Buffer As String)

  Dim udtData As InvoiceData

  udtData.Buffer = Buffer
  LSet mudtProps = udtData

End Sub

Public Function Save(ByVal Buffer As String, _
  TapesBuffer As String, FeesBuffer As String) As String

  Dim rsInvoice As Recordset
  Dim strSQL As String
  Dim objPersist As InvoiceItemsPersist

  On Error GoTo errh
  SetState Buffer
  strSQL = "SELECT * FROM Invoice WHERE InvoiceID=" & mudtProps.InvoiceID
  Set rsInvoice = New Recordset
  rsInvoice.Open strSQL, DB_CONNECT, adOpenKeyset, adLockOptimistic
  If udtProps.IsNew Then rsInvoice.AddNew

  With rsInvoice
    .Fields("CustomerID") = mudtProps.CustomerID
    .Fields("Subtotal") = mudtProps.SubTotal
    .Fields("Tax") = mudtProps.Tax
    .Fields("Total") = mudtProps.Total
    .Update
    If mudtProps.IsNew Then
      .Bookmark = .Bookmark
      mudtProps.InvoiceID = .Fields("InvoiceID")
```

```
      End If
      .Close
   End With

   strSQL = "SELECT NAME, PHONE FROM Customer " & _
      "WHERE CustomerID=" & mudtProps.CustomerID
   rsInvoice.Open strSQL, DB_CONNECT
   mudtProps.CustomerName = rsInvoice("Name")
   mudtProps.CustomerPhone = rsInvoice("Phone")
   rsInvoice.Close
   Set rsInvoice = Nothing
   Save = GetState

   Set objPersist = _
         mobjContext.CreateInstance("VideoServerMTS.InvoiceItemsPersist")
   TapesBuffer = objPersist.SaveTapes(mudtProps.InvoiceID, TapesBuffer)
   FeesBuffer = objPersist.SaveFees(FeesBuffer)
   Set objPersist = Nothing
   mobjContext.SetComplete

   Exit Function

errh:
   mobjContext.SetAbort
   With Err
      .Raise .Number, .Source, .Description
   End With

End Function
```

```
Public Sub DeleteObject(ByVal InvoiceID As Long)

   Dim cnVideo As Connection

   On Error GoTo errh
   Set cnVideo = New Connection
   cnVideo.Open DB_CONNECT
   cnVideo.Execute "DELETE FROM Invoice WHERE InvoiceID=" & InvoiceID
   cnVideo.Close
   Set cnVideo = Nothing
   mobjContext.SetComplete

   Exit Sub

errh:
   mobjContext.SetAbort
   With Err
      .Raise .Number, .Source, .Description
   End With

End Sub
```

```
Public Function Fetch(ByVal InvoiceID As Long) As String

   Dim rsInvoice As Recordset
   Dim strSQL As String

   On Error GoTo errh
   strSQL = "SELECT Invoice.*,Customer.Name,Customer.Phone " & _
```

```
         "FROM Invoice INNER JOIN Customer ON " & _
         "Invoice.CustomerID = Customer.CustomerID " & _
         "WHERE InvoiceID=" & CStr(InvoiceID)
      Set rsInvoice = New Recordset
      rsInvoice.Open strSQL, DB_CONNECT

      With rsInvoice
        mudtProps.InvoiceID = .Fields("InvoiceID")
        mudtProps.CustomerID = .Fields("CustomerID")
        mudtProps.CustomerName = .Fields("Name")
        mudtProps.CustomerPhone = .Fields("Phone")
        .Close
      End With

      Set rsInvoice = Nothing
      Fetch = GetState
      mobjContext.SetComplete

      Exit Function

errh:
      mobjContext.SetAbort
      With Err
        .Raise .Number, .Source, .Description
      End With

End Function
```

```
Private Function ObjectControl_CanBePooled() As Boolean

   ObjectControl_CanBePooled = False

End Function
```

```
Private Sub ObjectControl_Activate()

   Set mobjContext = GetObjectContext

End Sub
```

```
Private Sub ObjectControl_Deactivate()

   Set mobjContext = Nothing

End Sub
```

## The InvoiceItems Object

The scope of GetTapes, GetFees, SetTapes and SetFees is changed to Friend and we need to modify the ApplyEdit routine:

```
Public Sub ApplyEdit(InvoiceID As Long)

   'Dim objPersist As InvoiceItemsPersist
   Dim strTapes As String
   Dim strFees As String

   If Not mflgEditing Then Err.Raise 445
```

```
'Set objPersist = _
    CreateObject("VideoServerMTS.InvoiceItemsPersist", PERSIST_SERVER)
'strTapes = objPersist.SaveTapes(InvoiceID, GetTapes)
'strFees = objPersist.SaveFees(GetFees)
'Set objPersist = Nothing

Set mcolItems = Nothing
Set mcolItems = New Collection
'SetTapes strTapes
'SetFees strFees

mflgEditing = False

End Sub
```

## The InvoiceItemsPersist Object

```
Option Explicit

Implements ObjectControl

Private mobjContext As ObjectContext

Public Function FetchTapes(InvoiceID As Long) As String

    Dim rsItems As Recordset
    Dim strSQL As String
    Dim objBuffer As Buffer
    Dim udtProps As InvoiceTapeProps
    Dim objPersist As InvoiceTapePersist

    On Error GoTo errh
    strSQL = "SELECT ITEMID FROM INVOICETAPE " & _
      "WHERE INVOICEID=" & InvoiceID
    Set rsItems = New Recordset
    rsItems.Open strSQL, DB_CONNECT
    Set objBuffer = New Buffer
    objBuffer.Initialize Len(udtProps), 10
    Set objPersist = _
        mobjContext.CreateInstance("VideoServerMTS.InvoiceTapePersist")

    Do While Not rsItems.EOF
      objBuffer.Add objPersist.Fetch(rsItems("ItemID"))
    Loop

    rsItems.Close
    Set rsItems = Nothing
    FetchTapes = objBuffer.GetState
    mobjContext.SetComplete

    Exit Function

errh:
    mobjContext.SetAbort
    With Err
      .Raise .Number, .Source, .Description
    End With

End Function
```

```vb
Public Function FetchFees(CustomerID As Long) As String

  Dim rsItems As Recordset
  Dim strSQL As String
  Dim objBuffer As Buffer
  Dim udtProps As FeeProps
  Dim objPersist As InvoiceFeePersist

  On Error GoTo errh
  strSQL = "SELECT FEEID FROM LATEFEE " & _
    "WHERE DELETED=0 AND PAID=0 AND " & _
    "CUSTOMERID=" & CustomerID
  Set rsItems = New Recordset
  rsItems.Open strSQL, DB_CONNECT
  Set objBuffer = New Buffer
  objBuffer.Initialize Len(udtProps), 10
  Set objPersist = _
    mobjContext.CreateInstance("VideoServerMTS.InvoiceFeePersist")

  Do While Not rsItems.EOF
    objBuffer.Add objPersist.Fetch(rsItems("FeeID"))
    rsItems.MoveNext
  Loop

  rsItems.Close
  Set rsItems = Nothing
  FetchFees = objBuffer.GetState
  mobjContext.SetComplete

  Exit Function

errh:
  mobjContext.SetAbort
  With Err
    .Raise .Number, .Source, .Description
  End With

End Function


Public Function SaveTapes(InvoiceID As Long, Buffer As String) As String

  Dim objBuffer As Buffer
  Dim objUpdatedTapes As Buffer
  Dim objPersist As InvoiceTapePersist
  Dim lngIndex As Long
  Dim strBuffer As String

  On Error GoTo errh
  Set objBuffer = New Buffer
  Set objUpdatedTapes = New Buffer
  objBuffer.SetState Buffer
  objUpdatedTapes.Initialize objBuffer.Length, objBuffer.Count
  Set objPersist = _
    mobjContext.CreateInstance("VideoServerMTS.InvoiceTapePersist")

  For lngIndex = 1 To objBuffer.Count
    With objPersist
      strBuffer = .Save(InvoiceID, objBuffer.Item(lngIndex))
      If Len(strBuffer) > 0 Then _
```

```
            objUpdatedTapes.Add strBuffer
      End With
   Next

   Set objPersist = Nothing
   SaveTapes = objUpdatedTapes.GetState
   mobjContext.SetComplete

   Exit Function

errh:
   mobjContext.SetAbort
   With Err
     .Raise .Number, .Source, .Description
   End With

End Function
```

```
Public Function SaveFees(Buffer As String) As String

   Dim objBuffer As Buffer
   Dim objUpdatedFees As Buffer
   Dim objPersist As InvoiceFeePersist
   Dim lngIndex As Long
   Dim strBuffer As String

   On Error GoTo errh
   Set objBuffer = New Buffer
   Set objUpdatedFees = New Buffer
   objBuffer.SetState Buffer
   objUpdatedFees.Initialize objBuffer.Length, objBuffer.Count
   Set objPersist = _
       mobjContext.CreateInstance("VideoServerMTS.InvoiceFeePersist")

   For lngIndex = 1 To objBuffer.Count
     With objPersist
       strBuffer = .Save(objBuffer.Item(lngIndex))
       If Len(strBuffer) > 0 Then _
          objUpdatedFees.Add strBuffer
     End With
   Next

   Set objPersist = Nothing
   SaveFees = objUpdatedFees.GetState
   mobjContext.SetComplete

   Exit Function

errh:
   mobjContext.SetAbort
   With Err
     .Raise .Number, .Source, .Description
   End With

End Function
```

```
Private Function ObjectControl_CanBePooled() As Boolean

   ObjectControl_CanBePooled = False
```

```
      End Function

   Private Sub ObjectControl_Activate()

      Set mobjContext = GetObjectContext

   End Sub

   Private Sub ObjectControl_Deactivate()

      Set mobjContext = Nothing

   End Sub
```

## The InvoiceFeePersist Object

```
   Option Explicit

   Implements ObjectControl

   Private mobjContext As ObjectContext
   Private mudtProps As FeeProps

   Private Sub SetState(Buffer As String)

      Dim udtData As FeeData

      udtData.Buffer = Buffer
      LSet mudtProps = udtData

   End Sub

   Private Function GetState() As String

      Dim udtData As FeeData

      LSet udtData = mudtProps
      GetState = udtData.Buffer

   End Function

   Public Function Fetch(FeeID As Long) As String

      Dim rsLateFee As Recordset
      Dim strSQL As String

      On Error GoTo errh
      strSQL = "SELECT LateFee.*, Video.Title " & _
        "FROM (LateFee INNER JOIN Tape_ ON " & _
        "LateFee.TapeID = Tape_.TapeID) " & _
        "INNER JOIN Video ON Tape_.VideoID = Video.VideoID " & _
        "WHERE LateFee.FeeID=" & Format$(FeeID)
      Set rsLateFee = New Recordset
      rsLateFee.Open strSQL, DB_CONNECT

      With rsLateFee
        mudtProps.FeeID = .Fields("FeeID")
        mudtProps.VideoTitle = .Fields("Title")
```

```
        mudtProps.EnteredDate = .Fields("FeeDate")
        mudtProps.DaysOver = .Fields("DaysOver")
        mudtProps.Paid = .Fields("Paid")
        If Not IsNull(.Fields("PaidDate")) Then _
          mudtProps.PaidDate = .Fields("PaidDate")
        .Close
      End With

      Set rsLateFee = Nothing
      Fetch = GetState
      mobjContext.SetComplete

      Exit Function

    errh:
      mobjContext.SetAbort
      With Err
        .Raise .Number, .Source, .Description
      End With

    End Function
```

```
Private Sub DeleteObject(FeeID As Long)

    Dim rsLateFee As Recordset
    Dim strSQL As String

    On Error GoTo errh
    strSQL = "SELECT DELETED FROM LateFee WHERE FeeID=" & FeeID
    Set rsLateFee = New Recordset
    rsLateFee.Open strSQL, DB_CONNECT, , adLockOptimistic

    With rsLateFee
      .Fields("Deleted") = True
      .Update
      .Close
    End With
    mobjContext.SetComplete

    Exit Sub

  errh:  .
    mobjContext.SetAbort
    With Err
      .Raise .Number, .Source, .Description
    End With

End Sub
```

```
Public Function Save(Buffer As String) As String

    Dim rsLateFee As Recordset
    Dim strSQL As String

    On Error GoTo errh
    SetState Buffer
    If mudtProps.IsDeleted Then
      DeleteObject mudtProps.FeeID
      Exit Function
    End If
```

```
    strSQL = "SELECT * FROM LateFee WHERE FeeID=" & _
      mudtProps.FeeID
    Set rsLateFee = New Recordset
    rsLateFee.Open strSQL, DB_CONNECT, adOpenKeyset, adLockOptimistic
    If udtProps.IsNew Then rsLateFee.AddNew

    With rsLateFee
      .Fields("Paid") = mudtProps.Paid
      .Fields("PaidDate") = mudtProps.PaidDate
      .Update
      If mudtProps.IsNew Then
        .Bookmark = .Bookmark
        mudtProps.FeeID = .Fields("FeeID")
      End If
      .Close
    End With

    Set rsLateFee = Nothing
    Save = GetState
    mobjContext.SetComplete

    Exit Function

errh:
  mobjContext.SetAbort
  With Err
    .Raise .Number, .Source, .Description
  End With

End Function
```

```
Private Function ObjectControl_CanBePooled() As Boolean

  ObjectControl_CanBePooled = False

End Function
```

```
Private Sub ObjectControl_Activate()

  Set mobjContext = GetObjectContext

End Sub
```

```
Private Sub ObjectControl_Deactivate()

  Set mobjContext = Nothing

End Sub
```

## The InvoiceTapePersist Object

```
Option Explicit

Implements ObjectControl

Private mobjContext As ObjectContext
Private mudtProps As InvoiceTapeProps
```

```
Private Sub SetState(Buffer As String)

  Dim udtData As InvoiceTapeData

  udtData.Buffer = Buffer
  LSet mudtProps = udtData

End Sub
```

```
Private Function GetState() As String

  Dim udtData As InvoiceTapeData

  LSet udtData = mudtProps
  GetState = udtData.Buffer

End Function
```

```
Private Sub DeleteObject(ItemID As Long)

  Dim cnVideo As Connection

  On Error GoTo errh
  Set cnVideo = New Connection
  cnVideo.Open DB_CONNECT
  cnVideo.Execute "DELETE FROM InvoiceTape WHERE ItemID=" & _
    CStr(ItemID)
  cnVideo.Close
  Set cnVideo = Nothing
  mobjContext.SetComplete

  Exit Sub

errh:
  mobjContext.SetAbort
  With Err
    .Raise .Number, .Source, .Description
  End With

End Sub
```

```
Public Function Fetch(ItemID As Long) As String

  Dim rsInvoiceTape As Recordset
  Dim strSQL As String

  On Error GoTo errh
  strSQL = "SELECT InvoiceTape.*, Video.Title " & _
    "FROM (InvoiceTape INNER JOIN Tape ON " & _
    "InvoiceTape.TapeID = Tape.TapeID) " & _
    "INNER JOIN Video ON Tape.VideoID = Video.VideoID " & _
    "WHERE InvoiceTape.ItemID=" & ItemID
  Set rsInvoiceTape = New Recordset
  rsInvoiceTape.Open strSQL, DB_CONNECT

  With rsInvoiceTape
    mudtProps.ItemID = .Fields("ItemID")
    mudtProps.TapeID = .Fields("TapeID")
    mudtProps.Title = .Fields("Title")
```

```
          mudtProps.Price = .Fields("Price")
        .Close
      End With

      Set rsInvoiceTape = Nothing
      Fetch = GetState
      mobjContext.SetComplete

      Exit Function

  errh:
      mobjContext.SetAbort
      With Err
        .Raise .Number, .Source, .Description
      End With

  End Function
```

```
Public Function Save(InvoiceID As Long, Buffer As String) As String

    Dim rsInvoiceTape As Recordset
    Dim strSQL As String
    Dim objPersist As TapePersist

    On Error GoTo errh
    SetState Buffer
    If mudtProps.IsDeleted Then
      DeleteObject mudtProps.ItemID
      Exit Function
    End If

    strSQL = "SELECT * FROM InvoiceTape WHERE ItemID=" & _
      CStr(udtProps.ItemID)
    Set rsInvoiceTape = New Recordset
    rsInvoiceTape.Open strSQL, DB_CONNECT, adOpenKeyset, adLockOptimistic
    If mudtProps.IsNew Then rsInvoiceTape.AddNew

    With rsInvoiceTape
      .Fields("InvoiceID") = InvoiceID
      .Fields("TapeID") = mudtProps.TapeID
      .Fields("Price") = mudtProps.Price
      .Update
      If mudtProps.IsNew Then
        .Bookmark = .Bookmark
        mudtProps.ItemID = .Fields("ItemID")
      End If
      .Close
    End With

    Set objPersist = mobjContext.CreateInstance("VideoServerMTS.TapePersist")
    objPersist.CheckOut mudtProps.TapeID, InvoiceID
    Set objPersist = Nothing

    If mudtProps.IsNew Then
      strSQL = "SELECT Video.Title " & _
        "FROM Tape_ INNER JOIN Video ON " & _
        "Tape_.VideoID = Video.VideoID " & _
        "WHERE Tape_.TapeID=" & mudtProps.TapeID
      rsInvoiceTape.Open strSQL, DB_CONNECT
```

```
      mudtProps.Title = rsInvoiceTape("Title")
      rsInvoiceTape.Close
   End If

   Set rsInvoiceTape = Nothing
   Save = GetState
   mobjContext.SetComplete

   Exit Function

errh:
   mobjContext.SetAbort
   With Err
     .Raise .Number, .Source, .Description
   End With

End Function
```

```
Private Function ObjectControl_CanBePooled() As Boolean

   ObjectControl_CanBePooled = False

End Function
```

```
Private Sub ObjectControl_Activate()

   Set mobjContext = GetObjectContext

End Sub
```

```
Private Sub ObjectControl_Deactivate()

   Set mobjContext = Nothing

End Sub
```

### The CheckOut Routine on TapePersist

The CheckOut routine is pretty obviously a data-centric method. Looking at what it, we can see that it's basically only called when we are in the process of saving an Invoice, and then it just updates a couple fields in our Tape object.

In fact, once we've moved the routine to our data-centric TapePersist object, we can further simplify the routine. Rather than loading a lot of tape-related data, manipulating it and writing it back out, we can just work directly against the database and make the required changes there.

This is more efficient in terms of performance, and is also simpler code to read. Since the `TapePersist` object's entire purpose in life is to provide efficient data-oriented services for our application, this fits in nicely:

```
Public Sub CheckOut(TapeID As Long, InvoiceID As Long)

    Dim rsTape As Recordset
    Dim strSQL As String

    strSQL = "SELECT * FROM Tape_ WHERE TapeID=" & TapeID
    Set rsTape = New Recordset
    rsTape.Open strSQL, cnVideo, ,adLockOptimistic

    With rsTape
      .Fields("CheckedOut") = True
      .Fields("DateDue") = DateAdd("d", 2, Now)
      .Fields("InvoiceID") = InvoiceID
      .Update
      .Close
    End With

    Set rsTape = Nothing

End Sub
```

# Index

## Symbols

.asp, ASP scripts, 574
<%...%>, scripts, 574

## A

abstraction, 9
abstraction, object-oriented design, 30
Action property, VBXs, 48
Active Data Objects
  *see ADO*
Active Server Pages (ASP)
  *HTML user interface, 568, 570*
    (IIS) Internet Information Server, 573
    architecture, 569
    ASP objects, 576
    Microsoft Internet Service Manager, 571
    recursive HTML form, 587
    scripts, 570, 574
    threading, 580
    VideoObjects.dll, installing on server, 580
    VideoObjects/VideoPersistMTS, updating,
      579
  *IIS Application, 596*
    VideoObjects.dll, installing on server, 606
  *objects, 596*
  *Request object, 577*
    Request Form, 578
  *Response object, 578*
    Response Write, 579
  *Server object, 579*
  *Session object, 577*
  *user interface, HTML*
    video details display, 581
  *WebClass objects, 597, 607*
Active Server Pages (ASP), web based
  applications, 119, 120

ActiveX
  *ActiveX components, 19, 664*
    packaging objects, 664
  *ActiveX servers, 19, 50, 660, 664*
    GUID, 305
    VideoServer, 495
  *application architecture, 49, 117*
  *Component Object Model (COM), 24, 40*
    DCOM, 40
  *DHTML page, 635*
  *DLLs, in-process components, 24, 89, 664*
    compiling, 670
    creating, 669
    testing, 671
  *EXEs, out-of-process components, 22, 664*
    compiling, 667
    creating, 664
    testing, 667
  *Internet design, 569*
  *OCXs, controls, 24, 664*
    creating, 671
    method, adding to create an object, 673
    testing, 673
  *out-of-process servers*
    data-centric objects, 437
  *VideoObject project*
    ActiveX DLL, 416
    HTML interface, 579
  *VideoPersistMTS*
    HTML interface, 579
ActiveX Data Objects
  *see ADO*
Add method, Buffer object, 458
Add method, InvoiceItems object, 296
Add method, Tapes object
  *Tape object, adding to Tapes object, 260*
Add method, VideoEdit ListItem objects, 333
Address properties, Customer object, 205
AddTape method, InvoiceItems object, 298

**AddTape method, Tapes object, 263**
**ADO, 47, 66**
  *OLE DB, 47, 118, 368*
  *problems in using, 66*
  *Recordset object*
    connections, 535
    cursors, 549
  *transfers Recordset object, 48, 130, 133*
**ADO 2.0**
  *integrated with Visual Basic 6.0, 48*
**ADO library, VideoObjects**
  *persistence, 368*
**ADO, VB databases, 118**
**ADO, VideoServer, 442**
**AfterUpdate event, Visual Basic for**
  **Applications (VBA), 421**
  *replaces LostFocus event, 421*
**aggregate relationship, implementation, 100**
  *data, combining, 102*
  *object interfaces, combining, 101*
  *simple aggregation, 100*
**aggregation, static class diagram, 680**
**apartment model threading, VideoServer, 497**
**apartment model threading, VideoServerMTS**
  *supported in MTS 2.0, 531*
**application server, n-tier architecture, 26, 27,**
  **67, 116**
  *data-centric business objects, 117*
  *VideoServer*
    client, setting up, 511
    CLIREG32, 517
  *VideoServer project, 496, 497*
    binary compatibility, 500
    database, 501
    DCOM registration, 505
    installation, 502
    multi-threading, 497
    remote server files, 499
    TLB, VideoObjects, 510
    VideoServer permissions, 506
  *web-based applications, 120*
**application server, web-based applications, 27**
**applications**
  *application architecture, 26, 43*
    client/server, 26, 50
    components, 44
    controls, 48
    flexibility, 50
    logical architecture, 51
    reusability, 49
  *object-based or object-oriented design?, 30*
  *three-tier client/server, 26*

  *three-tier client/server applications*
    application server, 26
  *two-tier client/server, 26*
  *web-based applications, 27*
**applications, business objects, 25**
  *single-tier, 25*
**application-specific components, 21**
**Apply method, VideoUI Edit Form template,**
  **313**
**Apply, object implementation, 184**
  *object validity, 186*
**ApplyEdit method, InvoiceFee object, 280**
**ApplyEdit method, InvoiceItems object, 287,**
  **294**
**ApplyEdit method, object implementation, 184,**
  **185, 188, 189, 191, 192**
  *Customer object, creating, 201*
  *parent-child UI, Tape object, 241, 242*
**ApplyEdit method, Tape object**
  *updating, 490*
**ApplyEdit method, Tapes object, 257, 261**
  *updating, 487*
**ApplyEdit method, Video object persistence,**
  **473**
**ApplyEdit method, VideoUI Edit Form**
  **template, 313**
**ApplyEdit, Customer object**
  *calling Customer Persist, 452, 453*
  *Save method, 378*
**ApplyEdit, Tape object**
  *late fees, 267*
**ASP**
  *see Active Server Pages*
**atomic methods**
  *stateless objects, 555*
**Autonumber, object persistence, 366**
  *see also ObjectID, object persistence*

**B**

**BAS module, object persistence, 163**
  *TextChange routine, 319*
**BeginEdit method, InvoiceItems object, 293**
**BeginEdit method, object implementation, 184,**
  **185, 189**
  *Customer object, creating, 200*
  *parent-child UI, Tape object, 242*
**BeginEdit method, Tapes object, 255**
**BeginEdit method, VideoUI Edit Form**
  **template, 312**
**bidirectional updates, child objects, 478**
**binary components. see components**

**Broken Rules class**
*object implementation, 196*
*object -level validation, 147*
**BrokenRules object, object implementation**
*Valid event/IsValid property, 186*
**browser based applications, 28**
**browsers, HTML user interface, 568**
**Buffer class, Buffer object, 456**
**Buffer object, child object persistence, 470**
**Buffer object, list object persistence, 455**
*Add method, 458*
*Buffer class, 456*
*buffer extension, 458*
*element retrieval*
Count property, 461
Item property, 460
Length property, 461
*elements, updating*
Property Let Item, 461
*GetState method, 459*
Left$(), 459
*initializing, 456*
Initialize method, 457
variable declaration, 456
*object design, 455*
performance issues, 455
VB string handling, 455
*SetState method, 459*
**Business class, object implementation, 193**
*see also class templates*
**Business class, VideoUI Edit Form template, 311**
**business objects**
*adding properties, 585*
*application architecture, 43*
components, 44
logical architecture, 51
n-tier architecture, 62
*applications, 25*
object-based or object-oriented design, 30
single-tier, 25
three-tier client/server, 26
two-tier client/server, 26
web-based, 27
*building objects in VB, 653*
*building, in VB*
ActiveX components, packaging objects, 664
class modules, 653
classes, creating, 654
*business components, creating in VB, 22*
*compared to other objects, 17*
*component-oriented design, 18*

*components, 18*
business components, creating in VB, 22
*customer objects, implementation, 198*
Customer object, 198
Customers object, 211
*data-centric, 437*
see also data-centric objects and data-centric processing
*definition, 16*
*design*
defining objects, 72
functional decomposition, 74
functional use case, 76
identifying objects, 72
Internet, 568
object persistence, 162
object relationships, implementation, 93
requirements use case, 74
use case analysis, 73
use case formats, alternative, 93
*HTML user interface*
Active Server Pages (ASP), 568
*implementing, video rental example, 183*
common object interface, 184
Customer object, 198
Customers object, 211
Invoice object, 269
InvoiceFee object, 278
InvoiceItems object, 292
InvoiceTape object, 287
late fees, object interaction, 265
requirement overview, 197
Tape object, 236
Tapes object, 253
TextList object, 217
Videos object, 220, 222
*invoice objects, implementation, 265*
Invoice object, 269
InvoiceFee object, 278
InvoiceItem object, 275
InvoiceItems object, 292
InvoiceTape object, 287
*Microsoft Office, as interface, 415*
document, viewing objects, 426
Excel, 415
user forms, 416
VideoObjects, compiling, 416
*object-oriented design, 30*
*objects, introduction to, 7*
*reasons for using*
business processes, modeling, 16
flexibility, 50

modularity, 18
reusability, 17, 49, 73
*see also UI centric business objects & data*
   *centric business objects*
*see also components and objects*
*user interfaces*
   HTML/Active Server Pages, 567
*video objects, implementation*
   InvoiceItem object, 275
   Tape object, 236
   Tapes object, 253
   TextList object, 217
   Video object, 222
   Videos object, 220
**BusinessChild class, object implementation, 247**
**ByVal keyword, 216**
   *COM, data-centric objects, 448*

# C

**CallByName method**
   *not available with VBA, 422*
   *TextChange routine, 319*
**CanBePooled method, Object Control**
   *ObjectControl_Activate method, 548*
   *ObjectControl_CanBePooled method, 548*
   *ObjectControl_Deactivate method, 549*
**Cancel method, VideoUI Edit Form template,**
   **313**
**Cancel, object implementation, 184**
   *object validity, 186*
**CancelEdit method, InvoiceItems object, 294**
**CancelEdit method, object implementation,**
   **184, 185, 189**
   *Customer object, creating, 201*
   *parent-child UI, Tape object, 241, 242*
**CancelEdit method, Tapes object, 256**
**CancelEdit, Customer object, 379**
**Categories table, VideoOBjects database, 373**
**Category property, Video object, 230**
**CGI. see Common Gateway Interface (CGI)**
**Change event**
   *preferred to Validate event, 144*
   *removing code from, 153*
**CheckIn method, Tape object, 252, 265**
**CheckOut method, InvoiceTape objects, 402**
**CheckOut method, Tape object, 251, 266**
**child object, Tape object as, 387**
**child object, Tapes object as, 232, 236**
   *parent-child UI, 239*
**child objects**
   *Customers object persistence, 466*
   *Videos object persistence, 466*

**child objects, InvoiceItems**
   *InvoiceFee, 394*
   *InvoiceTape, 394*
**child objects, persistence, 469**
   *bidirectional updates, 478*
   *Buffer object, 470*
   *Customers object, 466*
   *Tape object, 470, 475*
   *Video object, 470*
   *Videos object, 466*
**ChildApplyEdit method, InvoiceFee object, 281**
**ChildApplyEdit method, InvoiceFee object**
   **persistence, 401**
**ChildApplyEdit method, object implementation**
   *parent-child UI, Tape object, 243*
**ChildApplyEdit method, Tape object, 246**
**ChildApplyEdit method, Tape object**
   **persistence, 388**
**ChildApplyEdit, Tape object**
   *late fees, 268*
**ChildBeginEdit method, object implementation**
   *parent-child UI, Tape object, 243*
**ChildBeginEdit method, Tape object, 245**
**ChildCancelEdit method, object**
   **implementation**
   *parent-child UI, Tape object, 243*
**ChildCancelEdit method, Tape object, 245**
**ChildLoad method, InvoiceFee object, 281**
**ChildLoad method, InvoiceFee object**
   **persistence, 400**
**ChildLoad method, Tape object, 244, 247**
**ChildLoad method, Tape object persistence,**
   **388**
**Class Builder wizard, 657**
**class ID (CLSID), 305**
**class modules, classes, 9, 653**
   *objects, creating, 9*
**class templates, object implementation, 193**
   *class modules, 193*
   *how the template works, 196*
   *saving template, 195*
   *see also user interface, object implementation*
   *template code, 193*
**Class_Initialize, BrokenRules class**
   *Customer object, creating, 202*
**Class_Initialize, BrokenRules object, 186, 190**
**Class_Initialize, InvoiceFee object, 282**
**Class_Initialize, Video object, 225**
**classes**
   *class ID (CLSID), 306*
**classes, objects, 8**
   *class modules, 9*

*creating classes in VB, 654*
   Class Builder wizard, 657
*instances, 8*
*see also objects*
*static class diagrams, UML, 678*
**Click event, VideoUI VideoEdit, 331**
**clients**
  *Active Server Pages (ASP), 569*
  *client/server applications, 50*
   n-tier, 67
   object persistence, 162
   three-tier, 26, 496
   three-tier, n-tier logical architecture, 116
   two-tier, 26
   two-tier, n-tier logical architecture, 114
   UI as business object client, 136
  *fat, 27*
   same as intelligent, 114
  *intelligent*
   same as fat, 114
  *out-of-process server, object manager as, 168*
  *thin, 27*
  *UI as business object client, 136*
  *UI-centric objects as, 441*
  *VideoServer*
   multiple clients, support for, 522
  *VideoUI, user interface, 304*
  *web-based applications, 27*
   Active Server Pages (ASP), 569
**client-side scripting, Internet design, 568**
**CLIREG32, ideoServer, 517**
**CLSID. see class ID (CLSID)**
**cnVideo, VideoObjects database connection, 368**
**code**
  *ignored even if present, 15, 36*
**Collection object, Buffer object, 460**
**Collection object, Customers object, 214**
  *creating, 214*
**Collection object, TextList object, 218**
**collections. see ownership relationship, implementation**
**COM. see Component Object Model (COM)**
**ComboBox controls, VideoUI VideoEdit, 329**
**Common Gateway Interface (CGI), limitations, 570**
**COMMON memory blocks, FORTRAN, 126**
  *see also User-Defined Types*
**common object interface, object implementation, 184**
**Common Object Request Broker Architecture (CORBA), 40**
**commonalities, generalization relationship, 106**

**Component method, VideoUI CustomerList, 343**
**Component method, VideoUI InvoiceEdit, 354**
**Component Object Model (COM), 24, 40**
  *ByVal keyword, 448*
  *data-centric objects, 438, 448*
  *DCOM, 40, 438, 448*
   DCOM registration, 505
   VideoServer, 496
  *out-of-process servers, 448*
  *physical architecture, 120*
   arguments, passing to a method, 121
   data, GetRows, 124
   data, User-Defined Types, 125
   single properties, calling, 120
**Component-based Scalable Logical Architecture**
  *see CSLA*
**component-oriented design, 30, 44, 367**
  *reusability, 19*
**components**
  *ActiveX, 24, 669, 670, 671*
  *application-specific components, 21*
  *business components, creating in VB, 22*
  *industry-specific components, 22*
  *interfaces, 20*
  *reusability, 19*
  *standard/general components, 21*
  *vs. objects, 19*
**components, business objects, 18**
  *application architecture, 44*
   controls, 48
   data access, 47
   event-driven programming, 44
   forms, 46
  *reusability, 49, 50*
**connection pooling, VideoServer, 524**
**Container, multiple interfaces, 15**
**containment, inheritance, 37, 108**
**context, MTS objects, 526**
  *security, 527, 546*
  *transactions, 526, 546*
   SetAbort method, 527
   SetComplete method, 527
**controls, ActiveX, 24**
  *creating, 671*
  *method, adding to create an object, 673*
  *testing, 673*
**controls, application architecture, 48**
  *ActiveX, 49*
  *VBXs, 48*
**cookie, client-side, 627, 633**
  *retrieving values from, 635, 644*

**CORBA. see Common Object Request Broker Architecture (CORBA)**
**Count method, Tapes object, 254**
**Count property, Buffer object, 461**
**Count property, Customers object, 214**
**CreateInstance method, MTS objects, 529**
**CreateInvoice method, Customer object, 208**
**CreateInvoice method, Customers object, 274**
**CreateObject method**
  *CustomerPersist object, 451*
**CreateObject method, MTS objects, 528**
  *preferred to New keyword, 532*
**CreateObject, MTS objects, 532**
**CSLA, 51, 72, 73, 114, 118, 137, 239, 526**
  *DHTML Applications, 623*
**CustEdit page**
  *DHTML page, 639*
**CustList page**
  *DHTML page, 634*
**Customer object, persistence, 376, 442**
  *CustomerData, 445*
  *data loading, 377*
  *data, adding/updating, 378*
  *data, deleting, 379*
  *GetState method, 443, 445*
  *IsDeleted property, 444*
  *IsDirty property, 444*
  *IsNew property, 444*
  *SetState method, 443, 446*
**Customer object, VideoUI, 310**
**Customer objects, object implementation, 198**
  *Customer object, 198*
    creating the object, 198
    testing the object, 209
  *Customers object*
    creating the object, 211
    using, 216
**Customer table, VideoOBjects database, 370**
**Customer, data-centric objects**
  *ApplyEdit, calling CustomerPersist,, 452, 453*
**CustomerData, Customer object persistence, 445**
**CustomerDisplay class, Customers object, 212**
**CustomerEdit, VideoUI, 316**
  *Form_Load, 318*
  *LostFocus event, 323*
  *template code, 317*
  *TextBox controls, 319*
  *txtName_Change event, 319*
  *VideoMain, adding code to, 324*
**CustomerEdit, VideoUI CustomerList, 345**
**CustomerID property, Customer object, 202**

**CustomerList, VideoUI List screens, 342**
  *code, 342*
  *Component method, 343*
  *controls code, 344*
  *VideoMain, adding code to, 344*
**CustomerPersist object, 466**
  *Fetch method, 467*
  *UDT, elements, 466*
**CustomerPersist, data-centric objects, 439**
  *calling from Customer object, 451*
  *CreateObject method, 451*
  *CustomerPersist class, 447*
  *DeleteObject method, 450*
  *Fetch method, 450*
  *GetState method, 447*
  *mudtProps, declaring, 447*
  *persistence, 446*
  *Save method, 448*
  *SetState method, 447*
**Customers class, Customers object, 214**
**Customers object, persistence, 405, 466, 468**
  *CustomersPersist object, 466*
    UDT, elements, 466
  *data, loading, 405*
  *DHTML user interface, 631*
  *CustomersPersist object, 467*
  *Item method, 407*
  *ListView control, DHTML, 636*
  *Load method, 468*
  *see also Buffer object*
  *SetState method, 468*
**CustomerSearch, VideoUI List screen, 339**
  *code, 340*
  *VideoMain, adding code to, 341*
**CustSearch page**
  *DHTML page, 631*
**CVDate(), Video object, 229**

**D**

**data**
  *shared selectively, 440*
**data access, application architecture, 47, 118**
  *JET engine, 47*
  *ODBCdirect, 47*
  *Open Database Connectivity (ODBC), 47*
  *Remote Data Objects (RDO), 47*
**data access, persistence, 362, 376**
  *Customer object, 376*
    data, adding/updating, 378
    data, deleting, 379
    data, loading, 377

*Customers objects, 405*
    data, loading, 405
    Item method, 407
*Invoice object, 392*
    DeleteObject method, 392
    Fetch method, 392
    Save method, 392
*InvoiceItems collection, 395*
    InvoiceFee object, 397
    InvoiceTape objects, 396, 401
    Load method, 396
    LoadFees method, 395
*read-only objects, 405*
*state, 362*
    Autonumber, 366
    DeleteObject method, 367
    Fetch method, 363
    Private Save, 365
*Tape object, 384*
    child object, Tape as, 387
    ChildApplyEdit method, 388
    ChildLoad method, 388
    DeleteObject method, 385
    Fetch method, 385
    late fee records, 389
    Save method, 384
    standalone object, Tape as, 386
*TextList object, 409*
*VideoObjects project, 367*
    ADO library, 368
    database connection, 368
*Videos object, 408*
    Fetch method, 408
    Item method, 409
    Load method, 408
*Video-Tapes object, parent-child relationship,
    379*
**data access, VideoObjects**
*database, setting up, 369*
    Categories table, 373
    Customer table, 370
    Invoice table, 374
    InvoiceTape table, 375
    LateFee table, 370
    Ratings table, 373
    Tape table, 372
    Video table, 371
*dbVideo, 368*
**data services, 61**
*n-tier architecture, 67*
**data, objects, 9**
*instance variables, 9*

*see also class modules, classes*
*state, 168*
**databases, application architecture, 47**
*JET engine, 47*
*ODBCdirect, 47*
*Open Database Connectivity (ODBC), VB*
    *databases, 47*
*Remote Data Objects (RDO), 47*
**data-centric business objects**
*analogous to object manager, 168*
*n-tier architecture, 117*
*object persistence, 167, 177*
**data-centric objects, 437**
*splitting from original object*
    UI-centric object as client, 441
*Customer*
    ApplyEdit, calling CustomerPersist,, 452, 453
*CustomerPersist, 446*
    calling from Customer object, 451
    CustomerPersist class, 447
    DeleteObject method, 450
    Fetch method, 450
    GetState method, 447
    mudtProps, declaring, 447
    Save method, 448
    SetState method, 447
*data-centric behaviors, isolating, 438*
*persistence, 446*
    CustomerPersist, 446
*splitting, from original object*
    CustomerPersist, 439
*state, moving between UI- and data-centric*
    *objects*
    SetState method, 440
*state, moving betwen UI- and data-centric*
    *objects, 440*
    GetState method, 440
*VideoServer, 441*
    ADO, using, 442
    database code, 442
**data-centric processing, 59, 60**
*n-tier architecture, 66*
    application server, 67
**DataFormat**
*object capability*
    Visual Basic 6.0, 120
**DateAcquired property, Tape object, 249**
*changed from Variant to Date data type, 476*
**DateDue property, Tape object, 266**
*changed from Variant to Date data type, 476*
**DaysOver property, InvoiceFee object, 283**
**DCOM. see Distributed COM (DCOM)**

delegation, inheritance, 37, 108, 109
Delete method, InvoiceItems object, 295
Delete method, object implementation, 188
Delete method, Tape object, 244
Delete method, Tapes object, 258
Delete method, Video object, 225
DeleteObject method, Customer object
  *ApplyEdit, calling the method from, 452*
DeleteObject method, CustomerPersist object,
  450
DeleteObject method, Invoice object
  persistence, 392
DeleteObject method, InvoiceFee object
  persistence, 399
DeleteObject method, InvoiceTape objects, 403
DeleteObject method, object persistence, 367
  *requires Connection object, 536*
DeleteObject method, Tape object persistence,
  385
DeleteObject method, TapePersist object, 486
design, business objects
  *defining objects, 72*
  *functional use case, 76*
    business objects, identifying, 78
    functionality, identifying, 77
    object events, 88
    object methods, 86
    object properties, 83
    object relationships, 78
  *identifying objects, 72*
  *Internet, 568*
    ActiveX, 569
    client-side scripting, 568
  *object persistence, 162*
    data-centric business objects, 167, 177
    form/BAS module, 163
    object manager, 166, 167
    self-saving objects, 163
  *object relationships, implementation, 93*
    aggregate relationship, 100
    generalization relationship, 105
    ownership relationship, 94
    user relationship, 99
  *requirements use case, 74*
    high-level objects, 76
    high-level requirements, 75
  *use case analysis, 73*
    functional decomposition, 74
  *use case formats, alternative, 93*
DHTML Applications, 28, 29, 623
  *advantages, 625*

  *CSLA, 623*
  *do not require web server, 639*
  *extension of HTML, 625*
  *page-oriented design, 626*
  *require Win32, 624*
  *Visual Basic 6.0, 624*
DHTML page
  *ActiveX, 635*
  *CustEdit page, 639*
  *CustList page, 634*
  *CustSearch page, 631*
DHTML user interface, 631
  *customers object, 631*
directly pasing
  *User-Defined Types, 122*
DisplayVideo object
  *VideoIIS, 616*
    hyperlinks, 617
Distributed COM, 117
  *physical architecture, 120*
    arguments, passing to a method, 121
    data, GetRows, 124
    data, User-Defined Types, 125
    single properties, calling, 120
Distributed COM (DCOM), 40, 448
  *COM, 40*
  *data-centric objects, 438*
  *DCOM registration, 505*
  *VideoServer, 496*
distributed object architecture. see logical
  architecture
Distributed Transaction Coordinator (DTC),
  MTS transactions, 562
DLLs
  *VideoObject project*
    ActiveX DLL, 416
    HTML interface, 579
  *VideoServer*
    MTS objects, 526
    multiple clients, support for, 523
DLLs, ActiveX components, 664
  *compiling, 670*
  *creating, 669*
  *testing, 671*
DLLs. see in-process servers (DLLs)
document, Microsoft Office interface
  *viewing objects, 426*
    report example, 426
DTC. see Distributed Transaction Coordinator
  (DTC)

# E

**early binding, polymorphism, 34**
**Edit screens, VideoUI, 310**
  *Customer object*
    VideoMain, adding code to, 324
  *CustomerEdit, 316*
    Form_Load, 318
    LostFocus event, 323
    template code, 317
    TextBox controls, 319
    txtName_Change event, 319
  *Edit Form template, 310*
  *TapeEdit, 337*
    Form_Load, 338
    txtAcquired control, 338, 339
  *VideoEdit, 325*
    Click event, 331
    ComboBox controls, 329
    date values, txtRelease control, 329
    Form_Load, 328, 330, 334
    ListView control, 327, 332
    LoadCombo, 331
    Tape objects, 332
    tape, adding, 335
    tape, editing, 336
    tape, removing, 336
    template code, 328
    TextBox controls, 328
    VideoMain, adding code to, 337
**encapsulation, object-oriented design, 10**
  *scope, 10*
**EnteredDate property, InvoiceFee object, 284**
**error handling**
  *Microsoft Transaction Server, 529*
**error raising, object and IU example, 144**
  *UI error trapping, 145*
**Event keyword, object interface, 10**
**Event, object events, 13, 91**
**event-driven programming, 44**
  *events, and objects, 45*
  *objects, and events, 45*
**events, object interface, 12**
**Excel. see Microsoft Excel**
**EXEs, ActiveX components, 664**
  *compiling, 667*
  *creating, 664*
  *testing, 667*
**EXEs. see out-of-process servers (EXEs)**

# F

**Fee property, InvoiceFee object, 283**
**Fetch method, TextListPersist object, 462**
**Fetch method, Customer object**
  *Load, calling the method from, 453*
**Fetch method, CustomerPersist object, 450**
**Fetch method, Invoice object persistence, 392**
**Fetch method, InvoiceFee object persistence, 398**
**Fetch method, InvoiceTape objects, 403**
**Fetch method, object persistence, 363**
  *ADO, 537*
**Fetch method, Tape object persistence, 385**
**Fetch method, TapePersist object, 483**
**Fetch method, TapesPersist object, 480**
**Fetch method, Videos object persistence, 408**
**field-level validation, object and UI example, 144**
**File_Check in, VideoUI InvoiceEdit, 357**
**For...Each, Customers object, 214**
**For...Each, Tapes object, 255**
**For...Each, TextList object, 219**
**form, object persistence, 163**
**Form_Load, VideoUI CustomerEdit, 318**
**Form_Load, VideoUI InvoiceEdit, 351**
**Form_Load, VideoUI TapeEdit, 338**
**Form_Load, VideoUI VideoEdit, 328, 330, 334**
**Format$(), Invoice object, 273**
**forms, application architecture, 46**
**forms, user interface, 303**
  *Edit screens, 310*
    CustomerEdit, 316
    Edit Form template, 310
    TapeEdit, 337
    VideoEdit, 325
  *InvoiceEdit, 350*
    child object support, 352
    File_Check in, menu option, 357
    Form_Load, 351
    menu option, 356
    VideoMain, adding code to, 356
  *List screens, 339*
    CustomerList, 342
    CustomerSearch, 339
    VideoList, 347
    VideoSearch, 346
  *VideoMain, 307*
  *VideoUI, 304*
**Friend keyword, 30, 213, 220, 241, 294, 660**

**Function, class modules, 9**
**functional decomposition, design, 74**
**functional use case, design, 76**
  *business objects, identifying, 78*
  *functionality, identifying, 77*
  *object events, 88*
  *object methods, 86*
  *object properties, 83*
  *object relationships, 78*
    consolidation, 81
    key objects, 80
    key relationships, 79

# G

**general components, 21**
  *applicability, 21*
**general relationships, static class diagram, 679**
**generalization relationship, implementation, 105**
  *commonalities, 106*
  *LineItem class, 107*
  *RentalItem class, 108*
**generalization, static class diagram, 680**
**GetPrice property, InvoiceTape object, 289**
**GetState method, Buffer object, 459**
  *Left$(), 459*
**GetState method, Customer object persistence, 443, 445**
**GetState method, CustomerPersist object, 447**
**GetState method, Tape object persistence, 475**
**GetState method, TapePersist object, 483**
**GetState method, Tapes object**
  *Tape object, persistence, 477*
**GetState method, Video object persistence, 474**
**GetState, data-centric objects, 440**
**GetTitle property, InvoiceTape object, 289**
**GetVideos object**
  *VideoIIS, 608*
    updating, 612
**global UDTs, Video object, 470**
  *see also User-Defined Types*
**global unique ID (GUID), 305**
  *when the GUID changes, 305*
**GUID. see global unique ID (GUID)**

# H

**HTML templates**
  *creating, 609*
  *WebClass objects*
    tag substitution, 604
  *WebItem objects, 602, 610*

**HTML user interface**
  *Active Server Pages (ASP), 568, 570*
    (IIS) Internet Information Server, 573
    architecture, 569
    ASP objects, 576
    Microsoft Internet Service Manager, 571
    recursive HTML form, 587
    scripts, 570, 574
    threading, 580
    video details display, 581
    VideoObjects.dll, installing on server, 580
    VideoObjects/VideoPersistMTS, updating, 579
  *IIS Application*
    video details display, 606
    VideoObjects.dll, installing on server, 606
**hyperlinks**
  *hyperlinked fields, 590*

# I

**IIS (Internet Information Server), 570**
  *HTML user interface, 573*
**IIS (Internet Information Server) Application, 27, 28, 29, 119, 120, 596**
  *Active Server Pages, 596*
  *creating, 607*
  *objects, 597*
  *Response object*
    WebClass objects, 599
  *user interface, HTML*
    video details display, 606
  *VideoIIS, 607*
  *WebClass objects, 597*
    WebItem objects, 607
  *WebItem objects, 601*
    WebClass objects, 607
**Implements keyword, interface inheritance, 30, 34, 35, 275**
**industry-specific components, 22**
**inheritance, object-oriented design, 35, 105**
  *containment, 37, 108*
  *delegation, 37, 108, 109*
  *interface inheritance, 35*
**Initialize method, Buffer object, 457**
**Initialize method, Invoice object, 274**
  *different from Class_Initialize routine, 209*
**Initialize method, InvoiceTape object, 290**
**in-process servers (DLLs), 24**
**in-process servers, ActiveX**
  *compiling, 670*
  *creating, 669*
  *testing, 671*

InputBox$(), VideoUI InvoiceEdit, 353
instance variables, 9
instances, classes, 8
intelligent client, two-tier client/server
    applications, 114
interface class, InvoiceItem object as, 275
interface inheritance, polymorphism, 33, 34, 35,
    275
interface, Microsoft Office
    *document, viewing objects, 426*
        report example, 426
    *user forms, 416*
        code, 420
        controls, adding, 419
        testing, 423
        user form, adding, 418
        user,making form available to, 424
        VBA editor, 417
        VideoObjects reference, adding, 418
    *VideoObjects project, 416*
interface, objects, 8, 10
    *common object interface, object*
        *implementation, 184*
        Broken Rules class, 196
        class templates, creating, 193
        OK, Cancel and Apply, 184
        persistence, 187
    *events, 12*
    *methods, 11*
    *multiple interfaces, 13*
        Container, 15
        Implements keyword, 14
        scope, 15
    *properties, 10*
        Property Get, 11
        Property Let, 11
        Property Set, 11
interfaces, components, 20
Internet Information Server
    *see IIS*
Internet Information Server Application
    *see IIS Application*
Internet Server Application Programming
    Interface (ISAPI), limitations, 570
Internet. see user interface, HTML
Internet. see web-based applications
Intranet applications, 118
    *n-tier logical architecture, 118*
Invoice object, persistence, 392
    *DeleteObject method, 392*
    *Fetch method, 392*
    *Save method, 392*
    *updating, 492*

Invoice objects, object implementation, 265
    *Invoice object, 269*
        creating, 274
    *InvoiceFee object, 278*
    *InvoiceItem object, 275*
    *InvoiceItems object, 292*
    *InvoiceTape object, 287*
Invoice property, Tape object, 250
    *load on demand, 250*
Invoice table, VideoOBjects database, 374, 375
InvoiceEdit, VideoUI, 350
    *child object support, 352*
        InvoiceTape objects, adding, 353
        LoadItems, 352
    *File_Check in, menu option, 357*
    *Form_Load, 351*
    *menu option, 356*
    *VideoMain, adding code to, 356*
InvoiceFee class, InvoiceFee object, 279
InvoiceFee object, InvoiceItems collection, 397
    *ChildApplyEdit method, 401*
    *ChildLoad method, 400*
    *DeleteObject method, 399*
    *Fetch method, 398*
    *Paid flag, 397*
    *Save method, 400*
InvoiceFee, InvoiceItem object, 275
InvoiceItem class, InvoiceItem object, 275
InvoiceItem interface, InvoiceFee object, 284
InvoiceItem interface, InvoiceTape object, 290
InvoiceItem, VideoUI InvoiceEdit, 355
InvoiceItems class, InvoiceItems object, 292
InvoiceItems collection, persistence, 395
    *InvoiceFee object, 397*
    *InvoiceTape objects, 396, 401*
    *Load method, 396*
    *LoadFees method, 395*
InvoiceTape class, InvoiceTape object, 287
InvoiceTape objects, persistence, 396, 401
    *CheckOut method, 402*
    *DeleteObject method, 403*
    *Fetch method, 403*
    *Save method, 401*
InvoiceTape objects, VideoUI InvoiceEdit, 353
InvoiceTape, InvoiceItem object, 275
InvoiceTapeEdit, VideoUI InvoiceEdit, 354
ISAPI. see Internet Server Application
    Programming Interface (ISAPI)
IsDate(), Video object, 229
IsDeleted property, Customer object
    persistence, 444
IsDeleted property, object implementation, 190

**IsDirty property, Customer object persistence,**
   **444**
**IsDirty property, object implementation, 191**
**IsNew property, Customer object persistence,**
   **444**
**IsNew property, object implementation, 190**
**IsNew property, Tapes object, 257**
**IsValid property, object implementation, 186**
   *BrokenRules object, 186*
**IsValid property, object-level validation, 146**
   *implementing, 151*
   *user interface, 152*
**IsValid property, VideoUI Edit Form template,**
   **314**
**Item method, Customers object, 215**
**Item method, Tapes object, 254**
**Item method, TextList object, 219**
**Item method, Videos object persistence, 409**
**Item property, Buffer object, 460**
**Item property, InvoiceItem object, 278**
**ItemDescription property, InvoiceItem object,**
   **277**
**ItemType property, InvoiceFee object, 286**
**ItemType property, InvoiceItems object, 293**

# J

**JET database**
   *switching to SQL Server database, 534*
**JET engine, VB databases, 47**

# K

**Key method, TextList object, 219, 230**

# L

**late binding, polymorphism, 33**
**late fees, data access**
   *LateFee table, 370*
**late fees, object interaction, 265**
**late fees, Tape object, 267**
**late fees, Tape object persistence**
   *SaveLateFee method, 389*
**late fees, Tape object persistence, 389**
**LateFee object, Customer object**
   *object interaction, 267*
**LateFee table, VideoOBjects database, 370**
**LenB, User-Defined Types (UDTs) and memory,**
   **129**
**Length property, Buffer object, 461**

**LineItem class, generalization relationship, 107**
**list object, Customers object as, 211**
**list objects, persistence, 454**
   *see also Buffer object*
**List screens, VideoUI, 339**
   *CustomerList, 342*
     code, 342
     Component method, 343
     controls code, 344
     VideoMain, adding code to, 344
   *CustomerSearch, 339*
     code, 340
     VideoMain, adding code to, 341
   *VideoList, 347*
   *VideoSearch, 346*
     main menu, 348
     TextBox controls, 346
**ListItem objects, VideoEdit ListView control,**
   **333**
   *Add method, 333*
**ListVideos object**
   *VideoIIS, 612*
     HTML template, 613
**ListView control, DHTML**
   *Customers object, 636*
**ListView control, VideoUI VideoEdit, 327**
   *care in using, 327*
   *Tape objects, displaying, 332*
     ListItem objects, 333
**ListView, VideoUI CustomerList, 343**
**Load method, Customers object, 216, 468**
**Load method, InvoiceItems collection, 396**
**Load method, InvoiceItems object, 296**
**Load method, object implementation, 188, 191**
   *Customer object, creating, 200*
**Load method, Tape object, 244**
   *updating, 491*
**Load method, Tapes object**
   *Tape objects, loading, 264*
   *updating, 487*
**Load method, Tapes object persistence, 382**
**Load method, TextList object, 220**
   *TextListPersist object, 464*
**Load method, Video object, 224**
**Load method, Video object persistence, 474**
**Load method, Videos object persistence, 408**
**load on demand, 250**
**LoadCombo, VideoUI VideoEdit, 331**
**LoadFees method, InvoiceItems collection, 395**
**LoadFees method, InvoiceItems object, 298**
**LoadItems, VideoUI InvoiceEdit, 352**

logical architecture, 51
  *n-tier architecture, 62*
    application server, 67
    data services, 67
    data-centric business objects, 66
    UI-centric business objects, 64
  *tiers in an application, 51*
    data-centric processing, 59, 60
    functionality, division of, 57, 58
    user interface, 57, 58, 59
  *user interface*
    On-Line Transaction Processing (OLTP), 58
**LostFocus event, VideoUI CustomerEdit, 321, 323**
**LSet and User-Defined Types (UDT), COM/DCOM, 438**
**LSet and User-Defined Types (UDTs), COM/DCOM, 125, 127, 129**
**LSet and User-Defined Types (UDTs), object manager, 168**

# M

**main menu, VideoUI VideoSearch, 348**
**mcolKeys collection, TextList object, 219**
**mcolList collection, TextList object, 218**
**mcolTapes, Tapes object, 254**
**MDI. see multiple document interface (MDI)**
**menu option, VideoUI InvoiceEdit, 356**
**menus, VideoMain, 308**
**methods, InvoiceItem object, 276**
**methods, InvoiceTape object, 289**
**methods, object interface, 11**
**mflgChild, Tape object, 241**
**mflgChildEditing, Tape object, 242**
**mflgDeleted, object implementation, 189**
**mflgDirty, object implementation, 192**
**mflgEditing, object implementation, 184**
**mflgLoading, VideoUI Edit Form template, 311, 315**
**mflgNew, object implementation, 190**
**Microsoft Excel**
  *interface, creating, 415, 416*
    reports, viewing objects, 426
    user forms, 417
**Microsoft Internet Service Manager**
  *Microsoft Management Console, 571*
**Microsoft Internet Service Manager, HTML user interface, 571**
**Microsoft Management Console (MMC)**
  *Microsoft Internet Service Manager, 571*
  *Microsoft Transaction Server, 539*

**Microsoft Office, as interface, 415**
  *document, viewing objects, 426*
    report example, 426
  *Excel, 415, 426*
  *user forms, 416*
    code, 420
    controls, adding, 419
    testing, 423
    user form, adding, 418
    user, making form available to, 424
    VBA editor, 417
    Video Objects reference, adding, 418
  *VideoObjects, compiling, 416*
**Microsoft Transaction Server (MTS), 496, 522**
  *components, 20*
  *error handling, 529*
  *Microsoft Management Console, 539*
  *VideoServer, 522*
    database connections, 524
    database transactions, 525
    MTS objects, 525
    MTS transactions, 545
    object request broker, 522
    objects numbers, limiting, 523
  *VideoServer project*
    preparing VideoServer, 529
    VideoServerMTS, 529
  *VideoServerMTS*
    running in MTS, 538
**Mid$(), VB string handling**
  *Buffer object design, 455, 458, 460*
  *mstrBuffer, 458*
**MMC**
  *see Microsoft Management Console*
**mnu..., VideoMain menus, 308**
**mobjBusiness, Business object, 312**
  *mobjInvoice, 351*
  *mobjInvoiceTape, 354*
**mobjContext, context object**
  *SetComplete method, MTS transactions, 556*
**mobjCustomer, Customer object, 317**
**mobjInvoice, Invoice object**
  *mobjBusiness, 351*
**mobjInvoiceTape, Invoice object**
  *mobjBusiness, 354*
**mobjValid object, 450**
  *RuleBroken method, 474*
**mobjValid, Invoice object, 271**
**modularity, business objects, 18**
**module level variables, 9**
  *scope, 9*
**mstrBuffer**
  *Mid$(), 458*

MTS. see Microsoft Transaction Server (MTS)
MTSTransactionMode property values
  *table, 560*
**mudtChild, Tape object, 245**
**mudtProps, declaring**
  *CustomerPersist, data-centric objects, 447*
**multiple document interface (MDI), 307**
**multiple interfaces, objects, 13**
  *Container, 15*
  *Implements keyword, 14*
  *objects, 275*
  *scope, 15*
**multiplicity, static class diagram, 680**
**multi-threading, VideoServer, 497**
  *advantages, 498*
  *fixed thread pool, 498*
  *options, 498*
  *thread per object, 498*

## N

**Name property, Customer object, 203**
**New keyword, MTS objects, 528, 533**
  *CreateObject method preferred, 532*
**NewEnum method, Customers object, 214**
**NewEnum method, Tapes object, 254**
**NewEnum method, TextList object, 219**
**n-tier architecture, 62**
  *data services, 67*
  *data-centric business objects, 66*
    *application server, 67*
  *UI-centric business objects, 64*
  *user interface, 62*

## O

**Object Linking and Embedding**
  *see OLE*
**object manager**
  *analogous to data-centric business objects, 168*
**object manager, object persistence, 166, 167**
  *out-of-process server, object manager as, 168*
**object persistence, design, 162**
  *data-centric business objects, 167, 177*
  *form/BAS module, 163*
  *object manager, 166, 167*
  *self-saving objects, 163*
**object persistence. see persistence, data access**
**object pooling**
  *not supported by MTS 2.0, 523*
**object request brokers (ORB)**
  *MTS, VideoServer, 522*
**ObjectControl_Activate method, 548**

**ObjectControl_CanBePooled method, 548**
**ObjectControl_Deactivate method, 549**
**ObjectID, object persistence, 363**
  *see also Autonumber, object persistence*
**object-level validation, object and UI example, 146**
  *BrokenRules class, 147*
  *canceled edits, 153*
  *IsValid property, 146*
    implementing, 151
  *methods, protecting, 159*
    disabling methods, 159
  *properties, protecting, 159*
    read-only properties, 159
    write-once properties, 160
    write-only properties, 161
**object-oriented design, 18**
  *abstraction, 30*
  *applications, 30*
  *defining objects, 73*
  *encapsulation, 31*
  *identifying objects, 73*
  *inheritance, 35, 105*
    containment, 37, 108
    delegation, 37, 108, 109
    interface inheritance, 35
  *Internet, 568*
    ActiveX, 569
    client-side scripting, 568
  *object persistence, 162*
    data-centric business objects, 167, 177
    form/BAS module, 163
    object manager, 166, 167
    self-saving objects, 163
  *object relationships, implementation, 93*
    aggregate relationship, 100
    generalization relationship, 105
    ownership relationship, 94
    user relationship, 99
  *polymorphism, 33*
    early binding, 34
    interface inheritance, 33, 34, 275
    late binding, 33
    persistence, 392
  *reusability, 18*
  *see also components, component-oriented design*
  *see also objects*
  *use case analysis, 73*
    functional decomposition, 74
    functional use case, 76
    requirements use case, 74
    use case formats, alternative, 93

objects
  *ActiveX components*
    packaging objects, 664
  *behaviour, 10, 86*
    identifying, 87
  *classes, 8*
    class modules, 9, 653
    creating in VB, 654
    instances, 8
    static class diagrams, UML, 678
  *definition, 8*
  *encapsulation, 10*
    scope, 10
  *event-driven programming, 45*
  *interface, 8, 10*
    events, 12
    methods, 11
    multiple interfaces, 13
    properties, 10
  *multiple interfaces, 13, 275*
    Container, 15
    Implements keyword, 14
    scope, 15
  *object data, 8, 9*
    instance variables, 9
    see also class modules
  *object-based or object-oriented design?, 30*
  *parent-child relationship, 85, 94, 222, 236*
    parent-child UI, Tape object, 239
    Tapes object, 253
  *see also components*
  *see also object-oriented design*
  *services, 10*
  *stateful and stateless compared, 526*
  *vs. components, 19*
objects, building in VB, 653
  *ActiveX components*
    packaging objects, 664
  *class modules, 653*
  *classes, creating, 654*
    Class Builder wizard, 657
OCXs, ActiveX components, 664
  *creating, 671*
  *method, adding to create an object, 673*
  *testing, 673*
OCXs. see controls, ActiveX
ODBC. see Open Database Connectivity
  (ODBC), VB databases
ODBCdirect, VB databases, 47
  *obsolete, 118*
ODBCDirect, VB databases, 118
Office. see Microsoft Office,
OK method, VideoUI Edit Form template, 313

OK, object implementation, 184
  *object validity, 186*
OLE, 40
OLE DB, 47, 66, 117
  *ADO, 47, 118, 368*
  *creates Recordset object, 364*
OLTP. see On-Line Transaction Processing
  (OLTP)
On  Error Resume Next, VideoUI InvoiceEdit,
  358
On Error GoTo ADDERR, VideoUI
  InvoiceEdit, 355
On-Line Transaction Processing (OLTP), 58
Open Database Connectivity (ODBC), VB
  databases, 47, 67
  *ODBC 3.5, VideoServer, 524*
optimistic locking, object persistence, 166
ORB. see object request brokers (ORB)
out-of-process server, object manager as, 168
out-of-process servers
  *data-centric objects, 437*
  *Microsoft Excel, 22*
out-of-process servers (EXEs), 22
out-of-process servers, ActiveX
  *compiling, 667*
  *creating, 664*
  *testing, 667*
ownership relationship, implementation, 94
  *calling program, 99*
  *invoice object, 94*
  *InvoiceItems collection, 95*
  *LineItem object, 98*

## P

package, MTS, 539
page-oriented design
  *DHTML Applications, 626*
Paid flag, InvoiceFee object persistence, 397
PAK, MTS, 543
parent object, Video object as, 232
parent-child relationship, objects, 85, 94, 222,
  236
  *parent-child UI, Tape object, 239*
  *persistence*
    Video-Tapes object, parent-child relationship,
      379
  *Tapes object, 253*
persistence
  *child objects, 469*
    bidirectional updates, 478
    Tape object, 470, 475
    Video object, 470

*Customers object, 466*
*list objects*
   see also read-only list objects
   TextList object, 461
*read-only list objects, 454*
   see also Buffer object
   TextList object, 461
*Videos object, 466*
**persistence, data access, 362, 376**
   *Customer object, 376*
      data loading, 377
      data, adding/updating, 378
      data, deleting, 379
   *Customers object, 405*
      data, loading, 405
      Item method, 407
   *Invoice object, 392*
      DeleteObject method, 392
      Fetch method, 392
      Save method, 392
   *InvoiceItems collection, 395*
      InvoiceFee object, 397
      InvoiceTape objects, 396, 401
      Load method, 396
      LoadFees method, 395
   *read-only objects, 405*
   *state, 362*
      Autonumber, 366
      DeleteObject method, 367
      Fetch method, 363
      Private Save, 365
   *Tape object, 384*
      child object, Tape as, 387
      ChildApplyEdit method, 388
      ChildLoad method, 388
      DeleteObject method, 385
      Fetch method, 385
      late fee records, 389
      Save method, 384
      standalone object, tape as, 386
   *TextList object, 409*
   *VideoObjects project, 367*
      ADO library, 368
      database connection, 368
   *Videos object, 408*
      Fetch method, 408
      Item method, 409
      Load method, 408
   *Video-Tapes object, parent-child relationship,*
   *379*
**persistence, data-centric objects, 446**
**persistence, object implementation, 187**
   *ApplyEdit method, 188*

   *Delete method, 188*
   *IsDirty property, 191*
   *IsNew property, 190*
   *Load method, 188*
   *see also user interface, object implementation*
**persistence, polymorphism, 392**
**persistence, UI-centric objects, 442**
**Person class example, object and UI, 138**
**PersonDemo example, object and UI, 141**
**pessimistic locking, object persistence, 166**
**Phone property, Customer object, 208**
**physical architectures, 113**
   *see also two- and three-tier applications, and*
   *   web-based applications, 113*
**PocessTag procedure**
   *WebItem object, 618*
**polymorphism, object-oriented design, 33, 275**
   *early binding, 34*
   *interface inheritance, 33, 34*
   *late binding, 33*
**polymorphism, persistence, 392**
**pool manager**
   *definition, 496*
**Price property, InvoiceTape object, 289**
**Private Save, object persistence, 365**
**Private scope, 9**
**properties, Invoice object, 271**
**properties, InvoiceFee object, 283**
**properties, InvoiceItem object, 276**
**properties, InvoiceTape object, 288**
**properties, object interface, 10**
   *Property Get, 11*
   *Property Let, 11*
   *Property Set, 11*
**Property Get, 11, 250, 655**
**Property Let, 11, 159, 249, 655**
**Property Let Item, Buffer object, 461**
**Property Set, 11, 159, 655**
**Property, class modules, 9**
**PropertyBag object, 134**
   *serializing data, 134*
**public classes, class ID (CLSID), 306**
**Public scope, 9**

# R

**RaiseEvent, object events, 13, 88, 91, 148**
**Rating property, Video object, 231**
**Ratings table, VideoObjects database, 373**
**RDO. see Remote Data Objects (RDO), VB**
   **databases**
**read-only list objects, persistence, 454**
   *see also Buffer object,*

read-only objects, persistence, **405**
read-only properties, object and UI example,
  **159**
**Recordset object**
  *ADO*
    connections, 535
    cursors, 549
  *connectionless*
    creating, 132
  *creating, 131, 365*
    by OLE DB, 364
  *transferred by ADO, 48, 130*
    creating, 133
  *Variant arrays, 124*
**ReleaseDate property, Video object, 227**
  *changed from Variant to Date data type, 471*
**Remote Automation server**
  *VideoServer project, application server, 503*
**Remote Data Objects (RDO), VB databases, 47,**
  **118**
remote server files, VideoServer, **499**
  *TLB, 500*
  *VBR, 500, 514*
**Remove method, InvoiceItems object, 298**
**Remove method, Tape object**
  *Tape object, removing from Tapes object, 263*
**Remove method, Tapes object, 257**
**RentalItem class, generalization relationship,**
  **108**
report, Excel
  *viewing objects, 426*
    building the report, 426
**Request object, ASP, 577**
  *Request.Form, 578*
requirements overview, object implementation
  *object structure, 197*
requirements use case, design, **74**
  *high-level objects, 76*
  *high-level requirements, 75*
**Response object, ASP, 578**
  *Response.Write, 579*
**Response object, IIS Application**
  *WebClass objects, 599*
reusability, business objects, **17**
  *components, 19, 49*
  *identifying and defining objects, 73*

**S**

**San Fransisco, IBM, 41**
**Save method, Customer object**
  *ApplyEdit, calling the method from, 453*

**Save method, Customer object ApplyEdit**
  **method, 378**
**Save method, CustomerPersist object, 448**
  *stateless objects, 450*
**Save method, Invoice object persistence, 392**
**Save method, InvoiceFee object persistence, 400**
**Save method, InvoiceTape objects, 401**
**Save method, object persistence, 365, 443**
  *Recordset object, 537*
**Save method, Tape object persistence, 384**
**Save method, TapePersist object, 484**
**Save method, TapesPersist object, 481**
**SaveChild method**
  *TapePersist object, 482, 486*
**SaveLateFee method, Tape object, 389**
**SaveLateFee method, TapePersist object, 485**
scope, **9**
  *encapsulation, 10*
  *instance variables, 9*
scripts, ASP
  *HTML user interface, 570*
  *video details display, 581*
    recursive HTML form, 587, 591
security, MTS objects, **527**
  *roles, 527*
serialiizing
  *data, 122*
    PropertyBag object, 134
**Server object, ASP, 579**
servers
  *Active Server Pages (ASP), 569*
  *ActiveX, 50, 117*
    VideoObjects, 579
    VideoPersistMTS, 579
  *ActiveX servers*
    GUID, 305
  *application server, 26, 27, 496*
  *client/server applications, 50*
    application server, 26, 27, 67, 116, 120, 496
    application server, data-centric business
      objects, 117
    n-tier, 67
    object persistence, 162
    three-tier, 26, 51, 496
    three-tier, n-tier logical architecture, 116
    two-tier, 26, 437, 441
    two-tier, n-tier logical architecture, 114
  *data-centric objects as, 441*
  *MicrosoftTransaction Server (MTS), 496*
  *out-of-process server, object manager as, 168*
  *out-of-process servers*
    data-centric objects, 437

*VideoObjects project, 418*
*web-based applications, 27, 119*
  Active Server Pages (ASP), 569
  application server, 120
**server-side scripting, ASP, 568**
**Session object, ASP, 577**
**SetAbort method, MTS objects, 527**
**SetAbort method, MTS transactions, 555, 559**
**SetAsChild method, Tape object, 241**
**SetAsChild method, Tapes object, 261**
**SetComplete method, MTS objects, 527**
**SetComplete method, MTS transactions, 555**
  *mobjContext, context object, 556*
**SetState method, Buffer object, 459**
**SetState method, Customer object persistence,
  443, 446**
**SetState method, CustomerPersist object, 447**
**SetState method, Customers object, 468**
**SetState method, Tape object persistence, 477**
**SetState method, TapePersist object, 483**
**SetState method, Tapes object**
*Tape object, persistence, 478*
**SetState method, TextListPersist object, 465**
**SetState method, Video object persistence, 475**
**SetState, data-centric objects, 440**
**simple aggregation, aggregate relationship, 100**
**single-tier applications, 25**
**Space$(), VB string handling**
*Buffer object design, 456, 458*
**SQL**
  *disadvantages, 26, 68*
**SQL Server database**
  *switching to JET database, 534*
**standard components. see general components**
**State property, Customer object, 206**
**state, object data, 168**
**state, object persistence, 362**
  *Autonumber, 366*
  *data-centric objects*
    state, moving betwen UI- and data-centric
      objects, 440
  *DeleteObject method, 367*
  *Fetch method, 363*
  *Private Save, 365*
**stateless objects**
  *atomic methods, 555*
**static class diagrams, UML, 677**
  *classes, 678*
    aggregation, 680
    general relationship, 679
    generalization, 680
    multiplicity, 680
    relationships between, 679

*methods, 679*
*properties, 678*
**string concatenation**
  *importance of avoiding, 455*
**string handling, VB**
  *Buffer object design, 455*
    Mid$(), 455
    Space$(), 456
**Structured Query Language**
  *see SQL*
**Sub Main routine**
  *eliminated from VOmain, 535*
**Sub, class modules, 9**
**SubTotal method, Invoice object, 272**
**SubTotal property, InvoiceItems object, 299**

# T

**tag substitution, HTML templates**
  *WebClass objects, 604*
**Tape class, Tape object, 236**
**Tape object, persistence, 384, 475**
  *child object persistence, 470*
  *child object, Tape as, 387*
  *ChildApplyEdit method, 388*
  *ChildLoad method, 388*
  *data-centric Tape objects, creating, 479*
  *DeleteObject method, 385*
  *Fetch method, 385*
  *GetState method, 475*
  *late fee records, 389*
  *Save method, 384*
  *see also Tapes object, persistence*
  *SetState method, 477*
  *standalone object, Tape as, 386*
  *TapePersist object, 482*
    DeleteObject method, 486
    Fetch method, 483
    GetState method, 483
    Save method, 484
    SaveChild method, 482, 486
    SaveLateFee method, 485
    SetState method, 483
  *Tapes object*
    GetState method, 477
    SetState method, 478
  *updating, 488*
    ApplyEdit method, 490
    Load method, 491
    TapePersist, making it public, 490
**Tape objects, VideoUI VideoEDit, 310, 332**
  *ListView control, displayng the objects, 332*
    ListItem objects, 333

Tape table, VideoOBjects database, 372
TapeEdit, VideoUI Edit screens, 337
  *Form_Load, 338*
  *txtAcquired control, 338, 339*
TapePersist object
  *updating*
    making the object public, 490
TapePersist object, persistence
  *DeleteObject method, 486*
  *Fetch method, 483*
  *GetState method, 483*
  *Save method, 484*
  *SaveChild method, 482, 486*
  *SaveLateFee method, 485*
  *SetState method, 483*
  *TapesPersist object, 482*
Tapes class, Tapes object, 254
Tapes object, persistence
  *see also Tape object, persistence*
  *Tape object, 477*
    Tapes object, GetState method, 477
    Tapes object, SetState method, 478
  *TapesPersist object, 479*
    Fetch method, 480
    Save method, 481
  *updating, 487*
    ApplyEdit method, 487
    Load method, 487
  *Video object, parent-child relationship, 379, 382*
    ChildLoad method, 382
    Load method, 382
Tapes property, Video object, 232
TapesPersist object, persistence
  *Fetch method, 480*
  *Save method, 481*
  *TapePersist object, 482*
TapesPersist object, Tapes object persistence, 479
TextBox controls, VideoUI CustomerEdit, 319
TextBox controls, VideoUI VideoEdit, 328
TextBox controls, VideoUI VideoSearch, 346
TextBox object
  *not recognized in VBA, 422*
TextChange routine, 319
  *CallByName method*
    Visual Basic 6.0, 319
  *date values, 329*
  *txtName_Change event, 321*
TextList class, TextList object, 218
TextList object, persistence, 461
  *Load method, 409*
  *see also Buffer object*

*TextListPersist object, 462*
  Fetch method, 462
  Load method, TextList, 464
  SetState method, 465
  UDT, adding, 462
TextList-based properties, Video object, 229
TextListPersist object, TextList object persistence, 462
  *Fetch method, 462*
  *Load method, TextList object, 464*
  *SetState method, 465*
  *UDT, adding, 462*
threads, HTML user interface, 580
three-tier client/server applications, 26
  *application server, 26*
  *logical architecture, 51*
  *n-tier logical architecture, 116*
  *VideoServer, 496*
tiers, applications, 51
  *data-centric processing, 59, 60*
  *functionality, division of, 57, 58*
  *user interface, 57, 58*
    On-Line Transaction Processing (OLTP), 58
    UI-centric processing, 59
Title field, Tape object, 239
TLB, remote server files, 500
Total method, InvoiceItem object, 276
Total property, InvoiceItem object, 276, 277
transactional methods, object implementation, 184
  *see also user interface, object implementation*
transactional ORB, MTS
  *see also object request broker (ORB)*
  *VideoServer*
    database transactions, 525
Trim$(), Customers object, 204
Trim$(), TextList object, 231
Trim(), Video object, 228
two-tier client/server applications, 26
  *n-tier logical architecture, 114*
    presentation objects, 116
  *VideoServer project, 437, 441*
txtAcquired control, VideoUI TapeEdit, 338, 339
txtName_Change event, VideoUI CustomerEdit, 319
  *TextChange routine, 320*
txtRelease control, VideoUI VideoEdit, 329
  *date values, 329*
type libraries, 306
type library, COM servers, 500

# U

**UCase$(), Customer object, 206**
**UDTs**
*see User-Defined Types*
**UI-centric business objects, common interface, 184**
**UI-centric business objects, n-tier architecture, 60, 64, 116**
*designing the objects, 136*
*object and UI example, 138*
canceled edits, 153
field-level validation, 144
field-level validation, error raising, 144
field-level validation, UI error trapping, 145
methods, protecting, 159
object-level validation, 146
properties, protecting, 159
*object support for UI, 137, 138*
*UI as client, 136*
**UI-centric objects**
*persistence, 442*
**UML. see Unified Modeling Language (UML)**
**Unified Modeling Language (UML), 80, 677**
*see also Appendix B*
*notations, 677*
*static class diagrams, 677*
**union keyword, C++, 126**
*see also User-Defined Types*
**use case analysis, design, 73**
*functional decomposition, 74*
*functional use case, 76*
business objects, identifying, 78
functionality, identifying, 77
object events, 88
object methods, 86
object properties, 83
object relationships, 78
*requirements use case, 74*
high-level objects, 76
high-level requirements, 75
*use case formats, alternative, 93*
**user forms, Microsoft Office interface, 416**
*code, 420*
*controls, adding, 419*
*testing, 423*
*user form, adding, 418*
*user, making form available to, 424*
*VBA editor, 417*
*VideoObjects reference, adding, 418*

**user interface, forms, 303**
*Edit screens, 310*
CustomerEdit, 316
Edit Form template, 310
TapeEdit, 337
VideoEdit, 325
*InvoiceEdit, 350*
child object support, 352
File_Check in, menu option, 357
Form_Load, 351
menu option, 356
VideoMain, adding code to, 356
*List screens, 339*
CustomerList, 342
CustomerSearch, 339
VideoList, 347
VideoSearch, 346
*VideoMain, 307*
*VideoUI, 304*
**user interface, HTML**
*Active Server Pages (ASP), 568, 570*
architecture, 569
ASP objects, 576
Microsoft Internet Service Manager, 571
recursive HTML form, 587
scripts, 570, 574
threading, 580
video details display, 581
VideoObjects.dll, installing on server, 580
VideoObjects/VideoPersistMTS, updating, 579
*IIS Application*
video details display, 606
VideoObjects.dll, installing on server, 606
**user interface, logical architecture, 57**
*n-tier architecture, 62*
*object and UI example, 138*
canceled edits, 153
field-level validation, 144
field-level validation, error raising, 144
field-level validation, UI error trapping, 145
methods, protecting, 159
object-level validation, 146
properties, protecting, 159
*object support for UI, 137, 138*
*On-Line Transaction Processing (OLTP), 58*
*UI as business object client, 136*
*UI-centric processing, 59*
**user interface, object implementation, 184**
*Broken Rules class, 196*

class templates, creating, 193
   class modules, 193
   how the template works, 196
   saving template, 195
   template code, 193
OK, Cancel and Apply, 184
   transactional methods, 184
   Valid event/IsValid property, 186
parent-child UI, Tape object, 240
persistence, 187
   ApplyEdit method, 188
   Delete method, 188
   IsDirty property, 191
   IsNew property, 190
   Load method, 188
**user relationship, implementation, 99**
**User-Defined Types (UDT), Video object**
   global UDTs, 470
**User-Defined Types (UDTs)**
   directly passing, 122
**User-Defined Types (UDTs), COM/DCOM, 125**
   LSet, VB implementation, 127
   memory alignment, 129
   memory alignment, LenB, 129
**User-Defined Types (UDTs), Customer object**
   customer objects, implementation
   Customer object, 199
**User-Defined Types (UDTs), object manager, 168**

## V

**Val(), VideoEdit, VideoUI**
   tape, editing, 336
**Valid event, object implementation, 186**
   BrokenRules object, 186
**Valid event, VideoUI Edit Form template, 314**
**Valid, object-level validation, 152**
   user interface, 152
**Validate event**
   prefer Change event, 144
**variables, object data, 9**
**Variant arrays, 123**
   Recordset object, 124
**VBA. see Visual Basic for Applications (VBA)**
**VBR, remote server files, 500**
   VideoServer project, application server, 514
**VBXs**
   application architecture, 48
   Action property, 48
**version compatibility, VideoObjects and VideoUI, 304**
   binary compatibility, 306

no compatibility, 306
project compatibility, 306
**vertical-market components, 22, 41**
**Video class, Video object, 223**
**Video object, persistence**
   child object persistence, 470
   Tapes object, parent-child relationship, 380
   data, adding, 381
   data, deleting, 381
   data, loading, 381
   data, updating, 381
   updating, 411
   VideoData UDT, 471
   VideoPersist object, 471
   Video object update, 473
   VideoProps UDT, 470
**Video object, VideoUI, 310**
**Video objects, object implementation**
   Tape object, 236
   Tapes object, 253
   TextList object, 217
   Video object, 222
   Videos object, 220
**video rental, Customer objects, 198**
   Customer object, 198
   creating the object, 198
   testing the object, 209
   Customers object
   creating the object, 211
   using, 216
**video rental, functional use case, 76**
**video rental, Invoice objects, 265**
   Invoice object, 269
   creating, 274
   InvoiceFee object, 278
   InvoiceItem object, 275
   InvoiceItems object, 292
   InvoiceTape object, 287
**video rental, requirements overview, 197**
**video rental, requirements use case, 74**
**video rental, Video objects**
   Tape object, 236
   Tapes object, 253
   TextList object, 217
   Video object, 222
   Videos object, 220
**Video table, VideoObjects database, 371**
**VideoData UDT, Video object persistence, 471**
**VideoDisplay object**
   VideoIIS, 614
   hyperlinks, 617
**VideoDisplay object, Videos object, 221**

**VideoEdit**
*updating, 412*
**VideoEdit, VideoUI, 325**
*Click event, 331*
*ComboBox controls, 329*
*date values, txtRelease control, 329*
*Form_Load, 328, 330, 334*
*ListView control, 327*
Tape objects, displaying, 332
*LoadCombo, 331*
*Tape objects, 332*
*tape, adding, 335*
*tape, editing, 336*
Val(), 336
*tape, removing, 336*
*template code, 328*
*TextBox controls, 328*
*VideoMain, adding code to, 337*
**VideoIIS**
*DisplayVideo object, 616*
hyperlinks, 617
*GetVideos object, 608*
updating, 612
*IIS Application, 607*
*ListVideos object, 612*
HTML template, 613
*VideoDisplay object, 614*
hyperlinks, 617
**VideoList, VideoUI List screens, 347**
**VideoMain, MDI form**
*menus, 308*
*see also forms, user interface*
**VideoObjects project**
*compiling, into an ActiveX DLL, 416*
see also Microsoft Office, as interface
*dependency file, VideoServer, 512*
*interface, creating*
Excel report, viewing objects, 426
HTML/ASP, 567
user forms, 416
*persistence, 367*
*see also VideoServer, application server*
*TLB, VideoServer, 510*
*VideoServerMTS, referencing, 543*
*VideoUI, user interface, 304*
version compatibility, 304
VideoObjects, referencing, 306
**VideoObjects.dll, VideoObjects compilation, 416**
*Package and Deployment Wizard, 580*
**VideoPersist object, object persistence**
*Save method*
changing, 550

*see also persistence*
**VideoPersist object, persistence, 471**
*Video object update, 473*
ApplyEdit method, 473
GetState method, 474
Load method, 474
SetState method, 475
**VideoProps UDT, Video object persistence, 470**
**Videos object, persistence, 408, 466**
*Fetch method, 408*
*Item method, 409*
*Load method, 408*
*see also Buffer object*
**VideoSearch, VideoUI List screens, 346**
*main menu, 348*
*TextBox controls, 346*
**VideoServer project**
*MTS objects, 526*
*database transactions, 525*
*Microsoft Transaction Server (MTS), 522*
database connections, 524
database transactions, 525
MTS objects, 525
MTS transactions, 545
preparing VideoServer, 529
*MTS objects, 525*
context, 526
CreateInstance method, 529
CreateObject method, 528, 532
New keyword, 528, 533
object lifetime, 527
*MTS transactions, 545*
Distributed Transaction Coordinator (DTC), 562
establishing a transaction, 560
ObjectContext objects, 545
ObjectControl interface, 547
transaction status, 555
*multiple clients, support for, 522*
database connections, 524
object request broker, 522
*multiple clients, supporting*
objects numbers, limiting, 523
*two-tier client/server applications, 437, 441*
*VideoServerMTS, 529*
running in MTS, 538
**VideoServer project, application server, 496, 497**
*binary compatibility, 500*
*client, setting up, 511*
VideoObjects, dependency file, 512
VideoServer setup, 515

*client, settng up*
  CLIREG32, 517
*database, 501*
*DCOM registration, 505*
*dependency file, 513, 514*
*Distributed COM (DCOM), 496*
*identity account, 509*
*installation, 502*
  Package and Deployment Wizard, 503, 512
  registration, manual, 504
*multi-threading, 497*
  apartment model, 497
  options, 498
*Remote Automation server, 503*
*remote server files, 499*
  TLB, 500
  VBR, 500, 514
*security, 508*
*see also VideoObjects project*
*TLB, VideoObjects, 510*
*VBR, remote server files*
  Package and Deployment Wizard, 515
*VideoServer permissions, 506*
**VideoServer, data-centric objects, 441**
*ADO, using, 442*
*database code, 442*
**VideoServerMTS, VideoServer, 529**
*creating, 529, 530*
*objects, creating, 532*
  CreateObject method, 532
  New keyword, 533
*running in MTS, 538, 543*
  client setup, 542
  server installation, 538
**VideoUI, user interface, 304**
*Edit screens, 310*
  CustomerEdit, 316
  Edit Form template, 310
  TapeEdit, 337
  VideoEdit, 325
*InvoiceEdit, 350*
  child object support, 352
  File_Check in, menu option, 357
  Form_Load, 351
  menu option, 356
  VideoMain, adding code to, 356
*List screens, 339*
  CustomerList, 342
  CustomerSearch, 339
  VideoList, 347
  VideoSearch, 346
*see also VideoMain*
*setup, VideoServer, 515*

*VideoObjects, referencing, 306*
**Visual Basic 6.0**
*DataFormat object capability, 120*
*integrated with ADO 2.0, 48*
**Visual Basic for Applications (VBA), 416**
*AfterUpdate event*
  replaces LostFocus event, 421
*CallByName method not available, 422*
*interface, creating, 416*
  code, 420
  controls, adding, 419
  Excel report, viewing objects, 427
  see also Microsoft Office, as interface
  testing, 423
  user form, adding, 418
  user, making form available to, 424
  VBA editor, 417
  VideoObjects reference, adding, 418
*TextBox object not recognozed, 422*

**W**

**web-based applications, 27**
*HTML user interface, 568*
*n-tier logical architecture, 118*
  application server, 120
**WebClass objects**
*Active Server Pages, 597, 607*
*HTML templates*
  tag substitution, 604
*IIS Application, 597*
*Response object, IIS Application, 599*
*updating, 612*
*Visual Basic 6.0*
  designers, 598
**WebItem objects**
*HTML templates, 602, 610*
*IIS Application, 601*
*ProcessTag procedure, 618*
**WithEvents keyword, 311**
**WithEvents, object events, 91, 143**
**write-once properties**
*risks of using, 161*
**write-once properties, object and UI example, 160**
**write-only properties, object and UI example, 161**

**Z**

**ZipCode property, Customer object, 207**